HALLIWELL'S GUIDE
TO THE BEST COMEDIES

By the same author

Halliwell's Filmgoer's Companion
Halliwell's Film Guide
Halliwell's Guide to the Best Children's Films

HALLIWELL'S GUIDE TO

THE BEST
COMEDIES

Edited by
John Walker

HarperCollins*Publishers*

HarperCollins*Publishers*
77–85 Fulham Palace Road,
Hammersmith, London W6 8JB

A Paperback Original 1994
1 3 5 7 9 8 6 4 2

A catalogue record for this book
is available from the British Library

ISBN 0 00 638116 2

Set in Meridien by
Rowland Phototypesetting Ltd, Bury St Edmunds, Suffolk

Printed in Great Britain by
HarperCollinsManufacturing, Glasgow

CONTENTS

INTRODUCTION

Film comedy is as old as the cinema itself. *Watering The Gardener*, probably the first ever comic movie, made in 1896, featured a simple practical joke: a man is watering a garden. A boy steps on the hose. As the gardener looks down the hose pipe to see what has happened to the water, the boy steps off. Swoosh! The man is soaked.

Such slapstick, refined and elaborated by Mack Sennett, creator of the Keystone Kops, had audiences rocking with laughter in the early days. Before long, Charlie Chaplin was the most famous figure in the world, only to be challenged a little later by Mickey Mouse.

Films were first seen in fairgrounds, nickelodeons, vaudeville and music-halls, which is where the first, and still much-loved, comics had learned their craft. Buster Keaton, Laurel and Hardy, W.C. Fields, Mae West, the Marx Brothers and others began by playing to live audiences. Perhaps that is why their films still have the ability to make us laugh. Even today, many of the screen's funny men, including Robin Williams, Steve Martin and Eddie Murphy, began as stand-up comedians.

This guide to comedies of the past and present includes films that are available on VHS video-cassette and on laser disk as well as those that are likely to turn up on television, often, in the case of black and white movies, late at night or early in the morning. (A word of warning: these days video releases quickly become unobtainable and it is impossible to be entirely up-to-date on what is still available and what has been deleted.)

The movies listed have been carefully selected from the

standard reference book *Halliwell's Film Guide*, now in its 9th edition, which contains details of nearly 20,000 films of all kinds. Biographical information on many of the stars and directors mentioned here can be found in the 10th edition of *Halliwell's Filmgoer's Companion*.

In tough times, comedy helps make life more bearable. In the good times that are just around the corner (where they tend to remain), it makes life even more fun. As someone once said, 'Laugh – and the world laughs with you. Cry – and you're watching the wrong movie.' Here you'll find the aids to brighten even the gloomiest day. Enjoy!

John Walker
January 1994

EXPLANATORY NOTES

Alphabetical Order

Unlike some books which take the complete title into account, as though there were no gaps between words, we have always persevered with the old-fashioned word-at-a-time arrangement. Thus, all titles starting with *In* are used up before one goes on to titles beginning *Incredible*. Hyphenated or apostrophized words are counted as one word. Compressions such as *Dr* and *St* are treated as though they had been spelled out, as *Doctor* and *Saint*. *Mac* and *Mc* are regarded as interchangeable under *Mac*. Titles consisting of initials, such as *C. C. and Company* or *D.O.A.* are dealt with at the beginning of each alphabetical section, except where they have become acronyms (i.e. pronounceable as one word, e.g. AWOL). In all cases the complete title is given as billed, though the definite and indefinite articles are not counted in the alphabetical arrangement where they occur as the first word of a title. The spelling of the country of origin is used, e.g. *My Favorite Blonde* and not *My Favourite Blonde*.

Individual Entries

All entries follow the same format and the notes are set out below in the order in which they will be encountered.

Publicity tags
These were used in the promotion of the film and, in the manner of trailers, precede the entry.

Ratings

These range from none to four stars. Four stars indicate a film outstanding in many ways, a milestone in cinema history, remarkable for acting, direction, writing, photography or some other aspect of technique. Three stars indicate a very high standard of professional excellence or great historical interest. Or, if you like, three strong reasons for admiring it. Two stars indicate a good level of competence and a generally entertaining film. One star indicates a film not very satisfactory as a whole; it could be a failed giant or a second feature with a few interesting ideas among the dross. No stars at all indicates a totally routine production or worse; such films may be watchable but are at least equally missable.

Country of origin

This is the first item on the second line.

Year of release

This comes after the country of origin and is intended to indicate the year when the film was first shown, which is not necessarily the year that it was made. Dating is sometimes an onerous task, and the result debatable.

Running time

This is given in minutes, signified by 'm'. So far as possible, this is the original release time. Very many films are cut as they appear in different countries, sometimes by twenty minutes or more. An engineering function of British television results in an imperceptible speeding-up of projection and a consequent loss of one minute in every twenty-five. A hundred-minute film, therefore, will run only ninety-six minutes on the box.

Colour

This is indicated by 'bw' for black and white films and 'colour' for the others. The colour process used, such as Technicolor, is given when known.

Other notable points
These are given at the end of the second line, indicating the use of a special process, such as Panavision.

Production credit
This is the central credit on the third line. To the left comes the name of the distributor, which is followed by the production company if different. To the right comes the name or names of the actual producer – in brackets, unless he has a stake in the production, in which case he follows an oblique. These days, many films tend to have more producers of one kind or another than actors. The credit here refers to the person bearing the title of producer rather than to the executive producer, associate producer, production executive and so on.

Video
'V' indicates that the film is available on VHS video-cassette.
   'V(W)' indicates that the film is available on VHS video-cassette in wide-screen format.
   'V(C)' indicates that the film is available on VHS video-cassette in a computer-colourized version.
   'L' indicates that the film is available on laser disc in either American NTSC format or British PAL format.

Alternative title
This is given on a separate line, usually with a note of the country in which it was used. If no such distinction exists, the formula aka (also known as) is used. Alternative titles are also listed individually, cross-referenced to the main entry for the film to which they belong.

Synopsis
This is a brief description of the film's plot.

Assessment
Again, this is brief and to the point.

Writer credit
(w) This appears first since the script precedes direction and is therefore, at least sometimes, more important than the director credit. The author of the screenplay is given; if this derives from a novel, play, musical, or story, this is given next, together with the original author.

Director credit
(d) This follows next. If the director is also the writer, then there will be a combined *'wd'* credit.

Photography credit
(ph) This indicates the cinematographer or lighting cameraman, otherwise known as the director of photography, rather than the actual camera operator.

Music credit
(m) This means the composer of the background music score. Sometimes there is only a music director *(md)* who orchestrates library or classical music. When noteworthy songs are performed in a film, or are specially written for it, those responsible are indicated by a credit for music and lyrics *(m/ly)* or simply *songs*.

Other credits
These include art director *(ad)*, choreographer *(ch)*, costume designer *(costume)*, film editor *(ed)*, production designer *(pd)* and special effects *(sp)*. They are given when they seem important and when they can be found. In some cases it has not been possible to track down all the credits one would wish.

Cast
A list of the principal actors is given, roughly in order of importance.

Italics
These denote a contribution of a particularly high standard.

Critical comments
Brief quotes from well-known professional critics are appended to many entries, sometimes because they wittily confirm the assessments and sometimes because they provide alternative opinions. The absence of a quote casts no reflection whatever on the film, only on the difficulty of finding an opinion worth quoting.

Additional notes
Any points of interest about the film are given after the symbol †.

Academy Awards
Awards (AA) and nominations (AAN) are listed for all principal categories, including best picture, acting, direction, photography, music score and songs, and some minor ones, such as sound and make-up, when they seem of interest.

'They're too wild for one world!'

Abbott and Costello Go to Mars
US 1953 76m bw
U-I (Howard Christie)

Two incompetents accidentally
launch a space ship and land first in
Louisiana, then on Venus.

Dismal knockabout, badly made.

w John Grant, D. D. Beauchamp
d Charles Lamont   ph Clifford
Stine   m Joseph Gershenson

Bud Abbott, Lou Costello, Mari
Blanchard, Robert Paige, Martha Hyer

Abbott and Costello in Hollywood*
US 1945 85m bw
MGM (Martin Gosch)

Two agents have hectic adventures in
a film studio.

Tolerable star romp on one of their
biggest budgets, climaxing in a roller
coaster ride.

w Nat Perrin, Lou Breslow   d S.
Sylvan Simon   ph Charles
Schoenbaum   m George Bassman

Bud Abbott, Lou Costello, Frances
Rafferty, Warner Anderson, Robert
Z. Leonard

**Abbott and Costello in the Foreign
Legion**
US 1950 80m bw
U-I (Robert Arthur)

Incompetent legionnaires become
heroes to the fury of their sergeant.

Dull star vehicle on ramshackle sets,
with no memorable routines.

w John Grant, Leonard Stern, Martin
Ragaway   d Charles Lamont
ph George Robinson   m Joseph
Gershenson

Bud Abbott, Lou Costello, Patricia
Medina, Walter Slezak, Douglass
Dumbrille

Abbott and Costello Lost in Alaska
US 1952 76m bw
U-I (Howard Christie)

Two San Francisco firemen take a
melancholy prospector back to
Alaska to find a gold mine.

Sub-standard comedy vehicle with
poor production.

w Martin Ragaway, Leonard Stern
d Jean Yarbrough   ph George
Robinson   m Joseph Gershenson

Bud Abbott, Lou Costello, *Tom Ewell*,
Mitzi Green, Bruce Cabot

**Abbott and Costello Meet Captain
Kidd***
US 1952 70m Supercinecolor
Warner/Woodley (Alex Gottlieb)

Two servants have a treasure map,
and a fearsome pirate wants it.

Crude knockabout: the stars are way

below their best, and a famous actor is embarrassed.

w Howard Dimsdale, John Grant
d Charles Lamont   ph Stanley Cortez   m Raoul Kraushaar

Bud Abbott, Lou Costello, Charles Laughton, Hillary Brooke, Leif Erickson

Abbott and Costello Meet Dr Jekyll and Mr Hyde*
US   1953   77m   bw
U-I (Howard Christie)

In Victorian London, two rookie policemen catch a monster.

Quite a lively spoof with some well-paced comedy sequences.

w John Grant, Lee Loeb   d Charles Lamont   ph George Robinson
m Hans Salter

Bud Abbott, Lou Costello, Boris Karloff, Reginald Denny, Craig Stevens, Helen Westcott, John Dierkes

'Gracious Boris Karloff is superior to his surroundings.' – MFB (Though it is doubtful whether he ever got behind the Hyde make-up.)

† In Britain, the film was given an 'X' certificate, though it later played on children's television.

'Jeepers! the creepers are after somebody – and guess who! More howls than you can shake a shiver at!!!'
Abbott and Costello Meet Frankenstein**
US   1948   83m   bw
U-I (Robert Arthur)
GB title: Abbott and Costello Meet the Ghosts

Two railway porters deliver crates containing the Frankenstein monster, Dracula, and the Wolf Man.

Fairly lively spoof which put an end to Universal's monsters for a while. Good typical sequences for the stars, a few thrills, and some good lines. Dracula to Costello, lovingly: 'What we need is young blood . . . and brains . . .'

w Robert Lees, Frederic I. Rinaldo, John Grant   d Charles Barton
ph Charles van Enger   m Frank Skinner

Bud Abbott, Lou Costello, Bela Lugosi, Lon Chaney Jnr, Glenn Strange, Lenore Aubert, Jane Randolph
  WOLF MAN: 'You don't understand. Every night when the moon is full, I turn into a wolf.'
  COSTELLO: 'You and fifty million other guys!'

† Probably the Abbott and Costello film which survives best.

Abbott and Costello Meet the Invisible Man*
US   1951   82m   bw
U-I (Howard Christie)

A boxer accused of murder makes himself invisible while two detectives clear him.

Quite a bright comedy with good trick effects.

w Robert Lees, Frederic I. Rinaldo, John Grant   d Charles Lamont
ph George Robinson   m Hans Salter

Bud Abbott, Lou Costello, Arthur Franz, Nancy Guild, Adele Jergens, Sheldon Leonard

'When every face wore a custard pie, and vamps broke hearts with a winking eye!'
Abbott and Costello Meet the Keystone Kops*
US   1954   79m   bw
U-I (Howard Christie)

In pioneer film days, two incompetents are sold a dud studio by a con man, but succeed as stunt men.

Flabby comedy which never seems to get going until the chase finale; notable chiefly for a guest appearance by Mack Sennett.

w John Grant   d Charles Lamont   ph Reggie Lanning m Joseph Gershenson

Bud Abbott, Lou Costello, Lynn Bari, Fred Clark, Frank Wilcox, Maxie Rosenbloom

'More ghoulish glee than when they met Frankenstein!'

Abbott and Costello Meet the Killer, Boris Karloff*
US   1948   84m   bw
U-I (Robert Arthur)

Two bellboys help to solve mysterious murders in a remote hotel.

This clumsily titled comedy really does not work until the last sequence in a cavern. Boris Karloff is not the killer and appears very little.

w Hugh Wedlock Jnr, Howard Snyder, John Grant   d Charles Barton   ph Charles van Enger md Milton Schwarzwald

Bud Abbott, Lou Costello, Boris Karloff, Gar Moore, Lenore Aubert, Alan Mowbray

'It has been said that a man's best friend is his mummy...'

Abbott and Costello Meet the Mummy*
US   1955   77m   bw
U-I (Howard Christie)

A missing medallion leads to a lost tomb and a living mummy.

The comedians show their age in this one, but there is some typical if predictable humour and a thrill or two.

w John Grant   d Charles Lamont   ph George Robinson m Hans Salter

Bud Abbott, Lou Costello, Kurt Katch, Marie Windsor, Michael Ansara, Dan Seymour

'How stupid can you get?'
– 'How stupid do you want me to be?'

Above Suspicion*
US   1943   91m   bw
MGM (Victor Saville)

Just before World War II, an Oxford professor on a continental honeymoon is asked to track down a missing agent.

Patchy, studio-bound spy comedy-drama with a couple of good sequences. Notable also for Mr MacMurray's impersonation of a professor who hails a Nazi as 'Hiya, dope!'

w Keith Winter, Melville Baker, Patricia Coleman   novel Helen MacInnes   d Richard Thorpe ph Robert Planck   m Bronislau Kaper

Fred MacMurray, Joan Crawford, Conrad Veidt, Basil Rathbone, Reginald Owen, Felix Bressart, Richard Ainley

'Will need more than strong support for passable biz.' – Variety

'Two roaring Romeos who thought even the dames were on lend lease!'

Abroad with Two Yanks*
US   1944   80m   bw
Edward Small

Adventures around the Pacific with two woman-chasing sailors.

This simple-minded farce with its

punny title was a great success in its day, and still generates a laugh or two.

w Charles Rogers, Wilkie Mahoney, Ted Sills   d Allan Dwan
ph Charles Lawton   m Lud Gluskin

Dennis O'Keefe, William Bendix, Helen Walker, John Abbott, John Loder

'It's all about a wacky prof who invents an anti-gravity goo that flew!'
The Absent-Minded Professor*
US   1961   97m   bw
Walt Disney (Bill Walsh)

A lighter-than-air substance called flubber enables its inventor to drive his Model-T through the sky and catch some spies.

Foolishly engaging fantasy comedy with goodish trick effects.

w Bill Walsh   d Robert Stevenson   ph Edward Colman
m George Bruns   sp Robert A. Mattey, Peter Ellenshaw, Eustace Lycett

Fred MacMurray, Tommy Kirk, Keenan Wynn, Nancy Olson, Leon Ames, Ed Wynn, Edward Andrews

† Sequel: *Son of Flubber* (1963).
AAN: Edward Colman

According to Mrs Hoyle
US   1951   60m   bw
Monogram

A retired schoolteacher lives in a hotel run by criminals, and becomes involved.

Uninspired sentimental comedy providing a rare star part for a well-liked character actress.

w W. Scott Darling and Barney Gerard   d Jean Yarbrough

Spring Byington, Anthony Caruso, Brett King, Tanis Chandler

Adam's Rib**
US   1949   101m   bw
MGM (Lawrence Weingarten)

Husband and wife lawyers are on opposite sides of an attempted murder case.

A superior star vehicle which also managed to introduce four promising personalities; slangily written and smartly directed, but perhaps a shade less funny than it once seemed.

w Ruth Gordon, Garson Kanin
d George Cukor   ph George J. Folsey   m Miklos Rozsa

Spencer Tracy, Katharine Hepburn, David Wayne, Tom Ewell, Judy Holliday, Jean Hagen, Hope Emerson, Clarence Kolb

'Hepburn and Tracy are again presented as the ideal US Mr and Mrs of upper-middle income. This time, as well as being wittily urbane, both are lawyers.' – *Time*
'It isn't solid food but it certainly is meaty and juicy and comically nourishing.' – *Bosley Crowther*

† A 1972 TV series of the same title provided a boring imitation, with Ken Howard and Blythe Danner.
AAN: Ruth Gordon and Garson Kanin

'Creepy. Kooky. Spooky. Ooky.'
The Addams Family*
US   1991   99m   DeLuxe
Columbia TriStar/Paramount/Orion (Scott Rudin)
V, L

An impostor turns up at the Addams family mansion, claiming to be a long-lost elder brother.

Owing more to the TV series of the 1960s than to the macabre wit of the original *New Yorker* cartoons, an ill-conceived, coarse-grained comedy that nevertheless was a success at the box-office.

w Caroline Thompson, Larry Wilson   *cartoons* based on characters created by Charles Addams   d Barry Sonnenfeld   ph Owen Roizman   m Marc Shaiman   pd Richard MacDonald   sp visual effects supervisor Alan Munro, Chuck Comisky   ed Dede Allen, Jim Miller

Anjelica Huston, Raul Julia, Christopher Lloyd, Dan Hedaya, Elizabeth Wilson, Judith Malina, Carel Struycken, Dana Ivey, Paul Benedict, Christopher Hart (whose hand appears as The Thing)

'Plays like a collection of sitcom one-liners augmented by feature-film special effects – a combination that is stretched well beyond its limits.' – *Variety*
'Misguided graveyard slapstick.' – *New Yorker*

'Motherhood just got a little stranger.'
Addams Family Values
US   1993   94m   colour
UIP/Paramount (Scott Rudin)

The older Addams children try to kill the new baby, but he is damage-proof, while the new nanny has murderous designs on Uncle Fester.

An elongated sit-com with a few good gags in a muddled narrative.

w Paul Rudnik   *cartoons* based on characters created by Charles Addams   d Barry Sonnenfield   ph Donald Peterman   m Marc Shaiman   pd Ken Adam

Angelica Huston, Raul Julia, Christopher Lloyd, Joan Cusack, *Christina Ricci*, Carol Kane, Jimmy Workman

'The film does not know when to stop, has little idea of how to begin, and moves forward by a process of "Quick, who's got the next gimmick" jolts and nudges.' – Nigel Andrews, *Financial Times*
'The storyline is almost too slim to recall and the cast simply earn their bread and butter doing revue turns.' –Derek Malcolm, *Guardian*

The Admiral Was a Lady
US   1950   87m   bw
Roxbury (Albert S. Rogell, Jack M. Warner)

Four ex-airmen and an ex-Wac try to live on their wits.

Unappealing comedy which gives the impression that it has tried to find a new style, and failed.

w Sidney Salkow, John O'Dea   d Albert S. Rogell   ph Stanley Cortez

Edmond O'Brien, Wanda Hendrix, Rudy Vallee, Johnny Sands, Steve Brodie, Richard Erdman, Hillary Brooke, Richard Lane

Adolf Hitler – My Part in His Downfall*
GB   1972   102m   Technicolor
UA/Norcon (Gregory Smith, Norman Cohen)

Episodes in the life of a conscript at the beginning of World War II.

Lumbering anarchic comedy based on Spike Milligan's own sidesplitting memoirs; an enfeebled British *M*A*S*H*.

w Johnny Byrne   d Norman Cohen   ph Terry Maher   m Wilfred Burns

Jim Dale, Spike Milligan (as his own father), Arthur Lowe, Bill Maynard, Windsor Davies, Pat Coombs, Tony Selby, Geoffrey Hughes

'A convincing period shabbiness and sleaziness which are endearing when they're not being overstated.' – *MFB*

Adorable Julia
Austria/France   1962   97m   bw
Wiener Mundus/Etoile
GB title: *The Seduction of Julia*

A middle-aged actress takes on a lover.

Moderately pleasing sex comedy, rather more heavily directed than Maugham would have liked.

w Johanna Sibelius, Eberhard Keindorff   *novel Theatre* by Somerset Maugham   *d* Alfred Weidenmann

Lilli Palmer, Charles Boyer, Jean Sorel, Jeanne Valeri

Adua e le Compagne
Italy   1960   150m   bw
Zebra Film
GB title: *Hungry for Love*

When brothels in Italy are officially closed, four of the old girls open a restaurant.

Immensely overlong comedy drama whose rewards come entirely from the actors.

w Ruggero Maccari, Ettore Scola, Antonio Pietrangeli, Tullio Pinelli   *d* Antonio Pietrangeli

Simone Signoret, Marcello Mastroianni, Sandra Milo, Emmanuelle Riva, Gina Rovere

'The script becomes increasingly episodic, and clichés abound.' – *MFB*

The Adventure of Sherlock Holmes' Smarter Brother
GB   1975   91m   DeLuxe
TCF/Jouer (Richard A. Roth)

More by good luck than good

management, Sherlock's younger brother solves one of his cases.

Infuriating parody with little sense of the original and a hit-or-miss style all of its own. Amusing moments fail to atone for the general waste of opportunity.

wd Gene Wilder   *ph* Gerry Fisher   *m* John Morris   *pd* Terry Marsh

Gene Wilder, Marty Feldman, Madeline Kahn, Leo McKern, Dom DeLuise, Roy Kinnear, John Le Mesurier, Douglas Wilmer, Thorley Walters

'Like a compilation of the kind of numbers actors like to do at parties.' – *Howard Kissel*
'He has bitten off more than he can chew or I can swallow.' – *John Simon*
'A few stray chuckles but nothing more.' – *Sight and Sound*
'There's no mystery, and since you can't have a parody of a mystery without a mystery, there's no comic suspense.' – *New Yorker, 1980*

The Adventures of Barry Mackenzie*
Australia   1972   114m   Eastmancolor
Columbia/Longford (Philip Adams)

A sex-hungry Australian gets into all kinds of trouble on a visit to the Old Country.

Occasionally funny, defiantly crude and tasteless, but poorly produced comedy-misadventure from the *Private Eye* comic strip. Australian slang combines with bad sound recording to make much of the film unintelligible.

w Barry Humphries, Bruce Beresford   *d* Bruce Beresford   *ph* Don McAlpine   *m* Peter Best

Barry Crocker, Barry Humphries (as Dame Edna Everage), Peter Cook, Spike Milligan, Dennis Price, Avice Landone, Dick Bentley, Joan Bakewell, William Rushton

'A wildly uneven concoction of antipodean bad taste, probably only fully appreciated by Earls Court exiles.' – *Sight and Sound*

† Sequel 1974: *Barry Mackenzie Holds His Own*

Adventures of Ford Fairlane
US 1990 104m DeLuxe
  Panavision
TCF (Joel Silver, Steve Perry)
V, L

A conceited rock 'n' roll detective solves the murder of a Los Angeles disc jockey.

Drearily vulgar comedy, featuring one of the more obnoxious stand-up comedians of the 90s and about as entertaining as stepping in something nasty in the street. It was a flop at the box-office, resulting in Fox's decision not to release Clay's concert film *Dice Rules* (qv).

w Daniel Waters, James Cappe, David Arnott *story* based on characters created by Rex Weiner *d* Renny Harlin *ph* Oliver Wood *m* Yello *pd* John Vallone *ed* Michael Tronick

Andrew Dice Clay, Wayne Newton, Priscilla Presley, Morris Day, Lauren Holly, Maddie Corman, Robert Englund, Ed O'Neill

'Surprisingly funny and expectedly rude.' – *Variety*
'What can you say about a movie whose comic highlight is the hanging of a koala bear?' – *Empire*

Affair with a Stranger*
US 1953 87m bw
RKO (Robert Sparks)

Five friends reminisce about a marriage which seems about to break up.

This would-be-smart comedy has a good idea unsatisfactorily worked out, and could have used a more sparkling cast.

w Richard Flournoy *d* Roy Rowland *ph* Harry J. Wild *m* Roy Webb

Jean Simmons, Victor Mature, Mary Jo Tarola, Monica Lewis, Jane Darwell, Nicholas Joy, Wally Vernon, Dabbs Greer

The Affairs of Dobie Gillis
US 1953 74m bw
MGM (Arthur M. Loew Jnr)

Adventures of an indolent and accident-prone university student.

Scatty comedy with good talent and musical numbers encased in a tatty production.

w Max Shulman *d* Don Weis *ph* William Mellor *md* Jeff Alexander

Bobby Van, Debbie Reynolds, Hans Conried, Barbara Ruick, Bob Fosse

'When it's after midnight in New York City, you don't have to look for love, laughter and trouble. They'll all find you!'
After Hours**
US 1985 97m DuArt Color
Warner/Geffen/Double Play (Amy Robinson, Griffin Dunne, Robert F. Colesberry)
V, L

Through a chapter of accidents, a mild-mannered computer programmer has a bad time in the night streets of New York.

An unsettling kind of black comedy with moments of malaise: nobody denies its touches of brilliance, but few people want to see it again.

w Joseph Minion   d Martin Scorsese   ph Michael Ballhaus   m Howard Shore   pd Jeffrey Townsend   ed Thelma Schoonmaker

Griffin Dunne, Rosanna Arquette, Verna Bloom, Thomas Chong, Teri Garr, Cheech Marin

'The cinema of paranoia and persecution reaches an apogee ... would have been pretty funny if it didn't play like a confirmation of everyone's worst fears about contemporary urban life.' – Variety
'A film so original, so particular, that one is uncertain from moment to moment exactly how to respond to it. Interesting.' – Roger Ebert

After the Fox*
US/Italy   1966   103m
   Technicolor   Panavision
UA/Nancy/CCM (John Bryan)

The Fox escapes from jail to execute a gold bullion caper and save his young sister from the streets.

Unlikeable and unfunny farce which sets its star among excitable Italians and hopes for the best, adding a few wild stabs at satire on movie-making styles.

w Neil Simon, Cesare Zavattini
d Vittorio de Sica   ph Leonida Barboni   m Burt Bacharach

Peter Sellers, Victor Mature (agreeably sending up his old image), Britt Ekland, Lilia Brazzi, Paola Stoppa, Akim Tamiroff, Martin Balsam

'Never even begins to get off the ground.' – MFB

A-Haunting We Will Go*
US   1942   68m   bw
TCF (Sol M. Wurtzel)
V

Gangsters dupe Laurel and Hardy into escorting a coffin, which is accidentally switched with one used in a magic act.

Nothing whatever to do with haunting: a poor comedy with no typical material for the stars, but interesting as a record of the touring show of Dante the Magician.

w Lou Breslow   d Alfred Werker   ph Glen MacWilliams   m Emil Newman

Stan Laurel, Oliver Hardy, Dante, Sheila Ryan, John Shelton, Elisha Cook Jnr

'The comedians' lack of enthusiasm for their material is rather evident.' – William K. Everson, 1967

Air Raid Wardens
US   1943   67m   bw
MGM (B. F. Zeidman)
V

Rejected by the armed services, two incompetent air raid wardens accidentally round up Nazi spies.

Well below par star comedy: their incomparable dignity has disappeared.

w Jack Jevne, Martin Rackin, Charles Rogers, Harry Crane   d Edward Sedgwick   ph Walter Lundin   m Nathaniel Shilkret

Stan Laurel, Oliver Hardy, Edgar Kennedy, Jacqueline White, Stephen McNally, Nella Walker, Donald Meek

Airplane**
US   1980   88m   Metrocolor
Paramount/Howard W. Koch (Jon Davison)
V, L

A former pilot gets his nerve back

when called upon to land a passenger plane because the crew all have food poisoning.

Arthur Hailey's play *Flight into Danger* and the film *Zero Hour* which was made from it get the zany parody treatment in this popular movie which is often funny but sometimes merely crude. It rang the box-office bell more loudly than most expensive epics of its year.

wd Jim Abrahams, David and Jerry Zucker   *ph* Joseph Biroc *m* Elmer Bernstein   *pd* Ward Preston

Robert Stack, Lloyd Bridges, Robert Hays, Julie Hagerty, Peter Graves, Leslie Nielsen, Lorna Patterson, Ethel Merman, Kareem Abdul-Jabbar

'Parody may be the lowest form of humour, but few comedies in ages have rocked the laugh meter this hard.' – *Variety*
'It keeps going, like a dervish with skids on.' – *Derek Malcolm, Guardian*
'Proof that the cinema is alive and well and bursting with ingenuity.' – *David Hughes, Sunday Times*
'It's compiled like a jokebook and has the kind of pacing that goes with a laugh track.' – *Pauline Kael*
'All pretty juvenile really, though the relentless pace and sheer poor taste make up for a lack of originality.' – *Time Out, 1984*
'Practically a satirical anthology of movie clichés . . . it compensates for its lack of original comic invention by its utter willingness to steal, beg, borrow and rewrite from anywhere.' – *Roger Ebert*

'Just when you thought it safe to go back into the departure lounge'
Airplane II: The Sequel
US   1982   85m   Metrocolor
Paramount (Howard W. Koch)
V, L

A space shuttle gets into trouble but is rescued in the nick of time.

Palsied sequel to a funny film, with some of the same cast and some of the same jokes.

wd Ken Finkleman   *ph* Joe Biroc   *m* Elmer Bernstein *pd* William Sandell   *ed* Dennis Virkler

Robert Hays, Julie Hagerty, Lloyd Bridges, Peter Graves, William Shatner, Chad Everett, Steven Stucker, Sonny Bono, Raymond Burr, Chuck Connors, Rip Torn, John Dehner, Kent McCord, John Vernon

'All the pleasure lies in the humour's weakness.' – *Observer*

The Alf Garnett Saga
GB   1972   90m   colour
Columbia/Associated London Films (Ned Sherrin, Terry Glinwood)

Bigoted Alf is exasperated by his council flat, his son-in-law, and the possibility that his daughter is pregnant by a black man.

Second inflation of the TV series, *Till Death Us Do Part*, even cruder and less funny than the first; listlessly written and developed.

w Johnny Speight   *d* Bob Kellett   *ph* Nic Knowland *m* Georgie Fame

Warren Mitchell, Dandy Nichols, Adrienne Posta, Mike Angelis, John Le Mesurier, Joan Sims, John Bird, Roy Kinnear

'One long, repetitive and unfunny diatribe.' – *MFB*

Alf's Button Afloat**
GB   1938   89m   bw
Gainsborough (Edward Black)

Six itinerants encounter a genie,

whose granting of their wishes brings riches and embarrassment.

Archetypal music hall farce descending at moments into surrealism (the lovers are eaten by a bear). All concerned are on top form.

w Marriott Edgar, Val Guest, Ralph Smart,   novel Alf's Button by W. A. Darlington   d Marcel Varnel   ph Arthur Crabtree   md Louis Levy

Bud Flanagan, Chesney Allen, Jimmy Nervo, Teddy Knox, Charles Naughton, Jimmy Gold (the six original members of the Crazy Gang), *Alastair Sim,* Wally Patch, Peter Gawthorne

Alias Jesse James*
US   1958   92m   DeLuxe
Hope Enterprises (Jack Hope)

An incompetent insurance salesman sells a policy to Jesse James and has to protect his client until he can get it back.

Ho-hum star comedy saved by a climax in which Hope is protected by every cowboy star in Hollywood.

w William Bowers, D. D. Beauchamp   d Norman Z. McLeod   ph Lionel Lindon   m Joseph J. Lilley

Bob Hope, Rhonda Fleming, Wendell Corey, Jim Davis, Will Wright

Alice*
US   1990   106m   Duart
Orion/Jack Rollins, Charles H. Joffe
V, L

A bored housewife indulges in a fantasy life.

Moderately amusing comedy of a search for individuality.

wd Woody Allen   ph Carlo di Palma   pd Santo Loquasto   ad Speed Hopkins

Mia Farrow, Joe Mantegna, Alec Baldwin, Blythe Danner, Judy Davis, William Hurt, Keye Luke, Bernadette Peters, Cybill Shepherd, Gwen Verdon

'A likable little pic that will please his fans.' – *Variety*
AAN: best original screenplay

Alive and Kicking*
GB   1958   94m   bw
ABP (Victor Skutezky)

Three old ladies escape from a home to an Irish island.

Agreeable minor comedy, a showcase for its elderly but vigorous stars.

w Denis Cannan   d Cyril Frankel   ph Gilbert Taylor   m Philip Green

Sybil Thorndike, Kathleen Harrison, Estelle Winwood, Stanley Holloway, Joyce Carey, Eric Pohlmann, Colin Gordon

'How Far Would You Go To Make A Wish Come True?'
All I Want For Christmas
US   1991   92m   Technicolor
Paramount (Marykay Powell)
V, L

The Christmas wish of two children is that their divorced parents should get together again.

Dim comedy that even the season of good-will cannot make palatable.

w Thom Eberhardt, Richard Kramer   d Robert Lieberman   ph Robbie Greenberg   m Bruce Broughton   pd Herman Zimmerman   ed Richard Berger, Dean Goodhill

Ethan Randall, Thora Birch, Harley

Jane Kozak, Jamey Sheridan, Lillian Brooks, Lauren Bacall

All in a Night's Work
US 1961 94m Technicolor
Paramount/Hal B. Wallis-Joseph Hazen
V

A publishing heir falls for a girl he suspects of having been his uncle's mistress.

Unpolished and not very amusing comedy which falters after an intriguing start.

w Edmund Beloin, Maurice Richlin, Sidney Sheldon   d Joseph Anthony   ph Joseph LaShelle   m André Previn

Shirley Maclaine, Dean Martin, Charles Ruggles, Cliff Robertson, Norma Crane, Gale Gordon, Jerome Cowan, Jack Weston

'Tame and aimless sex-and-big-business comedy.' – MFB

All of Me
US 1984 91m Technicolor
Thorn-EMI/Kings Road/Universal (Stephen Friedman)
V

A guru accidentally transfers a woman's soul after death into her lawyer's body.

Curiously vulgar sitcom with a familiar team trying and failing to go one better on The Man With Two Brains.

w Phil Alden Robinson   novel Me Two by Ed Davis   d Carl Reiner   ph Richard H. Kline   m Patrick Williams   pd Edward Carfagno   ed Bud Molin

Steve Martin, Lily Tomlin, Victoria Tennant, Madolyn Smith, Dana Elcar

All the Marbles . . .
US 1981 113m Metrocolor
MGM/Aldrich Company (William Aldrich)
GB title: The California Dolls

Problems of a women's wrestling team in the midwest.

Tasteless and tedious exploitation comedy with just a few flashes of the director's old flair.

w Mel Frohman   d Robert Aldrich   ph Joseph Biroc   m Frank de Vol   pd Carl Anderson   ed Irving C. Rosenblum, Richard Lane

Peter Falk, Vicki Frederick, Laurene Landon, Burt Young, Tracy Reed

All the Way Up*
GB 1970 97m Technicolor
Granada/EMI (Philip Mackie)

Social-climbing Dad makes his way by treachery and blackmail, but gets his come-uppance when his son takes after him.

Crudely farcical adaptation of a thoughtful comedy of its time; the treatment works in fits and starts but leaves one in no mood for the talkative finale.

w Philip Mackie   play Semi Detached by David Turner   d James MacTaggart   ph Dick Bush   m Howard Blake

Warren Mitchell, Pat Heywood, Elaine Taylor, Kenneth Cranham, Vanessa Howard, Richard Briers, Adrienne Posta, Bill Fraser

An Alligator Named Daisy
GB 1955 88m Technicolor Vistavision
Rank (Raymond Stross)

A young songwriter finds himself saddled with a pet alligator.

The ultimate in silly animal comedies, this does score a few laughs.

w Jack Davies   *novel* Charles Terrot   *d* J. Lee-Thompson
ph Reg Wyer   *m* Stanley Black

Donald Sinden, Diana Dors, Jean Carson, James Robertson Justice, Stanley Holloway, Roland Culver, Margaret Rutherford, Avice Landone, Richard Wattis, Frankie Howerd, Jimmy Edwards, Gilbert Harding

'Apart from a fairly Kafkaesque scene in which Daisy is discovered in an upright piano, the situation is treated with little wit or comic invention.' – *MFB*

Almost Summer
US   1978   88m   colour
Universal (Rob Cohen)

High-school students hold an election for their new president.

Mercifully short farcical comedy, aimed at a teenage audience.

w Judith Berg, Sandra Berg, Martin Davidson, Marc Reid Rubel
d Martin Davidson   *ph* Stevan Larner   *m* Ron Altbach, Charles Lloyd   *ad* William F. Hiney
ed Lynzee Klingman

John Friedrich, Bruno Kirby, Lee Purcell, Didi Conn, Thomas Carter, Tim Matheson, Patronia Paley

Alvin Purple
Australia   1973   97m   colour
Hexagon (Tim Burstall)

A young man who finds himself irresistible to women finally lands a job . . . as gardener in a convent.

Dismal sex farce which nevertheless helped to start the present world-wide popularity of Australian cinema. It

took over a million dollars at the Australian box-office.

w Alan Hopgood   *d* Tim Burstall

Graeme Blundell, Abigail, Lynette Curran, Christine Amor, Dina Mann

† A sequel *Alvin Rides Again* (qv) followed.

Alvin Rides Again
Australia   1974   89m   colour
Hexagon (Tim Burstall)

Alvin continues to be irresistible to women.

Dire sequel to dim comedy, but one that failed to find an appreciative audience.

w Alan Hopgood   *d* David Bilcock, Robin Copping

Graeme Blundell, Alan Finney, Frank Thring, Chantal Contouri, Abigail

Amazon Women on the Moon
US   1987   85m   colour
Universal (Robert K. Weiss)
L

A parody of a 1950s low-budget science fiction movie is interrupted by a series of supposedly comic sketches.

While the parody is precise and amusing, the surrounding material, which occupies the majority of the film, is weak and silly.

w Michael Barrie, Jim Mulholland
d Joe Dante, Carl Gottlieb, Peter Horton, John Landis, Robert K. Weiss   *ph* Daniel Pearl   *ed* Bert Lovitt, Marshall Harvey, Malcolm Campbell

Rosanna Arquette, Ralph Bellamy, Carrie Fisher, Griffin Dunne, Steve Guttenberg, Michelle Pfeiffer

The Ambassador's Daughter*
US   1956   102m   Technicolor
   Cinemascope
UA/Norman Krasna

An American senator in Paris decides that the presence of US forces in Paris constitutes a moral danger. The ambassador's daughter decides to investigate.

Thin comedy of the old-fashioned type: smart lines and intimate playing not helped by the vast screen.

wd Norman Krasna   *ph* Michael Kelber   *m* Jacques Metehen

Olivia de Havilland, John Forsythe, Edward Arnold, Adolphe Menjou, Myrna Loy, Francis Lederer, Tommy Noonan, Minor Watson

'An experienced cast approach the story's frivolities with poise and style.' – *MFB*

The Americanization of Emily*
US   1964   115m   bw
MGM/Filmways (John Calley)

World War II: just before the Normandy landings, a war widow driver falls for an American commander who is a self-confessed coward.

Bizarre comedy full of eccentric characters, an uneasy choice for its female star but otherwise successful in patches in its random distillation of black comedy, sex and the tumbling of old-fashioned virtues.

w Paddy Chayevsky   *novel* William Bradford Huie   *d* Arthur Hiller *ph* Philip Lathrop, Chris Challis *m* Johnny Mandel

Julie Andrews, James Garner, *Melvyn Douglas*, James Coburn, Liz Fraser, Joyce Grenfell, Edward Binns, Keenan Wynn, William Windom

'Out of it all there comes the definite feeling that Hitler's war is incidental to Paddy Chayevsky's war of ideas . . . no plot synopsis could begin to suggest how much the characters talk.' – *MFB*
AAN: Philip Lathrop

'The rollicking story of a ribald century that should have been ashamed of itself!'
The Amorous Adventures of Moll Flanders
GB   1965   125m   Technicolor
   Panavision
Paramount/Winchester (Marcel Hellman)

An ambitious servant girl loses her virtue to a succession of rich gentlemen but finally settles for a highwayman.

The aim was to make a female *Tom Jones*, but this bawdy romp never achieves the freewheeling fluency of that surprise success, and a vacuous central performance makes the constant couplings more boring than exciting.

w Dennis Cannan, Roland Kibbee *novel* Daniel Defoe   *d* Terence Young   *ph* Ted Moore   *m* John Addison   *pd* Syd Cain

Kim Novak, Richard Johnson, George Sanders, Lilli Palmer, Angela Lansbury, Leo McKern, Vittorio de Sica, Cecil Parker, Daniel Massey

'Further from Defoe than *Tom Jones* was from Fielding, but with much the same combination of crude table manners and clean sets to stand in for period flavour.' – *MFB*

The Amorous Prawn*
GB   1962   89m   bw
BL/Covent Garden (Leslie Gilliat)
US title: *The Playgirl and the War Minister*
   (an attempt to cash in on the Profumo
   case)

A hard-up general's wife invites American paying guests to their official highland home.

This film version of a stage success seems very mild, but the cast is eager to please: the result is a frantic high class farce.

w Anthony Kimmins, Nicholas Phipps   play Anthony Kimmins
d Anthony Kimmins   ph Wilkie Cooper   m John Barry

Joan Greenwood, Ian Carmichael, Cecil Parker, Dennis Price, Robert Beatty, Finlay Currie, Liz Fraser, Derek Nimmo

And Now for Something Completely Different**
GB   1971   88m   colour
Columbia/Kettledrum/Python (Patricia Casey)
L

Monty Python's Flying Circus perform again a selection of sketches from the BBC television series.

The first Monty Python film, intended to introduce the team's humour to an American audience. It lacks any overall coherence, but many of the individual sketches are a joy.

w Graham Chapman, John Cleese, Terry Gilliam, Eric Idle, Terry Jones, Michael Palin   d Ian Macnaughton   ph David Muir
ad Colin Grimes   ed Thom Noble

Graham Chapman, John Cleese, Terry Gilliam, Eric Idle, Terry Jones, Michael Palin, Carol Cleveland

'Very funny.' – MFB

'There's nothing but trouble in Paradise

when the bandleader tries to make love to a whole sister act – simultaneously!'

And the Angels Sing*
US   1943   95m   bw
Paramount (E. D. Leshin)

Four singing sisters have hectic adventures with a bandleader.

Mildly disarming romantic comedy with music, more firmly set in a recognizable social milieu than the usual fan product from this studio.

w Melvin Frank, Norman Panama, Claude Binyon   d George Marshall   ph Karl Struss
m Victor Young   m/ly Johnny Burke, Jimmy Van Heusen

Dorothy Lamour, Diana Lynn, Betty Hutton, Mimi Chandler, Fred MacMurray, Raymond Walburn, Eddie Foy Jnr, Frank Albertson, Mikhail Rasumny

'Slapstick sophistication in a sub-Sturges manner.' – MFB
'Cruel, soggily professional, over-elaborate, and inclined towards snobbish whimsy.' – James Agee

Animal Crackers***
US   1930   98m   bw
Paramount
V, L

Thieves covet a valuable oil painting unveiled at a swank party.

An excuse for the Marx Brothers, and a lively one in patches, though sedate and stage bound in treatment. The boys are all in top form, and many of the dialogue exchanges are classics.

w Morrie Ryskind   musical play Morrie Ryskind, George F. Kaufman   d Victor Heerman
ph George Folsey   m/ly Bert Kalmar, Harry Ruby

Groucho, Chico, Harpo, Zeppo, Margaret

Dumont, Lillian Roth, Louis Sorin, Robert Greig, Hal Thompson

GROUCHO: 'You're the most beautiful woman I've ever seen, which doesn't say much for you.'

GROUCHO: 'One morning I shot an elephant in my pajamas. How he got into my pajamas I'll never know.'

GUESTS: 'Hooray for Captain Spaulding, the African explorer!'

GROUCHO: 'Did someone call me schnorrer?'

GUESTS: 'Hooray, hooray, hooray!'

ZEPPO: 'He went into the jungle, where all the monkeys *throw* nuts.'

GROUCHO: 'If I stay here, I'll *go* nuts.'

GUESTS:
'Hooray, hooray, hooray!
He put all his reliance
In courage and defiance
And risked his life for science.'

GROUCHO: 'Hey, hey!'

MRS RITTENHOUSE: 'He is the only white man who covered every acre . . .'

GROUCHO: 'I think I'll try and make her . . .'

GUESTS: 'Hooray, hooray, hooray!'

'A hit on the screen before it opened, and in the money plenty.' – *Variety*

Annie Hall***
US   1977   93m   DeLuxe
UA/Jack Rollins-Charles H. Joffe (Fred T. Gallo)
V, L
Sub-title: *A Nervous Romance*

Against the neuroses of New York and Los Angeles, a Jewish comedian has an affair with a midwestern girl.

Semi-serious collage of jokes and bits of technique, some of the former very funny and some of the latter very successful. For no very good reason it hit the box-office spot and turned its creator, of whom it is very typical,

from a minority performer to a superstar.

w Woody Allen, Marshall Brickman   *d* Woody Allen
ph Gordon Willis   *m* various

Woody Allen, Diane Keaton, Tony Roberts, Carol Kane, Paul Simon, Shelly Duvall

ALLEN: 'Hey, don't knock masturbation. It's sex with someone I love.'

'The film's priceless vignettes about the difficulties in chitchatting with strangers, the awkward moments in family visits, and the frequent breakdowns in communication and failures in intimacy, its reminiscences about the palpable horrors of growing up in Brooklyn, and its comic encounters with lobsters in the kitchen or spiders in the bathroom, all seem like snapshots from Allen and Keaton's own romance.' – *Les Keyser, Hollywood in the Seventies*

† The narrative supposedly mirrors the real-life affair of the stars, who separated before the film came out. (Diane Keaton's family name is Hall.)

AA: best picture; script; direction; Diane Keaton
AAN: Woody Allen (as actor)

Another Fine Mess**
US   1930   30m   bw
Hal Roach

On the run from a cop, Stan and Ollie masquerade as master and maid.

Elaborate star comedy with spoken introduction instead of titles; very satisfying but not quite vintage.

w H. M. Walker, from a sketch by Stan Laurel's father   *d* James Parrott

Laurel and Hardy, James Finlayson, Thelma Todd, Charles Gerrard

Any Old Port*
US 1932 20m bw
Hal Roach
V

Stan and Ollie are sailors on leave, and Ollie enters Stan for a boxing match.

Minor star comedy with good moments but a weak finish.

w H. M. Walker   d James W. Horne

Laurel and Hardy, Walter Long

Any Wednesday*
US 1966 109m Technicolor
Warner (Julius J. Epstein)
GB title: Bachelor Girl Apartment

A millionaire businessman spends every Wednesday with his mistress, but complications arise when his young associate is accidentally sent to use the company flat.

Overlong screen version of a thinly scripted Broadway success in which yawns gradually overtake laughs.

w Julius J. Epstein   play Muriel Resnik   d Robert Ellis Miller
ph Harold Lipstein   m George Duning

Jane Fonda, Dean Jones, Jason Robards Jnr, Rosemary Murphy (a breath of air as the deceived wife who doesn't mind), Ann Prentiss, King Moody

Any Which Way You Can
US 1980 116m DeLuxe
Malpaso/Warner (Fritz Manes)
V

The hero of Every Which Way But Loose becomes involved in further brawls and car crashes, with the help of his friendly orang-utan.

A sequel designed entirely for the box-office, its tone set by the scene in which the villains on motorcycles are covered in tar.

w Stanford Sherman   d Buddy Van Horn   ph David Worth   md Steve Dorf   pd William J. Creber
ed Ferris Webster, Ron Spang

Clint Eastwood, Ruth Gordon, Sondra Locke, Geoffrey Lewis, William Smith, Harry Guardino

'This kind of thing is clearly beyond or beneath criticism.' – Variety
'Where the previous comedy set up a zany situation, this one ploughs it into the ground.' – Daily Mail

'Movie-wise, there has never been anything like it – laugh-wise, love-wise, or otherwise-wise!'

The Apartment**
US 1960 125m bw Panavision
UA/Mirisch (Billy Wilder)
V, L

A lonely, ambitious clerk rents out his apartment to philandering executives and finds that one of them is after his own girl.

Overlong and patchy but agreeably mordant and cynical comedy with a sparkling view of city office life and some deftly handled individual sequences.

w Billy Wilder, I. A. L. Diamond
d Billy Wilder   ph Joseph LaShelle   m Adolph Deutsch
ad Alexander Trauner   ed Daniel Mandell

Jack Lemmon (C. C. Baxter), Shirley Maclaine (Miss Kubelik), Fred MacMurray (Jeff D. Sheldrake), Ray Walston (Joe Dobisch), Jack Kruschen (Dr Dreyfuss), Joan Shawlee (Sylvia), Edie Adams (Miss Olsen), David Lewis (Al Kirkeby)

Baxter's opening narration: 'On November 1st, 1959, the population of New York City was 8,042,753. If you laid all these people end to end, figuring an average height of five feet six and a half inches, they would reach from Times Square to the outskirts of Karachi, Pakistan. I know facts like this because I work for an insurance company – Consolidated Life of New York. We are one of the top five companies in the country. Last year we wrote nine point three billion dollars worth of policies. Our home office has 31,259 employees, which is more than the entire population of Natchez, Mississippi, or Gallup, New Mexico. I work on the 19th floor – Ordinary Policy department – Premium Accounting division – Section W – desk number 861.'

BAXTER: 'Miss Kubelik, one doesn't get to be a second administrative assistant around here unless he's a pretty good judge of character, and as far as I'm concerned you're tops. I mean, decency-wise and otherwise-wise.'

BAXTER: 'You know, I used to live like Robinson Crusoe – shipwrecked among eight million people. Then one day I saw a footprint in the sand and there you were. It's a wonderful thing, dinner for two.'

MISS KUBELIK: 'Shut up and deal.' (*Last line of film.*)

'Without either style or taste, shifting gears between pathos and slapstick without any transition.' – *Dwight MacDonald*
'Billy Wilder directed this acrid story as if it were a comedy, which is a cheat, considering that it involves pimping and a suicide attempt and many shades of craven ethics.' – *New Yorker, 1980*

AA: best picture; Billy Wilder, I. A. L. Diamond (as writers); Billy Wilder (as director)
AAN: Joseph LaShelle; Jack Lemmon; Shirley Maclaine; Jack Kruschen; art direction; editing

'They came home with the milk!'
Appointment with Venus**
GB 1951 89m bw
GFD/British Film Makers (Betty E. Box)
US title: *Island Rescue*

During World War II, a pedigree cow is rescued from the German-occupied Channel Islands.

Curious but generally agreeable mixture of comedy and war adventure, pleasantly shot on Sark.

w Nicholas Phipps   *novel* Jerrard Tickell   d Ralph Thomas
ph Ernest Steward   m Benjamin Frankel

David Niven, Glynis Johns, George Coulouris, Barry Jones, Kenneth More, Noel Purcell, Bernard Lee, Jeremy Spenser

The April Fools*
US 1969 95m Technicolor Panavision
Cinema Center/Jalem (Gordon Carroll)

An unhappy New York husband elopes to Paris with an unhappy wife.

Whimsical romantic comedy which rather strains its resources without giving full value for money in romance, humour or simple charm. Good moments, though.

w Hal Dresner   d Stuart Rosenberg   ph Michel Hugo
m Marvin Hamlisch   pd Richard Sylbert

Jack Lemmon, Catherine Deneuve, Myrna Loy, Charles Boyer, Peter Lawford, Jack Weston, Harvey Korman, Sally Kellerman

'Painfully modish, from the opening party in an apartment filled with fashionable objets d'art to the final mad dash to the airport in an expensive sports car.' – *MFB*

Are You Being Served?

GB   1977   95m   Technicolor
EMI (Andrew Mitchell)
V

The staff of the clothing section of a department store go on holiday to the Costa Plonka.

Feeble enlargement of an old-fashioned but very popular TV series relying heavily on sexual badinage and ancient jokes.

w Jeremy Lloyd, David Croft
d Bob Kellett   *ph* Jack Atcheler
m various

John Inman, Frank Thornton, Mollie Sugden, Trevor Bannister, Wendy Richard, Arthur Brough, Nicholas Smith, Arthur English, Harold Bennett, Glyn Houston

'A withering selection of patent British puns.' – *John Pym, MFB*

Arsenic and Old Lace***

US   1942 (released 1944)   118m
  bw
Warner (Frank Capra)
V, L

Two dear, well-meaning old ladies invite lonely old men to their Brooklyn home, poison them with elderberry wine, and have their mad brother, who believes the corpses are yellow fever victims, bury them in the cellar. A homicidal nephew then turns up with bodies of his own.

A model for stage play adaptations, this famous black farce provided a frenzy of hilarious activity, and its flippant attitude to death was better received in wartime than would have been the case earlier or later. The director coaxes some perfect if overstated performances from his star cast, and added his own flair for perpetuating a hubbub.

w Julius J. and Philip G. Epstein, with help from Howard Lindsay, Russel Crouse   *play* Joseph Kesselring
d Frank Capra   *ph* Sol Polito
m Max Steiner

Cary Grant (Mortimer Brewster), *Josephine Hull* (Abby Brewster), *Jean Adair* (Martha Brewster), Priscilla Lane (Elaine Harper), Raymond Massey (Jonathan Brewster), *John Alexander* (Teddy Brewster), Peter Lorre (Dr Einstein), James Gleason (Lt Rooney), Jack Carson (officer O'Hara), Edward Everett Horton (Mr Witherspoon), Grant Mitchell (Reverend Harper)
  MORTIMER: 'Insanity runs in my family. It practically gallops.'
  MARTHA: 'One of our gentlemen found time to say "How delicious!" before he died. . . .'

'I race cars, I play tennis, I fondle women, but I have weekends off and I am my own boss!'
Arthur*

US   1981   97m   Technicolor
Warner/Orion (Robert Greenhut)
V, L

A rich New York layabout is forced to moderate his life style in order to qualify for his inheritance.

An unattractive excuse for the star to do his drunk act. In effect his thunder was stolen by Gielgud as the valet who is not above a few choice four-letter words; but over the whole enterprise hung a pall of desperation. It is a sign of its times that it made a lot of money.

wd Steve Gordon   *ph* Fred
Schuler   *m* Burt Bacharach
pd Stephen Hendrikson

Dudley Moore, *John Gielgud*, Liza
Minnelli, Geraldine Fitzgerald, Jill
Eikenberry, Stephen Elliott

'It comes as no surprise to find the
funniest sequences packed into the
first half-hour.' – *Martyn Auty, MFB*
'Gielgud may be the most poised and
confident funnyman you'll ever see.'
– *New Yorker*
'Arthur may be the surprise hit of
1981, but to me he's a pain in the
neck.' – *Margaret Hinxman, Daily Mail*

† In *Arthur II: On the Rocks* (1988,
113m, Bud Yorkin) the character tried
to sober up with the aid of Liza
Minnelli.

AA: John Gielgud (supporting actor);
song 'Best That You Can Do'(Burt
Bacharach, Carole Bayer Sager,
Christopher Cross, Peter Allen)
AAN: screenplay; Dudley Moore

Artists and Models*
US   1955   109m   Technicolor
    Vistavision
Paramount/Hal B. Wallis

A goonish young man receives
telepathic top secret information in
his nightmares, which are used by his
artist friend in comic strips; foreign
agents and the CIA get interested.

A good zany idea is worked into an
overlong dyspeptic comedy which
neither the stars nor frantic treatment
can hope to save.

w Frank Tashlin, Don McGuire
d Frank Tashlin   *ph* Daniel
Fapp   *m* Walter Scharf

Dean Martin, Jerry Lewis, Shirley
Maclaine, Dorothy Malone, Eddie
Mayehoff, Eva Gabor, Anita Ekberg,
George 'Foghorn' Winslow, Jack Elam

As Long as They're Happy*
GB   1955   91m   Eastmancolor
Rank/Regroup (Raymond Stross)

The suburban home of a London
stockbroker is invaded by an American
sob singer.

Frantic farce expanded from a stage
satire of the Johnnie Ray cult; a patchy
but sometimes funny star vehicle.

w Alan Melville   *play* Vernon
Sylvaine   *d* J. Lee-Thompson
ph Gilbert Taylor   *m* Stanley Black

Jack Buchanan, Brenda de Banzie,
Diana Dors, Jean Carson, Janette Scott,
Susan Stephen, Jerry Wayne, Hugh
McDermott

As You Like It*
GB   1936   96m   bw
TCF/Inter-Allied (Joseph M. Schenck, Paul
    Czinner)

The fortunes of an exiled king take a
turn in the Forest of Arden.

Stylized, rather effete but often
amusing version of Shakespeare's
pastoral comedy.

w J. M. Barrie, Robert Cullen
play William Shakespeare   *d* Paul
Czinner   *ph* Harold Rosson
m William Walton

Elisabeth Bergner, Laurence Olivier,
Sophie Stewart, Leon Quartermaine,
Henry Ainley, Richard Ainley, Felix
Aylmer, Mackenzie Ward, Aubrey
Mather, John Laurie, Peter Bull

'Rather too respectably lighthearted,
but by no means a contemptible
production.' – *New Yorker, 1978*
'There are far too many dull middle-
length shots from a fixed camera, so
that we might just as well be seated
in the circle above the deep wide stage
at Drury Lane.' – *Graham Greene*

Ask a Policeman**
GB   1938   82m   bw
Gainsborough (Edward Black)

In a small coastal village, incompetent policemen accidentally expose smugglers who are scaring the locals with a headless horseman legend.

One of the best comedies of an incomparable team, with smart dialogue, good situations and a measure of suspense.

w *Marriott Edgar, Val Guest, J. O. C. Orton*   d *Marcel Varnel*   ph Derek Williams   md Louis Levy

Will Hay, Moore Marriott, Graham Moffatt, Glennis Lorimer, *Peter Gawthorne, Herbert Lomas*, Charles Oliver

'A good laugh getter and safe second feature on any programme.' – *Variety*

The Assassination Bureau*
GB   1968   110m   Technicolor
Paramount/Heathfield (Michael Relph)

In 1906 a lady journalist breaks up an international gang of professional killers by falling in love with their leader.

Black comedy period pastiche which resolves itself into a series of sketches leading up to a spectacular zeppelin climax. Plenty going on, but the level of wit is not high.

w Michael Relph, Wolf Mankowitz   d Basil Dearden   ph *Geoffrey Unsworth*   m Ron Grainer

Oliver Reed, Diana Rigg, Telly Savalas, Curt Jurgens, Philippe Noiret, Warren Mitchell, Clive Revill, Beryl Reid, Kenneth Griffith

At the Circus**
US   1939   87m   bw
MGM (Mervyn Le Roy)
aka: *The Marx Brothers at the Circus*

A shyster lawyer and two incompetents save a circus from bankruptcy.

This film began the decline of the Marx Brothers; in it nothing is ill done but nothing is very fresh either apart from the rousing finale which shows just what professionalism meant in the old Hollywood. Highlights include Groucho singing about Lydia the tattooed lady, his seduction of Mrs Dukesbury, and the big society party.

w Irving Brecher   d Edward Buzzell   ph Leonard M. Smith   m Franz Waxman   m/ly Harold Arlen, E. Y. Harburg

Groucho, Chico, Harpo, Margaret Dumont, Florence Rice, Kenny Baker, Eve Arden, Nat Pendleton, Fritz Feld   *songs:* 'Lydia', 'Two Blind Loves', 'Step up and Take a Bow'
GROUCHO: 'I don't know what I'm doing here when I could be at home in bed with a hot toddy. That's a drink.'

'Rousing physical comedy and staccato gag dialogue . . . geared for fine b.o. and general audience appeal.' – *Variety*
'We must regretfully accept the fact that, thanks to the Metro millions, the Marx Brothers are finally imprisoned in the Hollywood world.' – *Graham Greene*

At War with the Army
US   1951   93m   bw
Paramount/Fred K. Finklehoffe
V

A couple of song and dance men

have trouble as army recruits.

American service farce, based on a play and confined largely to one set; rather untypical of Martin and Lewis, yet oddly enough the film which sealed their success.

w Fred K. Finklehoffe   play James Allardice   d Hal Walker   ph Stuart Thompson   m Joseph Lilley

Dean Martin, Jerry Lewis, Mike Kellin, Polly Bergen, Jimmie Dundee

Attack of the Killer Tomatoes
US 1978 87m colour
Four Square/NAI

Vegetables go berserk in the big city.

Apparently a cult film made deliberately as such, which is a contradiction in terms. Nothing for the ordinary audience, anyway.

w Costa Dillon, Steve Peace, John de Bello   d John de Bello

David Miller, George Wilson, Sharon Taylor, Jack Riley

'Though the idea sounds funny, actually sitting through nearly 90 minutes of it is enough to make anyone long for *Attack of the Fifty Foot Woman.' – Motion Picture Guide*

Auntie Mame*
US 1958 144m Technirama
Warner (Morton da Costa)

An orphan boy is adopted by his volatile extravagant aunt, whose giddy escapades fill his memory of the twenties and thirties.

A rather unsatisfactory star revue from a book and play later turned into a musical, *Mame.* A few splendid moments, otherwise rather dull and irritating.

w Betty Comden, Adolph Green

play Jerome Lawrence, Robert E. Lee   novel Patrick Dennis
d Morton da Costa   ph Harry Stradling   m Bronislau Kaper
ad Malcolm Bert   ed William Ziegler

Rosalind Russell, Forrest Tucker, Coral Browne, Fred Clark, Roger Smith, Patric Knowles, Peggy Cass, Lee Patrick, Joanna Barnes
AAN: best picture; Harry Stradling; Rosalind Russell; Peggy Cass; art direction; editing

Author, Author!*
US 1982 109m TVC Color
TCF (Irwin Winkler)

A Broadway playwright has worries about his wife's fidelity.

Like a sixties update of *All About Eve*, this thin but sometimes witty sex-behind-the-footlights comedy had nothing to offer the general audience of the eighties, and one can only speculate as to why it was made. The acting does help, but it's a long haul.

w Israel Horovitz   d Arthur Hiller   ph Victor J. Kemper
m Dave Grusin   pd Gene Rudolf
ed William Reynolds

Al Pacino, Dyan Cannon, Tuesday Weld, Bob Dishy, Bob Elliott

'In trying to dig a little deeper than the average Neil Simon comedy, it only prepares its own grave.' – Observer

'When someone knocks at your door and says "Permesso?", be careful before you say...'

Avanti!**
US 1972 144m DeLuxe
UA/Mirisch/Phalanx/Jalem (Billy Wilder)

A young American goes to Ischia to collect the body of his father who has died on holiday. He finds that the fatal accident had also killed his father's mistress, and amid overwhelming bureaucratic problems proceeds to fall in love with her daughter.

Absurdly overlong black comedy, with compensations in the shape of a generally witty script and some fine breakneck sequences of culminating confusion.

w Billy Wilder, I. A. L. Diamond, *play* Samuel Taylor *d* Billy Wilder *ph* Luigi Kuveiller *m* Carlo Rustichelli

Jack Lemmon, Juliet Mills, Clive Revill, Edward Andrews, Gianfranco Barra

Les Aventures de Rabbi Jacob

France/Italy 1973 94m
  Eastmancolor
Fox-Rank/Films Pomereu/Horse Film
  (Bernard Javal)
GB title: *The Mad Adventures of 'Rabbi' Jacob*

A French businessman with anti-Semitic views is forced by an Arab agitator on the run to impersonate a rabbi presiding at a Bar Mitzvah in Paris.

Broad comedy that raises a few laughs at the expense of xenophobia.

w Gérard Oury, Danielle Thompson, Josy Eisenberg *d* Gérard Oury *ph* Henri Decae *m* Vladimir Cosma *ad* Théo Meurisse *ed* Albert Jurgenson

Louis de Funès, Suzy Delair, Marcel Dalio, Claude Giraud, Claude Piéplu, Renzo Montagnani

'Much loved in France, this comedy of errors has not travelled well and turns up in Britain looking painfully unfunny.' – *David McGillivray*

The Awful Truth***

US 1937 90m bw
Columbia (Leo McCarey)

A divorcing couple endure various adventures which lead to reconciliation.

Classic crazy comedy of the thirties, marked by a mixture of sophistication and farce and an irreverent approach to plot.

w Vina Delmar *play* Arthur Richman *d* Leo McCarey *ph* Joseph Walker *md* Morris Stoloff *ed* Al Clark

Irene Dunne, Cary Grant, Ralph Bellamy, Alexander D'Arcy, Cecil Cunningham, Molly Lamont, Esther Dale, Joyce Compton
  IRENE DUNNE: 'You've come back and caught me in the truth, and there's nothing less logical than the truth.'
  CARY GRANT: 'In the spring a young man's fancy lightly turns to what he's been thinking about all winter.'

'Fast, smart comedy that will please everywhere and do strong general biz.' – *Variety*
'The funniest picture of the season.' – *Otis Ferguson*
'Among the ingredients the raising powder is the important thing and out of the oven comes a frothy bit of stuff that leaves no taste in the mouth and is easy on the stomach.' – *Marion Fraser, World Film News*
'Delightfully effective entertainment.' – *Time Out, 1985*

† Remade 1953 as *Let's Do It Again* (qv).

AA: Leo McCarey
AAN: best picture; script; Irene Dunne; Ralph Bellamy; Al Clark

Babes in Toyland**
US 1934 77m bw
Hal Roach
V, L
aka: Wooden Soldiers; March of the Wooden
 Soldiers; Laurel and Hardy in Toyland

Santa Claus's incompetent assistants
accidentally make some giant wooden
soldiers, which come in useful when
a villain tries to take over Toyland.

Comedy operetta in which the stars
have pleasant but not outstanding
material; the style and decor are
however sufficient to preserve the
film as an eccentric minor classic.

w Nick Grinde, Frank Butler
original book Glen MacDonough
d Gus Meins, Charles Rogers
ph Art Lloyd, Francis Corby
m Victor Herbert

Stan Laurel, Oliver Hardy, Charlotte
Henry, Henry Brandon, Felix Knight,
Florence Roberts, Johnny Downs,
Marie Wilson

'It is amusing enough to entertain
older persons who remember when
they were young.' – *Variety*

Babette Goes to War
France 1959 103m
 Eastmancolor Cinemascope
Iéna (Raoul Lévy)
original title: Babette S'en Va-t-en Guerre

In 1940 a French refugee girl is sent
by British intelligence from London
to Paris as bait in a plot to kidnap a
German general and delay the Nazi
invasion of England.

Witless war farce which goes on for
ever.

w Raoul Lévy, Gérard Oury
d Christian-Jaque ph Armand
Thirard m Gilbert Bécaud

Brigitte Bardot, Jacques Charrier,
Hannes Messemer, Yves Vincent,
Ronald Howard, Francis Blanche

'A kind of *Private's Progress* without
comedians.' – *MFB*

The Baby and the Battleship
GB 1956 96m Eastmancolor
British Lion/Jay Lewis

Two sailors hide an Italian baby on
their battleship.

Simple-minded lower decks farce,
with lots of confusion and cooing
over the baby, but not much to
laugh at.

w Jay Lewis, Gilbert Hackforth-
Jones, Bryan Forbes d Jay Lewis
ph Harry Waxman m James
Stevens

John Mills, Richard Attenborough,
André Morell, Bryan Forbes, Michael
Howard, Lisa Gastoni, Ernest Clark,
Lionel Jeffries, Thorley Walters

'In this British film the predicament
is made splendidly funny.' – *Dilys
Powell*

Baby Boom

US 1987 110m colour
UIP/MGM
V, L

The life of a busy executive changes when she acquires a small baby.

Moderately enjoyable comedy, though it lacks any particular distinction.

w Nancy Meyers, Charles Shyer d Charles Shyer ph William A. Fraker m Bill Conti pd Jeffrey Howard ed Lynzee Klingman

Diane Keaton, Harold Ramis, Sam Wanamaker, Sam Shepard, James Spader, Pat Hingle, Britt Leach

'If there were justice in the world of entertainment, *Baby Boom* would be unwatchable. But Diane Keaton gives a smashing, glamorous performance that rides over many of the inanities.' – *Pauline Kael, New Yorker*

Baby Face Morgan

US 1942 60m bw
Jack Schwartz/PRC

The son of a racketeer is made a figurehead by his father's old mob.

Curious comedy of non-violent crime; also non-entertaining.

w Edward Dein, Jack Rubin, Oscar Brodney d Arthur Dreifuss

Richard Cromwell, Mary Carlisle, Robert Armstrong, Chick Chandler, Warren Hymer, Vince Barnett

The Bachelor and the Bobbysoxer***

US 1947 95m bw
RKO (Dore Schary)
L
GB title: *Bachelor Knight*

A lady judge allows her impressionable young sister to get over her crush on an errant playboy by forcing them together.

Simple but unexpectedly delightful vehicle for top comedy talents, entirely pleasant and with several memorable moments.

w Sidney Sheldon d Irving Reis ph Robert de Grasse, Nicholas Musuraca m Leigh Harline

Cary Grant, Myrna Loy, Shirley Temple, Ray Collins, Rudy Vallee, Harry Davenport, Johnny Sands, Don Beddoe

'Sure-fire stuff guaranteed to do no conceivable harm . . . the audience laughed so loud I missed some of the lines.' – *Shirley O'Hara, New Republic*

AA: Sidney Sheldon

Bachelor Apartment

US 1931 77m bw
RKO (William Le Baron)

A virtuous working girl in New York falls for a rich woman-chasing bachelor.

Mildly agreeable early talking romantic comedy.

w J. Walter Ruben, John Howard Lawson d Lowell Sherman ph Leo Tover

Irene Dunne, Lowell Sherman, Mae Murray, Norman Kerry, Claudia Dell, Ivan Lebedeff

'It oversteps the reasonable limits of sophisticated art . . . thus the film is doubtful for small towns.' – *Variety*

Bachelor Flat

US 1961 91m DeLuxe
Cinemascope
TCF/Jack Cummings

An English professor at an American university is unrelentingly pursued by girls.

Flat one-joke comedy which simply hasn't the style to sustain itself.

w Frank Tashlin, Budd Grossman *play* Budd Grossman   *d* Frank Tashlin   *ph* Daniel L. Fapp *m* Johnny Williams

Terry-Thomas, Richard Beymer, Tuesday Weld, Celeste Holm, Francesca Bellini, Howard McNear

Bachelor in Paradise
US   1961   109m   Metrocolor
   Cinemascope
MGM/Ted Richmond

A famous writer of advice to the lovelorn settles incognito in a well-heeled Californian community to observe its social habits.

Mildly amusing satire is too frequently interrupted by unsuitable romantic interludes in this rather ill-considered star comedy.

w Valentine Davies, Hal Kanter *d* Jack Arnold   *ph* Joseph Ruttenberg   *m* Henry Mancini

Bob Hope, Lana Turner, Janis Paige, Don Porter, Paula Prentiss, Jim Hutton, Virginia Grey, Reta Shaw, John McGiver, Agnes Moorehead
AAN: title song (*m* Henry Mancini, *ly* Mack David)

'Just ten tiny fingers and ten tiny toes... Trouble? Scandal? Gosh, nobody knows!'
Bachelor Mother***
US   1939   82m   bw
RKO (B. G. De Sylva)
L

A shopgirl finds an abandoned baby and is thought to be its mother; the department store owner's son is then thought to be the father.

Blithely-scripted comedy which stands the test of time and provided several excellent roles.

w Norman Krasna,   story Felix Jackson   *d* Garson Kanin *ph* Robert de Grasse   *m* Roy Webb

Ginger Rogers, David Niven, Charles Coburn, Frank Albertson, E. E. Clive, Ernest Truex

'Carries some rather spicy lines aimed at the adult trade, but broad enough in implication to catch the fancy of general audiences . . . a surprise laugh hit that will do biz generally and overcome hot weather box office lethargy.' – *Variety*
'An excellent comedy, beautifully done.' – *Richard Mallett, Punch*
'This is the way farce should be handled, with just enough conviction to season its extravagances.' – *New York Times*

† Remade as *Bundle of Joy* (qv).
AAN: Felix Jackson

Bachelor of Hearts
GB   1958   94m   Technicolor
Rank/Independent Artists (Vivian A. Cox)

Adventures of a German student at Cambridge University.

Sometimes agreeable, sometimes annoying, especially when romance gets in the way of the possibilities for fun.

w Leslie Bricusse, Frederic Raphael   *d* Wolf Rilla *ph* Geoffrey Unsworth   *m* Hubert Clifford

Hardy Kruger, Sylvia Syms, Ronald Lewis, Eric Barker, Newton Blick

Bachelor Party
US   1984   105m   DeLuxe
Fox/Aspect Ratio/Twin Continental (Ron Moler, Bob Israel)

A bachelor party is beset by a series of disasters.

Crude, exploitative farce full of physical mess and tending to get most of its humour from the destruction of order and some teetering on the brink of pornography.

w Neal Israel, Pat Proft   story Bob Israel   d Neal Israel   ph Hal Trussell   m Robert Folk
ad Kevin Conlin, Martin Price
ed Tom Walls

Tom Hanks, Tawny Kitaen, Adrian Zmed, George Grizzard, Barbara Stuart, Robert Prescott

Back Roads
US   1981   95m   DeLuxe
  Panavision
CBS Theatrical/Meta Films (Ronald Shedlo)

A hooker and an ex-boxer hitch-hike to California.

Tiresomely with-it update of *It Happened One Night;* the humour and romance of the original are preferable to this dollop of bad language, boring people and bed-hopping.

w Gary Devore   d Martin Ritt
ph John A. Alonzo   m Henry Mancini

Sally Field, Tommy Lee Jones, David Keith, Miriam Colon, Michael Gazzo

'Decidedly sticky, and instantly forgettable.' – *Guardian*

Back Room Boy*
GB   1942   82m   bw
GFD/Gainsborough (Edward Black)
V

A timid meteorologist is sent to an Orkney lighthouse and unmasks a bunch of spies.

Fairly spirited star comedy of interest as a shameless rip-off of *The Ghost Train* and *Oh Mr Porter,* whose plotlines are milked but not improved: note also

that Askey took over Will Hay's discarded stooges.

w Val Guest, Marriott Edgar
d Herbert Mason   ph Jack Cox

Arthur Askey, Moore Marriott, Graham Moffatt, Googie Withers, Vera Frances, John Salew

Back to School
US   1986   94m   DeLuxe
Orion/Paper Clip (Chuck Russell)
V, L

A millionaire enrols in university as a freshman so as to teach his son the ropes.

Crass and ineptly made comedy vehicle for a star with distinct limitations.

w Steven Kampmann, Harold Ramis, Will Porter, Peter Torokvei   d Alan Metter   ph Thomas E. Ackerman   m Danny Elfman
pd David Snyder   ed David Rawlins

Rodney Dangerfield, Sally Kellerman, Burt Young, Keith Gordon, Paxton Whitehead

Bad Behaviour
GB   1993   104m   colour
First Independent/Channel Four/British
  Screen/Parallax (Sarah Curtis)

An Irish couple muddle through life.

A small-scale improvised comedy of minor interest.
d Les Blair   ph Witold Stok

Stephen Rea, Sinead Cusack, Philip Jackson, Clare Higgins, Phil Daniels

Bad Medicine
US   1985   96m   DeLuxe
TCF/Lantana (Alex Winitsky, Arlene Sellers)
V

A student goes to medical school in Mexico.

Condescending farce which the Mexicans certainly won't like. Nothing much in it for general audiences either.

wd Harvey Miller   *novel* Steven Horowitz   *ph* Kelvin Pike   *m* Lalo Schifrin   *pd* Les Dilley

Steve Guttenberg, Alan Arkin, Julie Hagerty, Bill Macy

'With the tone shifting constantly from realistic to slapstick, the film has no center and just sprawls on.' – *Variety*

The Bad News Bears
US   1976   103m   Movielab
Paramount (Stanley Jaffe)
L

An ex-baseball professional coaches a team of tough kids.

Rough-tongued, sentimental star comedy.

w Bill Lancaster   *d* Michael Ritchie   *ph* John A. Alonzo   *m* Jerry Fielding (after Bizet)

Walter Matthau, Tatum O'Neal, Vic Morrow, Joyce Van Patten

The Bad News Bears in Breaking Training
US   1977   100m   Movielab
Paramount/Leonard Goldberg (Fred T. Gallo)

The Bears are invited to play in the Houston Astrodome but have trouble finding a coach.

Dimwitted and alarmingly sentimental sequel to a raucously vulgar oncer which should have been left alone.

w Paul Brickman   *d* Michael

Pressman   *ph* Fred J. Koenekamp   *m* Craig Safan from Tchaikovsky's 1812 Overture   *ed* John W. Wheeler

William Devane, Clifton James, Jackie Earle Haley, Jimmy Baio, Chris Barnes

The Bad News Bears Go to Japan
US   1978   91m   Movielab
Paramount (Michael Ritchie)

Yet another unnecessary sequel with a self-explanatory title.

w Bill Lancaster   *d* John Berry   *ph* Gene Polito   *m* Paul Chihara

Tony Curtis, Jackie Earle Haley, Tomisaburo Wayakama, George Wyner

Bagdad Café***
West Germany   1988   91m   Eastmancolor
Mainline/Pelemele/Pro-Ject (Percy and Eleonore Adlon)
V
aka: *Out of Rosenheim*

A middle-aged Bavarian woman, left stranded in the Mojave desert by her husband, transforms a seedy motel she stumbles across.

High-spirited comedy, full of gentle wit and charm.

w Percy and Eleonore Adlon, Christopher Doherty   *d* Percy Adlon   *ph* Bernd Heinl   *m* Bob Telson   *ad* Bernt Amadeus Capra   *ed* Norbert Herzner

Marianne Sägebrecht, Jack Palance, C. C. H. Pounder, Christine Kaufmann, Monica Calhoun, Darron Flagg

† The success of the film resulted in an American TV series starring Whoopi Goldberg.

Ball of Fire*

US 1941 111m bw
Samuel Goldwyn
working title: *The Professor and the
Burlesque Queen*

Seven professors compiling a
dictionary give shelter to a stripteaser
on the run from gangsters.

Rather overstretched but fitfully
amusing romp inspired by *Snow White
and the Seven Dwarfs*.

w *Charles Brackett, Billy Wilder*
d Howard Hawks   ph Gregg
Toland   m Alfred Newman

Barbara Stanwyck, Gary Cooper,
Oscar Homolka, Henry Travers, S. Z.
Sakall, Tully Marshall, Leonid
Kinskey, Richard Haydn, Aubrey
Mather, Allen Jenkins, Dana
Andrews, Dan Duryea

'It's played as if it were terribly bright,
but it's rather shrill and tiresome.' –
New Yorker, 1982

† Ginger Rogers was first choice for
the Stanwyck role.
AAN: original story (Thomas Monroe,
Billy Wilder); Alfred Newman;
Barbara Stanwyck

The Ballad of Josie

US 1967 102m Techniscope
Universal (Marty Melcher)

Cleared of the manslaughter of her
husband, a Western widow renovates
a derelict ranch and sets up as a sheep
farmer.

Tediously whimsical, unsuitably cast
women's lib comedy with so few
laughs that it may require to be taken
seriously.

w Harold Swanton   d Andrew V.
McLaglen   ph Milton Krasner
m Frank de Vol

Doris Day, Peter Graves, George
Kennedy, William Talman, Andy
Devine, Audrey Christie

Bananas*

US 1971 81m DeLuxe
UA/Rollins and Joffe (Jack Grossberg)
V, L

A meek and mild product tester for a
New York corporation accidentally
becomes a South American rebel
hero.

Disjointed anarchic comedy with
a few good jokes typical of their
author.

w Woody Allen, Mickey Rose
d Woody Allen   ph Andrew M.
Costikyan   m Marvin Hamlisch

Woody Allen, Louise Lasser, Carlos
Montalban, Jacobo Morales

'Full of hilarious comic ideas and
lines, supplied by Allen and his
collaborator; then Allen, the director
and actor, murders them.' – *Stanley
Kauffmann*

† Asked why his film was called
Bananas, Allen replied: 'Because
there are no bananas in it.'

Band Waggon*

GB 1939 85m bw
GFD/Gainsborough (Edward Black)

Comedians running a pirate TV
station in a ghostly castle round up a
gang of spies.

Film version of a long-running radio
comedy series; quite a serviceable
record of a phenomenon.

w Marriott Edgar, Val Guest
d Marcel Varnel   ph Henry Harris

Arthur Askey, Richard Murdoch, Jack
Hylton and his band, Pat Kirkwood,
Moore Marriott, Peter Gawthorne,
Wally Patch, Donald Calthrop

The Bank Dick***
US   1940   73m   bw
Universal
GB title: *The Bank Detective*

In Lompoc, California, a ne'er-do-well accidentally stops a hold-up, is made a bank detective, acquires deeds to a worthless mine and interferes in the production of a film.

Imperfect, but probably the best Fields vehicle there is: the jokes sometimes end in mid-air, but there are delicious moments and very little padding. The character names are sometimes funnier than the script: they include Egbert Sousè (accent grave over the 'e'), J. Pinkerton Snoopington, Ogg Oggilbie and Filthy McNasty.

w Mahatma Kane Jeeves (W. C. Fields)   *d* Eddie Cline
ph Milton Krasner   *md* Charles Previn

W. C. Fields, Franklin Pangborn, Shemp Howard, Jack Norton, Grady Sutton, Cora Witherspoon

'One of the great classics of American comedy.' – *Robert Lewis Taylor*
'When the man is funny he is terrific . . . but the story is makeshift, the other characters are stock types, the only pace discernible is the distance between drinks or the rhythm of the fleeting seconds it takes Fields to size up trouble coming and duck the hell out.' – *Otis Ferguson*
'Individualistic display of broad comedy . . . adequate program supporter.' – *Variety*

† Fields's writing nom-de-plume was allegedly borrowed from noble characters in old English plays he squirmed through as a youth. They kept saying: 'M'hat, m'cane, Jeeves.'

Bank Holiday*
GB   1938   86m   bw
GFD/Gainsborough (Edward Black)
US title: *Three on a Weekend*

The lives of various people intertwine during a day out in Brighton.

Simple but effective slice-of-life comedy-drama, establishing several actors and a director. Still quite refreshing.

w Hans Wilhelm, Rodney Ackland, Roger Burford   *d* Carol Reed
ph Arthur Crabtree   *md* Louis Levy   *ad* Vetchinsky   *ed* R. E. Dearing, Alfred Roome

Margaret Lockwood, Hugh Williams, John Lodge, Kathleen Harrison, Wally Patch, Rene Ray, Linden Travers, Garry Marsh, Wilfrid Lawson

'Ranges from pathos to farce with a nice avoidance of overstatement.' – *Daily Telegraph*

'Break the rules! Make love! Fall over laughing!'
Barefoot in the Park**
US   1967   109m   Technicolor
Paramount/Hal B. Wallis
L

A pair of New York newlyweds rent a cold water flat at the top of a liftless building, and manage to marry the bride's mother to an eccentric neighbour.

Breezy but overlong adaptation of a stage play which succeeded through audience response to its one-liners, which on the screen sometimes fall flat. The people are nice, though.

w Neil Simon   *play* Neil Simon
d Gene Saks   *ph* Joseph LaShelle   *m* Neal Hefti

Robert Redford (Paul Bratter), Jane

Fonda (Corie Bratter), *Mildred Natwick* (Ethel Banks), *Charles Boyer* (Victor Velasco), Herb Edelman (Harry Pepper), Mabel Albertson (Aunt Harriet), Fritz Feld (restaurant owner)

ETHEL: 'Make him feel important. If you do that, you'll have a happy and wonderful marriage – like two out of every ten couples.'

ETHEL: 'I feel like we've died and gone to heaven – only we had to climb up.'

AAN: Mildred Natwick

The Bargee*

GB 1964 106m Techniscope
AB/Galton-Simpson (W. A. Whitaker)

A canal barge Casanova is trapped into marriage.

The long-awaited comedy which was supposed to make a film star out of TV's Young Steptoe turned out to be rough and vulgar but not very funny.

w Ray Galton, Alan Simpson
d Duncan Wood *ph* Harry Waxman *m* Frank Cordell

Harry H. Corbett, Ronnie Barker, Hugh Griffith, Eric Sykes, Julia Foster, Miriam Karlin, Eric Barker, Derek Nimmo, Norman Bird, Richard Briers

Barnacle Bill*

GB 1957 87m bw
Ealing (Michael Balcon)
US title: *All at Sea*

The last of a long line of sailors suffers from seasickness, and takes command of a decaying Victorian pier at an English seaside resort.

Quite an amusing comedy which had the misfortune to come at the tag-end of the Ealing classics and so seemed too mild and predictable. Perhaps it was a little staid.

w T. E. B. Clarke *d* Charles Frend *ph* Douglas Slocombe *m* John Addison

Alec Guinness, Irene Browne, Percy Herbert, Harold Goodwin, Maurice Denham, George Rose, Lionel Jeffries, Victor Maddern

The Battle of the Sexes*

GB 1960 83m bw
Prometheus (Monja Danischewsky)
V

A lady efficiency expert upsets the even tenor of life at an Edinburgh tweed manufactory, and the chief accountant plans to eliminate her.

Sub-Ealing black comedy which tends to misfire despite effort all round.

w Monja Danischewsky *story* The Catbird Seat by James Thurber
d Charles Crichton *ph* Freddie Francis *m* Stanley Black

Peter Sellers, Constance Cummings, Robert Morley, Jameson Clark, Moultrie Kelsall, Alex Mackenzie, Roddy McMillan, Donald Pleasence, Ernest Thesiger

Beau Hunks**

US 1931 40m bw
Hal Roach
V
GB title: *Beau Chumps*

A fool and his friend join the Foreign Legion to forget.

Patchy but amiable star comedy with memorable high spots. In-joke: the woman the whole legion wants to forget is Jean Harlow.

w H. M. Walker *d* James W. Horne

Laurel and Hardy, Charles Middleton

'She's got the biggest six-shooters in the west!'

The Beautiful Blonde from Bashful Bend*

US 1949 77m Technicolor
TCF (Preston Sturges)

A temperamental saloon entertainer accidentally shoots the sheriff and takes refuge as a school-mistress.

A dishevelled Western farce unworthy of its creator, but with the advantage of appearances by many of his usual repertory of players.

wd Preston Sturges   *ph* Harry Jackson   *m* Cyril Mockridge

Betty Grable, Cesar Romero, El Brendel, Hugh Herbert, Rudy Vallee, Olga San Juan, Sterling Holloway, Porter Hall, Esther Howard, Margaret Hamilton

'It erects a fabric of roaring slapstick on a conventional western foundation, and from time to time it succeeds in being very funny.' – *Richard Mallett, Punch*
'Somehow the ramshackle air of Bashful Bend itself seems to have permeated the whole film.' – *MFB*

The Bed Sitting Room*

GB 1969 91m DeLuxe
UA/Oscar Lewenstein (Richard Lester)

Surrealist romance; after a nuclear war, motley survivors in the waste lands turn into bed sitting rooms, cupboards and parakeets.

Arrogantly obscure fantasy, a commercial flop which kept its director in the wilderness for four years. Fans of Monty Python may salvage a joke or two.

w John Antrobus   *play* John Antrobus, Spike Milligan
d Richard Lester   *ph* David

Watkin   *m* Ken Thorne
pd Assheton Gorton

Ralph Richardson, Rita Tushingham, Michael Hordern, Arthur Lowe, Mona Washbourne, Peter Cook, Dudley Moore, Spike Milligan, Harry Secombe, Marty Feldman, Jimmy Edwards

Bedazzled*

GB 1967 96m DeLuxe
  Panavision
TCF/Stanley Donen
V, L

A short order cook is saved from suicide by Mr Spiggott, who offers him seven wishes in exchange for his soul.

A camped-up version of *Faust* which resolves itself into a series of threadbare sketches for the stars. All rather desperate apart from the leaping nuns.

w Peter Cook   *d* Stanley Donen
ph Austin Dempster   *m* Dudley Moore

Peter Cook, Dudley Moore, Michael Bates, Raquel Welch, Eleanor Bron

Bedtime for Bonzo

US 1951 83m bw
U-I (Michel Kraike)

To prove that environment determines character, a chimpanzee is brought up as a human baby.

Very moderate fun and games which proved successful enough for a sequel, *Bonzo Goes to College*.

w Val Burton, Lou Breslow
d Frederick de Cordova   *ph* Carl Guthrie   *m* Frank Skinner

Ronald Reagan, Diana Lynn, Walter Slezak, Lucille Barkley, Herbert Heyes

Bedtime Story*
US 1964 99m Eastmancolor
U-V/Lankershim/Pennebaker (Stanley
    Shapiro)

Two Riviera confidence tricksters
outwit each other.

A fairly lively script is defeated by dull
handling, but performances and
backgrounds are attractive.

w Stanley Shapiro, Paul Henning
d Ralph Levy   ph Clifford Stine
m Hans Salter

David Niven, Marlon Brando, Shirley
Jones, Dody Goodman, Aram
Stephan, Marie Windsor

'The most vulgar and embarrassing
film of the year.' – *Daily Express*

Beer
US 1985 82m DeLuxe
Orion (Robert Chartoff)
original title: *The Selling of America*

A lady executive on Madison Avenue
promotes a brand of beer by promoting
three honest Joes from the street and
turning them into macho media
figures.

Another shred of proof that satire is
what closes Saturday night. A few
smiles, but no release.

w Allan Weissbecker   d Patrick
Kelly   ph Bill Butler   m Bill
Conti   pd Bill Bordie   ed Alan
Heim

Loretta Swit, Rip Torn, Kenneth Mars,
David Alan Grier, William Russ, Dick
Shawn

'The head of the family is the one with the
tail.'

Beethoven
US 1992 87m DeLuxe
UIP/Universal (Joe Medjuck, Michael C.
    Gross)
V

A St Bernard dog causes havoc in a
family household to the delight of the
children and the annoyance of their
father.

Predictable comedy of the dreariest
kind.

w Edmond Dantes, Amy Holden
Jones   d Brian Levant   ph Victor
J. Kemper   m Randy Edelman
pd Alex Tavoularis   ed Sheldon
Kahn, William D. Gordean

Charles Grodin, Bonnie Hunt, Dean
Jones, Oliver Platt, Stanley Tucci,
David Duchovny, Patricia Heaton,
Laurel Cronin, O-Lan Jones

'Could be called harmless if it wasn't
so badly made and blandly
characterised.' – *Derek Malcolm,
Guardian*
'Laugh? We wait like locked-in dogs
whose noses are pressed to the
window for the first sign of life or
human interest coming up the
driveway. Wit we have already
despaired of in reel one.' – *Nigel
Andrews, Financial Times*

† Inevitably, a sequel is on its way.

Beetlejuice
US 1988 92m Technicolor
Warner Bros/Geffen (Michael Bender)
V, L

The newly dead at a New England
barn try to scare off objectionable
new buyers.

Mainly unpleasant and seldom funny
fantasy.

w Michael McDowell, Warren
Skaaren   d Tim Burton
ph Thomas Ackerman   m Danny
Elfman   pd Bo Welch

Alec Baldwin, Geena Davis, Michael
Keaton, Catherine O'Hara, Glenn
Shadix

Behave Yourself*
US   1951   81m   bw
RKO (Jerry Wald, Norman Krasna)

A young married couple and their dog get mixed up in a chain of murders.

Zany black comedy in the wake of *A Slight Case of Murder* and *The Thin Man*. The humour is spread too thin for success.

wd George Beck   *ph* James Wong Howe   *m* Leigh Harline

Farley Granger, Shelley Winters, William Demarest, Francis L. Sullivan, Margalo Gillmore, Lon Chaney, Hans Conried, Elisha Cook Jnr

'Getting there is half the fun; being there is all of it!'

Being There**
US   1979   130m   Metrocolor
Lorimar/North Star/CIP (Andrew Braunsberg)
L

An illiterate gardener is taken for a homespun philosopher and becomes a national celebrity.

Overlong serio-comic parable hinging on a somewhat dubious star performance. Chance made it a popular urban success, but few who saw it were enthused.

w Jerzy Kosinski   *novel* Jerzy Kosinski   *d* Hal Ashby
ph Dianne Schroeder   *m* John Mandel   *pd* Michael Haller

Peter Sellers, Shirley Maclaine, *Melvyn Douglas*, Jack Warden, Richard Dysart, Richard Basehart

'It pulls off its long shot and is a confoundingly provocative movie.' – *Roger Ebert*

AA: Melvyn Douglas

AAN: Peter Sellers

BFA: screenplay

'A bewitching comedy about an enchanting subject!'

Bell, Book and Candle*
US   1958   103m   Technicolor
Columbia/Phoenix (Julian Blaustein)

A publisher slowly becomes aware that his new girl friend is a witch.

A gossamer stage comedy has been fatally flattened in translation; most of the actors are miscast, and sentiment soaks the script. But it remains a civilized entertainment.

w Daniel Taradash   *play* John Van Druten   *d* Richard Quine
ph James Wong Howe   *m* George Duning   *ad* Cary Odell

James Stewart, Kim Novak, Jack Lemmon, Ernie Kovacs, *Hermione Gingold*, Elsa Lanchester, Janice Rule
AAN: art direction

The Bellboy*
US   1960   72m   bw
Paramount/Jerry Lewis Productions (Jerry Lewis)
V, L

An incompetent bellboy causes havoc in a Miami hotel.

Plotless essence of a comedian who divides opinion and will never be better than variable. This ragbag of old gags at least prevents his usual sentimental excesses, and is mercifully short.

wd Jerry Lewis   *ph* Haskell Boggs   *m* Walter Scharf

Jerry Lewis, Alex Gerry, Bob Clayton, Herkie Styles, Milton Berle

La Belle Américaine*

France · 1961 · 101m · bw
(colour finale)
CCFC/Film d'Art/Panorama/Corflor (Henri
Diamant-Berger, Arthur Lesser)
GB/US titles: What a Chassis; The American
Beauty

A Parisian factory worker gets into all
kinds of trouble when he buys an
American supercar for a ridiculously
low price.

Some brilliant gags are separated by
long dull spots of unnecessary
storytelling.

w Robert Dhéry, Pierre Tchernia,
Alfred Adam   d Robert Dhéry
ph Ghislain Cloquet   m Gérard
Calvi

Robert Dhéry, Louis de Funes, Colette
Brosset, Alfred Adam, Bernard
Lavalette, Annie Ducaux

The Belles of St Trinian's*

GB · 1954 · 91m · bw
BL/London Films/Launder and Gilliat
V

At an unruly and bankrupt school for
girls, more time is spent backing horses
than studying subjects, and the
headmistress's bookmaker brother
has a scheme or two of his own.

Fairly successful film version of
Ronald Searle's awful schoolgirl
cartoons, the emphasis shifted to a
grotesque older generation with the
star in drag. An enormous commercial
success, but the three sequels Blue
Murder at St Trinian's, The Pure Hell of
St Trinian's, The Great St Trinian's Train
Robbery went from bad to awful.

w Frank Launder, Sidney Gilliat, Val
Valentine   d Frank Launder
ph Stan Pavey   m Malcolm Arnold

Alastair Sim, George Cole, Joyce
Grenfell, Hermione Baddeley, Betty
Ann Davies, Renée Houston, Beryl
Reid, Irene Handl, Mary Merrall

'Not so much a film as an
entertainment on celluloid, a huge
charade, a rich pile of idiot and
splendidly senseless images.' – David
Robinson

Below Zero**

US · 1930 · 20m · bw
Hal Roach

Street musicians treat a policeman to
lunch on the contents of a found wallet
which turns out to be his.

Slow-paced but likeable star comedy
from their best period.

w H. M. Walker   d James Parrott

Laurel and Hardy, Frank Holliday,
Tiny Sandford

Benchley

The one-reel shorts in which Robert
Benchley, sitting behind a desk,
delivered nonsensical lectures on
aspects of modern life were very
popular with better-class audiences,
and launched Benchley onto his
movie career as a light actor. Here is
a list of them:

1928: THE TREASURER'S REPORT;
THE SEX LIFE OF THE
POLYP; THE SPELLBINDER.
1929: LESSON NUMBER ONE (2
reels); FURNACE TROUBLE
(2 reels); STEWED, FRIED
AND BOILED (2 reels).
1933: YOUR TECHNOCRACY AND
MINE (2 reels).
1935: HOW TO BREAK 90 AT
CROQUET; HOW TO SLEEP
(AA for best short).
1936: HOW TO BEHAVE; HOW TO
TRAIN A DOG; HOW TO VOTE;
HOW TO BE A DETECTIVE.
1937: THE ROMANCE OF

DIGESTION; HOW TO START THE DAY; A NIGHT AT THE MOVIES (AAN for best short).

1938: HOW TO FIGURE INCOME TAX; MUSIC MADE SIMPLE; AN EVENING ALONE; HOW TO RAISE A BABY; THE COURTSHIP OF THE NEWT; HOW TO READ; HOW TO WATCH FOOTBALL; OPENING DAY; MENTAL POISE; HOW TO SUBLET.

1939: AN HOUR FOR LUNCH; DARK MAGIC; HOME EARLY; HOW TO EAT; THE DAY OF REST; SEE YOUR DOCTOR.

1940: THAT INFERIOR FEELING; HOME MOVIES; THE TROUBLE WITH HUSBANDS.

1941: WAITING FOR BABY; CRIME CONTROL; THE FORGOTTEN MAN; HOW TO TAKE A VACATION.

1942: NOTHING BUT NERVES; THE WITNESS; KEEPING IN SHAPE; THE MAN'S ANGLE.

1943: MY TOMATO; NO NEWS IS GOOD NEWS.

1944: IMPORTANT BUSINESS; WHY, DADDY?

1945: BOOGIE WOOGIE (2 reels); I'M A CIVILIAN HERE MYSELF.

† In the late seventies a feature compilation was made under the title *Those Wonderful Benchley Shorts*.

Bernardine*

US   1957   95m   Eastmancolor Cinemascope
TCF (Samuel G. Engel)

A college student forced to swot for exams asks a friend's elder brother to look after his girl.

Henry Aldrich-style high school comedy, showing the lighter side of *Rebel without a Cause*. Notable for the clean-living hero played by a clean-living singing star, and the reappearance of Janet Gaynor for the only time since 1939, in a routine mother role.

w Theodore Reeves   *play* Mary Chase   d Henry Levin   ph Paul Vogel   m Lionel Newman

Pat Boone, Richard Sargent, Terry Moore, *Janet Gaynor*, Walter Abel, Dean Jagger, Natalie Schafer, James Drury

Bert Rigby, You're a Fool

USA   1989   94m   Metrocolor
Warner/Lorimar/A Clear Production (George Shapiro)
L

A former miner becomes a mostly unsuccessful song-and-dance man in Hollywood.

Dim comedy, intended as a showcase for the slight charm of Robert Lindsay.

wd Carl Reiner   ph Jan De Bont   m Ralph Burns   pd Terence Marsh   ad Dianne Wager, Michael Seirton   ed Bud Molin, Stephen Myers

Robert Lindsay, Anne Bancroft, Corbin Bernsen, Robbie Coltrane, Cathryn Bradshaw, Jackie Gayle, Bruno Kirby, Liz Smith, Lila Kaye

'Mixes sentimentality with vulgarity with reckless abandon.' – *John Pym, MFB*

Berth Marks

US   1929   20m   bw   silent
Hal Roach
V, V(C)

Stan and Ollie, on a train, have to share an upper berth.

Overstretched single-situation comedy, one of the team's poorest.

w Leo McCarey, H. M. Walker
d Lewis R. Foster

Laurel and Hardy

Best Defense

US 1984 94m Movielab
Paramount (Gloria Katz)
L

A US tank goes hopelessly out of control in Kuwait; intercut with this are some of the problems which confronted its designer two years earlier.

Weird, unappetizing and disjointed farce, composed mainly of irrelevancies.

w Gloria Katz, Willard Huyck
novel Easy and Hard Ways Out by Robert Grossbach *d* Willard Huyck
ph Don Peterman *m* Patrick Williams *pd* Peter Jamison

Dudley Moore, Eddie Murphy, Kate Capshaw, George Dzundza, Helen Shaver

'As bereft of charm and spontaneity as it is overburdened with tedious gesticulation.' – *Tim Pulleine, MFB*
'About as funny as getting hi-jacked by a group of kamikaze terrorists.' – *Derek Malcolm, Guardian*
'How did I get involved? The door opened, and four men came in carrying a cheque.' – *Eddie Murphy*

Best Friends*

US 1982 116m Technicolor
Warner/Joe Wizan/Norman Jewison
L

Two writers who have enjoyed a peaceful professional relationship find problems when they get married and visit their respective families.

Rather a heavy comedy which seems to have no real point, this gets by on enjoyable sequences and star performances.

w Valerie Curtin, Barry Levinson
d Norman Jewison *ph* Jordan Cronenweth *m* Michel Legrand
ad Joe Russo *ed* Don Zimmerman

Burt Reynolds, Goldie Hawn, Jessica Tandy, Barnard Hughes, Audra Lindley, Keenan Wynn

'A print-out of a script conference at which everyone collapsed at everyone else's contributory sally.' – *Sunday Times*
AAN: song 'How Do You Keep the Music Playing?' (Michel Legrand, Alan and Marilyn Bergman)

The Best House in London*

GB 1968 96m Eastmancolor
MGM/Bridge/Carlo Ponti (Philip Breen, Kurt Unger)

A Victorian publicity agent tries to organize a government-sponsored brothel.

Cheerful slam-bang historical send-up with as many dull thuds of banality as pleasant witticisms.

w Denis Norden *d* Philip Saville *ph* Alex Thompson
m Mischa Spoliansky *pd* Wilfrid Shingleton

David Hemmings, George Sanders, Joanna Pettet, Warren Mitchell, Dany Robin, William Rushton

The Best of Enemies

US/Italy 1961 104m colour
Technirama
Columbia/Dino de Laurentiis

During the Abyssinian campaign of 1941, an Italian and a British officer learn mutual respect.

Mild satirical comedy drama with a few points to make about war; the elements blend rather obviously and dispiritingly.

w Jack Pulman   *d* Guy Hamilton   *ph* Giuseppe Rotunno   *m* Nino Rota

David Niven, Alberto Sordi, Michael Wilding, Amedeo Nazzari, Harry Andrews, David Opatoshu, Kenneth Fortescue, Duncan Macrae

Betsy's Wedding*
US   1990   94m   Technicolor
Warner/Touchstone/Silver Screen Partners IV (Martin Bregman, Louis A. Stroller)
V, L

A father gives his daughter a no-expense-spared wedding.

Intermittently amusing comedy of domestic mishaps.

wd Alan Alda   *ph* Kelvin Pike   *m* Bruce Broughton   *pd* John Jay Moore   *ed* Michael Polakow

Alan Alda, Joey Bishop, Madeline Kahn, Anthony LaPaglia, Catherine O'Hara, Joe Pesci, Molly Ringwald, Ally Sheedy, Burt Young

'Surges ahead with tart one-liners, absurd spectacle, and ebullient side turns.' – *MFB*

Better Late Than Never
US   1983   87m   colour
Warner (Jack Haley Jnr, David Niven Jnr)

From two possibilities, an heiress selects her true grandfather. (Her grandmother wasn't sure.)

Would-be risqué comedy which fails to spark despite the talents involved.

wd Bryan Forbes   *m* Henry Mancini

David Niven, Art Carney, Maggie

Smith, Kimberley Partridge, Catherine Hicks, Lionel Jeffries

'As predictable as a rumbling stomach after a bowl of chilli.' – *Motion Picture Guide*

Better Off Dead
US   1985   98m   Technicolor
Warner/A&M (Michael Jaffe)
V, L

When his fickle girlfriend leaves him, a lonely teenager becomes despondent, but the sun shines when another girl shows interest.

Plotless, almost legless comedy drama with no direction whatever.

wd Savage Steve Holland   *ph* Isidore Mankovsky   *m* Rupert Hine   *pd* Herman Zimmerman

John Cusack, David Ogden Stiers, Kim Darby, Demian Slade, Scotter Stevens, Diane Franklin

'Kids deserve better than this.' – *Variety*

Beverly Hills Cop**
US   1984   105m   Technicolor
Paramount/Don Simpson/Jerry Bruckheimer
V, L

A Detroit cop races to Los Angeles to track down the killers of his best friend.

Filled with foul language and frenetic action, this rough-edged action comedy became one of the top box-office grossers of its year. So much for its year.

w Daniel Petrie Jnr   *d* Martin Brest   *ph* Bruce Surtees   *m* Harold Faltermeyer   *pd* Angelo Graham   *ed* Billy Weber, Arthur O. Coburn

Eddie Murphy, Judge Reinhold, Lisa

Eilbacher, John Ashton, Ronny Cox, Steven Berkoff

'The film's only function is to provide Murphy with the opportunity to work a dozen or so variations on his familiar and oddly endearing routine.' – *Time*

† The role was originally tailored for Sylvester Stallone.
AAN: original screenplay

Beverly Hills Cop 2
US 1987 102m Technicolor
  Panavision
UIP/Paramount/Don Simpson-Jerry
  Bruckheimer/Eddie Murphy
V, L

A cop returns to Beverly Hills to solve a series of crimes.

Further helpings from the same bowl. In no respect is the second film an improvement on the first.

w Larry Ferguson, Warren Skaaren, David Giler, Dennis Klein *story* Eddie Murphy, Robert D. Wachs *d* Tony Scott *ph* Jeffrey L. Kimball *m* Harold Faltermeyer *pd* Ken Davis *ed* Billy Weber, Chris Lebenzon, Michael Tronick

Eddie Murphy, Judge Reinhold, Jurgen Prochnow, Ronnie Cox, Allen Garfield, Brigitte Nielsen, Dean Stockwell, Paul Guilfoyle

'A noisy, numbing, unimaginative, heartless remake . . . all has gone sour and cold.' – *Daily Variety*

Big**
US 1988 102m DuArt/DeLuxe
TCF (James L. Brooks, Robert Greenhut, Anne Spielberg, Gary Ross)
V

A 13-year-old boy has his wish to grow 'big' granted by a carnival wishing machine.

Magic fun, better done than it has been since *Turnabout* in 1940.

w Gary Ross, Anne Spielberg *d* Penny Marshall *ph* Barry Sonnenfeld *m* Howard Shore *pd* Santo Loquasto

Tom Hanks, Elizabeth Perkins, John Heard, Jared Rushton, Robert Loggia, David Moscow
AAN: Tom Hanks; best original screenplay

The Big Bus
US 1976 88m Movielab
  Panavision
Paramount (Fred Freeman, Lawrence J. Cohen)

Misadventures of a giant atomic-powered bus on its first cross-country trip.

Rather feeble spoof on disaster pictures, with some good moments.

w Fred Freeman, Lawrence J. Cohen *d* James Frawley *ph* Harry Stradling Jnr *m* David Shire *pd* Joel Schiller

Joseph Bologna, Stockard Channing, John Beck, René Auberjonois, Ned Beatty, Bob Dishy, Jose Ferrer, Ruth Gordon, Harold Gould, Larry Hagman, Sally Kellerman, Richard Mulligan, Lynn Redgrave

'It's all fast, bright, surface stuff, almost obsessively intent on never letting a laugh get away, misfiring, backfiring, skidding and crashing gears gaily all the way, often quite as thrilling, if not always as ludicrous, as some of the films it mocks.' – *Alan Brien, Sunday Times*
'It has been produced with such consummate bad taste, schlock acting and feeble attempts at verbal and

visual humour that whatever laughs are engendered are at it rather than with it.' – *Dave Pomeroy, Film Information*

Big Business****
US   1929   20m   bw   silent
Hal Roach
V

Stan and Ollie fail to sell a Christmas tree to a belligerent householder.

Classic silent comedy consisting largely of a brilliant tit-for-tat routine of reciprocal destruction, to which scripting, acting and editing equally combine.

w Leo McCarey, H. M. Walker *d* James W. Horne   *ed* Richard Currier

Laurel and Hardy, James Finlayson

Big Business
US   1988   97m   Metrocolor
Buena Vista/Touchstone/Silver Screen
   Partners III (Steve Tisch, Michael Peyser)
V

Big business complexities are made more so by the fact that the principals are discovered to have been exchanged at birth.

Loud-shouting farce which just about gets by on star value.

w Dori Pierson, Marc Rubel   *d* Jim Abrahams   *ph* Dean Cundey *m* Lee Holdridge

Bette Midler, Lily Tomlin, Fred Ward, Edward Herrmann

The Big Noise
US   1944   74m   bw
TCF (Sol M. Wurtzel)

Two incompetent detectives accidentally round up a spy gang.

Very thin star vehicle consisting largely of poorly staged and warmed up versions of a few old routines.

w Scott Darling   *d* Mal St Clair *ph* Joe MacDonald   *m* Cyril Mockridge

Stan Laurel, Oliver Hardy, Doris Merrick, Arthur Space, Jack Norton

The Big Parade of Comedy**
US   1964   90m approx   bw
MGM (Robert Youngson)
aka: *MGM's Big Parade of Comedy*

A compilation by Robert Youngson, including material as diverse as *Ninotchka*, Laurel and Hardy and the Marx Brothers.

One is grateful for the excerpts but the assembly of them is somewhat graceless.

The Big Picture**
US   1988   101m   DeLuxe
Hobo/Columbia (Michael Varhol)
V, L

A student film maker goes to Hollywood.

Amusing satire of the movie business.

w Michael Varhol, Christopher Guest, Michael McKean   *d* Christopher Guest   *ph* Jeff Jur   *m* David Nichtern   *pd* Joseph T. Garrity *ad* Patrick Tagliaferro   *ed* Martin Nicholson

Kevin Bacon, Emily Longstreth, J. T. Walsh, Jennifer Jason Leigh, Martin Short, Michael McKean, Kim Miyori, Teri Hatcher

'He Wants The Key To Her Heart. They Want The Key To His Car.'
The Big Steal*
Australia   1990   100m   colour
Hobo/Cascade/Film Victoria/Australia Film
   Finance Corp. (David Parker, Nadia Tass)
V

An 18-year-old boy plots revenge against the car salesman who sold him a faulty Jaguar with which he had hoped to impress his new girl-friend.

Mildly amusing comedy of the eccentricity underlying suburban life.

w David Parker, Max Dunn
d Nadia Tass   ph David Parker
m Philip Judd   pd Paddy
Reardon   ed Peter Carrodus

Ben Mendelsohn, Claudia Karvan, Steve Bisley, Marshall Napier, Damon Herriman, Angelo D'Angelo, Tim Robertson, Maggie King

'Has a low-key charm that's appealing, and a couple of riotously funny scenes.' – Variety

The Big Store*
US   1941   83m   bw
MGM (Louis K. Sidney)
V

An eccentric private eye saves a department store from the hands of crooks.

Reckoned to be the Marx Brothers' weakest MGM vehicle, but it has its moments, especially the first reel and the bedding department scene, also Groucho's rendering of 'Sing While You Sell'.

w Sid Kuller, Hal Fimberg, Ray Golden   d Charles Reisner
ph Charles Lawton   m George Stoll

Groucho, Chico, Harpo, Margaret Dumont, Douglass Dumbrille, Tony Martin, Virginia Grey, Virginia O'Brien, Henry Armetta

Big Trouble
US   1984/86   93m   Metrocolor
Columbia/Delphi III (Michael Lobell)
L

Two incompetent con men try to swindle an insurance company.

Witless comic farrago apparently designed to cash in on the success of The In-Laws by utilizing the plot of Double Indemnity. Not a goer.

w Warren Bogle (Andrew Bergman)   d John Cassavetes
ph Bill Butler   m Bill Conti

Peter Falk, Alan Arkin, Beverly D'Angelo, Charles Durning, Paul Dooley, Robert Stack, Valerie Curtin

'Once … they made history. Now … they are history.'
Bill & Ted's Bogus Journey
US   1991   93m   DeLuxe
Columbia TriStar/Orion/Nelson
   Entertainment (Scott Kroopf)
V, L

Killed by robots designed to resemble them, two inept college boys trick Death, enlist the help of God and become heavy-metal heroes.

A sequel that, like the original, has attracted a cult following, though the joke, depending on the slang spoken by its dim heroes, remains a thin one.

w Ed Solomon, Chris Matheson
d Pete Hewitt   ph Oliver Wood
m David Newman   ed David Finfer

Alex Winter, Keanu Reeves, Jeff Miller, David Carrera, George Carlin, Joss Ackland, William Sadler

'A sequel that contrives another elaborate but non-excellent adventure.' – Variety

Bill and Ted's Excellent Adventure
US   1988   89m   Technicolor
 Panavision
Castle Premier/Interscope
 Communications/Soisson-Murphey
 Productions/ De Laurentiis Film Partners
 (Scott Kroopf, Michael S. Murphey, Joel
 Soisson)
V, L

In order to improve their essays, two
high-school students, with the aid of
a time machine, abduct famous
historical figures and take them to
modern-day America.

Mild comedy depending for its effect
on an understanding of teenage
Californian mores.

w Chris Matheson, Ed Solomon
d Stephen Herek   ph Timothy
Suhrstedt   m David Newman
pd Roy Forge Smith, Lynda
Paradise   ad Gordon White,
Pierluigi Basile   ed Larry Bock,
Patrick Rand

Keanu Reeves, Alex Winter, Robert V.
Barron, Terry Camilleri, Clifford David,
Al Leong, Ron Loomis, Dan Shor,
Tony Steedman, Jane Wiedlin

Billy Liar***
GB   1963   98m   bw
 Cinemascope
Vic Films (Joe Janni)
V

In a drab North Country town, an
undertaker's clerk lives in a world of
fantasy.

Flawed only by its unsuitable
Cinemascope ratio, this is a brilliant
urban comedy of its time, seminal in
acting, theme, direction and
permissiveness.

w *Keith Waterhouse, Willis Hall*
play Keith Waterhouse, Willis
Hall   *novel* Keith Waterhouse

inspired by Thurber's Walter Mitty
d *John Schlesinger   ph* Denys
Coop   m Richard Rodney Bennett

Tom Courtenay, Julie Christie, Wilfred
Pickles, Mona Washbourne, *Ethel
Griffies,* Finlay Currie, Rodney Bewes,
Leonard Rossiter

'John Schlesinger's direction, I am
delighted to say, is rich in wit.' – *Dilys
Powell*

† It was later turned into a TV series
and a successful stage musical, making
Billy a universal figure of the period.

Biloxi Blues*
US   1988   106m   colour
 Panavision
Universal/Rastar (Ray Stark)
V, L

Standard, quite pleasing version of a
Broadway comedy about a conscript
called up in 1945 when World War
Two was ending.

w Neil Simon   *play* Neil Simon
d Mike Nichols   ph Bill Butler
m Georges Delerue   pd Paul
Sylbert   ed Sam O'Steen

Matthew Broderick, Christopher
Walken, Matt Mulhern, Corey Parker

**The Bingo Long Traveling All-Stars
and Motor Kings**
US   1976   111m   Technicolor
Universal (Rob Cohen)

Adventures of a black baseball team
in the 1940s.

High-spirited japes and exhibitions of
athleticism which dramatically do not
add up to very much.

w Hal Barwood, Matthew Robbins
novel William Brashler   d John
Badham   ph Bill Butler
m William Goldstein

Billy Dee Williams, James Earl Jones, Richard Pryor, Rico Dawson

'Modest pleasures and dull stretches co-exist in equal abundance.' – *Frank Rich, New York Times*

Bird on a Wire

US   1990   111m   DeLuxe
UIP/Universal/Badham-Cohen-Interscope
   Communications (Ron Cohen)
V, L

A lawyer and her former lover run from their would-be assassins.

Chase comedy, too frenetic to be funny.

w David Seltzer, Louis Venosta, Eric Lerner   *d* John Badham
ph Robert Primes   *m* Hans Zimmer   *pd* Philip Harrison
ad Richard Hudolin   *ed* Frank Morriss, Dallas Puett

Mel Gibson, Goldie Hawn, David Carradine, Bill Duke, Stephen Tobolowsky, Joan Severance, Harry Caesar, Jeff Corey

'One of those star vehicles from deepest Hollywood for which there seems no adequate reason other than to pay someone's mortgage.' – *Derek Malcolm, Guardian*

The Bishop's Wife**

US   1947   108m   bw
Samuel Goldwyn

An angel is sent down to mend the ways of a bishop whose absorption with cathedral buildings has put him out of touch with his wife and parishioners.

Whimsical, stolid and protracted light comedy saved by its actors and its old-fashioned Hollywood style.

w Robert E. Sherwood, Leonardo Bercovici   *novel* Robert Nathan

d Henry Koster   *ph* Gregg Toland   *m* Hugo Friedhofer
ed Monica Collingwood

Cary Grant, Loretta Young, David Niven, Monty Woolley, James Gleason, Gladys Cooper, Elsa Lanchester, Sara Haden, Regis Toomey

'It is the Protestant comeback to the deadly successful RC propaganda of *Going My Way* and *The Bells of St Mary's*. It surpasses in tastelessness, equals in whimsy and in technique falls well below those crooning parables. It is really quite a monstrous film.' – *Richard Winnington, News Chronicle*
'When a film undertakes to bring audiences a spiritual message, we wonder whether the director doesn't owe it to us to clothe such messages in less muddled characterizations and to dispense with caricature.' – *Scholastic Magazine*
'A sophisticated *Christmas Carol*.' – *Philip Hartung*
'As cheerful an invasion of the realm of conscience as we have seen.' – *New York Times*

† Director William A. Seiter was replaced when the film was half complete; this caused nearly one million dollars to be wasted.
AAN: best picture; Henry Koster; Hugo Friedhofer; editing

Black and White in Colour*

France/Switzerland/Ivory Coast
   1976   100m   Eastmancolor
Reggance/SFP/Artco/Société Ivorienne de
   Production (Arthur Cohn, Jacques Perrin,
   Giorgio Silvagni)
original title: *La Victoire en Chantant*

In French West Africa in 1915, easy-going colonials learn of the outbreak of war and prepare to attack a neighbouring German garrison.

Curious mixture of Ealing-style comedy and mordant satire; interesting without being wholly engaging.

w Georges Conchon, Jean-Jacques Annaud   d Jean-Jacques Annaud   ph Claude Agostini, Eduardo Serra, Nanamoudou Magassouda   m Pierre Bachelet, Mat Camison

Jean Carmet, Jacques Dufilho, Catherine Rouvel, Jacques Spiesser, Dora Doll

AA: best foreign film

The Black Bird
US 1975 98m colour
Columbia/Rastar (Michael Levee, Lou Lombardo)

Sam Spade's son finds himself beset by crooks still after the Maltese falcon.

Dismal, witless, boring parody of a classic crime film, with none of the humour of the original.

wd David Giler   ph Philip Lathrop   m Jerry Fielding

George Segal, Stéphane Audran, Lee Patrick, Elisha Cook Jnr, Lionel Stander, John Abbott, Signe Hasso, Felix Silla

'A dumb comedy with an insecure tone and some good ideas mixed up with some terrible ones.' – Variety
'It doesn't work because it has nothing to say.' – Michael Billington, Illustrated London News

The Black Sheep of Whitehall*
GB 1941 80m bw
Ealing (S. C. Balcon)

An incompetent teacher is mistaken for an economics expert and saves the real expert from spies who run a nursing home.

Pretty good wartime star comedy, with a succession of briskly timed gags.

w Angus Macphail, John Dighton   d Basil Dearden, Will Hay   ph Gunther Krampf

Will Hay, John Mills, Basil Sydney, Frank Cellier, Felix Aylmer

'Murder, mistresses, madness and mayhem ... It's all part of the service.'
Blame It on the Bellboy
GB 1992 78m Technicolor
Warner/Bellboy/Hollywood Pictures (Jennifer Howarth)
V, L

At a hotel in Venice, a bellboy confuses the identities of a hitman, a timid estate agent and a mayor who has arranged a romantic assignation.

Tired and tepid farce, given the performances it deserves.

wd Mark Herman   ph Andrew Dunn   md Guy Dagel   pd Gemma Jackson   ed Mike Ellis

Dudley Moore, Bryan Brown, Richard Griffiths, Andreas Katsulas, Patsy Kensit, Alison Steadman, Penelope Wilton, Bronson Pinchot, Lindsay Anderson

'A lightweight ensemble comedy that should check out fast from most hospices. Ingenious plotting is let down by weak dialog and stop-go direction that largely squanders the talent involved.' – Variety

Blazing Saddles*
US 1974 93m Technicolor Panavision
Warner/Crossbow (Michael Herzberg)
V, L

A black railroad worker and an alcoholic ex-gunfighter foil a crooked attorney and his henchmen.

Wild Western parody in which the action eventually shifts to the Warner backlot, after which the actors repair to Grauman's Chinese Theatre to find out what happened at the end of the story. At least as many misses as hits, and all aimed squarely at film buffs.

w Norman Steinberg, Mel Brooks, Andrew Bergman, Richard Pryor, Alan Unger   d Mel Brooks   ph Joseph Biroc   m John Morris

Cleavon Little, Gene Wilder, Slim Pickens, Harvey Korman, Madeline Kahn, Mel Brooks, Burton Gilliam, Alex Karras

'One suspects that the film's gradual disintegration derives not from the makers' inability to end it, so much as from their inability to stop laughing at their own jokes.' – *Jan Dawson*
'A surfeit of chaos and a scarcity of comedy.' – *Judith Crist*
'"I just about got everything out of me," said Brooks, "all my furor, my frenzy, my insanity, my love of life and hatred of death." Audiences flocked to this insane affirmation of dancing girls, Hollywood production numbers, stomach gas around the campfire, and gallows humor. Brooks had found the perfect vehicle for the age.' – *Les Keyser, Hollywood in the Seventies*
AAN: Madeline Kahn; title song (*m* John Morris, *ly* Mel Brooks)

Bless This House
GB 1972 89m Eastmancolor
Rank/Peter Rogers

A suburbanite's multifarious frustrations culminate in preparations for his son's wedding.

This tedious spin-off from a TV sitcom virtually abandons plot in favour of an endless series of slapstick gags which could have been better presented.

w Dave Freeman   d Gerald Thomas

Sid James, Diana Coupland, Terry Scott, June Whitfield, Peter Butterworth, Sally Geeson, Robin Askwith, Bill Maynard

Blind Date*
US 1987 93m Metrocolor
Tri-Star/Blake Edwards (Tony Adams)
L

A company executive needs a date for a company function, and takes a remote relative who turns out to be an easy drunk.

One-note gag movie which spurs some laughs but wears out its welcome.

w Dale Launer   d Blake Edwards   ph Harry Stradling   m Henry Mancini

Kim Basinger, Bruce Willis, John Larroquette, William Daniels, Phil Hartman, Alice Hirson

'In short, hokey and hip – which in this case is a foolproof formula.' – *Daily Variety*

Bliss*
Australia 1985 111m colour
Entertainment (Anthony Buckley)

After a heart attack, an advertising executive realises the rottenness of his wife and children and seeks happiness elsewhere.

Energetic black comedy, intermittently entertaining, that won awards in its home country.

w Ray Lawrence, Peter Carey
novel Peter Carey   d Ray Lawrence   ph Paul Murphy   m Peter Best   ad Owen Paterson   ed Wayne Leclos

Barry Otto, Lynette Curran, Helen Jones, Miles Buchanan, Gia Carides, Tim Robertson, Jeff Truman, Bryan Marshall

Blithe Spirit*
GB   1945   96m   Technicolor
Two Cities/Cineguild (Anthony Havelock-Allan)
V

A cynical novelist's second marriage is disturbed when the playful ghost of his first wife materializes during a séance.

Direction and acting carefully preserve a comedy which on its first West End appearance in 1941 achieved instant classic status. The repartee scarcely dates, and altogether this is a most polished job of film-making.

w Noël Coward   play Noël Coward   scenario David Lean, Anthony Havelock-Allan, Ronald Neame   d David Lean ph Ronald Neame   m Richard Addinsell

Rex Harrison, Kay Hammond, Constance Cummings, Margaret Rutherford, Hugh Wakefield, Joyce Carey, Jacqueline Clark

† After seeing this, Noël Coward reputedly told Rex Harrison: 'After me you're the best light comedian in the world.'

Blockheads*
US   1938   60m   bw
Hal Roach/Stan Laurel
V, V(C)

Twenty years after World War I, Stan is still guarding a trench because nobody told him to stop. Olly takes him home to meet the wife, with disastrous consequences.

The last first-class Laurel and Hardy comedy is shapeless but hilarious, a fragmented reworking of earlier ideas, all of which work beautifully. Gags include encounters with a tip-up truck and an automatic garage, and a brilliantly worked out sequence up and down several flights of stairs.

w James Parrott, Harry Langdon, Felix Adler, Charles Rogers, Arnold Belgard   d John G. Blystone ph Art Lloyd   m Marvin Hatley

Stan Laurel, Oliver Hardy, Billy Gilbert, Patricia Ellis, Minna Gombell, James Finlayson

'Hodge-podge of old-fashioned slapstick and hoke.' – *Variety*
AAN: Marvin Hatley

Blotto*
US   1930   20m   bw
Hal Roach
V, V(C)

Ollie helps Stan escape his wife for a night on the town, but the lady takes revenge.

Palatable star comedy with a strained second half following a splendidly typical opening.

w Leo McCarey, H. M. Walker d James Parrott

Laurel and Hardy, Anita Garvin

Blue Murder at St Trinians*
GB   1957   86m   bw
British Lion/John Marvel (Launder and Gilliat)
V

The awful schoolgirls win a UNESCO prize trip which takes them to Rome where they become involved with a jewel thief.

Possibly the best of this series, which

isn't saying much. See *The Belles of St Trinians*.

w Frank Launder, Val Valentine, Sidney Gilliat   d Frank Launder   ph Gerald Gibbs   m Malcolm Arnold

Terry-Thomas, George Cole, Joyce Grenfell, Alastair Sim, Judith Furse, Sabrina, Lionel Jeffries, Lloyd Lamble, Thorley Walters, Kenneth Griffith, Eric Barker, Richard Wattis

The Blues Brothers
US 1980 133m Technicolor
Universal (Robert K. Weiss)
V, L

A massive car chase develops when two brothers collect money for their old orphanage without too much regard for law and order.

Fashionable chase comedy with so many stunts that its cost ran up to 33,000,000 dollars. The public stayed away, though it has gained a cult following since.

w Dan Aykroyd, John Landis   d John Landis   ph Stephen M. Katz   md Ira Newborn   pd John Lloyd

John Belushi, Dan Aykroyd, Kathleen Freeman, James Brown, Henry Gibson, Cab Calloway, Carrie Fisher

'It meanders expensively like some pedigreed shaggy dog through 70s/80s American cinema and 50s/60s American rock, cocking its leg happily at every popular landmark on the way.' – *Paul Taylor, MFB*
'There's not a *soupçon* of wit or ingenuity in this brainless exercise in overspending.' – *Daily Mail*
'There's even room, in the midst of the carnage and mayhem, for a surprising amount of grace, humor and whimsy.' – *Roger Ebert*

Bob and Carol and Ted and Alice**
US 1969 105m Technicolor
Columbia/M. J. Frankovich (Larry Tucker)
L

Two California couples, influenced by a group therapy session advocating natural spontaneous behaviour, decide to admit their extra-marital affairs and narrowly avoid a wife-swapping party.

Fashionable comedy without the courage of its convictions: it starts and finishes very bashfully, but there are bright scenes in the middle. An attempt to extend it into a TV series was a failure.

w Paul Mazursky, Larry Tucker   d Paul Mazursky   ph Charles E. Lang   m Quincy Jones

Natalie Wood, Robert Culp, Elliot Gould, Dyan Cannon, Horst Ebersberg

'An old-fashioned romantic comedy disguised as a blue picture.' – *Arthur Schlesinger Jnr*
AAN: Paul Mazursky, Larry Tucker; Charles E. Lang; Elliot Gould; Dyan Cannon

The Bobo
US 1967 105m Technicolor
Warner/Gina (Elliott Kastner, Jerry Gershwin) (David R. Schwarz)

An unsuccessful and timid bullfighter is offered a contract if within three days he can seduce the local belle.

Stylized, silly and boring comedy from an obviously dated play; Chaplinesque pathos was not this star's strong suit.

w David R. Schwarz   play David R. Schwarz   novel Olimpia by Burt Cole   d Robert Parrish   ph Gerry Turpin   m Francis Lai

Peter Sellers, Britt Ekland, Rossano Brazzi, Adolfo Celi, Hattie Jacques, Ferdy Mayne, Kenneth Griffith, John Wells

'The big comedy of nineteen sexty-sex!'
Boeing-Boeing
US   1965   102m   Technicolor
Paramount/Hal B. Wallis

By successfully juggling with plane schedules, a Paris journalist manages to live with three air hostesses at the same time.

Frenetic, paper-thin sex comedy from a one-joke play; film style generally undistinguished.

w Edward Anhalt   play Marc Camoletti   d John Rich
ph Lucien Ballard   m Neal Hefti

Tony Curtis, Jerry Lewis (his only 'straight' part), Dany Saval, Christiane Schmidtner, Suzanna Leigh, *Thelma Ritter*

'A sort of jet-age French farce.' – *Judith Crist*

Bonnie Scotland*
US   1935   80m   bw
MGM/Hal Roach
V

Two Americans journey to Scotland to collect a non-existent inheritance, then follow their friend in the army and wind up in India.

Generally disappointing star comedy which still contains excellent sequences when it is not vainly trying to preserve interest in a boring plot. An obvious parody on *Lives of a Bengal Lancer*, released earlier that year; Scotland has almost nothing to do with it.

w Frank Butler, Jeff Moffitt
d James Horne   ph Art Lloyd, Walter Lundin   ed Bert Jordan

Stan Laurel, Oliver Hardy, James Finlayson, Daphne Pollard, William Janney, June Lang

'Packed with Laurel and Hardy hokum and good for plenty of laughs' – *Boxoffice*

'A Player Who's About To Be Played.'
Boomerang
US   1992   117m   Technicolor
UIP/Paramount (Brian Grazer, Warrington Hudlin)

An executive in a cosmetics firm has an unsuccessful affair with his boss before finding true love.

Dim comedy that substitutes gloss for wit and deprives its star of everything except uncritical adulation.

w Barry W. Blaustein, David Sheffield   d Reginald Hudlin
ph Woody Omens   m Marcus Miller   pd Jane Musky   ed Earl Watson, John Carter, Michael Jablow

Eddie Murphy, Robin Givens, Halle Berry, David Alan Grier, Martin Lawrence, Grace Jones, Geoffrey Holder, Eartha Kitt, Melvin Van Peebles

'This Eddie Murphy vehicle tries hard to be positive. It's a pity that the movie isn't any good.' – *Michael Sragow, New Yorker*
'An ill-fitting comedy vehicle that's desperately in need of a reality check.' – *Variety*

Born in East L.A.
US   1987   87m   colour
Universal (Peter Macgregor-Scott)

An American Mexican is mistaken for an illegal immigrant and deported to Tijuana.

Mercifully short brain-dead comedy.

wd Cheech Marin   ph Alex

Phillips   *m* Lee Holdridge   *ed* Don Brochu

Cheech Marin, Daniel Stern, Paul Rodriguez, Jan Michael Vincent, Kamala Lopez, Tony Plana

Born to Sing
US   1941   82m   bw
Frederick Stephani/MGM

Kids put together a patriotic show.

Curiously undernourished family musical in the wake of *Babes in Arms*: lots of talent but no star.

w Franz Spencer, Harry Clork
d Edward Ludwig

Virginia Weidler, Douglas McPhail, Leo Gorcey, Ray McDonald, Rags Ragland, Sheldon Leonard, Margaret Dumont, Larry Nunn, Henry O'Neill

'A perfectly swell motion picture!'
Born Yesterday**
US   1950   103m   bw
Columbia (S. Sylvan Simon)
V

The ignorant ex-chorus girl mistress of a scrap iron tycoon takes English lessons, falls for her tutor, and politically outmanoeuvres her bewildered lover.

Pleasant film version of a cast-iron box-office play, subtle and intelligent in all departments yet with a regrettable tendency to wave the flag.

w Albert Mannheimer   *play* Garson Kanin   *d* George Cukor
ph Joseph Walker   *m* Frederick Hollander

Judy Holliday, Broderick Crawford, William Holden, Howard St John

† The original choices for the Judy Holliday role were Rita Hayworth and Jean Parker (who had played it on tour).

AA: Judy Holliday
AAN: best picture; Albert Mannheimer; George Cukor

Bottoms Up
GB   1960   89m   bw
ABPC (Mario Zampi)

A seedy schoolmaster passes off his bookie's son as an eastern prince.

Rambling film version of a successful TV series *Whacko!*, written by Frank Muir and Denis Norden.

w Michael Pertwee   *d* Mario Zampi   *ph* Gilbert Taylor
m Stanley Black   *ad* Ivan King *ed* Richard Best

Jimmy Edwards, Arthur Howard, Martita Hunt, Sidney Tafler, Raymond Huntley, Reginald Beckwith, Vanda

Boudu Sauvé des Eaux***
France   1932   87m   bw
Michel Simon/Jean Gehret
aka: *Boudu Saved from Drowning*

A scruffy tramp is not grateful for being rescued from suicide, and plagues the family who invite him to stay.

A minor classic of black comedy, interesting equally for its characterizations, its acting, and its film technique.

wd Jean Renoir,   *play* René Fauchois   *ph* Marcel Lucien
m from Raphael and Johann Strauss

Michel Simon, Charles Grandval, Marcelle Hainia, Séverine Lerczinska, Jean Dasté, Jacques Becker

'A beautifully rhythmed film that makes one nostalgic for the period when it was made.' – *New Yorker, 1977*

† Remade 1985, more or less, as *Down and Out in Beverly Hills.*

'No more bubble bath, she screamed!'

Boy, Did I Get a Wrong Number
US   1966   99m   DeLuxe
UA/Edward Small (George Beck)

Trying to phone his wife, an estate agent gets involved with a runaway actress.

Lifeless and generally resistible star comedy, the first of several hard and unfunny vehicles for an ageing Bob Hope seeming to hark back to the least attractive aspects of burlesque rather than the sympathetic wisecracking which suits him best.

w Burt Styler, Albert E. Lewin, George Kennett   d George Marshall   ph Lionel Lindon   m Richard Lasalle   ly By Dunham

Bob Hope, Elke Sommer, Phyllis Diller, Marjorie Lord, Cesare Danova, Benny Baker

Boy Meets Girl*
US   1938   86m   bw
Warner (George Abbott)

Two crazy Hollywood scenario writers make a star of an infant yet unborn.

Freewheeling film version of a hilarious play: fine crazy comedy and excellent Hollywood satire.

w Bella and Sam Spewack, play Bella and Sam Spewack   d Lloyd Bacon   ph Sol Polito   m Leo Forbstein

James Cagney, Pat O'Brien, Marie Wilson, Ralph Bellamy, Frank McHugh, Dick Foran, Bruce Lester, Ronald Reagan, James Stephenson

'Satisfactory, but not socko.' – Variety
'It bounces from one hilarious absurdity to another with all the resilience of a rubber ball.' – MFB

The Boys from Syracuse*
US   1940   74m   bw
Universal (Jules Levey)

The Comedy of Errors with modern wisecracks, and a few songs.

Predictable well-drilled confusion arises from master and slave having identical twins, but the general tone is a bit flat for an adaptation from a hilarious Broadway success. Still, the songs are lively and the chariot race finale shows spirit.

w Leonard Spigelgass, Charles Grayson, Paul Gerard Smith   play George Abbott, William Shakespeare   d Edward A. Sutherland   ph Joseph Valentine   md Charles Previn   m Frank Skinner   m/ly Richard Rodgers, Lorenz Hart   ad John Otterson

Allan Jones, Joe Penner, Charles Butterworth, Rosemary Lane, Irene Hervey, Martha Raye, Alan Mowbray   songs: 'Who Are You?'; 'This Can't be Love'; 'Falling in Love with Love'; 'The Greeks Have no Word for It'; 'Sing for Your Supper'; 'He and She'

† The writing credit on screen ends: 'After a play by William Shakespeare . . . long, long after!'
AAN: John Otterson

The Boys in Blue
GB   1983   91m   colour
Elstree/Rank

Village policemen catch art thieves.

Horribly incompetent remake of Ask a Policeman, with a totally untalented star team.

wd Val Guest

Tommy Cannon, Bobby Ball, Suzanne Danielle, Roy Kinnear, Eric Sykes,

Jack Douglas, Edward Judd, Jon Pertwee, Arthur English

'The perfect antidote to sweeping claims about the British renaissance.' – *Geoff Brown, MFB*

Boys Will Be Boys**
GB 1935 75m bw
Gaumont/Gainsborough (Michael Balcon)
V

An incompetent headmaster thwarts a jewel robber.

The first recognizable Will Hay vehicle, based in part on J. B. Morton's Narkover sketches.

w Will Hay, Robert Edmunds *d* William Beaudine *ph* Charles Van Enger *m* Louis Levy

Will Hay, Gordon Harker, Jimmy Hanley, Davy Burnaby, Norma Varden, Claude Dampier, Charles Farrell, Percy Walsh

'It is hard to see how his distinctive sketch writing could have found a satisfactory screen equivalent. Nevertheless, a good augury of the films to come.' – *Ray Seaton and Roy Martin, 1978*

Brain Donors
US 1992 79m colour
Paramount/Zucker (Gil Netter, James D. Brubaker)

A trio of idiots attempt to part a widow from her wealth by running a ballet company for her.

A misfiring farce and a leaden attempt to revive the Marx Brothers' style of comedy. Inspired by *A Night at the Opera*, it doesn't even approach the low level of *Love Happy*.

w Pat Proft *d* Dennis Dugan *ph* David M. Walsh *m* Ira

Newborn *pd* William J. Cassidy *ed* Malcolm Campbell

John Turturro, Bob Nelson, Mel Smith, Nancy Marchand, John Savident, George De La Pena

'Sounds like a horror film and for those expecting a comedy, it is.' – *Variety*

Brats*
US 1930 20m bw
Hal Roach

Stan and Ollie have trouble baby-sitting their own mischievous kids.

Fairly ambitious star comedy with trick sets and photography enabling Laurel and Hardy to play their own sons. About half the gags come off.

w Leo McCarey, H. M. Walker, Hal Roach *d* James Parrot *ph* George Stevens *ed* Richard Currier

Stan Laurel, Oliver Hardy

Brazil*
GB 1985 142m colour
Embassy (Arnon Milchan)
V

A comically pessimistic view of the future, seen through the eyes of a dutiful civil servant who is eventually crushed by the system.

An expensive, wild, overlong, hit-or-miss Orwellian satire: enough good jabs to please the intelligentsia, but a turnoff for patrons at the local Odeon.

w Terry Gilliam, Tom Stoppard, Charles McKeown *d* Terry Gilliam *ph* Roger Pratt *m* Michael Kamen *pd* Norman Garwood *ed* Julian Doyle

Jonathan Pryce, Robert de Niro, Michael Palin, Kim Greist, Katherine

Helmond, Ian Holm, Ian Richardson, Peter Vaughan, Bob Hoskins

'It will not be everybody's cup of poisoned tea.' – *Variety*
'Exuberantly violent, cruelly funny and sometimes sickeningly scatological . . . the whole is wrapped up in a melancholy wistfulness.' – *Sight and Sound*
AAN: original screenplay, art direction

Breaking Away*
US   1979   101m   DeLuxe
TCF (Peter Yates)
L

An imaginative teenager has trouble adjusting to adult life after high school.

Andy Hardy would have felt at home in this fragmented comedy of the American hinterland; 1979 audiences found it a welcome relief from the stronger brews to which they had become accustomed.

w Steve Tesich   *d* Peter Yates
ph Matthew F. Leonetti
md Lionel Newman   *m* Patrick Williams

Dennis Christopher, Dennis Quaid, Daniel Stern, Jackie Earle Haley, Barbara Barrie, Paul Dooley

'Affection for the middle classes, the landscapes of Indiana, and bicycle racing.' – *New Yorker*
'It is not devoid of pleasures . . . but it fatally lacks a clear purpose and identity.' – *Geoff Brown, MFB*
'Here's a sunny, goofy, intelligent little film about coming of age in Bloomington, Indiana.' – *Roger Ebert*

† An unsuccessful TV series followed in 1980.

AA: Steve Tesich

AAN: best picture; Peter Yates; Patrick Williams; Barbara Barrie

Breaking In*
US   1989   94m   colour
Castle Premier/Breaking In Productions/
   Sam Goldwyn Company (Harry Gittes)
V

A veteran safe-breaker teaches a teenager the tricks of the trade.

Mildly rewarding comedy of crooked manners.

w John Sayles   *d* Bill Forsyth
ph Michael Coulter   *pd* Adrienne Atkinson, John Willett   *ed* Michael Ellis

Burt Reynolds, Casey Siemaszko, Sheila Kelley, Lorraine Toussaint, Albert Salmi, Harry Carey, Maury Chaykin

'Less a barrel of laughs than elliptically funny in its observation of the unconscious discrepancy between word and deed.' – *Tom Milne, MFB*

Brewster McCloud
US   1970   105m   Metrocolor
   Panavision
MGM/Adler-Phillips/Lion's Gate (Lou Adler)

A man hides out under the roof of the Houston Astrodrome, prepares to learn to fly with man-made wings, and refuses all offers of help; when he launches himself, he falls to his death.

Anarchic, allegorical fantasy, a delight no doubt for connoisseurs of way-out humour. Everyone else, forget it.

w Doran William Cannon
d Robert Altman   *ph* Lamar Boren, Jordan Cronenweth
m Gene Page

Bud Cort, Sally Kellerman, Michael Murphy, William Windom, Shelley

Duvall, René Auberjonois, Stacy
Keach, John Shuck, Margaret
Hamilton

'Amorphous and rather silly . . . the
idea seems to be left over from a
Victorian fable, but the style is like a
Road Runner cartoon.' – *New Yorker*,
1974

Brewster's Millions*
GB   1935   84m   bw
British and Dominion (Herbert Wilcox)

If he can spend a million pounds
within two months, a playboy will
inherit many millions more.

Artless but lively version of a famous
comedy which provided a good role
for its star.

w Arthur Wimperis, Paul Gangelin,
Douglas Furber, Clifford Grey,
Donovan Pedelty, Wolfgang
Wilhelm   *play* George Barr
McCutcheon, Winchell Smith
novel George Barr McCutcheon
d Thornton Freeland   *ph* Henry
Harris, Barney McGill   *m* Ray
Noble   *ad* L. P. Williams
ed Merrill White

Jack Buchanan, Lili Damita, Nancy
O'Neil, Amy Veness, Sydney
Fairbrother, Fred Emney, Sebastian
Shaw

'As near 100% film entertainment as
can be expected.' – *Variety*

† There had been silent versions in
1916 (with Edward Abeles) and 1921
(with Roscoe Arbuckle).

Brewster's Millions*
US   1945   79m   bw
Edward Small

Competent American remake of the
above.

w Sig Herzig, Charles Rogers
d Allan Dwan   *ph* Charles Lawton
Jnr   *m* Hugo Friedhofer

Dennis O'Keefe, Eddie 'Rochester'
Anderson, Helen Walker, Gail
Patrick, Mischa Auer, June Havoc, Joe
Sawyer, Nana Bryant, John Litel,
Thurston Hall, Byron Foulger

† Remade as *Three on a Spree* (GB
1961).
AAN: Lou Forbes (music scoring)

Brewster's Millions
US   1985   97m   Technicolor
Universal (Lawrence Gordon, Joel Silver)

A baseball player learns that in order
to inherit 30 million dollars he must
spend one million a day for 30 days.

Frantically noisy remake of an old
chestnut.

w Herschel Weingrod, Timothy
Harris   *d* Walter Hill   *ph* Ric
Waite   *m* Ry Cooder   *pd* John
Vallone   *ed* Freeman Davis, Michel
Ripps

Richard Pryor, John Candy, Lonette
McKee, Stephen Collins, Jerry Orbach,
Pat Hingle, Tovah Feldshuh

The Bridal Path*
GB   1959   95m   Technicolor
Vale (Sidney Gilliat, Frank Launder)

A stalwart Hebridean islander
journeys to the mainland in search of
a wife.

Mild, episodic, very pleasant open-air
comedy set amid splendid locations.

w Frank Launder, Geoffrey
Willans   *novel* Nigel Tranter
d Frank Launder   *ph* Arthur
Ibbetson   *m* Cedric Thorpe Davie

Bill Travers, Fiona Clyne, George
Cole, Duncan Macrae, Gordon

Jackson, Dilys Laye, Bernadette
O'Farrell

The Bride Came C.O.D.*
US 1941 92m bw
Warner (Hal B. Wallis)

A charter pilot agrees to kidnap a
temperamental heiress, but is stuck
with her when they crashland in the
desert.

Feeble comedy with a script totally
unworthy of its stars. The mass of
talent does however provide a smile
or two towards the end.

w Julius J. and Philip G. Epstein
d William Keighley   ph Ernest
Haller   m Max Steiner

Bette Davis, James Cagney, Harry
Davenport, Stuart Erwin, Eugene
Pallette, Jack Carson, George Tobias,
William Frawley, Edward Brophy,
Chick Chandler

'Neither the funniest comedy ever
made, nor the shortest distance
between two points, but for the most
part a serviceable romp.' – *Theodore
Strauss*
'Both of them mug good-naturedly,
and it's pleasantly fast.' – *New Yorker*,
1977

The Bride Goes Wild
US 1948 98m bw
MGM (William H. Wright)

As his lady illustrator finds out, a
writer of children's books is not quite
the sober uncle she expected,
especially when he has to pretend to
adopt an unruly orphan.

Scatty comedy with farcical
interludes, quite pleasantly played but
lacking style.

w Albert Beich   d Norman
Taurog   ph Ray June   m Rudolf
Kopp

June Allyson, Van Johnson, Jackie
'Butch' Jenkins, Hume Cronyn,
Richard Derr

The Bride Walks Out
US 1936 81m bw
RKO (Edward Small)

A successful mannequin tries to
manage on her engineer husband's
lowly salary.

Thin, pleasant marital comedy with
no surprises.

w P. J. Wolfson, Philip G. Epstein
d Leigh Jason   ph J. Roy Hunt
m Roy Webb

Barbara Stanwyck, Gene Raymond,
Robert Young, Ned Sparks, Helen
Broderick, Willie Best, Robert
Warwick, Billy Gilbert, Hattie
McDaniel, Irving Bacon

Brighton Beach Memoirs*
US 1986 108m colour
Universal/Rastar (David Chasman)
V, L

In 1937 Brooklyn, a lower middle
class Jewish family has assorted crises.

Standard picturization of a Neil Simon
play, somewhat flattened out in the
process but with funny moments.

w Neil Simon   play Neil Simon
d Gene Saks   ph John Bailey
m Michael Small

Blythe Danner, Bob Dishy, Brian
Drillinger, Stacey Glick, Judith Ivey,
Lisa Waltz

Bringing Up Baby***
US 1938 102m bw
RKO (Howard Hawks)
L

A zany girl causes a zoology professor
to lose a dinosaur bone and a pet
leopard in the same evening.

Outstanding crazy comedy which barely pauses for romance and ends up with the whole splendid cast in jail.

*w Dudley Nichols, Hagar Wilde
d Howard Hawks   ph* Russell Metty   *m* Roy Webb

Katharine Hepburn, Cary Grant, May Robson, Charles Ruggles, Walter Catlett, Fritz Feld, Jonathan Hale, Barry Fitzgerald

'Harum-scarum farce comedy . . . definite box-office.' – *Variety*
'I am happy to report that it is funny from the word go, that it has no other meaning to recommend it . . . and that I wouldn't swap it for practically any three things of the current season.' – *Otis Ferguson*
'It may be the American movies' closest equivalent to Restoration comedy.' – *Pauline Kael*
'Crazy comedies continue to become crazier, and there will soon be few actors and actresses left who have no straw in their hair.' – *Basil Wright*

† The dog George was played by Asta from *The Thin Man* movies.

Britannia Hospital
GB   1982   116m   colour
EMI/Film and General/NFFC (Davina Belling, Clive Parsons)
V

Problems besetting a British hospital celebrating its 500th anniversary include strikes, demonstrators, and a mad doctor who transplants heads.

Looking as crummy as a Carry On at the end of its tether, this intended lampoon of the state of the nation never warms up and can only fire off stale jokes in all directions while repelling the eye with its Frankenstein scenes.

w David Sherwin   d Lindsay Anderson   *ph* Mike Fash
m Alan Price   *pd* Norris Spencer

Malcolm McDowell, Leonard Rossiter, Graham Crowden, Fulton Mackay, Vivian Pickles, Joan Plowright, Peter Jeffrey, Robin Askwith, Dandy Nichols, Valentine Dyall, Roland Culver, Alan Bates, Arthur Lowe, Marsha Hunt

'It has all the intensity, along with the flailing incoherence, of a soapbox jeremiah.' – *Richard Combs, MFB*
'Having once created a general shambles, the film is at a loss to clean it up.' – *Margaret Hinxman, Daily Mail*
'Inexplicably muddled and inconclusive.' – *Guardian*
'It mentholates the tubes and oxygenates the brain.' – *Sunday Telegraph*

Broadway Bill**
US   1934   104m   bw
Columbia (Frank Capra)
V
GB title: *Strictly Confidential*

A cheerful horse trainer finds he has a winner.

Easygoing romantic comedy with the energetic Capra style in fairly full bloom.

w Robert Riskin   story Mark Hellinger   *d Frank Capra*
ph Joseph Walker

Warner Baxter, Myrna Loy, Walter Connolly, Helen Vinson, Douglass Dumbrille, Raymond Walburn, Lynne Overman, Clarence Muse, Margaret Hamilton, Paul Harvey, Claude Gillingwater, Charles Lane, Ward Bond

'The effect of capable direction is discernible in every foot.' – *Variety*
'It will be a long day before we see so little made into so much: it is gay and

charming and will make you happy, and I am sorry to say I do not know recommendations much higher.' — *Otis Ferguson*

† Remade as *Riding High* (qv).

Broadway Danny Rose*
US 1984 84m DeLuxe
Orion (Robert Greenhut)
V, L

An artists' agent and former comic falls foul of the Mafia while promoting a client.

Generally appealing comedy-melodrama with rather less self-examination than has latterly been typical of its star.

wd Woody Allen   *ph* Gordon Willis   *md* Nick Hyman   *pd* Mel Bourne   *ed* Susan E. Morse

Woody Allen, Mia Farrow, Nick Apollo Forte, Craig Vandenbergh, Herb Reynolds
AAN: direction, original screenplay

BFA: original screenplay

Bronco Billy*
US 1980 116m DeLuxe
    Panavision
Warner/Second Street (Neal Dubrovsky, Dennis Hackin)
V, L

A New Jersey shoe salesman takes over a rundown wild west show.

Enjoyable, sentimental, satirical comedy which unaccountably let down its star's box-office record.

w Dennis Hackin   *d* Clint Eastwood   *ph* David Worth   *md* Snuff Garrett, Steve Dorff   *ad* Eugene Lourie

Clint Eastwood, Sondra Locke, Geoffrey Lewis, Scatman Crothers, Bill McKinney, Sam Bottoms

'Eastwood seems to have most enjoyed toying with some distinctly old-fashioned materials: a runaway heiress, a murder plot that isn't, some consequent punning on points of identity, and the most mischievously brittle set of greedy Eastern sophisticates since Frank Capra.' — *Richard Combs, MFB*

The Brother from Another Planet
US 1984 108m Movielab
A-Train Films

An alien lands in Harlem and is protected by locals from the horrors he finds there.

Moderately amusing combination of science fiction, farce and satire, which outstays its welcome by at least half an hour.

wd John Sayles

Joe Morton, Tom Wright, Caroline Aaron, Randy Sue Carter

Brothers in Law*
GB 1957 97m bw
British Lion/The Boultings (John Boulting)

A young barrister has comic misdemeanours in and out of court.

The lighter side of the law, from a bestseller by a judge; mechanically amusing and not in the same street as its predecessor *Private's Progress*, though it seemed hilarious at the time.

w Roy Boulting, Frank Harvey, Jeffrey Dell   *novel* Henry Cecil
d Roy Boulting   *ph* Max Greene
m Benjamin Frankel

Ian Carmichael, Terry-Thomas, Richard Attenborough, *Miles Malleson*, *Eric Barker*, Irene Handl, John Le Mesurier, Olive Sloane, Kynaston Reeves
FOREWORD: If all the characters in

this film were not fictitious – it would be alarming!

CLERK: 'You start with a blue robing bag, sir. Then if you do good work for counsel, he'll give you a red one. If at the end of seven years you haven't been given a red bag – use a suitcase.'

Buck Privates*

US 1941 84m bw
Universal (Alex Gottlieb)
GB title: *Rookies*

Two incompetents accidentally enlist in the army.

Abbott and Costello's first starring vehicle is a tired bundle of army jokes and old routines separated by plot and romance, but it sent the comedians right to the top, where they stayed for ten years.

w Arthur T. Horman   *d* Arthur Lubin   *ph* Milton Krasner
md Charles Previn

Bud Abbott, Lou Costello, Lee Bowman, Alan Curtis, Jane Frazee, *The Andrews Sisters, Nat Pendleton,* Samuel S. Hinds, Shemp Howard
AAN: Charles Previn; song 'The Boogie Woogie Bugle Boy of Company B' (*m* Hugh Prince, *ly* Don Raye)

Buck Privates Come Home

US 1946 77m bw
U-I (Robert Arthur)
GB title: *Rookies Come Home*

Incompetent war veterans are demobilized and find civilian life tough.

Thin star comedy with a good final chase.

w John Grant, Frederic I. Rinaldo, Robert Lees   *d* Charles T. Barton   *ph* Charles Van Enger

Bud Abbott, Lou Costello, Beverly Simmons, Tom Brown, Nat Pendleton

Buddy Buddy

US 1981 96m Metrocolor Panavision
MGM (Jay Weston)
V

A hit man on a job is hampered by a woebegone fellow intent on committing suicide.

Painful remake of the French *L'Emmerdeur* (A Pain in the A . . .). Lugubriously funny at times, but generally much less attractive than the original.

w Billy Wilder, I. A. L. Diamond *play* Francis Veber   *d* Billy Wilder   *ph* Harry Stradling Jnr
m Lalo Schifrin   *pd* Daniel A. Lomino

Walter Matthau, Jack Lemmon, Paula Prentiss, Klaus Kinski, Dana Elcar

'The saddest episode in Wilder's career.' – *Richard Combs, MFB*

Buffy the Vampire Slayer

US 1992 94m DeLuxe
TCF/Sandollar/Kuzui (Kaz Kasui, Howard Rosenman)
V

A Californian bimbo learns that her destiny is to be a killer of vampires.

Curiously ineffectual teen comedy.

w Joss Whedon   *d* Fran Rubel Kuzui   *ph* James Hayman
m Carter Burwell   *pd* Lawrence Miller   *ed* Camilla Toniolo, Jill Savitt, Richard Candib

Kristy Swanson, Donald Sutherland, Paul Reubens, Rutger Hauer, Luke Perry, Michele Abrams, Hilary Swank, Paris Vaughan, David Arquette

'A bloodless comic resurrection of the

undead that goes serious just when it should get wild and woolly.' – *Variety*
'To enjoy this moronic rubbish, you need to put your IQ into total unconsciousness.' – *Alexander Walker, Evening Standard*

The Bulldog Breed
GB 1960 97m bw
Rank (Hugh Stewart)
V

A grocer joins the navy.

Elementary raw recruit comedy with many familiar ruses.

w Jack Davies, Henry Blyth, Norman Wisdom *d* Robert Asher

Norman Wisdom, Edward Chapman, Ian Hunter, David Lodge, Robert Urquhart, Eddie Byrne, Peter Jones

'A farce which ought never to have put to sea.' – *MFB*

The Bullfighters*
US 1945 60m bw
TCF (William Girard)
V

Two detectives in Mexico find that one of them resembles a famous matador.

Laurel and Hardy's last American feature is poor enough as a whole, but at least has a few sequences in their earlier style.

w Scott Darling *d* Mal St Clair
ph Norbert Brodine *m* David Buttolph *ad* Lyle Wheeler, Chester Gore *ed* Stanley Rabjohn

Stan Laurel, Oliver Hardy, Richard Lane, Margo Woode, Carol Andrews

Bullseye!
US 1990 92m colour
Castle Premier/21st Century (Michael Winner)
V, L

Two con-men impersonate crooked nuclear scientists.

Tedious comedy with few laughs.

w Leslie Bricusse, Laurence Marks, Maurice Gran *story* Leslie Bricusse, Michael Winner, Nick Mead *d* Michael Winner
ph Alan Jones *pd* John Blezard
ad Alan Cassie *ed* Arnold Crust

Michael Caine, Roger Moore, Sally Kirkland, Deborah Barrymore, Lee Patterson, Mark Burns, Derren Nesbitt

'Wallowing in its excremental humour, *Bullseye!* is content to reinforce the crudest of racial and sexual stereotypes.' – *MFB*

Bullshot
GB 1983 88m Technicolor
HandMade (Ian La Frenais)

In the twenties, Bullshot Crummond is pitted against his arch enemy Count Otto von Bruno.

Very flat-footed spoof which belies the talents involved.

w Ron House, Diz White, Alan Shearman *d* Dick Clement
ph Alex Thomson *m* John Du Prez *pd* Norman Garwood

Alan Shearman, Diz White, Ron House, Frances Tomelty, Michael Aldridge, Ron Pember, Mel Smith, Billy Connolly, Geoffrey Bayldon, Bryan Pringle

'Unrelievedly ghastly . . . even canned laughter would be hard pressed to raise a titter.' – *Gilbert Adair, MFB*
'Behind every mannered line you can

hear technicians laughing the fun to death on the studio floor.' – *Sunday Times*

Bunny O'Hare
US 1971 92m Movielab
AIP (Gerd Oswald, Norman T. Herman)

A middle-aged widow and an ex-con plumber become bank robbers, dressed as hippies and escaping on a motor cycle.

Unappealing, ill-thought-out comedy with pretensions to satire, an unhappy venture for both stars.

w Stanley Z. Cherry, Coslough Johnson   *d* Gerd Oswald
ph Loyal Griggs, John Stephens
m Billy Strange

Bette Davis, Ernest Borgnine, Jack Cassidy, Joan Delaney, Jay Robinson, John Astin

The 'burbs**
US 1988 102m DeLuxe
UIP/Imagine (Michael Finnell, Larry Brezner)
V, L

Neighbours decide that there is something sinister about a new family on the block.

One-joke black comedy that has its moments.

w Dana Olsen   *d* Joe Dante
ph Robert Stevens   *m* Jerry Goldsmith   *pd* James Spencer
ed Marshall Harvey

Tom Hanks, Bruce Dern, Carrie Fisher, Rick Ducommun, Corey Feldman, Wendy Schaal, Henry Gibson, Brother Theodore, Courtney Gains, Gale Gordon

'For the most part, this is one of the most extraordinary major studio films of the late 80s.' – *Kim Newman, MFB*

Burglar
US 1987 102m Technicolor
Warner/Nelvana (Kevin McCormick, Michael Hirsch)
V

An ex-con turns tec to avoid arrest as a cat burglar.

Strained comedy which is too goofy to sustain its mystery elements.

w Joseph Loeb III, Matthew Weisman, Hugh Wilson
books Lawrence Block   *d* Hugh Wilson   *ph* William A. Fraker
m Sylvester Levay

Whoopi Goldberg, Bob Goldthwait, G. W. Bailey, Lesley Ann Warren, James Handy, Anne De Salvo

Bustin' Loose
US 1981 94m Technicolor
Universal/Richard Pryor (William Greaves)

A thief on parole learns to look after a school for maladjusted children en route to a mountain retreat.

A fairly nauseous compendium of pratfalls and sentiment, not too bad while it keeps on the move.

w Roger L. Simon   *d* Oz Scott
ph Dennis Dalzell   *m* Mark Davis, Roberta Flack

Richard Pryor, Cicely Tyson, Angel Ramirez, Jimmy Hughes

'The sort of forties-style warm experience I could well do without.' – *Derek Malcolm, Guardian*

Busy Bodies**
US 1933 20m bw
MGM/Hal Roach
V

Stan and Ollie are involved in various disasters in a sawmill.

Though not among their most

sympathetic comedies, this is a
sustained and brilliantly contrived
slapstick sequence.

w Anon (and Stan Laurel)   *d* Lloyd
French   *ph* Art Lloyd   *ed* Bert
Jordan

Laurel and Hardy, Tiny Sandford,
Charlie Hall

Bye Bye Braverman*
US 1968 92m Technicolor
Warner/Sidney Lumet

New Yorkers get drunk and
disillusioned on their way home from
the funeral of a friend.

Witty, downbeat Jewish comedy
which does not quite come off and
would in any case be caviare to the
general.

w Herbert Sargent   *novel To an
Early Grave* by Wallace Markfield
d Sidney Lumet   *ph* Boris
Kaufman   *m* Peter Matz

George Segal, Jack Warden, Joseph
Wiseman, Sorrell Booke, Jessica
Walter, Phyllis Newman, Zohra
Lampert, Alan King, Godfrey
Cambridge

'You don't have to be Jewish to love
it, but it helps a lot to be a New Yorker.'
– *Robert Hatch, The Nation*

C

Cactus Flower*
US 1969 103m Technicolor
Columbia/M. J. Frankovich
V

To deceive his mistress, a dentist
employs his starchy secretary to pose
as his wife, and falls for her when she
loosens up.

Amusing sophisticated comedy,
generally well handled.

w I. A. L. Diamond *play* Abe
Burrows, French original by Pierre
Barillet, Jean Pierre Gredy *d* Gene
Saks *ph* Charles E. Lang
m Quincy Jones *pd* Robert
Clatworthy

Ingrid Bergman, Walter Matthau,
Goldie Hawn, Jack Weston, Rick
Lenz, Vito Scotti, Irene Hervey

AA: Goldie Hawn

The Caddy
US 1953 95m bw
Paramount (Paul Jones)

A music hall comedy act recall how
they got together.

Less a feature than a series of short
sketches, this ragbag has its choice
moments, but they are few.

w Edmund Hartmann, Danny
Arnold *d* Norman Taurog
ph Daniel L. Fapp *m* Joseph L.
Lilley

Dean Martin, Jerry Lewis, Donna
Reed, Barbara Bates, Joseph Calleia,
Fred Clark, Clinton Sundberg,
Marshall Thompson
AAN: song 'That's Amore' (*m* Harry
Warren, *ly* Jack Brooks)

Caddyshack
US 1980 98m Technicolor
Warner/Orion (Douglas Kenney)
V, L

Misadventures at a golf club.

A relentlessly crude and lumbering
series of farcical incidents which
mainly fail to raise laughs.

w Brian Doyle-Murray, Harold
Ramis, Douglas Kenney *d* Harold
Ramis *ph* Stevan Larner
m Johnny Mandel *pd* Stan
Jolley *ed* William Carruth

Chevy Chase, Rodney Dangerfield,
Ted Knight, Michael O'Keefe

'There are jests about vomiting and
nose-picking, while the most
elaborate gag sequence involves a
chocolate bar falling into a swimming
pool and being mistaken for a turd . . .
a sustained exercise in tiresomeness.'
– *Tim Pulleine, MFB*

Caddyshack II
US 1988 99m colour
Warner (Neil Canton, Jon Peters, Peter
  Guber)

A self-made millionaire is persuaded
by his upwardly mobile daughter to

apply for membership of an exclusive golf club.

Dim sequel that reprises the central situation of the original without even managing its crude humour; this one is just crude.

w Harold Ramis, Peter Torokvei
d Allan Arkush   ph Harry
Stradling Jnr   m Ira Newborn
pd Bill Matthews   ed Bernard
Gribble

Jackie Mason, Robert Stack, Dian Merrill, Dyan Cannon, Jonathan Silverman, Randy Quaid, Chevy Chase, Dan Aykroyd

Cadillac Man
US   1990   97m   colour
Rank/Orion (Charles Roven, Roger Donaldson)
V, L

A car salesman is held hostage by a jealous husband.

Frenetic farce that is rarely funny.

w Ken Friedman   d Roger
Donaldson   ph David Gribble
m J. Peter Robinson   pd Gene
Rudolf   ed Richard Francis-Bruce

Robin Williams, Tim Robbins, Pamela Reed, Fran Drescher, Zack Norman, Annabella Sciorra, Lori Petty, Paul Guilfoyle, Bill Nelson, Eddie Jones

'A rarity among recent films – a comedy that is in touch with a recognizable reality.' – Richard Schickel, Time

La Cage aux Folles*
France/Italy   1978   91m
  Eastmancolor
UA/PAA/Da Ma (Marcello Danon)
V, L
aka: Birds of a Feather

A homosexual night-club owner is persuaded by his straight son to behave properly in front of his girl friend's parents, but chaos comes on the night of the party.

Internationally popular near-the-knuckle farce with excellent moments and some longueurs.

w .Francis Veber, Edouard Molinaro,
Marcello Danon, Jean Poiret
play Jean Poiret   d Edouard
Molinaro   ph Armando
Nannuzzi   m Ennio Morricone

Ugo Tognazzi, Michel Serrault, Michel Galabru, Claire Maurier, Remi Laurent
AAN: Edouard Molinaro (as director); script

La Cage aux Folles II
France/Italy   1980   99m
  Technicolor
UA/PAA/Da Ma (Marcello Danon)

An ageing homosexual tells his partner he is too old to be an effective female impersonator. Trying to prove the opposite, the partner becomes involved in a spy search for hidden microfilm.

Rather dimwitted sequel to a comedy which though deliberately 'naughty' showed some restraint; here, all is noise and excess.

w Jean Poiret, Francis Veber,
Marcello Danon   d Edouard
Molinaro   ph Armando
Nannuzzi   m Ennio Morricone

Ugo Tognazzi, Michel Serrault, Marcel Bozzuffi, Paola Borboni

'The juxtaposition of campy histrionics with the dreariest kind of espionage comedy offers quickly diminishing returns.' – Gilbert Adair, MFB

La Cage aux Folles III

France/Italy 1985 87m
  Eastmancolor
Da Ma/Columbia (Marcello Danon)

In order to inherit a fortune, Albin must marry and produce an heir.

Yawnworthy attempt to milk more gags out of a formula which exhausted itself with number one.

w Philippe Nicaud, Christine Carere, Marcello Danon, Jacques Audiard, Michel Audiard, Georges Lautner, Gerald Lamballe   d Georges Lautner   ph Luciano Tavoli   m Ennio Morricone   pd Mario Garbuglia   ed Michelle David, Elisabeth Guido, Lidia Pascolini

Ugo Tognazzi, Michel Serrault, Michel Galabru, Antonella Interlenghi

'Lots of cooks but not much broth.' – Variety

California Split*

US 1974 109m Metrocolor
  Panavision
Columbia/Persky-Bright/Reno (Robert Altman, Joseph Walsh)

Two cheerful gamblers get drunk, laid, cheated and happy.

Sporadically entertaining character comedy sunk in a sea of chatter.

w Joseph Walsh   d Robert Altman   ph Paul Lohmann   m Phyllis Shotwell

Elliott Gould, George Segal, Gwen Welles, Ann Prentiss, Joseph Walsh

'The film seems to be being improvised . . . we catch at events and personalities by the ends of threads.' – New Yorker

† An end title reads: FOR BARBARA, 1933–1973. This was Barbara Ruick, who played the barmaid and died on location.

California Suite*

US 1978 103m colour
Columbia/Ray Stark
V

Misadventures of four groups of guests at the Beverly Hills Hotel.

Two hits, two misses; closer intercutting might have helped. No doubt that Maggie Smith and Michael Caine come off best, with bitcheries about the Academy Awards.

w Neil Simon   play Neil Simon
d Herbert Ross   ph David M. Walsh   m Claude Bolling
pd Albert Brenner

Michael Caine, Maggie Smith, Walter Matthau, Elaine May, Alan Alda, Jane Fonda, Richard Pryor, Bill Cosby

'By turns silly and thoughtful, tedious and charming, broad and delicate.' – Frank Rich

AA: Maggie Smith
AAN: Neil Simon; art direction

Call Me Bwana*

GB 1962 93m Eastmancolor
Rank/Eon (Harry Saltzman, Albert R. Broccoli)

A fake African explorer is sent to the jungle to recover a space capsule.

Moderate star farce with occasional bright moments.

w Nate Monaster, Johanna Harwood   d Gordon Douglas   ph Ted Moore   m Monty Norman

Bob Hope, Anita Ekberg, Edie Adams, Lionel Jeffries, Percy Herbert, Paul Carpenter, Orlando Martins

Callaway Went Thataway*

US 1951 81m bw
MGM (Melvin Frank, Norman Panama)
GB title: The Star Said No

The old movies of a Hollywood cowboy become popular on TV, but the star has become a hopeless drunk and an actor is hired to pose as him for public appearances.

Reasonably engaging comedy using charm rather than acid.

wd Melvin Frank, Norman Panama   *ph* Ray June   *m* Marlin Skiles

Dorothy McGuire, Fred MacMurray, Howard Keel, Jesse White, Natalie Schafer

The Cameraman***
US 1928 78m approx (24 fps)
  bw silent
MGM (Lawrence Weingarten)

In order to woo a film star, a street photographer becomes a newsreel cameraman.

Highly regarded chapter of farcical errors, among the star's top features.

w Clyde Bruckman, Lex Lipton, Richard Schayer   *d* Edward Sedgwick   *ph* Elgin Lessley, Reggie Manning

Buster Keaton, Marceline Day, Harry Gribbon, Harold Goodwin

† The film was remade in 1948 for Red Skelton as *Watch the Birdie*, with Keaton sadly supervising the gags but getting no credit.

Cancel My Reservation
US 1972 99m Technicolor
Naho Enterprises

A TV talk show host retreats to his ranch and finds himself mixed up with murder.

Bob Hope's last film, though it reverted to farce and his bumbling coward persona, proved a sorry affair with egg on the face of everybody concerned.

w Arthur Marx, Robert Fisher
novel The Broken Gun by Louis L'Amour   *d* Paul Bogart

Bob Hope, Eva Marie Saint, Ralph Bellamy, Forrest Tucker, Anne Archer, Keenan Wynn, Doodles Weaver

The Cannonball Run
US 1980 95m Technicolor
Golden Harvest (Albert S. Ruddy)
V, L

The adventures of ill-assorted contestants in the illegal Cannonball coast-to-coast race.

Well-known stars are all at sea in this comedy/disaster extravaganza, which seems to have begun as a joke rather than a script.

w Brock Yates   *d* Hal Needham
ph Michael Butler   *md* Al Capps

Burt Reynolds, Roger Moore, Farrah Fawcett, Dom DeLuise, Dean Martin, Sammy Davis Jnr, Adrienne Barbeau, Jack Elam, Bert Convy, Jamie Farr, Peter Fonda, Molly Picon, Bianca Jagger

'Lacking any recognizable plot or characterization, or indeed incidental invention, it merely offers a parade of inept whimsy and lame intra-mural reference.' – *Tim Pulleine, MFB*
'Moviegoers who relish the screech of tyres taking a fast turn on a narrow bend should have a whale of a time.' – *Daily Mail*

Cannonball Run II
US 1983 108m Technicolor
Golden Harvest/Warner (Albert S. Ruddy)

An Arab sheik puts up a million-dollar prize for the Cannonball Run.

Dispirited rehash of number one, with

poor technique and non-performances by stars who should have known better than to get involved.

w Hal Needham, Albert S. Ruddy, Harvey Miller   d Hal Needham
ph Nick McLean   m Al Capps
ad Thomas E. Azzari   ed William Gordean, Carl Kress

Burt Reynolds, Dom DeLuise, Sammy Davis Jnr, Dean Martin, Jamie Farr, Telly Savalas, Shirley Maclaine, Frank Sinatra, Susan Anton, Catherine Bach, Richard Kiel, Tim Conway, Sid Caesar, Don Knotts, Ricardo Montalban, Jim Nabors, Henry Silva

Can't Buy Me Love
US   1987   94m   colour
Warner/Touchstone (Thom Mount)
L

A wimp hires a popular cheerleader to be his girlfriend for a month to improve his social standing.

Predictable comedy aimed at a teenage audience, and they are welcome to it.

w Michael Swerdlick   d James Foley   ph Peter Lyons Collister
m Robert Folk   pd D. J. Harris
ed Jeff Gourson

Patrick Dempsey, Amanda Peterson, Courtney Gains, Seth Green, Tina Caspary, Devin Devasquez, Darcy de Moss, Eric Bruskotter

The Captain's Paradise*
GB   1953   89m   bw
BL/London (Anthony Kimmins)
V

The captain of a steamer plying between Gibraltar and Tangier has a wife in each port, one to suit each of his personalities.

Over-dry comedy in which the idea is much funnier than the script. One is

left with the memory of a pleasant star performance.

w Alec Coppel, Nicholas Phipps
d Anthony Kimmins   ph Ted Scaife   m Malcolm Arnold

Alec Guinness, Celia Johnson, Yvonne de Carlo, Charles Goldner, Miles Malleson, Bill Fraser, Nicholas Phipps, Ferdy Mayne, George Benson
AAN: original story (Alec Coppel)

The Captain's Table*
GB   1958   89m   Eastmancolor
Rank (Joseph Janni)

A cargo skipper is given command of a luxury liner and has to watch his manners.

Lively adaptation of a frivolous book of obvious jokes, most of which come up quite funny amid the luxurious surroundings.

w John Whiting, Bryan Forbes, Nicholas Phipps   novel Richard Gordon   d Jack Lee
ph Christopher Challis   m Frank Cordell

John Gregson, Peggy Cummins, *Donald Sinden*, *Reginald Beckwith*, Nadia Gray, Richard Wattis, Maurice Denham, Nicholas Phipps, Joan Sims, Miles Malleson

Car Trouble
GB   1986   93m   colour
Thorn EMI/GTO/Goldfarb (Howard Malin, Gregory J. DeSantis)
V

A woman having an affair with a car salesman finds herself sexually locked to him in her husband's new vehicle.

This weird premise for a comedy rings up remarkably few laughs.

w James Whaley, A. J. Tipping

d David Green   *ph* Michael Garfath

Julie Walters, Ian Charleson, Stratford Johns, Vincenzo Ricotta

Car Wash
US   1976   96m   Technicolor
Universal
V

Various eccentrics congregate around the Dee Luxe Car Wash.

Zany ethnic (black) comedy with little rhyme or reason in its development but a certain vigour in some of its sketches. A subsequent TV series didn't last.

w Joel Schumacher   *d* Michael Schultz

Franklyn Ajaye, Sully Boyar, Richard Pryor, Ivan Dixon, Antonio Fargas, Tracy Reed

'Its specialty is yanking laughs by having blacks do dirtier versions of the standard pranks that naughty kids used to do in comedies.' – *Pauline Kael*

Carbon Copy
US   1981   91m   Metrocolor
Hemdale/RKO (Stanley Shapiro, Carter de Haven)
L

An executive is shocked when his long-lost son turns out to be black.

Stale comedy. The producers clearly think the basic idea worth ramming home a score of times; the characterization is thin and the production undernourished.

w Stanley Shapiro   *d* Michael Schultz   *ph* Fred J. Koenekamp *m* Bill Conti

George Segal, Susan Saint James, Jack Warden, Dick Martin, Denzel Washington, Paul Winfield

'It makes *Guess Who's Coming to Dinner?* look like a tract for the nineties.' – *Derek Malcolm, Guardian*

'He's the cheekiest man in town!'
The Card**
GB   1952   91m   bw
Rank/British Film Makers (John Bryan)
US title: *The Promoter*

A bright young clerk from the potteries finds many ingenious ways of improving his bank account and his place in society.

Pleasing period comedy with the star in a made-to-measure role and excellent production values.

w Eric Ambler   *novel* Arnold Bennett   *d Ronald Neame* *ph* Oswald Morris   *m* William Alwyn   *ad* T. Hopwell Ash

Alec Guinness, Glynis Johns, Petula Clark, *Valerie Hobson,* Edward Chapman, Veronica Turleigh, Gibb McLaughlin, Frank Pettingell

Cardboard Cavalier*
GB   1949   96m   bw
Rank/Two Cities (Walter Forde)

In Cromwellian England, royalists commission a barrow boy to carry a secret letter. Helped by Nell Gwynn, he succeeds after encounters with a castle ghost and custard pies.

A pantomime crossed with an Aldwych farce in a period setting. It failed at the time but now seems a brave try, with nice judgment all round.

w Noel Langley   *d Walter Forde* *ph* Jack Hildyard   *m* Lambert Williamson

Sid Field, Margaret Lockwood, Mary Clare, Jerry Desmonde, Claude Hulbert, Irene Handl, Brian Worth, Edmund Willard (as Cromwell)

Career Opportunities

US 1991 85m DeLuxe
Universal/Hughes Entertainment (John
  Hughes, A. Hunt Lowry)
V

A young nightwatchman outwits
thieves trying to rob a department
store.

Tired teen comedy that runs out of
jokes long before the end.

w John Hughes   d Bryan
Gordon   ph Don McAlpine
m Thomas Newman   pd Paul
Sylbert   ed Glenn Farr, Peck
Prior

Frank Whaley, Jennifer Connelly,
Dermot Mulroney, Kieran Mulroney,
John M. Jackson, Jenny O'Hara,
Noble Willingham, Barry Corbin, John
Candy (uncredited)

'Plenty of absorbing characters, smart,
snappy dialog and delightful stretches
of comic foolery.' – Variety

Carlton-Browne of the FO

GB 1958 88m bw
British Lion/Charter Films (John Boulting)
V
US title: Man in a Cocked Hat

When valuable mineral deposits are
found in a small British colony, the
diplomat sent to cement good
relations does quite the reverse.

Hit-or-miss farcical comedy several
rungs below the Ealing style, with all
concerned in poor form.

wd Jeffrey Dell, Roy Boulting
ph Max Greene   m John
Addison

Terry-Thomas, Peter Sellers, Ian
Bannen, Thorley Walters, Raymond
Huntley, John Le Mesurier, Luciana
Paluzzi, Miles Malleson, Kynaston
Reeves, Marie Lohr

Carnal Knowledge*

US 1971 97m Technicolor
  Panavision
Avco Embassy/Icarus (Mike Nichols)
L

A college student embarks on an
enthusiastic and varied sex life but by
middle age is bored and empty.

Hampered by an unsuitable wide
screen, this pretentious but
fragmented comedy drama is
embarrassingly conscious of its own
daring in subject and language, and
good performances are weighed
down by an unsubtle script and tricksy
direction.

w Jules Feiffer   d Mike Nichols
ph Giuseppe Rotunno   m various
songs   pd Richard Sylbert

Jack Nicholson, Arthur Garfunkel,
Candice Bergen, Ann-Margret, Rita
Moreno
AAN: Ann-Margret

Carry Me Back

New Zealand 1982 90m colour
Kiwi Films/New Zealand Film Commission
  (Graeme Crowley)

Two sons attempt to smuggle their
father's corpse from the city to their
farm in order to benefit from his
will.

Blackish comedy of mishaps and
misfits that occasionally amuses.

w Derek Morton, Keith Aberdeen,
John Reid   story Joy Cowley
d John Reid   ph Graeme
Cowley   m Tim Bridgewater,
James Hall   ad Jim Barr
ed Simon Reece, Michael Horton

Grant Tilley, Kelly Johnson, Dorothy
McKegg, Derek Hardwick, Joanne
Mildenhall

Carry On Abroad*
GB   1972   88m   Eastmancolor
Fox-Rank/Peter Rogers
V

A couple who go on a package holiday
to Spain find that their hotel is still
being built and there is a staff of no
more than three.

Every opportunity for bathroom jokes
is relished in what is otherwise an
average effort.

w Talbot Rothwell   d Gerald
Thomas   ph Alan Hume   m Eric
Rogers   ad Lionel Couch
ed Alfred Roome

Sidney James, Kenneth Williams,
Charles Hawtrey, Joan Sims, Bernard
Bresslaw, Darbara Windsor, Kenneth
Connor, Peter Butterworth, Jimmy
Logan, June Whitfield, Hattie Jacques

'Travelling well-trodden paths of
slapstick, *double entendre* and nudging
innuendo.' – *Nigel Andrews*

Carry On Again Doctor
GB   1969   89m   Eastmancolor
Rank/Adder (Peter Rogers)
V

A doctor, exiled to a tropical island,
returns to Britain with a special
slimming cure.

A slight air of desperation hangs over
the often-used setting of a hospital,
and most of the jokes remain in
intensive care.

w Talbot Rothwell   d Gerald
Thomas   ph Ernest Steward
m Eric Rogers   pd Jack Blezard
ed Alfred Roome

Sidney James, Kenneth Williams, Jim
Dale, Charles Hawtrey, Joan Sims,
Barbara Windsor, Hattie Jacques,
Patsy Rowlands, Peter Butterworth,
Pat Coombs

'Perhaps the team go that much

further than ever before. Their fans
will be delighted; those who aren't
won't care.' – *Richard Davis, Films and
Filming*

Carry On at Your Convenience
GB   1971   90m   Eastmancolor
Rank/Peter Rogers
V

A union leader at the firm of W. C.
Boggs, makers of fine toiletware, keeps
ordering the workers to come out on
strike.

No toilet joke is left unplumbed here,
and the result is dire.

w Talbot Rothwell   d Gerald
Thomas   ph Ernest Steward
m Eric Rogers   ed Alfred Roome

Sidney James, Kenneth Williams,
Charles Hawtrey, Joan Sims, Bernard
Bresslaw, Hattie Jacques, Kenneth
Cope, Patsy Rowlands, Jacki Piper,
Richard O'Callaghan

'One of the least funny of this
staggeringly successful series.' – *Eric
Braun*
'Even more scrappily assembled than
usual and, with the exception of a
fairly amusing parody of sex
education films, the level of humour,
though noticeably cleaner than of
late, is still rock bottom.' – *David
McGillivray*

Carry On Behind**
GB   1975   90m   Eastmancolor
Fox-Rank/Peter Rogers
V

Archaeologists arrive to search for
Roman remains at a caravan site full
of holiday-makers.

One of the best of the series and
certainly the last watchable film the
team produced.

w Dave Freeman   d Gerald

Thomas   *ph* Ernest Steward
m Eric Rogers   *ed* Alfred Roome

Elke Sommer, Kenneth Williams,
Joan Sims, Bernard Bresslaw, Kenneth
Connor, Peter Butterworth, Jack
Douglas, Windsor Davies, Liz Fraser,
Patsy Rowlands

'Emerges as the most consistently
funny *Carry On* in many years . . . a
strong vein of comedy is mined from
the simple situation of campsite
overcrowding, with some of the best
sight gags involving a lugubrious
Irish wolf-hound and a foul-mouthed
mynah bird.' – *Verina Glaessner, MFB*

Carry On Cabby*
GB   1963   91m   bw
Anglo Amalgamated/Peter Rogers
V

The neglected wife of the owner of a
taxi firm sets up a rival firm with
women drivers.

A deft farcical battle of the sexes.

w Talbot Rothwell   *d* Gerald
Thomas   *ph* Alan Hume   *m* Eric
Rogers   *ed* Archie Ludski

Sidney James, Charles Hawtrey,
Kenneth Connor, Hattie Jacques,
Esma Cannon, Liz Fraser, Bill Owen,
Milo O'Shea, Jim Dale

'The golden formula of the *Carry On*
series is back with a bang.' – *Variety*

Carry On Camping*
GB   1969   88m   Eastmancolor
Rank/Peter Rogers
V

Two men take their girlfriends on
holiday to a nudist camp in the hope
that it will make them less inhibited.

A partly successful attempt to provide
the characters with fewer sexual
repressions than usual.

w Talbot Rothwell   *d* Gerald
Thomas   *ph* Ernest Steward
m Eric Rogers   *ad* Lionel Couch
ed Alfred Roome

Sidney James, Kenneth Williams,
Joan Sims, Charles Hawtrey, Terry
Scott, Barbara Windsor

'Suffers somewhat in comparison to
some of its predecessors in that it lacks
a storyline, however slim.' – *Variety*

Carry On Cleo*
GB   1964   92m   Eastmancolor
Anglo Amalgamated/Peter Rogers
V

Ancient Britons are captured by the
Romans while Mark Antony carries
on with Cleopatra.

Sporadically amusing parody of the
Elizabeth Taylor epic, though it
should have been much funnier.

w Talbot Rothwell   *d* Gerald
Thomas   *ph* Alan Hume   *m* Eric
Rogers   *ad* Bert Davey   *ed* Archie
Ludski

Sidney James, Kenneth Williams,
Charles Hawtrey, Joan Sims,
Kenneth Connor, Jim Dale, Amanda
Barrie, E. V. H. Emmett, Sheila
Hancock, Jon Pertwee

'Gags, both verbal and visual, suffer
from repetition.' – *Variety*

† As a result of a court case for breach
of copyright brought by Twentieth
Century-Fox, the film's poster, which
parodied the advertising for *Cleopatra*,
had to be withdrawn.

'Up your anchor for a well crewed
voyage!!'
Carry On Columbus
GB   1992   91m   colour
Island World/Comedy House/Peter Rogers
  (John Goldstone)
V

Columbus's voyage to find a route to the East is sabotaged by spies in the pay of the Sultan of Turkey.

Ill-starred attempt, with a succession of single entendres and some inept performances, to revive a tired old formula.

w Dave Freeman   d Gerald Thomas   ph Alan Hume   m John Du Prez   pd Harry Pottle   ed Chris Blunden

Jim Dale, Bernard Cribbins, Maureen Lipman, Peter Richardson, Rik Mayall, Alexei Sayle, Charles Fleischer, Larry Miller, Leslie Phillips, Julian Clary, Sara Crowe, Rebecca Lacey, Nigel Planer, June Whitfield, Richard Wilson

'Painfully unfunny, lacking imagination and energy.' – *Philip French, Observer*

Carry On Constable*

GB   1960   86m   bw
Anglo Amalgamated/Peter Rogers
V

Four new and inept constables report for duty at their local police station.

In part a parody of the popular TV series *Dixon of Dock Green* and moderately amusing despite the absence of a plot.

w Norman Hudis   story Brock Williams   d Gerald Thomas   ph Ted Scaife   m Bruce Montgomery   ad Carmen Dillon   ed John Shirley

Sidney James, Kenneth Williams, Charles Hawtrey, Joan Sims, Kenneth Connor, Eric Barker, Leslie Phillips, Hattie Jacques, Shirley Eaton, Cyril Chamberlain, Irene Handl, Esma Cannon, Freddie Mills

'Simply an anthology of police gags and situations.' – *Variety*

Carry On Cowboy**

GB   1965   95m   Eastmancolor
Anglo Amalgamated/Peter Rogers
V

A sanitary engineer is given the task of cleaning up a town being terrorized by outlaws.

Amusing parody of *High Noon* and other classic Westerns.

w Talbot Rothwell   d Gerald Thomas   ph Alan Hume   m Eric Rogers   ad Bert Davey   ed Rod Keys

Sidney James, Kenneth Williams, Charles Hawtrey, Joan Sims, Jim Dale, Percy Herbert, Angela Douglas, Bernard Bresslaw, Peter Butterworth, Jon Pertwee

'Less a string of irrelevant situations than usual, giving the team more opportunity for comedy thesping.' – *Variety*

Carry On Cruising

GB   1962   89m   Eastmancolor
Anglo Amalgamated/Peter Rogers
V

The captain of a cruise liner finds his peace of mind threatened by new crew members and tourists.

Weak comedy that doesn't seem to know where it's going.

w Norman Hudis   story Eric Barker   d Gerald Thomas   ph Alan Hume   m Bruce Montgomery, Douglas Gamley   ad Carmen Dillon   ed John Shirley

Sidney James, Kenneth Williams, Kenneth Connor, Liz Fraser, Dilys Laye, Esma Cannon, Lance Perceval,

Ronnie Stevens, Cyril Chamberlain, Anton Rodgers

'Direction by Gerald Thomas is boisterously effective.' – *Variety*

Carry On Dick
GB 1974 91m Eastmancolor
Rank/Peter Rogers
V

Bow Street Runners ask a village clergyman to help them catch the highwayman Dick Turpin, better known as Big Dick.

Inspiration flags in a comedy where both cast and director seem hardly interested in what they were doing, probably because they had been doing it for too long.

w Talbot Rothwell *story* Lawrie Wyman, George Evans *d* Gerald Thomas *ph* Ernest Steward *m* Eric Rogers *ed* Alfred Roome

Sidney James, Kenneth Williams, Kenneth Connor, Barbara Windsor, Hattie Jacques, Bernard Bresslaw, Joan Sims, Peter Butterworth, Jack Douglas, Patsy Rowlands, Bill Maynard

'These tireless upholders of the "saucy" postcard tradition soldier on with their perennial rib-poking, elbow-nudging, albeit scarcely jaw-breaking esprit . . . Maybe their continuing appeal is beyond criticism – or according to taste, beneath it.' – *Nigel Gearing, MFB*

Carry On Doctor*
GB 1968 94m Eastmancolor
Rank/Peter Rogers
V

Hospital patients revolt against a tyrannical matron when their favourite doctor is sacked.

Occasionally amusing farce.

w Talbot Rothwell *d* Gerald Thomas *ph* Alan Hume *m* Eric Rogers *ed* Alfred Roome

Frankie Howerd, Sidney James, Kenneth Williams, Jim Dale, Charles Hawtrey, Joan Sims, Barbara Windsor, Hattie Jacques, Anita Harris, Bernard Bresslaw, Peter Butterworth

'Usual unabashed mixture of double-meanings, down-to-earth vulgarity, blue jokes.' – *Variety*

Carry On – Don't Lose Your Head
GB 1966 90m Eastmancolor
Rank/Peter Rogers
V
aka: *Don't Lose Your Head*

A foppish Briton, the Black Fingernail, rescues French aristocrats from the guillotine during the French Revolution.

A limp parody of *The Scarlet Pimpernel* causes no more than a few chuckles.

w Talbot Rothwell *d* Gerald Thomas *ph* Alan Hume *m* Eric Rogers *ed* Rod Keys

Sidney James, Kenneth Williams, Jim Dale, Charles Hawtrey, Joan Sims, Peter Butterworth, Dany Robin, Peter Gilmore

'A crazy debauch of duelling, doublecrossing and disaster. The troupers jump through their well-known hoops with agility.' – *Variety*

Carry On Emmannuelle
GB 1978 88m Technicolor
Hemdale/Peter Rogers
V

The wife of an impotent French ambassador to England seduces every man she meets.

A doomed attempt to update the formula for more sexually permissive times that resulted in the worst of the series, and the last for fourteen years, until it was revived in 1992.

w Lance Peters *d* Gerald Thomas *ph* Alan Hume *m* Eric Rogers *ad* Jack Shampan *ed* Peter Boita

Suzanne Danielle, Kenneth Williams, Kenneth Connor, Jack Douglas, Joan Sims, Peter Butterworth, Larry Dann, Beryl Reid, Eric Barker

'This one is rude, certainly, but the relentless phallic innuendo is as labored as makers' determination to show nothing to worry the censor. Leaden comic timing . . .' *Variety*
'It's rather like watching endearing elderly relatives disgracing themselves at a party.' – *Andy Medhurst, Sight and Sound*

Carry On England
GB 1976 89m colour
Rank/Peter Rogers
V

In 1940 the men and women who form an experimental anti-aircraft battery prefer to make love rather than war, to the annoyance of their new commanding officer.

One of the weakest of the series and a sign that the series was running out of energy, unable to find suitable replacements for its usual team and handicapped more than usual by a weak script.

w Jack Seddon, David Pursall *d* Gerald Thomas *ph* Ernest Steward *m* Max Harris *ad* Lionel Couch *ed* Richard Marden

Kenneth Connor, Windsor Davies, Patrick Mower, Judy Geeson, Jack Douglas, Diane Langton, Melvyn Hayes, Joan Sims, Peter Jones, Peter Butterworth, David Lodge

'Suffers from a particularly unfortunate hangup. It's not funny.' – *Variety*
'The laboured puns and overacting are as tiresome as ever.' – *MFB*

Carry On – Follow That Camel
GB 1966 90m Eastmancolor
Rank/Peter Rogers
V
aka: *Follow That Camel*

An English gentleman, accused of behaving badly at cricket, joins the Foreign Legion to regain his honour.

An ill-match between American and English styles of vaudeville and music-hall humour results in a direly unamusing movie.

w Talbot Rothwell *d* Gerald Thomas *ph* Alan Hume *m* Eric Rogers *ed* Alfred Roome

Phil Silvers, Kenneth Williams, Jim Dale, Charles Hawtrey, Joan Sims, Peter Butterworth, Anita Harris, Bernard Bresslaw, Angela Douglas, Peter Gilmore

'It all works with considerable bounce, with elements of parody of Beau Geste-style movies for those alert to them. All the regular comics are on first-rate form.' – *Variety*

Carry On Girls
GB 1973 88m Eastmancolor
Fox-Rank/Peter Rogers
V

The organizer of a seaside beauty contest annoys the local members of the Women's Liberation movement.

Below average romp.

w Talbot Rothwell *d* Gerald

Thomas *ph* Alan Hume   *m* Eric Rogers   *ed* Alfred Roome

Sidney James, Kenneth Connor, Joan Sims, Barbara Windsor, Bernard Bresslaw, Peter Butterworth, June Whitfield, Jack Douglas, Patsy Rowlands, Jimmy Logan, Joan Hickson, David Lodge

'Herculean efforts on the part of the entire cast do eventually pull off (in the context, I must insist this is not meant as a *double entendre*) some fairly effective slapstick.' – *Eric Braun*
'Thriving as ever on the sexual repression of its audience, Talbot Rothwell's windy, radio-style script . . . turns out the routine quota of puns on such words as bang, boob, bed, bust, bristol and bash, and makes such weary labour of it that every joke can be heard creaking into place long before the arrival of the punch-line.' – *Gareth Jones, MFB*

'A Great Guy With His Chopper!'
Carry On Henry**
GB 1971 89m Eastmancolor
Rank/Adder (Peter Rogers)
V

King Henry tries to get rid of his wife when he discovers she smells of garlic.

A coarsely successful parody of *Anne of the Thousand Days* and other period films.

w Talbot Rothwell   *d* Gerald Thomas   *ph* Alan Hume   *m* Eric Rogers   *ed* Alfred Roome

Sidney James, Kenneth Williams, Charles Hawtrey, Joan Sims, Terry Scott, Barbara Windsor, Kenneth Connor, Peter Butterworth, Peter Gilmore, Patsy Rowlands

'They have managed to come up with a bit of a winner . . . there is a delicious send up of that most boring and

perennial line of cinematic yawns, the historical romance.' – *Peter Buckley*
'The cast is the familiar stock company at full force; the script is from Talbot Rothwell at his most characteristic; and the film is at any rate better looking than most of its shoe-string predecessors.' – *John Pidgeon, MFB*

Carry On Jack
GB 1964 91m Eastmancolor
Anglo Amalgamated/Peter Rogers
V
US title: *Carry On Venus*

A midshipman finds himself at the mercy of a bullying captain and they are both put overboard after a mutiny.

Salty but unamusing parody of *Mutiny on The Bounty* and other sea-faring sagas.

w Talbot Rothwell   *d* Gerald Thomas   *ph* Alan Hume   *m* Eric Rogers   *ad* Jack Shampan   *ed* Archie Ludski

Bernard Cribbins, Kenneth Williams, Charles Hawtrey, Juliet Mills, Donald Houston, Percy Herbert, Peter Gilmore, Jim Dale, Anton Rogers, Cecil Parker, Patrick Cargill

'Gerald Thomas steers his cast through a maze of mixups and misadventures.' – *Variety*

Carry On Loving
GB 1970 88m Eastmancolor
Rank/Adder (Peter Rogers)
V

Assorted misfits try their luck at a computer dating agency.

Limp comedy for which the regulars show little enthusiasm.

w Talbot Rothwell   *d* Gerald Thomas   *ph* Ernest Steward   *m* Eric Rogers   *ad* Lionel Couch   *ed* Alfred Roome

Sidney James, Kenneth Williams, Charles Hawtrey, Joan Sims, Terry Scott, Hattie Jacques, Richard O'Callaghan, Bernard Bresslaw, Jacki Piper, Imogen Hassall, Patsy Rowlands, Bill Maynard

'Full of tired jokes, obvious situations and ludicrous performances, we have all been here at least three times before, but the crew have a way of working over the old material.' – *Peter Buckley, Films and Filming*
'Scrapings from the bottom of Talbot Rothwell's barrel of well-worn double entendre, delivered with mechanical efficiency by an equally well-worn cast.' – *MFB*

Carry On Matron*
GB 1972 87m Eastmancolor
Rank/Peter Rogers
V

A con-man persuades his son to dress as a nurse in order to infiltrate a maternity hospital to steal contraceptive pills.

Intermittently amusing comedy.

w Talbot Rothwell   *d* Gerald Thomas   *ph* Ernest Steward   *m* Eric Rogers   *ad* Lionel Couch   *ed* Alfred Roome

Sidney James, Kenneth Williams, Charles Hawtrey, Joan Sims, Hattie Jacques, Bernard Bresslaw, Terry Scott, Kenneth Cope, Barbara Windsor, Kenneth Connor, Jacki Piper, Patsy Rowlands, Jack Douglas

'A largely successful if slightly patchy addition to the series; its comic highlight involves Sid James, required to assume a medical alias, introducing himself as "Dr Zhivago".' – *Kenneth Thompson, MFB*

Carry On Nurse**
GB 1959 86m bw
Anglo Amalgamated/Peter Rogers
V

Male patients in a hospital rebel against the dictatorial matron.

The first true *Carry On*, done when the whole notion was still fresh and the cast responded with glee to its crudities.

w Norman Hudis   *story* Patrick Cargill, Jack Searle   *d* Gerald Thomas   *ph* Reg Wyer   *m* Bruce Montgomery   *ad* Alex Vetchinsky   *ed* John Shirley

Shirley Eaton, Kenneth Williams, Charles Hawtrey, Hattie Jacques, Joan Sims, Kenneth Connor, Terence Longden, Bill Owen, Leslie Phillips, Wilfrid Hyde-White, Irene Handl

'The yocks come thick and fast.' – *Variety*
'A seaside postcard come to life, a shameless procession of vulgarities. Utterly irresistible.' – *Andy Medhurst, Sight and Sound*

† The film topped the box-office in Britain and was surprisingly successful in the US where it ran for two-and-a-half years.

Carry On Regardless
GB 1960 90m bw
Anglo Amalgamated/Peter Rogers
V

A group of incompetent unemployed join an odd-job agency.

Less a film than a series of sketches, which are very variable in quality.

w Norman Hudis   *d* Ralph Thomas   *ph* Alan Hume   *m* Bruce Montgomery   *ed* John Shirley

Sidney James, Kenneth Williams, Charles Hawtrey, Joan Sims,

Kenneth Connor, Bill Owen, Liz Fraser, Terence Longden, Esma Cannon, Hattie Jacques, Fenella Fielding

'Ingenuity of scriptwriter Norman Hudis is sometimes a bit strained, but he has come up with some sound comedy situations.' − *Variety*

Carry On Screaming*
GB 1966 97m Eastmancolor
Anglo Amalgamated/Peter Rogers
V

Police investigate a mad doctor and his sister, who are turning young women into mannequins.

A send-up of Hammer horrors that manages to emulate the garishness of the originals.

w Talbot Rothwell *d* Gerald Thomas *ph* Alan Hume *m* Eric Rogers *ed* Rod Keys

Harry H. Corbett, Kenneth Williams, Jim Dale, Charles Hawtrey, Fenella Fielding, Joan Sims, Angela Douglas, Bernard Bresslaw, Peter Butterworth, Jon Pertwee

'Puts the skids under horror pix. Snag is that most horror films themselves teeter on the edge of parody and it is rather tough trying to burlesque a parody.' − *Variety*

Carry On Sergeant
GB 1958 83m bw
Anglo Amalgamated/Insignia (Peter Rogers)

An army training sergeant accepts a bet that his last platoon of raw recruits will win the Star Squad award.

Shabby farce with humdrum script and slack direction, saved by energetic performances.

w Norman Hudis *play The Bull Boys* by R. F. Delderfield *d* Gerald

Thomas *ph* Peter Hennessy *m* Bruce Montgomery

Bob Monkhouse, William Hartnell, Kenneth Williams, Charles Hawtrey, Shirley Eaton, Eric Barker, Dora Bryan, Bill Owen, Kenneth Connor

'They're At It Again − O.O.O.H!'
Carry On Spying
GB 1964 87m bw
Anglo Amalgamated/Peter Rogers
V

British spies are sent to recapture a secret formula stolen by the Total Extinction of Non-Conforming Humans, otherwise known as Stench.

A feeble parody of the Bond films.

w Talbot Rothwell, Sid Colin *d* Gerald Thomas *ph* Alan Hume *m* Eric Rogers *ed* Archie Ludski

Kenneth Williams, Bernard Cribbins, Charles Hawtrey, Barbara Windsor, Eric Pohlmann, Eric Barker, Dilys Laye, Jim Dale, Richard Wattis

'A dazzling return to form, milking every last drop from the ripe targets of espionage in general and Bond in particular.' − *Andy Medhurst, Sight and Sound*

Carry On Teacher*
GB 1959 86m bw
Anglo Amalgamated/Peter Rogers
V

Pupils at a school sabotage the headmaster's attempts to get another job because they don't want to lose him.

Amiable comedy that is less frenetic than many in the series, and all the better for it.

w Norman Hudis *d* Gerald

Thomas   *ph* Reginald Wyer
m· Bruce Montgomery   *ed* John
Shirley

Ted Ray, Kenneth Williams, Charles
Hawtrey, Leslie Phillips, Joan Sims,
Kenneth Connor, Hattie Jacques,
Rosalind Knight, Cyril Chamberlain

'The laughs come readily.' – *Variety*

Carry On up the Jungle
GB   1970   89m   Eastmancolor
Rank/Peter Rogers
V

An ornithologist journeys to Africa in
search of the rare Oozulum bird.

A tired parody of Tarzan and jungle
films; the jokes get lost in the
undergrowth.

w Talbot Rothwell   *d* Gerald
Thomas   *ph* Ernest Steward
m Eric Rogers   *ad* Alex
Vetchinsky   *ed* Alfred Roome

Frankie Howerd, Sidney James,
Charles Hawtrey, Joan Sims, Terry
Scott, Kenneth Connor, Bernard
Bresslaw, Jacki Piper

'The film is an assured success.' – *Films
and Filming*

Carry On up the Khyber***
GB   1968   88m   Eastmancolor
Rank/Adder (Peter Rogers)
V

A Scots regiment, the Third Foot and
Mouth, fails to defend British interests
in India.

The best of the series, a wonderfully
vulgar and ripe low comedy on an
imperial theme.

w Talbot Rothwell   *d* Gerald
Thomas   *ph* Alan Hume   *m* Eric
Rogers   *ed* Alfred Roome

Sidney James, Kenneth Williams,

Charles Hawtrey, Joan Sims, Roy
Castle, Bernard Bresslaw, Peter
Butterworth, Terry Scott, Angela
Douglas, Cardew Robinson, Julian
Holloway, Peter Gilmore

'Continues to rely primarily on low-
comedy visual and verbal gag
situations for its yocks.' – *Variety*

† The movie was filmed in Wales.

Casanova's Big Night
US   1954   86m   Technicolor
Paramount (Paul Jones)
V

In old Italy, the great lover is fleeing
from his creditors and changes places
with a tailor's apprentice.

The last of Bob Hope's big-budget,
big-studio burlesques is a lumbering
vehicle which wastes its star cast and
mistimes its laughs.

w Hal Kanter, Edmund Hartmann
d Norman Z. McLeod   *ph* Lionel
Lindon   *m* Lyn Murray

Bob Hope, Joan Fontaine (an
unhappy comedy foil), Basil
Rathbone, Vincent Price, Audrey
Dalton, Hugh Marlowe, John
Carradine, Primo Carnera, Arnold
Moss, Lon Chaney Jnr

Casino Royale
GB   1967   130m   Technicolor
    Panavision
Columbia/Famous Artists (Charles K.
    Feldman, Jerry Bresler)
V, L

The heads of the allied spy forces call
Sir James Bond out of retirement to
fight the power of *SMERSH*.

Woeful all-star kaleidoscope, a way-
out spoof which generates far fewer
laughs than the original. One of the
most shameless wastes of time and
talent in screen history.

w Wolf Mankowitz, John Law,
Michael Sayers *novel* Ian
Fleming *d* John Huston, Ken
Hughes, Val Guest, Robert Parrish, Joe
McGrath, Richard Talmadge
ph Jack Hildyard *m* Burt
Bacharach *pd* Michael Stringer

David Niven, Deborah Kerr, Orson
Welles, Peter Sellers, Ursula Andress,
Woody Allen, William Holden,
Charles Boyer, John Huston, Joanna
Pettet, Daliah Lavi, Kurt Kasznar,
Jacqueline Bisset, Derek Nimmo,
George Raft, Ronnie Corbett, Peter
O'Toole, Jean-Paul Belmondo,
Geoffrey Bayldon, Duncan Macrae

'One of those wild wacky
extravaganzas in which the audience
is expected to have a great time
because everybody making the film
did. It seldom works out that way, and
certainly doesn't here.' – *John Russell
Taylor*
'The dialogue is witless and
unhampered by taste, and the
interminable finale is a collection of
clichés in a brawl involving the
cavalry, parachuted Indians, split-
second appearances by George Raft
and Jean-Paul Belmondo, every
variety of mayhem, and Woody Allen
burping radiation as a walking atom
bomb.' – *Judith Crist*
'The worst film I ever enjoyed.' –
Donald Zec
AAN: song 'The Look of Love' (*m* Burt
Bacharach, *ly* Hal David)

The Cat and the Canary***
US 1939 72m bw
Paramount (Arthur Hornblow Jnr)

A superbly staged remake, briskly
paced, perfectly cast and lusciously
photographed.

The comedy-thriller par excellence,
with Bob Hope fresh and sympathetic
in his first big star part.

w *Walter de Leon, Lynn Starling*
d *Elliott Nugent* ph *Charles Lang*
m *Dr Ernst Toch* ad *Hans Dreier,*
Robert Usher

Bob Hope (Wally Campbell), *Paulette
Goddard* (Joyce Norman), *Gale
Sondergaard* (Miss Lu), Douglass
Montgomery (Charlie Wilder), John
Beal (Fred Blythe), *George Zucco*
(Lawyer Crosby), *Nydia Westman*
(Cicily), *Elizabeth Patterson* (Aunt
Susan), John Wray (Hendricks)

CICILY: 'Do you believe people come
back from the dead?'
WALLY: 'You mean like
republicans?'
CICILY: 'Don't these big empty
houses scare you?'
WALLY: 'Not me, I was in
vaudeville.'
WALLY: 'I get goose pimples. Even
my goose pimples have goose
pimples.'

'The objective is carried out briskly
and to our complete satisfaction.' –
New York Times
'A top programmer for upper-bracket
bookings in the keys, and will hit a
consistent stride down the line in the
subsequents.' – *Variety*
'Beautifully shot, intelligently
constructed.' – *Peter John Dyer,
1966*

The Cat and the Canary
GB 1979 98m Technicolor
Gala/Grenadier (Richard Gordon)

An overpoweringly cast but half-
heartedly scripted remake of the
above, which after a spirited
beginning bores more than it
thrills.

wd Radley Metzger ph Alex
Thomson m Steven Cagan

Honor Blackman, Michael Callan,

Edward Fox, Wendy Hiller, Beatrix Lehmann, Olivia Hussey, Daniel Massey, Carol Lynley, Peter McEnery, Wilfrid Hyde-White

'So mechanically are characters shunted through the indistinguishable rooms and corridors that one is surprised not to see the parquet marked off in neat little squares, as on a Cluedo board.' – *Gilbert Adair, MFB*

Cat Ballou**
US   1965   96m   Technicolor
Columbia (Harold Hecht)
V

Young Catherine Ballou hires a drunken gunfighter to protect her father from a vicious gunman, but despite her efforts he is shot, so she turns outlaw.

Sometimes lively, sometimes somnolent Western spoof which considering the talent involved should have been funnier than it is. The linking ballad helps.

w Walter Newman, Frank R. Pierson   *novel* Roy Chanslor
d Eliot Silverstein   *ph* Jack Marta   *m* Frank de Vol

Jane Fonda, *Lee Marvin*, Michael Callan, Dwayne Hickman, Nat King Cole, Stubby Kaye, Tom Nardini, John Marley, Reginald Denny

'Uneven, lumpy, coy and obvious.' – *Pauline Kael*

AA: Lee Marvin
AAN: Walter Newman, Frank R. Pierson; Frank de Vol; song 'The Ballad of Cat Ballou' (*m* Jerry Livingston, *ly* Mack David)

Catch 22*
US   1970   122m   Technicolor
Panavision
Paramount/Filmways (John Calley, Martin Ransohoff)
V, L

At a US Air Force base in the Mediterranean during World War II, one by one the officers are distressingly killed; a survivor paddles towards neutral Sweden.

Intensely black comedy, more so than *M*A*S*H* and less funny, effectively mordant in places but too grisly and missing several tricks.

w Buck Henry   *novel* Joseph Heller   *d* Mike Nichols   *ph* David Watkin   *m* none   *pd* Richard Sylbert

Alan Arkin, Martin Balsam, Richard Benjamin, Art Garfunkel, Jack Gilford, Buck Henry, Bob Newhart, Anthony Perkins, Paula Prentiss, Jon Voight, Martin Sheen, Orson Welles

'There are startling effects and good revue touches here and there, but the picture keeps going on and on, as if it were determined to impress us.' – *New Yorker, 1977*
'As hot and heavy as the original was cool and light.' – *Richard Schickel*
'It goes on so long that it cancels itself out, even out of people's memories; it was long awaited and then forgotten almost instantly.' – *Pauline Kael*
'Dr Strangelove out of Alice in Wonderland.' – *Daily Mail*

Catch Us If You Can
GB   1965   91m   bw
Anglo Amalgamated/Bruton (David Deutsch)
V
US title: *Having a Wild Weekend*

Freelance stuntmen have various adventures in the west of England.

The first film of a pretentious director is a bright but wearisomely high-spirited imitation of *A Hard Day's Night*.

w Peter Nichols   *d* John Boorman   *ph Manny Wynn*
m Dave Clark

The Dave Clark Five, Barbara Ferris, David Lodge, Robin Bailey, Yootha Joyce

'An uneven script, rather uncertainly making its point about disillusionment and capitulation to the sham; but – like Mr Boorman's direction – at its best well worth your attention.' – *Dilys Powell*

The Cat's Paw*
US 1936 101m bw
Harold Lloyd

The son of a Chinese missionary returns home and finds himself in the middle of a Tong war.

Very moderate star comedy from the time when he was considering himself a character comedian rather than a slapstick ace.

w Harold Lloyd, Sam Taylor
story Clarence Budington Kelland
d Sam Taylor

Harold Lloyd, George Barbier, Una Merkel, Nat Pendleton, Grant Mitchell, Vince Barnett

'The picture gets its laughs all right, but it approaches them at a crawl.' – *Variety*

Caveman
US 1981 91m Technicolor
UA (Lawrence Turman, David Foster)

Adventures of a prehistoric man.

Witless farrago of puns and farts on a lower level than Mel Brooks, if such a thing were possible.

w Rudy de Luca, Carl Gottlieb
d Carl Gottlieb   *ph* Alan Hume
m Lalo Schifrin   *pd* Philip M. Jeffries   *ed* Gene Fowler

Ringo Starr, Dennis Quaid, Jack Gilford, Barbara Bach, Avery Schreiber

'Too gross and leery for children and not nearly sprightly or sly enough for adults.' – *Daily Mail*
'Worth about half an hour of anybody's time. Unfortunately it runs 97 minutes.' – *Guardian*

The Chain*
GB 1984 100m Eastmancolor •
Quintet/County Bank/Channel 4 (Victor Glynn)

Seven groups of people, corresponding to the seven deadly sins, are involved in a house-moving chain.

Rather tedious and predictable 'all star' comedy with effective moments but no narrative command.

w Jack Rosenthal   *d* Jack Gold
ph Wolfgang Suschitzky
m Stanley Myers

Denis Lawson, Maurice Denham, Nigel Hawthorne, Billie Whitelaw, Judy Parfitt, Leo McKern, Warren Mitchell, Gary Waldhorn, Anna Massey

Charley's Aunt**
US 1941 81m bw
TCF (William Perlberg)
GB title: *Charley's American Aunt*

For complicated reasons, an Oxford undergraduate has to impersonate his friend's rich aunt from Brazil (where the nuts come from).

Very adequate version of the Victorian farce, with all concerned in excellent form.

w George Seaton   *play* Brandon
Thomas   *d* Archie Mayo
ph Peverell Marley   *m* Alfred
Newman   *ad* Richard Day, Nathan
Juran

Jack Benny, Kay Francis, James
Ellison, Anne Baxter, *Laird Cregar*,
Edmund Gwenn, Reginald Owen,
Richard Haydn, Arleen Whelan, Ernest
Cossart

† See also: *Where's Charley?*

Cheaper by the Dozen**
US   1950   86m   Technicolor
TCF (Lamar Trotti)

Efficiency expert Frank Gilbreth and
his wife Lillian have twelve children,
a fact which requires mathematical
conduct of all their lives.

Amusing family comedy set in the
twenties, unconvincing in detail
though based on a book by two of the
children. A great commercial success
and a Hollywood myth-maker.
Sequel: *Belles on their Toes* (qv).

w Lamar Trotti   *book* Frank B.
Gilbreth Jnr, Ernestine Gilbreth
Carey   *d* Walter Lang   *ph* Leon
Shamroy   *md* Lionel Newman
m Cyril Mockridge   *ad* Lyle
Wheeler, Leland Fuller

Clifton Webb, *Myrna Loy*, Jeanne Crain,
Edgar Buchanan, Barbara Bates,
Betty Lynn, Mildred Natwick, Sara
Allgood

Checking Out
GB   1988   95m   Technicolor
Virgin/Handmade (Ben Myron)
V

A successful advertising man becomes
a hypochondriac after the sudden
death of a friend.

Mildly amusing comedy.

w Joe Esterhas   *d* David Leland
ph Ian Wilson   *m* Carter Burwell
pd Barbara Ling   *ed* Lee Percy

Jeff Daniels, Melanie Mayron,
Michael Tucker, Kathleen York, Ann
Magnuson, Allan Harvey, Jo Harvey
Allen, Ian Wolfe

Cheech and Chong: Still Smokin'
US   1983   92m   colour
Paramount/Cheech & Chong's Comedy
    Film Festival Number One Inc (Peter
    MacGregor-Scott)

Two slobbish comedians attend a Burt
Reynolds-Dolly Parton film festival
in Amsterdam.

Dreary, plotless exercise in futility that
reaches its nadir in excerpts from the
duo's concert performance.

w Thomas Chong, Cheech Marin
d Thomas Chong   *ph* Harvey
Harrison   *m* George S. Clinton
ad Ruud Van Dijk   *ed* David
Ramirez, James Coblenz

Cheech Marin, Thomas Chong, Hans
Man In't Veld, Carol Van Herwijnen,
Shireen Strocker, Susan Hahn

Cheech and Chong's Next Movie
US   1980   95m   Technicolor
Howard Brown/Universal
V
GB title: *High Encounters of the Ultimate
    Kind*

Two dopers have various rude
adventures.

Totally repulsive comedy which gives
a bad name to self-indulgence.

w Cheech Marin, Thomas Chong
d Thomas Chong

Cheech Marin, Thomas Chong,
Evelyn Guerrero, Betty Kennedy, Sy
Kramer

Cheech and Chong's The Corsican Brothers
US 1984 90m colour
Orion (Peter MacGregor-Scott)

Twin brothers run amuck during the French Revolution.

Coarse and unfunny parody of a swashbuckling adventure.

w Cheech Marin, Thomas Chong
d Thomas Chong   ph Harvey Harrison   m GEO   ad Daniel Budin   ed Tom Avildsen

Cheech Marin, Thomas Chong, Roy Dotrice, Shelby Fiddis, Rikki Marin, Edie McClurg, Rae Dawn Chong, Robbi Chong

Chickens Come Home*
US 1931 30m bw
Hal Roach
V(C)

Stan helps his boss Ollie to evade the attentions of an old flame.

Rather heavy and untypical, but mainly very enjoyable star comedy, a remake of Love 'Em and Weep in which all three leading players had appeared four years earlier in different roles.

w H. M. Walker   story Hal Roach   d James W. Horne   ph Art Lloyd, Jack Stevens   ed Richard Currier

Laurel and Hardy, James Finlayson, Mae Busch, Thelma Todd

The Chiltern Hundreds*
GB 1949 84m bw
Rank/Two Cities (George H. Brown)
US title: The Amazing Mr Beecham

An aged earl is bewildered when his son fails to be elected to parliament as a socialist but his butler gets in as a Tory.

Satisfactory filming of an amusing stage comedy, with the aged A. E. Matthews repeating his delightful if irrelevant act as the dotty earl.

w William Douglas Home, Patrick Kirwan   play William Douglas Home   d John Paddy Carstairs   ph Jack Hildyard   m Benjamin Frankel

A. E. Matthews, Cecil Parker, David Tomlinson, Marjorie Fielding, Joyce Carey

The Chimp*
US 1932 30m bw
Hal Roach
V

Stan and Ollie try to get lodgings without revealing that their friend is a chimp, their share of a bankrupt circus.

The circus scenes are better than the rather tired farce which follows, especially as it is so similar to Laughing Gravy.

w H. M. Walker   d James Parrott   ph Walter Lundin   ed Richard Currier

Laurel and Hardy, James Finlayson, Billy Gilbert, Tiny Sandford

Christmas in Connecticut*
US 1945 101m bw Warner (William Jacobs)
GB title: Indiscretion

The spinster writer of a successful column about love and marriage has to conjure up a family for herself in the cause of publicity.

Predictable but fairly brisk comedy with excellent talent well deployed.

w Lionel Houser, Adele Commandini   d Peter Godfrey

ph Carl Guthrie   *m* Frederick Hollander

Barbara Stanwyck, Dennis Morgan, Sydney Greenstreet, Reginald Gardiner, S. Z. Sakall, Robert Shayne, Una O'Connor, Frank Jenks

'If you can't sleep at night, it isn't the coffee – it's the bunk!'

Christmas in July**
US   1940   67m   bw
Paramount

A young clerk and his girl win first prize in a big competition.

Slightly unsatisfactory as a whole, this Preston Sturges comedy has echoes of Clair and a dully predictable plot line, but is kept alive by inventive touches and a gallery of splendid character comedians.

wd Preston Sturges   *ph* Victor Milner   *m* Sigmund Krumgold

Dick Powell, Ellen Drew, Ernest Truex, *Al Bridge,* Raymond Walburn, William Demarest

'The perfect restorative for battered humors and jangled nerves.' – *Bosley Crowther*
'Agreeable enough, but it lacks the full-fledged Sturges lunacy.' – *New Yorker, 1977*

Chu Chu and the Philly Flash
US   1981   100m   colour
TCF (Jay Weston)

A one-woman band performer and a drunken ex-baseball player lay claim to the same lost briefcase.

Weird comedy which doesn't come off except at odd moments.

w Barbara Dana   *d* David Lowell Rich

Carol Burnett, Alan Arkin, Jack Warden, Danny Aiello, Adam Arkin, Ruth Buzzi

A Chump at Oxford**
US   1940   63m   bw
Hal Roach
V

Two street cleaners foil a bank hold-up and are presented with an Oxford education.

Patchy but endearing Laurel and Hardy romp, starting with an irrelevant two reels about their playing butler and maid, but later including Stan's burlesque impersonation of Lord Paddington.

w Charles Rogers, Harry Langdon, Felix Adler   *d* Alfred Goulding *ph* Art Lloyd   *m* Marvin Hatley *ed* Bert Jordan

Stan Laurel, Oliver Hardy, James Finlayson, Forrester Harvey, Wilfrid Lucas, Peter Cushing

'Ranks with their best pictures – which, to one heretic, are more agreeable than Chaplin's. Their clowning is purer; they aren't out to better an unbetterable world; they've never wanted to play Hamlet.' – *Graham Greene*

The Circus*
US   1928   72m (24 fps)   bw
  silent
(UA) Charles Chaplin
V

A tramp on the run from the police takes refuge in a circus and falls for an equestrienne.

Pathos often descends to bathos in this self-constructed star vehicle which has far too few laughs.

wd Charles Chaplin   ph Rollie Totheroh, Jack Wilson, Mark Marlott

Charles Chaplin, Merna Kennedy, Allan Garcia, Harry Crocker

AA: Special Award to Chaplin for acting, writing, directing and producing the film

City Lights***
US 1931 87m bw silent (with music and effects)
UA/Charles Chaplin
V, L

A tramp befriends a millionaire and falls in love with a blind girl.

Sentimental comedy with several delightful sequences in Chaplin's best manner.

wd/m Charles Chaplin   ph Rollie Totheroh   md Alfred Newman

Charles Chaplin, Virginia Cherrill, Florence Lee, Harry Myers

'Chaplin has another good picture, but it gives indications of being short-winded, and may tire fast after a bombastic initial seven days . . . he has sacrificed speed to pathos, and plenty of it.' – Variety
'Even while laughing, one is aware of a faint and uneasy feeling that Chaplin has been pondering with more than a bit of solemnity on conventional story values, and it has led him further than ever into the realms of what is often called pathetic.' – National Board of Review

'Three urban hombres heading west, seeking adventure, craving excitement . . . and longing for room service.'
City Slickers***
US 1991 114m CFI
First Independent/Castle Rock/Nelson/Face
(Irby Smith)
V, L

Three friends, all facing midlife crises,

decide to spend their vacation on a cattle drive.

A witty and engaging comedy for the most part, with some affectionate parodies of moments from classic Westerns.

w Lowell Ganz, Babaloo Mandel
d Ron Underwood   ph Dean Semler   m Marc Shaiman, Hummie Mann   pd Lawrence G. Paul
ed O. Nicholas Brown

Billy Crystal, Daniel Stern, Bruno Kirby, Patricia Wettig, Helen Slater, Jack Palance, Josh Mostel, David Paymer, Noble Willingham

'A deft blend of wry humour and warmth (albeit with a little too much thirty-something-esque angst for its own good).' – Variety

AA: Jack Palance

Class Act
US 1992 98m Technicolor
Warner/Wizan Black/Gordy de Passe
(Todd Black, Maynell Thomas)
V

Two high-school students – one an intellectual, the other a delinquent – swop identities.

Dim-witted teen comedy.

w John Semper, Cynthia Friedlob
story Michael Swerdlick, Wayne Rice, Richard Brenne   d Randall Miller   ph Francis Kenny
m Vassal Benford   pd David L. Snyder   ed John F. Burnett

Christopher Reid, Christopher Martin, Karyn Parsons, Alysia Rogers, Meshach Taylor, Doug E. Doug, Lamont Johnson

Clochemerle
France 1948 93m bw
Cinéma Productions (Ralph Baum)

The progressive mayor of a French village erects a gentlemen's convenience in the main street and shocks the local reactionaries.

Most of the book's political satire was ironed out in this cheap and opportunist production which got a few easy laughs but failed to sustain itself.

w Gabriel Chevalier *novel* Gabriel Chevalier *d* Pierre Chénal *ph* Robert Le Fèbvre *m* Henri Sauguet

Brochard, Maximilienne, Simone Michels, Jane Marken, Paul Demange, Felix Oudart, Saturnin Fabre

Clockwise*
GB 1986 97m Technicolor
EMI/Moment (Michael Codron)
V, L

A headmaster on his way to a conference is delayed by circumstance.

What was intended as an escalating climax of comic chaos falls away as the script runs out of steam, but the nation's need for comedy ensured box-office success.

w Michael Frayn *d* Christopher Morahan *ph* John Coquillon *m* George Fenton *pd* Roger Murray-Leach *ed* Peter Boyle

John Cleese, Alison Steadman, Penelope Wilton, Stephen Moore, Joan Hickson, Charon Maiden

Cockeyed Cavaliers
US 1934 72m bw
RKO

Two idiots have various adventures in medieval England.

Fairly tolerable slapstick from a team which never seemed quite at its best.

w Edward Kaufman, Ben Holmes *d* Mark Sandrich

Bert Wheeler, Robert Woolsey, Thelma Todd, Noah Beery, Dorothy Lee, Franklin Pangborn, Robert Greig

'With a fair quota of laughs, it eclipses their previous releases.' – *Variety*

The Cocoanuts**
US 1929 96m bw
Paramount (Walter Wanger, James R. Cowan)

A chiselling hotel manager tries to get in on the Florida land boom.

Considering its age and the dismal prints which remain, this is a remarkably lively if primitive first film by the Marxes, with some good routines among the excess footage.

w George S. Kaufman, Morrie Ryskind *d* Robert Florey, Joseph Santley *ph* George Folsey *m/ly* Irving Berlin

The Four Marx Brothers, Margaret Dumont, Oscar Shaw, Mary Eaton, Kay Francis, Basil Ruysdael

'The camerawork showed all the mobility of a concrete fire hydrant caught in a winter freeze.' – *Paul D. Zimmermann*

Cold Dog Soup
US 1989 88m Technicolor
Palace/HandMade/Aspen (Richard G. Abramson, William E. McEuen)
V

Given a dead dog to bury by his new girlfriend, a man attempts to sell it to a furrier and a Chinese restaurateur.

Dismal attempt at a black comedy.

w Thomas Pope *book* Stephen Dobyns *d* Alan Metter *ph* Frederick Elmes *m* Michael

Kamen, Mark Snow   *pd* David L.
Snyder   *ed* Kaja Fehr

Randy Quaid, Frank Whaley,
Christine Harnos, Sheree North, Nancy
Kwan

'Miserably unwatchable.' – *MFB*

'You'll graduate with a perpetual smile!'
College*
US   1927   65m (24 fps)   bw
  silent
Buster Keaton Productions (Joseph M.
  Schenck)
L

A brainy high school student becomes
a college football star.

Disappointing comedy from this great
stone-faced clown: the plums are
there, but few and far between.

w Carl Harbaugh, Bryan Foy
d James W. Horne   *ph* J.
Devereux Jennings, Bert Haines

Buster Keaton, Ann Cornwall, Harold
Goodwin, Snitz Edwards, Florence
Turner

Come Blow Your Horn*
US   1963   112m   Technicolor
  Panavision
Paramount/Lear and Yorkin

A country boy in New York is envious
of his older brother's sophisticated
life.

Amusing characters and funny lines
permeate this stolid transcription of
an early Neil Simon success; the big
screen is not the place for them.

w Norman Lear   *play* Neil Simon
d Bud Yorkin   *ph* William
Daniels   *m* Nelson Riddle

Frank Sinatra, Tony Bill, Lee J. Cobb,
Molly Picon, Jill St John, Barbara
Rush, Dan Blocker

Come Clean**
US   1931   20m   bw
Hal Roach

Two much-married men go out for
ice-cream and bring back a woman
of the streets they have saved from
suicide.

Splendid star comedy with the famous
characterizations fully rounded.

w H. M. Walker   *d* James W.
Horne   *ph* Art Lloyd   *ed* Richard
Currier

Laurel and Hardy, Mae Busch, Charlie
Hall, Gertrude Astor, Linda Loredo

† Remade in 1942 as *Brooklyn
Orchid*, with William Bendix and Joe
Sawyer.

Come on George*
GB   1939   88m   bw
ATP/Ealing (Jack Kitchin)
V

A stableboy calms a nervous racehorse
and rides him to victory.

Standard comedy vehicle, well
mounted, with the star at his box-
office peak.

w Anthony Kimmins, Leslie Arliss,
Val Valentine   *d* Anthony
Kimmins   *ph* Ronald Neame,
Gordon Dines   *m* Ernest Irving
ad Wilfred Shingleton   *ed* Ray
Pitt

George Formby, Pat Kirkwood, Joss
Ambler, Meriel Forbes, Cyril
Raymond, George Carney, Ronald
Shiner

Comfort and Joy*
GB   1984   106m   colour
Lake/EMI/STV (Davina Belling, Clive
  Parsons)
V

A Scottish radio disc jockey becomes

involved in a war between two ice-cream firms.

Heavy comedy, short of laughs and sympathy; a distinct descent from *Local Hero*, which was a comedown after *Gregory's Girl*.

wd Bill Forsyth   *ph* Chris Menges   *m* Mark Knopfler

Bill Paterson, Eleanor David, C. P. Grogan, Alex Norton

Coming to America

US   1988   116m   Technicolor
UIP/Paramount (George Folsey Jnr, Robert D. Wachs)
V

A wealthy African prince poses as a poor student in New York so he can find a bride who will love him for himself.

Tired comedy that fails to exploit Murphy's strengths, despite his popping up heavily disguised in several minor roles.

w David Sheffield, Barry W. Blaustein   *story* Eddie Murphy
d John Landis   *ph* Woody Omens   *m* Nile Rodgers
sp make-up: Rick Baker
ed Malcolm Campbell, George Folsey Jnr

Eddie Murphy, Arsenio Hall, John Amos, James Earl Jones, Shari Headley, Made Sinclair

'A true test for loyal fans.' – *Variety*

'Young ones! Parental units! We summon you!'

Coneheads

US   1993   83m   DeLuxe
Paramount (Lorne Michaels)
V

An illegal pointy-headed alien crash lands in the United States.

A one-joke, one laugh comedy, derived from a *Saturday Night Live* sketch.

w Tom Davis, Dan Akroyd, Bonnie Turner, Terry Turner   *d* Steve Barron   *ph* Francis Kenny
m David Newman   *pd* Gregg Fonseca

Dan Aykroyd, Jane Curtin, Michael McKean, Laraine Newman, Jason Alexander, Lisa Jane Persky, Chris Farley, David Spade, Michelle Burke

'Quite extraordinarily bad . . . worth renting only if you take a perverse pleasure in watching a very large amount of someone else's money going down the drain.' – Jonathan Ross. *Empire*

Confessions of a Pop Performer

GB   1975   91m   colour
Columbia-Warner/Swiftdown
V

A window cleaner joins a rock group and enjoys the groupies.

A broad and unsubtle slapstick comedy.

w Christopher Wood
novel Confessions from the Pop Scene by Timothy Lea   *d* Norman Cohen
ph Alan Hume   *m* Bugatti Musker   *pd* Robert Jones
ed Geoffrey Foot

Robin Askwith, Anthony Booth, Sheila White, Doris Hare, Bill Maynard, Bob Todd, Jill Gascoine, Peter Jones, Diane Langton, Ian Lavender

'Creaky gags, overly familiar slapstick routines, sniggering innuendo, grimly leaden mugging and a nervously regular injection of titillating sequences on the lines of the average German sex comedy.' – *Verina Glaessner, MFB*

□ □

Confessions of a Window Cleaner

GB   1974   90m   Eastmancolor
Columbia-Warner/Swiftdown (Greg
  Smith)
V

A window cleaner discovers many
amorous housewives on his round.

A broad, but not bawdy, comedy for
the sexually repressed. Despite its
low level, it did well enough at the
box-office to spawn several sequels.

w Christopher Wood, Val Guest
d Val Guest   ph Norman
Warwick   m Sam Sklair
pd Robert Jones   ed Bill Lenny

Robin Askwith, Anthony Booth,
Sheila White, Dandy Nicholls, Bill
Maynard, Linda Hayden, John Le
Mesurier, Joan Hickson, Richard
Wattis, Katya Wyeth, Sam Kydd

'The humour is of the sniggering,
innuendo-squeezing variety and is
aimed with unnerving mediocrity at a
particular kind of embarrassed – and
distinctly British – audience reaction.'
– Gareth Jones, MFB

The Constant Husband*

GB   1955   88m   Technicolor print
British Lion/London Films (Frank Launder,
  Sidney Gilliat)

An amnesiac discovers that he is a
multiple bigamist, still wanted by
each of his five wives.

Flimsy comedy which never really
gets going despite an attractive cast.

w Sidney Gilliat, Val Valentine
d Sidney Gilliat   ph Ted Scaife
m Malcolm Arnold

Rex Harrison, Kay Kendall, Margaret
Leighton, Cecil Parker, Nicole
Maurey, George Cole, Raymond
Huntley, Michael Hordern, Eric
Pohlmann, Robert Coote

Consuming Passions

GB/US   1988   100m   colour
Samuel Goldwyn/Euston Films (William
  Cartlidge)
V

By adding a new ingredient to
chocolate – human flesh – a young
man rises to the top of his profession.

Dire attempt to revive the tradition of
Ealing comedy.

w Paul D. Zimmerman, Andrew
Davies   play Secrets by Michael Palin,
Terry Jones   d Giles Foster
ph Roger Pratt   m Richard
Hartley   pd Peter Lamont
ed John Grover

Vanessa Redgrave, Freddie Jones,
Jonathan Pryce, Tyler Butterworth,
Sammi Davis, Thora Hird, Prunella
Scales

Cops and Robbers*

US   1973   89m   DeLuxe
UA/EK Corp (Elliott Kastner)

Two New York cops turn crook and
pull off a job for the Mafia.

Trendily anti-establishment comedy,
quite snappy and smart when you
can follow it.

w Donald E. Westlake   d Aram
Avakian   ph David L. Quaid
m Michel Legrand

Cliff Gorman, Joe Bologna, Dick
Ward, Shepperd Strudwick, Ellen
Holly, John P. Ryan

The Couch Trip*

US   1988   98m   colour
Rank/Orion (Lawrence Gordon)

A mental patient escapes to Los
Angeles where he becomes a success
as a radio doctor.

Sporadically amusing comedy that
mocks obvious targets.

□ □

w Stephen Kampmann, Will Port, Sean Stein   *novel* Ken Kolb
d Michael Ritchie   *ph* Donald E. Thorin   *m* Michel Colombier
pd Jimmy Bly   *ed* Richard A. Harris

Dan Aykroyd, Walter Matthau, Charles Grodin, Donna Dixon, Richard Romanus, Mary Gross, David Clennon

Count Your Blessings

US   1959   102m   Metrocolor
  Cinemascope
MGM (Karl Tunberg)

An English girl marries an aristocratic Frenchman, but the war and other considerations make them virtual strangers until their son is nine years old, when it becomes clear that daddy is a philanderer.

Slight upper-crust comedy, basically rather tedious but kept buoyant by Chevalier as commentator.

w Karl Tunberg   *novel* The Blessing by Nancy Mitford   *d* Jean Negulesco   *ph* Milton Krasner, George Folsey   *m* Franz Waxman

Deborah Kerr, *Maurice Chevalier*, Rossano Brazzi, Martin Stephens, Tom Helmore, Ronald Squire, Patricia Medina, Mona Washbourne

'Negulesco's aspirations to elegance are now familiar . . . this is far too absurd an example of Hollywood's infatuation with Old Europe to arouse much interest.' – *MFB*

A Countess from Hong Kong

GB   1967   120m   Technicolor
Universal (Jerome Epstein)

An American millionaire diplomat is followed from Hong Kong by his Russian émigrée girl friend, and complications mount when his wife boards the ship at Hawaii.

Flatulent comedy with neither the sparkle of champagne nor even the fizz of lemonade: Chaplin's writing, direction and music are alike soporific, and commiserations are due to the cast.

wd/m Charles Chaplin   *ph* Arthur Ibbetson   *pd* Don Ashton

Marlon Brando, Sophia Loren, *Patrick Cargill*, Margaret Rutherford, Charles Chaplin, Sydney Chaplin, Oliver Johnston, John Paul

'An unfunny, mindless mess.' – *Robert Windeler*
'So old-fashioned and dull that one can hardly believe it was made now.' – *Philip T. Hartung*

County Hospital**

US   1932   20m   bw
Hal Roach
V, V(C)

Ollie is in hospital; Stan brings him some hardboiled eggs and some nuts, and nearly wrecks the place.

Archetypal star comedy with brilliant character and slapstick sequences, let down by a badly processed car ride home.

w H. M. Walker   *d* James Parrott   *ph* Art Lloyd   *ed* Bert Jordan, Richard Currier

Laurel and Hardy, Billy Gilbert, William Austin, May Wallace

The Court Jester***

US   1955   101m   Technicolor
  Vistavision
Paramount/Dena (Melvin Frank, Norman Panama)
V, L

Opposition to a tyrannical king is provided by the Fox, but it is one of the rebel's meekest men who, posing as a jester, defeats the usurper.

One of the star's most delightful vehicles, this medieval romp has good tunes and lively action, not to mention an exceptional cast and the memorable 'chalice from the palace' routine.

wd Norman Panama, Melvin Frank *ph* Ray June *m/ly* Sylvia Fine, Sammy Cahn *ad* Hal Pereira, Roland Anderson

Danny Kaye, Glynis Johns, *Basil Rathbone*, Cecil Parker, *Mildred Natwick*, Angela Lansbury, Edward Ashley, Robert Middleton, Michael Pate, Alan Napier

The Courtship of Eddie's Father*
US 1962 117m Metrocolor Panavision
MGM/Joe Pasternak

The small son of a widower tries to interest Dad in another woman.

Fairly icky American-style sentimental comedy with most of the stops pulled out; way over-length and too self-indulgently solemn in the last part, but with professional touches.

w John Gay *novel* Muriel Toby *d* Vincente Minnelli *ph* Milton Krasner *m* George Stoll

Glenn Ford, Ronny Howard, Shirley Jones, Stella Stevens, Dina Merrill

† A TV series starring Bill Bixby followed in 1971.

Cousin, Cousine**
France 1975 95m Eastmancolor Pomereu/Gaumont (Bertrand Javal)

Various furtive love affairs centre on a family wedding.

Sprightly satirical comedy full of pleasing touches, mostly jibes at French bourgeois standards.

wd Jean-Charles Tacchella

ph Georges Lendi *m* Gerard Anfosso

Marie-France Pisier, Marie-Christine Barrault, Victor Lanoux, Guy Marchand, Ginette Garcin

'One of those rare delights you want to see again and again just to share the sheer joy of living, zest for love, genuine affection, all-too-human absurdity, and pure happiness of all those delicious people on screen.' – *Judith Crist, Saturday Review*
AAN: best foreign film; script; Marie-Christine Barrault

Cousins
US 1989 113m Technicolor UIP/Paramount (William Allyn)
V

Two couples, who meet at a relative's wedding, swop partners.

An adaptation of the French film *Cousin, Cousine* without the exuberant charm of the original.

w Stephen Metcalfe *d* Joel Schumacher *ph* Ralf Bode *m* Angelo Badalamenti *pd* Mark S. Freeborn *ed* Robert Brown

Ted Danson, Isabella Rossellini, Sean Young, William Petersen, Lloyd Bridges, Norma Aleandro, Keith Coogan, Gina DeAngelis, George Coe

'Combines satire, near-farce, and incipient fantasy with great dexterity.' – *Tim Pulleine, MFB*

Crackers
US 1984 92m Technicolor Universal/Edward Lewis

Incompetent crooks run a pawnshop.

Insufficiently rethought, San Francisco set, updating of Monicelli's 1956 comedy *Big Deal on Madonna*

Street (*I Soliti Ignoti*). No longer at all funny.

w Jeffrey Fiskin   *d* Louis Malle   *ph* Laszlo Kovacs   *m* Paul Chihara   *pd* John L. Lloyd

Donald Sutherland, Jack Warden, Sean Penn, Wallace Shawn, Larry Riley, Trinidad Silva, Charlaine Woodard, Irwin Corey

'One can sense that it would all sound much funnier in Italian.' – *Variety*

The Cracksman

GB   1963   112m   Technicolor   Cinemascope
ABPC
V

A master locksmith becomes the unwitting dupe of a gang of safecrackers.

The most elaborate vehicle devised for this diminutive star; despite bright moments, conventional mounting and over-generous length finally defeat it.

w Lew Schwartz, Charlie Drake   *d* Peter Graham Scott

Charlie Drake, George Sanders, Dennis Price, Nyree Dawn Porter, Eddie Byrne, Finlay Currie, Percy Herbert

Crazy House

US   1943   80m   bw
Universal (Erle C. Kenton)

Olsen and Johnson go to Hollywood to make a film.

Lame sequel to *Hellzapoppin*; after an explosively well edited first reel of panic in the studio, it degenerates into a slew of below-par variety turns.

w Robert Lees, Frederic I. Rinaldo   *d* Edward Cline   *ph* Charles Van

Enger   *md* George Hale, Milt Rosen

Ole Olsen, Chic Johnson, Martha O'Driscoll, Patric Knowles, Percy Kilbride, Cass Daley, Thomas Gomez, Edgar Kennedy

† Sherlock Holmes fans may or may not wish to record a two-line comic bit by Basil Rathbone and Nigel Bruce in character.

Crazy People

US   1990   92m   Technicolor
UIP/Paramount (Thomas Barad)
V, L

An ad-man runs his business from a rest home for mental patients.

Unsatisfactory would-be satire.

w Mitch Markowitz   *d* Tony Bill   *ph* Victor J. Kemper   *m* Cliff Eidelman   *ad* Steven Schwartz   *ed* Mia Goldman

Dudley Moore, Daryl Hannah, Paul Reiser, J. T. Walsh, Bill Smitrovich, Alan North, David Paymer

'Damp, indulgent squib of a film.' – *Geoff Brown, MFB*

The Crazy World of Laurel and Hardy**

US   1964   83m   bw
Hal Roach/Jay Ward

A compilation of Laurel and Hardy extracts from their classic period.

Although the material is in itself excellent and some of the build-up sequences well done, the clips are all too short to achieve maximum impact, and virtually none is identified.

w Bill Scott   *m* Jerry Fielding   *narrator* Garry Moore

The Criminal Life of Archibaldo de la Cruz*

Mexico 1955 91m bw
Alianza Cinematografica (Roberto Figueroa)
original title: *Ensayo de un Crimen*

A fantasist determines to kill all women who cross his path, but fate intervenes.

Cheaply made macabre joke, one of its director's throwaway oddities: not too smooth, but often amusing.

w Luis Buñuel, E. Ugarte   *d* Luis Buñuel   *ph* Augusto Jimenez *md* Jorge Perez

Ernesto Alonso, Ariadna Welter, Miroslava Stern, Rita Macedo

Critical Condition

US 1986 100m Technicolor
Paramount (Ted Field, Robert Cort)
V, L

Pretending to be mad in order to escape the Mafia, our hero is instead mistaken for a doctor.

Zany, hepped-up comedy which fails on all counts.

w Denis and John Hamill *d* Michael Apted   *ph* Ralf D. Bode   *m* Alan Silvestri   *pd* John Lloyd   *ed* Robert K. Lambert

Richard Pryor, Rachel Ticotin, Ruben Blades, Joe Mantegna, Bob Dishy

'Fans will find little to cheer about.' – *Daily Variety*

Crocodile Dundee*

Australia 1986 102m
  Kodacolour   Panavision
Paramount/Hoyts/Rimfire (John Cornell)
V

An outback hero goes to Manhattan and puts New Yorkers in their place.

Easygoing comedy with no real style, which astounded the industry by becoming one of America's most popular films in 1986.

w Paul Hogan, Ken Shadie   *d* Peter Faiman   *ph* Russell Boyd   *m* Peter Best

Paul Hogan, Linda Koslowski, John Meillon, Mark Blum

'*Romancing the Stone* combined with *Tarzan's New York Adventure*.' – *Sight and Sound*
'A movie doggedly designed to make you feel good.' – *Vincent Canby, New York Times*

† *Crocodile Dundee II* (V), which followed in 1988, offered very much the mixture as before.
AAN: best original screenplay

Crooks and Coronets

GB 1969 106m Technicolor
Warner Seven Arts/Herman Cohen
US title: *Sophie's Place*

American gangsters plan to rob a stately home but are taken over by the dowager in charge.

Overlong and mainly flatulent comedy, with a good climax involving a vintage plane.

wd Jim O'Connelly   *ph* Desmond Dickinson   *m* Patrick John Scott

Telly Savalas, Edith Evans, Warren Oates, Nicky Henson, Cesar Romero, Harry H. Corbett

Crooks Anonymous*

GB 1962 87m bw
Anglo Amalgamated (Nat Cohen)

A pretty thief joins an organization for reforming criminals, but is tempted again . . . and so are they.

Amusingly devised and plotted minor comedy with an exceptional cast.

w Jack Davies, Henry Blyth d Ken Annakin ph Ernest Steward m Muir Mathieson, Henry Martin

Leslie Phillips, Stanley Baxter, Wilfrid Hyde-White, Julie Christie, James Robertson Justice, Robertson Hare, Charles Lloyd Pack

Crooks in Cloisters

GB 1963 97m Technicolor Scope
ABPC

Forgers pose as monks but are reformed by the country life.

Busy comedy full of familiar faces; perhaps a small cut above the *Carry Ons*.

w Mike Watts d Jeremy Summers

Ronald Fraser, Barbara Windsor, Grégoire Aslan, Bernard Cribbins, Davy Kaye, Wilfred Brambell

Crooks' Tour*

GB 1940 84m bw
British National (John Corfield)

English tourists are mistaken for spies by Nazis in Baghdad.

Amusing vehicle for two comic actors who excelled at portraying the English abroad.

w John Watt, Max Kester
radio serial Sidney Gilliat, Frank Launder d John Baxter
ph James Wilson m Kennedy Russell

Basil Radford, Naunton Wayne, Greta Gynt, Abraham Sofaer, Gordon McLeod

'Their bland imperturbability in the face of extraordinary circumstances provides no little fun.' – *Picture Show*

'Big laughs come in small packages.'

Curly Sue

US 1991 101m Technicolor
Warner (John Hughes)
V, L

A con-man and a nine-year-old orphan win the heart of a successful woman lawyer.

Gruesomely sentimental and manipulative comedy.

wd John Hughes ph Jeffrey Kimball m Georges Delerue
pd Doug Kraner ed Peck Prior, Harvey Rosenstock

James Belushi, Kelly Lynch, Alisan Porter, John Getz

'With its mix of childish gags and shameless melodrama, *Curly Sue* could make off with a tidy box-office take.' – *Variety*
'John Hughes here graduates from the most successful comedy in film history to scripting and directing a large piece of non-biodegradable tosh.' – *Nigel Andrews, Financial Times*
'Lacks the charm, good jokes or vigour to hide its contrivances.' – *Geoff Brown, The Times*

Curse of the Pink Panther

GB 1983 110m Technicolor
Panavision
MGM-UA/Titan/Jewel (Blake Edwards, Gerald T. Nutting)
V

Inspector Clouseau has disappeared, and Dreyfus selects the world's worst detective to replace him.

Unspeakably awful attempt at prolonging a series whose star died two episodes ago. Crude, tasteless and unfunny throughout.

w Blake Edwards, Geoffrey Edwards d Blake Edwards

ph Dick Bush   *m* Henry Mancini   *pd* Peter Mullins

Ted Wass, Joanna Lumley, Herbert Lom, David Niven, Robert Wagner, Capucine, Harvey Korman, Burt Kwouk

'Another bout of film-making as grave robbing.' – *Sight and Sound*
'The ultimate version of deadpan humour . . . the most tedious of the whole series.' – *Richard Combs, MFB*

Curtain Up*
GB 1952 85m bw
Rank/Constellation (Robert Garrett)

A seaside repertory company runs into trouble when the producer is at loggerheads with the author of next week's play.

Fairly amusing farce which has now acquired historical value for the light it throws on the old weekly reps.

w Michael Pertwee, Jack Davies
play On Monday Next by Philip King   *d* Ralph Smart   *ph* Stanley Pavey   *m* Malcolm Arnold

Margaret Rutherford, Robert Morley, Olive Sloane, Joan Rice, Charlotte Mitchell, Kay Kendall, Liam Gaffney, Michael Medwin

Daddy's Dyin', Who's Got the Will?

US   1990   95m   DeLuxe
Palace/Propaganda Films/Artist Circle
    Entertainment (Sigurjon Sighvatsson,
    Steve Golin, Monty Montgomery)
V, L

Children gather at home after their
father has a stroke.

Raucous comedy of family
relationships that ends in
sentimentality.

w Del Shores   *play* Del Shores
d Jack Fisk   *ph* Paul Elliot
m David McHugh   *pd* Michelle
Minch   *ed* Edward A. Warschilka Jr

Beau Bridges, Beverly D'Angelo, Tess
Harper, Judge Reinhold, Amy Wright,
Patrika Darbo, Bert Remsen, Molly
McClure, Keith Carradine, Newell
Alexander

Dad's Army**

GB   1971   95m   Technicolor
Columbia/Norcon (John R. Sloan)
V

Misadventures of a number of elderly
gents in Britain's wartime Home
Guard.

Expanded big-screen version of the
long-running TV series, a pleasant
souvenir but rather less effective than
was expected because everything is
shown – the town, the Nazis, the
wives – and thus the air of gentle
fantasy disappears, especially in the
face of much coarsened humour.

w Jimmy Perry, David Croft
d Norman Cohen   *ph* Terry
Maher   *m* Wilfred Burns

*Arthur Lowe, John Le Mesurier, John
Laurie, James Beck,* Ian Lavender,
Arnold Ridley, Liz Fraser, *Clive Dunn,*
Bill Pertwee, Frank Williams, Edward
Sinclair

The Dancing Masters

US   1943   63m   bw
TCF (Lee Marcus)
V

Laurel and Hardy run a ballet school,
and get involved with gangsters and
inventors.

Insubstantial star comedy featuring
reworkings of old routines, and a back-
projected runaway bus climax.

w Scott Darling, George Bricker
d Mal St Clair   *m* Norbert
Brodine   *m* Arthur Lange
ad James Basevi, Chester Gore
ed Norman Colbert

Stan Laurel, Oliver Hardy, Trudy
Marshall, Bob Bailey, Margaret
Dumont, Matt Briggs, Robert
Mitchum

A Dangerous Game

US   1941   61m   bw
Universal

Various weird characters converge on
a lunatic asylum where a fortune is
hidden.

Failed attempt at black farce: the actors are game, but the material doesn't hold water.

w Larry Rhine, Ben Chapman, Maxwell Shane   d John Rawlins

Richard Arlen, Andy Devine, Jeanne Kelly, Edward Brophy, Marc Lawrence, Andrew Tombes, Tom Dugan

'For all its frantic, deafening slapstick it remains stubbornly humourless . . . if there's such a thing as a Class D picture, this is it.' – Variety

Dark Habits
Spain 1983 100m colour
Metro/Tesauro (Luis Calvo)
original title: Entre Tinieblas

A drug-addicted singer takes refuge from the police in a convent full of decadent nuns.

High spirited, but for the easily amused only.

wd Pedro Almodovar   ph Angel L. Fernandez   m Cam España
pd Pin Morales, Roman Arango
ed Jose Salcedo

Cristina S. Pascual, Marisa Paredes, Mari Carrillo, Lina Canalejas, Manuel Zarzo, Carmen Maura, Chus Lampreave

'A rather labored series of jokes.' – Pauline Kael, New Yorker

'The mission of the Strangelove generation!'
Dark Star*
US 1974 83m Metrocolor
Jack H. Harris (John Carpenter)
V, L

In the 22nd century, the bored crew of a starship on an intergalactic mission become a prey to their own phobias and to the alien mascot they are taking back to Earth.

A semi-professional film which turned out to be one of the screen's neatest low-budget entries in the pulp science fiction genre. That doesn't make it wholly entertaining, but its credentials are impeccable.

w John Carpenter, Dan O'Bannon
d John Carpenter   pd/ed Dan O'Bannon   ph Douglas Knapp
m John Carpenter

Brian Narelle, Dre Pahich, Cal Kuniholm, Dan O'Bannon

A Day at the Races****
US 1937 109m bw/blue-tinted
ballet sequence
MGM (Lawrence Weingarten)
V, L

The Marxes help a girl who owns a sanatorium and a racehorse.

Fashions in Marxism change, but this top quality production, though lacking their zaniest inspirations, does contain several of their funniest routines and a spectacularly well integrated racecourse climax. The musical and romantic asides are a matter of taste but delightfully typical of their time.

w Robert Pirosh, George Seaton, George Oppenheimer   d Sam Wood
ph Joseph Ruttenberg   m Franz Waxman   ch Dave Gould

Groucho, Chico, Harpo, Margaret Dumont, Maureen O'Sullivan, Allan Jones, Douglass Dumbrille, Esther Muir, Sig Rumann

'The money is fairly splashed about; the capitalists have recognized the Marx Brothers; ballet sequences, sentimental songs, amber fountains, young lovers. Easily the best film to be seen in London, but all the same

I feel a nostalgia for the old cheap rickety sets.' – *Graham Greene*
AAN: Dave Gould

Daydream Believer

Australia 1991 86m colour
Feature/View Films/Australian Film Finance Corp (Ben Gannon)

A would-be actress, who imagined as a child that she was a horse, proves to a stud-farm owner that she understands the needs of his unhappy mares.

Ludicrous comedy, which ranks among the silliest movies of the decade.

w Saturday Rosenberg   *d* Kathy Mueller   *ph* Andrew Lesnie, Ian Jones, Roger Lanser   *m* Todd Hunter, Johanna Pigott   *pd* Roger Ford   *ed* Robert Gibson

Miranda Otto, Martin Kemp, Anne Looby, Alister Smart, Gia Carides, Bruce Venables

'This insipid Australian comedy again prompts the question: what happened to their emerging film industry.' – *Ian Johnstone, Sunday Times*
'Truly abysmal.' – *Alexander Walker, London Evening Standard*

Days of Thrills and Laughter***

US 1961 93m bw
TCF (Robert Youngson)

Appealing if rather miscellaneous silent film compilation with the accent on action and thrills as well as comedy.

Like the other Youngson histories, a boon to film archivists despite a facetious commentary.   *m* Jack Shaindlin   *narrator* Jay Jackson

Stan Laurel, Oliver Hardy, Snub Pollard, Douglas Fairbanks, Charles Chaplin, Pearl White, Houdini, Harry Langdon, Ben Turpin, Charlie Chase, Boris Karloff, Warner Oland, Fatty Arbuckle, Keystone Kops

A Day's Pleasure*

US 1919 20m bw silent
First National/Charles Chaplin
V

Mishaps of a family picnic.

Very mild Chaplin, reaching for but not achieving a kind of lyric quality. Amusing bits rather than scenes.

wd Charles Chaplin   *ph* Rollie Totheroh

Charles Chaplin, Edna Purviance, Jackie Coogan, Henry Bergman, Babe London

Dead Men Don't Wear Plaid*

US 1982 88m bw
Universal/Aspen Film Society (David V. Picker, William E. McFuen)
V

A private eye is hired by a beautiful girl to find her father's murderer.

Ingenious but overstretched prank in which the hero apparently (by intercutting) gets involved with famous crime stars of the forties: Bogart, Ladd, Bacall, Stanwyck, etc. The basic script is simply not funny enough to support the superstructure, though the selection of lines from the oldies is often ingenious.

w Carl Reiner, George Gipe, Steve Martin   *d* Carl Reiner   *ph* Michael Chapman   *m* Miklos Rozsa *pd* John DeCuir   *ed* Bud Molin

Steve Martin, Rachel Ward, Carl Reiner, Reni Santoni

'The content is undergraduate facetiousness at its worst, but at least the excerpts themselves provide a pleasant *noir* anthology.' – *Sight and Sound*

Deal of the Century
US 1983 98m Technicolor
Warner (Bud Yorkin)
L

An arms dealer is urged not to sell a new weapon to a warmongering dictator.

Complex comedy, descending into farce when the visiting general is bribed by the availability of American women. Not a success.

w Paul Brickman *d* William Friedkin *ph* Richard H. Kline *m* Arthur B. Rubinstein *pd* Bill Malley *ed* Bud Smith

Chevy Chase, Sigourney Weaver, Gregory Hines, Vince Edwards, William Jarvis, William Marquez

'Your basic black comedy.'

Death Becomes Her
US 1992 104m colour
UIP/Universal (Robert Zemeckis, Steve Starkey)
V

An ageing Broadway star and a novelist, both rivals for the same man, take an elixir that gives eternal life.

A small comedy overwhelmed by its impressive special effects and suffering from its director's belief that louder and faster is funnier.

w Martin Donovan, David Koepp *d* Robert Zemeckis *ph* Dean Cundey *m* Alan Silvestri *pd* Rick Carter *sp* Industrial Light and Magic *ed* Arthur Schmidt

Meryl Streep, Goldie Hawn, Bruce Willis, Isabella Rossellini, Ian Ogilvy, Adam Storke, Nancy Fish, Alaina Reed Hall, Michelle Johnson, Mary Ellen Trainor

'A black comedy that is so pleased with its own blackness that it frequently forgets to be funny.' – *Kenneth Turan, Los Angeles Times*
AAN: Visual effects

Death in Brunswick**
Australia 1990 109m Eastmancolor
Meridian/Film Victoria/Australian Film Finance Corp (Timothy White)

The new cook in a sleazy night-club accidentally kills his drunken assistant and asks an old friend to help him get rid of the body.

w John Ruane, Boyd Oxlade *novel* Boyd Oxlade *d* John Ruane *ph* Ellery Ryan *m* Philip Judd *pd* Chris Kennedy *ed* Neil Thumpston

Sam Neill, Zoe Carides, John Clarke, Yvonne Lawley, Deborah Kennedy

'An unusual, intelligent black comedy. Some will find the film outrageous, but word-of-mouth should give the pic legs on the international art-house circuit.' – *Variety*

Decline and Fall
GB 1968 113m DeLuxe
TCF/Ivan Foxwell
aka: *Decline and Fall of a Birdwatcher*

An innocent, accident-prone Oxford undergraduate is expelled and after various adventures in high and low society is convicted as a white slaver.

Flabby, doomed attempt to film a satirical classic which lives only on the printed page. Odd moments amuse.

w Ivan Foxwell *novel* Evelyn Waugh *d* John Krish

ph Desmond Dickinson   *m* Ron Goodwin

Robin Phillips, Donald Wolfit, Genevieve Page, Robert Harris, Leo McKern, Colin Blakely, Felix Aylmer, Donald Sinden, Griffith Jones

'The British *Graduate*.' – *New Yorker*
'Literate, lavishly furnished, tastefully faithful.' – *Observer*

Defending Your Life**
US 1991 111m Technicolor
Warner/Geffen (Michael Grillo)
V, L

Killed in a car crash, an advertising executive finds himself in Judgement City where he must defend what he did with his life in a trial to decide his ultimate fate.

Enjoyable comedy of modern manners, less concerned with the afterlife than with the here-and-now.

wd Albert Brooks   *ph* Allen Daviau   *m* Michael Gore   *pd* Ida Random   *ed* David Finfer, Spencer Gross

Albert Brooks, Meryl Streep, Rip Torn, Lee Grant, Buck Henry, Michael Durrell, James Eckhouse, Gary Beach, Julie Cobb

'Original in concept, funny in spasms and pretty good about the American propensity to examine themselves in such minute detail that Judgement Day is likely to seem like just another spell on the analyst's couch.' – *Derek Malcolm, Guardian*

Delicatessen***
France 1990 99m colour
Electric/Constellation/UGC/Hachette Première (Claudie Ossard)
V

In a decaying city of the future, a butcher, who flourishes by killing his workers and selling their flesh, is attacked by underground vegetarian terrorists.

A gruesome theme given exuberant, witty, cartoon-like treatment.

wd Jean-Pierre Jeunet, Marc Caro   *ph* Darius Khondji   *m* Carlos D'Alessio   *ad* Marc Caro   *ed* Hervé Schneid

Dominique Pinon, Marie-Laure Dougnac, Jean-Claude Dreyfus, Karin Viard, Ticky Holgado, Anne-Marie Pisani, Jacques Mathou

'Beautifully textured, cleverly scripted and eerily shot . . . a zany little film that should get terrific word of mouth.' – *Variety*
'An impressive achievement and extremely funny.' – *Philip French, Observer*

The Demi-Paradise*
GB 1943 114m bw
Two Cities (Anatole de Grunwald)
US title: *Adventure for Two*

In 1939, a Russian inventor is sent to observe the British way of life.

Pleasant, aimless little satirical comedy in which this blessed plot seems to be peopled entirely by eccentrics.

w Anatole de Grunwald   *d* Anthony Asquith   *ph* Bernard Knowles   *m* Nicholas Brodszky

Laurence Olivier, Penelope Dudley Ward, *Margaret Rutherford*, Leslie Henson, Marjorie Fielding, Felix Aylmer, Guy Middleton, Michael Shepley, George Thorpe, Edie Martin, Muriel Aked, Joyce Grenfell

'A backhanded way of showing us poor juvenile-minded cinemagoers that the England of Mr Punch and Mrs

Malaprop lives forever.' – *Richard Winnington*

The Dentist**

US   1932   19m   bw
Paramount/Sennett

Classic star short with W. C. Fields working up briskly to a dentist sketch in which he deals summarily with a variety of patients.
d Leslie Pearce

The Desk Set**

US   1957   103m   Eastmancolor
    Cinemascope
TCF (Henry Ephron)
GB title: *His Other Woman*

Ladies in a broadcasting company's reference section are appalled when an electronics expert is sent to improve their performance.

Thin comedy, altered from a Broadway success; patchy as a whole, but with several splendid dialogue scenes for the principals.

w Phoebe and Henry Ephron
play William Marchant   *d* Walter Lang   *ph* Leon Shamroy   *m* Cyril Mockridge

Spencer Tracy, Katharine Hepburn, Joan Blondell, Gig Young, Dina Merrill, Neva Patterson

'They lope through this trifling charade like a couple of oldtimers who enjoy reminiscing with simple routines.' – *Bosley Crowther, New York Times*

The Devil and Miss Jones**

US   1941   97m   bw
RKO/Frank Ross, Norman Krasna

A millionaire masquerades as a clerk in his own department store to investigate worker complaints.

Attractive comedy with elements of the crazy thirties and the more socially conscious forties.

w Norman Krasna   *d* Sam Wood
ph Harry Stradling   *m* Roy Webb

Jean Arthur, *Charles Coburn*, Robert Cummings; Spring Byington, S. Z. Sakall, William Demarest
AAN: Norman Krasna; Charles Coburn

The Diary of Major Thompson

France   1955   83m   bw
SNE Gaumont/Paul Wagner
original title: *Les Carnets de Major Thompson*; US title: *The French They Are a Funny Race*

An Englishman married to a Frenchwoman keeps notes on the French way of life.

Tatty filming of a mildly amusing book; it falls away into a number of badly-timed and presented gags, and one can't believe that its creator was once the top comedy genius of Hollywood.

wd Preston Sturges   *ph* Maurice Barry, Christian Matras   *m* Georges Van Parys

Jack Buchanan, Martine Carol, Noel-Noel, Genevieve Brunet

'Even allowing for the appalling editing and the frequently incomprehensible dubbed soundtrack, there is little evidence to suggest that this film could ever have been anything but a shambles.' – *Peter John Dyer, MFB*

Dice Rules

US   1991   83m   Foto-Kem
Seven Arts/Fleebin Dabble (Fred Silverstein)

A 20-minute short on the emergence of the comedian is followed by footage of a concert performance in Madison Square Gardens.

Like strychnine, an acquired and less than enjoyable taste.

w Lenny Shulman, Andrew Dice Clay d Jay Dubin ph Michael Negrin ed Mitchell Sinoway

Andrew Dice Clay, Eddie Griffin, Sylvia Harman, Lee Lawrence, Noodles Levenstein, Maria Parkinson

'A pretty accurate snapshot of the comedian's standup act – crude, sexist, racist, homophobic and designed to shock.' – Variety

Die Laughing
US 1980 108m Technicolor
Orion/Warner (Jon Peters)

After the murder of a nuclear scientist, a young musician who knows too much is chased by the murderers and the FBI.

Witless black comedy rehash of The 39 Steps.

w Jerry Segal, Robby Benson, Scott Parker d Jeff Werner

Robby Benson, Linda Grovenor, Charles Durning, Elsa Lanchester, Bud Cort

Dirty Rotten Scoundrels
US 1988 110m DeLuxe
Rank/Orion (Bernard Williams)
V, L

Two con men compete in a contest of skills.

Heavy-handed remake of Ralph Levy's Bedtime Story, made in 1964.

w Dale Launer, Stanley Shapiro, Paul Henning d Frank Oz
ph Michael Ballhaus m Miles Goodman pd Roy Walker
ed Stephen A. Rotter, William Scharf

Steve Martin, Michael Caine, Glenne Headly, Anton Rodgers, Barbara Harris, Ian McDiarmid, Dana Ivey, Meagen Fay, Frances Conroy, Nicole Calfan

Dirty Work***
US 1933 20m bw
Hal Roach

Chimney sweeps cause havoc in the house of an eccentric scientist.

Hilarious star comedy with splendid timing and comedy touches.

w H. M. Walker d Lloyd French ph Kenneth Peach
ed Bert Jordan

Laurel and Hardy, Lucien Littlefield, Sam Adams

The Discreet Charm of the Bourgeoisie***
France/Spain/Italy 1972 105m Eastmancolor
Greenwich (Serge Silberman)
V
original title: Le Charme Discret de la Bourgeoisie

The efforts of a group of friends to dine together are continually frustrated.

A frequently hilarious, sometimes savage surrealist fable which makes all its points beautifully and then goes on twenty minutes too long. The performances are a joy.

w Luis Buñuel, Jean-Claude Carrière d Luis Buñuel ph Edmond Richard

Fernando Rey, Delphine Seyrig, Stéphane Audran, Bulle Ogier, Jean-Pierre Cassel, Paul Frankeur, Julien Bertheau

'A perfect synthesis of surreal wit and blistering social assault.' – Jan Dawson, MFB

AA: best foreign film
AAN: Luis Buñuel, Jean-Claude
Carrière (script)

The Disorderly Orderly
US   1964   89m   Technicolor
Paramount/York (Paul Jones)

A hospital orderly creates havoc by his
inefficiency and his sympathy for other
people's predicaments.

Spasmodic farce with far too much
pathos between its highlights.

wd Frank Tashlin   *ph* W. Wallace
Kelley   *m* Joseph Lilley

Jerry Lewis, Glenda Farrell, Everett
Sloane, Kathleen Freeman, Karen
Sharpe, Susan Oliver, Alice Pearce

'In America the ring costs two dollars to
put on – and a fortune to take off!'
Divorce American Style**
US   1967   109m   Technicolor
Columbia/Tandem (Norman Lear)

Well-heeled Los Angeles suburbanites
toy with divorce but eventually
resume their domestic bickering.

Rather arid and patchy but often
sharply sardonic comedy about a
society in which people can't afford to
divorce.

w Norman Lear   *d* Bud Yorkin
ph Conrad Hall   *m David Grusin*
pd Edward Stephenson

*Dick Van Dyke, Debbie Reynolds, Jean
Simmons,* Jason Robards Jnr, Van
Johnson, Joe Flynn, Shelley Berman,
Martin Gabel, Lee Grant, Tom
Bosley, Dick Gautier
AAN: Norman Lear

'A delightfully daring plan to give marriage
a surprise ending!'
Divorce Italian Style**
Italy   1961   108m   bw
Lux/Vides/Galatea (Franco Cristaldi)
original title: *Divorzio all'Italiana*

A Sicilian nobleman explains how,
wishing to be rid of his wife, he
arranged for her to be seduced and
later shot by a jealous lover.

Sardonic, stylized comedy which,
rather in the manner of *Kind Hearts
and Coronets,* manages while retailing
a black comedy plot to satirize Italian
manners and institutions.

*w Ennio de Concini, Pietro Germi,
Alfredo Gianetti   d Pietro Germi*
ph Leonida Barboni   *m* Carlo
Rustichelli

Marcello Mastroianni, Daniela Rocca,
Stefania Sandrelli, Leopoldo Trieste

AA: script
AAN: Pietro Germi; Marcello
Mastroianni

'What should a girl do when opportunity
knocks ... twice?'
Do Not Disturb
US   1965   102m   DeLuxe
   Cinemascope
TCF/Melcher/Arcola (Aaron Rosenberg,
   Martin Melcher)

An American wool executive is posted
to London; his dizzy wife makes him
jealous by flirting with a French
antique dealer.

Silly farce which paints a lunatic
picture of English and French life but
occasionally raises a wild laugh or
two. Thin script and production.

w Milt Rosen, Richard Breen
play William Fairchild   *d* Ralph
Levy   *ph* Leon Shamroy
m Lionel Newman

Doris Day, Rod Taylor, *Sergio Fantoni*, Reginald Gardiner, Hermione Baddeley, Leon Askin

Doc Hollywood*

US   1991   103m   Warner (Susan Solt, Deborah D. Johnson)
Technicolor
V, L

On the way to a new job as a plastic surgeon in Hollywood, a young doctor crashes his car in a small town and is sentenced to work at the local hospital.

Amiable, inoffensive comedy in a familiar vein.

w Jeffrey Price, Peter S. Seaman, Daniel Pyne   *novel What? . . . Dead Again* by Neil B. Shulman
d Michael Caton-Jones   *ph* Michael Chapman   *m* Carter Burwell
pd Lawrence Miller   *ed* Gregg London

Michael J. Fox, Julie Warner, Barnard Hughes, Woody Harrelson, David Ogden Stiers, Frances Sternhagen, George Hamilton, Bridget Fonda, Mel Winkler, Helen Martin, Roberts Blossom

'This serving of recycled Capracorn has no real taste of its own, but, in its mildness and predictability, offers the reassurance of a fast-food or motel chain.' – *Variety*

Doctor at Large

GB   1957   104m   Eastmancolor
Rank (Betty E. Box)

Simon Sparrow tries two country practices, but returns at last to St Swithin's.

Hit-or-miss medical comedy with honours about even.

w Nicholas Phipps   *novel* Richard Gordon   *d* Ralph Thomas

ph Ernest Steward   *m* Bruce Montgomery

Dirk Bogarde, Muriel Pavlow, James Robertson Justice, Donald Sinden, Shirley Eaton, Derek Farr, Michael Medwin, Edward Chapman, Barbara Murray, Gladys Henson, Lionel Jeffries, A. E. Matthews, Athene Seyler, George Coulouris

Doctor at Sea*

GB   1955   93m   Technicolor
VistaVision
Rank/Group Films (Betty E. Box)

Simon Sparrow becomes medical officer on a cargo steamer

Reasonably lively comedy of errors with nice seascapes and predictable jokes.

w Nicholas Phipps, Jack Davies
d Ralph Thomas   *ph* Ernest Steward   *m* Bruce Montgomery

Dirk Bogarde, Brigitte Bardot, Brenda de Banzie, James Robertson Justice, Maurice Denham, Michael Medwin, Hubert Gregg, Raymond Huntley, Geoffrey Keen, George Coulouris, Jill Adams, James Kenney

'Brisk professional humour has given way to the more elementary business of traditional British farce.' – *Penelope Houston, MFB*

Dr Heckyl and Mr Hype

US   1980   99m   Metrocolor
Golan-Globus

An ugly scientist is transformed into a handsome young sadist.

Would-be comic variation on a well-worn theme; the level of comedy is indicated by the title.

wd Charles B. Griffith

Oliver Reed, Sunny Johnson, Mel Wells, Maia Danziger

□ □

Doctor in Clover

GB   1966   101m   Eastmancolor
Rank/Betty E. Box-Ralph Thomas

Grimsdyke goes back to his old
hospital for a refresher course and
finds a rejuvenating drug useful in his
philandering.

Depressing mixture of smut and
slapstick.

w Jack Davies   *novel* Richard
Gordon   *d* Ralph Thomas
ph Ernest Steward   *m* John Scott

Leslie Phillips, James Robertson
Justice, Shirley Anne Field, Joan Sims,
John Fraser, Arthur Haynes, Fenella
Fielding, Noel Purcell, Jeremy Lloyd,
Eric Barker, Terry Scott, Alfie Bass

Doctor in Distress

GB   1963   102m   Eastmancolor
Rank/Betty E. Box-Ralph Thomas

Simon Sparrow goes back to work for
Sir Lancelot Spratt and finds his old
mentor in love.

Tedious flummery whose characters
fail to perform with the old pizazz.

w Nicholas Phipps, Ronald Scott
Thorn   *d* Ralph Thomas
ph Ernest Steward   *m* Norrie
Paramour

Dirk Bogarde, James Robertson
Justice, Mylene Demongeot,
Samantha Eggar, Barbara Murray,
Donald Houston, Jessie Evans, Ann
Lynn, Leo McKern, Dennis Price

Doctor in Love

GB   1960   97m   Eastmancolor
Rank/Betty E. Box-Ralph Thomas

Dr Burke and Dr Hare have various
adventures, mostly amorous, in city
and country practices.

Virtually plotless collection of weak
sketches based on schoolboy smut.

w Nicholas Phipps   *novel* Richard
Gordon   *d* Ralph Thomas
ph Ernest Steward   *m* Bruce
Montgomery

Michael Craig, Leslie Phillips, James
Robertson Justice, Virginia Maskell,
Nicholas Phipps, Reginald Beckwith,
Joan Sims, Liz Fraser, Ambrosine
Philpotts, Irene Handl

Doctor in the House**

GB   1954   91m   Eastmancolor
Rank (Betty E. Box)
V

Amorous and other misadventures of
medical students at St Swithin's
Hospital.

A comedy with much to answer for:
several sequels and an apparently
endless TV series. The original is not
bad, as the students, though plainly
over age, constitute a formidable mass
of British talent at its peak.

*w Nicholas Phipps   novel Richard
Gordon   d Ralph Thomas
ph Ernest Steward   m Bruce
Montgomery*

Dirk Bogarde, Kenneth More, Donald
Sinden, Donald Houston, Kay Kendall,
Muriel Pavlow, *James Robertson Justice,*
Geoffrey Keen

'Works its way with determined high
spirits through the repertoire of
medical student jokes.' – *MFB*
'An uproarious, devil-may-care,
almost wholly ruthless picture.' –
Dilys Powell

† Sequels, of increasing inanity and
decreasing connection with the
original characters, were: *Doctor at Sea,
Doctor at Large, Doctor in Love, Doctor in
Distress, Doctor in Clover* and *Doctor in
Trouble. Carry on Doctor* and *Carry on
Again Doctor* were horses of a different
colour.

□ □

Doctor in Trouble
GB   1970   90m   Technicolor
Rank/Betty E. Box

Dr Burke inadvertently becomes a
stowaway on an Atlantic cruise.

Witless tailpiece to the Doctor saga,
like a half-hearted wrapping-up of
discarded jokes from the other
episodes.

w Jack Davies   novel Doctor on Toast
by Richard Gordon   d Ralph
Thomas   ph Ernest Steward
m Eric Rogers

Leslie Phillips, Harry Secombe, Angela
Scoular, Irene Handl, Robert Morley,
Simon Dee, Freddie Jones, James
Robertson Justice, Joan Sims, John
Le Mesurier, Fred Emney

'The cinematic equivalent of an end-
of-the-pier summer show.' – Films and
Filming

Dr Knock*
France   1936   74m   bw
Pathé-Natan

A sly young doctor takes over a
country practice and turns the
townsfolk into hypochondriacs.

Amusing version of a modern French
comedy classic.

w Jules Romains   play Jules
Romains   d Louis Jouvet, Roger
Goupillières

Louis Jouvet, Palau, Le Vigan, Moor,
Alexandre Rignault

'Once under way it scoots along like
a Bermuda sloop, and holds right till
the surprise fadeout.' – Variety

'The hot line suspense comedy!'
**Dr Strangelove; or, How I Learned
to Stop Worrying and Love the
Bomb***
GB   1963   93m   bw
Columbia/Stanley Kubrick (Victor Lyndon)
V, L

A mad USAF general launches a
nuclear attack on Russia, and when
recall attempts fail, and retaliation is
inevitable, all concerned sit back to
await the destruction of the world.

Black comedy resolving itself into a
series of sketches, with the star
playing three parts (for no good
reason): the US president, an RAF
captain, and a mad German-
American scientist. Historically an
important film in its timing, its
nightmares being those of the early
sixties, artistically it clogs its
imperishable moments by untidy
narrative and unattractively contrasty
photography.

w Stanley Kubrick, Terry Southern,
Peter George   novel Red Alert by
Peter George   d Stanley Kubrick
ph Gilbert Taylor   m Laurie
Johnson   ad Ken Adam

Peter Sellers, George C. Scott, Peter Bull,
Sterling Hayden, Keenan Wynn, Slim
Pickens, James Earl Jones, Tracy Reed
   GENERAL (George C. Scott): 'I don't say
we wouldn't get our hair mussed, but
I do say no more than ten to twenty
million people killed.'

'Scarcely a picture of relentless
originality; seldom have we seen so
much made over so little.' – Joan
Didion
'The double-face of the story – serious
events broken up into farcical incidents
– is expressed in double-face acting of
a high order.' – Dilys Powell

† Fail Safe (qv), which took the same

theme more seriously, was released almost simultaneously.

AAN: best picture; script; Stanley Kubrick (as director); Peter Sellers

The Doctor Takes a Wife*
US 1940 89m bw
Columbia (William Perlberg)

A young doctor has to pretend to be the husband of a socialite.

Typical high life comedy of its period, quite brisk and diverting.

w George Seaton, Ken Englund
d Alexander Hall   ph Sid Hickox   md Morris Stoloff
m Frederick Hollander

Loretta Young, Ray Milland, Edmund Gwenn, Reginald Gardiner, Gail Patrick, Frank Sully, George Metaxa, Charles Halton, Chester Clute

Doctor You've Got to be Kidding
US 1967 93m Metrocolor
  Panavision
MGM/Trident (Douglas Laurence)

A girl arrives at a maternity hospital chased by three prospective husbands.

Wild and wacky farce which leaves little impression.

w Phillip Shuken   novel Patte Wheat Mahan   d Peter Tewkesbury   ph Fred Koenekamp   m Kenyon Hopkins

Sandra Dee, George Hamilton, Celeste Holm, Bill Bixby, Dwayne Hickman, Dick Kallman, Mort Sahl, Allen Jenkins

Dona Flor and Her Two Husbands
Brazil 1976 110m Eastmancolor
Carnaval (Luis Carlos Barreto)

A young widow remarries, and has to share her bed with her late husband's ghost.

Semi-pornographic comedy which achieved some fashionable success.

wd Bruno Barreto   novel Jorge Amado   ph Maurito Salles
m Chico Buarque de Holanda

Sonia Braga, Jose Wilker, Mauro Mendonca

Donovan's Reef
US 1963 108m Technicolor
Paramount (John Ford)

War veterans settle down on a South Sea island; when the daughter of one of them comes to visit, his reputation must be protected.

Good-humoured but finally enervating mixture of rough-house and slapstick, with the appearance of an old friends' benefit and the director in familiar sub-standard form.

w Frank Nugent, James Edward Grant   d John Ford   ph William H. Clothier   m Cyril Mockridge

John Wayne, Lee Marvin, Jack Warden, Elizabeth Allen, Dorothy Lamour, Cesar Romero, Mike Mazurki

Don't Bother to Knock
GB 1961 89m Technicolor
  Cinemascope
ABP/Haileywood (Frank Godwin)
V
US title: Why Bother to Knock

A Casanova travel agent gives each of his girl friends a key to his Edinburgh flat.

Poorly developed and self-conscious sex farce.

w Dennis Cannan, Frederick Gotfurt, Frederic Raphael   novel Clifford

Hanley   d Cyril Frankel
ph Geoffrey Unsworth
m Elisabeth Lutyens

Richard Todd, *Judith Anderson*, Elke
Sommer, June Thorburn, Nicole
Maurey, Rik Battaglia, Eleanor
Summerfield, John Le Mesurier

Don't Give Up the Ship
US   1959   89m   bw
Hal Wallis (Paramount)

A dim-witted naval lieutenant is
accused of stealing a destroyer.

Feeble American service farce.

w Herbert Baker, Edmund Beloin,
Henry Garson   d Norman Taurog

Jerry Lewis, Dina Merrill, Diana
Spencer, Mickey Shaughnessy, Robert
Middleton, Gale Gordon

Don't Go Near the Water*
US   1957   107m   Metrocolor
   Cinemascope
MGM/Avon (Lawrence Weingarten)

The US Navy sets up a public relations
unit on a South Pacific island.

Loosely cemented service farce full of
fumbling lieutenants and bumbling
commanders, a more light-hearted
*M*A*S*H*. Boring romantic
interludes separate some very funny
farcical sequences.

w Dorothy Kingsley, George Wells
novel William Brinkley   d Charles
Walters   ph Robert Bronner
m Bronislau Kaper

Glenn Ford, Fred Clark, Gia Scala,
Romney Brent, Mickey Shaughnessy,
Earl Holliman, Anne Francis, Keenan
Wynn, Eva Gabor, Russ Tamblyn,
Jeff Richards, Mary Wickes

'Drop everything! And see the cheekiest
comedy of the year!'

Don't Just Lie There, Say Something!
GB   1973   91m   Eastmancolor
Comocroft/Rank

By a strange chapter of accidents, a
politician finds himself in bed with his
under-secretary and a lady not his wife.

Stupefying from-the-stalls rendering
of a successful stage farce; in this form
it simply doesn't work.

w Michael Pertwee   *play* Michael
Pertwee   d Bob Kellett

Brian Rix, Leslie Phillips, Joan Sims,
Joanna Lumley, Derek Royle, Peter
Bland

Don't Just Stand There
US   1967   99m   Techniscope
Universal (Stan Margulies)

A mild-mannered watch smuggler
gets himself involved with kidnapping,
murder, and finishing a sex novel.

Frantic but ineffective farce which
keeps on the move but does not arrive
anywhere.

w Charles Williams   *novel The
Wrong Venus* by Charles Williams
d Ron Winston   ph Milton
Krasner   m Nick Perito

Mary Tyler Moore, Robert Wagner,
Barbara Rhoades, Glynis Johns, Harvey
Korman

'Paris locations might have helped,
but we're stuck with the San
Fernando Valley.' – *Robert Windeler*

Don't Look Now . . . We're Being Shot At!*
France   1966   130m
   Eastmancolor   Panavision
Les Films Corona (Robert Dorfmann)
original title: *La Grande Vadrouille*

During World War II three members of a British bomber crew bale out over Paris and make a frantic escape to the free zone by means of various wild disguises.

Freewheeling star farce, a shade lacking in control, but with some funny sequences.

wd Gérard Oury   *ph* Claude Renoir   *m* Georges Auric

Terry-Thomas, Bourvil, Louis de Funès, Claudio Brook, Mike Marshall

'Both the sight gags and the characters evoke pale echoes of Laurel and Hardy, but it is not familiarity that breeds contempt here so much as the debasement of the familiar.' – *MFB*

Don't Make Waves
US   1967   97m   Metrocolor
Panavision
MGM/Filmways (Julian Bercovici)

A swimming-pool salesman attempts to get his own back on an impulsive young woman who has wrecked his car.

Malibu beach farce for immature adults, made by professionals helpless in the face of a weak script, but boasting a funny climax with a house teetering on the edge of a cliff.

w Ira Wallach, George Kirgo
novel Muscle Beach by Ira Wallach
d Alexander Mackendrick
ph Philip Lathrop   *m* Vic Mizzy

Tony Curtis, Claudia Cardinale, Robert Webber, Joanna Barnes, Sharon Tate, Jim Backus, Mort Sahl

'The fun never sets on the British Empire!'
Don't Raise the Bridge, Lower the River
GB   1967   100m   Technicolor
Columbia/Walter Shenson

An American turns his English wife's home into a discotheque.

Dreary comedy apparently intent on proving that its star can be just as unfunny abroad as at home.

w Max Wilk   *d* Jerry Paris
ph Otto Heller   *m* David Whitaker

Jerry Lewis, Terry-Thomas, Jacqueline Pearce, Bernard Cribbins, Patricia Routledge, Nicholas Parsons, Michael Bates

Don't Take It to Heart*
GB   1944   90m   bw
GFD/Two Cities (Sydney Box)

A genial castle ghost is unleashed by a bomb and affects the love affair of a researcher with the daughter of the house.

Amiably lunatic British-upper-class extravaganza with eccentric characters and some felicitous moments.

wd Jeffrey Dell   *ph* Eric Cross
m Mischa Spoliansky

Richard Greene, *Edward Rigby*, Patricia Medina, Alfred Drayton, Richard Bird, Wylie Watson, Moore Marriott, Brefni O'Rourke, Amy Veness, Claude Dampier, Joan Hickson, Joyce Barbour, Ronald Squire, Ernest Thesiger

'A cheerful and rewarding entertainment.' – *Richard Mallett, Punch*
'Not funny accidental but funny deliberate, and nine times out of ten the joke comes off.' – *Observer*

Don't Tell Her It's Me
US   1990   102m   CFI
Rank/Sovereign (George Braunstein, Ron Hamady)
V

A romantic novelist persuades her

wimpish brother, who is recovering from radiation treatment, to pretend to be a biker in order to get a girlfriend.

Trivial, depressingly unsubtle comedy with matching performances.

w Sarah Bird novel The Boyfriend School by Sarah Bird d Malcolm Mowbray ph Reed Smoot m Michael Gore pd Linda Pearl, Daryl Kerrigan ed Marshall Harvey

Shelley Long, Steve Guttenberg, Jami Gertz, Kyle MacLachlan, Madchen Amick, Kevin Scannell

'Takes the germ of an amusing notion about the division between realistic and fantastic romantic hero and hammers it painfully into the ground.' – Kim Newman, Sight and Sound
'Grotesquely unfunny comedy.' – Variety

Don't Tell Mom the Babysitter's Dead

US 1991 105m DeLuxe
Warner/HBO/Cinema Plus/Outlaw/
  Mercury/Douglas (Robert Newmyer,
  Brian Reilly, Jeffrey Silver)
V

A young girl supports her siblings while their mother is away on holiday.

Lamentably silly comedy.

w Neil Landau, Tara Ison
d Stephen Herek ph Tim
Suhrstedt m David Newman, Brian
Nazarian pd Stephen Marsh
ed Larry Bock

Christina Applegate, Joanna Cassidy, John Getz, Josh Charles, Keith Coogan, Concetta Tomei, David Duchovny, Kimmy Robertson

'Starts with the enjoyable, if crude, black comedy situation promised by the title, but then it turns into an

incredibly dumb teenage girl's fantasy of making it in the business world. Even backward teenagers won't fall for this knuckle-headed release.'
–Variety

Double Bunk

GB 1961 92m bw
British Lion/Bryanston (George H. Brown)

Newlyweds live in an old houseboat.

Thin comedy which turns out not to be leakproof.

wd C. M. Pennington-Richards

Ian Carmichael, Janette Scott, Liz Frazer, Sid James, Dennis Price, Reginald Beckwith, Irene Handl, Noel Purcell, Naunton Wayne

Double Dynamite

US 1951 (produced 1948) 80m
  bw
RKO (Irving Cummings Jr)
aka: It's Only Money

A bank teller wins a fortune at the race track but is afraid his winnings will be thought the proceeds of a bank robbery.

Insultingly mild comedy, nearly saved by a few quips from Groucho.

w Melville Shavelson, Harry Crane, Leo Rosten d Irving Cummings ph Robert de Grasse m Leigh Harline

Frank Sinatra, Jane Russell, Groucho Marx, Don McGuire, Howard Freeman

Double Whoopee**

US 1928 20m bw silent
Hal Roach

Incompetent doormen at a swank hotel cause havoc.

Simple-minded but pleasing star farce.

w Leo McCarey, H. M. Walker
d Lewis R. Foster   ph George
Stevens, Jack Roach   ed Richard
Currier

Laurel and Hardy, Jean Harlow,
Charlie Hall

Doughboys*
US   1930   80m approx   bw
MGM/Buster Keaton (Lawrence
   Weingarten)
GB title: Forward March

A young eccentric joins the army.

Simple-minded farce with a few good
routines for the star.

w Richard Schayer   d Edward
Sedgwick   ph Leonard Smith

Buster Keaton, Sally Eilers, Cliff
Edwards, Edward Brophy

'Keaton's first talker is comedy with a
kick.' – Variety

The Doughgirls*
US   1944   102m   bw
Warner (Mark Hellinger)

In a crowded wartime Washington
hotel, a honeymoon is frustrated by
constant interruption, not to mention
the discovery that the wedding was
not legal.

Frantic farce, generally well adapted,
and certainly played with gusto.

w James V. Kern, Sam Hellman
play Joseph Fields   d James V.
Kern   ph Ernest Haller
m Adolph Deutsch

Alexis Smith, Jane Wyman, Jack
Carson, Ann Sheridan, Irene Manning,
Eve Arden, Charlie Ruggles, John
Alexander, John Ridgely, Craig
Stevens, Alan Mowbray, Donald
MacBride

'There's nothing so good in it that you

must attend, just as there is nothing
bad enough to keep you away.' –
Archer Winsten

Down and Out in Beverly Hills*
US   1985   97m   Technicolor
Touchstone (Paul Mazursky)
V

A wandering con artist is taken in by
an insecure Beverly Hills family.

Somewhat bumbling but sporadically
effective rehash of Renoir's Boudu
Sauvé des Eaux (qv), with a few
modern jabs and effectively eccentric
performances.

w Paul Mazursky, Leon Capetanos
play René Fauchois   d Paul
Mazursky   ph Donald McAlpine
m Andy Summers   pd Pato Guzman

Nick Nolte, Richard Dreyfuss, Bette
Midler, Little Richard, Tracy Nelson,
Elizabeth Pena

Down by Law*
US   1986   107m   bw
Island Pictures/Black Snake/Grokenburger
Films (Alan Kleinberg)
V

A disc jockey and a pimp, framed for
crimes they did not commit, escape
from jail with an Italian who has a
minimal grasp of English.

Engaging lowlife comedy.

wd Jim Jarmusch   ph Robby
Müller   m John Lurie, Tom
Waits   ed Melody London

Tom Waits, John Lurie, Roberto
Benigni, Ellen Barkin, Billie Neal,
Rockets Redgrave, Vernel Bagneris,
Nicoletta Braschi

Down Memory Lane*
US   1949   70m   bw
Aubrey Schenck

A kaleidoscope of Mack Sennett comedy shorts, linked by Steve Allen as a disc jockey. Much Bing Crosby; Fields in *The Dentist;* an appearance by Sennett himself.
d Phil Karlson

Dragnet
US   1987   106m   DeLuxe
Universal/Applied Action/Bernie Brillstein

The nephew of Sgt Joe Friday gets involved in a murder case.

Overlong parody with some obvious amusements before the whole thing becomes tiresome.

w Dan Aykroyd, Alan Zweibel, Tom Mankiewicz   d Tom Mankiewicz   ph Matthew F. Leonetti   m Ira Newborn
pd Robert F. Boyle

Dan Aykroyd, Tom Hanks, Christopher Plummer, Harry Morgan, Alexander Paul, Elizabeth Ashley, Dabney Coleman

The Dream Team*
US   1989   113m   DeLuxe
    Panavision
UIP/Imagine Entertainment (Christopher
    W. Knight)
V, L

On a day trip to New York, four inmates of a psychiatric hospital foil a murder plot.

Enjoyable sentimental comedy that avoids most of the pitfalls of its subject matter.

w Jon Connolly, David Loucka
d Howard Zieff   ph Adam Holender   m David McHugh
pd Todd Hallowell   ad Christopher Nowak   ed C. Timothy O'Meara

Michael Keaton, Christopher Lloyd, Peter Boyle, Stephen Furst, Dennis Boutsikaris, Lorraine Bracco, Milo

O'Shea, Philip Bosco, James Remar

'Sharp and punchily acted.' – *John Pym, MFB*

Dream Wife
US   1953   99m   bw
MGM (Dore Schary)

An executive leaves his ambitious wife for a sheik's daughter schooled in the art of pleasing men, but naturally finds drawbacks.

Very moderate comedy with strained situations and few laughs. The stars work hard.

w Sidney Sheldon, Herbert Baker, Alfred L. Levitt   d Sidney Sheldon   ph Milton Krasner
m Conrad Salinger

Cary Grant, Deborah Kerr, Walter Pidgeon, Betta St John, Eduard Franz, Buddy Baer, Les Tremayne

Dreamboat*
US   1952   83m   bw
TCF (Sol C. Siegel)

A romantic star of the silent film era is embarrassed when his old movies turn up on television.

Hollywood rather blunderingly makes fun of its arch enemy in this sometimes sprightly but often disappointing comedy which should have been a bull's-eye.

wd Claude Binyon   ph Milton Krasner   m Cyril Mockridge

Clifton Webb, Ginger Rogers, Anne Francis, Jeffrey Hunter, Elsa Lanchester, Fred Clark, Ray Collins, Paul Harvey

'A merry comedy filled with uproarious laughter from beginning to end.' – *Hollywood Reporter*

Drive-in

US 1976 96m Technicolor
Columbia (George Litto)

In Texas, various illicit activities find their climax at a drive-in movie.

Mild sex-and-destruction comedy which raises few laughs and makes little sense.

w Bob Peete   d Rod Amateau
ph Robert Jessup   m various

Lisa Lemole, Glen Morshower, Gary Cavagnaro, Billy Milliken, Lee Newsome, Regan Kee

Drop Dead Darling

GB 1966 100m Technicolor
Panavision
Seven Arts (Ken Hughes)
US title: Arrivederci Baby

A con man who marries and murders rich women meets a con lady with similar intentions.

Loud, restless black comedy which squanders its moments of genuine inventiveness among scenes of shouting, confusion and action for action's sake.

wd Ken Hughes   story The Careful Man by Richard Deming   ph Denys Coop   m Dennis Farnon

Tony Curtis, Rosanna Schiaffino, Lionel Jeffries, Zsa Zsa Gabor, Nancy Kwan, Fenella Fielding, Anna Quayle, Warren Mitchell, Mischa Auer

'He creates the havoc. She takes the blame.'

Drop Dead Fred

US 1991 99m colour
Rank/Working Title/Polygram (Paul Webster)
V

A young woman in difficulties is revisited by her imaginary, destructive childhood friend.

Singularly tasteless comedy, lacking any vestige of wit or even humour.

w Carlos Davis, Anthony Fingleton   story Elizabeth Livingston   d Ate de Jong
ph Peter Deming   m Randy Edelman   pd Joseph T. Garrity
ed Marshall Harvey

Phoebe Cates, Rik Mayall, Marsha Mason, Tim Matheson, Bridget Fonda, Carrie Fisher, Keith Charles, Ashley Peldon, Daniel Gerroll

'Harvey reimagined for the Beetlejuice generation, with strident gags standing in for magic and relentless obviousness overriding the disturbing ambiguity that might have made the film work.' – Kim Newman, Sight and Sound
'This celebration of mental retardation is where the nadirs of two current Hollywood cycles – the regression to childhood/life swap movie and the ghost/revenant picture – intersect.' – Philip French, Observer

Dry Rot

GB 1956 87m bw
Romulus (Jack Clayton)

Three bookmakers plot to make a fortune by substituting a doped horse for the favourite.

Flat filming of a long-running theatrical farce.

w John Chapman   play John Chapman   d Maurice Elvey
ph Arthur Grant   m Peter Akister

Ronald Shiner, Brian Rix, Sid James, Michael Shepley, Joan Haythorne, Joan Sims, Heather Sears, Lee Patterson, Peggy Mount

'If the rustlers didn't get you ... the hustlers did!'

The Duchess and the Dirtwater Fox
US 1976 104m DeLuxe
Panavision
TCF (Melvin Frank)

A Barbary Coast con man and a saloon singer have various hectic adventures.

Wild and woolly spoof Western which fires off aimlessly in a variety of styles and becomes merely tiresome despite good scenes.

w Melvin Frank, Barry Sandler
d Melvin Frank ph Joseph Biroc
m Charles Fox

George Segal, Goldie Hawn, Conrad Janis, Thayer David, Roy Jenson, Bob Hoy, Bennie Dobbins

'The classic Western has now been shot to death by Sam Peckinpah, laughed to death by Mel Brooks and pondered to death by Arthur Penn, and Frank is like a scavenger picking up stray relics from its body.' – *Newsweek*
'The relentless vulgarity of the enterprise suggests that Mr Frank, having been so long constrained by the Hollywood Production Code when churning out vehicles for Bob Hope and Danny Kaye, is still making up for lost time.' – *Philip French*

Duck Soup****
US 1933 68m bw
Paramount
L

An incompetent becomes President of Fredonia and wages war on its scheming neighbour.

The satirical aspects of this film are fascinating but appear to have been unintentional. Never mind, it's also the most satisfying and undiluted

Marx Brothers romp, albeit the one without instrumental interludes. It does include the lemonade stall, the mirror sequence, and an endless array of one-liners and comedy choruses.

w Bert Kalmar, Harry Ruby, Arthur Sheekman, Nat Perrin d Leo McCarey ph Henry Sharp m/ly Bert Kalmar, Harry Ruby ad Hans Dreier, Wiard Ihnen

The Four Marx Brothers, Margaret Dumont, Louis Calhern, Edgar Kennedy, Raquel Torres

'Practically everybody wants a good laugh right now, and this should make practically everybody laugh.' – *Variety*
'So much preliminary dialogue is necessary that it seems years before Groucho comes on at all; and waiting for Groucho is agony.' – *E. V. Lucas, Punch*
'The most perfect of all Marxist masterpieces.' – *Time Out, 1984*

The Duke Wore Jeans
GB 1958 89m bw
Insignia (Peter Rogers)

An aristocrat persuades his cockney double to woo a princess on his behalf.

Moderately lively comedy with songs, tailored for Britain's new musical star.

w Norman Hudis d Gerald Thomas

Tommy Steele, June Laverick, Michael Medwin, Alan Wheatley, Eric Pohlmann

Dutch
US 1991 107m DeLuxe
TCF (John Hughes, Richard Vane)
V, L
GB title: *Driving Me Crazy*

An arrogant and snobbish twelve-year-old boy is reformed by his divorced mother's working-class boyfriend.

Inert comedy of class warfare, part of the cycle of buddy-buddy movies in which antagonists at the beginning become friends by the end.

w John Hughes   *d* Peter Faiman

ph Charles Minsky   *m* Alan Silvestri   *pd* Stan Jolley   *ed* Paul Hirsch, Adam Bernardi

Ed O'Neill, Ethan Randall, Christopher McDonald, Ari Meyers, E. G. Daily, L. Scott Caldwell, Kathleen Freeman

The Eagle**
US 1925 80m approx (24 fps)
bw silent
United Artists/Joseph M. Schenck
L

A Cossack lieutenant turns masked
outlaw when his father's lands are
annexed.

Enjoyable romp in the wake of Robin
Hood, the Scarlet Pimpernel and Zorro;
the eye-flashing star is somewhere
near his best.

w Hans Kraly   *story* Dubrowsky by
Alexander Pushkin   *d* Clarence
Brown   *ph* George Barnes

Rudolph Valentino, Vilma Banky,
Louise Dresser

The Early Bird
GB 1965 98m Eastmancolor
Rank/Hugh Stewart
V

A milkman gets involved in an inter-
company war.

Star farcical comedy; not the worst of
Wisdom, but overlong and mainly
uninventive.

w Jack Davies, Norman Wisdom,
Eddie Leslie, Henry Blyth   *d* Robert
Asher   *ph* Jack Asher   *m* Ron
Goodwin

Norman Wisdom, Edward Chapman,
Jerry Desmonde, Paddie O'Neil, Bryan
Pringle, Richard Vernon, John Le
Mesurier, Peter Jeffrey

Early to Bed
US 1928 20m bw silent
Hal Roach

Stan becomes Ollie's butler but rebels
when his friend's fortune goes to his
head.

One of the most untypical and seldom
seen of the stars' comedies, with both
prankishly out of character. On its
own account however it is mainly
very funny.

w H. M. Walker   *d* Emmett
Flynn   *ph* George Stevens
ed Richard Currier

Laurel and Hardy

Earthworm Tractors
US 1936 69m bw
Warner
GB title: *A Natural Born Salesman*

A salesman whose fiancée wants him
to think big turns to tractors.

One of the star's livelier comedies.

w Richard Macauley, Joe Traub,
Hugh Cummings   *d* Ray Enright

Joe E. Brown, June Travis, Guy
Kibbee, Dick Foran

'Where there's smoke, there must be
somebody smoking!'

Easy Living**
US 1937 91m bw
Paramount (Arthur Hornblow Jnr)
L

A fur coat is thrown out of a window and lands on a typist . . .

Amusing romantic comedy with farcical trimmings; it now stands among the semi-classic crazy comedies of the thirties.

w Preston Sturges   *d* Mitchell Leisen   *ph* Ted Tetzlaff   *md* Boris Morros

Jean Arthur, Ray Milland, *Edward Arnold*, Luis Alberni, Mary Nash, Franklin Pangborn, William Demarest, Andrew Tombes

'Slapstick farce which does not fulfil the box office possibilities of its stars.' – *Variety*
'Secretaries, millionaires, jokes, sight gags, furies, attacks of cool sense – there are always three things going on at once.' – *New Yorker, 1977*

Easy Money
US   1983   100m   bw
Orion
L

A baby photographer is left a fortune provided that he totally reforms.

Overlong and increasingly feeble comedy with a star who quickly outstays his welcome.

w Rodney Dangerfield, Michael Endler, P. J. O'Rourke, Dennis Blair
d James Signorelli

Rodney Dangerfield, Joe Pesci, Geraldine Fitzgerald, Candy Azzara, Val Avery

Easy Street****
US   1917   22m approx   bw
  silent
Mutual/Charles Chaplin

In a slum street, a tramp is reformed by a dewy-eyed missionary, becomes a policeman, and tames the local bully.

Quintessential Chaplin, combining sentimentality and social comment with hilarious slapstick.

wd Charles Chaplin   *ph* William C. Foster, Rollie Totheroh

Charles Chaplin, Edna Purviance, Albert Austin, Eric Campbell

Eat the Peach*
Eire   1986   95m   Technicolor
Strongbow/Film Four International (David Collins)
V

Out-of-work Irish devise a mad scheme to construct a motorcycle Wall of Death.

Fairly amusing comedy, like an Irish version of an Ealing movie.

w Peter Ormrod, John Kelleher
d Peter Ormrod   *ph* Arthur Wooster   *m* Donal Lummy

Stephen Brennan, Eamon Morrissey, Catherine Byrne, Niall Toibin, Joe Lynch, Tony Doyle

Eating Raoul*
US   1982   83m   Pacific Color
Bartel Film (Anne Kimmel)

A restaurateur kills a drunken swinger, and finds that he has a profitable sideline on his hands . . .

Black comedy with insufficient humour to offset tastelessness.

w Richard Blackburn, Paul Bartel
d Paul Bartel   *ph* Gary Thieltges   *m* Arlon Ober

Paul Bartel, Mary Woronov, Robert Beltran, Susan Saiger, Richard Blackburn

'I wanted to make a film about two greedy, uptight people who are at the

same time not so unlike you and me
and Nancy and Ronnie, to keep it
funny and yet communicate
something about the psychology and
perversity of these values . . . My
movie touches on many things: the
perversion of middle class values, the
resurgence of Nixonism, machismo
versus WASP fastidiousness, *film
noir* . . .' – *Paul Bartel*

Eddie Holm's Second Life**
Denmark   1985   95m   colour
Scenograf (Poul Arnt Thomsen)
original title: *Eddie Holms Andet Liv*

A suicidal musician is taken back
through his life to discover what
drove him to end it.

Witty, black comedy of love, death
and family life.

w Bjarne Henriksen, Gert
Henriksen   *d* Esben Hùilund
Carlsen   *ph* Ole Schultz   *m* Bo
Lykke Jùrgensen   *ed* Jette Allarp

Kristian Halken, Pernille Hansen,
Lisbet Lundquist, Claus Nissen,
Holger Boland, Karen Marie Lowert,
Frederik Esbensen

Educated Evans
GB   1936   86m   bw
Warner (Irving Asher)

A racetrack bookie becomes a trainer.

Rather unyielding vehicle for a fast-
talking star.

w Frank Launder and Robert
Edmunds   *story* Edgar Wallace
d William Beaudine   *ph* Basil
Emmott   *ad* Peter Proud

Max Miller, Nancy O'Neil, Clarice
Mayne, Albert Whelan, Hal Walters

† A sequel followed in 1938: *Thank
Evans.*

The Egg and I*
US   1947   104m   bw
U-I (Chester Erskine)

A city couple try to become gentleman
farmers.

Mild, pleasant comedy notable chiefly
for introducing a hillbilly couple, Ma
and Pa Kettle, who went on, in the
personae of Main and Kilbride, to
make several later features. (See
under *Kettles*.)

w Chester Erskine, Fred
Finklehoffe   *novel* Betty
Macdonald   *d* Chester Erskine
ph Milton Krasner   *m* Frank
Skinner

Claudette Colbert, Fred MacMurray,
Marjorie Main, Percy Kilbride, Louise
Allbritton, Richard Long, Billy House,
Ida Moore, Donald MacBride

'Marjorie Main, in an occasional fit of
fine, wild comedy, picks the show up
and brandishes it as if she were
wringing its neck. I wish to God she
had.' – *James Agee*
AAN: Marjorie Main

Eight on the Lam
US   1966   107m   DeLuxe
United Artists/Hope Enterprises (Bill
    Lawrence)
GB title: *Eight on the Run*

A bank teller is suspected of
embezzlement and goes on the run
with his seven children.

Feeble comedy punctuated by even
feebler chases; the star had lost his
comic character.

w Albert E. Lewin, Burt Styler, Bob
Fisher, Arthur Marx   *d* George
Marshall   *ph* Alan Stensvold
m George Romanis

Bob Hope, Phyllis Diller, Jonathan
Winters, Shirley Eaton, Jill St John

18 Again!

US   1988   100m   DeLuxe
Entertainment/New World (Walter
  Coblenz)

After a car crash, the mind of an 81-
year-old grandfather is switched into
the body of his 18-year-old grandson.

Feeblest of the body-swap cycle of
films, with little to entertain.

w Josh Goldstein, Jonathan Prince
d Paul Flaherty   ph Stephen M.
Katz   m Billy Goldenberg
pd Dena Roth   ed Danford B.
Greene

George Burns, Charlie Schlatter, Tony
Roberts, Anita Morris, Miriam Flynn,
Jennifer Runyon, Red Buttons

Electric Dreams

GB   1984   112m   Metrocolor
Virgin/MGM-UA (Rusty Lemorande, Larry
  de Waay)
V

A computer becomes jealous of its
owner's love affair.

Gruesomely extended revue sketch
which totally fails to develop its
characters and offers instead a very
sparing amount of cleverness.

w Rusty Lemorande   d Steve
Barron   ph Alex Thomson
m Giorgio Moroder   pd Richard
MacDonald

Lenny Von Dohlen, Virginia Madsen,
Maxwell Caulfield, Bud Cort, Don
Fellows

Eliza Fraser

Australia   1976   127m   colour
Hexagon (Tim Burstall)

A shipwrecked couple have to live
with Aborigines; later she becomes a
fairground attraction.

Would-be bawdy historical romp on

the lines of *Tom Jones;* it seldom
works.

w David Williamson   d Tim
Burstall

Susannah York, Trevor Howard, Noel
Ferrier, John Waters, Charles Tingwell

Ella Cinders**

US   1926   83m approx   bw
  silent
First National

A servant girl wins a trip to
Hollywood.

Famous and still pleasing comedy
from the comic strip *Cinderella in the
Movies.*

w Frank Griffin, Mervyn Le Roy
d Alfred E. Green

Colleen Moore, Lloyd Hughes, Vera
Lewis, Doria Baker

Elstree Calling*

GB   1930   95m   bw/Pathécolour
Wardour/BIP (John Maxwell)

A film studio mounts a television
show.

Slender excuse for an all-star revue
which luckily preserves much light
entertainment talent of the time.

w Adrian Brunel, Walter C. Mycroft,
Val Valentine   d Adrian Brunel,
Alfred Hitchcock, Jack Hulbert, André
Charlot, Paul Murray   ph Claude
Friese-Greene   m Reg Casson,
Vivian Ellis, Chick Endor, Ivor Novello,
Jack Strachey   ed Émile de Ruelle,
A. C. Hammond

Tommy Handley, Jack Hulbert, Cicely
Courtneidge, Will Fyffe, Lily Morris,
Teddy Brown, Anna May Wong,
Gordon Harker, Donald Calthrop,
John Longden, Jameson Thomas,
Bobbie Comber

Elvira, Mistress of the Dark

US 1988 96m CFI color
Entertainment/New World/NBC/Queen B
  (Eric Gardner, Mark Pierson)
V, L

The hostess of a TV horror show discovers that she has magic powers.

Camp nonsense, limply performed.

w Sam Egan, John Paragon, Cassandra Peterson d James Signorelli ph Hanania Baer m James Campbell pd John DeCuir Jnr ed Battle Davis

Cassandra Peterson, W. Morgan Shepherd, Daniel Greene, Susan Kellermann, Jeff Conaway, Edie McClurg, Kurt Fuller, Pat Crawford Brown

Encino Man

US 1992 88m Technicolor
Warner/Hollywood Pictures/Touchwood
  Pacific Partners I (George Zaloom)
V
GB title: California Man

Two high-school students revive a frozen prehistoric youth who quickly adapts to the prevailing life-style.

A depressing youth comedy, though those with a Neanderthal sense of humour may be amused.

w Shawn Schepps story George Zaloom, Shawn Schepps d Les Mayfield ph Robert Brickmann m J. Peter Robinson pd James Allen ed Eric Sears, Jonathan Siegel

Sean Astin, Brendan Fraser, Pauly Shore, Megan Ward, Robin Tunney, Michael DeLuise, Patrick Van Horn, Dalton James, Rick Ducommun

'Mindless would-be comedy . . . insulting even within its own no-effort parameters.' – Variety

'Less funny than your own funeral.'
– Washington Post

'A comedy for you and your next of kin!'
The End

US 1978 100m DeLuxe
UA/Lawrence Gordon (Hank Moonjean)

A selfish man finds he is dying and unsuccessfully tries to change what remains of his life.

Presumably intended as an ironic black comedy, this comes over as tasteless ham; nobody involved, least of all the director-star, has any idea how to handle it.

w Jerry Belson d Burt Reynolds ph Bobby Byrne m Paul Williams pd Jan Scott

Burt Reynolds, Dom de Luise, Sally Field, Strother Martin, David Steinberg, Joanne Woodward, Norman Fell, Myrna Loy, Pat O'Brien, Robby Benson, Carl Reiner

English without Tears*

GB 1944 89m bw
GFD/Two Cities (Anatole de Grunwald, Sydney Box)
US title: Her Man Gilbey

During World War II a rich ATS girl falls for her butler who has become a lieutenant.

Wispy satirical comedy with amusing moments, chiefly interesting for the pre-war League of Nations sequences.

w Terence Rattigan, Anatole de Grunwald d Harold French ph Bernard Knowles

Lilli Palmer, Michael Wilding, Margaret Rutherford, Penelope Dudley Ward, Albert Lieven, Roland Culver, Peggy Cummins

Ensign Pulver

US   1964   104m   Technicolor
Panavision
Warner (Joshua Logan)

Further naval misadventures of the
character from *Mr Roberts*.

Threadbare naval comedy with every
expected cliché.

w Joshua Logan, Peter S.
Feibleman   *play* Joshua Logan,
Thomas Heggen   d Joshua
Logan   ph Charles Lawton
m George Duning

Robert Walker, Burl Ives, Walter
Matthau, Tommy Sands, Millie
Perkins, Kay Medford, Larry Hagman,
James Farentino, James Coco, Al
Freeman Jnr

Enter Laughing*

US   1967   111m   Technicolor
Columbia/Acre/Sajo (Carl Reiner, Joseph
Stein)

In New York in the thirties, a young
man about to train as a pharmacist
decides to become an actor instead.

Strident Jewish comedy based on the
writer-director's own youthful
experiences, which might have been
more effectively strained by another
hand. The talent is there, though.

w Joseph Stein, Carl Reiner
play Carl Reiner   d Carl Reiner
ph Joseph Biroc   m Quincy Jones

Reni Santoni, Jose Ferrer, Shelley
Winters, Elaine May, Jack Gilford,
Janet Margolin, David Opatoshu,
Michael J. Pollard

Entertaining Mr Sloane*

GB   1969   94m   Technicolor
Pathe/Canterbury (Douglas Kentish)
V

A lodger attracts the amorous
attention of both the middle-aged
daughter and older son of the house.

A Gothic *tour de force* of bad taste
which worked better on the stage but
has its moments.

w Clive Exton   *play* Joe Orton
d Douglas Hickox   ph Wolfgang
Suschitsky   m Georgie Fame

Beryl Reid, Harry Andrews, Peter
McEnery, Alan Webb

The Errand Boy

US   1961   92m   bw
Paramount/Jerry Lewis (Ernest D.
Glucksman)
V

A dimwit paperhanger causes havoc
in a Hollywood studio but is
eventually signed up as a comic to
rival Jerry Lewis.

Feeble comedy with the star at his
self-satisfied worst.

wd Jerry Lewis   ph W. Wallace
Kelley   m Walter Scharf

Jerry Lewis, Brian Donlevy, Sig
Rumann, Fritz Feld, Isobel Elsom, Iris
Adrian

Eternally Yours*

US   1939   95m   bw
Walter Wanger

A magician's wife thinks he is too
interested in his tricks.

Slightly scatty romantic comedy,
amiable if not quite good enough to
stand the test of time, but with a great
cast.

w Gene Towne, Graham Baker
d Tay Garnett   ph Merritt
Gerstad   m Werner Janssen

Loretta Young, David Niven,
Broderick Crawford, Hugh Herbert,
Billie Burke, C. Aubrey Smith,
Raymond Walburn, Zasu Pitts, Virginia

Field, Eve Arden, Herman the Rabbit

'Will have to depend on the name power to get it by.' – *Variety*
'An amusing and irresponsible picture, though on the whole more irresponsible than amusing.' – *New York Times*
AAN: Werner Janssen

Every Day's a Holiday*
US   1937   79m   bw
Paramount (Emmanuel Cohen)

A confidence girl in the old Bowery sells Brooklyn Bridge to suckers.

The most satisfactory example of post-Legion of Decency Mae West, the smut being replaced by a lively cast of comedians.

w Mae West   *d* A. Edward Sutherland   *ph* Karl Struss   *m/ly* various   *ad* Wiard Ihnen

Mae West, Edmund Lowe, Charles Butterworth, Charles Winninger, Walter Catlett, Lloyd Nolan, Herman Bing, Roger Imhof, Chester Conklin

'A lively, innocuously bawdy, and rowdy entertainment.' – *Variety*
AAN: Wiard Ihnen

Every Girl Should be Married
US   1948   84m   bw
RKO (Don Hartman, Dore Schary)

A determined girl sets her cap at a bachelor pediatrician.

Woefully thin star comedy with few laughs.

w Stephen Morehouse Avery, Don Hartman   *d* Don Hartman   *ph* George E. Diskant   *m* Leigh Harline

Cary Grant, Betsy Drake, Franchot Tone, Diana Lynn, Alan Mowbray, Elizabeth Risdon, Richard Gaines

'In the past, Cary Grant has shown a talent for quietly underplaying comedy. In this picture, he has trouble finding comedy to play.' – *Time*

Every Home Should Have One
GB   1970   94m   Eastmancolor
British Lion/Example (Ned Sherrin)
V

An advertising man goes berserk when he tries to think up an erotic way of selling porridge.

Tiresomely frenetic star comedy with the emphasis on smut.

w Marty Feldman, Barry Took, Denis Norden   *d* James Clark   *ph* Ken Hodges   *m* John Cameron

Marty Feldman, Shelley Berman, Judy Cornwell, Julie Ege, Patrick Cargill, Jack Watson, Patience Collier, Penelope Keith, Dinsdale Landen

Every Little Crook and Nanny
US   1972   92m   Metrocolor
MGM (Leonard J. Ackerman)

A Mafia chief finds his child's new nanny has a grudge against him.

Sporadically amusing farce.

w Cy Howard, Jonathan Axelrod, Robert Klane   *d* Cy Howard   *ph* Philip Lathrop   *m* Fred Karlin

Victor Mature, Lynn Redgrave, Paul Sand, Maggie Blye, Austin Pendleton, John Astin, Dom De Luise

Every Which Way but Loose
US   1978   114m   DeLuxe
Warner/Malpaso
V, L

A Los Angeles trucker wins an orang-utan in a prize fight and becomes involved in sundry brawls and chases.

Easy-going, shambling star vehicle

which was liked by nobody but the public.

w Jeremy Joe Kronsberg   d James Fargo   ph Rexford Metz   md Steve Dorff

Clint Eastwood, Sondra Locke, Ruth Gordon, Geoffrey Lewis, Walter Barnes

† The 1980 sequel, almost indistinguishable, was *Any Which Way You Can*.

Everything You Always Wanted to Know about Sex*

US   1972   87m   DeLuxe
UA (Charles H. Joffe)
V, L

Seven sketches on sexual themes.

Dishevelled revue with a reasonable number of laughs for broadminded audiences.

wd Woody Allen   book Dr David Reuben   ph David M. Walsh   m Mundell Lowe   pd Dale Hennesy

Woody Allen, Lynn Redgrave, Anthony Quayle, John Carradine, Lou Jacobi, Louise Lasser, Tony Randall, Burt Reynolds, Gene Wilder

Everything's Ducky

US   1961   81m   bw
Barboo/Columbia

Two naval ratings adopt a talking duck.

Anything-goes service farce, with material below the standard of the talent available.

w John Fenton Murray, Benedict Freedman   d Don Taylor

Mickey Rooney, Buddy Hackett, Jackie Cooper, Joanie Summers, Roland Winters

The Experts

US   1989   83m   Alpha Cine colour
Paramount (James Keach)

Two trendy New Yorkers think they have been hired to open a night-club in Nebraska; in reality, they are transported to the USSR to teach American manners to Russian spies living in a replica of a US town.

Feeble and simple-minded comedy that is almost enough to restart the Cold War.

w Nick Thiel, Stephen Greene, Eric Alter   d Dave Thomas   ph Ronnie Taylor   m Marvin Hamlisch   pd David Fischer   ed Bud Molin

John Travolta, Arye Gross, Kelly Preston, Deborah Foreman, James Keach, Jan Rubes, Brian Doyle Murray, Mimi Maynard, Eve Brent, Charles Martin Smith

'Johnny never had it so good – or lost it so fast!'

Expresso Bongo*

GB   1959   111m   bw   Dyaliscope
BL/Britannia/Conquest (Val Guest)
V

A Soho agent turns a nondescript teenage singer into an international star.

Heavily vulgarized version of a stage skit on the Tommy Steele rock phenomenon, divested of most of its satirical barbs and only intermittently amusing.

w Wolf Mankowitz   play Wolf Mankowitz   d Val Guest   ph John Wilcox   md Robert Farnon   m/ly David Heneker, Monty Norman

Laurence Harvey, Sylvia Syms, Yolande Donlan, Cliff Richard, *Meier Tzelniker*, Gilbert Harding, Ambrosine Philpotts, Eric Pohlmann, Wilfrid Lawson, Hermione Baddeley, Reginald Beckwith, Martin Miller

'What the cinema offers is a sardonic rattle with music . . . The approach may be satirical or flippant; and yet one finds oneself half-beginning to believe in the subject; even minding about it.' – *Dilys Powell*

The Extra Girl*
US 1923 69m bw silent
Mack Sennett

A small town girl wins a beauty contest and goes to Hollywood.

A comparatively restrained comedy with slapstick interludes, this charming film shows its star at her best and admirably illustrates Hollywood in the early twenties.
d Mack Sennett *m* Jack Ward

Mabel Normand, Max Davidson, Ralph Graves, George Nicholls

F

The Facts of Life*
US   1960   103m   bw
UA/HLP (Norman Panama)

Two middle-aged married
suburbanites have an abortive affair.

Star comedy with muted slapstick and
earnest acting, a good try, but less
effective than their normal pratfalls.

w Norman Panama, Melvin Frank
d Melvin Frank   *ph* Charles Lang
Jnr   *m* Leigh Harline   *ad* Joseph
McMillan Johnson, Kenneth A. Reid

Bob Hope, Lucille Ball, Ruth Hussey,
Don Defore, Louis Nye, Philip Ober

'Random shots of mockery aimed
effectively at the American middle-
class way of life.' – *Peter John Dyer*
AAN: Norman Panama, Melvin Frank
(script); Charles Lang Jnr; title song
(*m/ly* Johnny Mercer); art direction

Family Business
US   1989   110m   colour
Palace/Tri-Star (Lawrence Gordon)
V, L

Three generations of crooks take part
in a robbery.

Dull comedy that never convinces and
certainly doesn't amuse.

w Vincent Patrick   *novel* Vincent
Patrick   *d* Sidney Lumet
ph Andrzej Bartowiak   *m* Cy
Coleman   *pd* Philip Rosenberg
ed Andrew Mondshein

Sean Connery, Dustin Hoffman,
Matthew Broderick, Rosana DeSoto,
Janet Carroll, Victoria Jackson, Bill
McCutcheon, Deborah Rush,
Marilyn Cooper

The Family Jewels
US   1965   100m   Technicolor
Paramount/York/Jerry Lewis

A child heiress chooses a new father
from among her five uncles.

Unfunny star farce with multiple
impersonations.

w Jerry Lewis, Bill Richmond
d Jerry Lewis   *ph* W. Wallace
Kelley   *m* Pete King

Jerry Lewis, Donna Butterworth,
Sebastian Cabot, Robert Strauss

The Family Way*
GB   1966   115m   Eastmancolor
BL/Jambox (John Boulting)
V

There is consternation in a Lancashire
family when the son cannot
consummate his marriage.

Overstretched domestic farce-drama.
Good scenes and performances, but
it was all much sharper as a one-hour
TV play.

w Bill Naughton   *play Honeymoon
Deferred* by Bill Naughton   *d* Roy
Boulting   *ph* Harry Waxman
m Paul McCartney

John Mills, *Marjorie Rhodes*, Hywel

Bennett, Hayley Mills, *Avril Angers*, Murray Head, Wilfred Pickles, Barry Foster, Liz Fraser

Fancy Pants**
US   1950   92m   Technicolor
Paramount (Robert Welch)

A British actor stranded in the far west poses as a butler.

Lively Western comedy remake of *Ruggles of Red Gap* (qv), one of the star's better vehicles.

w Edmund Hartman, Robert O'Brien   *d* George Marshall
ph Charles Lang Jnr   *m* Van Cleave

Bob Hope, Lucille Ball, Bruce Cabot, Jack Kirkwood, Lea Penman, Eric Blore, John Alexander, Norma Varden

Fandango
US   1985   91m   Technicolor
Warner/Amblin (Tim Zinnemann)

In the early 1970s, a group of college friends drive across Texas for a final weekend of fun before graduation and army service in Vietnam looms.

Slight but enjoyable movie that began life as a small student film before being expanded under the auspices of Steven Spielberg's production company.

wd Kevin Reynolds   *ph* Thomas Del Ruth   *m* Alan Silvestri
ad Peter Lansdown Smith
ed Arthur Schmidt, Stephen Semel

Kevin Costner, Judd Nelson, Sam Robards, Chuck Bush, Brian Cesak, Marvin J. McIntyre, Suzy Amis, Glenne Headly

Fanfan la Tulipe*
France   1951   98m   bw
Filmsonor-Ariane-Amato

Recruited into the army of Louis XV by a prophecy that he will marry the king's daughter, a young braggart does everything he can to live up to it.

Rather like a spoof Errol Flynn effort, this likeable swashbuckler can't quite summon up enough buckle or swash to be the minor classic it clearly intends.

w René Wheeler, Jean Fallet
d Christian-Jaque   *ph* Christian Matras   *m* Georges Van Parys, Maurice Thiriet

Gérard Philipe, Gina Lollobrigida, Noel Roquevert, Marcel Herrand

'A daring and delightful piece of work.' – *Times*

'Now she's raising eyebrows instead of corn!'
The Farmer's Daughter**
US   1947   97m   bw
RKO (Dore Schary)

The Swedish maid of a congressman becomes a political force.

Well-made Cinderella story with a touch of asperity and top notch production values and cast.

w Allen Rivkin, Laura Kerr   *d* H. C. Potter   *ph* Milton Krasner   *m* Leigh Harline

Loretta Young, Joseph Cotten, Ethel Barrymore, Charles Bickford, Rose Hobart, Rhys Williams, Harry Davenport, Tom Powers

'Patricians, politicians, even peasants are portrayed with unusual perception and wit.' – *James Agee*

AA: Loretta Young
AAN: Charles Bickford

The Fast Lady**

GB 1962 95m Eastmancolor
Rank/Group Films (Teddy Baird)

A bashful suitor buys an old Bentley,
becomes a roadhog, passes his test,
captures some crooks and gets the girl.

Spirited if aimless farcical comedy
which crams in all the jokes about cars
anyone can think of.

w Jack Davies, Henry Blyth   d Ken
Annakin   ph Reg Wyer   m Norrie
Paramor

Stanley Baxter, James Robertson
Justice, Leslie Phillips, Julie Christie,
Dick Emery

Fast Times at Ridgemont High

US 1982 92m Technicolor
Universal/Refugee (C. O. Erickson)

Students at a California high school
aim to lose their virginity.

The tiresome content of this teen
comedy is slightly offset by bright
handling. But only slightly.

w Cameron Crowe   book Cameron
Crowe   d Amy Heckerling
ph Matthew F. Leonetti   m/
songs Rob Fahey

Sean Penn, Jennifer Jason Leigh,
Judge Reinhold, Phoebe Cates, Brian
Backus, Robert Romanus, Ray
Walston

Fast-Walking

US 1981 116m Metrocolor
Lorimar

Racial disharmony and violence
prevail at a midwest state prison.

Curious black comedy dealing entirely
with unpleasant types.

wd James B. Harris   novel The Rap
by Ernest Brawley

James Woods, Tim McIntire, Kay
Lenz, Robert Hooks, M. Emmet Walsh

'What do people think of when they
write a script these days? Don't they
have any sense of human values or
human decency?' – Arthur Knight

The Fatal Glass of Beer*

US 1933 18m bw
Paramount/Sennett

The prodigal son returns to a
snowbound cabin in the Yukon.

Absurd star comedy with appeal to
addicts only: most of the humour
consists of repeats of one line, ' 'Taint
a fit night out for man nor beast.'

w W. C. Fields   d Clyde Bruckman

W. C. Fields, Rosemary Theby,
Rychard Cramer, George Chandler

Father Goose*

US 1964 116m Technicolor
U-I/Granox (Robert Arthur)
V

During World War II a South Seas
wanderer is compelled by the
Australian navy to act as sky observer
on a small island, where he finds
himself in charge of six refugee
schoolchildren and their
schoolmistress.

Eager-to-please but unsatisfactory
film which wanders between farce,
adventure and sex comedy, taking too
long about all of them.

w Peter Stone, Frank Tarloff
d Ralph Nelson   ph Charles Lang
Jnr   m Cy Coleman

Cary Grant, Leslie Caron, Trevor
Howard
    CARY GRANT: 'Let me tell you I am
not a father figure. I am not a brother
figure or an uncle figure or a cousin
figure. In fact, the only figure I intend
being is a total stranger figure.'

'Reasoning would indicate a made-to-order Christmas package for the family trade. However, the more sophisticated may be bored and exasperated after some of the initial brightness wears off.' – *Cue*

'Cary Grant wrings what there is to be wrung from the role, but never quite enough to conceal the fact that *Father Goose* is a waste of his talent and the audience's time.' – *Arthur Knight*

AA: Peter Stone, Frank Tarloff

'The bride gets the thrills! Father gets the bills!'

Father of the Bride**
US 1950 93m bw
MGM (Pandro S. Berman)
V, L

A dismayed but happy father surveys the cost and chaos of his daughter's marriage.

Fragmentary but mainly delightful suburban comedy which finds Hollywood in its best light vein and benefits from a strong central performance.

w Frances Goodrich, Albert Hackett
novel Edward Streeter   *d* Vincente Minnelli   *ph* John Alton
m Adolph Deutsch

Spencer Tracy, Joan Bennett, Elizabeth Taylor, Don Taylor, Billie Burke, Moroni Olsen, Leo G. Carroll, Taylor Holmes, Melville Cooper

'The idealization of a safe sheltered existence, the good life according to MGM: 24 carat complacency.' – *New Yorker, 1980*

† Jack Benny badly wanted the role but was thought unsuitable.
AAN: best picture; Frances Goodrich, Albert Hackett; Spencer Tracy

'Love is wonderful. Until it happens to your only daughter.'

Father of the Bride
US 1991 105m Technicolor
Touchstone/Touchwood Pacific Partners I
(Nancy Myers, Carol Baum, Howard Rosenman)
V, L

A father is upset by his daughter's announcement that she is engaged – and even more horrified by the arrangements for an expensive wedding.

Lacklustre remake with flat or exaggerated performances, few jokes and a great deal of sentimentality.

w Frances Goodrich, Albert Hackett, Nancy Myers, Charles Shyer
novel Edward Streeter   *d* Charles Shyer   *ph* John Lindley   *m* Alan Silvestri   *pd* Sandy Veneziano
ed Richard Marks

Steve Martin, Diane Keaton, Kimberley Williams, Martin Short, Kieran Culkin, George Newbern, B. D. Wong, Peter Michael Goetz

'Little more than a mildly entertaining diversion.' – *Empire*

Father's Doing Fine
GB 1952 83m Technicolor
Marble Arch/ABP

An impoverished lady has trouble with her daughters, one of whom is pregnant.

Agreeable madcap farce from a long-running stage success (so why did they change the title?).

w Anne Burnaby   *play Little Lambs Eat Ivy* by Noel Langley   *d* Henry Cass

Heather Thatcher, Richard Attenborough, Susan Stephen, Noel Purcell, George Thorpe

Father's Little Dividend

US 1951 81m bw
MGM (Pandro S. Berman)

Sequel to *Father of the Bride*, in which the newlyweds have a baby.

A very flat follow-up, palatable enough at the time but quite unmemorable.

w Frances Goodrich, Albert Hackett *d* Vincente Minnelli *ph* John Alton *m* Albert Sendrey

Spencer Tracy, Joan Bennett, Elizabeth Taylor, Don Taylor, Billie Burke, Moroni Olsen, Frank Faylen, Marietta Canty, Russ Tamblyn

Fatso

US 1980 93m DeLuxe
TCF/Brooksfilms

A fat man fails to make much headway at slimming, and gives up.

Unappealing mixture of sentiment, satire, shouting and crude humour.

wd Anne Bancroft

Dom DeLuise, Anne Bancroft, Ron Carey, Candice Azzara

'As bumbling and sluggish as its title might suggest, a lamentable affair which ricochets uncontrollably between attempts at hilarity and pathos.' – *Variety*

'A romantic comedy beyond normal experience.'

The Favour, the Watch & the Very Big Fish

France/GB 1991 87m colour
Rank/Sovereign/Ariane/Fildebroc/Umbrella (Michelle de Broca)

A religious photographer, who gets an ex-criminal to pose as Christ for him, falls in love with an actress who dubs pornographic films.

Flaccid farce in which most of the cast give the impression that they would rather be somewhere else.

wd Ben Lewin *story Rue Saint-Sulpice* by Marcel Ayme *ph* Bernard Zitzermann *m* Vladimir Cosma *pd* Carlos Conti *ed* John Grover

Bob Hoskins, Jeff Goldblum, Natasha Richardson, Michel Blanc, Jacques Villeret, Jean-Pierre Cassel, Angela Pleasance

'Mildy intriguing title, stultifyingly dull film.' – *Empire*

The Fearless Vampire Killers, or Pardon Me, Your Teeth Are in My Neck*

US 1967 124m Metrocolor Panavision
MGM/Cadre Films/Filmways (Gene Gutowski)
aka: *Dance of the Vampires*

A professor and his assistant stake a Transylvanian vampire.

Heavy, slow spoof of *Dracula*, most of which shows that sense of humour is very personal; a few effective moments hardly compensate for the prevailing stodge.

w Gerard Brach, Roman Polanski *d* Roman Polanski *ph* Douglas Slocombe *m* Krzystof Komeda *pd* Wilfrid Shingleton

Jack MacGowran, Roman Polanski, Alfie Bass, Sharon Tate, *Ferdy Mayne*, Iain Quarrier, Terry Downes

'An engaging oddity . . . long stretches might have been lifted intact from any Hammer horror.' – *Tom Milne*

† A credit ran: Fangs by Dr Ludwig von Krankheit.

Feather Your Nest*
GB   1937   86m   bw
ATP (Basil Dean)

A gramophone record technician substitutes his own voice for a star and becomes world famous.

The star in less farcical vein than usual; this is the one in which he sings 'Leaning on a Lamp-post'.

w Austin Melford, Robert Edmunds, Anthony Kimmins   story Ivar and Sheila Campbell   d William Beaudine   ph Ronald Neame   m Leslie Sarony, Leslie Holmes and others   ad R. Holmers Paul   ed Ernest Aldridge

George Formby, Polly Ward, Enid Stamp Taylor, Val Rosing, Davy Burnaby

'A thrill a minute! A laugh a second! A comedy cyclone!'

Feet First*
US   1930   88m   bw
Harold Lloyd

A shoe salesman gets entangled with crooks and has a narrow escape when hanging from the side of a building.

Very funny early talkie comedy, probably the comedian's last wholly satisfactory film.

w Lex Neal, Felix Adler, Paul Gerard Smith   d Clyde Bruckman   ph Walter Ludin, Henry Kohler

Harold Lloyd, Robert McWade, Barbara Kent

'That Lloyd was a bit pressed for laughs may be guessed from the fact that he is again dangling from the front of a skyscraper.' – Variety

La Femme du Boulanger**
France   1938   110m   bw
Marcel Pagnol
aka: The Baker's Wife

Villagers put a stop to the infidelity of the baker's wife because her husband no longer has the heart to make good bread.

Best-known of Pagnol's rustic fables, this rather obvious and long-drawn-out joke is important because international critics hailed it as a work of art (which it isn't) and because it fixed an image of the naughty bucolic French.

wd Marcel Pagnol   novel Jean Le Bleu by Jean Giono   ph Georges Benoit, R. Lendruz, N. Daries   m Vincent Scotto   ed Suzanne de Troeye

Raimu, Ginette Leclerc, Charles Moulin, Charpin, Maximilienne

'It is a long film with a small subject, but the treatment is so authentic that it seems over far too soon, and the acting is superb.' – Graham Greene

Ferris Bueller's Day Off*
US   1986   103m   Metrocolor   Panavision
Paramount/John Hughes, Tom Jacobson
V, L

A teenage student enjoys an aimless day playing truant.

Aimless it is, and juvenile, but people have found pleasing things in it.

wd John Hughes   ph Tak Fujimoto   m Ira Newborn   pd John W. Corso   ed Paul Hirsch

Matthew Broderick, Alan Ruck, Mia Sara, Jeffrey Jones, Cindy Pickett, Jennifer Grey

Fiddlers Three*
GB   1944   87m   bw
Ealing (Robert Hamer)

Sailors struck by lightning on Salisbury Plain are transported back to ancient Rome.

Sequel to *Sailors Three;* despite a harsh and unattractive look, every conceivable joke about old Romans is deftly mined and the good humour flows free.

w Diana Morgan, Angus Macphail *d* Harry Watt   *ph* Wilkie Cooper *m* Spike Hughes

Tommy Trinder, Sonnie Hale, Frances Day, Francis L. Sullivan, Ernest Milton, Diana Decker, Elizabeth Welch, Mary Clare

The Fiendish Plot of Dr Fu Manchu
US   1980   108m   Technicolor
Warner/Orion/Playboy (Hugh Hefner)
L

The 'yellow peril' returns to the western world to mastermind diamond thefts.

Feeble spoof with a history of production troubles; clearly the only thing in anybody's mind was to get it over with.

w Jim Moloney, Rudy Dochtermann   *d* Piers Haggard *ph* Jean Tournier   *m* Marc Wilkinson   *pd* Alexander Trauner

Peter Sellers, Helen Mirren, David Tomlinson, Sid Caesar, Simon Williams, Steve Franken, Stratford Johns, John Le Mesurier, Clive Dunn

Fifth Avenue Girl*
US   1939   83m   bw
RKO (Gregory La Cava)

An unemployed girl is persuaded by a millionaire to pose as a gold digger and annoy his avaricious family.

Brightish comedy of the Cinderella kind.

w Allan Scott   *d* Gregory La Cava   *ph* Robert de Grasse

Ginger Rogers, Walter Connolly, Verree Teasdale, Tim Holt, James Ellison, Franklin Pangborn, Kathryn Adams, Louis Calhern

'Substantial comedy drama for top grosses.' – *Variety*

Finders Keepers
US   1984   96m   Technicolor
CBS (Sandra Marsh, Terence Marsh)

On a train from California to New York, various factions try to grab stolen money hidden in a coffin.

Yawnworthy comedy-thriller with a zany streak; all the elements have been better done in other movies.

w Ronny Graham, Charles Dennis, Terence Marsh   *novel* The Next to Last Train Ride by Charles Dennis *d* Richard Lester   *ph* Brian West *m* Ken Thorne   *pd* Terence Marsh

Michael O'Keefe, Beverly D'Angelo, Lou Gossett Jnr, Pamela Stephenson, Ed Lauter, David Wayne, Brian Dennehy, John Schuck

A Fine Madness*
US   1966   104m   Technicolor
Warner Seven Arts (Jerome Hellman)

A frustrated New York poet has outbursts of violence.

Patchy, interesting, with-it comedy which suffers from too many changes of mood.

w Elliot Baker   *novel* Elliot Baker   *d* Irvin Kershner   *ph* Ted McCord   *m* John Addison

Sean Connery, Jean Seberg, Joanne Woodward, Patrick O'Neal, Colleen Dewhurst, Clive Revill

'Straddling a no man's land somewhere between the *nouvelle vague* and the crazy comedies of Old Hollywood.' – *Tom Milne*

A Fine Mess

US 1985 88m DeLuxe
Panavision
Columbia/BEE/Delphi V (Tony Adams)
L

Two private eyes who accidentally know too much chased by gangsters.

Not enough plot for a feature, and not enough comedy talent for a comedy, despite the dedication to Laurel and Hardy.

wd Blake Edwards *ph* Harry Stradling *m* Henry Mancini *pd* Rodger Maus *ed* John F. Burnett

Ted Danson, Howie Mandel, Richard Mulligan, Stuart Margolin, Paul Sorvino

'Word of mouth is unlikely to be favourable . . . mechanically contrived funny business, most of which falls pretty flat.' – *Variety*
'The plot needn't be the thing, but then the gags and setpieces aren't much either.' – *Sight and Sound*

Finian's Rainbow*

US 1968 140m Technicolor
Panavision 70
Warner Seven Arts (Joseph Landon)
V(W), L

A leprechaun tries to retrieve a crock of gold from an old wanderer who has taken it to America.

Musical whimsy-whamsy, a long way after a 1947 Broadway success; in this overlong and overblown screen version the elements and the style do not jell and there is too much sentimental chat, but moments of magic shine through.

w E. Y. Harburg, Fred Saidy *play* E. Y. Harburg, Fred Saidy *d* Francis Ford Coppola *ph* Philip Lathrop

md Ray Heindorf *pd* Hilyard M. Brown *m/ly* Burton Lane, E. Y. Harburg

Fred Astaire, Petula Clark, Tommy Steele, Don Francks, Keenan Wynn, Barbara Hancock, Al Freeman Jnr
AAN: Ray Heindorf

The Finishing Touch*

US 1928 20m bw silent
Hal Roach

Stan and Ollie accidentally destroy the house they are building.

Excellent early star slapstick with predictable but enjoyable gags.

w H. M. Walker *d* Clyde Bruckman *ph* George Stevens *ed* Richard Currier

Laurel and Hardy, Edgar Kennedy, Dorothy Coburn

Fireman Save My Child

US 1954 80m bw
U-I (Howard Christie)

In 1910 San Francisco, incompetent firemen accidentally catch a gang of crooks.

Slapstick farce intended for Abbott and Costello, taken over by a new team which did not catch on, played like the Keystone Kops. Mildly funny during the chases.

w Lee Loeb, John Grant *d* Leslie Goodwins *ph* Clifford Stine *m* Joseph Gershenson

Buddy Hackett, Spike Jones and the City Slickers, Hugh O'Brian, Adèle Jergens

First Lady*

US 1937 82m bw
Warner (Hal B. Wallis)

The President's wife is a power behind the scenes.

Solidly entertaining Washington comedy.

w Rowland Leigh   play George S. Kaufman, Katherine Dayton
d Stanley Logan   ph Sid Hickox
m Max Steiner

Kay Francis, Preston Foster, Anita Louise, Walter Connolly, Verree Teasdale, Victor Jory, Marjorie Rambeau, Louise Fazenda

'Smart stuff but generally palatable.' – Variety

The First Time
US   1968   90m   DeLuxe
UA/Mirisch/Rogallan (Roger Smith, Allan Carr)
GB title: You Don't Need Pajamas at Rosie's

Three teenage boys who fantasize about sex help a stranded girl under the impression that she is a prostitute.

Embarrassingly sentimental teenage sex comedy, all the more irritating by its restraint. Not a patch on Summer of '42.

w Jo Heims, Roger Smith   d James Nielson   ph Ernest Laszlo
m Kenyon Hopkins

Jacqueline Bisset, Wes Stern, Rick Kelman, Wink Roberts, Sharon Acker

A Fish Called Wanda**
US   1988   108m   Technicolor
MGM (Michael Shamberg)
V, L

Diamond-heist comedy depending on Anglo-American rivalries for its laughs.

Monty Python fans found it disappointing, but it went down well in the US.

w John Cleese, Charles Crichton
d Charles Crichton   ph Alan

Hume   m John Du Prez
pd Roger Murray-Leach

John Cleese, Jamie Lee Curtis, Kevin Kline, Michael Palin, Maria Aitken

AA: Kevin Kline
AAN: Charles Crichton; best original screenplay

The Fish that Saved Pittsburgh
US   1979   104m   colour
United Artists (David Dashev, Gary Stromberg)

An inept baseball team improves its performance by recruiting players born under the sign of Pisces.

Uninteresting comedy to a disco beat.

w Jaison Starkes, Edmond Stevens
d Gilbert Moses   ph Frank Stanley   m Thom Bell
ad Herbert Spencer Deverill
ed Peter Zinner

Julius Erving, Jonathan Winters, Meadowlark Lemon, Jack Kehoe, Margaret Avery, James Bond III, Michael V. Gazzo, M. Emmet Walsh, Stockard Channing, Flip Wilson

Fitzwilly*
US   1967   102m   DeLuxe
Panavision
UA/Dramatic Features Inc/Walter Mirisch
GB title: Fitzwilly Strikes Back

A New York butler, in order to keep his lady in style, has to organize the staff into a crime syndicate.

Moderately inventive, good-looking comedy with rather too much plot and not enough funny lines.

w Isobel Lennart   novel A Garden of Cucumbers by Poyntz Tyler   d Delbert Mann   ph Joseph Biroc
m Johnny Williams

Dick Van Dyke, Edith Evans, Barbara Feldon, John McGiver, Harry

Townes, John Fiedler, Norman Fell, Cecil Kellaway, Anne Seymour, Sam Waterston, Billy Halop

Five Golden Hours

GB/Italy 1960 90m bw
Columbia/Anglofilm/Fabio Jegher (Mario Zampi)

A con man tries to murder three widows who have invested money in one of his schemes.

Ill-judged black comedy, sadly lacking style.

w Hans Wilhelm   d Mario Zampi   ph Christopher Challis   m Stanley Black

Ernie Kovacs, Cyd Charisse, Kay Hammond, George Sanders, Dennis Price, Reginald Beckwith, Martin Benson, Ron Moody, Finlay Currie, Avis Landone, Sidney Tafler, John Le Mesurier, Clelia Matania

The Flamingo Kid

US 1984 100m DeLuxe
Palace/Mercury/ABC (Michael Phillips)
L

In 1963, a teenager comes of age while working at a beach club.

Innocent but unexciting comedy-drama about matters which scarcely concern grown-ups.

w Neal Marshall, Garry Marshall (no relation)   d Garry Marshall   ph James A. Kontner   pd Lawrence Miller   ed Priscilla Nedd

Matt Dillon, Richard Crenna, Hector Elizondo, Jessica Walter, Fisher Stevens

A Flea in Her Ear*

US/France 1968 94m
DeLuxe Panavision
TCF (Fred Kohlmar)

Various suspicious wives and husbands converge on the notorious Hotel Coq d'Or.

Disappointing filming of a Feydeau farce, which needs to be much more cleverly handled to come over with its full theatrical force.

w John Mortimer   play La Puce à l'Oreille by Georges Feydeau   d Jacques Charon   ph Charles Lang   m Bronislau Kaper   pd Alexander Trauner

Rex Harrison, Rachel Roberts, Rosemary Harris, Louis Jourdan, John Williams, Grégoire Aslan, Edward Hardwicke, Frank Thornton, Victor Sen Yung

'The plunge into madness never comes, and one is left with the sight of a group of talented players struggling with alien material.'
– Michael Billington, Illustrated London News

Fletch*

US 1985 96m Technicolor
Universal/Douglas/Greisman
V, L

A newspaper columnist with a penchant for disguise tracks down a nefarious con man.

A lightness of touch unusual for the eighties makes this comedy mystery more welcome than most.

w Andrew Bergman   novel Gregory McDonald   d Michael Ritchie   ph Fred Schuler   m Harold Faltermeyer

Chevy Chase, Dana Wheeler-Nicholson, Tim Matheson, Joe Don Baker, Richard Libertini, Kenneth Mars, M. Emmet Walsh

Fletch Lives
US 1989 95m colour
UIP/Universal/Greisman/Douglas)
V, L

An investigative reporter inherits trouble along with a Southern mansion.

Dire comedy with nothing to recommend it.

w Leon Capetanos   d Michael Ritchie   ph John McPherson   m Harold Flatermyer, Buckwheat Zydeco   ed Richard A. Harris

Chevy Chase, Hal Holbrook, Julianne Phillips, R. Lee Ermey, Richard Libertini, Randall 'Tex' Cobb, Cleavon Little

The Flim Flam Man*
US 1967 104m DeLuxe
  Panavision
TCF/Lawrence Turman
GB title: One Born Every Minute

An army deserter joins forces with an elderly con man.

Folksy comedy in a small-town setting; none of it really comes to the boil after a couple of early chase sequences.

w William Rose   novel Guy Owen   d Irvin Kershner, Yakima Canutt   ph Charles Lang   m Jerry Goldsmith

George C. Scott, Michael Sarrazin, Sue Lyon, Harry Morgan, Jack Albertson, Alice Ghostley, Albert Salmi

The Flying Deuces*
US 1939 67m bw
Boris Morros
V

Laurel and Hardy join the Foreign Legion.

Patchy comedy from the end of the comedians' period of glory, and showing signs of decline.

w Ralph Spence, Harry Langdon, Charles Rogers, Alfred Schiller
d Edward Sutherland   ph Art Lloyd, Elmer Dyer   md Edward Paul   m Leo Shuken   ed Jack Dennis

Stan Laurel, Oliver Hardy, Jean Parker, James Finlayson, Reginald Gardiner, Charles Middleton

'Mechanical stuff . . . seemed like Beau Hunks and Bonnie Scotland all over again.' – William K. Everson

Flying Elephants
US 1927 20m bw silent
Hal Roach

A caveman has the toothache.

Fragmentary and generally unsatisfactory comedy starring Laurel and Hardy before they properly teamed, but released after their joint success.

w Hal Roach, H. M. Walker
d Frank Butler

Laurel and Hardy, James Finlayson, Viola Richard, Dorothy Coburn

Folks!
US 1992 106m Technicolor
First Independent/Penta (Victor Drai, Malcolm R. Harding)

At his ailing mother's suggestion, a businessman tries to kill her and his senile father for the insurance money.

Embarrassingly bad comedy, not merely tasteless but, what is worse, devoid of humour.

w Robert Klane   d Ted Kotcheff   ph Larry Pizer   m Michel Colombier   pd William J. Creber   ed Joan E. Chapman

Tom Selleck, Don Ameche, Anne Jackson, Christine Ebersole, Wendy Crewson, Robert Pastorelli, Michael Murphy

'Marking severe career setbacks for Ameche and Selleck, *Folks!* obviously miscalculates the low intelligence of the mass audience.' – *Variety*

Follow a Star

GB 1959 104m bw
Rank (Hugh Stewart)

A shy amateur singer allows a fading star to mime to his voice.

Star comedy with an antique plot and a superfluity of pathos.

w Jack Davies, Henry Blyth, Norman Wisdom *d* Robert Asher
ph Jack Asher *m* Philip Green

Norman Wisdom, Jerry Desmonde, June Laverick, Hattie Jacques, Richard Wattis, John Le Mesurier, Fenella Fielding, Ron Moody

'Such comedy as there is is mostly muffed by the lack of any sense of comic timing.' – *MFB*

Follow That Dream

US 1962 110m DeLuxe
Panavision
UA/Mirisch (David Weisbart)
V

A wandering family sets up house on a Florida beach.

Tiresomely cute comedy vehicle for a resistible star.

w Charles Lederer *novel Pioneer Go Home* by Richard Powell *d* Gordon Douglas *ph* Leo Tover *m* Hans Salter

Elvis Presley, Arthur O'Connell, Joanna Moore, Anne Helm, Jack Kruschen

Folly to be Wise*

GB 1952 91m bw
London Films/Launder and Gilliat

A brains trust at an army unit starts off a battle of the sexes.

Typical James Bridie comedy which starts brightly and whimsically, then peters out and is saved by the acting.

w Frank Launder, John Dighton
play It Depends What You Mean by James Bridie *d* Frank Launder
ph Jack Hildyard *m* Temple Abady

Alastair Sim, Roland Culver, Elizabeth Allan, Martita Hunt, Colin Gordon

'It seems to get funnier the longer it's spun out.' – *Pauline Kael, 70s*

Football Crazy

Italy 1974 106m colour
Documento Films (Gianni Hecht Lucara)

A small-town football referee, who dreams of making the big time, has an affair with a glamorous journalist.

An ineffectual comedy that requires an audience to believe that referees are heroes in their community and that Joan Collins offers erotic promise.

w G. Scarniaci, R. Vianello, S. Continenza, Luigi Filipo D'Amico
d Luigi Filipo D'Amico *ph* Sergio D'Offizi *m* Guido and Maurizio de Angelis *pd* Walter Patriarca
ed Marisa Mengoli

Lando Buzzanca, Joan Collins, Gabriella Pallotta, Ignazio Leone, Daniele Vargas

For Love of Ivy

US 1968 100m Perfectcolor
Cinerama/Palomar (Edgar J. Scherick, Jay Weston)

An invaluable coloured maid gives notice, and the family blackmails a likeable black ne'er-do-well to make love to her so that she will stay.

Unhappy whimsy with an extremely laboured script and no jokes, notable only as Hollywood's first bow towards a black love affair.

w Robert Alan Aurthur
story Sidney Poitier   d Daniel Mann   ph Joseph Coffey
m Quincy Jones

Sidney Poitier, Abby Lincoln, Beau Bridges, Carroll O'Connor, Nan Martin, Lauri Peters
AAN: title song (m Quincy Jones, ly Bob Russell)

For Pete's Sake*
US   1974   90m   Eastmancolor
Columbia/Rastar/Persky-Bright-Barclay
  (Martin Erlichmann, Stanley Shapiro)

A New York taxi driver's wife borrows money and finds herself heavily committed to work off the debt.

Involved farcical comedy with amusing passages.

w Stanley Shapiro, Martin Richlin
d Peter Yates   ph Laszlo Kovacs
m Artie Butler

Barbra Streisand, Michael Sarrazin, Estelle Parsons, William Redfield, Molly Picon

'Revives memories of how much more inventively they used to do it thirty years ago.' – Sight and Sound

A Foreign Affair**
US   1948   116m   bw
Paramount (Charles Brackett)

A deputation of American politicians goes to visit post-war Berlin and a congresswoman finds herself in an emotional triangle with a captain and his German mistress.

Bleakly sophisticated comedy from

this team's headline-grabbing period; full of interest and amusement, it never quite sparkles enough to remove the doubtful taste.

w Charles Brackett, Billy Wilder, Richard Breen,   story David Shaw   d Billy Wilder   ph Charles Lang Jnr
m Frederick Hollander

Jean Arthur, Marlene Dietrich, John Lund, Millard Mitchell, Peter Von Zerneck, Stanley Prager

'This deliberately cynical political farce . . . often seems on the verge of being funny, but the humour is too clumsily forced.' – New Yorker, 1980
AAN: script; Charles Lang Jnr

Forever Darling
US   1956   91m   Eastmancolor
MGM/Zanra (Desi Arnaz)

A couple's matrimonial difficulties are solved by her guardian angel.

Cutesy-pie comedy with all concerned embarrassed by their material.

w Helen Deutsch   d Alexander Hall   ph Harold Lipstein
m Bronislau Kaper

Lucille Ball, Desi Arnaz, James Mason (as the angel), John Emery, Louis Calhern, John Hoyt, Natalie Schafer

Forsaking All Others*
US   1934   84m   bw
MGM (Bernard H. Hyman)

A woman almost marries the wrong man twice.

Star power carries this thin comedy drama.

w Joseph L. Mankiewicz
play Edward Barry Roberts, Frank Morgan Cavett   d W. S. Van Dyke   ph Gregg Toland, George Folsey   m William Axt

Clark Gable, Joan Crawford, Robert Montgomery, *Charles Butterworth*, Billie Burke, Frances Drake, Rosalind Russell, Arthur Treacher

'Stock romantic comedy despite some messy hokum.' – *Variety*
'Contrary to expectation, sophistication is at a minimum.' – *Time*

The Fortune

US 1975 88m Technicolor Panavision
Columbia (Hank Moonjean)

A twenties heiress elopes with her lover and his dim-witted friend but discovers that they mean to murder her for her money.

Bungled black comedy with top talent over-confident of carrying it.

w Adrien Joyce (Carol Eastman)
d Mike Nichols   ph John A. Alonzo   m various songs
pd Richard Sylbert

Jack Nicholson, Warren Beatty, Stockard Channing, Florence Stanley, Richard B. Shull, John Fiedler

'Like the ill-assorted styles of the film generally, the stars themselves frequently seem to belong in different movies.' – *Richard Combs*
'A silly, shallow, occasionally enjoyable comedy trifle . . . classy 20's production values often merit more attention than the plot.' – *Variety*

The Fortune Cookie*

US 1966 125m bw Panavision
UA/Mirisch/Phalanx/Jalem (Billy Wilder)
L
GB title: *Meet Whiplash Willie*

A crooked lawyer forces his slightly injured client to sue for a million dollars.

Flat, stretched-out, only occasionally

effective comedy which relies too much on mordant attitudes and a single star performance.

w Billy Wilder, I. A. L. Diamond
d Billy Wilder   ph Joseph LaShelle   m André Previn

Walter Matthau, Jack Lemmon, Ron Rich, Cliff Osmond, Lurene Tuttle

'A jackhammer of a film savagely applied to those concrete areas of human spirit where cupidity and stupidity have been so long entrenched.' – *Richard Schickel*

AA: Walter Matthau
AAN: Billy Wilder, I. A. L. Diamond (script); Joseph LaShelle

Forty Carats*

US 1973 109m Metrocolor
Columbia/M. J. Frankovich

A 40-year-old divorcee on holiday in Greece has a brief affair with a 22-year-old man.

Curiously miscast and mishandled comedy for the smart set; scores a laugh or two but never really takes off.

w Leonard Gershe   play Pierre Barillet, Jean-Pierre Gredy
d Milton Katselas   ph Charles Lang Jnr   m Michel Legrand

Liv Ullmann, Edward Albert, Gene Kelly, Billy 'Green' Bush, Binnie Barnes, Nancy Walker, Deborah Raffin, Don Porter, Natalie Schafer, Rosemary Murphy

48 Hours

US 1982 96m Movielab
Paramount/Lawrence Gordon
V, L

A cop and a criminal on parole combine to track down the latter's former associates.

Reasonable action melodrama with comedy asides and San Francisco locations; but too violent for its own good.

w Roger Spottiswoode, Walter Hill, Larry Gross, Steven E. de Souza *d* Walter Hill *ph* Ric Waite *m* James Horner *pd* John Vallone

Nick Nolte, Eddie Murphy, Annette O'Toole, Frank McRae

'It's like *The French Connection, Dirty Harry* and *Butch Cassidy* all put in a compactor and pressed into cartoon form.' – *New Yorker*

† It was followed, after a long gap, by a sequel *Another 48 Hours* (qv).

Forty Pounds of Trouble*
US 1963 105m Eastmancolor Panavision
U-I/Curtis Enterprises (Stan Margulies)

A casino manager is chased by his ex-wife's detective for alimony payments, and also has to look after an abandoned six-year-old girl.

Standard sentimental comedy with some verve and a lively climactic chase through Disneyland.

w Marion Hargrove *d* Norman Jewison *ph* Joe MacDonald *m* Mort Lindsey

Tony Curtis, Phil Silvers, Suzanne Pleshette, Edward Andrews

Foul Play*
US 1978 116m Movielab
Paramount/Thomas L. Miller, Edward K. Milkis
V, L

Two innocents in San Francisco get involved in a plot to assassinate the visiting pope.

Sometimes sprightly, sometimes tired rehash of Hitchcock elements, rather on the level of the similar *Silver Streak*.

wd Colin Higgins *ph* David M. Walsh *m* Charles Fox

Goldie Hawn, Chevy Chase, Burgess Meredith, Rachel Roberts, Eugene Roche, Dudley Moore, Billy Barty
AAN: song, 'Ready to Take a Chance Again' (*m* Charles Fox, *ly* Norman Gimbel)

Four Clowns**
US 1970 96m bw
Robert Youngson Productions (Herb Gelbspan)

Studies of four silent comedians. Laurel and Hardy in excerpts from *Putting Pants on Philip, The Second Hundred Years, Their Purple Moment, Big Business, Two Tars* and *Double Whoopee;* Charley Chase in *Us, What Price Goofy, Fluttering Hearts, The Family Group* and *Limousine Love;* Buster Keaton in *Seven Chances.*

An essential compendium, especially for the Charley Chase revaluation which was long overdue.

w Robert Youngson *m* Manny Alban

Narrator: Jay Jackson

Francis*
US 1950 90m bw
U-I (Robert Arthur)

An army private makes friends with a talking mule who causes him some embarrassment.

Simple-minded, quite agreeable if rather slow-moving fantasy farce which was popular enough to spawn several sequels and later a TV series called *Mister Ed.*

w David Stern *novel* David Stern *d* Arthur Lubin *ph* Irving Glassberg *m* Frank Skinner

Donald O'Connor, Patricia Medina, Zasu Pitts, Ray Collins, John McIntire, Eduard Franz, Robert Warwick, and Chill Wills as Francis' voice. Sequels (the first six with Donald O'Connor):

1951: FRANCIS GOES TO THE RACES
1952: FRANCIS GOES TO WEST POINT
1953: FRANCIS COVERS BIG TOWN
1954: FRANCIS JOINS THE WACS
1955: FRANCIS IN THE NAVY
1956: FRANCIS IN THE HAUNTED HOUSE (with Mickey Rooney)

'Today they demolished 23 cars, four motor cycles and one apartment building. But don't call the cops. They *are* the cops!'

Freebie and the Bean*
US   1974   113m   Technicolor Panavision
Warner (Richard Rush)

Two vaguely incompetent cops try to link a mobster with the numbers racket.

Violent comedy melodrama with a high mortality rate, amoral outlook, and the usual seventies reliance on incoherent plot, bumbled dialogue and excessive background noise. Occasionally funny all the same.

w Richard Kaufman   *d* Richard Rush   *ph* Laszlo Kovacs   *m* Dominic Frontière

Alan Arkin, James Caan, Loretta Swit, Jack Kruschen, Mike Kellin

'It summarizes Hollywood's favourite thematic elements of the early seventies: platonic male love affair, police corruption, comic violence, cynicism in high places, San Francisco, gay villains, the car chase. A return to the Keystone Kops, with character trimmings and lashings of sado-masochistic mayhem.' – *Clyde Jeavons*

'A tasteless film from a spitball script.' – *Variety*

'There is a beating or a killing, or at least a yelling scene, every couple of minutes.' – *New Yorker, 1980*

French Dressing
GB   1963   86m   bw
ABP/Kenwood (Kenneth Harper)

A deckchair attendant and a local reporter believe that what Bardot can do for St Tropez they can do for Gormleigh-on-Sea.

Cinema's *enfant terrible* directs this his first theatrical film at breakneck speed with echoes of Tati, Keaton and the Keystone Kops. Alas, lack of star comedians and firm control make its exuberance merely irritating.

w Peter Myers, Ronald Cass, Peter Britt   *d* Ken Russell   *ph* Ken Higgins   *m* Georges Delerue

James Booth, Roy Kinnear, Marisa Mell, Bryan Pringle

A French Mistress
GB   1960   98m   bw
British Lion/Charter (John Boulting)

An attractive new mistress causes havoc at a boys' school.

Sloppy, predictable comedy with practised performers getting a few easy laughs. The producers tried to excuse its imperfections by promoting it as 'a romp'.

w Roy Boulting, Jeffrey Dell *play* Robert Monro (Sonnie Hale)   *d* Roy Boulting   *ph* Max Greene   *m* John Addison

James Robertson Justice, Cecil Parker, Raymond Huntley, Ian Bannen, Agnes

Laurent, Thorley Walters, Edith
Sharpe, Athene Seyler, Kenneth
Griffith

French without Tears
GB 1939 85m bw
Paramount/Two Cities (David E. Rose)

Young Britons at a French crammer
fall for the young sister of one of their
number.

Pleasant light comedy from a
successful West End play.

w Terence Rattigan, Anatole de
Grunwald, Ian Dalrymple
play Terence Rattigan   d Anthony
Asquith   ph Bernard Knowles,
Jack Hildyard   m Nicholas
Brodszky   ad Paul Sheriff, Carmen
Dillon   ed David Lean

Ray Milland, Ellen Drew, Guy
Middleton, Ronald Culver, David Tree,
Jim Gerald, Janine Darcy, Kenneth
Morgan

'There is always something a little
shocking about English levity. The
greedy exhilaration of these blithe
young men when they learn that
another fellow's girl is to join them at
the establishment where they are
learning French, the scramble over
her luggage, the light-hearted
badinage, the watery and libidinous
eye – that national mixture of
prudery and excitement – would be
unbearable if it were not for Mr
Asquith's civilized direction.' –
Graham Greene

† Incredibly, Paramount had
purchased the property as a vehicle
for Marlene Dietrich.

The Freshman**
US 1925 75m (24 fps) bw
  silent
Harold Lloyd
V

An awkward college student
accidentally becomes a star football
player.

A rather slow but striking star vehicle
with assured set-pieces. The football
game climax was later used as the first
reel of Mad Wednesday.

w Sam Taylor, Ted Wilde, Tim
Whelan, John Grey   d Fred
Newmeyer, Sam Taylor   ph Walter
Lundin, Henry Kohler

Harold Lloyd, Jobyna Ralston, Brooks
Benedict

'Next time they make you an offer you
can't refuse ... refuse!'
The Freshman**
US 1990 102m Technicolor
Tri-Star/Mike Lobell, Andrew Bergman
V

A student of gangster movies goes to
work for a real-life criminal.

A genial spoof of The Godfather films,
with Brando parodying his own
performance as an ageing patriarch of
crime.

wd Andrew Bergman   ph William
A. Fraker   m David Newman
ed Barry Malkin

Marlon Brando, Matthew Broderick,
Bruno Kirby, Penelope Ann Miller,
Frank Whaley, Jon Polito, Paul
Benedict, Richard Gant, Kenneth
Welsh, Pamela Payton-Wright

The Frisco Kid
US 1979 108m Technicolor
Warner (Howard W. Koch Jnr)
V

In the old west, a rabbi heading for
San Francisco makes friends with an
outlaw.

Unsuccessful episodic comedy,

unreasonably alternating farce with
sentimentality.

w Michael Elias, Frank Shaw
d Robert Aldrich   ph Robert B.
Hauser   m Frank De Vol

Gene Wilder, Harrison Ford, Ramon
Bieri, Leo Fuchs, Penny Peyser

'A very forced comedy, made all the
worse by the fact that Aldrich seems
to time and edit comedy as though it
were a melodrama only played a little
slower.' – Richard Combs, MFB

Fritz the Cat**

US   1971   78m   DeLuxe
Fritz Productions/Aurica (Steve Krantz)

An alleycat student in New York seeks
new and varied experience.

Cartoon feature which applies the old
anthropomorphism to the
contemporary scene, and whips up
more obscenity and violence than
Disney ever dreamed of. A fast-
moving orgy of outrage which could
never have got by in live form.

wd/animator Ralph Bakshi   comic
strip R. H. Crumb   m Ed Bogas,
Ray Shanklin

'A bitter and snarling satire that
refuses to curl up in anyone's lap.' –
Bruce Williamson

From Soup to Nuts*

US   1928   20m   bw   silent
Hal Roach

Two temporary waiters wreck a
dinner party.

Very funny slapstick which the stars
subsequently reworked into A Chump
at Oxford.

w H. M. Walker   story Leo
McCarey   d Edgar Kennedy
ph Len Powers   ed Richard Currier

Laurel and Hardy, Anita Garvin, Tiny
Sandford

The Front Page***

US   1931   101m   bw
Howard Hughes

A Chicago reporter wants to retire and
marry, but is tricked by his scheming
editor into covering one last case.

Brilliant early talkie perfectly
transferring into screen terms a stage
classic of the twenties. Superficially a
shade primitive now, its essential
power remains.

w Bartlett Cormack, Charles
Lederer   play Charles MacArthur, Ben
Hecht   d Lewis Milestone   ph Glen
MacWilliams

Adolphe Menjou (Walter Burns), Pat
O'Brien (Hildy Johnson), Mary Brian
(Peggy), Edward Everett Horton
(Bensinger), Walter Catlett (Murphy),
George E. Stone (Earl Williams), Mae
Clarke (Molly), Slim Summerville
(Pincus), Matt Moore (Kruger), Frank
McHugh (McCue)

'Sure money-getter . . . it will
universally entertain and please.' –
Variety
'The most riproaring movie that ever
came out of Hollywood.' – Pare Lorentz
'It excelled most of the films of its day
by sheer treatment. The speedy
delivery of lines and business and the
re-emphasis upon cutting as a prime
structural element made the film a
model of mobility for confused
directors who did not know yet how
to handle sound.' – Lewis Jacobs, The
Rise of the American Film

† Remade in 1940 as His Girl Friday
(qv) and in 1988 as Switching Channels
(qv). And see below.
AAN: best picture; Lewis Milestone;
Adolphe Menjou

The Front Page**

US   1974   105m   Technicolor
  Panavision
U-I (Paul Monash)

Disappointing Billy Wilder remake,
relying overmuch on bad language
and farcical intrusions, while tending
to jettison the plot in the latter half.
Some laughs nevertheless.

w Billy Wilder, I. A. L. Diamond
d Billy Wilder   ph Jordan S.
Cronenweth   m Billy May

Walter Matthau, Jack Lemmon, Susan
Sarandon, David Wayne, Carol Burnett,
Vincent Gardenia, Allen Garfield,
Herb Edelman, Charles Durning,
Austin Pendleton

'The signs of coarsening in Wilder's
comedy technique are unmistakable.'
– MFB
'I can't think of a better tonic for the
winter glooms.' – Michael Billington,
Illustrated London News

The Frozen Limits*

GB   1939   84m   bw
Gainsborough (Edward Black)

Six impecunious comedians hear of
the Yukon gold rush, and join it . . .
forty years too late.

The Crazy Gang not quite at its best,
but working hard, with a few hilarious
moments and a special assist from
Moore Marriott.

w Marriott Edgar, Val Guest, J. O. C.
Orton   d Marcel Varnel
ph Arthur Crabtree   md Louis
Levy   ad Vetchinsky   ed R. E.
Dearing, Alfred Roome

Flanagan and Allen, Nervo and Knox,
Naughton and Gold, Moore Marriott,
Eileen Bell, Anthony Hulme, Bernard
Lee, Eric Clavering

'The funniest English picture yet
produced . . . it can bear comparison
with Safety Last and The General.' –
Graham Greene

Fuddy Duddy Buddy**

US   1952   7m   Technicolor
UPA

Mr Magoo mistakes a walrus for his
friend the colonel.

Top drawer Magoo adventure
climaxing with the celebrated line: 'I
don't care if he is a walrus. I like him.
I like him!'.

wd John Hubley   m William Lava

A Full Day's Work*

France   1973   90m   Eastmancolor
President/Cinetel/Euro International
  (Jacques-Eric Strauss)
original title: Une Journée Bien Remplie

A baker sets out to kill in one day the
jurors who found his son guilty of
murder.

Mildly amusing black comedy, though
it is too self-conscious for its own good.

wd Jean-Louis Trintignant
ph William Lubtchansky   m Bruno
Nicolai   ed Nicole Lubtchansky

Jacques Dufilho, Luce Marquand,
Denise Peron, Antoine Marin,
Jacques Doniol-Valcroze, Vittorio
Caprioli

Full Moon in Blue Water

US   1988   95m   Technicolor
Entertainment/Trans World Entertainment
  (Lawrence Turman, David Foster, John
  Turman)

A Texan restaurateur foils plans by
property developers to buy his diner.

Weak and sentimental comedy,
resembling a TV sitcom.

w Bill Bozzone *d* Peter Masterson *ph* Fred Murphy *m* Phil Marshall *ed* Jill Savitt

Gene Hackman, Teri Garr, Burgess Meredith, Elias Koteas, Kevin Cooney, David Doty, Gil Glasgow, Becky Gelke, Marietta Marich, Lexie Masterson

'A comedy as soft-centered as they come . . . just about insufferable' – *MFB*

The Fuller Brush Girl*
US 1950 85m bw
Columbia (S. Sylvan Simon)
GB title: *Affairs of Sally*

A cosmetics saleslady gets involved in murder.

Fairly amusing slapstick mystery with the star in good form.

w Frank Tashlin *d* Lloyd Bacon *ph* Charles Lawton *m* Heinz Roemheld

Lucille Ball, Eddie Albert, Carl Benton Reid, Gale Robbins, Jeff Donnell, John Litel, Jerome Cowan, Lee Patrick

The Fuller Brush Man*
US 1948 93m bw
Columbia (S. Sylvan Simon)
GB title: *That Mad Mr Jones*

A door-to-door salesman gets involved in homicide.

Bright star comedy with slow patches.

w Frank Tashlin, Devery Freeman *d* S. Sylvan Simon *ph* Leslie White *m* Heinz Roemheld

Red Skelton, Janet Blair, Don McGuire, Adele Jergens

Fun with Dick and Jane
US 1976 100m Metrocolor
Columbia/Peter Bart, Max Pelevsky

When an aerospace executive is fired, in order to keep up with the Joneses he and his wife embark on a life of crime.

This being a 1970s satire, they actually get away with it, providing some, but not enough, fun on the way.

w David Giler, Jerry Belson, Mordecai Richler *story* Gerald Gaiser *d* Ted Kotcheff *ph* Fred J. Koenekamp *m* Ernest Gold

George Segal, Jane Fonda, Ed McMahon, Dick Gautier, Alan Miller

'A nitwit mixture of counterculture politics, madcap comedy and toilet humour.' – *New Yorker*

† The sequence in which the heroine discusses the family predicament while sitting on a toilet was later deleted, reducing the running time by two minutes.

The Funniest Man in the World*
US 1967 102m bw
Funnyman Inc

Moderately intelligent compilation of sequences from the films of Charlie Chaplin, including *Making a Living*, *Kid Auto Races at Venice*, *Tillie's Punctured Romance*, *The Tramp*, *A Night Out*, *The Rink*, *The Immigrant* and *Easy Street*. The later shorts and features, on which Chaplin himself claimed full copyright, are not included.

wd Vernon P. Becker

A Funny Thing Happened on the Way to the Forum**
GB 1966 99m DeLuxe
UA/Quadrangle (Melvin Frank)
V, L

In ancient Rome, a conniving slave schemes to win his freedom.

Bawdy farce from a Broadway musical inspired by Plautus but with a New York Jewish atmosphere. The film pays scant attention to the comic numbers that made the show a hit, but adds some style of its own, including a free-for-all slapstick climax.

w Melvin Frank, Michael Pertwee *musical comedy* Burt Shevelove, Larry Gelbart   *d Richard Lester*
ph Nicolas Roeg   md Ken Thorne *pd* Tony Walton   *titles* Richard Williams   *m/ly Stephen Sondheim*

Zero Mostel, Phil Silvers, Michael Crawford, Jack Gilford, *Michael Hordern*, Buster Keaton, Patricia Jessel, Leon Greene, Beatrix Lehmann

'Actors have to be very fast and very sly to make themselves felt amid the flash and glitter of a characteristic piece of Lester film-mosaic.' – *John Russell Taylor*
'He proceeds by fits and starts and leaves jokes suspended in mid-air . . . like coitus interruptus going on forever.' – *Pauline Kael*

AA: Ken Thorne

Funnyman
US   1967   100m   bw/colour
Korty Films (Hugh McGraw, Stephen Schmidt)

A satirical comedian seeks some better occupation in life, but finally agrees he's best as a comic.

One suspects Korty has seen *Sullivan's Travels* several times; but even though his film tries hard, it finally provides more yawns than appreciative chuckles.

w John Korty, Peter Bonerz   *d John Korty   ph* John Korty   *m* Peter Schickele

Peter Bonerz, Sandra Archer, Carol Androsky, Gerald Hiken

'It has its dull patches, but it made me laugh louder and more often than any other film this year.' – *Michael Billington, Illustrated London News*

The Further Perils of Laurel and Hardy***
US   1967   99m   bw
TCF/Robert Youngson

A compilation of longish extracts from the stars' silent comedies, including *Early to Bed, The Second Hundred Years, Should Married Men Go Home, You're Darn Tootin', Habeas Corpus, That's My Wife*, and *Leave 'Em Laughing*. The producer is to be congratulated on refurbishing so many deteriorating negatives, though the commentary leaves much to be desired.

w/ed Robert Youngson   *m* John Parker

Futtock's End*
GB   1969   49m   Eastmancolor
Paradine/Gannet/British Lion

Adventures of a weekend in an English country mansion.

A collection of visual gags, rather thinly spread, with dialogue replaced by squeaks and mumblings. Like all Barker's subsequent comedies on similar lines (*The Picnic, By the Sea*, etc) one chuckles in constant anticipation of guffaws which never come.

w Ronnie Barker   *d* Bob Kellett

Ronnie Barker, Michael Hordern, Roger Livesey, Julian Orchard, Kika Markham, Mary Merrall, Richard O'Sullivan

Fuzz*
US   1972   93m   DeLuxe
UA/Filmways/Javelin (Jack Farren)

Detectives of Boston's 87th precinct
try to catch a rapist.

A black farce devoted to police
incompetence, though taken from a
straight 'Ed McBain' story. Brisk and
sometimes funny.

w *Evan Hunter* ('Ed McBain')
d Richard A. Colla   *ph* Jacques
Marquette   *m* Dave Grusin

Burt Reynolds, Raquel Welch, Jack
Weston, Yul Brynner, Tom Skerritt,
James McEachin

G

The Galloping Major*

GB 1951 82m bw
British Lion/Romulus (Monja
  Danischewsky)

A group of suburbanites form a
syndicate to buy a racehorse.

Rather contrived and imitative sub-
Ealing comedy which fails to generate
much steam.

w Monja Danischewsky, Henry
Cornelius   *d* Henry Cornelius
ph Stan Pavey   *m* Georges
Auric

Basil Radford, Janette Scott, Hugh
Griffith, Jimmy Hanley, René Ray,
Joyce Grenfell, Sidney Tafler, Charles
Victor, A. E. Matthews

Gambit**

US 1966 109m Technicolor
Universal (Leo L. Fuchs)

A cockney thief conspires with a
Eurasian girl to rob a multi-
millionaire of a prize statue.

An enjoyably light pattern of cross
and double cross is well sustained to
the end.

w Jack Davies, Alvin Sargent
d Ronald Neame   *ph* Clifford
Stine   *m* Maurice Jarre

Michael Caine, Shirley Maclaine,
Herbert Lom, John Abbott, Roger C.
Carmel, Arnold Moss

The Gang That Couldn't Shoot Straight

US 1971 96m Metrocolor
MGM (Robert Chartoff, Irwin Winkler)

Members of the New York Mafia
organize a cycle race and start
antagonisms that end in mass
murder.

Unfunny black comedy with all
concerned gesticulating wildly.

w Waldo Salt   *novel* Jimmy
Breslin   *d* James Goldstone
ph Owen Roizman   *m* Dave Grusin

Jerry Orbach, Leigh Taylor-Young, Jo
Van Fleet, Lionel Stander, Robert de
Niro, Herve Villechaize, Joe Santos

Garbo Talks*

US 1984 103m Technicolor
MGM-UA/Elliott Kastner (Burtt Harris)

A dying woman's last obsession is to
meet her idol Greta Garbo.

New Yorkish wry comedy which
doesn't seem entirely clear of its point
but is smartly acted and produced.

w Larry Grusin   *d* Sidney
Lumet   *ph* Andrzej Bartkowiak
m Cy Coleman   *pd* Philip
Rosenberg   *ed* Andrew Mondshein

Anne Bancroft, Ron Silver, Carrie
Fisher, Catherine Hicks, Steven Hill,
Howard Da Silva, Harvey Fierstein,
Dorothy Loudon, Hermione Gingold

'A sweet and sour film clearly not for all tastes.' – *Variety*

Gasbags*
GB   1940   77m   bw
Gainsborough (Edward Black)

Airmen stranded in Germany by a barrage balloon return in a captured secret weapon.

Fast-moving knockabout from the Crazy Gang; often inventive despite reach-me-down script and production.

w Val Guest, Marriott Edgar *d* Marcel Varnel *ph* Arthur Crabtree *md* Louis Levy

Flanagan and Allen, Nervo and Knox, Naughton and Gold, Moore Marriott, Wally Patch, Peter Gawthorne, Frederick Valk

The Gazebo*
US   1959   102m   bw
MGM/Avon (Lawrence Weingarten)

A TV writer kills a blackmailer (he thinks) and hides his body in the garden.

Frenetic black comedy which must have worked better on the stage but produces a few laughs.

w George Wells *play* Alec Coppel *d* George Marshall *ph* Paul C. Vogel *m* Jeff Alexander

Glenn Ford, Debbie Reynolds, Carl Reiner, John McGiver, Mabel Albertson, Doro Merande, Zasu Pitts, Martin Landau

The Geisha Boy
US   1958   98m   Technicolor
   Vistavision
Paramount (Jerry Lewis)

A third-rate magician joins a USO entertainment tour in Japan.

Disconnected farce which amuses only fitfully, and actively displeases when it becomes sentimental with the star drooling over a baby.

wd Frank Tashlin *ph* Haskell Boggs *m* Walter Scharf

Jerry Lewis, Marie MacDonald, Barton MacLane, Sessue Hayakawa, Suzanne Pleshette

'Everybody laughs but Buster!'
The General****
US   1926   80m approx (24 fps)
   bw   silent
UA/Buster Keaton (Joseph M. Schenck)
V, L

A confederate train driver gets his train and his girl back when they are stolen by Union soldiers.

Slow-starting, then hilarious action comedy, often voted one of the best ever made. Its sequence of sight gags, each topping the one before, is an incredible joy to behold.

w Al Boasberg, Charles Smith *d* Buster Keaton, Clyde Bruckman *ph* J. Devereux Jennings, Bert Haines

Buster Keaton, Marion Mack, Glen Cavander

'It has all the sweet earnestness in the world. It is about trains, frontier America, flower-faced girls.' – *New Yorker*, 1977
'The production itself is singularly well mounted, but the fun is not exactly plentiful . . . here he is more the acrobat than the clown, and his vehicle might be described as a mixture of cast iron and jelly.' – *Mordaunt Hall, New York Times*

† The story is based on an actual incident of the Civil War, treated more seriously in *The Great Locomotive Chase* (qv).

†† The screenplay with 1,400 freeze frames was issued in 1976 in the Film Classics Library (editor, Richard Anobile).

Generation
US 1969 104m Technicolor
Avco Embassy/Frederick Brisson
GB title: A Time for Giving

A Denver advertising executive is horrified by his daughter's ideas of modern marriage.

Lame generation-gap comedy centring on a couple who intend to deliver their own baby.

w William Goodhart   play William Goodhart   d George Schaefer
ph Lionel Lindon   m Dave Grusin

David Janssen, Kim Darby, Carl Reiner, Pete Duel, Andrew Prine, James Coco, Sam Waterston, Don Beddoe

'Slightly too sticky for comfort.' – MFB

Genevieve****
GB 1953 86m Technicolor
GFD/Sirius (Henry Cornelius)

Two friendly rivals engage in a race on the way back from the Brighton veteran car rally.

One of those happy films in which for no very good or expected reason a number of modest elements merge smoothly to create an aura of high style and memorable moments. A charmingly witty script, carefully pointed direction, attractive actors and locations, an atmosphere of light-hearted British sex and a lively harmonica theme turned it, after a slowish start, into one of Britain's biggest commercial hits and most fondly remembered comedies.

w William Rose   d Henry Cornelius   ph Christopher Challis
md Muir Mathieson   m Larry Adler

(who also played it)   ad Michael Stringer

Dinah Sheridan, John Gregson, Kay Kendall, Kenneth More, Geoffrey Keen, Joyce Grenfell, Reginald Beckwith, Arthur Wontner

'One of the best things to have happened to British films over the last five years.' – Gavin Lambert

† On American prints, Muir Mathieson was credited as the composer and with the Oscar nomination rather than Larry Adler, who was blacklisted at the time.
AAN: William Rose; Larry Adler

Geordie*
GB 1955 99m Technicolor
British Lion/Argonaut (Sidney Gilliat, Frank Launder)
US title: Wee Geordie

A weakly Scottish boy takes a physical culture course and becomes an Olympic hammer-thrower.

Slight comic fable, good to look at but without the necessary style to follow it through.

w Sidney Gilliat, Frank Launder
novel David Walker   d Frank Launder   ph Wilkie Cooper
m William Alwyn

Bill Travers, Alastair Sim, Norah Gorsen, Raymond Huntley, Brian Reece, Miles Malleson, Stanley Baxter

George and Margaret
GB 1940 77m bw
Warner

The frictions of a suburban family come to boiling point.

Fairly spruce film version of a stage comedy in which the title pair were much talked of but never seen.

w Brock Williams, Rodney Ackland   *play* Gerald Savory   *d* George King

Judy Kelly, Marie Lohr, Oliver Wakefield, Noel Howlett, Ann Casson, Arthur Macrae

George and Mildred
GB   1980   93m   colour
Chips/ITC (Roy Skeggs)

A suburban husband on a weekend package holiday is mistaken for a hired killer.

Abysmal TV spinoff, seeming even more lugubrious since it was released after the death of the female star.

w Dick Sharples   *d* Peter Frazer Jones   *ph* Frank Watts   *m* Philip Martell   *ad* Carolyn Scott   *ed* Peter Weatherley

Yootha Joyce, Brian Murphy, Stratford Johns, Norman Eshley, Sheila Fearn, Kenneth Cope

'Flaccid entertainment even by routine sit-com standards.' – *Martyn Auty, MFB*

George in Civvy Street
GB   1946   79m   bw
Columbia (Marcel Varnel, Ben Henry)

A soldier returns to his country pub and finds himself in the middle of a beer war.

The star's last film was oddly lacklustre and compared very badly with his earlier successes.

w Peter Fraser, Ted Kavanagh, Max Kester, Gale Pedrick   *d* Marcel Varnel   *ph* Phil Grindrod

George Formby, Rosalyn Boulter, Ronald Shiner, Ian Fleming, Wally Patch

Georgy Girl*
GB   1966   100m   bw
Columbia/Everglades (Otto Plaschkes, Robert A. Goldston)
V, L

An unattractive girl is fancied by her middle-aged employer but escapes to look after the illegitimate baby of her ungrateful friend.

Frantic black farce which seems determined to shock, but has a few good scenes once you get attuned to the mood. A censorship milestone.

w Margaret Forster, Peter Nichols
novel Margaret Forster   *d* Silvio Narizzano   *ph* Ken Higgins
m Alexander Faris

James Mason, Lynn Redgrave, Charlotte Rampling, Alan Bates, Bill Owen, Clare Kelly, Rachel Kempson

'Another swinging London story filled with people running through London late at night, dancing madly in the rain, and visiting deserted children's playgrounds to ride on the roundabouts.' – *MFB*
'So glib, so clever, so determinedly kinky that everything seems to be devalued.' – *Pauline Kael*
'Its barrage of fashionable tricks proves exhausting.' – *Sight and Sound*
AAN: Ken Higgins; James Mason; Lynn Redgrave; title song (*m* Tom Springfield, *ly* Jim Dale)

Gerald McBoing Boing***
US   1951   7m   Technicolor
UPA

A small boy becomes famous because he can't speak words: 'he goes boing-boing instead'.

Highly influential cartoon in what was then a new style; told with a light touch which is still extremely funny. Followed less successfully by *Gerald*

McBoing Boing's Symphony and *Gerald McBoing Boing On Planet Moo*.

w *Dr Seuss* (Theodore Geisel)
d *Robert Cannon*   m *Gail Kubik*
    pd pd John Hubley

AA: best cartoon

Get Cracking*
GB   1942   96m   bw
Columbia (Ben Henry)

George joins the home guard.

Adequate star comedy.

w L. DuGarde Peach   d Marcel
Varnel   ph Stephen Dade
md Harry Bidgood

George Formby, Edward Rigby, Frank
Pettingell, Dinah Sheridan, Ronald
Shiner, Wally Patch, Irene Handl

Get off My Foot
GB   1935   83m   bw
Warner (Irving Asher)

A Smithfield porter becomes a butler,
and later finds himself heir to a
fortune.

The nearest Max Miller came to being
a genuine film star was in this first of
eight Warner comedies, but the screen
simply couldn't contain him.

w Frank Launder, Robert
Edmunds   play *Money By Wire* by
Edward Paulton   d William
Beaudine   ph Basil Emmott
ad Peter Proud

Max Miller, Chili Bouchier, Morland
Graham, Jane Carr, Norma Varden,
Reginald Purdell, Wally Patch

Getting it Right
US   1989   102m   Fujicolor

A hairdresser becomes involved with
three contrasting women.

Mildly amusing, old-fashioned, romp.

w Elizabeth Jane Howard
novel Elizabeth Jane Howard
d Randal Kleiser   ph Clive
Tickner   pd Caroline Amies
ad Frank Walsh   ed Chris Kelly

Jesse Birdsall, Helena Bonham Carter,
Peter Cook, John Gielgud, Jane
Horrocks, Lynn Redgrave, Shirley
Ann Field, Pat Heywood, Bryan
Pringle, Nan Munro

'A contemporary London romance
that vacillates between the relishable
and the acutely embarrassing.' – *Kim
Newman, MFB*

'Doin' what comes supernaturally ... it's
the man-woman affair that's like nothing
on earth!'
The Ghost and Mrs Muir*
US   1947   104m   bw
TCF (Fred Kohlmar)
L

A widow refuses to be frightened
away from her seaside home by the
ghost of a sea captain, with whom she
falls in love.

Charming sentimental fable in
Hollywood's best style.

w Philip Dunne   novel R. A.
Dick   d Joseph L. Mankiewicz
ph Charles Lang   m Bernard
Herrmann   ad Richard Day, George
Davis

Gene Tierney, Rex Harrison, George
Sanders, Edna Best, Vanessa Brown,
Anna Lee, Robert Coote, Natalie
Wood, Isobel Elsom

'A not at all disagreeable piece of
whimsy.' – *News Chronicle*
'A jolly caper, gently humorous and
often sparkling.' – *New York Times*

† A half-hour TV series followed in
1968.
AAN: Charles Lang

The Ghost Breakers***
US   1940   85m   bw
Paramount (Arthur Hornblow Jnr)

A girl inherits a West Indian castle and finds herself up to her neck in ghosts, zombies and buried treasure.

Archetypal comedy horror, very well done; a follow-up to the success of *The Cat and the Canary*, and just about as entertaining.

*w Paul Dickey, Walter de Leon
play Paul Dickey, Charles W. Goddard   d George Marshall
ph Charles Lang   m Ernst Toch
ad Hans Dreier*

Bob Hope, Paulette Goddard, Paul Lukas, Willie Best, Richard Carlson, Lloyd Corrigan, Anthony Quinn, Noble Johnson, Pedro de Cordoba

'Bob Hope can joke, apparently, even with a risen corpse.' – *MFB*
'Paramount has found the fabled formula for making audiences shriek with laughter and fright at one and the same time.' – *New York Times*

† Previously filmed in 1914 with H. B. Warner; in 1922 with Wallace Reid; and remade in 1953 as *Scared Stiff*.

The Ghost Goes West***
GB   1935   85m   bw
London Films (Alexander Korda)
V

When a millionaire buys a Scottish castle and transports it stone by stone to America, the castle ghost goes too.

Amusing whimsy which is always pleasant but never quite realizes its full potential; fondly remembered for its star performance.

*w Robert E. Sherwood, Geoffrey Kerr   story Eric Keown   d René Clair   ph Harold Rosson
m Mischa Spoliansky*

Robert Donat, Jean Parker, Eugene Pallette, Elsa Lanchester, Ralph Bunker, Patricia Hilliard, Morton Selten

'Fine business likely in the keys, but not for the tanks.' – *Variety*
'Although the film is not cast in the fluid, rapidly paced style of Clair's typical work, it has a sly wit and an adroitness of manner that make it delightful.' – *André Sennwald, New York Times*
'It is typical of the British film industry that M. René Clair should be brought to this country to direct a Scottish film full of what must to him be rather incomprehensible jokes about whisky and bagpipes, humorous fantasy without any social significance, realistic observation, or genuine satire.' – *Graham Greene*

The Ghost of St Michael's**
GB   1941   82m   bw
Ealing (Basil Dearden)

A school is evacuated to the Isle of Skye, and the local ghost turns out to be an enemy agent.

The star's schoolmaster character is here at its seedy best, and he is well supported in a comedy-thriller plot.

*w Angus Macphail, John Dighton
d Marcel Varnel   ph Derek Williams*

Will Hay, Claude Hulbert, Felix Aylmer, Raymond Huntley, Elliot Mason, Charles Hawtrey, John Laurie, Hay Petrie, Roddy Hughes, Manning Whiley

The Ghost Train**
GB   1931   72m   bw
Gainsborough (Michael Balcon)

Passengers stranded at a haunted station in Cornwall include a detective posing as a silly ass in order to trap smugglers.

Excellent early sound version of a comedy-thriller play which has not only been among the most commercially successful ever written but also provided the basic plot for many another comedy: *Oh Mr Porter, The Ghost of St Michael's, Back Room Boy, Hold That Ghost*, etc. Previously filmed as a silent in 1927, with Guy Newall.

w Angus Macphail, Lajos Biro *play* Arnold Ridley   *d* Walter Forde *ph* Leslie Rowson   *ad* Walter Murton   *ed* Ian Dalrymple

Jack Hulbert, Cicely Courtneidge, Donald Calthrop, Ann Todd, Cyril Raymond, Angela Baddeley, Allan Jeayes

The Ghost Train*
GB   1941   85m   bw
Gainsborough (Edward Black)

Adequate remake with the lead split into two characters, which doesn't work quite so well.

w Marriott Edgar, Val Guest, J. O. C. Orton   *d* Walter Forde   *ph* Jack Cox

Arthur Askey, Richard Murdoch, Kathleen Harrison, Morland Graham, Linden Travers, Peter Murray Hill, *Herbert Lomas*

Ghostbusters*
US   1984   105m   Metrocolor
  Panavision
Columbia/Delphi (Ivan Reitman)
V, L

Unemployed academic parapsychologists set themselves up as ghostbusters and destroy several monstrous apparitions on the streets of New York.

Crude farce with expensive special effects. It took more money – millions more – than *Indiana Jones and the Temple of Doom*, which must say something about the age we live in.

w Dan Aykroyd, Harold Ramis *d* Ivan Reitman   *ph* Laszlo Kovacs, Herb Wagreitch   *m* Elmer Bernstein   *pd* John DeCuir *ed* Sheldon Kahn, David Blewitt

Bill Murray, Dan Aykroyd, Harold Ramis, Sigourney Weaver, Rick Moranis, Annie Potts, William Atherton
AAN: title song (*m/ly* Ray Parker)

Ghostbusters II
US   1989   108m   DeLuxe
  Panavision
Columbia TriStar (Ivan Reitman)
V, L

The disbanded Ghostbusters reform to deal with supernatural threats to New York.

Rambling, disjointed sequel of little amusement.

w Harold Ramis, Dan Aykroyd *d* Ivan Reitman   *ph* Michael Chapman   *m* Randy Edelman *pd* Bo Welch   *ed* Sheldon Kahn, Donn Cambern

Bill Murray, Dan Aykroyd, Sigourney Weaver, Harold Ramis, Rick Moranis, Ernie Hudson, Annie Potts, Peter MacNichol, Harris Yulin, David Margulies

Gidget
US   1959   95m   Eastmancolor
  Cinemascope
Columbia (Lewis J. Rachmil)

A 16-year-old girl falls for a surfer; her parents disapprove until he turns out to be the son of their best friend.

Commercial mixture of domestic comedy and beach athletics, for nice teenagers and their moms and pops.

w Gabrielle Upton   *novel* Frederick Kohner   *d* Paul Wendkos *ph* Burnett Guffey   *md* Morris Stoloff   *m* George Duning

Sandra Dee, Cliff Robertson, James Darren, Arthur O'Connell

† Sequels include *Gidget Goes Hawaiian* (1961) with Deborah Walley; *Gidget Goes to Rome* (1962) with Cindy Carol; and two TV movies.

Ginger and Fred***
Italy/France/West Germany   1986   126m   colour
PEA/Revcom/Stella/RAI (Alberto Grimaldi)

An ageing pair of dancers is brought out of retirement to appear on a TV show.

Melancholy comedy with resonances, chiefly taking the side of age against youth, with 'Fred' as an image of Fellini himself.

w Federico Fellini, Tonino Guerra, Tullio Pinelli   *d* Federico Fellini *ph* Tonino Delli Colli, Ennio Guarnieri   *m* Nicola Piovani *pd* Dante Ferretti

Giulietta Masina, Marcello Mastroianni, Franco Fabrizi, Frederick Von Ledenberg

A Girl, a Guy and a Gob
US   1941   91m   bw
RKO/Harold Lloyd
GB title: *The Navy Steps Out*

A secretary and her sailor boy friend teach her stuffy boss how to enjoy life.

Did producer Lloyd intend himself for the role played by O'Brien? If so, he would have needed a stronger script to prevent this Capraesque comedy from falling flat.

w Frank Ryan, Bert Granet *d* Richard Wallace   *ph* Russell Metty   *m* Roy Webb

Lucille Ball, Edmond O'Brien, George Murphy, George Cleveland, Henry Travers, Franklin Pangborn, Marguerite Churchill, Lloyd Corrigan

The Girl Can't Help It*
US   1956   97m   Eastmancolor Cinemascope
TCF (Frank Tashlin)
V, L

A theatrical agent grooms a gangster's dumb girl friend for stardom.

Scatty, garish pop scene spoof with a plot borrowed from *Born Yesterday* and a lot of jokes about its new star's superstructure. Some scenes are funny, and it puts the first rock and roll stars in pickle for all time.

w Frank Tashlin, Herbert Baker *story Do Re Mi* by Garson Kanin *d* Frank Tashlin   *ph* Leon Shamroy   *md* Lionel Newman

Jayne Mansfield, Tom Ewell, Edmond O'Brien, Henry Jones, John Emery; and Julie London, Ray Anthony, Fats Domino, Little Richard, The Platters

The Girl from Missouri*
US   1934   75m   bw
MGM (Bernard H. Hyman)
aka: *100% Pure*

original titles: *Born to be Kissed; Eadie was a Lady*

A chorus girl determines to remain virtuous until the right millionaire comes along.

Smart, amusing comedy very typical of its period.

w Anita Loos, John Emerson   *d* Jack Conway   *ph* Ray June   *m* William Axt

Jean Harlow, Franchot Tone, Lionel Barrymore, Lewis Stone, Patsy Kelly, Alan Mowbray, Clara Blandick, Henry Kolker

'It's going to be in the money . . . one that plenty of purity crusaders will see and like.' – *Variety*
'Noisily defiant, rip-roaring and raucous in spots . . . fast and furious adult fare.' – *Photoplay*

A Girl Must Live**
GB   1939   92m   bw
Gainsborough-20th Century (Edward Black)

A runaway schoolgirl falls among chorus girls planning to marry into the nobility.

Light, peppery comedy with a strong cast.

w Frank Launder, Michael Pertwee   *novel* Emery Bonnet
d Carol Reed   *ph* Jack Cox
md Louis Levy   *m/ly* Eddie Pola, Manning Sherwin
ad Vetchinsky   *ed* R. E. Dearing

Margaret Lockwood, Renée Houston, Lilli Palmer, George Robey, Hugh Sinclair, Naunton Wayne, Moore Marriott, Mary Clare, David Burns, Kathleen Harrison, Martita Hunt, Helen Haye

'An unabashed display of undressed femininity, double-meaning dialogue alternating between piquancy and vulgarity, and hearty knockabout involving scantily attired young viragos who fight furiously in a whirligig of legs and lingerie.' – *Kine Weekly*

Girl Stroke Boy
GB   1971   88m   Eastmancolor
Hemdale/Virgin (Ned Sherrin, Terry Glinwood)

A well-to-do couple try to find out whether their son's house guest is male or female.

Initially funny but appallingly extended one-joke comedy which many will find merely embarrassing.

w Caryl Brahms, Ned Sherrin
play Girlfriend by David Percival
d Bob Kellett   *ph* Ian Wilson
m John Scott

Joan Greenwood, Michael Hordern, Clive Francis, Patricia Routledge, Peter Bull, Rudolph Walker, Elizabeth Welch

'Underwater . . . undercover . . . under any circumstances . . . you must see the wildest, funniest new comedy!'

The Glass Bottom Boat
US   1966   110m   Metrocolor
      Panavision
MGM/Arwin-Reame (Martin Melcher)

A young widow gets involved with spies.

Frantic spy spoof, pleasantly set on the Californian coast, but overflowing with pratfalls, messy slapstick and pointless guest appearances.

w Everett Freeman   *d* Frank Tashlin   *ph* Leon Shamroy
m Frank de Vol

Doris Day, Rod Taylor, Arthur Godfrey, Paul Lynde, John McGiver, Edward Andrews, Eric Fleming, Dom De Luise

A Global Affair
US   1963   84m   bw
Seven Arts/Hall Bartlett

A United Nations official has to look after an abandoned baby.

Flat sentimental farce which embarrassingly tries to say something about the UN.

w Arthur Marx, Bob Fisher, Charles Lederer   *d* Jack Arnold
ph Joseph Ruttenberg   *m* Dominic Frontière

Bob Hope, Lilo Pulver, Michèle Mercier, Yvonne de Carlo

'Squaresville incarnate, with a side trip into Leersville.' – *Judith Crist, 1973*

Go to Blazes

GB   1961   84m   Technicolor
   Cinemascope
ABP (Kenneth Harper)
V

Ex-convicts become firemen, intending to use the engine for smash and grab raids.

Mild comedy ruined by wide screen.

w Patrick Campbell, Vivienne Knight   *d* Michael Truman
ph Erwin Hillier   *m* John Addison

Dave King, Daniel Massey, Norman Rossington, Wilfrid Lawson, Maggie Smith, Robert Morley, Coral Browne

'Laughter is what it has nothing else but!'

Go West*

US   1925   70m (24 fps)   bw
   silent
Metro-Goldwyn/Buster Keaton (Joseph M. Schenck)

A tenderfoot makes friends with a cow and takes it everywhere.

Disappointingly slow star comedy with splendid moments.

w Raymond Cannon   *d* Buster Keaton   *ph* Bert Haines, E. Lessley

Buster Keaton, Howard Truesdall, Kathleen Myers

Go West**

US   1940   82m   bw
MGM (Jack Cummings)
V

Three zanies tackle a Western villain.

Minor Marx comedy with a good start (the ticket office sketch) and a rousing finale as they take a moving train to bits, but some pretty soggy stuff in between.

w Irving Brecher   *d* Edward Buzzell   *ph* Leonard Smith
md Georgie Stoll   *m* Bronislau Kaper

Groucho Marx, Harpo Marx, Chico Marx, John Carroll, Diana Lewis, Robert Barrat

The Gods Must Be Crazy

South Africa   1980   109m
   colour   Panavision
New Realm/Mimosa/CAT (Jamie Uys)
V, L

A Coca Cola bottle falls from a plane and becomes a religious object to Kalahari bushmen.

Unexpected throwback farce with the blacks behaving almost as stupidly as Mantan Moreland in an old Charlie Chan movie. One for the Race Relations Board.

wd Jamie Uys   *ph* Jamie Uys, Buster Reynolds   *m* John Boshoff   *ad* Caroline Burls

N'xau, Marius Weyers, Sandra Prinsloo, Nic de Jager, Michael Thys

The Gods Must Be Crazy II

South Africa   1988   98m   colour
Fox/Elrina Investment Corp (Boet Troskie)
V

A bushman searching for his lost children finds a New York lawyer in the desert.

Implausible tale, as condescending as the first film to its black cast.

wd Jamie Uys   *ph* Buster

Reynolds   *m* Charles Fox
ed Renee Engelbrecht, Ivan Hall

N'xau, Lena Farugia, Hans Strydom,
Eiros, Nadies, Erick Bowen, Treasure
Tshabalala, Pierre Van Pletzen,
Lournes Swanepoel, Richard Loring

Going Bye Bye**
US   1934   20m   bw
Hal Roach

A violent convict escapes to take
vengeance on the two innocents
whose evidence sent him up.

Splendid star comedy displaying most
of the team's most endearing aspects.

w Anon   *d* Charles Rogers
ph Francis Corby   *ed* Bert Jordan

Laurel and Hardy, Walter Long, Mae
Busch

Going in Style
US   1979   97m   Technicolor
Warner/Tony Bill

Three bored elderly men decide to
plan a bank robbery.

Curiously aimless sentimental
comedy-drama which is simply
neither funny enough, thrilling
enough or moving enough to hold
the interest.

wd Martin Brest   *ph* Billy
Williams   *m* Michael Small

George Burns, Art Carney, Lee
Strasberg

'Mae's a lady now and she'll lick anyone in
the house who says she ain't!'
Goin' To Town*
US   1935   74m   bw
Paramount (William Le Baron)

A Western oil heiress moves into
society.

Reasonably satisfactory Mae West

vehicle, but not in the old bawdy
style.

w Mae West   *d* Alexander Hall
ph Karl Struss   *md* Andrea
Setaro   *m/ly* Sammy Fain, Irving
Kahal

Mae West, Paul Cavanagh, Ivan
Lebedeff, Tito Coral, Marjorie
Gateson, Fred Kohler Snr, Monroe
Owsley

'No amount of epigrammatic hypoing
can offset the silly story.' – *Variety*

The Gold Rush***
US   1925   72m (sound version
   1942)   bw
Charles Chaplin
L

A lone prospector in the Yukon
becomes rich after various adventures.

Essentially a succession of slowly but
carefully built visual gags, this is
Chaplin's finest example of comedy
drawn from utter privation; as such it
appealed vastly to the poor of the
world. As a clown, Chaplin himself is
near his best, though as usual there is
rather too much straining for pathos.

wd/m Charles Chaplin   ph Rollie
Totheroh   *md* Max Terr (1942
version)   *ad* Charles D. Hall
ed Harold McGhean (1942 version)

Charles Chaplin, Georgia Hale, Mack
Swain, Tom Murray
AAN: Max Terr

The Golden Age of Buster Keaton**
US   1975   97m   bw
Jay Ward (Raymond Rohauer)

A useful introductory package to the
shorts and features of Buster Keaton,
with most of the great silent scenes
present.

commentary: Bill Scott

The Golden Age of Comedy****
US   1957   78m   bw
Robert Youngson Productions

First of the scholarly compilations of
silent comedy which saved many
negatives from destruction, this is a
fast-paced general survey which
despite a facetious sound track does
provide a laugh a minute.

It particularly brought Laurel and
Hardy back into public notice, and
includes sections from *Two Tars* and
The Battle of the Century.

wd Robert Youngson
narrators Dweight Weist, Ward
Wilson   *m* George Steiner

Stan Laurel, Oliver Hardy, Harry
Langdon, Ben Turpin, Will Rogers,
Billy Bevan, Charlie Chase, Andy
Clyde

Good Morning Boys**
GB   1937   79m   bw
GFD/Gainsborough (Edward Black)

A schoolmaster takes his troublesome
pupils to Paris and becomes involved
with an art theft.

Sprightly vehicle for the star's seedy
schoolmaster persona: it established
him as a major draw in British
films.

w Marriott Edgar, Val Guest, Anthony
Kimmins   *d* Marcel Varnel
ph Arthur Crabtree   *md* Louis
Levy   *ad* Vetchinsky   *ed* R. E.
Dearing, Alfred Roome

Will Hay, Graham Moffatt, Lilli
Palmer, Mark Daly, Peter
Gawthorne, Martita Hunt, Charles
Hawtrey, Will Hay Jnr

† Remade with Ronald Shiner as *Top
of the Form*.

Good Neighbour Sam
US   1964   130m   Eastmancolor
Columbia/David Swift

A prissy suburban advertising man
becomes innocently involved in a
pretence to be the husband of the
divorcee next door.

A promising comic idea is here ruined
by lengthiness, lack of funny lines, and
no apparent idea of how to film a
farce. The actors are driven to
repeating every trick a dozen times.

w James Fritzell, Everett Greenbaum,
David Swift   *novel* Jack Finney
d David Swift   *ph* Burnett
Guffey   *m* Frank de Vol

Jack Lemmon, Romy Schneider,
Dorothy Provine, Senta Berger,
Edward G. Robinson, Mike Connors,
Edward Andrews, Louis Nye

Goodbye Charlie*
US   1964   116m   DeLuxe
    Cinemascope
TCF/Venice (David Weisbart)

A philandering gangster, shot dead by
an irate husband, is reincarnated in his
friend's house as a dishy blonde.

Overlong but amusing Broadway
comedy for wisecrackers,
uninventively adapted.

w Harry Kurnitz   *play* George
Axelrod   *d* Vincente Minnelli
ph Milton Krasner   *m* André
Previn

Debbie Reynolds, Pat Boone, Walter
Matthau, Tony Curtis

'Every father's daughter is a virgin!'
Goodbye Columbus**
US   1969   105m   Technicolor
Paramount/Willow Tree (Stanley Jaffe)

A young Jewish librarian has an affair
with the wilful daughter of a *nouveau
riche* family.

An amusing and well-observed
delineation of two kinds of Jewish
life in New York; the story, despite its
frank talk of penises and diaphragms,
leaves much to be desired, and the
style is post-*Graduate*.

w Arnold Schulman   *novel* Philip
Roth   *d Larry Peerce   ph* Gerald
Hirschfeld   *m* Charles Fox

Richard Benjamin, Ali MacGraw, Jack
Klugman, Nan Martin, Michael
Meyers, Lori Shelle
AAN: Arnold Schulman

'Every man she ever loved thought a
permanent relationship was a three-day
weekend!'
The Goodbye Girl*
US   1977   110m   Metrocolor
Warner/Rastar (Ray Stark)
V, L

A misunderstanding about the lease
of an apartment results in a girl dancer
agreeing to share it with a would-be
actor.

A very moderate script assisted by
excellent acting and the usual array
of Neil Simon one-liners. Nothing at
all new, but enjoyable.

w Neil Simon   *d* Herbert Ross
ph David M. Walsh   *m* Dave Grusin

Richard Dreyfuss, Marsha Mason,
Quinn Cummings, Paul Benedict,
Barbara Rhoades

AA: Richard Dreyfuss
AAN: best picture; Neil Simon;
Marsha Mason; Quinn Cummings

The Goose Steps Out*
GB   1942   79m   bw
Ealing (S. C. Balcon)

To steal a secret weapon, an
incompetent teacher is sent into
Germany in place of his Nazi double.

Quite amusing star vehicle, not up to
his best standards.

w Angus Macphail, John Dighton
d Will Hay, Basil Dearden
ph Ernest Palmer   m Bretton Byrd

Will Hay, Charles Hawtrey, Frank
Pettingell, Julien Mitchell, Peter Croft,
Jeremy Hawk, Peter Ustinov,
Raymond Lovell, Barry Morse

The Gorilla*
US   1939   66m   bw
TCF (Harry Joe Brown)

A murderer blames an escaped gorilla
for his crimes.

Spooky house mystery comedy
revamped as a Ritz Brothers vehicle;
not much suspense, but it all looks
good and the cast is highly
satisfactory.

w Rian James, Sid Silvers
play Ralph Spence   *d Allan Dwan*
ph Edward Cronjager   md David
Buttolph

The Ritz Brothers, Bela Lugosi, Lionel
Atwill, Patsy Kelly, Joseph Calleia,
Anita Louise, Edward Norris, Wally
Vernon

'A good programmer that will get by
for normal biz where the Ritzes can
attract.' – *Variety*

† There were two previous versions,
in 1927 with Charlie Murray and
1931 with Joe Frisco.

'This is Benjamin ... he's a little worried
about his future!'
The Graduate***
US   1967   105m   Technicolor
    Panavision
UA/Embassy (Lawrence Turman)
V, L

A rich Californian ex-student is led
into an affair with the wife of his

father's friend, then falls in love with her daughter.

Richly reflecting the anything-goes mood of the late sixties, this lushly-filmed sex comedy opened a few new doors, looked ravishing, was well acted and had a popular music score, so that few people noticed that only the first half was any good.

w Calder Willingham, Buck Henry
novel Charles Webb   d Mike
Nichols   ph Robert Surtees   m Dave
Grusin   pd Richard Sylbert   m/
ly Paul Simon (sung by Simon and Art
Garfunkel)

Dustin Hoffman, Anne Bancroft,
Katharine Ross, Murray Hamilton,
William Daniels, Elizabeth Wilson
    BENJAMIN: 'Mrs Robinson, if you
don't mind my saying so, this
conversation is getting a little strange.'

'Seeing The Graduate is a bit like
having one's most brilliant friend to
dinner, watching him become more
witty and animated with every
moment, and then becoming aware
that what one may really be
witnessing is the onset of a nervous
breakdown.' – Renata Adler
'Yes, there are weaknesses . . . But in
cinematic skill, in intent, in sheer
connection with us, The Graduate is a
milestone in American film history.'
– Stanley Kauffmann

AA: Mike Nichols
AAN: best picture; script; Robert
Surtees; Dustin Hoffman; Anne
Bancroft; Katharine Ross

Le Grand Blond avec une Chaussure Noire (dubbed)*
France   1972   89m   Eastmancolor
Fox-Rank/Gaumont International/
    Productions de la Guéville/Madeleine
    (Alain Poire, Yves Robert)
aka: Follow That Guy with the One Black Shoe

A disaster-prone violinist is the victim of a set-up by the head of the secret service who is attempting to discredit his second-in-command.

Mildly amusing comedy that makes fun of spies and their suspicious attitudes, though it suffers from being dubbed.

w Yves Robert, Francis Véber
d Yves Robert   ph René
Mathelin   m Vladimir Cosma
ed Ghislaine Desjonquères

Pierre Richard, Bernard Blier, Jean
Rochefort, Mireille Darc, Jean
Carmet, Colette Castel

Grandma's Boy*
US   1922   50m approx (24 fps)
    bw   silent
Associated Exhibitors

Inspired by the heroism of his own grandpa, a meek and mild young fellow subdues a terrifying tramp.

Modest second-feature-length comedy of a burgeoning star, no great shakes by his later standards.

d Fred Newmeyer

Harold Lloyd, Dick Sutherland, Anna
Townsend

The Grass Is Greener*
GB   1960   104m   Technirama
Grandon (Stanley Donen)
V

The wife of an English earl falls for an American millionaire tourist.

Heavy-going and unsuitably widescreened version of an agreeable piece of West End fluff. Performances just about save it.

w Hugh and Margaret Williams
play Hugh and Margaret Williams
d Stanley Donen   ph Christopher

Challis   md Muir Mathieson   m/
ly Noël Coward

Cary Grant, Deborah Kerr, Robert
Mitchum, *Jean Simmons, Moray Watson*

'It's too bad Coward couldn't have
written the wisecracks too.' – *Philip T.
Hartung*
'The stars do not glitter or even glow.
Instead of being liberated and
propelled by the screenplay, they are
chained and sunk. It is one of the
year's most disappointing films.' –
James Powers, Hollywood Reporter

The Great Chase
US   1963   82m   bw
Continental

A compendium of chase sequences
from silent films.

w Harvey Kort, Paul Killiam, Saul
Turrell

William S. Hart, Douglas Fairbanks
Snr and Buster Keaton (in *The General*)

The Great Dictator**
US   1940   129m   bw
United Artists/Charles Chaplin
V

A Jewish barber is mistaken for
dictator Adenoid Hynkel.

Chaplin's satire on Hitler has a few
funny moments, but the rest is heavy
going, the production is cheeseparing,
and the final speech to the world is a
grave mistake.

wd Charles Chaplin   *ph* Karl Struss,
Rollie Totheroh   *m* Meredith
Willson   *ad* J. Russell Spencer
ed Willard Nico

Charles Chaplin, Paulette Goddard,
Jack Oakie (as Napaloni), Reginald
Gardiner, Henry Daniell, Billy Gilbert,
Maurice Moscovich

'For this film he takes on more than

a mimed representation of common
humanity; he states, and accepts, the
responsibility of being one of
humanity's best and most widely-
known representatives.' – *Basil Wright*
'The last impassioned speech about
peace and serenity still wrecks
everything that has gone before:
Chaplin mawkish can always overrule
Chaplin the innocent mime.' – *New
Yorker, 1978*
'You must go back to *Intolerance* for
another motion picture that is so
completely one man's personal
expression of his attitude on
something about which he feels
deeply and passionately.' – *James
Shelley Hamilton, National Board of
Review*
'No time for comedy? Yes, I say, time
for comedy. Time for Chaplin
comedy. No time ever for Chaplin to
preach as he does in those last six
minutes, no matter how deeply he
may feel what he wrote and says. He
is not a good preacher. Indeed, he is
frighteningly bad.' – *John O'Hara*
'Some moments actually work, but
they are very few and far between.' –
Time Out, 1984
AAN: Charles Chaplin (as writer and
actor); Meredith Willson; Jack Oakie

Great Guns*
US   1941   74m   bw
TCF (Sol M. Wurtzel)
V

A young millionaire's retainers join
the army with him.

Disappointing Laurel and Hardy
comedy, their first for Fox and the
beginning of their decline. A few good
jokes, but no overall control or
inventiveness.

w Lou Breslow   *d* Monty Banks
ph Glen MacWilliams   *m* Emil
Newman   *ed* Al de Gaetano

Stan Laurel, Oliver Hardy, Sheila
Ryan, Dick Nelson, Edmund
Macdonald, Charles Trowbridge,
Ludwig Stossel, Mae Marsh

The Great Lover*
US   1949   80m   bw
(Paramount) Hope Enterprises (Edmund
   Beloin)

On a transatlantic liner, a timid
scoutmaster catches a strangler.

Amusing suspense comedy, a good
star vehicle.

w Edmund Beloin, Melville
Shavelson, Jack Rose   d Alexander
Hall   ph Charles Lang   m Joseph
J. Lilley

Bob Hope, Rhonda Fleming, Roland
Young, Jim Backus, Roland Culver,
George Reeves

'He'll give you the biggest heart sock, laugh
shock you ever thrilled to!'
The Great McGinty**
US   1940   83m   bw
Paramount (Paul Jones)
GB title: Down Went McGinty

A hobo and a crook have a hectic
political career.

Lively comedy-drama which signalled
the arrival as director of a new and
stimulating Hollywood talent.

wd Preston Sturges   ph William C.
Mellor   m Frederick Hollander

Brian Donlevy, Akim Tamiroff, Muriel
Angelus, Louis Jean Heydt, Arthur
Hoyt

   PROLOGUE: 'This is the story of two
men who met in a banana republic.
One of them never did anything
dishonest in his life except for one
crazy minute. The other never did
anything honest in his life except for
one crazy minute. They both had to
leave the country.'

'This is his first directing job and
where has he been all our lives? He
has that sense of the incongruous
which makes some of the best gaiety.'
– Otis Ferguson
'The tough dialogue is matched by
short, snappy scenes; the picture
seems to have wasted no time, no
money.' – Gilbert Seldes
'A director as adroit and inventive as
any in the business . . . it starts like a
five-alarm fire and never slackens
pace for one moment until its
unexpected conclusion.' – Pare Lorentz
'Sturges takes the success ethic and
throws it in the face of the audience.'
– James Orsini
'Capra with the gloves off.' – Raymond
Durgnat

AA: script

The Great McGonagall
GB   1974   89m   Eastmancolor
Darlton

An unemployed Scot aims to become
Queen Victoria's Poet Laureate.

Appalling tribute to a minor figure of
sub-literature.

w Joe McGrath, Spike Milligan
d Joe McGrath

Spike Milligan, Peter Sellers, Julia
Foster, Julian Chagrin, John Bluthal,
Valentine Dyall, Victor Spinetti

'They booed him to greatness!'
The Great Moment**
US   1944   83m   bw
Paramount

How anaesthetics may have been
invented.

Curious biopic of Dr W. T. G. Morgan,
poised somewhere between utter
seriousness and pratfall farce. The
beginning of its director's decline, but
always interesting in itself.

wd Preston Sturges   book Triumph
over Pain by René Fulop-Miller
ph Victor Milner   m Victor Young

Joel McCrea, Betty Field, William
Demarest, Harry Carey, Franklin
Pangborn, Porter Hall, Grady Sutton

'Mr Sturges has triumphed over
stiffness in screen biography.' — New
York Times
'The careless, careful authority is
there . . . the contrivance is smart
enough.' — Sunday Times

The Great Muppet Caper**
GB   1981   97m   Technicolor
ITC (David Lazer, Frank Oz)

Kermit and Fozzie are reporters sent
to solve a jewel robbery.

Considerably livelier than The Muppet
Movie but a badly timed flop at the
box-office, this genial caper has a
pleasant collection of guest stars as well
as showing the familiar puppets at
their most typical.

w Tom Patchett, Jay Tarses, Jerry
Juhl, Jack Rose   d Jim Henson
ph Oswald Morris   m Joe Raposo
pd Harry Lange

Diana Rigg, Charles Grodin, John
Cleese, Robert Morley, Trevor Howard,
Peter Ustinov, Jack Warden

'Large chunks are pleasingly daft.' —
Sight and Sound
AAN: song 'The First Time It
Happened' (m/ly Joe Raposo)

The Great Outdoors
US   1988   90m   CFI   Panavision
Universal/Hughes Entertainment (Arne L.
   Schmidt)
V

A family's holiday in the woods is
disrupted by a surprise visit from their
wealthy in-laws.

Broad and tiresome comedy in which
its participants flail around noisily to
no particular purpose.

w John Hughes   d Howard
Deutch   ph Ric Waite   m Thomas
Newman   pd John W. Corso
ed Tom Rolf, William Gordean, Seth
Flaum

Dan Aykroyd, John Candy, Stephanie
Faracy, Annette Bening, Chris Young,
Ian Giatti, Hilary Gordon, Rebecca
Gordon, Robert Prosky

'The greatest comedy ever made!'
The Great Race***
US   1965   163m   Technicolor
   Super Panavision
Warner/Patricia/Jalem/Reynard (Martin
   Jurow)
L

In 1908, the Great Leslie and Professor
Fate are leading contenders in the first
New York to Paris car race.

Elaborate comedy spectacular with
many good moments, notably the
early disasters, a Western saloon
brawl, and a custard pie fight.
Elsewhere, there is more
evidence of an oversize budget than
of wit or finesse, and the entire
Prisoner of Zenda spoof could have
been omitted. Excellent
production detail and general
good humour.

w Arthur Ross   d Blake
Edwards   ph Russell Harlan
m Henry Mancini   pd Fernando
Carrere

Jack Lemmon, Tony Curtis, Peter Falk,
Natalie Wood, George Macready, Ross
Martin, Vivian Vance, Dorothy
Provine
AAN: Russell Harlan; song 'The
Sweetheart Tree' (m Henry Mancini, ly
Johnny Mercer)

The Great St Trinian's Train Robbery

GB   1966   94m   Eastmancolor
British Lion/Braywild (Leslie Gilliat)
V

The staff of St Trinian's is infiltrated by would-be train robbers.

Flat-footed farce with a sense of strain evident from first to last shot.

w Frank Launder, Ivor Herbert
d Frank Launder, Sidney Gilliat
ph Ken Hodges   m Malcolm Arnold

Frankie Howerd, Dora Bryan, Reg Varney, Desmond Walter-Ellis, Raymond Huntley, Richard Wattis, George Benson, Eric Barker, Godfrey Winn, George Cole, Colin Gordon, Barbara Couper, Elspeth Duxbury

The Great Stone Face*

US   1968   93m   bw
Funnyman Productions

A very acceptable biography of Buster Keaton, with unusual emphasis on the very early films.

wd Vernon P. Becker

A Great Wall

US   1987   102m   colour
Mainline/W and S/Nanhai (Shirley Sun)
V, L

A Chinese-American executive takes his family to visit China and the sister he has not seen for twenty years.

The first American film to be made in China since the revolution turns out to be a small and pleasant comedy of cultural misunderstandings.

w Peter Wang, Shirley Sun   d Peter Wang   ph Peter Stein, Robert Primes   m David Laing, Ge Ganru   ad Wing Lee, Feng Yuan, Moing Ming Cheung   ed Graham Weinbren

Peter Wang, Sharon Iwai, Kelvin Han Yee, Li Qinqin, Hu Xiaoguang, Shen Guanglan

Green Card*

Australia/France   1991   108m
Technicolor
Touchstone (Peter Weir)
V, L

A Frenchman marries a New Yorker in order to stay in the United States.

Amiable romantic tale of an odd couple.

wd Peter Weir   ph Geoffrey Simpson   m Hans Zimmer
pd Wendy Stites   ad Christopher Nowak   ed William Anderson

Gérard Depardieu, Andie MacDowell, Bebe Neuwirth, Gregg Edelman, Robert Prosky, Jessie Keosian, Ethan Phillips, Mary Louise Wilson, Lois Smith, Conrad McLaren

Green for Danger***

GB   1946   93m   bw
Rank/Individual (Frank Launder, Sidney Gilliat)

A mysterious murderer strikes on the operating table at a wartime emergency hospital.

Classic comedy-thriller, with serious detection balanced by excellent jokes and performances, also by moments of fright.

w Sidney Gilliat, Claud Guerney
novel Christianna Brand   d Sidney Gilliat   ph Wilkie Cooper
m William Alwyn   pd Peter Proud   ed Thelma Myers

Alastair Sim, Sally Gray, Rosamund John, Trevor Howard, Leo Genn, Megs Jenkins, Judy Campbell, Ronald Ward, Moore Marriott

'Slick, witty and consistently entertaining.' – *Daily Telegraph*
'Launder and Gilliat have told an exciting story excitingly.' – *Times*

The Green Man*

GB 1956 80m bw
BL/Grenadier (Frank Launder, Sidney Gilliat)

A professional assassin stalks a pompous politician.

Cheerful but not very subtle black comedy, suffering from the attempt to make a star part out of a very minor character.

w Sidney Gilliat, Frank Launder *play* Meet a Body *by* Sidney Gilliat, Frank Launder   *d* Robert Day
ph Gerald Gibbs   *m* Cedric Thorpe Davie

Alastair Sim, George Cole, Jill Adams, Terry-Thomas, Avril Angers, John Chandos, Dora Bryan, Colin Gordon, Raymond Huntley

Greetings*

US 1968 88m Eastmancolor
West End Films
L

A draftee tries every which way to be exempted, then subjects himself to a whirl of physical experience.

Kaleidoscopic stringing together of fleeting satirical bits; talent undeniable but equally uncontrolled.

w Charles Hirsch, Brian de Palma
d Brian de Palma   *ed* Brian de Palma

Jonathan Warden, Robert de Niro, Gerrit Graham, Megan McCormick

Gregory's Girl**

GB 1980 91m colour
Lake/NFFC/STV (Davina Belling, Clive Parsons)
V

In a Scottish new town, a school footballer becomes aware of sex.

Curiously diverting comedy peopled by dreamers but handicapped by impenetrable accents. An unexpected world-wide success.

wd Bill Forsyth   *ph* Michael Coulter   *m* Colin Tully

Gordon John Sinclair, Dee Hepburn, Jake D'Arcy, Claire Grogan

BFA: best script

'He's having the day of his life . . . over and over again.'

Groundhog Day****

US 1993 101m Technicolor Panavision
Columbia TriStar/Columbia (Trevor Albert, Harold Ramis)
V

A cynical weatherman, sent to cover an annual small-town Ground Hog ceremony, finds himself reliving his day over and over again until he becomes a better person.

A 90s version of *It's A Wonderful Life*: tougher, smarter, more knowing and successfully avoiding corn to provide a unexpectedly witty and warming comedy.

w Danny Rubin, Harold Ramis
d Harold Ramis   *ph* John Bailey
m George Fenton   *pd* David Nichols   *ed* Pembroke J. Herring

Bill Murray, Andie MacDowell, Chris Elliott, Stephen Tobolowsky, Brian Doyle-Murray, Marita Geraghty, Angela Paton, Rick Ducommun

'A major studio Hollywood comedy

that both delights and surprises.' –
Sight and Sound

Guest Wife

US 1945 90m bw
UA/Greentree (Jack H. Skirball)

For business purposes a man allows
his wife to pretend to be the wife of
another.

Stereotyped star farce which seemed
tolerable at the time.

w Bruce Manning, John Klorer
d Sam Wood   *ph* Joseph
Valentine   *md* Daniele
Amfitheatrof

Claudette Colbert, Don Ameche, Dick
Foran, Charles Dingle, Grant Mitchell

'Mr Wood is a big gun to be trained
on so trivial a target, but the result
justifies the choice.' – *Richard Mallett,
Punch*
AAN: Daniele Amfitheatrof

'For the married man who's thinking single
– or the single man who's just thinking!'
A Guide for the Married Man**
US 1967 91m DeLuxe
  Panavision
TCF (Frank McCarthy)

A practised wolf explains to a perfect
husband how to be unfaithful.

Generally funny revue with as many
hilarious moments as flat spots.

w Frank Tarloff   *d* Gene Kelly
ph Joe Macdonald   *m* Johnny
Williams

Walter Matthau, Inger Stevens, *Robert
Morse*, Sue Anne Langdon, Lucille
Ball, Art Carney, Jack Benny, Polly
Bergen, Joey Bishop, Sid Caesar,
Wally Cox, Jayne Mansfield, Carl
Reiner, Phil Silvers, Jeffrey Hunter,
Terry-Thomas, Ben Blue

'One of the funniest films of the last
several seasons . . . it has sense enough
to sit down when it's through.' –
Robert Windeler

Gumshoe**

GB 1971 85m Eastmancolor
Columbia/Memorial (David Barber)
V

A Liverpool bingo caller dreams of
becoming a Bogart-like private eye and
finds himself in the middle of a
murder case.

A likeable spoof which is never quite
as funny as it means to be. *Billy Liar*
did it better, but there's plenty of
amusing detail.

w Neville Smith   *d* Stephen
Frears   *ph* Chris Menges
m Andrew Lloyd Webber

Albert Finney, Billie Whitelaw, Fulton
Mackay, Frank Finlay, Janice Rule

Gung Ho

US 1986 111m Technicolor
  Panavision
Paramount (Tony Ganz, Deborah Blum)

Japanese management takes over an
American small town.

Basically old-fashioned hands-across-
the-sea stuff, without any very clear
attitude except gentle fun. It rapidly
led to a TV series, which folded, and
that's about its level.

w Lowell Ganz, Babaloo Mandel
d Ron Howard   *ph* Don
Peterman   *m* Thomas Newman
pd James Schoppe   *ed* Daniel
Hanley, Michael Hill

Michael Keaton, Gedde Watanabe,
George Wendt, Mimi Rogers, John
Turturro

'A film that's not much of anything
except two hours long.' – *People*

Habeas Corpus*
US 1928 20m bw silent
Hal Roach

A mad professor sends two vagabonds out to look for a body.

Unusual star comedy, more grotesque and pantomimish than any of the others.

w H. M. Walker *story* Leo McCarey *d* James Parrott *ph* Len Powers *ed* Richard Currier

Laurel and Hardy, Richard Carle

Hail the Conquering Hero***
US 1944 101m bw
Paramount (Preston Sturges)

An army reject is accidentally thought a hero when he returns to his small-town home.

Skilfully orchestrated Preston Sturges romp, slightly marred by an overdose of sentiment but featuring his repertory of comic actors at full pitch.

wd Preston Sturges ph John Seitz m Werner Heymann

Eddie Bracken, William Demarest, Ella Raines, *Franklin Pangborn,* Elizabeth Patterson, *Raymond Walburn, Alan Bridge,* Georgia Caine, Freddie Steele, Jimmy Conlin, Torben Meyer

'Mob scenes, rough-houses and sharply serious passages are played for all the pantomime they are worth . . . one of the happiest, heartiest comedies in a twelvemonth.' – *Otis L. Guernsey Jnr*

'First rate entertainment, a pattern of film making, not to be missed.' – *Richard Mallett, Punch*

'The energy, the verbal density, the rush of Americana and the congestion seen periodically in *The Miracle of Morgan's Creek* stagger the senses in this newest film.' – *James Ursini*

'It tells a story so touching, so chock-full of human frailties and so rich in homely detail that it achieves a reality transcending the limitations of its familiar slapstick.' – *James Agee*

'He uses verbal as well as visual slapstick, and his comic timing is so quirkily effective that the dialogue keeps popping off like a string of firecrackers.' – *New Yorker, 1977*

AAN: Preston Sturges (as writer)

Hairspray
US 1988 90m colour
Palace (Rachel Talalay)
V, L

A fat teenager becomes the star of a local TV dance show.

Drear and campy comedy, set in the early days of rock and beehive hair-styles.

wd John Waters ph David Insley m Kenny Vance pd Vincent Peranio ed Janice Hampton

Sonny Bono, Ruth Brown, Divine, Colleen Fitzpatrick, Jo Ann Havrilla,

Michael St Gerard, Debbie Harry, Ricki Lake, Leslie Ann Powers

Half Shot at Sunrise*
US 1930 78m bw
RKO

Allegedly one of the best representations of a star comedy duo who went into a decline after 1932.

w James Ashmore Creelman
d Paul Sloane

Bert Wheeler, Robert Woolsey, Edna May Oliver, Dorothy Lee, John Rutherford

'Laugh programmer beyond ordinary . . . it will do business, including de luxers.' – Variety

Hammersmith Is Out*
US 1972 114m DuArt Color
Cinerama/J. Cornelius Cream (Alex Lucas)

With the help of a male nurse, a homicidal mental inmate escapes and becomes the most influential man in the country.

Pretentious updating of Faust into a kind of black farce that seldom amuses but is interesting in fits and starts.

w Stanford Whitmore   d Peter Ustinov   ph Richard Kline
m Dominic Frontière

Richard Burton, Elizabeth Taylor, Peter Ustinov, Beau Bridges, Leon Ames, John Schuck, George Raft

Hands Up*
US 1926 65m (24 fps) bw
   silent
Paramount

General Lee assigns a spy to prevent a Union man from getting his hands on a gold cache.

Pleasant Civil War comedy with a curious Mormon happy ending.

w Monty Brice, Lloyd Corrigan
d Clarence Badger

Raymond Griffith, Marion Nixon, Virginia Lee Corbin, Mack Swain, Montagu Love

Hanky Panky
US 1982 107m Metrocolor
Columbia (Martin Ransohoff)
L

A girl on a spy mission is pursued by assassins and enlists the reluctant aid of an architect she meets in a taxi.

Frantic spoof of North by Northwest, which was itself as spoofy as all get out. This strained effort lacks wit, substituting shouting, violence and an exasperating hero.

w Henry Rosenbaum, David Taylor   d Sidney Poitier
ph Arthur Ornitz   m Tom Scott
pd Ben Edwards   ed Harry Keller

Gene Wilder, Gilda Radner, Kathleen Quinlan, Richard Widmark

'The plot, rather like Mr Wilder, rushes hither and yon at the slightest excuse without ever adding up to very much. Even McGuffins are supposed to make more sense than this.' – Richard Combs, MFB
'A comedy thriller designed solely as a vehicle for Wilder's uninhibited hysteria is bad enough; one that so thoroughly submerges everyone else is so much worse.' – Sight and Sound
'One long screech.' – Ibid.

Hannah and Her Sisters***
US 1986 106m Technicolor
Orion/Charles R. Joffe, Jack Rollins (Robert Greenhut)
V

Relationships intermingle for a New

York family over a two-year period between Thanksgiving dinners.

Even though it has nowhere in particular to go, and certain scenes are over the top, this is a brilliantly assembled and thoroughly enjoyable mélange of fine acting and New Yorkish one-liners, with particularly sharp editing and a nostalgic music score.

wd Woody Allen   ph Carlo di Palma   m popular and classical extracts   *pd* Stuart Wurtzel *ed Susan E. Morse*

Woody Allen, Mia Farrow, Dianne Wiest, Michael Caine, Carrie Fisher, Barbara Hershey, Maureen O'Sullivan, Lloyd Nolan, Max von Sydow, Daniel Stern, Sam Waterston, Tony Roberts

'A loosely knit canvas of Manhattan interiors and exteriors.' – *Sight and Sound*
'One of Woody Allen's great films.' – *Variety*

AA: best original screenplay; Dianne Wiest; Michael Caine
AAN: best picture; Woody Allen (as director); Susan E. Morse; art direction

The Happening
US   1967   101m   Technicolor
Columbia/Horizon/Dover (Jud Kinberg)

Four young hippies kidnap a wealthy businessman and don't know what to do with him; he turns the tables.

Freewheeling irresponsible comedy which even at the time of swinging cities seemed very irritating.

w Frank R. Pierson, James D. Buchanan, Ronald Austin   *d* Eliot Silverstein   *ph* Philip Lathrop *m* Frank de Vol   *pd* Richard Day

Anthony Quinn, George Maharis, Michael Parks, Faye Dunaway, Robert Walker, Oscar Homolka, Martha Hyer, Milton Berle, Jack Kruschen

'A wacky comedy à la mode, oddly mixed and only spasmodically effective.' – *Variety*

Happidrome
GB   1943   87m   bw
Aldwych

A play intended seriously becomes a comedy hit.

A theme later used by *The Producers* forms the background for this naive screen version of a wartime radio series.

w Tom Arnold, James Seymour *d* Phil Brandon

Harry Korris, Robbie Vincent, Cecil Frederick, Bunty Meadows, Lisa Lee, 'Hutch', the Cairoli Brothers

The Happiest Days of Your Life***
GB   1950   81m   bw
British Lion/Individual (Frank Launder)

A ministry mistake billets a girls' school on a boys' school.

Briskly handled version of a semi-classic postwar farce, with many familiar talents in excellent form.

w Frank Launder, John Dighton *play* John Dighton   *d* Frank Launder   *ph* Stan Pavey *m* Mischa Spoliansky

Alastair Sim, Margaret Rutherford, Joyce Grenfell, Richard Wattis, Edward Rigby, Guy Middleton, Muriel Aked, John Bentley, Bernadette O'Farrell

'Absolutely first rate fun.' – *Richard Mallett, Punch*
'Launder couldn't have knocked another laugh out of the situation if he'd used a hockey stick.' – *Sunday Express*
'The best mixed comedy pairing since

Groucho Marx and Margaret Dumont.'
— *Sunday Chronicle*

Happy Ever After*

GB   1954   87m   Technicolor
ABP/Mario Zampi
V
US title: *Tonight's the Night*

Irish villagers draw lots for the
privilege of murdering their rascally
squire.

Fairly hilarious black comedy with a
good cast entering into the spirit of
the thing.

w Jack Davies, Michael Pertwee, L. A.
G. Strong   *d* Mario Zampi
ph Stan Pavey   *m* Stanley Black

David Niven, Yvonne de Carlo, A. E.
Matthews, Michael Shepley, George
Cole, Barry Fitzgerald

The Happy Hooker

US   1975   98m   Movielab
Double H/Cannon-Happy (Fred Caruso)

A Dutch girl in New York starts a
career as a prostitute and finds she
enjoys it.

Glum sex comedy based on the
supposed exploits of a real madam;
crude and not very funny. If this is
emancipation, Shirley Temple seems
more attractive by the minute.

w William Richert   *book* Xaviera
Hollander   *d* Nicholas Sgarro
ph Dick Kratina   *m* Don Elliott

Lynn Redgrave (hilariously miscast),
Jean-Pierre Aumont, Lovelady Powell,
Nicholas Pryor, Elizabeth Wilson,
Tom Poston, Conrad Janis, Richard
Lynch

† Follow-ups: *The Happy Hooker
Goes to Washington* (1977), *The
Happy Hooker Goes to Hollywood*
(1980).

Happy New Year*

France/Italy   1973   115m
Eastmancolor
Films 13/Rizzoli (Claude Lelouch)
original title: *La Bonne Année*

A thief is paroled on New Year's Eve
in the hope that he will lead police to
his confederates. In fact he learns a lot
about the world and himself.

Bitter comedy apparently intended to
distance the director from the
romantic fervour of *A Man and a
Woman*, a clip from which is screened
for the convicts at the beginning.

wd/ph Claude Lelouch   *m* Francis Lai

Lino Ventura, Françoise Fabian,
Charles Gérard, André Falcon

Happy New Year*

US   1987   85m   DeLuxe
Columbia/Delphi IV (Jerry Weintraub)

Two middle-aged jewel thieves head
for a big score in Florida.

Loose remake of Lelouch's *La Bonne
Année*, quite watchable in its familiar
way.

w Warren Lane   *d* John G.
Avildsen   *ph* James Crabe
m Bill Conti   *pd* William J.
Cassidy   *ed* Jane Kuson

Peter Falk, Charles Durning, Wendy
Hughes, Tom Courtney, John
Copeland

Happy Together

US   1990   96m   Metrocolor
Seymour Borde (Jere Henshaw)
V, L

Due to a mix-up, a prudish college
student finds himself sharing a room
with an attractive girl.

Predictable teenage wish-fulfilment
comedy unlikely to interest anyone
over school-going age.

w Craig J. Nevius   *d* Mel
Damski   *ph* Joe Pennella
m Robert Folk   *pd* Marcia Hinds
ed O. Nicholas Brown

Patrick Dempsey, Helen Slater, Dan
Schneider, Kevin Hardesty, Marius
Weyers, Barbara Babcock

A Hard Day's Night****
GB   1964   85m   bw
UA/Proscenium (Walter Shenson)
V. L

Harassed by their manager and Paul's
grandpa, the Beatles embark from
Liverpool by train for a London TV
show.

Comic fantasia with music; an
enormous commercial success with
the director trying every cinematic
gag in the book, it led directly to
all the kaleidoscopic swinging
London spy thrillers and comedies
of the later sixties, and so has a
lot to answer for; but at the time it
was a sweet breath of fresh air, and
the Beatles even seemed willing
and likeable.

w Alun Owen   *d* Richard Lester
ph Gilbert Taylor   *md* George
Martin   *m/ly* The Beatles

The Beatles, Wilfrid Brambell, Norman
Rossington, *Victor Spinetti*

'A fine conglomeration of madcap
clowning . . . with such a dazzling use
of camera that it tickles the intellect
and electrifies the nerves.' – *Bosley
Crowther*
'All technology was enlisted in the
service of the gag, and a kind of
nuclear gagmanship exploded.' – *John
Simon*
'The *Citizen Kane* of Jukebox movies'
– *Andrew Sarris*
AAN: Alun Owen; George Martin

The Hard Way*
US   1991   111m   DeLuxe
UIP/Universal/Badham/Cohen (William
   Sackheim)
V. L

A Hollywood actor who plans to play
a cop in his new film teams up with a
real-life New York policeman who is
obsessed with catching a serial killer.

Amusing comedy that pokes fun at
buddy-buddy and cop movies while
being both itself.

w Daniel Pyne, Lem Dobbs
story Lem Dobbs, Michael Kozoll
d John Badham   *ph* Robert Primes,
Don McAlpine   *m* Arthur B.
Rubinstein   *pd* Philip Harrison
ed Frank Morris, Tony Lombardo

Michael J. Fox, James Woods,
Stephen Lang, Annabella Sciorra,
Delroy Lindo, Luis Guzman, Mary
Mara, Penny Marshall

'Proves that sometimes the system,
fuelled here by self-mocking jibes, can
turn out films appreciable and
enjoyable without adding anything to
the cinema.' – *Kim Newman, Sight and
Sound*

Harold and Maude*
US   1971   92m   Technicolor
Paramount/Mildred Lewis/Colin Higgins
L

A repressed young man, fixated on
death and funerals, has an affair with
an 80-year-old woman.

Often hilarious black comedy for
those who can stand it; the epitome
of bad taste, splashed around with wit
and vigour, it became a minor cult.

w Colin Higgins   *d* Hal Ashby
ph John A. Alonzo   *m* Cat Stevens

Bud Cort, Ruth Gordon, Vivian Pickles,
Cyril Cusack

Harold Lloyd's Funny Side of Life***
US   1963   99m   bw
Harold Lloyd (Duncan Mansfield)

Excerpts from twenties comedies plus a shortened version of *The Freshman* (1925).

Excellent compilation, though the mini-feature makes it a little unbalanced.

w Arthur Ross   *m* Walter Scharf

Harold Lloyd

Harold Lloyd's World of Comedy****
US   1962   97m   bw
Harold Lloyd

Generous clips from the comic climaxes of Lloyd's best silent and sound comedies including *Safety Last, The Freshman, Hot Water, Why Worry, Girl Shy, Professor Beware, Movie Crazy* and *Feet First*.

As Lloyd's work lends itself well to extract, this can hardly fail to be a superb anthology capsuling the appeal of one of America's greatest silent comedians. The timing is just perfect.

w Walter Scharf

commentary: Art Ross

Harper Valley P.T.A.
US   1978   93m   colour
April Fools (George Edwards)

An independent woman takes her revenge on those who disapprove of her free-wheeling ways.

A feeble-minded comedy that cannot sustain interest for any longer than the hit song of the 1960s on which it is based.

w George Edwards, Barry Schneider   *d* Richard Bennett

ph Willy Kurant   *m* Nelson Riddle   *ed* Michael Economu

Barbara Eden, Ronny Cox, Nanette Fabray, Susan Swift, Louis Nye, Pat Paulsen

Harry and Walter Go to New York
US   1976   120m   Metrocolor Panavision
Columbia (Don Devlin, Harry Gittes)
V, L

In oldtime New York, two carnival entertainers get involved with suffragettes and a safecracker.

Extended period romp in which the high humour soon palls and a general lack of talent makes itself felt.

w John Byrum, Robert Kaufman
d Mark Rydell   *ph* Laszlo Kovacs   *m* David Shire   *pd* Harry Horner

James Caan, Elliott Gould, Michael Caine, Diane Keaton, Charles Durning, Lesley Ann Warren, Jack Gilford

'A charmless mishmash.' – *Sight and Sound*
'This film fails to work as a light comedy, as a period piece, as a jigsaw puzzle . . . mainly, it just sits there and dies.' – *Frank Rich, New York Post*
'Strictly for those who'll laugh at anything.' – *Kevin Thomas, Los Angeles Times*

Harry in Your Pocket
US   1973   103m   DeLuxe Panavision
UA/Cinema Video (Bruce Geller)

Adventures of a young, a middle-aged and an old pickpocket.

Partly pleasant but rather aimless comedy drama, agreeably set in Seattle and Salt Lake City.

w Ron Austin, James Buchanan

d Bruce Geller *ph* Fred Koenekamp *m* Lalo Schifrin

James Coburn, *Walter Pidgeon*, Michael Sarrazin, Trish Van Devere

Harvey***
US 1950 104m bw
U-I (John Beck)
V

A middle-aged drunk has an imaginary white rabbit as his friend, and his sister tries to have him certified.

An amiably batty play with splendid lines is here transferred virtually intact to the screen and survives superbly thanks to understanding by all concerned, though the star is as yet too young for a role which he later made his own.

w Mary Chase (with Oscar Brodney) *play* Mary Chase *d* Henry Koster *ph* William Daniels *m* Frank Skinner

James Stewart, Josephine Hull, Victoria Horne, Peggy Dow, *Cecil Kellaway*, Charles Drake, *Jesse White*, Nana Bryant, Wallace Ford

VETA LOUISE (Josephine Hull): 'Myrtle Mae, you have a lot to learn, and I hope you never learn it.'

ELWOOD (James Stewart): 'I've wrestled with reality for 35 years, and I'm happy, doctor, I finally won out over it.'

ELWOOD: 'Harvey and I have things to do . . . we sit in the bars . . . have a drink or two . . . and play the juke box. Very soon the faces of the other people turn towards me and they smile. They say: "We don't know your name, mister, but you're all right, all right." Harvey and I warm ourselves in these golden moments. We came as strangers – soon we have friends. They come over. They sit with us. They drink with us. They talk to us. They tell

us about the great big terrible things they've done and the great big wonderful things they're going to do. Their hopes, their regrets. Their loves, their hates. All very large, because nobody ever brings anything small into a bar. Then I introduce them to Harvey, and he's bigger and grander than anything they can offer me. When they leave, they leave impressed. The same people seldom come back.'

ELWOOD (describing his first meeting with Harvey): 'I'd just helped Ed Hickey into a taxi. Ed had been mixing his drinks, and I felt he needed conveying. I started to walk down the street when I heard a voice saying: "Good evening, Mr Dowd". I turned, and there was this big white rabbit leaning against a lamp-post. Well, I thought nothing of that! Because when you've lived in a town as long as I've lived in this one, you get used to the fact that everybody knows your name . . .'

AA: Josephine Hull
AAN: James Stewart

Haunted Honeymoon
US 1986 82m Rank Colour
Orion/Susan Ruskin
L

A radio actor takes his fiancée to the family's gloomy country estate, where werewolves and transvestites are some of the creatures which abound.

Mainly unfunny spoof: all concerned should have taken a closer look at *The Cat and the Canary*.

w Gene Wilder, Terence Marsh *d* Gene Wilder *ph* Fred Schuler *m* John Morris *pd* Terence Marsh *ed* Christopher Greenbury

Gene Wilder, Gilda Radner, Dom DeLuise, Jonathan Pryce, Peter Vaughan, Bryan Pringle

'Faintly amusing but singularly uncompelling.' – *Variety*

Having Wonderful Time

US   1938   70m   bw
RKO (Pandro S. Berman)

A New York girl falls in love at a summer camp.

Mild comedy which, robbed of its original Jewish milieu, falls resoundingly flat.

w Arthur Kober   *play* Arthur Kober   *d* Alfred Santell   *ph* Robert de Grasse   *m* Roy Webb

Ginger Rogers, Douglas Fairbanks Jnr, Peggy Conklin, Lucille Ball, Lee Bowman, Eve Arden, Red Skelton, Donald Meek, Jack Carson

Hawmps

US   1976   127m   colour
Mulberry Square

The Texas cavalry experiments with the use of camels in the south-western desert.

Incredibly overstretched and tedious period comedy with some bright patches.

w William Bickley, Michael Warren   *d* Joe Camp

James Hampton, Christopher Connelly, Slim Pickens, Denver Pyle, Jennifer Hawkins, Jack Elam

Head Over Heels

US   1980   97m   Technicolor
UA/Triple Play (Mark Metcalf, Allen Joseph, Griffin Dunne)
aka: *Chilly Scenes of Winter*

A government office worker thinks back on his on-again off-again relationship with the woman he loves.

Quirky comedy drama without the

zest of *Annie Hall*, which it much resembles; too much like a television play for box-office success.

wd Joan Macklin Silver
novel Chilly Scenes of Winter by Ann Beattie   *ph* Bobby Byrne   *m* Ken Lauber   *pd* Peter Jamison
ed Cynthia Scheider

John Heard, Mary Beth Hurt, Peter Riegert, Kenneth McMillan, Gloria Grahame

Hear My Song**

GB   1991   105m   Fujicolor
Palace/Film Four/Vision/Limelight/British Screen/Windmill Lane (Alison Owen-Allen)
V, L

To revive his flagging business, a 1980s Liverpudlian night-club manager hires a singer who may, or may not, be Joseph Locke, a romantic tenor who was once a variety theatre headliner and fled to Ireland to avoid charges of tax evasion.

A small-scale delight, a film of charm and wit.

w Peter Chelsom, Adrian Dunbar
d Peter Chelsom   *ph* Sue Gibson   *m* John Altman
pd Caroline Hanania   *ed* Martin Walsh

Ned Beatty, Adrian Dunbar, Shirley Anne Field, Tara Fitzgerald, William Hootkins, Harold Berens, David McCallum, John Dair, Stephen Marcus

'One of the year's most delightful films.' – *Kevin Thomas, Los Angeles Times*
'Far from making an innovative contribution to British cinema, *Hear My Song* relies for the most part on nostalgia, whimsy and sleight of hand.' – *Tom Charity, Sight and Sound*

Heart Condition
US 1990 95m DeLuxe
Enterprise/New Line Cinema (Steve Tisch)
V, L

A bigoted white cop who has a heart transplant is haunted by the organ's donor, a suave black lawyer.

Dire comedy, despite likeable performances by its stars.

wd James D. Parriott *ph* Arthur Albert *m* Patrick Leonard *pd* John Muto *ed* David Finfer

Bob Hoskins, Denzel Washington, Chloe Webb, Robert Apisa, Jeffrey Meek, Frank R. Roach, Kieran Mulroney, Lisa Stahl, Ray Baker, Eva Larue, Roger E. Mosley

Heart of the West*
US 1975 103m Metrocolor
MGM/Bill-Zieff (Tony Bill)
GB title: *Hollywood Cowboy*

In the early thirties a naïve midwesterner almost accidentally becomes a Hollywood star.

Overstretched comedy poking gentle fun at old Hollywood: likeable but finally disappointing, as it obviously needed a Buster Keaton.

w Rob Thompson *d* Howard Zieff *ph* Mario Tosi *m* Ken Lauber

Jeff Bridges, Alan Arkin, Andy Griffith, Blythe Danner, Donald Pleasence, Richard B. Shull, Herb Edelman

The Heartbreak Kid*
US 1972 106m DeLuxe
(TCF) Palomar (Edgar J. Scherick)
V, L

Disappointed with his honeymoon, a sporting goods salesman promptly sets his cap at a richer, prettier prospective spouse.

Heartless modern comedy reminiscent of *The Graduate;* quite well done but unsympathetic and somehow too American to export satisfactorily.

w Neil Simon *story A Change of Plan* by Bruce Jay Friedman *d* Elaine May *ph* Owen Roizman *m* Garry Sherman

Charles Grodin, Cybill Shepherd, Jeannie Berlin, Eddie Albert, Audra Lindley, William Prince, Art Metrano

'The latest in a relatively new kind of American film – glittery trash.' – *Stanley Kauffmann*
AAN: Jeannie Berlin; Eddie Albert

Heathers
US 1988 103m DeLuxe
Premier Releasing/New World/
   Cinemarque Entertainment (Denise Di
   Novi)
V, L

A high-school student begins to systematically murder his fellow students.

Black joke that rapidly runs out of interest.

w Daniel Waters *d* Michael Lehmann *ph* Francis Kenny *m* David Newman *pd* Jon Hutman *ed* Norman Hollyn

Winona Ryder, Christian Slater, Shannen Doherty, Lisanne Falk, Kim Walker, Penelope Milford, Glenn Shadix

'The film is not seriously a comedy about high school as a metaphor for society – its false values, its power-hungry cliques, its emotional exploitation.' – *Richard Coombs, MFB*

Heaven Can Wait***
US 1943 112m Technicolor
TCF (Ernst Lubitsch)

On arrival in Hades, an elderly playboy reports his peccadilloes to Satan, who sends him Upstairs.

Charming period piece with fantasy bookends; the essence of the piece is its evocation of American society in the nineties, and in its director's waspish way with a funny scene.

w Samson Raphaelson   play Birthday by Lazlo Bus-Fekete   d Ernst Lubitsch   ph Edward Cronjager m Alfred Newman   ad James Basevi, Leland Fuller

Don Ameche, Gene Tierney, Laird Cregar, Charles Coburn, Marjorie Main, Eugene Pallette, Allyn Joslyn, Spring Byington, Signe Hasso, Louis Calhern

'It was so good I half believed Lubitsch could still do as well as he ever did, given half a chance.' – James Agee AAN: best picture; Ernst Lubitsch; Edward Cronjager

Heaven Can Wait*
US   1978   100m   Movielab Paramount/Warren Beatty (Howard W. Koch Jnr, Charles H. McGuire)
L

A football star finds himself accidentally in heaven after a car accident; when he is allowed to return, his body has been cremated, so he has to find another.

Unexpectedly commercially successful (the late seventies clearly needed religion) remake of 1941's Here Comes Mr Jordan. It lacks the sharpness and style of its predecessor, and despite amusing moments is often merely tacky.

w Warren Beatty, Elaine May play Harry Segall   d Warren Beatty, Buck Henry   ph William A. Fraker   m Dave Grusin   pd Paul Sylbert

Warren Beatty, Julie Christie, James Mason (as Mr Jordan), Jack Warden, Charles Grodin, Dyan Cannon, Buck Henry, Vincent Gardenia, Joseph Maher
AAN: best picture; script; direction; photography; music; Warren Beatty (as actor); Jack Warden; Dyan Cannon

Heaven Help Us
US   1985   104m   Metrocolor Tri-Star/HBO/Silver Screen (Dan Wigutow, Mark Carliner)

In mid-sixties Brooklyn, a new priest has trouble with teenagers at a Catholic boys' school.

Lively if rather wearing exploration of teenage sex pranks and Catholic guilt, treated rather uncertainly as comedy.

w Charles Purpura   d Michael Dinner   ph Miroslav Ondricek m James Horner   pd Michael Molly   ed Stephen A. Rotter

Donald Sutherland, John Heard, Andrew McCarthy, Mary Stuart Masterson, Kevin Dillon, Kate Reid

The Heavenly Body
US   1943   93m   bw MGM (Arthur Hornblow Jnr)

An astronomer is too busy to notice his wife, so she takes up astrology and meets a dark handsome stranger as predicted.

Thin romantic comedy which despite crazy touches never actually makes one laugh.

w Michael Arlen, Walter Reisch d Alexander Hall   ph Robert Planck   m Bronislau Kaper

William Powell, Hedy Lamarr, James Craig, Fay Bainter, Henry O'Neill, Spring Byington, Morris Ankrum, Connie Gilchrist

Heavens Above*

GB 1963 118m bw
British Lion/Charter (Roy Boulting)
V

A northern parson with proletarian sympathies is accidentally appointed to a snobby village where he converts the dowager aristocrat to works of absurd charity. Eventually he has the whole country in an uproar and takes the place of an astronaut.

Patchy satirical comedy which takes unsteady aim at too many targets but scores some predictable laughs.

w Frank Harvey, John Boulting
d John Boulting   ph Max
Greene   m Richard Rodney
Bennett

Peter Sellers, Isabel Jeans, Cecil Parker, Brock Peters, Ian Carmichael, Irene Handl, Eric Sykes, Bernard Miles

Hello Again

US 1987 96m colour
Warner/Touchstone (Frank Perry)
V, L

A year after dying, a housewife is brought back by her sister, a medium, to discover that life has changed in her absence.

Moribund comedy that fails to get much mileage from its material.

w Susan Isaacs   d Frank Perry
ph Jan Weincke   m William
Goldstein   pd Edward Pisoni
ed Peter C. Frank, Trudy Ship

Shelly Long, Judith Ivey, Thor Fields, Corbin Bernsen, Gabriel Byrne, Sela Ward, Austin Pendleton, Carrie Nye

Hellzapoppin***

US 1942 84m bw
Universal/Mayfair (Glenn Tryon, Alex Gottlieb)

Two incompetent comics make a picture.

Zany modification of a smash burlesque revue; the crazy jokes are toned down and a romantic interest is added (and tentatively sent up). The result is patchy but often hilarious, and the whole is a handy consensus of forties humour and pop music.

w Nat Perrin, Warren Wilson   d H.
C. Potter   ph Woody Bredell
md Charles Previn   m Frank
Skinner

Ole Olsen, Chic Johnson, Hugh Herbert, Martha Raye, Mischa Auer, Robert Paige, Jane Frazee, Shemp Howard, Elisha Cook Jnr, Richard Lane

'Alive with good gags, mechanical surprise effects, and novelty touches.'
– CEA Report

† The Frankenstein monster and Man Who Falls into Pool were played by Dale Van Sickel.

Help!*

GB 1965 92m Eastmancolor
UA/Walter Shenson/Suba Films
V, L

An oriental high priest chases the Beatles around the world because one of them has a sacred ring.

Exhausting attempt to outdo A Hard Day's Night in lunatic frenzy, which goes to prove that some talents work better on low budgets. The humour is a frantic cross between Hellzapoppin, the Goons, Bugs Bunny and the shade of Monty Python to come. It looks good but becomes too tiresome to entertain.

w Charles Wood, Marc Behm
d Dick Lester   ph David Watkin
m The Beatles   ad Ray Simm

The Beatles, Leo McKern, Eleanor Bron, Victor Spinetti

Helter Skelter

GB 1949 75m bw
GFD/Gainsborough (Anthony Darnborough)

An heiress with hiccups is helped by the staff of the BBC.

Scatty comedy which tries everything, from custard pies and guest stars to a clip from a silent Walter Forde comedy. It isn't the British *Hellzapoppin* it sets out to be, but hardened buffs will find it worth a look.

w Patrick Campbell   *d* Ralph Thomas   *ph* Jack Asher
m Francis Chagrin

Carol Marsh, David Tomlinson, Mervyn Johns, Peter Hammond, Jimmy Edwards, Richard Hearne, Jon Pertwee, Terry-Thomas

Her Alibi

US 1989 94m colour
Warner (Keith Barish)
V, L

A thriller writer provides a false alibi for a woman accused of murder.

A romantic comedy without laughs or much love.

w Charlie Peters   *d* Bruce Beresford   *ph* Freddie Francis
m Georges Delerue   *pd* Henry Bumstead   *ed* Anne Goursaud

Tom Selleck, Paulina Porizkova, William Daniels, James Farentino, Hurd Hatfield, Ronald Guttman, Victor Argo, Patrick Wayne, Tess Harper

'Lacking a script able to go beyond the obvious, and direction able to make up for the lack of wit and sophistication.' – *MFB*

Hercules in New York

US 1969 91m Eastmancolor
RAF Industries (Aubrey Wisberg)
aka: *Hercules Goes Bananas; Hercules – the Movie*

Hercules drops in on modern-day New York and becomes involved with wrestlers and gamblers.

Schwarzenegger's first film, a dim comedy – and one that no doubt returns to haunt him, particularly his dubbed all-American high tenor voice and the way his muscles do the acting.

w Aubrey Wisberg   *d* Arthur A. Seidelman   *ph* Leo Lebowitz
m John Balamos   *ad* Perry Watkins   *ed* Donald Finamore

Arnold Stang, Arnold Strong (Schwarzenegger), Deborah Loomis, James Karen, Ernest Graves, Tanny McDonald, Tania Elg, Michael Lipton

'Schwarzenegger as Herc wrestled with a man in a bear suit and when I tell you that the suit was a better actor you will have some conception.' – *Nancy Banks Smith, Guardian*

Here Come the Coeds

US 1945 88m bw
Universal (John Grant)

Janitors help to forestall a mortgage foreclosure on a college for women.

Routine star vehicle with few highlights.

w Arthur T. Horman, John Grant
d Jean Yarbrough   *ph* George Robinson   *m/ly* Jack Brooks, Edgar Fairchild

Bud Abbott, Lou Costello, Lon Chaney Jnr, Peggy Ryan, Martha

O'Driscoll, Donald Cook, June
Vincent, Charles Dingle

Here Come the Girls*
US   1953   78m   Technicolor
Paramount/Hope Enterprises (Paul Jones)
original title: *Champagne for Everybody*

In the nineties an ageing chorus boy
traps a mysterious murderer.

Spotty, ineptly titled star comedy with
music; in fact among the last of his
passable vehicles, with excellent
production backing.

w Edmund Hartmann, Hal Kanter
d Claude Binyon   *ph* Lionel
Lindon   *md* Lyn Murray   *ad* Hal
Pereira, Roland Anderson

Bob Hope, Rosemary Clooney, Tony
Martin, Arlene Dahl, Millard Mitchell,
Fred Clark, William Demarest, Robert
Strauss

Here Come the Huggetts*
GB   1948   93m   bw
Rank/Gainsborough (Betty Box)

A suburban family has its ups and
downs.

Cosy domestic comedy drama, a
presage of TV soap operas to come, or
Britain's answer to the Hardys,
depending how you look at it.
Tolerable at the time.

w Mabel and Denis Constanduros,
Muriel and Sydney Box, Peter
Rogers   *d* Ken Annakin   *ph* Reg
Wyer   *m* Anthony Hopkins

Jack Warner, Kathleen Harrison, Jane
Hylton, Susan Shaw, Petula Clark,
Jimmy Hanley, David Tomlinson,
Diana Dors, Peter Hammond, John
Blythe

† The Huggetts had actually
originated in *Holiday Camp* the
previous year, and appeared again in

Vote for Huggett and *The Huggetts Abroad;*
Warner and Harrison became an
inseparable duo for many years.

Here Comes Mr Jordan***
US   1941   93m   bw
Columbia (Everett Riskin)
V, L

A prizefighter who is also an amateur
saxophonist crashes in his private
plane and goes to heaven by mistake:
he was supposed to survive and live
another forty years. Unfortunately
when he goes back for his body it has
been cremated, so he has to find
another one, recently deceased . . .

Weird heavenly fantasy which
succeeded because of its novelty and
because heaven in wartime was a
comforting vision. As a movie taken
on its own merits, it suffers from
illogicalities, a miscast star and a
wandering plot, but scene for scene
there is enough firmness and control
to make it memorable. It certainly had
many imitations, including *Angel on My
Shoulder*, *Down to Earth*, *A Guy Named
Joe*, *Heaven Only Knows*, *The Horn Blows
at Midnight* and *That's the Spirit.*

w Seton I. Miller, Sidney Buchman
play *Halfway to Heaven* by Harry
Segall   *d* Alexander Hall
ph Joseph Walker   *md* Morris
Stoloff   *m* Frederick Hollander

Robert Montgomery, Evelyn Keyes,
Rita Johnson, *Claude Rains*, James
Gleason, *Edward Everett Horton*, John
Emery, *Donald MacBride*, Halliwell
Hobbes, Don Costello

'There is something about this original
so sweet-spirited and earnest that it
transcends its plot devices and shines
through its comedic asides to become
a true morality play without once
becoming either preachy or
mawkish.' – *Kit Parker catalogue, 1980*

'Audiences loved this chunk of whimsy ... the slickly hammy Rains gives Mr Jordan a sinister gloss, as if he were involved in some heavenly racket, like smuggling Chinese.' – *Pauline Kael, 70s*

† Remade 1978 as *Heaven Can Wait.*

AA: original story (Harry Segall); script
AAN: best picture; Alexander Hall; Joseph Walker; Robert Montgomery; James Gleason

Here We Go Round the Mulberry Bush*
GB 1967 96m Technicolor
UA/Giant (Larry Kramer, Clive Donner)

A school-leaver is obsessed by sex and determines to lose his virginity.

Repetitive comedy which certainly opened new avenues in British humour and seemed pretty permissive at the time (pre-*Graduate*). In itself, however, more modish than sympathetic.

w Hunter Davies, Larry Kramer
novel Hunter Davies   *d* Clive Donner   *ph* Alex Thomson
m various groups

Barry Evans, Judy Geeson, Angela Scoular, Adrienne Posta, Sheila White, Vanessa Howard, Denholm Elliott, Maxine Audley, Moyra Fraser, Michael Bates

'The only incongruity is that it should have been made by adults, so completely does it enter into the teenager's view of himself.' – *MFB*

Hero at Large
US 1980 98m Metrocolor
MGM (Stephen Freedman)
V

An actor playing Captain Avenger accidentally becomes a real-life hero, but his fans turn against him when they find he's just an ordinary guy.

Muddled satirical comedy-melodrama with too many pauses for love interest.

w A. J. Carothers   *d* Martin Davidson

John Ritter, Anne Archer, Bert Convy, Kevin McCarthy, Harry Bellaver

Hi, Mom!*
US 1969 86m Movielab
West End Films

Adventures of a young porno film maker and of the eccentrics who live in the same building.

Busy comedy of the drop-out life, full of random satirical jabs and *hommages* to other film makers.

wd Brian de Palma

Robert de Niro, Allen Garfield, Gerrit Graham, Jennifer Salt

High Anxiety*
US 1977 94m DeLuxe
TCF/Crossbow (Mel Brooks)
V, L

A psychologist taking up a new appointment suspects that his predecessor may have been murdered.

Elementary but somewhat entertaining spoof of various Hitchcock movies (*Spellbound, North by Northwest, The Birds*), with the level of humour as unsubtle and lavatorial as one has come to expect.

w Mel Brooks, Ron Clark, Rudy DeLuca, Barry Levinson   *d* Mel Brooks   *ph* Paul Lohmann
m John Morris

Mel Brooks, Madeline Kahn, Cloris

Leachman, Harvey Korman, Ron Carey, Howard Morris, Dick Van Patten

'It basically just shambles along, in search of the next big set-piece to send up.' – *Richard Combs, MFB*
'Brooks has no idea of how to build a sequence, how to tell a story, when to leave well enough (or ill enough) alone.' – *Philip French, Observer*
'A child's idea of satire – imitations, with a comic hat and a leer.' – *New Yorker*

High Hopes
GB   1988   112m   Eastmancolor
Palace/Portman/Film Four International/
    British Screen (Simon Channing-Williams,
    Victor Glynn)
V

A family of contrasting types gather to celebrate their mother's birthday.

A comedy of caricatures.

wd Mike Leigh   *m* Andrew Dixon   *pd* Diana Charnley
ed Jon Gregory

Philip Davis, Ruth Sheen, Edna Dore, Philip Jackson, Heather Tobias, Lesley Manville, David Bamber, Jason Watkins, Judith Scott

High Season
GB   1987   92m   colour
Curzon/British Screen/Film Four/Michael
    White/Hemdale (Clare Downs)
L

A female photographer meets strange friends in Rhodes.

Spies, thieves and tourists make an odd lightweight mixture in a movie best suited to TV.

w Mark and Clare Peploe   *d* Clare Peploe   *ph* Chris Menges
m Jason Osborn   *pd* Andrew McAlpine   *ed* Gabriella Cristiani

Jacqueline Bisset, James Fox, Irene Papas, Sebastian Shaw, Kenneth Branagh, Robert Stephens

High Spirits
GB   1988   96m   colour
Palace/Vision PDG (Stephen Woolley,
    David Saunders)
V, L

In order to attract tourists, the owner of an Irish castle fakes ghosts and then discovers that he has summoned up some real ones.

Insubstantial comedy that lurches unsuccessfully into supernatural romance.

wd Neil Jordan   *ph* Alex Thomson   *m* George Fenton
pd Alex Furst   *ed* Michael Bradsell

Peter O'Toole, Donald McCann, Mary Koughlan, Liz Smith, Steve Guttenberg, Beverly D'Angelo, Jennifer Tilly, Peter Gallagher, Daryl Hannah, Liam Neeson, Ray McAnally

Hips Hips Hooray
US   1934   68m   bw
RKO

Two salesmen pitch flavoured lipstick to a beauty parlour chain.

Tired star comedy.

w Harry Ruby, Bert Kalmar
d Mark Sandrich

Bert Wheeler, Robert Woolsey, Ruth Etting, Thelma Todd, Dorothy Lee, George Meeker

'Femme display chief asset.' – *Variety*

His Double Life*
US   1933   63m   bw
Paramount (Eddie Dowling)

A famous painter, when his valet dies, takes his identity.

Adequate transcription of a novel later redone as *Holy Matrimony*.

w Arthur Ellis   *novel* Arnold Bennett   *d* Arthur Hopkins

Roland Young, Lillian Gish, Lumsden Hare, Lucy Beaumont

'Pleasant little film; big grosses unlikely.' – *Variety*

His Girl Friday**
US   1940   92m   bw
Columbia (Howard Hawks)

A remake of *The Front Page* (qv), with Hildy Johnson turned into a woman.

Frantic, hilarious black farce with all participants at their best; possibly the fastest comedy ever filmed, and one of the funniest.

w *Charles Lederer   play* The Front Page *by* Charles MacArthur, Ben Hecht   *d* *Howard Hawks*
ph Joseph Walker   *md* Morris Stoloff   *m* Sydney Cutner

Rosalind Russell, Cary Grant, Ralph Bellamy, Gene Lockhart, Porter Hall, *Ernest Truex*, Cliff Edwards, *Clarence Kolb*, Roscoe Karns, *Frank Jenks*, Abner Biberman, Frank Orth, John Qualen, Helen Mack, *Billy Gilbert*, Alma Kruger

'The kind of terrific verbal slam-bang that has vanished from current film-making.' – *New Yorker, 1975*
'One of the fastest of all movies, from line to line and from gag to gag.' – *Manny Farber, 1971*
'Overlapping dialogue carries the movie along at breakneck speed; word gags take the place of the sight gags of silent comedy, as this vanished race of brittle, cynical, childish people rush around on corrupt errands.' – *Pauline Kael, 1968*
'The main trouble is that when they made *The Front Page* the first time, it stayed made.' – *Otis Ferguson*

† The Rosalind Russell role had first been turned down by Jean Arthur, Ginger Rogers, Claudette Colbert and Irene Dunne.

The History of Mr Polly*
GB   1949   94m   bw
GFD/Two Cities (John Mills)

A draper's assistant buys a small shop but tires of his nagging wife and decides the time has come for a change.

Patchy but generally amusing version of a popular comic novel, very English and rather appealingly done.

w Anthony Pelissier   *novel* H. G. Wells   *d* *Anthony Pelissier*
ph Desmond Dickinson   *m* William Alwyn

John Mills, Sally Ann Howes, Megs Jenkins, Finlay Currie, Betty Ann Davies, Edward Chapman

History of the World Part One
US   1981   92m   DeLuxe
Panavision
Brooksfilms (Mel Brooks)
V, L

Episodes from world history are presented with the author's usual lack of taste or wit: a woeful collection of schoolboy scatology.

wd Mel Brooks   *ph* Woody Omens, Paul Wilson   *m* John Morris

Mel Brooks, Dom De Luise, Madeline Kahn, Cloris Leachman, Harvey Korman, Ron Carey, Sid Caesar, Pamela Stephenson, Henny Youngman

'Most of the time it's just expensive sets sitting around waiting for Brooks to do something funny in front of them.' – *Roger Ebert*

Hobson's Choice***

GB 1953 107m bw
British Lion/London (Norman Spencer)
V

In the 1890s a tyrannical Lancashire
bootmaker is brought to heel by his
plain-speaking daughter and her
simple-minded husband.

Brilliantly played version of a
famous working-class comedy,
memorably set and photographed;
one regrets only the slight
decline of the predictable
third act.

w Norman Spencer, Wynard
Browne   play Harold Brighouse
d David Lean   ph Jack Hildyard
m Malcolm Arnold   ad Wilfrid
Shingleton

Charles Laughton, Brenda de Banzie,
John Mills, Richard Wattis, Helen
Haye, Daphne Anderson, Prunella
Scales

† Previously filmed in 1931 by
Thomas Bentley for BIP from a
screenplay by Frank Launder, with
James Harcourt, Viola Lyel and Frank
Pettingell.

Hog Wild***

US 1930 20m bw
Hal Roach
V

Stan helps Ollie to put a radio aerial
on the roof of his house.

Brilliantly sustained slapstick makes
this one of the best star comedies of
Laurel and Hardy.

w H. M. Walker, Leo McCarey
d James Parrott   ph George
Stevens   ed Richard Currier

Laurel and Hardy, Fay Holderness,
Dorothy Granger

Hold That Blonde

US 1945 75m bw
Paramount (Paul Jones)

A psychiatrist suggests that romance
may cure a kleptomaniac, but the
patient unfortunately chooses a jewel
thief.

Thin comedy which erupts into frantic
farce, with some energetic slapstick
and a Harold Lloyd style finale.

w Walter de Leon, Earl Baldwin, E.
Edwin Moran   d George
Marshall   ph Daniel L. Fapp
m Werner Heymann

Eddie Bracken, Veronica Lake, Albert
Dekker, Frank Fenton, George Zucco,
Donald MacBride, Norma Varden,
Willie Best

Hold That Ghost*

US 1941 86m bw
Universal (Burt Kelly, Glenn Tryon)

A group of strangers are stranded in
an apparently haunted house.

Long thought of as Abbott and
Costello's best comedy, this now seems
pretty strained and slow to start, but
it has its classic moments.

w Robert Lees, Fred Rinaldo, John
Grant   d Arthur Lubin
ph Elwood Bredell, Joe Valentine
m Hans Salter

Bud Abbott, Lou Costello, Joan Davis, the
Andrews Sisters, Richard Carlson, Ted
Lewis and his band, Evelyn Ankers,
Marc Lawrence, Mischa Auer

A Hole in the Head*

US 1959 120m DeLuxe
    Cinemascope
UA/Sincap (Frank Sinatra)

A Miami hotelier is threatened with
foreclosure and tries to raise the
money from his provident elder
brother.

Easy-going comedy without much point, but various amusing facets artfully deployed.

w Arnold Shulman   play Arnold Shulman   d Frank Capra
ph William H. Daniels   m Nelson Riddle

Frank Sinatra, Edward G. Robinson, Eleanor Parker, Eddie Hodges, Carolyn Jones, Thelma Ritter, Keenan Wynn, Joi Lansing

AA: song 'High Hopes' (m Jimmy Van Heusen, ly Sammy Cahn)

Holiday*
US   1930   99m   bw
Pathe (E. B. Derr)

A bright-minded rich girl steals her sister's fiancé, a struggling young lawyer.

Competent early talkie version of a hit play.

w Horace Jackson   play Philip Barry   d Edward H. Griffith
ph Norbert Brodine   m Josiah Zuro

Ann Harding, Robert Ames, Mary Astor, Edward Everett Horton, Hedda Hopper, Monroe Owsley, William Holden

'A comedy of wide appeal in a finished style.' – Variety
AAN: Horace Jackson; Ann Harding

'So daring – so tender – so human – so true – that everyone in love will want to see it!'

Holiday***
US   1938   93m   bw
Columbia (Everett Riskin)
V, L
GB titles: Free to Live; Unconventional Linda

Elegant, highly successful remake of the above; still a stage play on film,
but subtly devised to make the very most of the lines and performances.

w Donald Ogden Stewart   d George Cukor   ph Franz Planer
m Sidney Cutner   ad Stephen Goosson, Lionel Banks

Katharine Hepburn, Cary Grant, Doris Nolan, Edward Everett Horton (same role), Ruth Donnelly, Lew Ayres, Henry Kolker, Binnie Barnes

'Corking comedy . . . exhibitors will pencil in some extra days.' – Variety
'The comedy is full of the best of humour, edged with pathos never allowed to drop into sentimentality. It is played with the greatest cheerfulness and a winning skill.' – Arthur Pollock, Brooklyn Daily Eagle
'I suppose actually it is a neat and sometimes elegant job, but under its surface of too much brightness and too many words it seems so deadly bored and weary. Hell, save your money and yawn at home.' – Otis Ferguson
'Played with the greatest cheerfulness and a winning skill.' – Brooklyn Daily Eagle
AAN: art direction

Holiday Camp*
GB   1947   97m   bw
GFD/Gainsborough (Sydney Box)

At a summer holiday camp, a murderer on the prowl affects people's enjoyment in various ways.

Seminal compendium comedy drama, a bore in itself but establishing several post-war norms of the British cinema, including the Huggetts.

w Muriel and Sidney Box, Ted Willis, Peter Rogers, Mabel and Denis Constanduros   story Godfrey Winn   d Ken Annakin   ph Jack Cox   m Bob Busby

Jack Warner, Kathleen Harrison, Flora Robson, Dennis Price, Hazel Court, Emrys Jones, Yvonne Owen, Esmond Knight, Jimmy Hanley, Peter Hammond, Esma Cannon, John Blythe, Susan Shaw

'It is real – and true – and it will be a smash at the box office.' – *Sunday Chronicle*

Hollywood Boulevard
US 1977 83m colour
New World (Jon Davison)

An inexperienced actress goes to work for makers of low-budget exploitation movies with violent results.

Bizarre action film spoof, with dialogue and a slim narrative added to action sequences taken from previous Roger Corman movies; it will mainly interest fans of Corman or of the other talents involved.

w Patrick Hobby   *d* Allan Arkush, Joe Dante   *ph* Jamie Anderson
m Andrew Stein   *ad* Jack DeWolfe   *ed* Allan Arkush, Joe Dante, Amy Jones

Candice Rialson, Mary Woronov, Rita George, Jeffrey Kramer, Dick Miller, Paul Bartel, Jonathan Kaplan, Charles B. Griffith

† The film began as a bet which Davison made with Roger Corman that he could produce a picture for $90,000, which was less than any other New World movie, providing he could use stock footage from other Corman productions. It was shot in ten days at a cost of $80,000.

Hollywood or Bust
US 1956 95m Technicolor
  Vistavision
Paramount/Hal Wallis

Two halfwits win a car and drive across country to Hollywood.

Dopey comedy with more misses than hits; the last film of Martin and Lewis as a team.

w Erna Lazarus   *d* Frank Tashlin   *ph* Daniel Fapp
m Walter Scharf

Dean Martin, Jerry Lewis, Pat Crowley, Maxie Rosenbloom, Anita Ekberg

Hollywood Party
US 1934 68m bw/Technicolor
  sequence
MGM (Harry Rapf, Howard Dietz)

A mad Russian throws a party which ends in disaster.

Dismal 'all-star' comedy relieved by guest appearances.

w Howard Dietz, Arthur Kober
d (uncredited) Richard Boleslawski, Allan Dwan, Roy Rowland, George Stevens   *ph* James Wong Howe
m/ly Rodgers, Hart and others
ed George Boemier

Laurel and Hardy, Jimmy Durante, Lupe Velez, Charles Butterworth, Eddie Quillan, Ted Healy and the Stooges, Polly Moran

'A big short . . . averagely passable screen divertissement.' – *Variety*
'The picture hardly rates the time and money that MGM has expended.' – *Hollywood Reporter*

† The film was dogged by disaster and was in production for a year. At least eight directors were involved, but no one wanted a credit on the finished film.

Hollywood Shuffle*

US   1987   82m   colour
Samuel Goldwyn Company/Conquering
   Unicorn (Robert Townsend)

A young black actor looks for work in
films.

A loosely connected series of satirical
sketches that provide fun at the
expense of current movie genres and
the stereotyping of black actors as
gangsters or pimps.

w Robert Townsend, Keenen Ivory
Wayans   d Robert Townsend
ph Peter Deming   m Patrice
Rushen, Udi Harpaz   ad Melba
Katzman Farquhar   ed W. O.
Garrett

Robert Townsend, Anne-Marie
Johnson, Starletta Dupois, Helen
Martin, Craigus R. Johnson, John
Witherspoon, Keenen Ivory Wayans,
Jimmy Woodard

'Scattershot humor misses as much as
it hits.' – Variety

Holy Matrimony*

US   1943   87m   bw
TCF (Nunnally Johnson)

A famous painter comes back from
exile for a knighthood; but when his
valet dies of pneumonia, has him
buried as himself in Westminster
Abbey.

Slightly stilted but generally warmly
amusing version of a favourite novel,
with excellent star performances.

w Nunnally Johnson   novel Buried
Alive by Arnold Bennett   d John
Stahl   ph Lucien Ballard   m Cyril
Mockridge

Monty Woolley, Gracie Fields, Laird
Cregar, Eric Blore, Una O'Connor

'A pleasant hour and a half, very well
produced and acted.' – James Agate
AAN: Nunnally Johnson

Home Alone*

US   1990   102m   DeLuxe
TCF/John Hughes
V, L

A young boy, inadvertently left
behind at Christmas when his
parents go on holiday, foils some inept
house-breakers.

Swinging uneasily between heavy-
handed slapstick and sentimental
domestic comedy, this unpretentious
movie was, inexplicably, the biggest
box-office success of 1990.

w John Hughes   d Chris
Columbus   ph Julio Macat
m John Williams   pd John
Muto   ed Raja Gosnell

Macaulay Culkin, Joe Pesci, Daniel
Stern, Catherine O'Hara, John Heard,
Roberts Blossom, John Candy

'What is astonishing is that a cute
family comedy which takes over an
hour really to get going should have
provoked such an enthusiastic
audience response and gained such a
phenomenal word-of-mouth
reputation.' – MFB
AAN: John Williams; best song
'Somewhere In My Memory'

'He's Up Past His Bedtime In The City That
Never Sleeps!'

Home Alone 2: Lost in New York

US   1992   120m   colour
TCF (John Hughes)

Separated from his family after
boarding the wrong plane, a young boy
alone in New York thwarts the same
two robbers he met at home.

Virtually a re-make of the first film,
though the humour has a far more
unpleasantly sadistic edge to it. This
undistinguished comedy was among
the biggest box-office successes of
1992.

w John Hughes   *d* Chris
Columbus   *ph* Julio Macat
m John Williams   *pd* Sandy
Veneziano   *ed* Raja Gosnell

Macaulay Culkin, Joe Pesci, Daniel
Stern, Catherine O'Hara, John
Heard, Devin Ratray, Hillary Wolf,
Maureen Elisabeth Shay, Brenda
Fricker

'An interesting example of formula
film-making, making use of a higher
budget than before but even lower
expectations.' – *Derek Malcolm,
Guardian*

Honey, I Blew Up the Kid
US   1992   89m   Technicolor
Buena Vista/Walt Disney (Dawn Steel,
   Edward S. Feldman)

An inventor inadvertently exposes his
two-year-old son to a ray that causes
him to grow to 50 feet tall.

Predictable and dull comedy that fails
to develop its central notion in
interesting ways.

w Thom Eberhardt, Peter Elbling,
Garry Goodrow   *d* Randal
Kleiser   *ph* John Hora   *m* Bruce
Broughton   *pd* Leslie Dilley
ed Michael A. Stevenson, Harry
Hitner, Tina Hirsch

Rick Moranis, Marcia Strassman,
Robert Oliveri, Daniel Shalikar,
Joshua Shalikar, Lloyd Bridges, John
Shea, Keri Russell, Ron Canada, Amy
O'Neill

'A romp, escapism at its breeziest.' –
Variety
'Proclaims in its every move that
particular blend of crassness and
technical expertise that is so often
used for Hollywood's more down-
market popular successes.' – *Derek
Malcolm, Guardian*

Honey, I Shrunk the Kids*
US   1989   93m   Metrocolor
Warner/Walt Disney/Doric (Penny
   Finkelman Cox)
V

An inventor inadvertently
miniaturises his children and dumps
them in the garden.

Amusing comedy with Disney's
winsomeness kept at bay for the most
part, apart from a brave little ant.

w Ed Naha, Tom Schulman
story Stuart Gordon, Brian Yuzna, Ed
Naha   *d* Joe Johnston   *ph* Hiro
Narita   *pd* Gregg Fonseca
ed Michael A. Stevenson

Rick Moranis, Matt Frewer, Marcia
Strassman, Kristine Sutherland,
Thomas Brown, Jared Rushton, Amy
O'Neil, Robert Oliveri, Carl Steven

'You are cordially invited to a perfectly
elegant case of murder!'
The Honey Pot*
US   1966   150m   Technicolor
UA/Famous Artists (Charles K. Feldman)
   (Joseph L. Mankiewicz)

A millionaire pretends to be dying in
order to trick three former mistresses;
but one of them is murdered.

Uneasy variation, via two other
variations, on Ben Jonson's *Volpone;*
despite bright moments, the mood is
fatally inconsistent, and a cloud of
pseudo-sophisticated dialogue hangs
over the whole thing like a pall.

wd Joseph L. Mankiewicz   *play Mr
Fox of Venice* by Frederick Knott
novel The Evil of the Day by Thomas
Sterling   *ph* Gianni di Venanzo
m John Addison   *pd* John DeCuir

Rex Harrison, Susan Hayward, *Maggie
Smith*, Cliff Robertson, Capucine, Edie
Adams, Adolfo Celi, Herschel
Bernardi

'One of the talkiest pictures ever made.' – *Stephen Farber*

Honeymoon Hotel

US 1964 98m Metrocolor Cinemascope
MGM/Avon (Lawrence Weingarten)

A jilted swain goes off with a philandering friend on what was to have been his honeymoon trip . . . only to be followed by his repentant fiancée.

Rather unattractive farce with insufficient funny moments.

w R. S. Allen, Harvey Bulloch
d Henry Levin   ph Harold Lipstein   m Walter Scharf

Nancy Kwan, Robert Goulet, Robert Morse, Jill St John, Elsa Lanchester, Keenan Wynn

'A comedy about one bride, two grooms, and 34 flying Elvises.'

Honeymoon in Vegas*

US 1992 96m Technicolor
First Independent/Castle Rock/New Line/Lobell/Bergman (Mike Lobell)

In a poker game a Las Vegas gambler wins a weekend with the fiancée of a New York detective.

Moderately enjoyable comedy, with an amusing running gag about Elvis impersonators.

wd Andrew Bergman   ph William A. Fraker   m David Newman
pd William A. Elliott   ed Barry Malkin

James Caan, Nicolas Cage, Sarah Jessica Parker, Pat Morita, Johnny Williams, Anne Bancroft, Peter Boyle

'A virtually nonstop scream of benign delirium, pop entertainment as revivifying as anything you're likely to see this year.' – *Vincent Canby, New York Times*
'A very good comedy indeed, a dynamite throwback to those 40s screwball numbers.' – *Jeff Dawson, Empire*

Honky Tonk Freeway

US 1981 107m Technicolor
EMI/Kendon/HTF Company (Don Boyd, Howard W. Koch Jnr)
V

The mayor of a small Florida resort town has it painted pink to attract tourists . . . but too many of the wrong kind come in.

Zany farce, rather like It's a Mad Mad Mad Mad World without a proper hook to the story. Not an audience-pleaser, and very expensive.

w Edward Clinton   d John Schlesinger   ph John Bailey
m George Martin, Elmer Bernstein

William Devane, Beau Bridges, Teri Garr, Beverly D'Angelo, Hume Cronyn, Jessica Tandy, Howard Hesseman, Geraldine Page, George Dzundza

'A shambles, and a more convincing one than the half-hearted affair which brings it to a close.' – *Richard Combs, MFB*
'A film for "now" which seems almost endearingly bereft of any real ideas about the messed-up contemporary world it inhabits.' – *Guardian*

Hook Line and Sinker

US 1930 72m bw
RKO
L

Two insurance agents run a derelict hotel.

Feeble comedy vehicle.

w Tim Whelan, Ralph Spence
d Eddie Cline

Bert Wheeler, Robert Woolsey, Hugh
Herbert, Dorothy Lee, Jobyna
Howland, Ralf Harolde

'Will tickle most in those spots where
the price is least.' – *Variety*

Hook, Line and Sinker
US   1968   92m   Technicolor
Columbia/Jerry Lewis

A salesman who thinks he is dying
goes on a spending spree; when he
learns the truth, he has to disappear
because of his huge debts.

Miserable comedy with frantic
slapstick interludes. The plot might
have served Preston Sturges.

w Rod Amateau   d George
Marshall   ph W. Wallace Kelley
m Dick Stabile

Jerry Lewis, Peter Lawford, Anne
Francis, Pedro Gonzales Gonzales

The Hoosegow**
US   1929   20m   bw
Hal Roach

Stan and Ollie, in prison, contrive to
fell a tree on the cook's tent and to
smother the governor in boiled rice.

Splendid slapstick leading up to one
of their best tit-for-tat routines.

w Leo McCarey, H. M. Walker
d James Parrott   ph George Stevens,
Len Powers, Glenn Robert
Kershner   ed Richard Currier

Laurel and Hardy, James Finlayson,
Tiny Sandford

Hoots Mon*
GB   1939   77m   bw
Warner

A cockney comedian starts a

popularity contest with a female
impressionist.

Tolerable comedy whose value is that
it preserves, albeit in cleaned-up
form, portions of Max Miller's variety
act. Florence Desmond isn't bad either.

w Roy William Neill, Jack Henley,
John Dighton   d Roy William
Neill   ph Basil Emmott
md Bretton Byrd   ad Norman
Arnold   ed Leslie Norman

Florence Desmond, Max Miller, Hal
Walters, Davina Craig, Garry Marsh

The Horn Blows at Midnight*
US   1945   80m   bw
Warner (Mark Hellinger)

An angel is sent to earth to destroy
the planet with Gabriel's horn.

Wacky comedy inspired by *Here Comes
Mr Jordan*, but on a broader slapstick
level; much better than its star always
pretended.

w Sam Hellman, James V. Kern
d Raoul Walsh   ph Sid Hickox
m Franz Waxman

Jack Benny, Alexis Smith, Dolores
Moran, Allyn Joslyn, Guy Kibbee,
Reginald Gardiner, *Franklin Pangborn*,
John Alexander, Margaret Dumont

'A scandalous record of low Marx at
college – or life among the thirsty co-eds!'
Horse Feathers***
US   1932   69m   bw
Paramount (Herman J. Mankiewicz)

A college needs to win at football, and
its corrupt new president knows just
how to do it.

Possibly the Marxes' wildest yet most
streamlined kaleidoscope of high jinks
and irreverence, with at least one
bright gag or line to the minute and

lively musical interludes to boot. A classic of zany comedy.

w Bert Kalmar, Harry Ruby, S. J. Perelman, Will B. Johnstone
d Norman Z. McLeod   ph Ray June   m/ly Bert Kalmar, Harry Ruby

Groucho, Chico, Harpo, Zeppo, Thelma Todd, Robert Greig

GROUCHO: 'You have the brain of a four-year-old child, and I'll bet he was glad to get rid of it.'

CHICO: 'There's a man outside with a big black moustache.'

GROUCHO: 'Tell him I've got one.'

GROUCHO (to Zeppo): 'You're a disgrace to our family name of Wagstaff, if such a thing is possible.'

GROUCHO:
'For years before my son was born
I used to yell from night till morn
Whatever it is – I'm against it!
And I've been yelling since I first commenced
it – I'm against it!'

'The current Marx comedy is the funniest talkie since the last Marx comedy, and the record it establishes is not likely to be disturbed until the next Marx comedy comes along. As for comparisons, I was too busy having a good time to make any.' – Philip K. Scheuer

The Horse's Mouth*
GB 1958 93m Technicolor
UA/Knightsbridge (John Bryan)

An obsessive painter is a liability to his friends.

Thin but fitfully amusing light study of a social outcast, with a background of London river and streets. Too slight for real success.

w Alec Guinness   novel Joyce Cary   d Ronald Neame   ph Arthur Ibbetson   m K. V. Jones from Prokofiev   paintings John Bratby

Alec Guinness, Kay Walsh, Renée Houston, Robert Coote, Arthur Macrae, Michael Gough, Ernest Thesiger

'Immensely and joyously successful at what it sets out to do.' – Evening Standard
'A work of genius.' – News of the World
AAN: Alec Guinness (as writer)

Hot Pursuit
US 1987 93m Metrocolor
Paramount/RKO (Theodore R. Parvin, Pierre David)

Delayed at the start of a Caribbean holiday, a student tries to catch up with his girlfriend and her family who have gone on ahead.

Predictable and uninteresting teen comedy that veers into unexpected and unnecessary violence at its climax.

w Stephen Lisberger, Steven Carabatsos   d Stephen Lisberger   ph Frank Tidy   m Rareview   pd William J. Creber   ed Mitchell Sinoway

John Cusack, Robert Loggia, Wendy Gazelle, Jerry Stiller, Monte Markham, Shelley Fabares

The Hot Rock***
US 1972 105m DeLuxe Panavision
TCF (Hal Landers, Bobby Roberts)
GB title: How to Steal a Diamond in Four Uneasy Lessons

Four crooks plan to rob the Brooklyn Museum of a priceless diamond.

Enjoyable variation on the caper theme, with relaxed comic performances and highly skilled technical back-up. It's refreshing to come across a film which hits its targets so precisely.

w William Goldman   novel Donald
E. Westlake   *d* Peter Yates   *ph* Ed
Brown   *m* Quincy Jones

Robert Redford, George Segal, Zero
Mostel, Paul Sand, Ron Leibman,
Moses Gunn, William Redfield

'A funny, fast-paced, inventive and
infinitely clever crime comedy, almost
as if *The French Connection* had been
remade as a piece of urban humour.'
– *Michael Korda*

'There's Something Funny In The Air.'
Hot Shots!
US   1991   85m   DeLuxe
TCF (Bill Badalato)
V

A young disturbed pilot joins an élite
group to take part in a raid on a nuclear
plant or, as secondary target, an
accordion factory.

A hit-and-miss send-up of *Top Gun*
and other Hollywood hits, in which
most of the targets are missed.

w Jim Abrahams, Pat Proft   *d* Jim
Abrahams   *ph* Bill Butler
m Sylvester Levay   *pd* William A.
Elliott   *ed* Jane Kurson, Eric Sears

Charlie Sheen, Cary Elwes, Valeria
Golino, Lloyd Bridges, Jon Cryer,
Kevin Dunn, Bill Irwin, William
O'Leary, Kristy Swanson, Efrem
Zimbalist Jnr

Hot Stuff
US   1979   91m   Metrocolor
Columbia/Rastar/Mort Engleberg
V, L

Members of a Burglary Task Force
need convictions, so they set up fences
in order to lure criminals, and are
embarrassed by the results.

Slightly unusual but rather frantically
assembled comedy which wears out its
welcome long before the end.

w Michael Kane, Donald E.
Westlake   *d* Dom DeLuise
ph James Pergola   *m* Patrick
Williams

Dom DeLuise, Suzanne Pleshette,
Ossie Davis, Jerry Reed, Luis Avalos,
Marc Lawrence

'Heavy farce in which a bright comedy
is struggling to escape.' – *Tom Milne,
MFB*

Hotel Paradiso*
US   1966   99m   Metrocolor
   Panavision
MGM (Peter Glenville)

Various romantic affairs come to a
head one evening at a seedy hotel.

A famous boulevard farce seems
jellied in aspic in this good-looking
but very flatly handled film version,
in which famous artists are left to
caper about on an unsuitable wide
screen with no help from the
director.

w Peter Glenville, Jean-Claude
Carrière   *play* Georges Feydeau
d Peter Glenville   *ph* Henri Decaë
m Laurence Rosenthal   *pd* François
de Lamothe

Alec Guinness, Gina Lollobrigida,
Robert Morley, Peggy Mount,
Douglas Byng, Akim Tamiroff,
Robertson Hare

The Hound of the Baskervilles
GB   1977   85m   Technicolor
Hemdale/Michael White Ltd (John
   Goldstone)

A pointless, pitiful and vulgar spoof of
an enjoyable original.

w Dudley Moore, Peter Cook, Paul
Morrissey   *d* Paul Morrissey
ph Dick Bush, John Wilcox
m Dudley Moore

Peter Cook (Sherlock Holmes), Dudley Moore (Watson), Denholm Elliott (Stapleton), Terry-Thomas (Mortimer), Joan Greenwood, Max Wall, Irene Handl, Kenneth Williams, Hugh Griffith, Roy Kinnear, Penelope Keith, Dana Gillespie, Prunella Scales, Jessie Matthews, Spike Milligan

House Calls*

US   1978   98m   Technicolor
Universal/Jennings Lang (Alex Winitsky, Arlene Sellers)
L

A middle-aged doctor finds himself widowed and seeks a new mate.

Spotty comedy which tries to combine conventional romantic spats with medical satire, and comes off only in fits and starts.

w Max Shulman, Julius J. Epstein, Alan Mandel, Charles Shyer
d Howard Zieff   ph David M. Walsh   m Henry Mancini

Walter Matthau, Glenda Jackson, Art Carney, Richard Benjamin, Candice Azzara, Thayer David, Dick O'Neill

Houseboat

US   1958   110m   Technicolor
   Vistavision
Paramount/Scribe (Jack Rose)
V, L

A widower with three children engages a maid who is really a socialite, and they all set up house on a boat.

Artificial sentimental comedy with A-1 credits but little style or bite.

w Melville Shavelson, Jack Rose
d Melville Shavelson   ph Ray June   m George Duning

Cary Grant, Sophia Loren, Martha Hyer, Eduardo Ciannelli, Harry Guardino

'The kind of picture to which you can take your stuffy maiden aunt, your wicked sophisticated uncle and your ten-year-old child, and they will all have a wonderful time.' – *Ruth Waterbury, Los Angeles Examiner*
AAN: script; song 'Almost In Your Arms' (*m/ly* Jay Livingston, Ray Evans)

The Housekeeper's Daughter*

US   1939   71m   bw
Hal Roach

A gangster's moll returns to mama for a visit and falls in love with the stuffy son of the household.

Zany crime farce which too often lets its zip fade, but atones in a crazy firework finale.

w Rian James, Gordon Douglas
novel Donald Henderson Clarke
d Hal Roach   ph Norbert Brodine   m Amedeo de Filippi

Joan Bennett, John Hubbard, Adolphe Menjou, William Gargan, George E. Stone, Peggy Wood, Donald Meek, Marc Lawrence, Lilian Bond, Victor Mature, Luis Alberni

'A smacko laugh generator due for profitable biz up and down the line.' – *Variety*

Housesitter

US   1992   102m   DeLuxe
UIP/Imagine/Universal (Brian Grazer)
V

After a one-night stand with an architect, a waitress decides to move into his new house, claiming to be his wife.

A farcical comedy that is too leisurely to provoke laughter.

w Mark Stein, Brian Grazer
d Frank Oz   ph John A. Alonzo

m Miles Goodman   *pd* Ida
Random   *ed* John Jympson

Steve Martin, Goldie Hawn, Dana
Delany, Julie Harris, Donald Moffat,
Peter MacNicol, Richard B. Shull,
Laurel Cronin

'A tediously unfunny screwball
comedy . . . a career misstep both for
Steve Martin and Goldie Hawn.' –
Variety

How I Got Into College
US   1989   89m   colour
TCF (Michael Shamberg)
V, L

Dim student applies to go to the same
difficult-to-enter college as the girl
he loves.

Mildy amusing teenage comedy.

w Terrel Seltzer   *d* Savage Steve
Holland   *m* Joseph Vitarelli
pd Ida Ransom   *ed* Sonya Sones
Tramer, Kaja Fehr

Anthony Edwards, Corey Parker, Lara
Flynn Boyle, Finn Carter, Charles
Rocket, Christopher Rydell, Brian-
Doyle Murray

How I Won the War
GB   1967   110m   Eastmancolor
UA/Petersham (Richard Lester)

During World War II an earnest
young man becomes an officer and
survives many tribulations including
the death of his comrades.

Appalling kaleidoscope of black
comedy and the director's own brand
of uncontrolled cinematic zaniness,
with echoes of *Candide* and *Oh What
a Lovely War!* Just the way to alienate
a paying audience.

w Charles Wood   *novel* Patrick
Ryan   *d* Richard Lester
ph David Watkin   *m* Ken Thorne

Michael Crawford, John Lennon, Roy
Kinnear, Lee Montague, Jack
McGowran, Michael Hordern, Jack
Hedley, Karl Michael Vogler, Ronald
Lacey, James Cossins, Alexander
Knox

'Pretentious tomfoolery.' – *John Simon*
'One feels that Lester has bitten off
more than he can chew . . . the ideas
misfire, lost somewhere between the
paper on which they were conceived
and the celluloid on which they
finally appear.' – *MFB*

How Sweet It Is*
US   1968   98m   Technicolor
  Panavision
Warner/Cherokee/National General
  (Garry Marshall, Jerry Belson)

Suspicious of their son's intentions
towards his girl friend on a European
holiday, a middle-aged American
couple decide to follow.

Good-looking, rather silly comedy,
plain spoken in the modern manner
but without much entertainment
value except when farce gets the upper
hand.

w Garry Marshall, Jerry Belson
novel The Girl in the Turquoise Bikini by
Muriel Resnik   *d* Jerry Paris
ph Lucien Ballard   *m* Pat Williams

James Garner, Debbie Reynolds,
Maurice Ronet, Paul Lynde, Marcel
Dalio, Terry-Thomas, Donald Losby,
Hilarie Thompson

'One of those slender marital farces in
which the behaviour of the adults is
consistently more juvenile than that
of the teenagers.' – *MFB*

How to Be Very Very Popular
US   1955   89m   DeLuxe
  Cinemascope
TCF (Nunnally Johnson)

Two belly dancers on the run from gangsters hide out in a co-ed college.

Wacky remake of *She Loves Me Not* (qv); tries hard for a vein of freewheeling lunacy but only occasionally achieves it. A few numbers might have helped.

wd Nunnally Johnson *ph* Milton Krasner *m* Cyril Mockridge

Betty Grable, Sheree North, *Charles Coburn*, Robert Cummings, Orson Bean, Fred Clark, Tommy Noonan

How to Commit Marriage
US 1969 98m Technicolor
Cinerama/Naho (Bill Lawrence)

A couple decide to divorce, with repercussions on their family and in-laws.

Tiresome generation-gap comedy.

w Ben Starr, Michael Kanin *d* Norman Panama *ph* Charles Lang *m* Joseph J. Lilley

Bob Hope, Jackie Gleason, Jane Wyman, Leslie Nielsen, Maureen Arthur, Paul Stewart, Tina Louise

How to Get Ahead In Advertising
GB 1989 94m colour
Virgin/HandMade Films (David Wimbury)

An advertising man, in revolt against salesmanship, grows a boil that turns into an alternative head.

Unsuccessful diatribe on the consumer society.

wd Bruce Robinson *ph* Peter Hannan *m* David Dundas, Rick Wentworth *pd* Michael Pickwood *ed* Alan Strachan

Richard E. Grant, Rachel Ward, Richard Wilson, Jacqueline Tong, John Shrapnel, Susan Wooldridge, Mick Ford, Jacqueline Pearce, Roddy Maude-Roxby

How to Marry a Millionaire**
US 1953 96m Technicolor
Cinemascope
TCF (Nunnally Johnson)
V, L

Three girls rent an expensive New York apartment and set out to trap millionaires.

Cinemascope's first attempt at modern comedy was not quite as disastrous as might have been expected, largely because of the expensiveness of everything and the several stars still brightly twinkling, but the handling of this variation on the old *Golddiggers* theme, while entirely amiable, is dramatically very slack.

w Nunnally Johnson *d* Jean Negulesco *ph* Joe MacDonald *md* Alfred Newman *m* Cyril Mockridge

Lauren Bacall, Marilyn Monroe, Betty Grable, *William Powell*, Cameron Mitchell, David Wayne, Rory Calhoun, Alex D'Arcy, Fred Clark

'Not only educational, but great fun.' – *Star*

† The film has an eight-minute pre-credits concert sequence, which is pretty unnerving when it unspools on TV.

'The last word in do-it-yourself!'
How to Murder a Rich Uncle
GB 1957 80m bw
Cinemascope
Columbia/Warwick (Ronald Kinnoch)

An impoverished nobleman decides to murder his rich old uncle.

Feebly-handled black comedy which

does not come off at all despite a highly talented cast.

w John Paxton   play Il Faut Tuer Julie by Didier Daix   d Nigel Patrick   ph Ted Moore

Nigel Patrick, Charles Coburn, *Katie Johnson*, Wendy Hiller, Anthony Newley, Athene Seyler, Michael Caine, Noel Hood, Kenneth Fortescue

How to Save a Marriage and Ruin Your Life

US   1968   102m   Technicolor Panavision
Columbia/Nob Hill (Stanley Shapiro)

An attorney takes it upon himself to convince his friend of the infidelity of the friend's mistress . . .

Tedious sex antics without any sex; a few smiles are not enough to endear it.

w Stanley Shapiro, Nate Monaster d Fielder Cook   ph Lee Garmes m Michel Legrand

Dean Martin, Eli Wallach, Stella Stevens, Anne Jackson, Betty Field, Jack Albertson, Katharine Bard

'Another variation on Hollywood's patent version of the Restoration comedy, which as usual abandons the lustiness of its 17th-century prototype in favour of guilt-ridden lechery and a fundamental respect for the married state.' – *MFB*

How to Steal a Million*

US   1966   127m   DeLuxe Panavision
TCF/World Wide (Fred Kohlmar)

The daughter of an art forger mistakenly involves a private detective in a robbery.

High-class but rather boring romantic comedy; the credits promise much but interest wanes quickly owing to uncertain handling.

w Harry Kurnitz   d William Wyler   ph Charles Lang m Johnny Williams

Audrey Hepburn, Peter O'Toole, Charles Boyer, Hugh Griffith, Eli Wallach, Fernand Gravet, Marcel Dalio

'Terribly wordy and slow . . . Wyler hasn't got the touch nowadays.' – *Sight and Sound*
'The picture isn't offensive, and it's handsome enough, but it's just blah.' – *Pauline Kael, New Yorker*

Hue and Cry***

GB   1946   82m   bw
Ealing (Michael Balcon)

East End boys discover that their favourite boys' paper is being used by crooks to pass information.

The first 'Ealing comedy' uses vivid London locations as background for a sturdy comic plot with a climax in which the criminals are rounded up by thousands of boys swarming over dockland.

w T. E. B. Clarke   d Charles Crichton   ph Douglas Slocombe, John Seaholme   m Georges Auric

Alastair Sim, Jack Warner, Harry Fowler, Valerie White, Frederick Piper

'Refreshing, bloodtingling and disarming.' – *Richard Winnington*

Hurry Up, or I'll Be 30*

US   1973   88m   colour
Avco Embassy (Joseph Jacoby)

A failure attempts to find success and love before he reaches the beginning of middle age.

Gentle and sometimes perceptive comedy of manners.

w Joseph Jacoby, David Wiltse
d Joseph Jacoby   ph Burleigh Wartes   m Stephen Lawrence
ed Stan Warnow

John Lefkowitz, Linda De Coff, Ronald Anton, Maureen Byrnes, Danny DeVito, David Kirk, Frank Quinn

'A comedy about love, death, and freedom!'

Husbands*
US   1970   154m   DeLuxe
Columbia/Faces Music Inc (Al Ruban)

Three married men, shocked by the death of their friend, impulsively get drunk, fly to London and set out on a weekend of dissipation.

Irritatingly rough hewn and insanely overlong, this half-improvised tragi-comedy forces three good actors to overplay embarrassingly; but its best moments are memorable.

wd John Cassavetes   ph Victor Kemper   m none

Peter Falk, John Cassavetes, Ben Gazzara

Husbands and Wives***
US   1992   108m   DuArt
Columbia TriStar/TriStar (Jack Rollins, Charles H. Joffe)

After their best friends announce that they are splitting up, a writer and his wife decide to separate and he becomes infatuated with a young student.

One of Allen's best films, a clever and insightful examination of the insecurities and often self-destructive behaviour of couples, though the nervy camera-work irritates.

wd Woody Allen   ph Carlo Di Palma   pd Santo Loquasto
ed Susan E. Morse

Woody Allen, *Judy Davis*, Mia Farrow, Juliette Lewis, Liam Neeson, Blythe Danner, Sydney Pollack, Lysette Anthony

'The thing that moviegoers will realize decades hence is that *Husbands and Wives* is a damn fine film.' – *Richard Corliss, Time*
'Rich in characterisation, waspishly witty and profound in its observations about the frailty and fallibilities of modern marriage.' – *Ian Johnstone, Sunday Times*
AAN: Judy Davis; Woody Allen (as writer)

I Hired a Contract Killer

Finland/Sweden 1990 79m Metrocolor

Electric/Contemporary/Villealfa/Swedish Film Institute (Aki Kaurismäki)

An unhappy man hires someone to kill him, and then decides he wants to live.

Lacklustre comedy.

wd Aki Kaurismäki *ph* Timo Salminen *pd* John Ebden *ed* Aki Kaurismäki

Jean-Pierre Léaud, Margi Clarke, Kenneth Colley, Trevor Bowen, Imogen Clare, Angela Walsh, Cyril Epstein, Nicky Tesco

I Love My Wife

US 1970 95m Technicolor

Universal (Robert Kaufman)

The affairs of a successful doctor with a guilt complex about sex.

Frantic, fashionable comedy drama with wildly erratic treatment and performances.

w Robert Kaufman *d* Mel Stuart *ph* Vilis Lapenieks *m* Lalo Schifrin

Elliott Gould, Brenda Vaccaro, Angel Tompkins

'A leer-laden, anti-feminist tract disguised as a comedy.' – *Judith Crist*

I Love You, Alice B. Toklas*

US 1968 93m Technicolor

Warner Seven Arts/Paul Mazursky, Larry Tucker

An asthmatic Los Angeles lawyer escapes his bullying fiancée by joining the flower people.

Quite amusing satirical farce about the dangers of marijuana, Gertrude Stein and Jewish mothers, thrown together with no great sense of style but achieving hilarious moments among the longueurs.

w Paul Mazursky, Larry Tucker *d* Hy Averback *ph* Philip Lathrop *m* Elmer Bernstein *pd* Pato Guzman

Peter Sellers, Jo Van Fleet, Joyce Van Patten, Leigh Taylor-Young, David Arkin, Herb Edelman

I Love You to Death

US 1990 97m Technicolor

Columbia TriStar/Chestnut Hill (Jeffrey Lurie, Ron Moler)

V, L

Discovering her husband's philandering, a wife decides to have him killed.

Black comedy that runs out of jokes.

w John Kostmayer *d* Lawrence Kasdan *ph* Owen Roizman *m* James Horner *pd* Lilly Kilvert *ed* Anne V. Coates

Kevin Kline, Tracey Ullman, Joan

Plowright, River Phoenix, William Hurt, Keanu Reeves, James Gammon, Jack Kehler, Victoria Jackson

'Over-the-top farce.' – *David Robinson, The Times*
'A stillborn attempt at black comedy that wastes considerable acting talent.' – *Variety*

'She knows all about love potions ... and lovely motions!'

I Married a Witch***
US 1942 82m bw
UA/Cinema Guild/René Clair

A Salem witch and her sorcerer father come back to haunt the descendant of the Puritan who had them burned.

Delightful romantic comedy fantasy which shows all concerned at the top of their form. Hollywood moonshine, impeccably distilled.

w Robert Pirosh, Marc Connelly novel The Passionate Witch by Thorne Smith *d René Clair ph* Ted Tetzlaff *m* Roy Webb

Fredric March, Veronica Lake, Cecil Kellaway, Robert Benchley, Susan Hayward, Elizabeth Patterson, Robert Warwick

'A delightful sense of oddity and enchantment.' – *New York World Telegram*
AAN: Roy Webb

I Married a Woman
US 1956 85m bw/colour
  sequence RKOscope
RKO

A nervous young advertising executive neglects his wife, who determines to make him jealous.

Simple-minded comedy tailored to unsympathetic stars.

w Goodman Ace *d* Hal Kanter

ph Lucien Ballard *m* Cyril Mockridge

George Gobel, Diana Dors, Adolphe Menjou, Jessie Royce Landis, Nita Talbot

I Met Him in Paris*
US 1937 86m bw
Paramount (Wesley Ruggles)

A fashion designer spends five years' savings on a fling in Paris and finds herself pursued to Switzerland by two philanderers.

Not very witty but likeable romantic comedy with polished performers near their best.

w Claude Binyon *d* Wesley Ruggles *ph* Leo Tover *md* Boris Morros *m* John Leopold

Claudette Colbert, Melvyn Douglas, Robert Young, Lee Bowman, Mona Barrie

'A money picture ... laughs are piled on laughs.' – *Variety*
'At least half the footage is a perfect scream, and if you miss it you are an old sobersides, and who cares.' – *Otis Ferguson*

I Ought to Be in Pictures*
US 1982 107m DeLuxe
TCF (Herbert Ross, Neil Simon)

A young actress hitch-hikes to Hollywood to break into pictures and also to see her estranged scriptwriter father.

Fairly agreeable comedy-drama in the Neil Simon manner, with the studio background an extra plus.

w Neil Simon *play* Neil Simon *d* Herbert Ross *ph* David M. Walsh *m* Marvin Hamlisch *pd* Albert Brenner

Walter Matthau, Ann-Margret, Dinah Manoff, Lance Guest, Lewis Smith

I Wanna Hold Your Hand
US 1978 104m Technicolor
Universal/Steven Spielberg (Tamara Asseyev, Alex Rose)

A day in 1964 finds assorted New Jersey teenagers eagerly awaiting the Beatles' appearance on the Ed Sullivan Show.

Modest period comedy utilizing fresh young talent.

w Robert Zemeckis, Bob Gale
d Robert Zemeckis   ph Donald M. Morgan   m Meredith Willson

Nancy Allen, Bobby diCicco, Marc McClure, Susan Kendall Newman

I Was a Male War Bride**
US 1949 105m bw
TCF (Sol C. Siegel)
GB title: You Can't Sleep Here

A WAC in Europe marries a French officer and can't get him home.

High-spirited farce against realistic backgrounds of war-torn Europe, which scarcely accord with Cary Grant's pretending to be a Frenchman (and later a Frenchwoman). Funny, though.

w Charles Lederer, Hagar Wilde, Leonard Spigelgass   d Howard Hawks   ph Norbert Brodine, Osmond Borradaile   md Lionel Newman   m Cyril Mockridge

Cary Grant, Ann Sheridan, Marion Marshall, Randy Stuart

'It is excellent light entertainment but it is not likely to appeal to the prudish and some discretion should be exercised in booking it.' – CEA Film Report

I Will . . . I Will . . . for Now
US 1975 108m Technicolor
Brut (C. O. Erickson)

Divorcees with sex problems eventually get together again.

Witless soft-core farrago of coy jokes, as clumsy and unappealing as its title.

w Norman Panama, Albert E. Lewin   d Norman Panama
ph John A. Alonzo   m John Cameron   pd Fernando Carrere

Elliott Gould, Diane Keaton, Paul Sorvino, Victoria Principal, Warren Berlinger, Candy Clark, Robert Alda

The Icicle Thief**
Italy 1989 85m colour
Metro/Bambú/Reitalia (Ernesto Di Sarro)
V, L
original title: Ladri Di Saponette

Watching the television screening of his new film, a director enters the movie when he discovers his characters are changing their lines and leaving the action to appear in commercials.

Witty parody of neo-realistic cinema (the title recalls de Sica's classic Bicycle Thieves), commercialism and TV's treatment of films.

w Maurizio Nichetti, Mauro Monti   d Maurizio Nichetti
ph Maria Battistoni   m Manuel De Sica   pd Ada Legori   ed Rita Rossi, Anna Missoni

Maurizio Nichetti, Caterina Sylos Labini, Federico Rizzo, Renato Scarpa, Heidi Komarex, Carlina Torta, Massimo Sacilotto, Claudio G. Fava

'An unqualified treat . . . This sophisticated satire on the undifferentiated tap-flow of television is also a passionate declaration of love for the movies.' – *David Robinson, The Times*

If I Had a Million**
US 1932 88m bw
Paramount (Benjamin Glazer, Louis D. Lighton)

Various people each receive a million dollars from an eccentric who wants to test their reactions.

Interesting, dated multi-part comedy drama remembered chiefly for the brief sequence in which Laughton blows a raspberry to his boss and Fields chases road hogs. As an entertainment it's patchy, lacking an overall style.

w Claude Binyon, Whitney Bolton, Malcolm Stuart Boylan, John Bright, Sidney Buchman, Lester Cole, Isabel Dawn, Boyce DeGaw, Walter de Leon, Oliver H. P. Garrett, Harvey Gates, Grover Jones, Ernst Lubitsch, Lawton Mackaill, Joseph L. Mankiewicz, William Slavens McNutt, Seton I. Miller, Tiffany Thayer *story* Robert D. Andrews d Ernst Lubitsch, Norman Taurog, Stephen Roberts, Norman Z. McLeod, James Cruze, William A. Seiter, H. Bruce Humberstone

W. C. Fields, *Charles Laughton, May Robson,* Richard Bennett, Alison Skipworth, Gary Cooper, Wynne Gibson, George Raft, Jack Oakie, Frances Dee, Charles Ruggles, Mary Boland, Roscoe Karns, Gene Raymond, Lucien Littlefield

'Not uninteresting, but spotty in retrospect . . . the cinematic porridge is naturally replete with a diversity of seasonings.' – *Variety*
'It develops an obvious idea in an obvious way.' – *Time*

If It's Tuesday, This Must Be Belgium*
US 1969 98m DeLuxe
UA/Wolper (Stan Margulies)

A group of American tourists have various adventures during a lightning tour of Europe.

Amusing comedy which does pretty well by a good idea.

w David Shaw   d Mel Stuart
ph Vilis Lapenieks   m Walter Scharf

Suzanne Pleshette, Ian McShane, Mildred Natwick, Murray Hamilton, Michael Constantine, Sandy Baron, Norman Fell, Peggy Cass, Marty Ingels, Pamela Britton, Luke Halpin, Aubrey Morris

I'll Never Forget Whatshisname*
GB 1967 96m Technicolor
Universal/Scimitar (Michael Winner)

An advertising executive gives up power and money for integrity on a small literary magazine, but is won back by a mogul.

Vivid yet muddled tragi-comedy of the sixties, with splashes of sex and violence in trendy settings, a hero one really doesn't believe in, and a title which seems to have no meaning whatsoever.

w Peter Draper   d Michael Winner   ph Otto Heller
m Francis Lai

Oliver Reed, Orson Welles, Carol White, Harry Andrews, Michael Hordern, Wendy Craig, Marianne Faithfull

I'm All Right Jack***
GB 1959 104m bw
British Lion/Charter (Roy Boulting)

A world-innocent graduate takes a job in industry; by starting at the bottom he provokes a national strike.

Satirical farce which manages to hit most of its widespread targets and finds corruption in high, low and middle places. A not inaccurate picture of aspects of British life in the fifties, and a presage of the satire boom to come with *Beyond the Fringe* and *That Was the Week That Was*.

w Frank Harvey, John Boulting *novel Private Life* by Alan Hackney d John Boulting   *ph* Max Greene   *m* Ken Hare

Ian Carmichael, Peter Sellers, Irene Handl, Richard Attenborough, Terry-Thomas, Dennis Price, Margaret Rutherford, Liz Fraser, John Le Mesurier, Sam Kydd

I'm Gonna Git You, Sucka
US   1988   89m   DeLuxe
UIP/United Artists/Ivory Way/Raymond Katz/Front Films (Peter McCarthy, Carl Craig)

Black heroes are recruited to overthrow a white gangster.

Good-natured parody of black action movies such as *Shaft*.

wd Keenen Ivory Wayans   *ph* Tom Richmond   *m* David Michael Frank   *pd* Melba Farquhar, Catherine Hardwicke   *ed* Michael R. Miller

Keenen Ivory Wayans, Bernie Casey, Antonio Fargas, Steve James, Isaac Hayes, Jim Brown, Janet DuBois, Dawnn Lewis, John Vernon, Clu Gulagher

'Just a sensitive gal who climbed the ladder of success ... wrong by wrong! A story about a gal who lost her reputation – and never missed it!'

I'm No Angel***
US   1933   88m   bw
Paramount (William Le Baron)

A carnival dancer gets off a murder charge, moves into society and sues a man for breach of promise.

The star's most successful vehicle, credited with saving the fortunes of Paramount, remains a highly diverting side show with almost a laugh a minute. Released before the Legion of Decency was formed, it also contains some of Mae's fruitiest lines.

w Mae West   d Wesley Ruggles *ph* Leo Tover   *m/ly* Harvey Brooks, Gladys Dubois

Mae West, Edward Arnold, Cary Grant, Gregory Ratoff, Ralf Harolde, Kent Taylor, Gertrude Michael

'The most freewheeling of all Mae's screen vehicles, and the most satisfying of the lot.' – *James Robert Parish*
'A quality of balance and proportion which only the finest films attain.' – *Views and Reviews*

The Immigrant**
US   1917   20m approx   bw
    silent
Mutual

A penniless immigrant befriends a girl on the boat and later helps her in a café.

One of the most inventive early Chaplins, with touches of sentiment and social comment which for once only strengthen and do not antagonize.

wd Charles Chaplin   *ph* William C. Foster, Rollie Totheroh

Charles Chaplin, Edna Purviance, Albert Austin, Henry Bergman, Eric Campbell

'In its roughness and apparent simplicity it is as much a jewel as a story by O. Henry.' – *Photoplay*

The Importance of Being Earnest**
GB 1952 95m Technicolor
Rank/Javelin/Two Cities (Teddy Baird)

Two wealthy and eligible bachelors of
the 1890s have problems with their
marriage prospects.

Disappointingly stagey rendering
(when compared, say, with *Occupe-toi
d'Amélie*) of Britain's most
wondrously witty lighter-than-air
comedy of manners. As a record of a
theatrical performance, however, it is
valuable.

w Anthony Asquith   *play* Oscar
Wilde   d Anthony Asquith
ph Desmond Dickinson
m Benjamin Frankel   ad Carmen
Dillon

*Michael Redgrave, Michael Denison,
Edith Evans, Margaret Rutherford, Joan
Greenwood, Miles Malleson,* Dorothy
Tutin, Walter Hudd

'A more positive decision on style
should have been taken. A film of this
kind must be either an adaptation or
a piece of filmed theatre. This one,
being partially both, is not wholly
either.' – *Gavin Lambert*

The Impossible Years
US 1968 98m Metrocolor
  Panavision
MGM/Marten (Lawrence Weingarten)

A university psychiatrist has trouble
controlling his nubile 17-year-old
daughter.

Wacky farce which veers between the
tasteless and the ludicrous, and is
never more than momentarily
entertaining.

w George Wells   *play* Bob Fisher,
Arthur Marx   d Michael
Gordon   ph William H. Daniels
m Don Costa

David Niven, Lola Albright, Chad
Everett, Ozzie Nelson, Cristina Ferrare,
Don Beddoe

'A comedy of the generation gap
which didn't bridge it but fell right
into it.' – *Gerald Garrett*

In God We Trust
US 1980 97m Technicolor
Universal

A monk leaves his monastery to raise
some ready cash.

Dismal and tasteless attempt at
religious satire.

w Marty Feldman, Chris Allen
d Marty Feldman

Marty Feldman, Peter Boyle, Louise
Lasser, Richard Pryor, Wilfrid Hyde
White

'A rare achievement – a comedy with
no laughs. Its energy is prodigious.
But only rarely is it matched by
invention.' – *Variety*

The Incredible Shrinking Woman
US 1981 88m Technicolor
Universal/Lija (Hank Moonjean)

A housewife finds herself shrinking
after using a new perfume . . .

Hamfisted spoof on *The Incredible
Shrinking Man*, with flat jokes and
rather poor trick photography.

w Jane Wagner   d Joel
Schumacher   ph Bruce Logan
m Suzanne Ciani

Lily Tomlin, Charles Grodin, Ned
Beatty, Henry Gibson, Elizabeth
Wilson

'Leaden satire on consumerism . . .
even the special effects are barely
passable.' – *Time Out, 1984*

□ □

'Through one indiscretion ... a woman with a future became a woman with a past!'

Indiscreet

US   1931   92m   bw

Art Cinema Corporation (Joseph M. Schenck)

A socialite endangers her own romance when she tries to protect her younger sister.

Embarrassing and slow-moving farce which helped to kill its star's career.

w/songs Brown, de Sylva and Henderson   *d* Leo McCarey   *ph* Ray June, Gregg Toland   *m* Alfred Newman

Gloria Swanson, Ben Lyon, Monroe Owsley, Barbara Kent, Arthur Lake, Maude Eburne, Henry Kolker

'How dare he make love to me – and not be a married man!'

Indiscreet**

GB   1958   100m   Technicolor

Grandon (Stanley Donen)

V

An American diplomat in London falls in love with an actress but protects himself by saying he is married.

Affairs among the ultra rich, amusing when played by these stars but with imperfect production values which the alarmingly thin plot allows one too much time to consider.

w Norman Krasna   *play Kind Sir* by Norman Krasna   *d* Stanley Donen   *ph* Frederick A. Young   *m* Richard Bennett, Ken Jones

Cary Grant, Ingrid Bergman, Phyllis Calvert, Cecil Parker, David Kossoff, Megs Jenkins

'One is often on the point of being bored, but one never is, quite.' – *Richard Roud*

'A film to which you would not hesitate to take your jeweller, your architect, your home decorator, your dressmaker and your domestic staff.' – *Alexander Walker*

Inspector Clouseau

GB   1968   105m   Eastmancolor Panavision

UA/Mirisch (Lewis J. Rachmil)

V

An incompetent French policeman is brought to London to investigate the aftermath of the Great Train Robbery.

Tiresome charade with all the jokes well telegraphed, and a background of swinging London.

w Tom and Frank Waldman   *d* Bud Yorkin   *ph* Arthur Ibbetson   *m* Ken Thorne

Alan Arkin, Delia Boccardo, Frank Finlay, Patrick Cargill, Beryl Reid, Barry Foster

The Inspector General**

US   1949   101m   Technicolor

Warner (Jerry Wald)

aka: *Happy Times*

An assistant elixir salesman with a travelling fair is mistaken by villagers for the dreaded inspector general.

Well wrought but basically boring version of a basically boring classic farce full of rhubarbing Old Russians. Nice production and hilarious moments do not quite atone for the dull stretches.

w Philip Rapp, Harry Kurnitz   *play* Nikolai Gogol   *d* Henry Koster   *ph* Elwood Bredell   *m* John Green   *songs* Sylvia Fine   *ad* Robert Haas

Danny Kaye, Walter Slezak, Barbara Bates, Elsa Lanchester, Gene Lockhart, Alan Hale, Benny Baker, Walter Catlett

□ □

The Intelligence Men
GB   1965   104m   Eastmancolor
Rank/Hugh Stewart
US title: *Spylarks*

Two incompetent spies blunder
through a series of adventures.

Inept and rather embarrassing big-
screen debut for two excellent
television comedians.

w S. C. Green, R. M. Hills   *d* Robert
Asher   *ph* Jack Asher   *m* Phillip
Green

Eric Morecambe, Ernie Wise, William
Franklyn, April Olrich, Richard
Vernon, David Lodge, Warren
Mitchell, Francis Matthews

'Stars of stage, screen, radio and boudoir
throw a party for your entertainment!'

International House*
US   1933   73m   bw
Paramount

A weird variety of travellers are
quarantined in a Shanghai hotel where
a local doctor has perfected television.

Madcap farce which succeeds in hits
and misses.

w Francis Martin, Walter de Leon,
Lou Heifetz, Neil Brant   *d* Edward
Sutherland   *ph* Ernest Haller   *m/
ly* Ralph Rainger, Leo Robin

W. C. Fields, George Burns, Gracie Allen,
Peggy Hopkins Joyce, Stuart Erwin,
Sari Maritza, Bela Lugosi, Edmund
Breese, Lumsden Hare, Rose Marie,
Rudy Vallee, Sterling Holloway, Cab
Calloway and his band, Colonel
Stoopnagle and Budd

'Cast includes enough names to offset
the effects of an otherwise second-
rate picture.' – *Variety*
'Constructed along the lines of a
mammoth vaudeville show, the
motivating story often is sidetracked

entirely to permit a lot of unrelated
hokum comedy.' – *Motion Picture
Herald*

The Invisible Woman
US   1941   72m   bw
Universal (Burt Kelly)

A mad scientist turns a model
invisible.

Screwball comedy with a
deteriorating star at his hammiest:
generally very laboured, but with
some funny moments.

w Robert Lees, Fred Rinaldo,
Gertrude Purcell   *d* A. Edward
Sutherland   *ph* Elwood Bredell
md Charles Previn

John Barrymore, Charles Ruggles,
Virginia Bruce, John Howard, Oscar
Homolka, Donald MacBride, Edward
Brophy, Shemp Howard, Margaret
Hamilton, Maria Montez

Invitation to the Wedding
GB   1985   90m   colour
    widescreen
Chancery Lane (Joseph Brooks)

An aristocratic wedding causes
trouble when the bride's uncle, the
bishop, marries her to the wrong man
at rehearsal.

A situation which could have been
mildly amusing in the *Quiet Wedding*
vein is botched by an unfunny script
and wildly eccentric casting.

w William Fairchild   *d* Joseph
Brooks   *ph* Freddie Young
m Joseph Brooks

Ralph Richardson, John Gielgud (as
an American evangelist), Paul
Nicholas, Elizabeth Shepherd, Ronald
Lacey (as two people for some reason),
John Standing, Susan Brooks

'A story of bloodshed, passion, desire and death ... everything in fact that makes life worth living!'

Irma La Douce*

US   1963   146m   Technicolor
Panavision
UA/Phalanx/Mirisch/Edward L. Alperson
(Billy Wilder)

A Paris policeman falls for a prostitute and becomes her pimp.

A saucy yarn originally presented inventively as a small-scale stage musical becomes a tasteless yawn on the big screen, especially when presented at such length and without the songs. Minor compensations abound but are insufficient.

w Billy Wilder, I. A. L. Diamond
d Billy Wilder   *ph* Joseph LaShelle   *md* André Previn
m Marguerite Monnot
ad Alexander Trauner

Shirley Maclaine, Jack Lemmon, Lou Jacobi, Herschel Bernardi, Joan Shawlee, Bruce Yarnell

AA: André Previn
AAN: Joseph LaShelle; Shirley Maclaine

Ishtar

US   1987   107m   Technicolor
Columbia/Delphi V (Warren Beatty)
V

Two untalented songwriters get involved with Middle Eastern turmoil.

Bitty rehash of old jokes and situations, vaguely resembling a Hope-Crosby Road picture of long ago, but far less funny despite costing 50 million dollars.

wd Elaine May   *ph* Vittorio Storaro   *pd* Paul Sylbert

Dustin Hoffman, Warren Beatty,
Isabelle Adjani, Charles Grodin, Jack Weston, Tess Harper

'One can't help but wonder whether the camel was the only blind creature who had something to do with this picture.' – *Daily Variety*

It*

US   1927   72m (24 fps)   bw
silent
Famous Players-Lasky/Paramount (B. P. Schulberg)

A shopgirl tries to live by the tenets of Elinor Glyn's book, and finally marries her boss.

In its day a fast and funny spoof, and the years have not dealt too unkindly with it.

w Hope Loring, Louis D. Lighton
adaptation Elinor Glyn   *d* Clarence Badger   *ph* H. Kinley Martin

Clara Bow, Antonio Moreno, William Austin, Jacqueline Gadsdon, Gary Cooper, Elinor Glyn

It Ain't Hay

US   1943   79m   bw
Universal (Alex Gottlieb)
GB title: *Money for Jam*

When a racehorse dies, a New York cabbie and his friend try to find a new one for the impecunious owners.

Formula Abbot and Costello with a small injection of sentiment and Runyonese. Not their best by a mile.

w Allen Boretz, John Grant
story Princess O'Hara by Damon Runyon   *d* Erle C. Kenton
ph Charles Von Enger   *m/ly* Harry Revel, Paul Francis Webster

Bud Abbott, Lou Costello, Grace McDonald, Cecil Kellaway, Patsy O'Connor, Eugene Pallette, Shemp Howard, Eddie Quillan

'Together For The First Time!'
It Happened One Night***
US   1934   105m   bw
Columbia (Frank Capra)
V, L

A runaway heiress falls in love with
the reporter who is chasing her across
America.

Highly successful and influential
romantic comedy, the first to use buses
and motels as background and still
come up sparkling; it remains
superlative in patches, but overall has
a faded, dated air.

w Robert Riskin,   *story* Night Bus by
Samuel Hopkins Adams   *d* Frank
Capra   *ph* Joseph Walker
md Louis Silvers

Clark Gable, *Claudette Colbert*, Walter
Connolly, Roscoe Karns, Alan Hale,
Ward Bond, Jameson Thomas, Arthur
Hoyt

'A laughing hit that will mean
important coin.' – *Variety*
'It will be a long day before we see so
little made into so much.' – *Otis
Ferguson*
'Something to revive your faith in a
medium which could belong among
the great arts.' – *Robert Forsythe*
'We may look askance at Capra's
sententious notions about the
miserable rich and the happy poor,
but there's no doubting the chord he
struck in depression audiences.' –
Time Out, 1980
'It made audiences happy in a way
that only a few films in each era do.
In the mid-30s, the Colbert and Gable
of this film became Americans'
idealized view of themselves – breezy,
likeable, sexy, gallant, and maybe just
a little harebrained. It was the *Annie
Hall* of its day – before the invention
of anxiety.' – *Pauline Kael, 70s*
'One of the most entertaining films

that has ever been offered to the
public.' – *Observer*

† Remade 1956 (badly) as *You Can't
Run Away From It*.

†† Robert Montgomery was the first
choice for the Gable role, but he
refused it because he had been on a
bus in *Fugitive Lovers*. The Colbert role
was first offered to Myrna Loy,
Margaret Sullavan and Constance
Bennett. Colbert was lured by a
40,000-dollar fee.

AA: best picture; Robert Riskin; Frank
Capra; Clark Gable; Claudette Colbert

It Happened to Jane
US   1959   98m   Technicolor
   Cinemascope
Columbia/Arwin (Richard Quine)

A lady lobster dealer becomes
involved in a battle with the railroad
whose inefficiency affects her
business.

Witless, wholesome farce which
promises more than it delivers.

w Norman Katkov   *d* Richard
Quine   *ph* Charles Lawton Jnr
m George Duning

Doris Day, Jack Lemmon, *Ernie
Kovacs*, Steve Forrest

It Started with Eve**
US   1941   93m   bw
Universal (Joe Pasternak)

A dying millionaire wants to see his
grandson engaged, so a waitress
obliges for an hour . . . but the old
man recovers.

Charming comedy which was
probably the star's best film; remade as
I'd Rather be Rich (qv).

w Norman Krasna, Leo Townsend
d Henry Koster   *ph* Rudolph

Maté   *md* Charles Previn, Hans Salter

Deanna Durbin, Charles Laughton, Robert Cummings, Margaret Tallichet, Guy Kibbee, Walter Catlett, Catherine Doucet

'The perfect 8 to 80 picture.' – *Variety*
AAN: Charles Previn, Hans Salter

An Italian Straw Hat***
France   1927   74m (24 fps)   bw
  silent
Albatross
original title: *Un Chapeau de Paille d'Italie*

The hero is prevented from getting to a wedding when his horse chews up a lady's straw hat and her escort demands that it be replaced.

Lively but gentle comedy of errors, a stage farce expanded for the screen and filled with visual gags. A very influential and still amusing piece.

wd René Clair,   *play* Eugène Labiche   *ph* Maurice Desfassiaux, Nicolas Roudakoff   *ad* Lazare Meerson

Albert Préjean, Olga Tschekowa, Marise Maia, Alice Tissot

'The very springtime of screen comedy.' – *Tatler*
'One of the funniest films ever made.' – *Tribune, 1945*
'Still one of the funniest films in the world.' – *Sunday Times, 1948*

It's a Mad Mad Mad Mad World**
US   1963   192m   Technicolor
  Ultra Panavision 70
UA/Stanley Kramer
V, L

An assortment of people including a frustrated cop are overcome by greed when they hear of buried loot.

Three hours of frantic chasing and violent slapstick is too much even when done on this scale and with this cast, but one must observe that scene for scene it is extremely well done and most of the players are in unusually good form though they all outstay their welcome and are upstaged by the stunt men.

w William and Tania Rose
d Stanley Kramer   *ph* Ernest Laszlo   *m* Ernest Gold,
stunts Carey Loftin   *titles* Saul Bass

Spencer Tracy, Jimmy Durante, *Milton Berle*, Sid Caesar, Ethel Merman, Buddy Hackett, Mickey Rooney, Dick Shawn, *Phil Silvers, Terry-Thomas*, Jonathan Winters, Edie Adams, Dorothy Provine, Eddie Anderson, Jim Backus, William Demarest, Peter Falk, Paul Ford, Leo Gorcey, Ben Blue, Edward Everett Horton, Buster Keaton, Joe E. Brown, Carl Reiner, the Three Stooges, Zasu Pitts, Sterling Holloway, Jack Benny, Jerry Lewis

'To watch on a Cinerama screen in full colour a small army of actors inflict mayhem on each other with cars, planes, explosives and other devices for more than three hours with stereophonic sound effects is simply too much for the human eye and ear to respond to, let alone the funny bone.' – *Dwight MacDonald*
AAN: Ernest Laszlo; Ernest Gold; title song (*m* Ernest Gold, *ly* Mack David)

It's a Wonderful Life****
US   1946   129m   bw
RKO/Liberty Films (Frank Capra)
V, V(C), L

A man is prevented from committing suicide by an elderly angel, who takes him back through his life to show him what good he has done.

Superbly assembled small-town comedy drama in a fantasy

framework; arguably Capra's best and
most typical work.

*w Frances Goodrich, Albert Hackett,
Frank Capra   d Frank Capra
ph Joseph Walker, Joseph Biroc
m Dimitri Tiomkin   ed William
Hornbeck*

*James Stewart, Henry Travers, Donna
Reed, Lionel Barrymore, Thomas
Mitchell, Beulah Bondi, Frank Faylen,
Ward Bond, Gloria Grahame, H. B.
Warner, Frank Albertson, Samuel S.
Hinds, Mary Treen*
   CLARENCE (Henry Travers): 'Every time
you hear a bell ring, it means that some
angel's just got his wings.'

'One of the most efficient sentimental
pieces since *A Christmas Carol*.' – *James
Agee*
'The most brilliantly made motion
picture of the 1940s, so assured, so
dazzling in its use of screen narrative.'
– *Charles Higham*
'In its own icky, bittersweet way, it's
terribly effective.' – *New Yorker, 1977*
AAN: best picture; Frank Capra;
James Stewart; editing

It's a Wonderful World*
US 1939 86m bw
MGM (Frank Davis)

Kidnapped by a suspected murderer,
a girl helps him track down the real
criminal.

Madcap comedy mystery which now

seems much fresher and funnier than
it did at the time. A highlight of the
crazy comedy cycle.

*w Ben Hecht, Herman J.
Mankiewicz   d W. S. Van Dyke
II   ph Oliver Marsh   m Edward
Ward*

Claudette Colbert, James Stewart,
Guy Kibbee, Nat Pendleton, Frances
Drake, Edgar Kennedy, Ernest Truex,
Richard Carle, Sidney Blackmer,
Andy Clyde, Cliff Clark, Hans Conried

'It's right down the alley for general
audiences.' – *Variety*
'One of the few genuinely comic
pictures in a dog's age.' – *Otis Ferguson*

It's That Man Again**
GB 1942 84m bw
GFD/Gainsborough (Edward Black)

The Mayor of Foaming-at-the-Mouth
puts on a show to save a bombed
theatre.

Smart, fast-moving comedy which no
longer seems particularly funny in
itself but is an invaluable record of the
characters and wisecracks of a radio
show which proved a prime morale
booster during World War II.

*w Howard Irving Young, Ted
Kavanagh   d Walter Forde*

Tommy Handley, Jack Train, Greta
Gynt, Dino Galvani, Dorothy
Summers, Horace Percival, Sidney
Keith, Clarence Wright

□ □ □ □ □

Jabberwocky
GB 1977 101m Technicolor
Umbrella (John Goldstone, Sandy
  Lieberson)
L

A medieval cooper's apprentice is
mistaken for a prince and slays the
dragon which is terrorizing the
neighbourhood.

An intellectual Carry On film, with
very little more taste and a great deal
more unpleasant imagery. Despite
much re-editing, the laughs are very
intermittent.

w Charles Alverson, Terry Gilliam
d Terry Gilliam   *ph* Terry
Bedford   *m* De Wolfe   *pd* Roy
Smith

Michael Palin, Max Wall, Deborah
Fallender, Warren Mitchell, John Le
Mesurier, Harry H. Corbett, Rodney
Bewes, Bernard Bresslaw

'The constant emphasis on blood,
excrement, dismemberment and filth
ultimately becomes rather wearing.' –
*Michael Billington, Illustrated London
News*

'A Film Where Women Eat Men And Men
Eat Ham.'

Jamón Jamón*
Spain 1992 91m colour
Metro Tartan/Lolafilms/Ovideo/Sogepaq
  (Andreás Vincente Gómez)
V(W)

A wealthy mother decides she wants

a local stud for herself after hiring him
to seduce her son's girlfriend.

Broad and enjoyable comedy of sex
and male virility, not to be taken
seriously despite its downbeat,
partner-swapping finale.

w Cuca Canals, Bigas Luna, Quim
Monzó   *d* Bigas Luna   *ph* José
Luis Alcaine   *m* Nicola Piovani

Stefania Sandrelli, Anna Galiena,
Juan Diego, Penélope Cruz, Javier
Bardem, Jordi Molla

'Racy and surreal farce.' – *Empire*

Jinxed!
US 1982 103m Technicolor
MGM-UA/Herb Jaffe

A frustrated blackjack dealer seduces
the girl of a frequent winner.

Unfunny gambling comedy which
never begins to cohere.

w Bert Blessing, David Newman
d Don Siegel   *ph* Vilmos
Zsigmond   *m* Bruce Roberts, Miles
Goodman

Bette Midler, Ken Wahl, Rip Torn, Val
Avery, Jack Elam, Benson Fong,
Jacqueline Scott

Jit*
Zimbabwe 1990 92m bw
ICA/FilmAfrica/Makuvisi (Rory Kilalea)

A youth takes various jobs in order to

□ □

raise the money he needs to buy the bride he wants.

Lively low-budget comedy, the first feature film to be made in Zimbabwe, with an engaging soundtrack of local popular music.

wd Michael Raeburn   *ph* João Costa   *m* Oliver Mtukudzi
pd Lindie Pankiv   *ed* Justin Krish

Dominic Makuvachuma, Sibongile Nene, Farai Sevenzo, Winnie Ndemera, Oliver Mtukudzi, Lawrence Simbarashe

Jitterbugs*
US   1943   75m   bw
TCF (Sol M. Wurtzel)

Laurel and Hardy help a night-club singer to fight off gangsters.

The last Laurel and Hardy film to contain any good scenes, and almost the only one of their TCF films that did.

w Scott Darling   *d* Mal St Clair
ph Lucien Andriot   *md* Emil Newman   *m/ly* Charles Newman, Lew Pollack   *ed* James Basevi, Chester Gore

Stan Laurel, Oliver Hardy, Vivian Blaine, Bob Bailey, Douglas Fowley, Noel Madison, Lee Patrick

Joe versus the Volcano
US   1990   102m   Technicolor
  Panavision
Warner/Amblin Entertainment (Teri Schwartz)
V, L

Told that he has only a few months to live, a man agrees to jump into a volcano to prevent an eruption and save an island for an entrepreneur.

Weak whimsy, directed without flair.

wd John Patrick Shanley

ph Stephen Goldblatt   *pd* Bo Welch   *ed* Richard Halsey

Tom Hanks, Meg Ryan, Lloyd Bridges, Robert Stack, Abe Vigoda, Dan Hedaya, Barry McGovern, Amanda Plummer, Ossie Davis, Jayne Haynes

'A Smooth Comedy...'
Johnny Suede*
US/Switzerland/France   1991
  97m   Fujicolor
Artificial Eye/Vega/Balthazar/Starr/Arena
  (Yoram Mandel, Ruth Waldburger)
V

After a pair of suede shoes drops on top of a phone booth he's using, an ineffectual young man with an exaggerated quiff puts them on and tries to become a rock star.

Stylish exploration of pop style, although a certain tedium sets in before the end.

wd Tom DiCillo   *ph* Joe DeSalvo   *m* Jim Farmer, Link Wray   *pd* Patricia Woodbridge
ed Geraldine Peroni

Brad Pitt, Catherine Keener, Calvin Levels, Alison Moir, Nick Cave, Peter McRobbie, Ashley Gardner, Dennis Parlato, Ron Vawter, Tina Louise

'There are moments of quirky charm and humor in this odd, stylized fable.'
– *Stephen Farber, Movieline*

A Jolly Bad Fellow*
GB   1964   95m   bw
British Lion/Pax/Tower/Michael Balcon
  (Donald Taylor)
US title: *They All Died Laughing*

A brash chemistry don tries a new poison on his enemies.

Interesting but finally irritating comedy of murders with a punnish rather than a donnish script and only moments of genuine sub-Ealing hilarity.

w Robert Hamer, Donald Taylor
novel Don Among the Dead Men by C. E. Vulliamy   d Don Chaffey
ph Gerald Gibbs   m John Barry

Leo McKern, Janet Munro, Maxine Audley, Duncan Macrae, Dennis Price, Miles Malleson, Leonard Rossiter

'The epic love story in which everybody has a great role and a big part.'

Joseph Andrews
GB   1977   104m   Eastmancolor
UA/Woodfall (Neil Hartley)

Adventures of a naïve 18th-century footman.

Woebegone attempt to restage Tom Jones.

w Allan Scott, Chris Bryant
d Tony Richardson   ph David Watkin   m John Addison
pd Michael Annals

Peter Firth, Ann-Margret, Michael Hordern, Beryl Reid, Jim Dale, Peter Bull, John Gielgud, Hugh Griffith, Timothy West, Wendy Craig, Peggy Ashcroft, James Villiers, Karen Dotrice, Ronald Pickup

'Even the incidental pleasures cannot offset the sense of déjà vu which pervades this musty enterprise.' – John Pym, MFB

Jour de Fête*
France   1948   87m   bw
Francinex (Fred Orain)
V, L

A village postman sees a film about the efficiency of the American postal service and decides to smarten himself up.

First, and some say best, of Tati's

comedy vehicles: two-thirds superb local colour, one-third hilarious slapstick.

w Jacques Tati, Henri Marquet
d Jacques Tati   ph Jacques Mercanton   m Jean Yatove

Jacques Tati, Guy Decomble, Paul Fankeur, Santa Relli

'You could watch it with a bout of toothache and it would make you laugh.' – Daily Express

† A reissue version had colour items hand-painted in each frame, and proved quite effective.

Jumpin' Jack Flash
US   1986   100m   DeLuxe
TCF (Lawrence Gordon-Joel Silver)
V, L

A black office worker finds herself plunged into espionage.

Tiresome, dirty-talking, would-be wild and woolly comedy which fails to establish itself.

w David H. Franzoni, J. W. Melville, Patricia Irving, Christopher Thompson   d Penny Marshall
ph Matthew F. Leonetti
m Thomas Newman   pd Robert Boyle   ed Mark Goldblatt

Whoopi Goldberg, Stephen Collins, John Wood, Carol Kane, Annie Potts, Roscoe Lee Browne

Jumping Jacks*
US   1952   96m   bw
Paramount/Hal B. Wallis

Two cabaret comedians join the paratroops.

Standard star farce, one of Martin and Lewis' best.

w Robert Lees, Fred Rinaldo, Herbert Baker   d Norman Taurog *ph* Daniel L. Fapp   *m* Joseph J. Lilley

Dean Martin, *Jerry Lewis*, Mona Freeman, Robert Strauss, Don Defore

Just Like a Woman
GB   1966   89m   Eastmancolor
Dormar (Bob Kellett)

A TV director's wife leaves him and gets ideas above her station.

Curious comedy which aims at sophistication but starts flagging in the first five minutes. Familiar performers just about keep it afloat.

wd Bob Fuest   *ph* Billy Williams *m* Ken Napper

Wendy Craig, Francis Matthews, John Wood, Dennis Price, Miriam Karlin, Peter Jones, Clive Dunn, Ray Barrett

'She stole his heart. He stole her clothes.'
Just Like a Woman
GB   1992   106m   Eastmancolor
Rank/Zenith/LWT/British Screen (Nick Evans)

An American living in London moves into lodgings after his wife throws him out, and reveals to his landlady that he is a transvestite.

Tedious comedy of minimal interest, even to cross-dressers.

w Nick Evans   *novel Geraldine, for the Love of a Transvestite* by Monica Jay   *d* Christopher Monger *ph* Alan Hume   *m* Michael Storey   *pd* John Box   *ed* Nicolas Gaster

Julie Walters, Adrian Pasdar, Paul Freeman, Susan Woolridge, Gordon Kennedy, Ian Redford, Shelley Thompson

'The film remains poky, parochial, and its message is clear – no sex, please, we're British.' – *Geoff Brown, The Times*
'A tepid comedy of Anglo-Saxon inhibition.' – *Philip French, Observer*

Just You and Me, Kid
US   1979   93m   Metrocolor
Columbia/Irving Fein-Jerome M. Zeitman

An elderly comedian reluctantly takes care of a naked teenager on the run from a dope pusher.

Virtually a one-set comedy which quickly tires the eye and ear; not a good idea despite the veteran star.

w Oliver Hailey, Leonard Stern *d* Leonard Stern   *ph* David Walsh   *m* Jack Elliott

George Burns, Brooke Shields, Burl Ives, Lorraine Gary, John Schuck, Keye Luke, Leon Ames, Ray Bolger, Carl Ballantine

K

K-9
US 1988 102m DeLuxe
UIP/Universal (Lawrence Gordon, Charles Gordon)
V, L

A narcotics cop teams up with an Alsatian.

A not-so-shaggy dog story with a couple of laughs.

w Steven Siegel, Scott Myers
d Rod Daniel   ph Dean Semler
m Miles Goodman   pd George Costello   ed Lois Freeman-Fox

James Belushi, Mel Harris, Kevin Tighe, Ed O'Neill, Jerry Lee, James Handy, Daniel Davis, Cotter Smith, John Snyder, Pruitt Taylor Vince

Keep Smiling*
GB 1938 91m bw
TCF (Robert T. Kane)
US title: Smiling Along

Problems of a touring concert party.

Pretty good star vehicle, though with unfortunate signs of an attempt to glamorize Our Gracie.

w Val Valentine, Rodney Ackland
story Sandor Farago, Alexander G. Kemedi   d Monty Banks
ph Max Greene   md Bretton Byrd   ad Oscar Werndorff
ed James B. Clark

Gracie Fields, Roger Livesey, Mary Maguire, Peter Coke, Jack Donohue, Tommy Fields, Eddie Gray, Edward Rigby, Hay Petrie

Keep Your Seats Please*
GB 1936 82m bw
ATP (Basil Dean)

A prospective heir seeks a fortune hidden in one of six chairs.

Good star comedy on a theme later reworked in It's in the Bag (qv) and The Twelve Chairs (qv).

w Tom Geraghty, Ian Hay, Anthony Kimmins   play Twelve Chairs by Elie Ilf, Eugene Petrov   d Monty Banks   ph John W. Boyle   m/ly Harry Parr-Davies, Harry Gifford, Fred E. Cliffe   ad R. Holmes Paul   ed Jack Kitchin

George Formby, Florence Desmond, Alastair Sim, Gus McNaughton, Harry Tate

The Kentucky Fried Movie
US 1977 90m colour
Alpha/Kentucky Fried Theatre (Robert K. Weiss)
V

Comedy sketches from the University of Wisconsin parodying television programmes and commercials.

The writers later gave us Airplane. Enough said?

w David and Jerry Zucker, Jim Abrahams   d John Landis

ph Stephen M. Katz   *ad* Rick Harvel   *ed* George Folsey Jr

Marilyn Joi, Saul Kahan, Marcy Goldman, Joe Medalis

The Kid***
US   1921   52m approx (24 fps)   bw   silent
First National/Charles Chaplin
V

A tramp brings up an abandoned baby, and later loses him to his mother; but there is a happy ending.

Sentimental comedy set in the slums. The comedy is very sparingly laid on, but the effect of the whole is much less painful than the synopsis would suggest, the production is comparatively smooth, the child actor is sensational, and the film contains much of the quintessential Chaplin.

wd Charles Chaplin   *ph* Rollie Totheroh

Charles Chaplin, Jackie Coogan, Edna Purviance

The Kid Brother****
US   1927   83m   bw   silent
Paramount/Lloyd (Harold Lloyd)

The youngest son in the family proves that he is more than the household drudge.

Lively, slapstick comedy with the star at his best.

w John Grey, Tom Crizer, Ted Wilde   *d* Ted Wilde, J. A. Howe, Lewis Milestone   *ph* Walter Lundin, Henry N. Kohler   *ad* Liell K. Vedder   *ed* Allen McNeil

Harold Lloyd, Jobyna Ralston, Walter James, Leo Willis, Olin Francis, Constantine Romanoff

'As gaggy a gag picture as he has ever done.' – Variety

The Kid from Brooklyn
US   1946   114m   Technicolor
Samuel Goldwyn

A timid milkman becomes a prizefighter.

Yawn-provoking comedy, a remake of Harold Lloyd's The Milky Way; the first indication that Danny Kaye could be a bore.

w Grover Jones, Frank Butler, Richard Connell   *d* Norman Z. McLeod   *ph* Gregg Toland *md* Carmen Dragon   *m/ly* Jule Styne, Sammy Cahn

Danny Kaye, Virginia Mayo, Vera-Ellen, Steve Cochran, Eve Arden, Walter Abel, Lionel Stander, Fay Bainter, Clarence Kolb

† Lionel Stander played the same role in The Milky Way.

Killing Dad
GB   1989   93m   Technicolor
Panavision
Palace/Scottish TV Film Enterprises/British Screen/Applecross (Iain Smith)
V

When a down-at-heel father tries to return to the family he abandoned more than twenty years before, his ineffectual son decides to kill him.

Limp, forced and unfunny attempt at a black comedy.

wd Michael Austin   *novel* Berg by Anna Quinn   *d* Michael Austin *ph* Gabriel Beristain   *m* Chaz Jankel, David Storrs   *pd* Adrienne Atkinson   *ed* Edward Marner, Derek Trigg

Denholm Elliott, Julie Walters, Richard E. Grant, Anna Massey, Laura De Sol

'Signally fails to amuse.' – MFB

The Killing of Sister George*

US   1969   138m   Metrocolor
Associates and Aldrich/Palomar
V

An ageing lesbian actress is fired from a TV serial and her life collapses around her.

Heavily handled film version of an amusing and moving play; everything is clumsily spelt out, including the love scenes, and the actresses are forced to repeat themselves.

w Lukas Heller   play Frank Marcus   d Robert Aldrich
ph Joseph Biroc   m Gerald Fried

Beryl Reid, Susannah York, Coral Browne, Roland Fraser, Patricia Medina, Hugh Paddick, Cyril Delevanti

'The play was second-rate, but with its nice blend of the homely and the chilling, the absurdist and the perverse, it had the quality of a Kraft-Ebbing comic book. Aldrich and Heller have turned this material into a crawling tear-jerker, the lines spoken at a speed adjusted to non-English or non-language-speaking audiences.' – John Simon

'A clumpingly archaic piece of film-making.' – New Yorker, 1982

Kind Hearts and Coronets***

GB   1949   106m   bw
Ealing (Michael Relph)
V

An impecunious heir eliminates eight D'Ascoynes who stand between him and the family fortune.

Witty, genteel black comedy well set in the stately Edwardian era and quite deserving of its reputation for wit and style; yet the effect is curiously muffled and several opportunities are missed.

w Robert Hamer, John Dighton, novel Noblesse Oblige by Roy Horniman   d Robert Hamer
ph Douglas Slocombe   md Ernest Irving

Dennis Price, Alec Guinness (in eight roles), Valerie Hobson, Joan Greenwood, Miles Malleson, Arthur Lowe

'A brilliant misfire for the reason that its plentiful wit is literary and practically never pictorial.' – Richard Winnington
'Enlivened with cynicism, loaded with dramatic irony and shot through with a suspicion of social satire.' – Daily Telegraph
'The film in general lacks a visual style equal to its script . . . All the same, Kind Hearts and Coronets is a very funny film and it gets away with a great deal. With so much, in fact, that its makers deserve salutation as pioneers in the little-explored territory of adult British cinema.' – Lindsay Anderson
'A film which can be seen and seen again with undiminished pleasure.' – Basil Wright, 1972

Kindergarten Cop

US   1990   110m   colour
Universal (Ivan Reitman, Brian Grazer)
V, L

A cop, attempting to catch a drug dealer, works undercover as a teacher.

Muscle-bound would-be comedy, with an undercurrent of brutality and objectionable morality.

w Murray Salem, Herschel Weingrod, Timothy Harris   d Ivan Reitman   ph Michael Chapman
m Randy Edelman   pd Bruno Rubeo   ed Sheldon Kahn, Wendy Bricmont

Arnold Schwarzenegger, Penelope Ann Miller, Pamela Reed, Linda Hunt, Richard Tyson, Carroll Baker, Joseph Cousins, Christian Cousins

King Ralph

US 1991 97m Eastmancolor
UIP/Universal/Mirage/Ibro (Jack Brodsky)
V, L

A Las Vegas entertainer becomes King of England when the Royal Family is electrocuted.

Witless farce, set in an England that even P.G. Wodehouse would have found quaintly old hat.

wd David S. Ward novel Headlong by Emlyn Williams ph Kenneth MacMillan m James Newton Howard pd Simon Holland ed John Jympson

John Goodman, Peter O'Toole, John Hurt, Camille Coduri, Richard Griffiths, Leslie Phillips, James Villiers, Joely Richardson, Niall O'Brian, Julian Glover, Judy Parfitt

'As the man who wouldn't be King if he could help it, Goodman redeems what might have been just another high-concept comedy for the party of humanity.' — Richard Schickel, Time

Kipps***

GB 1941 112m bw
TCF (Edward Black)
US title: The Remarkable Mr Kipps

In 1906, a draper's assistant comes into money and tries to crash society.

Charming, unassuming film of a well-loved novel, later musicalized as Half a Sixpence.

w Sidney Gilliat novel H. G. Wells d Carol Reed ph Arthur Crabtree m Charles Williams

Michael Redgrave, Phyllis Calvert,

Diana Wynyard, Arthur Riscoe, Max Adrian, Helen Haye, Michael Wilding, Lloyd Pearson, Edward Rigby, Hermione Baddeley, Frank Pettingell, Beatrice Varley, Kathleen Harrison, Felix Aylmer

'It has the old fashioned charm of wax roses under a glass bell.' — New York Times

Kiss Me Goodbye

US 1982 101m DeLuxe
TCF/Boardwalk/Burt Sugarman/Keith Barish (Robert Mulligan)

A widow planning to marry again is harassed by the ghost of her first husband.

It worked in Blithe Spirit, but this is on a different level, a toned-down rendering of the heavy-breathing Brazilian farce Donna Flor and Her Two Husbands, and it doesn't work on any level.

w Charlie Peters d Robert Mulligan ph Donald Peterman m Ralph Burns pd Philip M. Jefferies ed Sheldon Kahn

James Caan, Sally Field, Jeff Bridges, Paul Dooley, Claire Trevor, Mildred Natwick, William Prince

Kiss Me Stupid*

US 1964 124m bw Panavision
UA/Mirisch/Phalanx/(Billy Wilder)
V, L

A womanizing pop singer stops overnight in a small California desert town and shows interest in an unsuccessful songwriter in order to get at his wife.

Draggy, tasteless, surprisingly unamusing smoking room story, with the actors behaving as though driven against their will (apart from Dean Martin, ideally cast as the idol who gets a headache if he doesn't have sex every night). Some good wisecracks, but it should have been much faster and funnier.

w Billy Wilder, I. A. L. Diamond *play* L'oro della fantasia by Anna Bonacci *d* Billy Wilder *ph* Joseph LaShelle *m* André Previn *pd* Alexander Trauner *m/ly* George and Ira Gershwin

Dean Martin, Kim Novak, Ray Walston, Cliff Osmond

'A work of ferocious tastelessness . . . Swiftian in its relentless disgust.' – *Peter Barnes*

Kiss Them for Me
US 1957 105m Eastmancolor Cinemascope
TCF (Jerry Wald)

Three navy pilots spend a weekend's unofficial leave in San Francisco, and get into various kinds of trouble.

Based on a novel which also served as source for the musical Hit the Deck, this very heavy-footed comedy with serious asides is most unsuitably cast and generally ill-timed and unattractive.

w Julius Epstein *novel* Shore Leave by Frederick Wakeman *d* Stanley Donen *ph* Milton Krasner *m* Lionel Newman

Cary Grant, Jayne Mansfield, Suzy Parker, Ray Walston, Larry Blyden, Leif Erickson, Werner Klemperer

Kisses for My President
US 1964 113m bw
Warner/Pearlayne (Curtis Bernhardt)

America's first woman president causes problems for her husband.

Solidly-carpentered comedy with too few ideas for its length.

w Claude Binyon, Robert G. Kane *d* Curtis Bernhardt *ph* Robert Surtees *m* Bronislau Kaper

Polly Bergen, Fred MacMurray, Arlene Dahl, Eli Wallach, Edward Andrews

The Knack***
GB 1965 84m bw
UA/Woodfall (Oscar Lewenstein)

A sex-starved young teacher lets one room of his house to a successful womanizer, another to an innocent girl from the north.

An excuse for an anarchic series of visual gags, a kaleidoscope of swinging London in which anything goes. Brilliantly done in the style of A Hard Day's Night.

w Charles Wood *play* Ann Jellicoe *d* Richard Lester *ph* David Watkin *m* John Barry

Michael Crawford, Ray Brooks, Rita Tushingham, Donal Donnelly

'The whole film has the anarchic quality modish today and at all times appealing to a new generation understandably bent on overturning the ideas which have hardened in the minds of their elders.' – *Dilys Powell*
'The running jokes and gags never come off.' – *Pauline Kael*

Knave of Hearts*
GB 1954 103m bw
Transcontinental (Paul Graetz)
aka: Monsieur Ripois et Son Nemesis

US title: Lover Boy

A born philanderer confesses all his affairs to his wife.

Well-observed though strangely flat and disappointing sex comedy, something of a pioneer in its time and therefore perhaps too diffident in its approach.

w René Clément, Hugh Mills
d René Clément   *ph* Oswald Morris   *m* Roman Vlad

Gérard Philipe, Margaret Johnston, Joan Greenwood, Natasha Parry, Valerie Hobson

Knock on Wood**

US   1954   103m   Technicolor
Paramount (Norman Panama, Melvin Frank)

Stolen plans are hidden inside the dummy of an unsuspecting ventriloquist.

Excellent star comedy with good script and production (but some strange ideas of London's geography).

wd Norman Panama, Melvin Frank
ph Daniel Fapp   *m* Leith Stevens   *ch* Michael Kidd   *m/ly* Sylvia Fine

Danny Kaye, Mai Zetterling, David Burns, Torin Thatcher, Leon Askin, Abner Biberman, Steve Geray
AAN: Norman Panama, Melvin Frank (script)

Kotch*

US   1971   114m   Metrocolor
ABC/Kotch Company (Richard Carter)

An eccentric 72-year-old widower is at odds with his family and helps a pregnant babysitter.

Variously amusing, moving and sentimental, this generally likeable film about a crotchety grandpa is sustained by its star performance.

w John Paxton   *novel* Katherine Topkins   *d* Jack Lemmon
ph Richard H. Kline   *m* Marvin Hamlisch

Walter Matthau, Deborah Winter, Felicia Farr, Charles Aidman
AAN: Walter Matthau; song 'Life Is What You Make It' (*m* Marvin Hamlisch, *ly* Johnny Mercer)

'When you have attitude, who needs experience?'
Kuffs

US   1992   101m   Technicolor
Universal/EvansGideon (Raynold Gideon)
V, L

A high-school dropout inherits his murdered brother's private police business and sets out to avenge his death.

Messily coarse comedy not helped by the star's direct addresses to the camera.

w Bruce A. Evans, Raynold Gideon   *d* Bruce A. Evans
ph Thomas Del Ruth   *m* Harold Faltermeyer   *pd* Victoria Paul, Armin Ganz   *ed* Stephen Semel

Christian Slater, Tony Goldwyn, Milla Jovovich, Bruce Boxleitner, Troy Evans, George de la Pena, Leon Rippy

'Film veers from ultra-violence to slapstick comedy in an arbitrary and irritating fashion. Hokey camera angles and flashy dissolves fail to pump up the action.' – *Variety*
'The film comes to resemble the bastard child of *Miami Vice* and an especially bad movie-of-the-week.' – *New York Times*

L

◘ ◘ ◘ ◘ ◘

'Something Funny Is Happening In L.A.'
L.A. Story*
US 1991 95m Technicolor
Guild/Rastar (Daniel Melnick, Michael
    Rachmil)
V, L

A TV weather forecaster in Los
Angeles falls for a visiting English
journalist.

A pleasant romantic comedy, though
the love affair is mainly with Los
Angeles itself.

w Steve Martin   d Mick Jackson
ph Andrew Dunn   m Peter
Melnick   pd Lawrence Miller
ed Richard A. Harris

Steve Martin, Victoria Tennant,
Richard E. Grant, Marilu Henner,
Sarah Jessica Parker, Susan Forristal,
Kevin Pollak, Patrick Stewart

'A light-headed joyride for an
audience.' – *Pauline Kael, New Yorker*

Ladies' Man
US 1961 106m Technicolor
Paramount/York (Jerry Lewis)

The adventures of an accident-prone
houseboy at a Hollywood hotel for
aspiring actresses.

Hit-or-miss collection of comic scraps
which might have benefited from
being put together on a less grandiose
scale.

w Jerry Lewis, Bill Richmond

d Jerry Lewis   ph W. Wallace
Kelley   m Walter Scharf

Jerry Lewis, Helen Traubel, Jack
Kruschen, Doodles Weaver, Gloria
Jean

'Regression into infantilism cannot be
carried much further than this.' – *MFB*

Ladies Who Do
GB 1963 85m bw
British Lion/Bryanston/Fanfare (George H.
    Brown)

Charladies form a successful company
from tips they salvage from
wastepaper baskets.

Mild farce sustained by familiar actors.

w Michael Pertwee   d C. M.
Pennington-Richards   ph Geoffrey
Faithfull   m Ron Goodwin

Peggy Mount, Miriam Karlin, Robert
Morley, Harry H. Corbett, Dandy
Nichols

'Eve Sure Knows Her Apples!'
The Lady Eve*
US 1941 97m bw
Paramount (Paul Jones)

A lady cardsharper and her father are
outsmarted on a transatlantic liner by
a millionaire simpleton; she plans an
elaborate revenge.

Hectic romantic farce, the first to show
its director's penchant for mixing up
sexual innuendo, funny men and
pratfalls. There are moments when the

◘ ◘

pace drops, but in general it's scintillating entertainment, especially after viewing its weak remake *The Birds and the Bees* (qv).

wd Preston Sturges, *play* Monckton Hoffe *ph* Victor Milner *m* Leo Shuken, Charles Bradshaw *ad* Hans Dreier, Ernest Fegte *ed* Stuart Gilmore

Barbara Stanwyck, Henry Fonda, Charles Coburn, Eugène Pallette, William Demarest, Eric Blore, Melville Cooper, Martha O'Driscoll, Janet Beecher, Robert Greig, Luis Alberni, Jimmy Conlin

'The whole theme, with all its variations of keys, is played to one end, to get laughs, and at several different levels it gets them.' – *National Board of Review*
'Preston Sturges, they tell me, is known in Hollywood as "the streamlined Lubitsch". This needn't put you off, because if he goes on producing films as lively as this one he will one day come to be known as Preston Sturges.' – *William Whitebait*
'This time Preston Sturges has wrapped you up another package that is neither very big nor very flashy, but the best fun in months.' – *Otis Ferguson*
'A mixture of visual and verbal slapstick, of high artifice and pratfalls . . . it represents the dizzy high point of Sturges' writing.' – *New Yorker, 1977*
'The brightest sort of nonsense, on which Preston Sturges' signature is written large. The result has a sustained comic flavour and an individual treatment that are rarely found in Hollywood's antic concoctions.' – *New York Herald Tribune*
'A more charming or distinguished gem of nonsense has not occurred since *It Happened One Night*.' – *New York Times*

AAN: Monckton Hoffe (original story)

Lady for a Day***
• US 1933 95m bw
Columbia (Frank Capra)
V, L

Gangsters help an old apple seller to pose as a rich woman when her daughter visits.

Splendid sentimental comedy full of cinematic resource; the best translation of Runyon to the screen.

w Robert Riskin *story* Madame La Gimp by Damon Runyon *d* Frank Capra *ph* Joseph Walker

May Robson, Warren William, Guy Kibbee, Glenda Farrell, Ned Sparks, Jean Parker, Walter Connolly, Nat Pendleton

'Exceptionally adroit direction and scenario . . . sell it with plenty of adjectives as it will please everybody.' – *Variety*
AAN: best picture; Robert Riskin; Frank Capra; May Robson

Lady Killer***
US 1933 76m bw
Warner (Henry Blanke)

A cinema usher turns to crime, flees to Hollywood, and becomes a movie star.

Hectic slam-bang action comedy with melodramatic moments. Great fun.

w Ben Markson *novel* The Finger Man by Rosalind Keating Shaffer *d* Roy del Ruth *ph* Tony Gaudio *md* Leo F. Forbstein

James Cagney, Mae Clarke, Leslie Fenton, Margaret Lindsay, Henry O'Neill, Willard Robertson, Raymond Hatton, Russell Hopton

'An all-time high in roughneck

character work even for this rough-and-tumble star.' – *Variety*
'A kind of résumé of everything he has done to date in the movies.' – *New York Evening Post*
'Sprightly, more or less daring, thoroughly entertaining.' – *New York World Telegram*

'A Comedy With Balls.'
Ladybugs
US 1992 90m DeLuxe
Warner/Morgan Creek (Albert S. Ruddy, Andre E. Morgan)
V

A salesman takes over managership of a women's soccer team and has his son join it in drag.

Dismayingly stupid comedy that is embarrassing to watch.

w Curtis Burch   d Sidney J. Furie   m Richard Gibbs   pd Robb Wilson King   ed John W. Wheeler, Timothy N. Board

Rodney Dangerfield, Jackée, Jonathan Brandis, Ilene Graff, Vinessa Shaw, Tom Parks

'This picture doesn't deserve any respect. Sexist, homophobic and woefully unfunny to boot, Rodney Dangerfield's latest starring effort is a waste of comic talent.' – *Variety*
'This week's candidate for the worst film in history.' – *Geoff Brown, The Times*

The Ladykillers*
GB 1955 97m Technicolor
Ealing (Seth Holt)
V

An old lady takes in a sinister lodger, who with his four friends commits a robbery. When she finds out, they plot to kill her, but are hoist with their own petards.

Overrated comedy in poor colour; those who made it quite clearly think it funnier than it is.

w William Rose   d Alexander Mackendrick   ph Otto Heller   m Tristam Cary

Alec Guinness, *Katie Johnson*, Peter Sellers, Cecil Parker, Herbert Lom, Danny Green, Jack Warner, Frankie Howerd, Kenneth Connor

'To be frivolous about frivolous matters, that's merely boring. To be frivolous about something that's in some way deadly serious, that's true comedy.' – *Alexander Mackendrick*
AAN: William Rose

Last Holiday*
GB 1950 88m bw
ABPC/Watergate (Stephen Mitchell, A. D. Peters, J. B. Priestley)

A man with a short time to live has a thoroughly enjoyable and useful final fling.

Slight, amusing and moving comedy drama spoiled by an unnecessary double twist.

w J. B. Priestley   d Henry Cass   ph Ray Elton   m Francis Chagrin

Alec Guinness, Kay Walsh, Beatrice Campbell, Grégoire Aslan, Bernard Lee, Wilfrid Hyde White, Helen Cherry, Sidney James, Muriel George

The Last Married Couple in America
US 1979 102m Technicolor
Universal/Cates Brothers (John Shaner)

A Los Angeles couple resist the efforts of their friends to involve them in the swinging life.

Tolerable sex comedy of modern mores, a shade too long delayed after *Bob and Carol and Ted and Alice*.

w John Herman Shaner   d Gilbert

Cates   ph Ralph Woolsey
m Charles Fox   pd Gene Callahan

Natalie Wood, George Segal, Richard Benjamin, Arlene Golonka, Alan Arbus, Marilyn Sokol, Dom DeLuise, Valerie Harper

Last of the Red Hot Lovers*
US   1972   98m   Technicolor
Paramount (Howard W. Koch)

A middle-aged fish restaurateur feels the need for an extra-marital spree.

Modest, plainly-filmed sex comedy from a reliable stable.

w Neil Simon   play Neil Simon
d Gene Saks   ph Victor J. Kemper   m Neal Hefti

Alan Arkin, Paula Prentiss, Sally Kellerman, Renée Taylor

'A different kind of love story!'
The Last Remake of Beau Geste
US   1977   85m   Technicolor
Universal (William S. Gilmore Jnr)

The Geste brothers find themselves in the Foreign Legion after the theft of the Blue Water sapphire.

Woebegone spoof of a romantic original, with most of the jokes totally irrelevant to the purpose and seldom at all funny.

w Marty Feldman, Chris J. Allen
d Marty Feldman   ph Gerry Fisher   m John Morris

Marty Feldman, Michael York, Ann-Margret, Peter Ustinov, Trevor Howard, James Earl Jones, Henry Gibson, Terry-Thomas, Roy Kinnear, Spike Milligan, Hugh Griffith, Irene Handl

'A ragbag of a film which looks like nothing so much as a Monty Python extravaganza in which inspiration has run dry and the comic timing gone sadly awry.' – Tom Milne, MFB

Laugh with Max Linder**
France   1963   88m   bw
Films Max Linder
original title: En Compagnie de Max Linder

Excerpts from three of the dapper comedian's most famous American comedies: Be My Wife (1921), The Three Must-Get-Theres (1922), Seven Years' Bad Luck (1923).

A compilation which must serve as a consensus of this almost forgotten comedian's work. The gag with a broken mirror in particular was borrowed by innumerable other comedians, notably the Marx Brothers in Duck Soup. Audiences new to Linder's work will find him not especially sympathetic but capable of many felicities. He wrote, produced and directed all three films.
compiler Maud Max Linder

Laughing Gravy***
US   1931   20m   bw
Hal Roach
V(C)

Stan and Ollie retrieve their dog when the landlord throws it out into the snow.

One of the most endearing comedies of these stars, and one of the simplest.

w H. M. Walker   d James W. Horne

Laurel and Hardy, Charlie Hall

Laughter in Paradise*
GB   1951   93m   bw
Transocean (Mario Zampi)

An eccentric leaves in his will a fortune for each of his relations providing they will perform certain embarrassing or criminal acts.

A funny idea gets half-hearted treatment, but the good bits are hilarious.

w Michael Pertwee, Jack Davies
d Mario Zampi   ph William
McLeod   m Stanley Black

*Alastair Sim, Joyce Grenfell, Hugh
Griffith, Fay Compton, John Laurie,
George Cole, Guy Middleton, Ronald
Adam, Leslie Dwyer, A. E. Matthews,
Beatrice Campbell*

† Remade 1972 as *Some Will, Some Won't.*

Laughterhouse*
GB 1984 93m colour
Greenpoint/Film Four International (Ann Scott)

A Norfolk farmer decides to walk his fattened geese to market.

An attempt to revive the tradition of Ealing comedy lands up somewhere on the wrong side of Group Three. Not enough plot, almost no jokes, and the geese are almost the only pleasant creatures.

w Brian Glover   d Richard Eyre
ph Clive Tickner   m Dominic
Muldowney

Ian Holm, Penelope Wilton, Bill Owen, Richard Hope, Stephen Moore, Rosemary Martin

The Laurel and Hardy Murder Case
US 1930 30m bw
Hal Roach

Heirs to a fortune are menaced by a mad murderer.

Empty spoof on *The Cat and the Canary* which affords little scope to Laurel and Hardy.

w H. M. Walker   d James Parrott

Laurel and Hardy's Laughing Twenties**
US 1965 90m bw
MGM/Robert Youngson
V, L

Excerpts from lesser comedians of the period – Max Davidson, Charlie Chase – are interspersed with highlights from Laurel and Hardy's silent two-reelers.

A hilarious and craftsmanlike compilation, perhaps a little too long for its own good.

w/ed Robert Youngson   m Skeets
Alquist   commentator Jay Jackson

† Films extracted include *Putting Pants on Philip, From Soup to Nuts, Wrong Again, The Finishing Touch, Liberty, Double Whoopee, Leave 'Em Laughing, You're Darn Tooting* and the custard pie climax from *The Battle of the Century.*

The Lavender Hill Mob****
GB 1951 78m bw
Ealing (Michael Truman)
V, L

A timid bank clerk conceives and executes a bullion robbery.

Superbly characterized and inventively detailed comedy, one of the best ever made at Ealing or in Britain.

w T.E.B. Clarke   d Charles
Crichton   ph Douglas Slocombe
m Georges Auric

*Alec Guinness, Stanley Holloway, Sidney
James, Alfie Bass, Marjorie Fielding,
Edie Martin, John Gregson, Gibb
McLaughlin*

'Amusing situations and dialogue are well paced and sustained throughout: the climax is delightful.' – *MFB*

AA: T. E. B. Clarke
AAN: Alec Guinness

Laxdale Hall
GB 1952 77m bw
Group Three (Alfred Shaughnessy)
US title: *Scotch on the Rocks*

MPs are sent to investigate a tiny
Hebridean island which refuses to pay
road tax.

Thin rehash of *Whisky Galore* put
together without the Ealing style.
Minor compensations can be found.

w John Eldridge, Alfred
Shaughnessy   d John Eldridge
ph Arthur Grant   m Frank Spencer

Raymond Huntley, Ronald Squire,
Sebastian Shaw, Fulton Mackay,
Kathleen Ryan, Kynaston Reeves

'Constantly amusing in its quiet and
wry fashion.' – *Cinema*

The League of Gentlemen***
GB 1960 112m bw
Rank/Allied Film Makers (Michael Relph)

An ex-army officer recruits high-class
misfits with guilty secrets to help him
in a bank robbery.

Delightfully handled comedy
adventure, from the days (alas) when
crime did not pay; a lighter ending
would have made it a classic.

w Bryan Forbes,   novel John
Boland   d Basil Dearden
ph Arthur Ibbetson   m Philip
Green

Jack Hawkins, Richard Attenborough,
Roger Livesey, *Nigel Patrick*, Bryan
Forbes, Kieron Moore, Terence
Alexander, *Norman Bird*, Robert
Coote, Melissa Stribling, Nanette
Newman, Gerald Harper, Patrick
Wymark, David Lodge, Doris Hare,
Lydia Sherwood

'Once in a lifetime you get a chance to do
something different.'

A League of Their Own*
US 1992 128m Technicolor
Columbia/Parkway
V

During the Second World War,
women are recruited to play in an all-
female baseball league.

A comedy that trundles along in a
predictable fashion, settling for
sentimentality rather than humour.

w Lowell Ganz, Babaloo Mandel
story Kim Wilson, Kelly Candaele
d Penny Marshall   ph Miroslav
Ondricek   m Hans Zimmer
pd Bill Groom   ed George Bowers

Tom Hanks, Geena Davis, Madonna,
Lori Petty, Jon Lovitz, David
Strathairn, Gerry Marshall, Bill
Pullman, Megan Cavanagh, Tracy
Reiner, Rosie O'Donnell, Ann Cusack

'This movie aims for the tear ducts and
the funny bone as ruthlessly as the
summer's big action-fantasy hits go
after the viscera. It unfolds in field-of-
dreams land – complete with
cornstalks.' – *Michael Sragow, New
Yorker*
'Awash in sentimentality and manic
energy but only occasionally bubbling
over with high humor.' – *Variety*

Leave 'Em Laughing*
US 1928 20m bw silent
Hal Roach

Stan has toothache, visits the dentist,
and accidentally causes all concerned
to inhale an overdose of laughing gas.

The earlier sequences are only mildly
funny, but the laughing finale is
irresistible.

w Hal Roach and Reed Heustis
d Clyde Bruckman

Laurel and Hardy, Edgar Kennedy, Charlie Hall

'Top of the poll for laughs!'

Left Right and Centre*
GB 1959 95m bw
Vale/Launder and Gilliat

A TV personality becomes Tory candidate at a by-election.

Scrappy political comedy with the saving grace of a large number of comic talents.

w Sidney Gilliat, Val Valentine
d Sidney Gilliat   ph Gerald Gibbs
m Humphrey Searle

Ian Carmichael, Alastair Sim, Patricia Bredin, Richard Wattis, Eric Barker, Gordon Harker, George Benson, Frederick Leister

The Lemon Drop Kid*
US 1951 91m bw
Paramount (Robert A. Welch)

A gangster forces a bookie to find the money which he has lost on a horse through the bookie's incompetence.

Amusing Bob Hope/Runyon vehicle despite heavy sentiment about an old folks' home. The Santa Claus sequences are memorable.

w Edmund Hartmann, Frank Tashlin, Robert O'Brien   story Damon Runyon   d Sidney Lanfield
ph Daniel L. Fapp   m Victor Young

Bob Hope, Marilyn Maxwell, Lloyd Nolan, Jane Darwell, Andrea King, Fred Clark, Jay C. Flippen, William Frawley, Harry Bellaver

† The previous 1934 version starred Lee Tracy, Helen Mack and William Frawley; ran 60m; and was directed by Marshall Neilan for Paramount

'Somewhere in the tundra lived the worst rock'n'roll band in the world...'

Leningrad Cowboys Go America**
Finland/Sweden 1989 78m
Artificial Eye/Villealfa/Swedish Film Institute/
    Finnish Film Foundation (Aki Kaurismäki,
    Klas Olofsson, Katinka Farago)
V, L

An inept rock band travels through America in search of fame and fortune, which prove elusive.

Engagingly ramshackle comedy, with keen observation of the underside of the American dream.

wd Aki Kaurismäki   story Sakke Järvenpää, Aki Kaurismäki, Mato Valtonen   ph Timo Salminen
m Mauri Sumén   ed Raija Talvio

Matti Pellonpää, Kari Väänänen, Sakke Jarvenpää, Hiekki Keskinen, Pimme Oinonen, Silu Seppälä, Mauri Sumén, Mato Valtonen, Pekka Virtanen, Jim Jarmusch

Leon the Pig Farmer
GB 1992 104m colour
Electric/Leon the Pig Farmer Production
    (Gary Sinyor, Vadim Jean)

A Jewish estate agent discovers that his real father is a Yorkshire pig farmer.

Laboured low-budget comedy of racial stereotypes.

w Gary Sinyor, Michael Norman
d Vadim Jean, Gary Sinyor
ph Gordon Hickie   m John Murphy
pd Simon Hicks   ed Ewa Lind

Mark Frankel, Gina Bellman, Janet Suzman, Brian Glover, Connie Booth, Maryam D'Abo

'Overall, flashes of inspiration are outweighed by laboured skits that fall somewhat flat, but this is a worthy and promising effort.' – Empire

'The comedy has wit and pace. It has originality that Mel Brooks might envy.' – *Alexander Walker, London Evening Standard*

† The film was made on a budget of £160,000. It won the International Critics' Prize at the Venice Film Festival and an award for best first film at the Edinburgh Film Festival.

Let George Do It**

GB 1940 82m bw
Ealing (Basil Dearden)

A ukelele player accidentally goes to Bergen instead of Blackpool and is mistaken for a spy.

Generally thought to be the best George Formby vehicle, with plenty of pace, good situations and catchy tunes.

w John Dighton, Austin Melford, Angus MacPhail, Basil Dearden d Marcel Varnel ph Gordon Dines, Ronald Neame

George Formby, Phyllis Calvert, Garry Marsh, Romney Brent, Bernard Lee, Coral Browne, Torin Thatcher, Hal Gordon

Let's Do It Again

US 1975 113m Technicolor
Warner/First Artists/Verdon (Melville Tucker, Pembroke J. Herring)

Three Atlanta workers conceive a zany plan to raise money for their church by hypnotizing a boxer into winning a big fight.

Lively but overlong farce reassembling the black talents of *Uptown Saturday Night.*

w Richard Wesley d Sidney Poitier ph Donald M. Morgan m Curtis Mayfield

Sidney Poitier, Bill Cosby, Calvin Lockhart, John Amos, Denise Nicholas, Ossie Davis, Jimmy Walker

Let's Face It

US 1943 76m bw
Paramount (Fred Kohlmar)

A smart-alec soldier has a plot involving a ladies' health camp, but finds himself up to his neck in spies.

Tepid star comedy which unaccountably ditches almost all the numbers from the musical on which it was based.

w Harry Tugend *musical play* Dorothy and Herbert Fields, Cole Porter *play Cradle Snatchers* by Norma Mitchell, Russell Medcraft d Sidney Lanfield ph Lionel Lindon *songs* Cole Porter

Bob Hope, Betty Hutton, Eve Arden, Phyllis Povah, Dona Drake, Zasu Pitts, Marjorie Weaver, Raymond Walburn, Joe Sawyer

Let's Hope It's a Girl*

Italy/France 1985 119m colour
Artificial Eye/Clemi Cinematografica/
    Producteurs Associes/Soprofilms/A2
    (Raimondo Castelli, Bruno Ridolfi)
original title: *Speriamo Che Sia Femmina*

A countess strives, with the help of other women of the household, to keep running the family farm.

Gently amusing, rambling comedy.

w Leo Benvenuti, Tullio Pinelli, Suso Cecchi D'Amico, Piero De Bernardi, Mario Monicelli d Mario Monicelli ph Camillo Bazzoni m Nicola Piovani ad Enrico Fiorentini ed Ruggero Mastroianni

Liv Ullmann, Catherine Deneuve, Philippe Noiret, Bernard Blier, Giuliana De Sio, Stefania Sandrelli,

Athina Cenci, Lucrezia Lante Della
Rovere

Let's Make It Legal
US   1951   77m   bw
TCF

An attractive grandmother divorces
her gambler husband and takes up
with an old boy friend.

Unremarkable but competent star
comedy.

w F. Hugh Herbert, I. A. L.
Diamond   d Richard Sale

Claudette Colbert, Zachary Scott,
Macdonald Carey, Barbara Bates,
Robert Wagner, Marilyn Monroe

A Letter to Brezhnev**
GB   1985   95m   colour
Yeardream/Film Four International/Palace
   Productions (Janet Goddard)
V

Two girls from Liverpool spend a busy
night with Russian sailors; when one
of them receives no subsequent
letters, she writes to Brezhnev and is
invited to Moscow.

Vivid it is, but also raucous and seedy
until true love enters as a redeeming
factor. The critics loved it, thinking it
about unemployment and urban
decline; it certainly paints a low
picture of Liverpool.

w Frank Clarke   d Chris
Bernard   ph Bruce McGowan
m Alan Gill   ed Lesley Walker

Alfred Molina, Peter Firth, Margi
Clarke, Tracy Lea, Alexandra Pigg

'Fast-moving, funny, entertaining
and poignant . . . in short how to make
a British film.' – Jill Forbes, MFB

'A peek into the other woman's male!'
A Letter to Three Wives**
US   1949   102m   bw
TCF (Sol C. Siegel)
L

Three wives on a picnic receive word
from a friend that she has run off with
one of their husbands.

Amusing short-story compendium
which seemed more revelatory at the
time than it does now, and paved
the way for its writer-director's
heyday.

wd Joseph L. Mankiewicz,
novel John Klempner   ph Arthur
Miller   m Alfred Newman

Jeanne Crain, Ann Sothern, Linda
Darnell, Jeffrey Lynn, Kirk Douglas,
Paul Douglas, Barbara Lawrence,
Connie Gilchrist, Florence Bates,
Hobart Cavanaugh, and the voice of
Celeste Holm

'A mere shadow of those acid
Hollywood comedies of the thirties . . .
over-written and under-directed . . .
but it has a supply of ironies and
makes a certain alkaline comment on
present-day American customs and
manners.' – Richard Winnington
'Replete with sharp dialogue. He aims
barbed darts at the country's
favourite institutions, and makes
them score with telling effect.' –
Variety

AA: Joseph L. Mankiewicz (as writer);
Joseph L. Mankiewicz (as director)
AAN: best picture

Liberty**
US   1929   20m   bw   silent
Hal Roach
V

Two convicts escape and have
adventures high on a construction
site.

Amusing gags are succeeded by breathtaking thrills in the Harold Lloyd style.

w Leo McCarey and H. M. Walker
d Leo McCarey

Laurel and Hardy, James Finlayson

The Lieutenant Wore Skirts
US 1955 99m Eastmancolor
Cinemascope
TCF (Buddy Adler)

When a TV writer joins the service, his wife enlists to be near him; but he is rejected on medical grounds.

Raucous, tasteless farce which tries far too hard to raise laughs.

w Albert Beich, Frank Tashlin
d Frank Tashlin   ph Leo Tover
m Cyril Mockridge

Tom Ewell, Sheree North, Rita Moreno, Rick Jason, Les Tremayne

Life Is a Circus
GB 1958 84m bw
Vale Film (M. Smedley Aston)

An odd-job man in a rundown circus finds Aladdin's lamp.

Feeble comedy by the Crazy Gang in a state of geriatric disrepair, simply going through the motions, which is an understandable reaction given the script. Chesney Allen makes a brief appearance to sing 'Underneath the Arches' with his old partner, Bud Flanagan.

wd Val Guest   m Philip Green
ad Tony Masters   ed Bill Lenny

Bud Flanagan, Nervo and Knox, Naughton and Gold, Monsewer Eddie Gray, Shirley Eaton, Michael Holliday, Joseph Tomelty, Lionel Jeffries

Life Stinks
US 1991 95m DeLuxe
TCF/Brooks Films/Le Studio Canal Plus (Mel Brooks)
V

A rich property developer takes a bet that he can survive on his own on the streets of a slum for thirty days.

Crass, tasteless comedy in which the jokes are poor.

w Mel Brooks, Rudy De Luca, Steve Haberman   story Mel Brooks, Ron Clark, Rudy De Luca, Steve Haberman   d Mel Brooks
ph Steven Poster   m John Morris   pd Peter Larkin   ed David Rawlins

Mel Brooks, Lesley Ann Warren, Jeffrey Tambor, Stuart Pankin, Howard Morris, Rudy De Luca, Teddy Wilson, Billy Barty

'Antic comedy has more laughs than the filmmaker's last couple of efforts, and presents an amiably sympathetic, if unreliable, look at the homeless.' – Variety

'Take your cookie to see the picture that takes the cake for laughs!'

Life with Father*
US 1947 118m Technicolor
Warner (Robert Buckner)

Turn-of-the-century anecdotes of an irascible well-to-do paterfamilias who won't be baptized.

Well-upholstered screen version of a long-running play; oddly tedious considering the talent involved.

w Donald Ogden Stewart
play Howard Lindsay, Russel Crouse   d Michael Curtiz
ph Peverell Marley, William V. Skall   m Max Steiner   ad Robert Haas

William Powell, Irene Dunne,

Edmund Gwenn, Zasu Pitts, Elizabeth Taylor, Martin Milner, Jimmy Lydon, Emma Dunn, Moroni Olsen, Elizabeth Risdon

'Everybody seems to be trying too hard ... the director is totally out of his element in this careful, deadly version.' – *New Yorker, 1978*

† Censorship of the day absurdly clipped Father's famous last line: 'I'm going to be baptized, damn it!'
AAN: Peverell Marley, William V. Skall; Max Steiner; William Powell; Robert Haas

Like Father Like Son
US 1987 98m Technicolor
Grazer-Valdes/Tri-Star
L

A surgeon and his son find themselves in each other's bodies.

Role-reversal comedy at the beginning of a trend; in itself a bore.

w Lorne Cameron, Steven L. Bloom *d* Rod Daniel *ph* Jack N. Green *m* Miles Goodman *pd* Dennis Gassner *ed* Lois Freeman-Fox

Dudley Moore, Kirk Cameron, Sean Astin, Patrick O'Neal, Margaret Colin

The Likely Lads*
GB 1976 90m bw
EMI (Aida Young)
V

Two Geordie friends, with wife and mistress, go on a touring holiday.

Valuable as a record of an excellent and long-running TV series, this big-screen version finds most of the humour regrettably broadened.

w Dick Clement, Ian La Frenais *d* Michael Tuchner *ph* Tony Imi *m* Mike Hugg

Rodney Bewes, James Bolam, Brigit Forsyth, Mary Tamm, Sheila Fearn, Zena Walker

Limelight***
US 1952 144m bw
Charles Chaplin
V

A broken-down music hall comedian is stimulated by a young ballerina to a final hour of triumph.

Sentimental drama in a highly theatrical London East End setting. In other hands it would be very hokey, but Chaplin's best qualities, as well as his worst, are in evidence, and in a way the film sums up his own career.

wd Charles Chaplin *ph* Karl Struss *m* Charles Chaplin, Raymond Rasch, Larry Russell *ad* Eugene Lourié *photographic consultant* Rollie Totheroh

Charles Chaplin, Claire Bloom, Buster Keaton, Sydney Chaplin, Nigel Bruce, Norman Lloyd

'From the first reel it is clear that he now wants to talk, that he loves to talk ... where a development in the story line might easily be conveyed by a small visual effect, he prefers to make a speech about it ... it is a disturbing rejection of the nature of the medium itself.' – *Walter Kerr*
'Surely the richest hunk of self-gratification since Huck and Tom attended their own funeral.' – *New Yorker, 1982*
'His exhortations about life, courage, consciousness and "truth" are set in a self-pitying, self-glorifying story.' – *Pauline Kael, 70s*

AA: Charles Chaplin, Raymond Rasch, Larry Russell

Limit Up

US 1989 88m colour
Medusa/Management Company
  Entertainment (Jonathan D. Krane)

A woman sells her soul to an apparent demon in exchange for a successful career on the stock exchange.

A dull fantasy, dimly directed.

w Richard Martini, Luana Anders
d Richard Martini   ph Peter Lyons
Collier   m John Tesh   pd R.
Clifford Searcy   ed Sonny Baskin

Nancy Allen, Dean Stockwell, Brad Hall, Danitra Vance, Ray Charles, Rance Howard, Sandra Bogan

Little Darlings

US 1980 92m Metrocolor
Paramount/Stephen J. Friedman
L

Teenage girls at a summer camp take bets on who will lose her virginity first.

Crass and tasteless comedy with only prurient appeal.

w Kimi Peck, Dalene Young
d Ronald F. Maxwell   ph Fred
Batka   m Charles Fox
pd William Hiney   ed Pembroke J.
Herring

Tatum O'Neal, Kristy McNichol, Krista Errickson, Armand Assante

'From homicide to house parties – from dames to debutantes!'

Little Giant

US 1946 91m bw
Universal (Joseph Gershenson)
GB title: On the Carpet

Misadventures of a vacuum cleaner salesman.

Curious, unsatisfactory Abbott and Costello comedy in which the boys play separate characters instead of working as a team. They should have waited for a better script before experimenting.

w Paul Jarrico, Richard Collins,
Walter de Leon   d William A.
Seiter   ph Charles van Enger
m Edgar Fairchild

Bud Abbott, Lou Costello, Brenda Joyce, George Cleveland, Elena Verdugo

Little Murders

US 1971 108m DeLuxe
TCF/Brodsky-Gould (Jack Brodsky)

A young photographer rises above all the urban horror of New York life, but when his wife is killed by a sniper he takes to violence.

This adaptation of an ultrablack comedy would have worked better as a comic strip, for its characters are satirical puppets, and when played by human beings the whole thing seems violently silly.

w Jules Feiffer   play Jules
Feiffer   d Alan Arkin   ph Gordon
Willis   m Fred Kaz

Elliott Gould, Marcia Rodd, Elizabeth Wilson, Vincent Gardenia, Alan Arkin

A Little Romance

US 1979 108m Technicolor
Warner/Orion (Patrick Kelley)
L

A French teenager elopes with an American girl, encouraged by a garrulous old pickpocket.

Treacly juvenile romance enriched by in-jokes and an enjoyably over-the-top star performance.

w Allan Burns   novel Patrick
Cauvin   d George Roy Hill
ph Pierre William Glenn

m Georges Delerue   *pd* Henry Bumstead

Laurence Olivier, Diane Lane, Thelonious Bernard, Arthur Hill, Sally Kellerman, Broderick Crawford, David Dukes

AA: Georges Delerue
AAN: Allan Burns

A Little Sex
US   1982   94m   Technicolor
Universal/MTM (Robert de Laurentiis, Bruce Paltrow)

A young husband has a wandering eye.

Very thin comedy drama more suitable for TV if it were a little less outspoken.

w Robert de Laurentiis   *d* Bruce Paltrow   *ph* Ralf D. Bode
m Georges Delerue

Tim Matheson, Kate Capshaw, Edward Herrmann, John Glover

The Little World of Don Camillo*
France/Italy   1952   106m   bw
Rizzoli-Amato-Francinex (Giuseppe Amato)

In a small Italian village the parish priest and the communist mayor are in a constant state of amiable feud.

Slightly lethargic character comedy with a mild message for its times, popular enough to warrant several sequels.

w Julien Duvivier, René Barjavel
novel Giovanni Guareschi
d Julien Duvivier   *ph* Nicolas Hayer   *m* Alessandro Cicognini

Fernandel, Gino Cervi, Sylvie, Manara, Vera Talqui, Franco Interlenghi

'Cute and cosy.' – *MFB*

The Live Ghost
US   1934   20m   bw
Hal Roach

Two reluctant sailors think they have murdered one of their mates.

Somewhat unyielding material for Stan and Ollie, but still funnier than any of their rivals at the time.

w H. M. Walker   *d* Charles Rogers

Laurel and Hardy, Walter Long, Arthur Housman

Live Now, Pay Later
GB   1962   104m   bw
(Regal) Woodlands/Jay Lewis (Jack Hanbury)

A credit store salesman is himself heavily in debt, and his private life is in ruins; but even after a chapter of unexpected and tragic events he remains irrepressibly optimistic.

A satirical farce melodrama which lets fly in too many directions at once and has a cumulatively cheerless effect despite funny moments.

w Jack Trevor Story   *d* Jay Lewis   *ph* Jack Hildyard   *m* Ron Grainer

Ian Hendry, John Gregson, June Ritchie, Geoffrey Keen, Liz Fraser

Local Hero**
GB   1983   111m   colour
Enigma/Goldcrest (David Puttnam)
V, L

A young American executive meets various difficulties when he is sent to a Scottish coastal village to arrange for the building of a new refinery.

Reminiscent of various Ealing comedies, especially *Whisky Galore* and *The Maggie*, this ambitious comedy is really not funny enough for its great length.

wd Bill Forsyth　*ph* Chris Menges　*m* Mark Knopfler

Burt Lancaster, Peter Riegert, *Denis Lawson*, Peter Capaldi, Fulton Mackay, Jenny Seagrove

'Little in the way of obvious commercial hooks . . . dominated by a constantly surprising sense of whimsicality.' – *Variety*

BFA: direction

'The restoration comedy about what cannot be restored!'

Lock Up Your Daughters

GB 1969 103m Technicolor
Columbia/Domino (David Deutsch)

In 18th-century London an aristocratic rake and various lower orders are all in search of female companionship and get their wires crossed.

Noisy, vulgar, ill-acted version (without music) of a successful musical based on two old theatrical warhorses.

w Keith Waterhouse, Willis Hall *play* Bernard Miles based on *Rape upon Rape* by Henry Fielding and *The Relapse* by John Vanbrugh　*d* Peter Coe *ph* Peter Suschitzky　*m* Ron Grainer　*pd* Tony Woollard

Christopher Plummer, Roy Kinnear, Georgia Brown, Susannah York, Glynis Johns, Ian Bannen, Tom Bell, Elaine Taylor, Jim Dale, Kathleen Harrison, Roy Dotrice, Vanessa Howard, Fenella Fielding, Peter Bayliss, *Richard Wordsworth*, Peter Bull, Fred Emney

'Subtlety is neither required nor displayed.' – *Jack Ibberson*

London Belongs to Me**

GB 1948 112m bw
GFD/Individual (Frank Launder, Sidney Gilliat)
US title: *Dulcimer Street*

A young boy is arrested on a murder charge and his boarding-house friends rally to his defence.

Unconvincing but highly entertaining sub-Dickensian comedy-drama with a rousing finish and an abundance of character roles.

w Sidney Gilliat, J. B. Williams *novel* Norman Collins　*d* Sidney Gilliat　*ph* Wilkie Cooper *m* Benjamin Frankel

Alastair Sim, Stephen Murray, Richard Attenborough, Fay Compton, Wylie Watson, Susan Shaw, Ivy St Helier, Joyce Carey, Andrew Crawford, Eleanor Summerfield, Hugh Griffith, Gladys Henson

'Memorable for its character-drawing and for the excellence of its writing and acting.' – *Dilys Powell*

The Lonely Guy

US 1984 90m Technicolor
Universal (Arthur Hiller)
V

After being thrown out by his girlfriend, a writer discovers a secret society of single men.

Glossy but heavy-handed comedy, attempting satire but not succeeding in its aim.

w Ed Weinberger, Stan Daniels, Neil Simon　*book* The Lonely Guy's Book of Life by Bruce J. Friedman　*d* Arthur Hiller　*ph* Victor J. Kemper *m* Jerry Goldsmith　*pd* James D. Vance　*ed* William Reynolds

Steve Martin, Charles Grodin, Judith Ivey, Steven Lawrence, Robyn

Douglass, Merv Griffin, Dr Joyce
Brothers

'Generally likeable, but it makes you
feel as though you were watching
television.' – *Pauline Kael, New Yorker*

Lonesome Cowboys
US   1968   105m   colour
Andy Warhol Films
V
aka: *Andy Warhol's Lonesome Cowboys*

A gang of outlaws rides into town,
where the only inhabitants are a
wealthy woman, her male nurse and
a transvestite sheriff.

A sort of improvised and inspired
home movie, a gay Western made by
city lovers who regard wide-open
spaces and horses with great
suspicion.

wd Paul Morrissey

Viva, Taylor Mead, Tom Hompertz,
Louis Waldron, Joe Dallesandro, Eric
Emerson

'A classic of the bashful age!'
Long Pants*
US   1927   58m (24 fps)   bw
   silent
First National/Harry Langdon

A country bumpkin has trouble in the
city.

Far from the best Langdon comedy,
but funny in flashes.

w Arthur Ripley   *d* Frank Capra
ph Elgin Lessley

Harry Langdon, Gladys Brockwell,
Alan Roscoe, Alma Bennett

Look Up and Laugh*
GB   1935   82m   bw
ATP (Basil Dean)

Market stallholders defy a big chain
store.

Good star comedy with music.

w Gordon Wellesley   *story* J. B.
Priestley   *d* Basil Dean
ph Robert G. Martin   *md* Ernest
Irving

Gracie Fields, Douglas Wakefield,
Harry Tate, Alfred Drayton, Morris
Harvey, Vivien Leigh, Robb Wilton

Look Who's Laughing
US   1941   75m   bw
RKO (Allan Dwan)
See also: Here We Go Again

Fibber McGee and Molly act as
unexpected hosts to Edgar Bergen
and Charlie McCarthy.

Exploitation of radio sitcoms,
acceptable at the time. With Lucille
Ball.

w James V. Kern and others
d Allan Dwan

Look Who's Talking
US   1989   96m   Technicolor
Columbia TriStar (Jonathan D. Krane)
V, L

A baby comments on the growing
relationship between his unmarried
mother and a taxi driver.

Indifferent comedy that enjoyed a
great success through the novelty of
adult speech and attitudes issuing
from the mouth of a baby.

wd Amy Heckerling   *ph* Thomas
Del Ruth   *m* David Kitay
ad Reuben Freed, Graeme Murray
ed Debra Chiate

John Travolta, Kirstie Alley, Olympia
Dukakis, George Segal, Abe Vigoda,
Bruce Willis, Twink Caplan, Joy
Boushel, Don S. Davis

'Carelessly put together, ugly to look
at and mawkish and stupid in turn.' –
Derek Malcolm, Guardian

Look Who's Talking Too
US 1990 81m Technicolor
Columbia TriStar (Jonathan D. Krane)
V, L

Small babies comment on the
disagreements between a husband
and wife.

All that this sad comedy has to
recommend it is the novelty of adult
voices issuing from the mouths of
babes, a joke that quickly outstays its
welcome.

w Amy Heckerling, Neal Israel
d Amy Heckerling   ph Thomas Del
Ruth   m David Kitay   pd Reuben
Freed   ed Debra Chiate

John Travolta, Kirstie Alley,
Olympia Dukakis, Elias Koteas,
Twink Caplan and voices of Bruce
Willis, Roseanne Barr, Damon
Wayans, Mel Brooks

'Whenever Heckerling runs out
of inspiration, which is every
couple of minutes, she slaps an old
rock 'n' roll record on the turntable
and transforms the film
into a music-video.' – *Philip
French, Observer*

Lookin' to Get Out
US 1982 105m colour
Lorimar/North Star/Voight-Schaffel
  (Robert Schaffel)

A couple of inveterate gamblers take
on the Las Vegas establishment.

Fairly pleasant, mindless, quite
forgettable comedy.

w Al Schwartz, Jon Voight   d Hal
Ashby   ph Haskell Wexler
m Johnny Mandel   pd Robert
Boyle

Jon Voight, Ann-Margret, Burt
Young, Bert Remsen, Jude Farese,
Richard Bradford

Looking on the Bright Side*
GB 1931 81m bw
ATP (Basil Dean)

A songwriter gets ideas above his
station but eventually returns to the
manicurist who loves him.

Dated but lively musical which helped
confirm Gracie's stardom.

w Basil Dean, Archie Pitt, Brock
Williams   d Basil Dean
ph Robert G. Martin   md Carroll
Gibbons

Gracie Fields, Richard Dolman, Julian
Rose, Wyn Richmond

Loose Connections*
GB 1983 96m colour
Umbrella/Greenpoint (Simon Perry)

Adventures on a drive to Munich.

Thin, easy-going road comedy.
Pleasant enough, but no *Genevieve*.

w Maggie Brooks   d Richard
Eyre   ph Clive Tickner
m Dominic Muldowney

Lindsay Duncan, Stephen Rea, Carole
Harrison, Frances Low

Loot*
GB 1970 101m Eastmancolor
Performing Arts Ltd (Arthur Lewis)
V

A crook hides his mother's body and
uses the coffin to carry the proceeds
of a robbery.

Breakneck black farce which still can't
move quite fast enough to cover up its
bad taste, though well done by all
concerned.

w Ray Galton, Alan Simpson
play Joe Orton   d Silvio
Narizzano   ph Austin Dempster
m Keith Mansfield, Richard Willing-
Denton   ad Anthony Pratt

Richard Attenborough, Lee Remick,

Hywel Bennett, Milo O'Shea, Dick Emery

Lord Love a Duck*
US 1966 105m bw
UA/Charleston (George Axelrod)

A senior Los Angeles student practises hypnotism on his girl friend.

Rather sloppy satire on American culture and fancies, dressed up as crazy comedy; occasional laughs.

w Larry H. Johnson, George Axelrod   novel Al Hine
d George Axelrod   ph Daniel Fapp   m Neal Hefti ·

Roddy McDowall, Tuesday Weld, Lola Albright, Ruth Gordon, Harvey Korman, Max Showalter

Lost and Found
US 1979 105m Technicolor Panavision
Columbia/Gordon (Melvin Frank)
V

A widowed American professor meets an English divorcee on a skiing holiday, but after marriage they prove to be incompatible.

Unattractive romantic comedy-drama which despite capable stars degenerates into a series of wounding slanging matches.

w Melvin Frank, Jack Rose
d Melvin Frank   ph Douglas Slocombe   m John Cameron ·
pd Trevor Williams

Glenda Jackson, George Segal, Maureen Stapleton, Paul Sorvino, John Cunningham, Hollis McLaren

Lost in a Harem**
US 1944 89m bw
MGM (George Haight)

Two travelling entertainers in the Middle East get mixed up with a conniving sultan, who hypnotizes them.

Lively, well-staged romp which shows the comedians at their best and uses astute borrowings from burlesque, pantomime, and Hollywood traditions of fantasy and running jokes.

w Harry Ruskin, John Grant, Harry Crane   d Charles Reisner
ph Lester White   m David Snell

Bud Abbott, Lou Costello, Douglass Dumbrille, Marilyn Maxwell, John Conte, Jimmy Dorsey and his Orchestra

Lost in America*
US 1985 91m Technicolor Panavision
Warner/Geffen Company (Marty Katz)
L

A successful couple drop out of their expensive life-style to discover that poverty has its disadvantages.

Witty demolition of yuppie attitudes to the simple life.

w Albert Brooks, Monica Johnson
d Albert Brooks   ph Eric Saarinen   m Arthur B. Rubinstein   pd Richard Sawyer
ed David Finfer

Albert Brooks, Julie Hagerty, Michael Greene, Garry K. Marshall, Maggie Roswell, Tom Tarpey

Love and Death*
US 1975 85m DeLuxe Panavision
UA/Jack Rollins, Charles H. Joffe
V, L

In 1812 Russia, a man condemned reviews the follies of his life.

Personalized comedy fantasia inspired

by *War and Peace*, Ingmar Bergman and S. J. Perelman. Basically only for star fans.

wd Woody Allen　*ph* Ghislain Cloquet　*m* Prokofiev

Woody Allen, Diane Keaton, Georges Adel, Despo, Frank Adu

'I have a feeling that one of these days Allen will get it most dreadfully together and make a film which is more than a string of funny one-liners and set-pieces. He hasn't quite done it here.' – *Benny Green, Punch*

Love at First Bite*
US 1979 96m colour
Simon (Joel Freeman)
V

Count Dracula flees from the communists and settles in New York.

Energetic spoof, with jokes on the sexy side; good work all round.

w Robert Kaufman　*d* Stan Dragoti　*ph* Edward Rosson　*m* Charles Bernstein　*pd* Serge Krizman

George Hamilton, Susan St James, Richard Benjamin, Dick Shawn, Arte Johnson

'Love is so hard to find you have to hire a detective'

Love at Large*
US 1990 97m DeLuxe
Rank/Orion (David Blocker)
V, L

A private eye checks on the wrong man, while a female detective is hired by his girlfriend to check on him.

Enjoyably light-hearted treatment of an intricate plot of double-cross and double lives.

wd Alan Rudolph　*ph* Elliot Davis　*m* Mark Isham

pd Stephen Legler　*ed* Lisa Churgin

Tom Berenger, Elizabeth Perkins, Anne Archer, Kate Capshaw, Annette O'Toole, Ted Levine, Ann Magnuson, Kevin J. O'Connor, Ruby Dee, Barry Miller, Neil Young

Love Crazy*
US 1941 100m bw
MGM (Pandro S. Berman)

When his wife threatens to divorce him, a businessman hatches all manner of crazy schemes, including disguising himself as his own sister.

Zany romantic comedy, over-stretched but with a fair share of hilarity.

w William Ludwig, Charles Lederer, David Hertz　*d* Jack Conway　*ph* Ray June　*m* David Snell

William Powell, Myrna Loy, Gail Patrick, Jack Carson, Florence Bates, Sidney Blackmer, Vladimir Sokoloff, Donald MacBride, Sig Rumann, Sara Haden, Elisha Cook Jnr, Kathleen Lockhart

Love Happy*
US 1949 85m bw
Lester Cowan/Mary Pickford
V, L

A group of impoverished actors accidentally gets possession of the Romanov diamonds.

The last dismaying Marx Brothers film, with Harpo taking the limelight and Groucho loping in for a couple of brief, tired appearances. A roof chase works, but Harpo tries too hard for sentiment, and the production looks shoddy.

w Ben Hecht, Frank Tashlin, Mac Benoff　*d* David Miller

ph William Mellor   *m* Ann Ronell

Groucho, Harpo, Chico, Eric Blore, Ilona Massey, Marilyn Monroe, Vera-Ellen

'A big comedy about life's little heartaches'

Love Hurts

US   1990   115m   CFI

Vestron/Love Hurts Production (Bud Yorkin, Doro Bachrach)

V

Returning home for his sister's wedding, a philanderer puts his past behind him.

A botched attempt, with unsympathetic characters, to return to comic style of Capra.

w Ron Nyswaner   *d* Bud Yorkin *ph* Adam Greenberg   *m* Frank DeCaro   *pd* Armin Ganz   *ed* John C. Horger

Jeff Daniels, Judith Ivey, John Mahoney, Cynthia Sikes, Amy Wright, Cloris Leachman, Mary Griffin, Thomas Allen

Love in the Afternoon

US   1957   126m   bw

AA (Billy Wilder)

The daughter of a private detective warns an American philanderer in Paris that an enraged husband is en route to shoot him.

Tired and dreary romantic sex comedy, miscast and far too long. With the talent around, there are of course a few compensations.

w Billy Wilder, I. A. L. Diamond *novel* Ariane by Claude Anet   *d* Billy Wilder   *ph* William Mellor *m* Franz Waxman   *ad* Alexander Trauner

Gary Cooper, Audrey Hepburn, Maurice Chevalier, John McGiver

Love, Life and Laughter*

GB   1934   83m   bw

ATP (Basil Dean)

A film actress catches the eye of a Ruritanian prince.

Lively star vehicle ranging from sentiment to slapstick.

w Robert Edmunds   *d* Maurice Elvey

Gracie Fields, John Loder, Norah Howard, Allan Aynesworth, Esme Percy, Robb Wilton, Fred Duprez, Horace Kenney, Veronica Brady

The Love Lottery

GB   1953   83m   Technicolor.

Ealing (Monja Danischewsky)

A British film star is persuaded to offer himself as first prize in a lottery.

Satirical farce which doesn't come off, mainly owing to paucity of comedy ideas.

w Harry Kurnitz   *d* Charles Crichton   *ph* Douglas Slocombe   *m* Benjamin Frankel *pd* Tom Morahan

David Niven, Herbert Lom, Peggy Cummins, Anne Vernon, Charles Victor, Gordon Jackson, Felix Aylmer, Hugh McDermott

The Love Match*

GB   1955   85m   bw

British Lion/Beaconsfield (Maclean Rogers)

A North Country train driver's enthusiasm for his local football team lands him in trouble at home and work.

A regional farce, full of stock characters and situations, but given some individuality by the likeable performances of its cast.

w Godfrey Orme, Glenn Melvyn *play* Glenn Melvyn   *d* David

Paltenghi   *ph* Arthur Grant
m Wilfred Burns   *ad* Bernard
Robinson   *ed* J. M. Sterling

Arthur Askey, Thora Hird, Glenn
Melvyn, Robb Wilton, Shirley Eaton,
Edward Chapman, William Franklyn,
Patricia Hayes, Maurice Kaufmann

Love Thy Neighbour
GB   1973   85m   Technicolor
EMI/Hammer (Roy Skeggs)
V

A prejudiced white worker has
coloured neighbours.

Elongated screen version of the
popular TV series in which the West
Indians smile through all the insults
and come out top in the end. It might
have been worse, but not much.

w Vince Powell, Harry Driver
d John Robins   *ph* Moray
Grant   *m* Albert Elms

Jack Smethurst, Kate Williams,
Rudolph Walker, Nina Baden-Semper,
Bill Fraser, Charles Hyatt, Keith
Marsh, Patricia Hayes, Arthur English

The Loved One*
US   1965   118m   bw
MGM/Filmways (Neil Hartley)

A young English poet in California
gets a job at a very select burial
ground.

A pointed satire on the American way
of death has been allowed to get out
of hand, with writer and actors alike
laying it on too thick; but there are
pleasantly waspish moments in a
movie advertised as 'the motion
picture with something to offend
everybody'.

w Terry Southern, Christopher
Isherwood   *novel* Evelyn Waugh
d Tony Richardson   *ph* Haskell

Wexler   *m* John Addison
pd Rouben Ter-Arutunian

Robert Morse, John Gielgud, Rod
Steiger, *Liberace*, Anjanette Comer,
Jonathan Winters, Dana Andrews,
Milton Berle, James Coburn, Tab
Hunter, Margaret Leighton, Roddy
McDowall, Robert Morley, Lionel
Stander

'Even a chaotic satire like this is
cleansing, and it's embarrassing to
pan even a bad movie that comes out
against God, mother and country.' –
Pauline Kael, 1968
'A spineless farrago of collegiate gags.'
– *Stanley Kauffmann*
'A sinking ship that makes it to port
because everyone on board is too
giddy to panic.' – *New Yorker, 1978*

Lover Come Back
US   1946   90m   bw
Universal (Howard Benedict)

When a war correspondent returns,
his wife discovers that he hasn't been
so lonely overseas as he might have
been.

Very tolerable star comedy which at
the time seemed quite fresh.

w Michael Fessier, Ernest Pagano
d William A. Seiter   *ph* Joseph
Valentine   *m* Hans J. Salter

George Brent, Lucille Ball, Vera
Zorina, Charles Winninger, Carl
Esmond, Raymond Walburn, Franklin
Pangborn, Louise Beavers

'Should chalk up good grosses in most
situations.' – *Variety*

Lover Come Back**
US   1961   107m   Eastmancolor
U-I/Seven Pictures/Nob Hill/Arwin (Stanley
Shapiro, Marty Melcher)

Rival executives find themselves
advertising a non-existent product.

Fairly sharp advertising satire disguised as a romantic comedy; the most entertaining of the Day-Hudson charmers.

w *Stanley Shapiro, Paul Henning*
d Delbert Mann   ph Arthur E. Arling   m Frank de Vol

Doris Day, Rock Hudson, *Tony Randall*, Jack Oakie, Edie Adams
AAN: Stanley Shapiro, Paul Henning

Loverboy
US   1989   99m   Technicolor
Columbia TriStar/Crescent Film
    Enterprises (Gary Foster, Willie Hunt)
V, L

A pizza delivery boy pays his way through college by becoming a lover to his female customers.

Feeble comedy with little wit or sense.

w Robin Schiff, Tom Ropelewski, Leslie Dixon   d Joan Micklin Silver   ph John Davis   m Michel Colombier   pd Dan Leigh
ed Rick Shaine

Patrick Dempsey, Kate Jackson, Kirstie Alley, Carrie Fisher, Robert Ginty, Nancy Valen, Charles Hunter Walsh, Barbara Carrera

'The material often suggests a crude and juvenile variation on *The Graduate*.' – *MFB*

The Lovers
GB   1972   89m   Eastmancolor
British Lion/Gildor (Maurice Foster)

A Manchester bank clerk with a prim girl friend finds it difficult to lose his virginity.

Well-written but rather arch comedy which seemed much funnier and fresher as a TV series.

w Jack Rosenthal   d Herbert Wise   ph Bob Huke   m Carl Davis

Richard Beckinsale, Paula Wilcox, Joan Scott, Susan Littler, John Comer, Stella Moray, Nikolas Simmonds

Lovers and Other Strangers***
US   1970   104m   Metrocolor
ABC/David Susskind

After living together for eighteen months, Susan and Mike decide to get married, and find their parents have sex problems of their own.

Wise, witty and well-acted sex farce, with many actors making the most of ample chances under firm directorial control.

w *Renée Taylor, Joseph Bologna, David Zelag Goodman*   d *Cy Howard*
ph *Andrew Laszlo*   m Fred Karlin

Gig Young, Anne Jackson, *Richard Castellano*, Bonnie Bedelia, Michael Brandon, *Beatrice Arthur*, Robert Dishy, Harry Guardino, Diane Keaton, Cloris Leachman, Anne Meara, *Marian Hailey*

'An extremely engaging comedy.' – *Gillian Hartnoll*

AA: song 'For All We Know' (m Fred Karlin, ly Robb Wilson, Arthur James)
AAN: script, Richard Castellano

Lovesick
US   1983   96m   Technicolor
Warner/Ladd (Charles Okun)
L

A New York psychiatrist in love with a patient is guided by the ghost of Sigmund Freud.

Depressing comedy with a non-star and supporting players who must have been embarrassed.

wd Marshall Brickman   ph Gerry Fisher   m Philippe Sarde
pd Philip Rosenberg

Dudley Moore, Elizabeth McGovern, Alec Guinness (as Freud), John Huston, Larry Rivers, Gene Saks, Renee Taylor, Alan King

'Flat, lamebrained and indigestible.' – *Geoff Brown, MFB*

Loving Couples

US   1980   98m   Metrocolor
Time Life (Renee Valente)

Man-and-wife doctors decide to liven up their lives by having affairs.

Embarrassingly with-it romantic charade.

w Martin Donovan   *d* Jack Smight   *ph* Philip Lathrop *m* Fred Karlin

Shirley Maclaine, James Coburn, Susan Sarandon, Stephen Collins, Sally Kellerman

Lucky Jim**

GB   1957   95m   bw
British Lion/Charter (Roy Boulting)
V

At a provincial university, an accident-prone junior lecturer has a disastrous weekend with his girl friend and his professor.

Quite funny in its own right, this is a vulgarization of a famous comic novel which got its effects more subtly, with more sense of place, time and character.

w Jeffrey Dell, Patrick Campbell *novel* Kingsley Amis   *d* John Boulting   *ph* Max Greene *m* John Addison

Ian Carmichael, Hugh Griffith, Terry-Thomas, Sharon Acker, Jean Anderson, Maureen Connell, Clive Morton, John Welsh, Reginald Beckwith, Kenneth Griffith

'An almost endless ripple of

comfortable laughter.' – *News Chronicle*

Lucky Partners*

US   1940   101m   bw
RKO (George Haight)

Two strangers share a sweepstake ticket and fall in love.

A very thin comedy kept afloat by its stars.

w Allan Scott, John Van Druten *story Bonne Chance* by Sacha Guitry *d* Lewis Milestone   *ph* Robert de Grasse   *m* Dimitri Tiomkin

Ronald Colman, Ginger Rogers, Jack Carson, Spring Byington, Cecilia Loftus, Harry Davenport

Lunch on the Grass**

France   1959   91m   Eastmancolor
Compagnie Jean Renoir
original title: *Déjeuner sur l'Herbe*

An international scientist hears the pipes of Pan, embarks on a country idyll and impregnates a housemaid whom he later marries.

Charming if overlong frolic with ideas, a harking back to earlier Renoir themes such as in *Boudu Sauvé des Eaux.*

wd Jean Renoir   *ph* Georges Leclerc   *m* Joseph Kosma

Paul Meurisse, Catherine Rouvel, Fernand Sardou, Ingrid Nordine

'A warm, loving, garrulous, undisciplined film.' – *Penelope Houston, MFB*

Lust in the Dust

US   1984   87m   CFI colour
Fox Run (Allan Glaser, Tab Hunter)
V

In the old west, a strong silent man and a drag queen beat the baddies to the gold.

Fitfully funny spoof for adults.

w Philip Taylor   *d* Paul Bartel
ph Paul Lohmann   *m* Peter Matz
ed Alan Toomayan

Tab Hunter, Divine, Lainie Kazan,
Geoffrey Lewis, Henry Silva, Cesar
Romero, Woody Strode

Luv

US 1967 95m Technicolor
   Panavision
Columbia/Jalem (Martin Manulis)

When a man prevents an old friend
from jumping off the Brooklyn Bridge
and brings him home, a sexual square
dance develops.

A modern comedy that should have
stayed in the theatre.

w Elliott Baker   *play* Murray
Shisgal   *d* Clive Donner
ph Ernest Laszlo   *m* Gerry
Mulligan

Jack Lemmon, Peter Falk, Elaine May,
Nina Wayne, Eddie Mayehoff, Paul
Hartman, Severn Darden

'A light but incisive comedy about the
patterns and language of love in a
Freud-ridden society has become an
inept and lethally unamusing film
farce.' – *MFB*

Mad about Men

GB 1954 90m Technicolor
GFD/Group Films (Betty Box)

By mutual agreement, a sports
mistress and a mermaid change places
for a while.

Laborious rehash of *Miranda* with
familiar jokes.

w Peter Blackmore   *d* Ralph
Thomas   *ph* Ernest Steward
m Benjamin Frankel

Glynis Johns, Donald Sinden, Anne
Crawford, Margaret Rutherford,
Dora Bryan, Nicholas Phipps, Irene
Handl

Mad Wednesday*

US 1947 77m bw
Howard Hughes

A middle-aged book-keeper is sacked
and goes on the town.

Woolly and unattractive farce which
proved something of a disaster for all
the talents concerned but historically
is of considerable interest. It begins
with an excerpt from *The Freshman*
and continues to comic adventures
with a lion.

wd/pd Preston Sturges (re-edited by
others)   *ph* Robert Pittack
m Werner Richard Heymann

Harold Lloyd, Jimmy Conlin, Raymond
Walburn, Franklin Pangborn, Al
Bridge, Margaret Hamilton, Edgar
Kennedy

'At the sperm-bank, she asked for a tall,
intelligent, black man. One out of three
ain't bad.'

Made in America

US 1993 110m Technicolor
Warner/Stonebridge/Kalola/Regency/
   Canal+ (Arnon Milchan, Michael
   Douglas, Rick Bieber)

A black teenager, born by artificial
insemination, discovers that her
father is a white car-salesman with a
crass manner.

An occasionally amusing comedy, due
more to the performances than the
script which skirts all the racial issues
it raises to settle for a comforting
situation comedy.

w Holly Goldberg Sloan
story Marcia Brandwynne, Nadine
Schiff, Holly Goldberg   *d* Richard
Benjamin   *ph* Ralph Bode
m Mark Isham   *pd* Evelyn
Sakash   *ed* Jacqueline Cambas

Whoopi Goldberg, Ted Danson, Will
Smith, Nia Long, Paul Rodriguez,
Jennifer Tilly, Peggy Rae, Clyde
Kusatsu

'It's a likeable effort, good enough for
a sultry summer evening at the
multiplex when the film you came to
see is sold out.' – *Sight and Sound*

Madhouse

US 1990 90m colour
Rank/Orion/A Boy of the Year (Leslie Dixon)
V

Unwanted friends and neighbours move in as house guests of a young couple.

Remarkably unfunny domestic comedy, directed with a heavy hand.

wd Tom Ropelewski *ph* Denis Lewiston *m* David Newman *pd* Dan Leigh *ed* Michael Jablow

John Larroquette, Kirstie Alley, Alison LaPlaca, John Diehl, Jessica Lundy, Bradley Gregg, Dennis Miller, Robert Ginty, Wayne Tippit

The Maggie**

GB 1953 93m bw
Ealing (Michael Truman)
US title: *High and Dry*

An American businessman is tricked into sending his private cargo to a Scottish island on an old puffer in need of repair.

Mildly amusing comedy about the wily Scots; not the studio at its best, but pretty fair.

w William Rose d Alexander Mackendrick ph Gordon Dines *m* John Addison

Paul Douglas, *Alex Mackenzie*, James Copeland, Abe Barker, Dorothy Alison, Hubert Gregg, Geoffrey Keen, Andrew Keir, Tommy Kearins

The Magic Christian

GB 1969 95m Technicolor
Commonwealth United/Grand Films (Dennis O'Dell)
V, L

An eccentric millionaire spends his wealth deflating those who pursue money or power.

A series of variably funny but always unpleasant sketches, climaxing with citizens delving for spoils in a vat of blood and manure. In its aim to be satirical, very typical of its time.

w Terry Southern, Joseph McGrath, Peter Sellers *novel* Terry Southern *d* Joseph McGrath *ph* Geoffrey Unsworth *m* Ken Thorne *pd* Assheton Gorton

Peter Sellers, Ringo Starr, Richard Attenborough, Laurence Harvey, Christopher Lee, Spike Milligan, Yul Brynner, Roman Polanski, Raquel Welch, Wilfrid Hyde White, Fred Emney, John Le Mesurier, Dennis Price, Patrick Cargill, John Cleese, Graham Chapman

The Magnet

GB 1950 79m bw
Ealing (Sidney Cole)

A small boy steals a magnet and accidentally becomes a hero.

Very mild Ealing comedy, not really up to snuff.

w T. E. B. Clarke *d* Charles Frend *ph* Lionel Banes *m* William Alwyn

Stephen Murray, Kay Walsh, William Fox, Meredith Edwards, Gladys Henson, Thora Hird, Wylie Watson

The Magnificent Seven Deadly Sins

GB 1971 107m colour
Tigon (Graham Stark)
V

Compendium of comedy sketches, a very variable ragbag of old jokes.

w Bob Larbey, John Esmonde, Dave Freeman, Barry Cryer, Graham Chapman, Graham Stark, Marty

Feldman, Alan Simpson, Ray Galton, Spike Milligan   *d* Graham Stark *ph* Harvey Harrison Jnr   *m* Roy Budd

Bruce Forsyth, Joan Sims, Roy Hudd, Harry Secombe, Leslie Phillips, Julie Ege, Harry H. Corbett, Ian Carmichael, Alfie Bass, Spike Milligan, Ronald Fraser

The Magnificent Two

GB 1967 100m Eastmancolor
Rank (Hugh Stewart)

One of two incompetent travelling salesmen in a Latin American banana republic is persuaded to pose as a dead rebel leader.

More or less a Bob Hope vehicle, adapted for the less realistic Morecambe and Wise with unhappy results: too few sight gags and a curious emphasis on violence. The third and last of their attempts to find film vehicles.

w S. C. Green, R. M. Hills, Michael Pertwee, Peter Blackmore   *d* Cliff Owen   *ph* Ernest Steward *m* Ron Goodwin

Eric Morecambe, Ernie Wise, Margit Saad, Cecil Parker, Virgilio Texeira, Isobel Black, Martin Benson

Maid's Night Out

US 1937 65m bw
RKO

A wealthy girl falls for the milkman, who is really a rich man who thinks she's the maid.

Skittish second-feature comedy which helped to build a new star.

w Bert Granet   *d* Ben Holmes

Joan Fontaine, Allan Lane, Billy Gilbert, Cecil Kellaway, Hedda Hopper

The Main Event

US 1979 112m Technicolor
Warner/First Artists/Barwood (Jon Peters, Barbra Streisand)
V, L

A lady entrepreneur takes on a prizefighter.

Thin and very patchy comedy for confirmed addicts of its star.

w Gail Parent, Andrew Smith *d* Howard Zieff   *ph* Mario Tosi *m* Michael Melvoin   *pd* Charles Rosen

Barbra Streisand, Ryan O'Neal, Paul Sand, Whitman Mayo, James Gregory

Main Street to Broadway*

US 1953 102m bw
Lester Cowan Productions

After several reverses a young playwright sees his work through to a Broadway opening night; it fails, but he has learned several lessons.

Curious, flat attempt to show the public how Broadway works, with big stars playing themselves in cameo roles.

w Samson Raphaelson   *d* Tay Garnett   *ph* James Wong Howe

Tom Morton, Mary Murphy, Ethel Barrymore, Lionel Barrymore, Shirley Booth, Rex Harrison, Lilli Palmer, Helen Hayes, Henry Fonda, Tallulah Bankhead, Mary Martin, Louis Calhern, John Van Druten, Cornel Wilde, Joshua Logan, Agnes Moorehead, Gertrude Berg

Maisie

US 1939 74m bw
MGM (J. Walter Ruben)

Adventures of a Brooklyn showgirl.

Acceptable programmer which led to

a series, all quite watchable and absolutely forgettable.

w Mary McCall Jnr *novel Dame* by Wilson Collison *d* Edwin L. Marin *ph* Leonard Smith

Ann Sothern, Robert Young, Ian Hunter, Ruth Hussey, Anthony Allan (John Hubbard), Cliff Edwards
The succeeding titles, mostly written by Mary McCall and directed by Marin or Harry Beaumont or Roy del Ruth, were:

1940: CONGO MAISIE (with John Carroll; a remake of RED DUST), GOLD RUSH MAISIE (with Lee Bowman), MAISIE WAS A LADY (with Lew Ayres, Maureen O'Sullivan)
1941: RINGSIDE MAISIE (with George Murphy; GB title CASH AND CARRY)
1942: MAISIE GETS HER MAN (with Red Skelton; GB title SHE GOT HER MAN)
1943: SWING SHIFT MAISIE (with James Craig; GB title THE GIRL IN OVERALLS)
1944: MAISIE GOES TO RENO (with John Hodiak; GB title YOU CAN'T DO THAT TO ME)
1946: UP GOES MAISIE (with George Murphy; GB title UP SHE GOES)
1947: UNDERCOVER MAISIE (with Barry Nelson; GB title UNDERCOVER GIRL)

'Is she a kid – or is she kidding?'
The Major and the Minor**
US 1942 100m bw
Paramount (Arthur Hornblow Jnr)

A girl poses as a child in order to travel half fare on a train, and is helped by an officer who falls for her.

Moderately smart comedy showing the writer-director's emergent style.

Remade as *You're Never Too Young* (qv).

w Charles Brackett, Billy Wilder *d* Billy Wilder *ph* Leo Tover *m* Robert Emmett Dolan

Ginger Rogers, Ray Milland, Rita Johnson, Robert Benchley, Diana Lynn, Edward Fielding, Frankie Thomas, Charles Smith
  OSBORNE (Robert Benchley): 'Why don't you get out of that wet coat and into a dry martini?'

'The script seems to have been concocted after the title.' – *New Yorker, 1977*

Major Barbara***
GB 1941 121m bw
Gabriel Pascal

The daughter of an armaments millionaire joins the Salvation Army but resigns when it accepts her father's donation.

Stagey but compulsive version of a play in which the author takes typical side swipes at anything and everything within reach, allowing for some gorgeous acting (and overacting) by an impeccable cast.

w Anatole de Grunwald, Gabriel Pascal *play Bernard Shaw* *d* Gabriel Pascal, Harold French, David Lean *ph* Ronald Neame *m* William Walton *ad* Vincent Korda, John Bryan *ed* Charles Frend *costumes* Cecil Beaton

Wendy Hiller, Rex Harrison, Robert Morley, Robert Newton, Marie Lohr, Emlyn Williams, Sybil Thorndike, Deborah Kerr, David Tree, Felix Aylmer, Penelope Dudley Ward, Walter Hudd, Marie Ault, Donald Calthrop

'Shaw's ebullience provides an unslackening fount of energy . . . his all-star cast of characters are outspoken as no one else is in films except the Marx Brothers.' — *William Whitebait*

'To call it a manifest triumph would be an arrant stinginess with words.' — *New York Times*

Major League

US 1989 106m Technicolor
Braveworld/Fox (Mark Rosenberg)
V, L

A hopeless baseball team turn winners when they learn their owner wants them to lose.

Broad and often tasteless comedy, too predictable to be funny.

wd David S. Ward   *ph* Reynaldo Villalobos   *m* James Newton Howard   *pd* Jeffrey Howard   *ed* Dennis M. Hill, Tony Lombardo

Tom Berenger, Charlie Sheen, Corbin Bernsen, Margaret Whitton, James Gammon, Rene Russo, Wesley Snipes, Charles Cyphers

Make Mine a Million

GB 1959 82m bw
British Lion/Elstree Independent/Jack
  Hylton (John Baxter)

A TV make-up man strikes it rich by showing advertisements on non-commercial television.

Amiable, low-key comedy, relying heavily on the personality of its star.

w Peter Blackmore, Arthur Askey, Talbot Rothwell   *story* Jack Francis   *d* Lance Comfort   *ph* Arthur Grant   *m* Stanley Black   *ad* Dennis Wreford   *ed* Peter Pitt

Arthur Askey, Sidney James, Dermot Walsh, Olga Lindo, Clive Morton, Sally Barnes, Leigh Madison, Bernard

Cribbins, Gillian Lynee, The Penge Formation Dancers

Make Mine Mink**

GB 1960 101m bw
Rank (Hugh Stewart)

Members of a high-class boarding establishment steal furs to give the proceeds to charity.

Enjoyable comedy, expertly performed.

w Michael Pertwee, Peter Blackmore   *play Breath of Spring* by Peter Coke   *d* Robert Asher   *ph* Reginald Wyer   *m* Philip Green   *ad* Carmen Dillon   *ed* Roger Cherrill

Terry-Thomas, Athene Seyler, Hattie Jacques, Billie Whitelaw, Raymond Huntley, Irene Handl, Kenneth Williams, Noel Purcell, Sydney Tafler

† The film was reissued with 21m cut.

Making Mr Right

US 1987 98m colour
Rank/Orion (Mike Wise, Joel Tuber)

An android falls in love with a public relations consultant.

Slight comedy that soon runs out of anywhere to go.

w Floyd Byars, Laurie Frank   *d* Susan Seidelman   *ph* Edward Lachman   *m* Chaz Jankel   *pd* Barbara Ling   *ed* Andrew Mondshein

Ann Magnuson, John Malkovich, Glenne Headly, Ben Masters, Laurie Metcalf, Polly Bergen, Harsh Nayyar, Hart Bochner

The Male Animal*

US 1942 101m bw
Warner (Wolfgang Reinhardt)

A dry college professor emancipates

himself when his wife becomes attracted to a football star.

Stagebound but amusing college comedy with pleasant humour and good performances. Remade as *She's Working Her Way through College* (qv).

w Julius J. and Philip G. Epstein, Stephen Morehouse Avery *play* James Thurber and Elliott Nugent *d* Elliott Nugent *ph* Arthur Edeson *m* Heinz Roemheld

Henry Fonda, Olivia de Havilland, Jack Carson, Joan Leslie, Eugene Pallette, Don Defore, Herbert Anderson, Hattie McDaniel

A Man about the House
GB 1974 90m colour
EMI/Hammer (Roy Skeggs)
V

Two young women, their male flatmate and their landlords combine forces to prevent the terrace from being razed for redevelopment.

Mild and rather exhausting sex comedy from the TV series, as relentlessly single-minded as a 'Carry On'.

w Johnnie Mortimer, Brian Cooke *d* John Robins *ph* Jimmy Allen *m* Christopher Gunning

Richard O'Sullivan, Paula Wilcox, Sally Thomsett, Yootha Joyce, Brian Murphy, Peter Cellier, Patrick Newell, Spike Milligan, Arthur Lowe

The Man in the White Suit****
GB 1951 81m bw
Ealing (Sidney Cole)
V, L

A scientist produces a fabric that never gets dirty and never wears out. Unions and management are equally aghast.

Brilliant satirical comedy played as farce and put together with meticulous cinematic counterpoint, so that every moment counts and all concerned give of their very best.

w Roger Macdougall, John Dighton, Alexander Mackendrick *d* Alexander Mackendrick *ph* Douglas Slocombe *m* Benjamin Frankel

Alec Guinness, Joan Greenwood, Cecil Parker, Vida Hope, Ernest Thesiger, Michael Gough, Howard Marion Crawford, Miles Malleson, George Benson, Edie Martin

'The combination of an ingenious idea, a bright, funny and imaginative script, skilful playing and perceptive brisk direction has resulted once more in a really satisfying Ealing comedy.' – *Richard Mallett, Punch*
AAN: script

The Man on the Flying Trapeze*
US 1935 65m bw
Paramount (William Le Baron)
GB title: *The Memory Expert*

Adventures of an oppressed family man who is useful to his boss because of his prodigious memory.

Plotless rigmarole of shapeless comedy sketches, for star fans.

w Ray Harris, Sam Hardy, Jack Cunningham, Bobby Vernon *story* Charles Bogle (W. C. Fields) *d* Clyde Bruckman *ph* Al Gilks

W. C. Fields, Kathleen Howard, Mary Brian, Grady Sutton, Vera Lewis, Lucien Littlefield, Oscar Apfel

'A series of gags unrelated to the title. Under average.' – *Variety*

The Man Who Came to Dinner***
US 1941 112m bw
Warner (Jack Saper, Jerry Wald)

An acid-tongued radio celebrity breaks his hip while on a lecture tour, and terrorizes the inhabitants of the suburban home where he must stay for several weeks.

Delightfully malicious caricature of Alexander Woollcott which, though virtually confined to one set, moves so fast that one barely notices the lack of cinematic variety, and certainly provides more than a laugh a minute, especially for those old enough to understand all the references.

w Julius J. and Philip G. Epstein *play George S. Kaufman, Moss Hart* d William Keighley   ph Tony Gaudio   m Frederick Hollander

Monty Woolley, Bette Davis, Ann Sheridan, *Jimmy Durante* (spoofing Chico Marx), *Reginald Gardiner* (spoofing Noël Coward), Richard Travis, *Billie Burke, Grant Mitchell, Ruth Vivian, Mary Wickes,* George Barbier, Elisabeth Fraser

WHITESIDE (Monty Woolley) to his nurse, who won't let him eat chocolates: 'I had an aunt who ate a box of chocolates every day of her life. She lived to be a hundred and two, and when she had been dead three days, she looked healthier than you do now!'

NURSE (Mary Wickes): 'I am not only walking out on this case, Mr Whiteside, I am leaving the nursing profession. I became a nurse because all my life, ever since I was a little girl, I was filled with the idea of serving a suffering humanity. After one month with you, Mr Whiteside, I am going to work in a munitions factory. From now on, anything I can do to help exterminate the human race will fill me with the greatest of pleasure. If Florence Nightingale had ever nursed YOU, Mr Whiteside, she would have married Jack the

Ripper instead of founding the Red Cross!'

WHITESIDE (introducing his secretary): 'This ageing debutante, Mr Jefferson, I retain in my employ only because she is the sole support of her two-headed brother.'

BANJO (Jimmy Durante): 'Did you ever get the feeling that you wanted to stay, and still get the feeling that you wanted to go?'

BEVERLY CARLTON (Reginald Gardiner impersonating Noël Coward): 'Don't tell me how you are, Sherry, I want none of the tiresome details. I've very little time, and so the conversation will be entirely about me, and I shall love it. Shall I tell you how I glittered through the South Seas like a silver scimitar, or would you rather hear how I finished a three-act play with one hand and made love to a maharaja's daughter with the other?'

'Deciding which woman in the world he loved most is driving him out of his mind!'

The Man Who Loved Women
France . 1977 119m Eastmancolor
Les Films du Carrosse/PAA (Marcel Bebert)
L

A man spends his life in pursuit of women and dies in the chase.

Sour comedy which doesn't quite come off.

w François Truffaut, Michel Fermaud, Suzanne Schiffman   d François Truffaut   ph Nestor Almendros   m Maurice Jaubert

Charles Denner, Brigitte Fossey, Leslie Caron, Nelly Borgeaud, Nathalie Baye

The Man Who Loved Women
US 1983 110m Metrocolor
Columbia/Delphi/Blake Edwards (Blake Edwards, Tony Adams)

An American remake of the above, with even less success.

w Blake Edwards, Milton Wexler, Geoffrey Edwards *d* Blake Edwards *ph* Haskell Wexler *m* Henry Mancini

Burt Reynolds, Julie Andrews, Kim Basinger, Marilu Henner, Cynthia Sikes, Jennifer Edwards

The Man with Two Brains
US 1983 93m colour
Warner/Aspen (David V. Picker, William E. McEuen)

A surgeon, trapped in a frustrating marriage, falls in love with a brain in a jar.

Offbeat, broad comedy that is never as funny as it promises to be.

w Carl Reiner, Steve Martin, George Gipe *d* Carl Reiner *ph* Michael Chapman *m* Joel Goldsmith *ad* Polly Platt *ed* Bud Molin

Steve Martin, Kathleen Turner, David Warner, Paul Benedict, Richard Brestoff, James Cromwell, Sissy Spacek (voice)

'Indefensible by any known standard of comedy form – or formlessness. It's not much of anything, but it moves along enjoyably.' – *Pauline Kael, New Yorker*

Manhattan***
US 1979 96m bw Panavision
UA/Jack Rollins/Charles H. Joffe
V, L

Episodes in the sex life of a TV comedy writer with an obsession about New York.

As close to a summation of Woody Allen's views and *oeuvre* as anybody needs; some smart jabs about the lives we lead are sometimes bogged down in earnestness and half-comic despair.

w Woody Allen, Marshall Brickman *d* Woody Allen *ph* Gordon Willis *md* Tom Pierson

Woody Allen, Diane Keaton, Meryl Streep, Mariel Hemingway, Michael Murphy

'Given that the identity of his films has increasingly been determined by his compulsion to talk about the things he finds important, but also by his fear of having them come out as anything but a joke, it is not surprising that he has scarcely been able to decide on a form for his "art": from the anything-for-a-laugh skittering of his early films, to the broad parodies and pastiches of his middle period, to the recent confessional/psychoanalytical mode.' – *Richard Combs, MFB*
'A masterpiece that has become a film for the ages by not seeking to be a film of the moment.' – *Andrew Sarris*
AAN: script; Mariel Hemingway

Manifesto
US 1988 94m colour
Cannon/Menahem Golan, Yoram Globus

In an Eastern European village in the 1920s, a lecherous secret policeman waylays revolutionaries before a visit by a king.

Sex-obsessed black comedy that muffs its climaxes.

wd Dusan Makavejev *story For a Night of Love* by Emile Zola *ph* Tomislav Pinter *m* Nicola Piovani *pd* Velijo Despotovic *ed* Tony Lawson

Alfred Molina, Camilla Soeberg, Simon Callow, Lindsay Duncan, Eric Stoltz, Rade Serbedzija, Chris Haywood, Linda Marlowe, Ronald Lacey

Mannequin
US 1987 89m DuArt
TCF/Gladden (Art Levinson)
V, L

A window dresser falls in love with a
mannequin who changes into a real
live girl.

Feeble and never less than idiotic
fantasy.

w Edward Rugoff, Michael
Gottlieb d Michael Gottlieb
ph Tim Suhrstedt m Sylvester
Levay pd Josan Russo
ed Richard Halsey, Frank Jiminez

Andrew McCarthy, Kim Cattrall,
Estelle Getty, James Spader, G. W.
Bailey, Carole Davis, Stephen
Vinovich, Christopher Maher,
Meshach Taylor

Mannequin Two: On the Move
US 1991 95m colour
Rank/Gladden (Edward Rugoff)
V, L

A window dresser discovers that a
mannequin holds the imprisoned
spirit of a bewitched peasant girl.

Even less enjoyable than the original,
if that's possible.

w Edward Rugoff, David Isaacs, Ken
Levine, Betty Israel d Stewart
Raffill ph Larry Pizer m David
McHugh ad Norman B. Dodge
Jnr ed Joan Chapman

Kristy Swanson, William Ragsdale,
Meshach Taylor, Terry Kizer, Stuart
Pankin, Cynthia Harris, Andrew Hill
Newman

'If this stiff ever shows any life, it will
be a wonder indeed.' – Variety
'A messy rehash of clichés and tired
jokes.' – Empire

Man's Favourite Sport?*
US 1963 120m Technicolor
Universal/Gibraltar/Laurel (Howard
  Hawks)

A star salesman of fishing tackle finds
his bluff called when he has to enter a
fishing competition.

Over-extended romantic farce drawn
by the director from memories of older
and better films, such as Libeled Lady
and his own Bringing Up Baby.

w John Fenton Murray d Howard
Hawks ph Russell Harlan
m Henry Mancini

Rock Hudson, Paula Prentiss, Maria
Perschy, Charlene Holt, John McGiver,
Roscoe Karns

'Hawks' deadpan documentation of a
physical gag is as effective as ever, but
the overall pace of his direction is
curiously contemplative, as though he
were savoring all his past jokes for the
last time.' – Andrew Sarris

The Marriage Circle**
US 1924 78m (24 fps) bw
  silent
Warner

A bachelor on the loose becomes
amorously involved in two marriages.

Feather-light comedy of manners
which began a whole new American
school, heavily influenced by various
European masters.

w Paul Bern play Only a Dream by
Lothar Schmidt d Ernst
Lubitsch ph Charles Van Enger

Monte Blue, Florence Vidor, Marie
Prevost, Adolphe Menjou, Creighton
Hale

'A vanished world of roses, kisses and
embraces, of whispers and sighs, of a
woman's shadowed arm encased in
georgette beckoning across a moonlit

□ □

garden . . . and hand-kissing all over the place.' – *Herman G. Weinberg*

'At once perfect cinematography and perfect conventional drama.' – *Iris Barry, The Spectator*

'So slim a plot, so hackneyed if you will, is told with gaiety and a wit that lift it into the very first rank of screen comedy.' – *National Board of Review*

† Remade as *One Hour with You,* also by Lubitsch.

'It's the most hilarious proposition a wife ever had!'

The Marriage Go Round
US 1961 98m DeLuxe
    Cinemascope
TCF (Leslie Stevens)

A Swedish girl suggests to a married American professor that she borrow his body for mating purposes, believing they would produce the perfect child.

Silly, unfunny sex comedy.

w Leslie Stevens *play* Leslie Stevens *d* Walter Lang *ph* Leo Tover *m* Dominic Frontière

James Mason, Susan Hayward, Julie Newmar, Robert Paige, June Clayworth

'As tedious as it is tasteless.' – *Evening Standard*

'It offers James Mason, an actor who couldn't crack a joke if it was a lichee nut, and Susan Hayward, a bargain basement Bette Davis whose lightest touch as a comedienne would stun a horse.' – *Time*

The Marriage of a Young Stockbroker**
US 1971 95m DeLuxe
TCF/Lawrence Turman

A stockbroker who finds his life and his marriage dull tries voyeurism and extramarital sex.

Sardonic adult comedy of the battle between the sexes, pretty lively from start to finish.

w Lorenzo Semple Jnr, *novel* Charles Webb *d* Lawrence Turman *ph* Laszlo Kovacs *m* Fred Karlin

Richard Benjamin, Joanna Shimkus, Elizabeth Ashley, Adam West, Patricia Barry

Married to the Mob**
US 1988 103m DuArt
Rank/Orion/Mysterious Arts (Kenneth Utt, Edward Saxon)
V, L

The wife of a murdered gangster tries to live an honest life after her husband's death.

Effervescent comedy-thriller that bubbles merrily along.

w Barry Strugatz, Mark R. Burns *d* Jonathan Demme *ph* Tak Fujimoto *m* David Byrne *pd* Kristi Zea *ed* Craig McKay

Michelle Pfeiffer, Matthew Modine, Dean Stockwell, Mercedes Ruehl, Alec Baldwin, Trey Wilson, Joan Cusack
AAN: Dean Stockwell

The Marrying Man
US 1991 116m Technicolor
Warner/Hollywood Pictures/Silver Screen Partners IV/Odyssey (David Permut)
GB title: *Too Hot To Handle*

A playboy, forced to marry a gangster's girlfriend, finds himself repeating the experience several times.

A misfiring romantic comedy, both involved and uninvolving.

w Neil Simon *d* Jerry Rees *ph* Donald E. Thorin *m* David

□ □

Newman   pd William F.
Matthews   ed Michael Jablow

Kim Basinger, Alec Baldwin, Elisabeth
Shue, Armand Assante, Paul Reiser,
Fisher Stevens, Peter Dobson, Steve
Hytner

'A still-born romantic comedy of
staggering ineptitude. Industry bad-
mouthing of the stars during
production was just a preview of the
terrible picture.' – Variety
'A comedy that bounces skittishly
down a lane that memory has not
travelled in a while. Maybe it's silly.
But it does awaken a nostalgic
fondness for an era when celebrity
dreaming was goofier, giddier and less
consequential than it is now.' –
Richard Schickel, Time

M*A*S*H***
US   1970   116m   DeLuxe
   Panavision
TCF/Aspen (Ingo Preminger, Leon
   Ericksen)
V, L

Surgeons at a mobile hospital in Korea
spend what spare time they have
chasing women and bucking
authority.

Savage comedy of man's rebellion in
the face of death, alternating sex farce
with gory operation scenes; hailed as
the great anti-everything film, and
certainly very funny for those who
can take it. It led to a television series
which for once did not disgrace its
original.

w Ring Lardner Jnr   novel Richard
Hooker   d Robert Altman
ph Harold E. Stine   m Johnny
Mandel

Donald Sutherland, Elliott Gould,
Tom Skerritt, Sally Kellerman, Robert
Duvall, Jo Ann Pflug, René
Auberjonois, Gary Burghof

'Bloody funny. A hyper-acute wiretap
on mankind's death wish.' – Joseph
Morgenstern
'The laughter is blood-soaked and the
comedy cloaks a bitter and terrible
truth.' – Judith Crist
'A foul-mouthed, raucous, anti-
establishment comedy, combining
gallows humour, sexual slapstick and
outrageous satire.' – Les Keyser,
Hollywood in the Seventies

AA: Ring Lardner Jnr
AAN: best picture; Robert Altman;
Sally Kellerman

Maxie
US   1985   98m   DeLuxe
Carter De Haven/Ellsboy/Aurora/Orion
L

The ghost of a twenties starlet revisits
her old apartment and takes over the
body of the wife of the tenant.

Heavenly comedy which would have
been funnier in the forties.

w Patricia Resnick   novel Marion's
Wall by Jack Finney   d Paul Aaron

Glenn Close, Mandy Patinkin, Ruth
Gordon, Barnard Hughes, Valerie
Curtin

Me and Him
US   1988   90m   colour
Columbia/Egmont/Neue Constantin (Bernd
Eichinger)
V, L

A New Yorker's penis begins to talk
back to him.

A comedy about male chauvinism
that fails to raise a smile.

w Warren D. Leight, Michael Junker,
Doris Dörrie   novel Io e Lui by
Alberto Moravia   d Doris Dörrie
ph Helge Weindler   ed Raimund
Barthelmes

Griffin Dunne, Ellen Greene, Steven Marcus, Craig T. Nelson, Kelly Bishop, Carey Lowell, Kara Glover, Kim Flowers

Me and My Pal*
US 1933 20m bw
Hal Roach

Ollie becomes engrossed in a jigsaw puzzle and forgets to get married.

Oddball star comedy which nearly comes off but simply doesn't provide enough jokes.

w Stan Laurel   d Charles Rogers, Lloyd French

Laurel and Hardy, James Finlayson, Eddie Dunn

The Meanest Man in the World
US 1943 57m bw
TCF

An easy-going small-town lawyer finds that business picks up when he becomes tough and mean.

Very minor star comedy with a muddled opening followed by strictly rationed laughs.

w George Seaton, Allan House
play George M. Cohan   d Sidney Lanfield

Jack Benny, Priscilla Lane, Rochester, Edmund Gwenn, Anne Revere

Meatballs
Canada 1979 92m Sonolab Color
Paramount
L

Adventures at an ineptly run summer camp.

Adolescent fun and games for the easily pleased adolescent. (By 1987, Meatballs 3 had been reached.)

w Len Blum, Dan Goldberg, Harold Ramis, Janis Allen   d Ivan Reitman

Bill Murray, Harvey Atkin, Russ Banham, Ron Barry

Meet Mr Lucifer*
GB 1953 81m bw
Ealing (Monja Danischewsky)

The Demon King in a tatty provincial pantomime dreams he is the devil preventing people from wasting time watching television.

Clean and occasionally amusing piece of topical satire on tellymania; but the prologue is funnier than the sketches.

w Monja Danischewsky
play Beggar My Neighbour by Arnold Ridley   d Anthony Pelissier
ph Desmond Dickinson   m Eric Rogers

Stanley Holloway, Peggy Cummins, Jack Watling, Barbara Murray, Joseph Tomelty, Gordon Jackson, Jean Cadell, Kay Kendall, Ian Carmichael, Gilbert Harding, Charles Victor, Humphrey Lestocq

'The human race is about to be destroyed by people who wouldn't hurt a fly'

Meet the Applegates
US 1990 82m DuArt
Castle Premier/New World (Denise Di Novi)
V, L
US title: The Applegates

Giant insects, whose habitat in the Brazilian rain forests has been destroyed, disguise themselves as humans and go to America to wreck a nuclear power plant.

Ineffectual slapstick satire aimed at suburban life-styles.

w Redbeard Simmons, Michael

Lehmann   *d* Michael Lehmann
ph Mitchell Dubin   *m* David
Newman   *pd* John Hutman
ad Kara Lindstrom, Adam Lustig
ed Norman Hollyn

Ed Begley Jr, Stockard Channing,
Dabney Coleman, Bobby Jacoby, Cami
Cooper, Glenn Shadix, Susan Barnes,
Adam Bieski

'This wayward movie has a great deal
of charm.' – *MFB*

Melvin and Howard*
US   1980   95m   Technicolor
Universal (Terry Nelson)

The life of a factory worker is changed
when a man he picks up in the Nevada
desert claims to be Howard Hughes.

Eccentric comedy which has been
compared to the work of Preston
Sturges, but has an agreeable style of
its own.

w Bo Goldman   *d* Jonathan
Demme   *ph* Tak Fujimoto
m Bruce Langhorne

Paul Le Mat, Jason Robards Jnr, Mary
Steenburgen, Elizabeth Cheshire,
Michael J. Pollard, Gloria Grahame

'An almost flawless act of sympathetic
imagination . . . it's what might have
happened if Jean Renoir had directed
a comedy script by Preston Sturges.' –
New Yorker

AA: Bo Goldman; Mary Steenburgen
AAN: Jason Robards Jnr (supporting
actor)

'Women want him for his wit. The C.I.A.
wants him for his body. All Nick wants is
his molecules back.'

'An adventure like you've never
seen.'

Memoirs of an Invisible Man*
US   1992   99m   Technicolor
    Panavision
Warner/Le Studio Canal Plus/Regency
    Enterprises/Alcor (Bruce Bodner, Dan
    Kolsrud)
V

A CIA agent pursues a stock analyst
who has turned invisible after an
accident.

Clever special effects fail to
compensate for the lacklustre script
and uninspired performances.

w Robert Collector, Dana Olsen,
William Goldman   *novel* H. F.
Saint   *d* John Carpenter
ph William A. Fraker   *m* Shirley
Walker   *pd* Lawrence G. Paull
sp Industrial Light and Magic
ed Marion Rothman

Chevy Chase, Daryl Hannah, Sam
Neill, Michael McKean, Stephen
Tobolowsky, Jim Norton

'Where's the wit? It fades into
invisibility while you're watching it.'
– *Los Angeles Times*

Men o' War*
US   1929   20m   bw
Hal Roach
V

Two sailors and two girls have
adventures in a park.

Simple-minded early talkie star
comedy featuring their famous soda
fountain routine.

w H. M. Walker   *d* Lewis R. Foster

Laurel and Hardy, James Finlayson

Mermaids

US 1990 110m colour
Rank/Orion (Lauren Lloyd, Wallis Nichita,
    Patrick Palmer)
V, L

A daughter, torn between becoming a
nun and her feelings for a handsome
boy, resolves her difficulties with her
flirtatious mother.

A romantic comedy uncertain
whether it is trying for laughs or tears;
it attempts, unsuccessfully, to settle
for both.

w June Roberts novel Patty
Dann d Richard Benjamin
ph Howard Atherton m Jack
Nitzsche pd Stuart Wurtzel
ed Jacqueline Cambas

Cher, Bob Hoskins, Winona Ryder,
Michael Schoeffling, Christina Ricci,
Caroline McWilliams, Jan Miner,
Betsey Townsend

'It wavers between arch comedy and
hollow melodrama, each desperately
over-pitched.' – Sight and Sound

† Lasse Halstrom was replaced by
Frank Oz as director before filming
began. Two weeks after filming
started, Richard Benjamin replaced
Frank Oz. Winona Ryder's role as
Cher's daughter was to have been
played by Emily Lloyd until Cher
objected that Lloyd did not look like
her.

Merry Andrew

US 1958 103m Metrocolor
    Cinemascope
MGM/Sol C. Siegel

A stuffy teacher in search of an
ancient statue joins a travelling
circus.

Deliberately charming star comedy
which plumps too firmly for whimsy
and, despite its professionalism,
provokes barely a smile, let alone a
laugh.

w Isobel Lennart, I. A. L. Diamond
story Paul Gallico d/ch Michael
Kidd ph Robert Surtees m Saul
Chaplin ly Johnny Mercer

Danny Kaye, Pier Angeli, Baccaloni,
Noel Purcell, Robert Coote, Patricia
Cutts, Rex Evans, Walter Kingsford,
Tommy Rall, Rhys Williams

Mexican Spitfire

A series of second feature comedies
nominally about a young businessman
and his temperamental Mexican wife
(Donald Woods and Lupe Velez),
whose interest shifted firmly to the
young man's accident-prone uncle
Matt and his aristocratic boss Lord
Epping, both of whom were played
by the rubber-legged Ziegfeld comic
Leon Errol at something near the top
of his form. The plots made little
sense, but the hectic situations
provoked hearty roars of laughter.
The films were all made by RKO, and
all directed by Leslie Goodwins.

1939: THE GIRL FROM MEXICO,
      MEXICAN SPITFIRE
1940: MEXICAN SPITFIRE OUT
      WEST
1941: MEXICAN SPITFIRE'S BABY,
      MEXICAN SPITFIRE AT SEA
1942: MEXICAN SPITFIRE SEES A
      GHOST, MEXICAN SPITFIRE'S
      ELEPHANT
1943: MEXICAN SPITFIRE'S

      BLESSED EVENT

Micki and Maude*

US 1984 118m Metrocolor
    Panavision
Columbia/Delphi III/B.E.E. (Tony Adams)

A TV show host accidentally gets his

wife and his mistress pregnant at the same time.

Wild and overlong farce with some undeniably funnier scenes than have been noted in the participants' work for some years.

w Jonathan Reynolds   d Blake Edwards   ph Harry Stradling Jr m Lee Holdridge   pd Roger Maus   ed Ralph E. Winters

Dudley Moore, Amy Irving, Ann Reinking, Richard Mulligan, George Gaynes, Wallace Shawn, John Pleshette

Midnight***

US   1939   95m   bw
Paramount (Arthur Hornblow Jnr)

A girl stranded in Paris is hired by an aristocrat to seduce the gigolo paying unwelcome attention to his wife.

Sparkling sophisticated comedy which barely flags until a slightly disappointing ending; all the talents involved are in excellent form.

w Billy Wilder, Charles Brackett, story Edwin Justus Mayer, Franz Schultz   d Mitchell Leisen ph Charles Lang   m Frederick Hollander

Claudette Colbert, Don Ameche, John Barrymore, Francis Lederer, Mary Astor, Elaine Barrie, Hedda Hopper, Rex O'Malley

'Leisen's masterpiece, one of the best comedies of the thirties.' – John Baxter, 1968
'One of the authentic delights of the thirties.' – New Yorker, 1976
'It has the elements of an American La Règle du Jeu.' – John Gillett
'Just about the best light comedy ever caught by the camera.' – Motion Picture Daily

'Three centuries in the making!'
A Midsummer Night's Dream***

US   1935   133m   bw
Warner (Max Reinhardt)
L

Two pairs of lovers sort out their problems with fairy help at midnight in the woods of Athens.

Shakespeare's play is treated with remarkable respect in this super-glamorous Hollywood adaptation based on the Broadway production by Max Reinhardt. Much of it comes off, and visually it's a treat.

w Charles Kenyon, Mary McCall Jnr   play William Shakespeare d Max Reinhardt, William Dieterle ph Hal Mohr, Fred Jackman, Byron Haskin, H. F. Koenekamp   md Erich Wolfgang Korngold   ch Bronislawa Nijinska   m Mendelssohn ad Anton Grot   ed Ralph Dawson

James Cagney, Dick Powell, Jean Muir, Ross Alexander, Olivia de Havilland, Joe E. Brown, Hugh Herbert, Arthur Treacher, Frank McHugh, Otis Harlan, Dewey Robinson, Victor Jory, Verree Teasdale, Mickey Rooney, Anita Louise, Grant Mitchell, Ian Hunter, Hobart Cavanaugh

'General b.o. chances could be improved by judicious pruning and appreciative selling . . . a fine prestige picture not only for Warners but for the industry as a whole.' – Variety
'You must see it if you want to be in a position to argue about the future of the film!' – Picturegoer
'The publicity push behind the film is tremendous – it is going to be a success or everyone at Warner Brothers is going to get fired.' – Robert Forsythe
'Its assurance as a work of film technique is undoubted.' – John Baxter, 1968

'Its worst contradiction lies in the way Warners first ordered up a whole batch of foreign and high-sounding names to handle music, dances, general production – and then turned around and handed them empty vessels for actors.' – *Otis Ferguson*

AA: photography; editing
AAN: best picture

A Midsummer Night's Sex Comedy*
US 1982 88m Technicolor
Warner/Orion/Rollins-Joffe (Robert Greenhut)
V

Around the turn of the century, a Wall Street broker expects various weekend guests at his country retreat.

Subdued, melancholy and rather uninventive Woody Allen variation on *Smiles of a Summer Night*.

wd Woody Allen   *ph* Gordon Willis   *m* from Mendelssohn
pd Mel Bourne   *ed* Susan E. Morse

Woody Allen, Mia Farrow, Jose Ferrer, Julie Hagerty, Tony Roberts, Mary Steenburgen

The Milky Way*
US 1936 88m bw
Paramount/Harold Lloyd (Edward Sheldon)

A milkman becomes a prizefighter and overcomes a gang of crooks.

Modest Harold Lloyd comedy towards the end of his career; remade as *The Kid from Brooklyn* (qv).

w Grover Jones, Frank Butler, Richard Connell   *play* Lynn Root, Harry Clork   *d* Leo McCarey
ph Alfred Gilks

Harold Lloyd, Adolphe Menjou, Verree Teasdale, Helen Mack, William Gargan, George Barbier, Lionel Stander

'The work of many hands, all laid on expertly.' – *Otis Ferguson*
'One is more amazed than ever at the good fortune of this youngish man whose chief talent is not to act at all, to do nothing, to serve as a blank wall for other people to scrawl their ideas on.' – *Graham Greene*

Le Million****
France 1931 89m bw
Tobis (Frank Clifford)

An artist and an ingratiating crook search Paris for a lost lottery ticket.

With its delicate touch, perfect sense of comedy timing and infectious use of recitative and song, this is superb screen entertainment using most of the medium's resources.

wd René Clair,   *musical comedy* Georges Berr, M. Guillemaud   *ph* Georges Périnal
m Georges Van Parys, Armand Bernard, Philippe Parès   *ad* Lazare Meerson

Annabella, René Lefèvre, *Paul Olivier*, Louis Allibert, Vanda Gréville, Raymond Cordy

'A good musical farce that ought to do well everywhere . . . it has speed, laughs, splendid photography and a good cast.' – *Variety*
'René Clair at his exquisite best; no one else has ever been able to make a comedy move with such delicate inevitability.' – *New Yorker, 1978*
'I wanted an atmosphere of foolishness . . . we put gauze between the actors and the sets, which created an illusion of unreality.' – *René Clair*

† The style of this film was developed and expanded in Hollywood by Lubitsch in *One Hour with You* and by Mamoulian in *Love Me Tonight*.

'Roaring laughs in a story built of goofer dust and frog fur!'

Million Dollar Legs*

US 1932 64m bw
Paramount

A mythical sport-ridden country decides to enter the Olympic Games.

The good gags in this film are weighted down by plodding treatment, and the general effect is more doleful than funny.

w Harry Myers, Nick Barrows, Joseph L. Mankiewicz d Edward Cline ph Arthur Todd

W. C. Fields, Jack Oakie, Andy Clyde, Lyda Roberti, Ben Turpin, Hugh Herbert, Billy Gilbert, George Barbier, Susan Fleming

'One of the silliest and funniest pictures ever made.' – New Yorker, 1977

The Million Pound Note*

GB 1954 91m Technicolor
GFD/Group Films (John Bryan)
US title: Man with a Million

A man is given a million pounds in the form of a single banknote and finds it difficult to spend.

Fairly pleasing period comedy which wears its one joke pretty thin but is nicely decorated and acted.

w Jill Craigie story Mark Twain d Ronald Neame ph Geoffrey Unsworth m William Alwyn

Gregory Peck, Jane Griffiths, Ronald Squire, Joyce Grenfell, A. E. Matthews, Reginald Beckwith, Hartley Power, Wilfrid Hyde White

'From naughty, notorious George Bernard Shaw, the sultry story of the beautiful babe in the Balmain gowns who pants for romance ...!'

The Millionairess*

GB 1960 90m DeLuxe Cinemascope
TCF/Dimitri de Grunwald (Pierre Rouve)

The richest woman in the world falls for a poor Indian doctor.

Messy travesty of a Shavian comedy that was never more than a star vehicle to begin with. Hardly any of it works despite the star cast, who are mostly miscast.

w Wolf Mankowitz play Bernard Shaw d Anthony Asquith ph Jack Hildyard m Georges Van Parys

Sophia Loren, Peter Sellers, Alastair Sim, Vittorio de Sica, Dennis Price, Gary Raymond, Alfie Bass, Miriam Karlin, Noel Purcell

'The result, lacking any sort of dramatic cohesion or continuity and seemingly planned less as a film than as a series of haphazard effects, is merely tiring.' – Peter John Dyer

Minnie and Moskowitz*

US 1971 115m Technicolor
Universal (Al Rubin)

Two lonely Los Angeles misfits have a bumpy courtship.

Enjoyably aimless character comedy.

wd John Cassavetes ph Arthur J. Ornitz m Bob Harwood

Gena Rowlands, Seymour Cassel

The Miracle of Morgan's Creek*

US 1943 99m bw
Paramount (Preston Sturges)

Chaos results when a stuttering hayseed tries to help a girl accidentally pregnant by a soldier she met hazily at a dance.

Weird and wonderful one-man assault on the Hays Office and sundry other American institutions such as motherhood and politics; an indescribable, tasteless, roaringly funny mêlée, as unexpected at the time as it was effective, like a kick in the pants to all other film comedies.

wd Preston Sturges   ph John Seitz   *m* Leo Shuken, Charles Bradshaw

Betty Hutton, Eddie Bracken, William Demarest, Diana Lynn, Porter Hall, Akim Tamiroff, Brian Donlevy, Alan Bridge

OFFICER KOCKENLOCKER (William Demarest): 'Daughters. They're a mess no matter how you look at 'em. A headache till they get married – *if* they get married – and after that they get worse . . . Either they leave their husbands and come back with four kids and move into your guest room or the husband loses his job and the whole caboodle comes back. Or else they're so homely that you can't get rid of them at all and they sit around like Spanish moss and shame you into an early grave.'

EMILY KOCKENLOCKER (Diana Lynn): 'If you don't mind my mentioning it, father, I think you have a mind like a swamp.'

'Like taking a nun on a roller coaster.' – *James Agee*
'This film moves in a fantastic and irreverent whirl of slapstick, nonsense, farce, sentiment, satire, romance, melodrama – is there any ingredient of dramatic entertainment except maybe tragedy and grand opera that hasn't been tossed into it?' – *National Board of Review*
'Bad taste, or no bad taste, I

thoroughly enjoyed it.' – *Richard Mallett, Punch*
AAN: Preston Sturges (as writer)

Miracle on 34th Street***
US   1947   94m   bw
TCF (William Perlberg)
V, L
GB title: *The Big Heart*

A department store Santa Claus claims to be the real thing.

Mainly charming comedy fantasy which quickly became an American classic but does suffer from a few dull romantic stretches.

wd George Seaton,   story Valentine Davies   *ph* Charles Clarke, Lloyd Ahern   *m* Cyril Mockridge

Edmund Gwenn, Maureen O'Hara, John Payne, Natalie Wood, Gene Lockhart, Porter Hall, William Frawley, Jerome Cowan, Thelma Ritter

'Altogether wholesome, stimulating and enjoyable.' – *Motion Picture Herald*

AA: George Seaton (as writer); Valentine Davies; Edmund Gwenn
AAN: best picture

Miranda*
GB   1947   80m   bw
GFD/Gainsborough/Sydney Box (Betty Box)

A doctor on holiday in Cornwall catches a mermaid and takes her to London disguised as an invalid.

Simple-minded comedy which scores a few easy laughs on obvious targets.

w Peter Blackmore   *play* Peter Blackmore   *d* Ken Annakin
ph Ray Elton   *m* Temple Abady

Glynis Johns, Griffith Jones, Googie Withers, *Margaret Rutherford*, David

Tomlinson, Sonia Holm, John McCallum

† Sequel 1949, *Mad about Men*.

Miss Grant Takes Richmond*
US 1949 87m bw
Columbia (S. Sylvan Simon)
GB title: *Innocence Is Bliss*

A dumb secretary helps defeat crooks and improve the local housing situation.

Mildly amusing star comedy.

w Nat Perrin, Devery Freeman, Frank Tashlin   *d* Lloyd Bacon
ph Charles Lawton Jnr   *md* Morris Stoloff   *m* Heinz Roemheld

Lucille Ball, William Holden, Janis Carter, James Gleason, Gloria Henry, Frank McHugh, George Cleveland

'One of the more delightful comedies of the season.' – *Lawrence J. Quirk*

The Missionary*
GB 1983 86m colour
   Panavision
HandMade Films (Michael Palin)

In 1906, a clergyman returns from darkest Africa and sets up a Mission to Fallen Women in the East End of London.

Sporadically amusing comedy of a reformer being tempted; the decoration is funnier than the central theme.

w Michael Palin   *d* Richard Loncraine   *ph* Peter Hannan
m Mike Moran   *ad* Norman Garwood

Michael Palin, Maggie Smith, Michael Hordern, Trevor Howard, Denholm Elliott, Graham Crowden, Phoebe Nichols, Roland Culver

'It leaves one with a half-frozen smile, in anticipation of a comic fulfilment which never quite happens.' – *Nick Roddick, MFB*
'A deliciously straight-faced acceptance of the palpably absurd.' – *Daily Mail*

Mr Belvedere Goes to College*
US 1949 88m bw
TCF (Samuel G. Engel)

A self-styled genius goes back to school and helps a college widow.

Flat follow up to *Sitting Pretty* (qv), with only a few laughs.

w Richard Sale, Mary Loos, Mary McCall Jnr   *d* Elliott Nugent
ph Lloyd Ahern   *m* Alfred Newman

Clifton Webb, Shirley Temple, Alan Young, Tom Drake, Jessie Royce Landis, Kathleen Hughes, Taylor Holmes

Mr Belvedere Rings the Bell*
US 1951 87m bw
TCF (André Hakim)

Imperturbable Mr Belvedere enters an old folk's home under false pretences to test his theories of ageing.

A not unagreeable star vehicle for those who can stand the sentiment.

w Ranald MacDougall   *play The Silver Whistle* by Robert E. McEnroe
d Henry Koster   *ph* Joseph LaShelle   *m* Cyril Mockridge

Clifton Webb, Joanne Dru, Hugh Marlowe, Zero Mostel, Doro Merande

Mr Blandings Builds His Dream House***
US 1948 84m bw
RKO (Norman Panama, Melvin Frank)
L

A New York advertising man longs to

live in the Connecticut countryside, but finds the way to rural satisfaction is hard.

It hasn't the lightness and brightness of the book, but this is a fun film for the middle-aged who like to watch three agreeable stars doing their thing.

w Norman Panama, Melvin Frank, novel Eric Hodgins   d H. C. Potter ph James Wong Howe md Constantin Bakaleinikoff m Leigh Harline

Cary Grant, Myrna Loy, Melvyn Douglas, Reginald Denny, Louise Beavers, Ian Wolfe, Harry Shannon, Nestor Paiva, Jason Robards

'A bulls-eye for middle-class middlebrows.' – *James Agee* 'I loved it. That was really a pleasure to make.' – *H. C. Potter, 1973*

Mr Deeds Goes to Town***
US   1936   118m   bw
Columbia (Frank Capra)
V, L

A small-town poet inherits a vast fortune and sets New York on its heels by his honesty.

What once was fresh and charming now seems rather laboured in spots, and the production is parsimonious indeed, but the courtroom scene still works, and the good intentions conquer all.

w Robert Riskin,   story Opera Hat by Clarence Budington Kelland *d Frank Capra   ph* Joseph Walker   *md* Howard Jackson *m* Adolph Deutsch

Gary Cooper, Jean Arthur, Raymond Walburn, Lionel Stander, Walter Catlett, George Bancroft, Douglass Dumbrille, H. B. Warner, Ruth Donnelly, *Margaret Seddon, Margaret McWade*

'I have an uneasy feeling he's on his way out. He's started to make pictures about themes instead of people.' – *Alistair Cooke* 'Everywhere the picture goes, from the endearing to the absurd, the accompanying business is carried through with perfect zip and relish.' – *Otis Ferguson* 'A comedy quite unmatched on the screen.' – *Graham Greene* 'The film culminates in a courtroom sequence that introduced the word "pixilated" to just about every American home, and set people to examining each other's casual scribbles or sketches – their "doddles".' – *Pauline Kael, 70s*

AA: Frank Capra
AAN: best picture; Robert Riskin; Gary Cooper

Mr Destiny
US   1990   105m   colour
Buena Vista/Touchstone/Silver Screen
    Partners IV (James Orr, Jim Cruikshank)
L

A 35-year-old failure is given the chance to re-live his life as a success.

Dim comedy with the dimmer moral that everyone gets the life they deserve.

w James Orr, Jim Cruikshank d James Orr   ph Alex Thomson *m* David Newman   *pd* Michael Seymour   *ed* Michael R. Miller

James Belushi, Linda Hamilton, Michael Caine, Jon Lovitz, Hart Bochner, Bill McCutcheon, René Russo

'A heavy-handed by-the-numbers fantasy.' – *Variety*

Mr Drake's Duck**
GB   1950   85m   bw
Daniel M. Angel/Douglas Fairbanks

A duck lays a uranium egg, and a gentleman farmer finds himself at the centre of international military disagreement.

Brisk and amusing minor comedy deploying British comic types to good purpose.

wd Val Guest,   *radio play* Ian Messiter   *ph* Jack Cox   *m* Philip Martell

Douglas Fairbanks Jnr, Yolande Donlan, Wilfrid Hyde White, A. E. Matthews, Jon Pertwee, Reginald Beckwith, Howard Marion-Crawford, Peter Butterworth, Tom Gill

'One of the funniest films I have ever seen.' – *News of the World*

Mr Hobbs Takes a Vacation*
US · 1962 116m DeLuxe
  Cinemascope
TCF (Jerry Wald)

A city dweller takes a seaside house for a family holiday, but it turns out to be a crumbling ruin.

Overlong, sloppy comedy which devotes too much time to teenage romance but manages occasional smiles.

w Nunnally Johnson
novel Edward Streeter   *d* Henry Koster   *ph* W. C. Mellor
m Henry Mancini

James Stewart, Maureen O'Hara, Fabian, John Saxon, Marie Wilson, Reginald Gardiner, *John McGiver*

Mr North*
US 1988 93m Metrocolor
Columbia TriStar/Heritage Entertainment/
  Showcase Productions (Steven Haft,
  Skip Steloff)
L

In the wealthy society of Newport in the 1920s, a young man angers the local doctor by gaining a reputation as a miracle healer.

Gentle, amusing fable, peopled by some engaging eccentrics.

w Joanet Roach, John Huston, James Costigan   *novel Theophilus North* by Thornton Wilder   *d* Danny Huston   *ph* Robin Vidgeon
m David McHugh   *pd* Eugene Lee   *ed* Roberto Silvi

Anthony Edwards, Robert Mitchum, Lauren Bacall, Harry Dean Stanton, Anjelica Huston, Mary Stuart Masterson, Virginia Madsen, Tammy Grimes, David Warner

Mr Peabody and the Mermaid
US 1948 89m bw
U-I (Nunnally Johnson)

A middle-aged husband imagines an affair with a mermaid.

Bone-headed quick-cash-in on *Miranda* (qv); it never begins to work.

w Nunnally Johnson   *novel* Guy and Constance Jones   *d* Irving Pichel   *ph* Russell Metty
m Robert Emmett Dolan

William Powell, Ann Blyth, Irene Hervey, Andrea King, Clinton Sundberg

Mister Roberts**
US 1955 123m Warnercolor
  Cinemascope
Warner/Leland Hayward

Life aboard a World War II cargo ship yearning for action.

A mixture of comedy and sentimentality which has become an American minor classic as a play; this film version is a shambling affair but gets most of the effects over.

w Frank Nugent, Joshua Logan *play* Thomas Heggen and Joshua Logan *novel Thomas Heggen* d John Ford, Mervyn Le Roy *ph* Winton Hoch *m* Franz Waxman

Henry Fonda, James Cagney, William Powell, Jack Lemmon, Betsy Palmer, Ward Bond, Phil Carey, Ken Curtis, Harry Carey Jnr

AA: Jack Lemmon
AAN: best picture

'It's lonely at the middle.'

Mr Saturday Night*

US 1992 119m colour
Columbia/Castle Rock/New Line (Billy Crystal)

In his dotage, a successful comedian looks back over his long career.

Intermittently amusing comedy, not helped by over-generous dollops of sentimentality.

w Billy Crystal, Lowell Ganz, Babaloo Mandel *d* Billy Crystal *ph* Don Peterman *m* Marc Shaiman *pd* Albert Brenner *ed* Kent Beyda

Billy Crystal, David Paymer, Julie Warner, Helen Hunt, Ron Silver

'What's so special about this movie is that the funny parts are so funny, with gags coming too fast and too good to be assimilated on first hearing. At such moments, the main reaction is exhausted gratitude. It's as if you hired a painter to do your bathroom and he gave you the Sistine Chapel at no extra cost.' – *Richard Corliss, Time*
AAN: David Paymer

Mrs Doubtfire*

US 1993 125m DeLux Panavision
TCF/Blue Wolf (Marcia Garces Williams, Robin Williams, Mark Radcliffe)

An unemployed actor disguises

himself as a nanny so that he can spend more time with his children.

If you can accept Williams as an Englishwoman, there is occasional slapstick amusement to be found in this over-long and sickly sweet comedy.

w Randi Mayem Singer, Leslie Dixon *novel Alias Madam Doubtfire* by Anne Fine *d* Chris Columbus

Robin Williams, Sally Field, Pierce Brosnan, Harvey Fierstein, Polly Holiday

Mo' Money

US 1992 90m colour
Columbia TriStar/Columbia/A Wife N'Kids (Michael Rachmil)

After trying and failing to go straight, a hustler and his brother make money with a stolen credit card but also expose a big-time crook.

A vehicle of dubious morality, with some street-wise comedy, expertly delivered, from its star.

w Damon Wayans *d* Peter Macdonald *ph* Don Burgess *m* Jay Gruska *pd* William Arnold *ed* Hubert C. de La Bouillerie

Damon Wayans, Stacey Dash, Joe Santos, John Diehl, Harry J. Lennix, Marlon Wayans, Mark Beltzman

'The comedy is, in truth, pretty feeble – rancid without the redeeming virtue of wit.' – *Sheila Johnston, Independent*
'If this is grown-up cinema, give me Peter Rabbit.' – *Geoff Brown, The Times*

'You'll never laugh as long and as loud again as long as you live! The laughs come so fast and so furious you'll wish it would end before you collapse!'

Modern Times*

US 1936 87m bw

Charles Chaplin

V, L

An assembly-line worker goes berserk but can't get another job.

Silent star comedy produced in the middle of the sound period; flashes of genius alternate with sentimental sequences and jokes without punch.

wd Charles Chaplin   ph Rollie Totheroh, Ira Morgan   m Charles Chaplin

Charles Chaplin, Paulette Goddard, Henry Bergman, Chester Conklin, Tiny Sandford

'A natural for the world market . . . box office with a capital B.' – *Variety*
'A feature picture made out of several one- and two-reel shorts, proposed titles being *The Shop, The Jailbird, The Singing Waiter.*' – *Otis Ferguson*

Mon Oncle*

France 1956 116m Eastmancolor

Specta/Gray/Alterdel-Centaure (Louis Dolivet)

V

A small boy has less affection for his parents than for his vague, clumsy uncle.

Tiresomely long star vehicle, with Tati harping on his theory of detachment, i.e. keeping his comic character on the fringes of the action. It really doesn't work in a film of this length, and the jokes are thin.

w Jacques Tati, Jacques Lagrange   d Jacques Tati   ph Jean Bourgoin   m Alain Romains, Franck Barcellini

Jacques Tati, Jean-Pierre Zola, Adrienne Servatie, Alain Becourt, Yvonne Arnaud

'Deft, elusive, full of heart.' – *Brenda Davies, MFB*
'Cinema humour at its brilliant best.' – *Daily Worker*

AA: best foreign film

The Money Pit

US 1986 91m DuArt Color

Universal/Steven Spielberg (Frank Marshall, Kathleen Kennedy, Art Levinson)

V, L

New Yorkers take on an old suburban house, and find it was no bargain.

Witless semi-remake of *Mr Blandings Builds His Dream House*, with screams instead of subtlety and no real humour at all.

w David Giler   d Richard Benjamin   ph Gordon Willis   m Michel Colombier   pd Patrizia von Brandenstein   ed Jacqueline Cambas

Tom Hanks, Shelley Long, Alexander Godunov, Maureen Stapleton, Joe Mantegna, Philip Bosco, Josh Mostel

'It begins unpromisingly and slides irrevocably downward from there.' – *Variety*

'The 1931 nut crop is ready!'

Monkey Business*

US 1931 81m bw

Paramount (Herman J. Mankiewicz)

V, L

Four ship's stowaways crash a society party and catch a few crooks.

The shipboard part of this extravaganza is one of the best stretches of Marxian lunacy, but after the Chevalier impersonations it runs out of steam. Who's grumbling?

w S. J. Perelman, Will B. Johnstone, Arthur Sheekman *d Norman Z. McLeod. ph Arthur L. Todd*

Groucho, Chico, Harpo, Zeppo, Thelma Todd, Rockcliffe Fellowes, Ruth Hall, Harry Woods

'Surefire for laughs despite working along familiar lines . . . picture has started off by doing sweeping business all over, and no reason why it shouldn't continue to tickle wherever it plays.' — *Variety*

Monkey Business*
US 1952 97m bw
TCF (Sol C. Siegel)
original title: *Darling I Am Growing Younger*

A chimpanzee in a research lab accidentally concocts an elixir of youth.

Remarkably laboured comedy by and with top people; it can't fail to have funny moments, but they are few and far between.

w Ben Hecht, Charles Lederer, I.A.L. Diamond d Howard Hawks ph Milton Krasner m Leigh Harline

Cary Grant, Ginger Rogers, *Charles Coburn,* Marilyn Monroe, Hugh Marlowe
CHARLES COBURN to Marilyn Monroe (playing his secretary): 'Find someone to type this.'

Monsieur Hulot's Holiday****
France 1953 91m bw
Cady/Discina (Fred Orain)
V, L
original title: *Les Vacances de Monsieur Hulot*

An accident-prone bachelor arrives at a seaside resort and unwittingly causes havoc for himself and everyone else.

Despite lame endings to some of the jokes, this is a film to set the whole

world laughing, Hulot himself being an unforgettable character and some of the timing magnificent. One feels that it could very nearly happen.

w Jacques Tati, Henri Marquet d Jacques Tati ph Jacques Mercanton, Jean Mouselle m Alain Romans

Jacques Tati, Nathalie Pascaud, Michèle Rolla, Valentine Camax

'The casual, amateurish air of his films clearly adds to their appeal: it also appears to explain their defects.' — *Penelope Houston, MFB*
'It had me laughing out loud with more enjoyment than any other comedy film this year.' — *Daily Express*
AAN: script

Monsieur Verdoux**
US 1947 125m bw
Charles Chaplin
V

A bank cashier marries and murders rich women to support his real wife.

Interesting but unsatisfactory redrafting of the Landru case; the star is more dapper than funny, the moral is unconvincing, and the slapstick sequences too often raise yawns.

wd Charles Chaplin ph Rollie Totheroh m Charles Chaplin

Charles Chaplin, Martha Raye, Isobel Elsom

'The cleverest and most brilliant film I have yet made.' — *Charles Chaplin*
'The result is pure Chaplin; and his genius alone has perfected the astonishing central portrait, among the few which, owing nothing to stage or fiction, belong entirely to the cinema.' — *Dilys Powell*
'Even today it will seem a failure to anyone who has taken half a dozen

lessons in film technique.' – *Andrew Sarris, 1970*

AAN: Charles Chaplin (as writer)

'Makes *Ben-Hur* look like an epic!'
Monty Python and the Holy Grail**
GB   1975   90m   Technicolor
EMI/Python (Monty) Pictures/Michael White (Mark Forstater)
V, L

King Arthur and his knights seek the Holy Grail.

Hellzapoppin-like series of linked sketches on a medieval theme; some slow bits, but often uproariously funny and with a remarkable visual sense of the Middle Ages.

w Graham Chapman, John Cleese, Terry Gilliam, Eric Idle, Michael Palin   *d* Terry Gilliam, Terry Jones   *ph* Terry Bedford
animation Terry Gilliam   *m* Neil Innes   *pd* Roy Smith

Graham Chapman, John Cleese, Terry Gilliam, Eric Idle, Michael Palin

'The team's visual buffooneries and verbal rigmaroles are piled on top of each other with no attention to judicious timing or structure, and a form which began as a jaunty assault on the well-made revue sketch and an ingenious misuse of television's fragmented style of presentation, threatens to become as unyielding and unfruitful as the conventions it originally attacked.' – *Geoff Brown*

Monty Python's Life of Brian**
GB   1979   93m   Eastmancolor
Hand Made Films (John Goldstone)
V, L

A contemporary of Jesus is mistaken for him and crucified.

Controversial middle-eastern romp which left its creators battered but extremely wealthy. In the face of such an onslaught of bad taste, criticism seems irrelevant.

w and starring John Cleese, Graham Chapman, Eric Idle, Michael Palin, Terry Gilliam, Terry Jones   *d* Terry Jones   *ph* Peter Biziou
m Geoffrey Burgon   *ad* Roger Christian   *ed* Julian Doyle

Monty Python's The Meaning of Life
GB   1983   90m   Technicolor
Universal/Celandine/The Monty Python Partnership (John Goldstone)
V, L

A series of sketches in questionable taste.

Subjects include organ transplants, sex, death and the results of overeating.

w and starring Graham Chapman, John Cleese, Terry Gilliam, Eric Idle, Michael Palin, Terry Jones   *d* Terry Jones   *ph* Peter Hannan
m various   *pd* Harry Lange

The Moon Is Blue*
US   1953   99m   bw
Otto Preminger
L

A spry young girl balances the attractions of a middle-aged lover against her young one.

Paper-thin comedy partly set on top of the Empire State Building (and thereafter in a dowdy set); mildly amusing in spots, it gained notoriety, and a Production Code ban, by its use of such naughty words as 'virgin' and 'mistress'.

w F. Hugh Herbert   *play* F. Hugh Herbert   *d* Otto Preminger
ph Ernest Laszlo   *m* Herschel Burke Gilbert   *ed* Otto Ludwig

Maggie McNamara, David Niven, William Holden, Tom Tully, Dawn Addams

PATTY (Maggie McNamara): 'Men are usually bored with virgins. I'm so glad you're not . . . Have you a mistress?'

DONALD: 'Don't you think it's better for a girl to be preoccupied with sex than occupied with it?'

'It adds nothing to the art of cinema and certainly does not deserve the attention it will get for flouting the Production Code.' – *Philip T. Hartung*

† The film was made simultaneously in German, as *Die Jungfrau auf dem Dach*, with Hardy Kruger, Johanna Matz and Johannes Heesters.
AAN: Maggie McNamara; title song (*m* Herschel Burke Gilbert, *ly* Sylvia Fine); editing

Moon over Parador
US   1988   104m   DeLuxe
UIP/Universal (Paul Mazursky)
V, L

An actor is kidnapped and forced to impersonate the president of a Caribbean country.

Occasionally amusing, but the joke is too thin to bear much watching.

w Leon Capetanos, Paul Mazursky
story Charles G. Booth   *d* Paul Mazursky   *ph* Donald McAlpine
m Maurice Jarre   *pd* Pato Guzman   *ed* Stuart Pappe

Richard Dreyfuss, Raul Julia, Sonia Bragg, Jonathan Winters, Fernando Rey, Sammy Davis Jr, Michael Greene, Polly Holliday, Milton Goncalves, Charo, Marianne Sagebrecht

Moonstruck*
US   1987   102m   Technicolor
Patrick Palmer/Norman Jewison
V, L

Young widow falls for the estranged brother of her husband-to-be.

Noisy, sometimes heavy-handed romantic comedy of Italian-American manners.

w John Patrick Shanley   *d* Norman Jewison   *ph* David Watkin
m Dick Hyman   *pd* Philip Rosenberg

Cher, Nicolas Cage, Vincent Gardenia, Olympia Dukakis, Danny Aiello

AA: Cher; John Patrick Shanley
AAN: best picture; Norman Jewison; Vincent Gardenia; Olympia Dukakis

The More the Merrier*
US   1943   104m   bw
Columbia (George Stevens)

In crowded Washington during World War II, a girl allows two men to share her apartment and falls in love with the younger one.

Thoroughly amusing romantic comedy with bright lines and situations; remade less effectively as *Walk Don't Run* (qv).

w Robert Russell, Frank Ross, Richard Flournoy, Lewis R. Foster   *d* George Stevens   *ph* Ted Tetzlaff
md Morris Stoloff   *m* Leigh Harline

Jean Arthur, Joel McCrea, Charles Coburn, Richard Gaines, Bruce Bennett

'The gayest comedy that has come from Hollywood in a long time. It has no more substance than a watermelon, but is equally delectable.' – *Howard Barnes*
'Farce, like melodrama, offers very special chances for accurate observation, but here accuracy is avoided ten times to one in favour of the easy burlesque or the easier idealization which drops the bottom out of farce. Every good

moment frazzles or drowns.' – *James Agee*

† Garson Kanin has claimed to have written virtually all the script.

AA: Charles Coburn
AAN: best picture; script; original story (Frank Ross, Robert Russell); George Stevens; Jean Arthur

Morgan – A Suitable Case for Treatment**
GB 1966 97m bw
British Lion/Quintra (Leon Clore)
V
US title: *Morgan!*

A young woman determines to leave her talented but half-mad artist husband, who has a fixation on gorillas and behaves in a generally uncivilized manner.

Archetypal sixties marital fantasy, an extension of *Look Back in Anger* in the mood of swinging London. As tiresome as it is funny – but it is funny.

w David Mercer,   *play* David Mercer   *d* Karel Reisz   *ph* Larry Pizer, Gerry Turpin   *m* Johnny Dankworth

Vanessa Redgrave, *David Warner*, Robert Stephens, Irene Handl, Newton Blick, Nan Munro

'Poor Morgan: victim of a satire that doesn't bite, lost in a technical confusion of means and ends, and emerging like an identikit photograph, all bits and pieces and no recognizable face.' – *Penelope Houston*
'The first underground movie made above ground.' – *John Simon*
'I think Morgan is so appealing to college students because it shares their self-view: they accept this mess of cute infantilism and obsessions and aberrations without expecting the writer and director to resolve it and without themselves feeling a necessity to sort it out.' – *Pauline Kael*
AAN: Vanessa Redgrave

Morons from Outer Space
GB 1985 91m colour
Thorn EMI (Barry Hanson)

Dopey space travellers arrive on Earth.

Spoofy comedy which, apart from staging a spectacular motorway landing and mocking various popular film genres, never decides where to go.

w Griff Rhys Jones, Mel Smith   *d* Michael Hodges   *ph* Phil Meheux   *m* Peter Brewis

Mel Smith, Griff Rhys Jones, Paul Bown, Joanne Pearce, Jimmy Nail, Dinsdale Landen, James B. Sikking

'It remains stuck on the launch pad.' – *Variety*

Moscow on the Hudson*
US 1984 117m Metrocolor
Columbia/Delphi (Paul Mazursky)
V

A Soviet circus artiste defects in New York but has second thoughts.

Not so much a political comedy as an immigrant one, with the Big Apple shown at its worst. As such, occasionally funny in a desperate way, but overlong.

w Paul Mazursky, Leon Capetanos   *d* Paul Mazursky   *ph* Donald McAlpine   *m* David McHugh   *pd* Pato Guzman

Robin Williams, Maria Conchita Alonso, Cleavant Derricks, Alejandro Rey, Savely Kramarov

Mother, Jugs and Speed

US 1976 98m DeLuxe
Panavision
TCF (Joseph R. Barbera)
V

Comic and tragic events in the lives of
Los Angeles drivers of private
commercial ambulances.

Black comedy of incidents ranging
from farcical to sentimental,
sometimes funny but basically
unacceptable in either vein.

w Tom Mankiewicz   d Peter
Yates   ph Ralph Woolsey   md Joel
Sill   m various

Bill Cosby, Raquel Welch, Harvey
Keitel, *Allen Garfield*, Bruce Davison,
Larry Hagman

'The writer has found a way to get
into the underbelly of a city, to survey
the twilight territory where tragedy
and comedy trip over each other and
make an unsightly mess.' – *Time*

Mother Riley Meets the Vampire

GB 1952 74m bw
Renown (John Gilling)
US title: *My Son the Vampire*

An old washerwoman accidentally
catches a robot-wielding crook called
The Vampire.

Childish farce notable for Lucan's last
appearance in his dame role, and
Lugosi's last substantial appearance of
any kind – two pros at the end of
their tether.

w Val Valentine   d John Gilling
ph Stan Pavey   m Linda
Southworth

Arthur Lucan, Bela Lugosi, Dora
Bryan, Richard Wattis

'Stupid, humourless and repulsive.' –
MFB

The Mouse on the Moon

GB 1963 85m Eastmancolor
UA/Walter Shenson

The tiny duchy of Grand Fenwick
discovers that its home-made wine
makes excellent rocket fuel.

Piddling sequel to *The Mouse that
Roared*, suffering from a hesitant
script, too few jokes, and overacting.

w Michael Pertwee   d Richard
Lester   ph Wilkie Cooper
m Ron Grainer

Margaret Rutherford, Ron Moody,
Bernard Cribbins, David Kossoff,
Terry-Thomas, Michael Crawford

The Mouse that Roared**

GB 1959 85m Technicolor
Columbia/Open Road (Carl Foreman)
V

The tiny duchy of Grand Fenwick is
bankrupt, and its minister decides to
declare war on the United States, be
defeated, and receive Marshall Aid.

Lively comedy which sounds rather
better than it plays, but has bright
moments.

w Roger Macdougall, Stanley
Mann   novel Leonard Wibberley
d Jack Arnold   ph John Wilcox
m Edwin Astley

Peter Sellers (playing three parts),
Jean Seberg, David Kossoff, William
Hartnell, Leo McKern, Macdonald
Parke, Harold Kasket

'The kind of irrepressible topical satire
whose artistic flaws become
increasingly apparent but whose
merits outlast them.' – *Peter John
Dyer*

Move Over Darling**

US 1963 103m DeLuxe
Cinemascope
TCF/Arcola/Arwin (Aaron Rosenberg,
Marty Melcher)
V

A wife who has spent five years
shipwrecked on a desert island returns
to find that her husband has just
remarried.

Thin but fitfully amusing remake of
My Favorite Wife; sheer professionalism
gets it by.

w Hal Kanter, Jack Sher   d Michael
Gordon   ph Daniel L. Fapp
m Lionel Newman

Doris Day, James Garner, Polly
Bergen, Thelma Ritter, Chuck
Connors, Fred Clark

Movers and Shakers

US 1985 79m Metrocolor
MGM-UA/BHC (Charles Grodin, William
Asher)

A Hollywood writer tries to cope with
a difficult project while having
personal problems with his wife.

Mishmash of unrealized anecdotes
with pauses for studio in-jokes.
Despite the talent, it could never have
worked, not even under the
previously announced title *Dreamers*.

w Charles Grodin   d William
Asher   ph Robbie Greenberg
m Ken and Mitzie Welch

Walter Matthau, Charles Grodin,
Vincent Gardenia, Tyne Daly, Bill
Macy, Gilda Radner, Steve Martin,
Nita Talbot

'Only occasionally amusing: faces a
bleak box-office future.' – *Variety*

Movie Crazy**

US 1932 82m bw
Harold Lloyd

A filmstruck young man is mistakenly
invited to Hollywood for a film
test.

The silent comedian is not quite at his
best in this early sound comedy, but it
contains his last really superb
sequences and its picture of
Hollywood is both amusing and
nostalgic.

w Harold Lloyd and others   d Clyde
Bruckman   ph Walter Lundin

Harold Lloyd, Constance Cummings

'A corking comedy, replete with wow
belly laughs. Sure-fire.' – *Variety*

Movie Movie**

US 1978 106m part colour
ITC (Stanley Donen)
V

A pastiche of a thirties double bill,
including a boxing yarn (*Dynamite
Hands*) and a Busby-Berkeley style
girlie show (*Baxter's Beauties of 1933*).

Unfortunately there weren't enough
paying customers to appreciate the
spoofs, which are pretty patchy
anyway; but golden moments stay in
the mind.

w Larry Gelbart, Sheldon Keller
d Stanley Donen   ph Chuck Rosher
Jnr, Bruce Surtees   m Ralph
Burns   ch Michael Kidd

George C. Scott, Trish Van Devere,
Red Buttons, Eli Wallach, Michael
Kidd, Barbara Harris, Barry Bostwick,
Art Carney, Jocelyn Brando

'*Camp*, which has to do with a switch
of vision from one era to another,
cannot be created, and where it is, as
this and previous attempts testify, it is
immediately swallowed in its own
idiocy.' – *Richard Combs, MFB*

Moving

US 1988 89m Technicolor
Warner (Stuart Cornfeld)

A traffic engineer runs into all kinds of trouble when he decides to move his family from New Jersey to Idaho.

Disappointingly predictable comedy, making all the obvious jokes in a leaden way.

w Andy Breckman   d Alan Metter   ph Donald McAlpine   m Howard Shore   pd David L. Snyder   ed Alan Balsam

Richard Pryor, Beverly Todd, Randy Quaid, Dave Thomas, Dana Carvey, Stacey Dash, Gordon Jump, Morris Day

Mumsy, Nanny, Sonny and Girly

GB 1959 102m Eastmancolor
CIRO/Brigitte (Ronald J. Kahn)
aka: Girly

Two adolescents bring home lonely people as playthings for a homicidal family.

Revolting black comedy for masochists, representing the British cinema at its lowest ebb.

w Brian Comport   play Maisie Mosco   d Freddie Francis   ph David Muir   m Bernard Ebbinghouse

Michael Bryant, Ursula Howells, Pat Heywood, Howard Trevor, Vanessa Howard

The Muppet Christmas Carol*

US 1992 86m colour
Buena Vista/Walt Disney/Jim Henson (Brian Henson, Martin G. Baker)

A Christmas-hating miser is reformed by the visitations of five ghosts.

Cheerful adaptation of the perennial story, in a version that should appeal to the young.

w Jerry Juhl   story A Christmas Carol by Charles Dickens   d Brian Henson   ph John Fenner   m Miles Goodman   pd Val Strazovec   m/ly Paul Williams   sp The Computer Film Company   ed Michael Jablow

Michael Caine, Steven MacKintosh, Meredith Brown, Robin Weaver, Kermit the Frog, Miss Piggy, The Great Gonzo, Fozzie Bear

'The film sinks into a quagmire of sentimentality; the Muppets withdraw discreetly during Scrooge's ghostly visitations and the dominant flavour is more saccharine than humbug. Nice try, though.' – Sheila Johnston, Independent

'More entertainment than humanly possible!'

The Muppet Movie**

GB 1979 97m Eastmancolor
ITC (Jim Henson)

Kermit the Frog and friends travel across America to Hollywood and are offered a film contract by Lew Lord, the famous impresario.

Technically an adroit transfer of the celebrated puppets from their TV backstage milieu to a wider canvas; but the latter tends to dwarf them, the material is very variable, the guest stars look embarrassed and the show goes on too long.

w Jerry Juhl, Jack Burns   d James Frawley   ph Isidore Mankofsky   m Paul Williams, Kenny Ascher   pd Joel Schiller

Charles Durning, Edgar Bergen, Bob Hope, Milton Berle, Mel Brooks, James Coburn, Dom DeLuise, Elliott Gould, Cloris Leachman, Telly Savalas, Orson Welles
AAN: Paul Williams, Kenny Ascher; song 'The Rainbow Connection'

The Muppets Take Manhattan*
US   1984   94m   Technicolor
Tri-Star (David Lazer)
L

The Muppets' varsity show is promised a New York opening.

Probably the best of the Muppet features, but by the time of its arrival the early brilliance had been forgotten and even Miss Piggy had worn out her welcome.

w Frank Oz, Tom Patchett, Jay Tarses   d Frank Oz
AAN: Jeffrey Moss (music)

The Music Box****
US   1932   30m   bw
Hal Roach
V

Two delivery men take a piano to a house at the top of a flight of steps.

Quintessential Laurel and Hardy, involving almost all their aspects including a slight song and dance. With Billy Gilbert.

w H. M. Walker   d James Parrott

AA: best short

My Blue Heaven
US   1990   95m   Technicolor
Warner (Herbert Ross, Anthea Sylbert)
V, L

Relocated in a small town, a gangster who has turned state's evidence decides not to go straight.

Dull comedy, broadly acted and directed.

w Nora Ephron   d Herbert Ross
ph John Bailey   m Ira Newborn   pd Charles Rosen
ed Stephen A. Rotter, Robert Reitano

Steve Martin, Rick Moranis, Joan Cusack, Melanie Mayron, William Irwin, Carol Kane, William Hickey, Deborah Rush, Daniel Stern, Jesse Bradford

My Cousin Vinny*
US   1992   119m   DeLuxe
TCF/Peter V. Miller Investment Corp.
  (Dale Launer, Paul Schiff)
V

An inexperienced New York lawyer goes to Alabama to defend his cousin who is charged with murder.

Ramshackle comedy that raises an occasional smile and one or two laughs.

w Dale Launer   d Jonathan Lynn   ph Peter Deming   m Randy Edelman   pd Victoria Paul
ed Tony Lombardo

Joe Pesci, Ralph Macchio, Marisa Tomei, Mitchell Whitfield, Fred Gwynne, Lane Smith, Austin Pendleton, Bruce McGill, Maury Chaykin

'The bits and pieces never quite add up. Somewhere during this film's making I suspect that half the script was mysteriously lost down a street grating.' – Nigel Andrews, Financial Times

AA: Marisa Tomei

My Dear Secretary
US   1948   96m   bw
Cardinal/UA

A secretary marries her boss and becomes jealous of his new secretary.

Slow-paced, frivolous romantic comedy.

wd Charles Martin

Kirk Douglas, Laraine Day, Keenan Wynn, Rudy Vallee, Helen Walker, Florence Bates, Alan Mowbray

My Favorite Blonde***

US 1942 78m bw
Paramount (Paul Jones)

A burlesque comic travelling by train helps a lady in distress and lives to regret it.

Smartly paced spy comedy thriller, one of its star's best vehicles.

w Don Hartman, Frank Butler, Melvin Frank, Norman Panama   d Sidney Lanfield   ph William Mellor *m* David Buttolph

Bob Hope, Madeleine Carroll, Gale Sondergaard, George Zucco, Lionel Royce, Walter Kingsford, Victor Varconi

My Favorite Brunette*

US 1947 87m bw
Paramount/Hope Enterprises (Daniel Dare)
L

A photographer gets mixed up with mobsters.

Pretty fair star vehicle which half-heartedly spoofs *Farewell My Lovely.*

w Edmund Beloin, Jack Rose *d* Elliott Nugent *ph* Lionel Lindon *m* Robert Emmett Dolan

Bob Hope, Dorothy Lamour, Peter Lorre, Lon Chaney Jnr, John Hoyt, Charles Dingle, Reginald Denny

My Favorite Spy*

US 1951 93m bw
Paramount (Paul Jones)

A burlesque comic is asked by the US government to pose as an international spy who happens to be his double.

Moderately funny star vehicle with more willing hands than good ideas. The chase finale however is worth waiting for.

w Edmund Hartmann, Jack Sher *d* Norman Z. McLeod *ph* Victor Milner *m* Victor Young

Bob Hope, Hedy Lamarr, Francis L. Sullivan, Arnold Moss, Mike Mazurki, Luis Van Rooten

'The funniest, fastest honeymoon ever screened!'

My Favorite Wife***

US 1940 88m bw
RKO (Leo McCarey)
L

A lady explorer returns after several shipwrecked years to find that her husband has married again.

A well-worn situation gets its brightest treatment in this light star vehicle.

w Sam and Bella Spewack, Leo McCarey   *d Garson Kanin ph* Rudolph Maté   *m* Roy Webb *ad* Van Nest Polglase, Mark-Lee Kirk

Cary Grant, Irene Dunne, Randolph Scott, Gail Patrick, Ann Shoemaker, Donald MacBride

'One of those comedies with a glow on it.' *– Otis Ferguson*

† Other variations (qv): *Too Many Husbands, Our Wife, Three for the Show, Move Over Darling.*
AAN: story; Roy Webb; art direction

'I can't go on *live!* I'm a movie star, not an actor!'

My Favorite Year**

US 1982 92m Metrocolor
MGM-UA/Brooksfilms/Michael Gruskoff
V

In 1954, a legendary Hollywood star noted for wine and women is unwisely invited to star in a television series.

A good-humoured and well-researched romp with a central character not too far removed from Errol Flynn.

w Norman Steinberg, Dennis Palumbo   *d* Richard Benjamin *ph* Gerald Hirschfeld   *m* Ralph Burns   *pd* Charles Rosen *ed* Richard Chew

Peter O'Toole, Mark Linn-Baker, Jessica Harper, Joseph Bologna, Bill Macy, Lainie Kazan, Lou Jacobi, Cameron Mitchell

'A field day for a wonderful bunch of actors.' – *Variety*
AAN: Peter O'Toole

My Geisha
US   1962   120m   Technirama
Paramount/Steve Parker

A director makes a film in Japan; his wife disguises herself as a geisha and gets the leading role.

Silly, overstretched comedy with pretty locations.

w Norman Krasna   *d* Jack Cardiff   *ph* Shunichuro Nakao *m* Franz Waxman

Shirley Maclaine, Yves Montand, Robert Cummings, Edward G. Robinson, Yoko Tani

My Learned Friend***
GB   1943   76m   bw
Ealing (Robert Hamer)

A shady lawyer is last on a mad ex-convict's murder list of those who helped get him convicted.

Madcap black farce, plot-packed and generally hilarious; the star's last vehicle, but one of his best, with superbly timed sequences during a pantomime and on the face of Big Ben.

w John Dighton, Angus Macphail

d Basil Dearden, Will Hay   *ph* Wilkie Cooper   *m* Ernest Irving

Will Hay, Claude Hulbert, Mervyn Johns, Ernest Thesiger, Charles Victor, Lloyd Pearson, Maudie Edwards, G. H. Mulcaster, Gibb McLaughlin

My Little Chickadee*
US   1939   83m   bw
Universal (Lester Cowan)

A shady lady and an incompetent cardsharp unmask a villain in the old West.

A clash of comedy personalities which is affectionately remembered but in truth does not play very well apart from the odd line.

w Mae West, W. C. Fields   *d* Edward Cline   *ph* Joseph Valentine *md* Charles Previn   *m* Frank Skinner

Mae West, W. C. Fields, Joseph Calleia, Dick Foran, Margaret Hamilton

'It obstinately refuses to gather momentum.' – *The Times*
'A classic among bad movies . . . the satire never really gets off the ground. But the ground is such an honest mixture of dirt, manure and corn that at times it is fairly aromatic.' – *Pauline Kael, 1968*

My Man Godfrey***
US   1936   90m   bw
Universal (Gregory La Cava)

A zany millionaire family invite a tramp to be their butler and find he is richer than they are.

Archetypal Depression concept which is also one of the best of the thirties crazy sophisticated comedies, though its pacing today seems somewhat unsure.

w Morrie Ryskind, Eric Hatch, Gregory

La Cava   *d Gregory La Cava*
ph Ted Tetzlaff   *m* Charles Previn

Carole Lombard, William Powell, Alice Brady, Mischa Auer, Eugene Pallette, Gail Patrick, Alan Mowbray, Jean Dixon

AAN: script; Gregory La Cava (as director); Carole Lombard; William Powell; Alice Brady; Mischa Auer

'The butler did it! He made every lady in the house oh so very happy!'
My Man Godfrey
US   1957   92m   Technicolor
  Cinemascope
U-I (Ross Hunter)

Tepid remake which without the period background, and in unsuitable wide screen, raises very few laughs.

w Everett Freeman, Peter Berneis, William Bowers   *d* Henry Koster
ph William Daniels   *m* Frank Skinner

June Allyson, David Niven, Jessie Royce Landis, Jay Robinson, Robert Keith, Martha Hyer, Eva Gabor

My Stepmother Is an Alien
US   1988   108m   The Film House
Columbia TriStar/Weintraub
  Entertainment (Ronald Parker, Franklin R. Levy)
V, L

A scientist marries a beautiful woman from another planet.

Feeble comedy with little point and no taste.

w Jerico, Herschel Weingrod, Timothy Harris, Jonathan Reynolds   *d* Richard Benjamin
ph Richard H. Kline   *pd* Charles Rosen   *ed* Jacqueline Cambas, Brian Chambers

Dan Aykroyd, Kim Basinger, Jon

Lovitz, Alyson Hannigan, Joseph Maher, Seth Green, Ann Prentiss, Wesley Mann, Tony Jay, Peter Bromilow

My Tutor
US   1982   97m   DeLuxe
Crown

Two teenage boys try to lose their virginity.

As woeful as it sounds.

w Joe Roberts   *d* George Bowers

Matt Lattanzi, Caren Kaye, Kevin McCarthy, Arlene Golonka

'At last, the book that couldn't be written is now the motion picture that couldn't be made!'
Myra Breckinridge
US   1970   94m   DeLuxe
  Panavision
TCF (Robert Fryer)
V

After a sex-change operation a film critic goes to Hollywood to accomplish the deflation of the American male.

A sharply satirical novel has been turned into a sleazy and aimless picture which became a watershed of permissiveness; after international outcry it was shunned even by its own studio. A few good laughs do emerge from the morass, but even the old clips are misused.

w Mike Sarne, David Giler
novel Gore Vidal   *d* Mike Sarne
ph Richard Moore   *md* Lionel Newman   *m* John Philips

Mae West, Raquel Welch, John Huston, Rex Reed, Jim Backus, John Carradine, Andy Devine

'Whatever the novel may be like, it surely cannot be this sort of witless, lip-smacking, continuously inept cop-out.' – *John Simon*

'About as funny as a child molester.' – *Time*

'A disjointed patchwork of leers, vulgarity and general ineptness.' – *Cue*

'An incompetent attempt at exploitation by an industry that knew once, at the very least, how to make a dishonest buck.' – *Newsweek*

'I don't want subtlety. I want vulgarity.' – *Michael Sarne*

N

Nadine

US 1987 88m Metrocolor
Columbia TriStar/ML Delphi (Arlene
  Donovan)
V, L

Husband and wife on the brink of
divorce are drawn together by a
suspicious killing.

Unresolvedly old-fashioned comedy
which seems to need the Cary Grant
touch.

wd Robert Benton   *ph* Nestor
Almendros   *m* Howard Shore
pd Paul Sylbert   *ed* Sam O'Steen

Jeff Bridges, Kim Basinger, Rip Torn,
Gwen Verdon, Glenne Headly, Jerry
Stiller

The Naked Gun: From the Files of Police Squad*

US 1988 85m Technicolor
UIP/Paramount (Robert K. Weiss)
V, L

A bungling detective foils attempts to
assassinate the Queen in Los Angeles.

A barrage of gags, some good, some
dreadful, is harnessed to a limp
narrative. Not as funny as it should
be.

w Jerry Zucker, Jim Abrahams, David
Zucker, Pat Profit   *d* David
Zucker   *ph* Robert Stevens   *m* Ira
Newborn   *pd* John J. Lloyd
ed Michael Jablow

Leslie Nielsen, Priscilla Presley,
Ricardo Montalban, George Kennedy,
O. J. Simpson, Susan Beaubian,
Nancy Marchand, Raye Birk,
Jeannette Charles

'Quickly and efficiently establishes its
pattern of wildly escalating absurdity
within each scene, combined with a
series of gags related to each character
throughout the film.' – *Philip Strick,
MFB*

Naked Gun 2½: The Smell of Fear

US 1991 85m Technicolor
UIP/Paramount/Zucker/Abrahams/Zucker
  (Robert K. Weiss)
V, L

A clumsy police lieutenant
investigates an attempt to kill a solar
energy expert.

The mixture as before, although this
time around the slapstick comedy is
enlivened with fewer good jokes.

w David Zucker, Pat Proft   *d* David
Zucker   *ph* Robert Stevens
m Ira Newborn   *pd* John J.
Lloyd   *ed* James Symons, Chris
Greenbury

Leslie Nielsen, Priscilla Presley,
George Kennedy, O.J. Simpson,
Robert Goulet, Richard Griffiths,
Jacqueline Brookes, Anthony James,
Lloyd Bochner

'At least two-and-a-half times less
funny than its hilarious progenitor.' –
Variety
'An appealing rag-bag of the ribald

and the ridiculous, showing only the slightest signs of running out of steam.' – *Philip Strick, Sight and Sound*

The Naked Truth*
GB   1957   92m   bw
Rank/Mario Zampi
US title: *Your Past is Showing*

Celebrities band together to kill a blackmailer who threatens to expose unsavoury aspects of their lives.

Frenzied black farce, quite a lot of which comes off.

w Michael Pertwee   *d* Mario Zampi   *ph* Stan Pavey   *m* Stanley Black

Peter Sellers, Terry-Thomas, Peggy Mount, Dennis Price, Shirley Eaton, Georgina Cookson

Nasty Habits*
GB   1976   92m   Technicolor
Brut/Bowden (Robert Enders)

An abbess dies and the nuns vie for succession.

Satirical comedy rather obviously based on the Watergate scandals; initially amusing, but very tiresome by the end.

w Robert Enders   *novel* The Abbess of Crewe by Muriel Spark   *d* Michael Lindsay-Hogg   *ph* Douglas Slocombe   *m* John Cameron

Glenda Jackson, Melina Mercouri, Geraldine Page, Sandy Dennis, Anne Jackson, Anne Meara, Edith Evans, Susan Penhaligon, Rip Torn, Eli Wallach, Jerry Stiller

'The sort of material just about fit for a half-hour TV sketch.' – *Richard Combs, MFB*

The National Health*
GB   1973   97m   Eastmancolor
Columbia (Ned Sherrin, Terry Glinwood)

Life in the general men's ward of a large antiquated hospital.

Acerbic comedy from a National Theatre play which mixes tragedy and farce into a kind of *Carry on Dying*.

w Peter Nichols,   *play* Peter Nichols   *d* Jack Gold   *ph* John Coquillon   *m* Carl Davis   *pd* Ray Simm

Jim Dale, Lynn Redgrave, Eleanor Bron, Sheila Scott-Wilkinson, Donald Sinden, Colin Blakely, Clive Swift

National Lampoon's Animal House*
US   1978   109m   Technicolor
Universal (Matty Simmons, Ivan Reitman)
V

On an American campus around 1962, scruffy newcomers challenge the elegant élite.

A ragbag of college gags, of interest only to those who have had the experience; but its success caused much imitation, especially in American television.

w Harold Ramis, Douglas Kenney, Chris Miller   *d* John Landis   *ph* Charles Correll   *m* Elmer Bernstein

John Belushi, Tim Matheson, John Vernon, Donald Sutherland, Verna Bloom, Cesare Danova, Mary Louise Weller

National Lampoon's Christmas Vacation
US   1989   97m   colour
Warner/Hughes Entertainment (John Hughes, Tom Jacobson)
V, L

A father decides to give the family an old-fashioned Christmas at home.

Unsubtle comedy that always goes for the easy laugh.

w John Hughes   *d* Jeremiah S. Chechik   *ph* Thomas Ackerman   *m* Angelo Badalmenti   *pd* Stephen Marsh   *ed* Jerry Greenberg

Chevy Chase, Beverly D'Angelo, Randy Quaid, Diane Ladd, E. G. Marshall, Doris Roberts, Julia Louis-Dreyfus, Mae Questel, William Hickey

National Lampoon's Class Reunion
US   1982   85m   Metrocolor
Fox/ABC Productions (Matty Simmons)
L

The class of '72 foregathers at Lizzie Borden High, where a murderer is lurking.

An entertainment in which the presentation is better than the material, which is a vague spoof of high school and horror films.

w John Hughes   *d* Michael Miller   *ph* Phil Lathrop   *m* Peter Bernstein, Mark Goldenberg   *pd* Dean Edward Mitzner   *ed* Richard C. Meyer, Ann Mills

Gerrit Graham, Michael Lerner, Fred McCarren, Miriam Flynn, Stephen Furst

National Lampoon's European Vacation
US   1985   94m   Technicolor
Warner (Matty Simmons)
V, L

An American family determines to see Europe.

Hopelessly unfunny and simple-minded comedy, lacking even the usual schoolboy smut.

w John Hughes, Robert Klane

d Amy Heckerling   *ph* Bob Paynter   *m* Charles Fox   *pd* Bob Cartwright   *ed* Paul Herring

Chevy Chase, Beverly D'Angelo, Jason Lively, Dana Hill, Eric Idle

National Lampoon's Movie Madness
US   1981   89m   Technicolor
  Panavision
UA (Matty Simmons)
aka: *National Lampoon Goes to the Movies*

Three parodies of movie genres: an insurance salesman seeks personal growth; a stripper becomes First Lady in three days; a young cop learns how to be tough.

Cinema audiences were spared this inept and witless display, though it turns up on late-night TV to bore the unwary.

w Tod Carroll, Shary Flenniken, Pat Mephitis, Gerald Sussman, Ellis Weiner   *d* Bob Giraldi, Henry Jaglom   *ph* Charles Correll, Tak Fujimoto   *m* Andy Stein   *ad* Alexander A. Mayer   *ed* James Coblentz, Bud S. Isaacs

Robby Benson, Richard Widmark, Diane Lane, Candy Clark, Christopher Lloyd, Peter Riegert, Ann Dusenberry, Elisha Cook, Robert Culp

National Lampoon's Vacation
US   1983   98m   Technicolor
Warner (Matty Simmons)
V

An inventor drives his family on a holiday starting in Chicago and ending in California, but the journey is fraught with disaster.

Episodic, more or less straight black comedy, with detail more often boring or repellent than funny.

w John Hughes   *d* Harold

Ramis   *ph* Victor J. Kemper
m Ralph Burns   *pd* Jack Collis
ed Paul Herring

Chevy Chase, Imogene Coca, Beverly
D'Angelo, Randy Quaid, Eddie
Bracken

The Naughty Nineties
US   1945   72m   bw
Universal (Edward L. Hartmann, John
  Grant)

Two incompetents help an old
showboat owner.

Dim star comedy apart from the
team's rendition of their most famous
routine, 'Who's On First'.

w Edmund L. Hartmann, John Grant,
Edmund Joseph, Hal Fimburg
d Jean Yarborough   *ph* George
Robinson

Bud Abbott, Lou Costello, Henry
Travers, Alan Curtis, Rita Johnson,
Joe Sawyer

The Navigator***
US   1924   63m approx (24 fps)
   bw   silent
Metro-Goldwyn/Buster Keaton (Joseph M.
  Schenck)
V

A millionaire and his girl are the only
people on a transatlantic liner
marooned in mid-ocean.

A succession of hilarious sight gags:
the star in top form.

w Jean Havez, Clyde Bruckman, J. A.
Mitchell   *d* Buster Keaton, Donald
Crisp   *ph* Elgin Lessley, Byron
Houck

Buster Keaton, Kathryn McGuire

'Studded with hilarious moments and
a hundred and one adroit gags.' –
Photoplay

Nearly a Nasty Accident
GB   1961   91m   bw
British Lion/Britannia/Marlow (Bertram
  Ostrer)

A mild-mannered aircraftman causes
disaster wherever he goes.

Familiar faces just about save from
disaster this underscripted comedy for
indulgent audiences.   ›

w Jack Davies, Hugh Woodruff
play Touch Wood by David Stringer,
David Carr   *d* Don Chaffey
ph Paul Beeson   *m* Ken Jones

Kenneth Connor, Jimmy Edwards,
Shirley Eaton, Richard Wattis, Ronnie
Stevens, Jon Pertwee, Eric Barker,
Peter Jones, Jack Watling, Joyce
Carey, Terry Scott

Necessary Roughness
US   1991   104m   Technicolor
UIP/Paramount (Mace Neufeld, Robert
  Rehme)

After a college football team has been
dismissed for corruption, a coach
attempts to create a new squad from
unathletic students.

Drear movie that is never less than
predictable and never more than
tedious.

w Rick Natkin, David Fuller   *d* Stan
Dragoti   *ph* Peter Stein   *m* Bill
Conti   *pd* Paul Peters   *ed* John
Wright, Steve Mirkovich, Wayne
Wahrman

Scott Bakula, Robert Loggia, Hector
Elizondo, Harley Jane Kozack, Larry
Miller, Sinbad, Fred Dalton Thompson

'All the expected clichés of the losers-
make-a-comeback plot.' – *Variety*
'As phoney as the Astroturf on which
most of it takes place.' – *Philip French,
Observer*

Neighbors*

US   1981   94m   Technicolor
Columbia/Zanuck-Brown
L

A staid suburbanite is first irritated,
then taken over by his splashy
neighbours.

Hit-or-miss but generally quite funny
comedy in a style familiar to viewers
of American late night television.

w Larry Gelbart   novel Thomas
Berger   d John G. Avildsen
ph Gerald Hirschfeld   m Bill
Conti   pd Peter Larkin   ed Jan
Kurson

John Belushi, Dan Aykroyd, Kathryn
Walker, Cathy Moriarty, Igors Gavon,
Dru-Ann Chukron

Never Give a Sucker an Even Break*

US   1941   70m   bw
Universal
GB title: What a Man

W. C. Fields dives off an aeroplane
into the lap of a young woman who
has never seen a man; she falls in love
with him.

Stupefyingly inept in its scripting and
pacing, this comedy is often irresistibly
funny because of the anti-everything
personality of its writer-star. No one
else could have got away with it, or
would have been likely to try.

w John T. Neville, Prescott
Chaplin   story Otis Criblecoblis (W.
C. Fields)   d Edward Cline
ph Charles Van Enger   m Frank
Skinner

W. C. Fields, Gloria Jean, Leon Errol,
Butch and Buddy, Franklin
Pangborn, Anne Nagel, Mona Barrie,
Susan Miller, Margaret Dumont

'A beautifully timed exhibition of
mock pomposity, puzzled
ineffectualness, subtle
understatement and true-blue
nonchalance.' – James Agee

A New Kind of Love

US   1963   110m   Technicolor
Paramount/Llenroc (Melville Shavelson)

An American dress designer in Paris is
softened by a boorish newspaper
columnist.

Very thin sex comedy, dressed to kill
but with nowhere to go.

wd Melville Shavelson   ph Daniel
Fapp   m Leith Stevens

Paul Newman, Joanne Woodward,
Maurice Chevalier, Thelma Ritter,
George Tobias
AAN: Leith Stevens

A New Leaf*

US   1970   102m   Movielab
Paramount/Aries/Elkins (Joe Manduke)

A middle-aged playboy, close to
bankruptcy, thinks of acquiring a
wealthy wife.

Agreeably mordant comedy which
sparkles in patches rather than as a
whole.

wd Elaine May,   story The Green
Heart by Jack Ritchie   ph Gayne
Rescher   m John Mandel, Neal
Hefti   pd Richard Fried

Walter Matthau, Elaine May, Jack
Weston, George Rose, William
Redfield, James Coco

'Unashamedly a thirties fairy tale in
modern, but not fashionable, dress.'
– Jan Dawson

A New Life

US   1988   104m   Technicolor
    Panavision
Paramount (Martin Bregman)
L

A middle-aged couple divorce and find new partners and problems.

Occasionally wry, but more often sentimental, romantic comedy.

wd Alan Alda   *ph* Kelvin Pike
m Joseph Turrin   *pd* Barbara Dunphy   *ed* William Reynolds

Alan Alda, Ann-Margret, Hal Linden, Veronica Hamel, John Shea, Mary Kay Place

New York Stories**
US   1989   124m   Technicolor
Warner/Touchstone (Robert Greenhut)
L

Anthology of three stories: 'Life Lessons', dealing with a painter's attitude to life and art; 'Life Without Zoë', in which a 12-year-old girl brings her parents back together; and 'Oedipus Wrecks', in which a son is tyrannized by his mother materializing in the sky over New York.

Worth watching for Scorsese's sharp look at the art world and Allen's ultimate Jewish mother joke. Sandwiched between them is Coppola at his most disastrously winsome.

w Richard Price, Francis Coppola, Sofia Coppola, Woody Allen
d Martin Scorsese, Francis Coppola, Woody Allen   *ph* Nestor Almedros, Vittorio Storaro, Sven Nykvist
m Carmine Coppola, Kid Creole and the Coconuts   *pd* Kristi Zea, Dean Tavoularis, Santo Loquasto
ed Thelma Schoonmaker, Barry Malkin, Susan E. Morse

Nick Nolte, Patrick O'Neal, Rosanna Arquette, Heather McComb, Talia Shire, Gia Coppola, Giancarlo Giannini, Woody Allen, Marvin Chatinover, Mae Questel, Mia Farrow

Next to No Time
GB   1958   93m   Eastmancolor
British Lion/Montpelier (Albert Fennell)

A meek-and-mild engineer crossing the Atlantic gains confidence when told that anything is possible during the hour 'lost' every day.

Whimsical comedy which never gains momentum.

wd Henry Cornelius   *story* The Enchanted Hour by Paul Gallico
ph Freddie Francis   *m* Georges Auric

Kenneth More, Betsy Drake, Bessie Love, Harry Green, Roland Culver, Reginald Beckwith, John Welsh, John Laurie, Howard Marion-Crawford

Nickelodeon*
US/GB   1976   122m   Metrocolor
Columbia/EMI/Chartoff-Winkler (Frank Marshall)
V

In 1910, various characters come together to make movies, finally attending the 1915 opening in Hollywood of *The Birth of a Nation*.

What should have been a hugely entertaining chunk of comic nostalgia is killed stone dead by embarrassed acting, poor timing, and a general lack of funny ideas, despite having so much to borrow from.

w W. D. Richter, Peter Bogdanovich   *d* Peter Bogdanovich   *ph* Laszlo Kovacs
md Richard Hazard

Ryan O'Neal, Burt Reynolds, Tatum O'Neal, Brian Keith, Stella Stevens, John Ritter, Jane Hitchcock

'Ponderous slapstick and a pathetic parody of Harold Lloyd.' – *Sight and Sound*
'Another collection of scenes from

other people's films.' – *Howard Kissel, Women's Wear Daily*

'The slightest familiarity with the early works of Hal Roach – not to mention D. W. Griffith, here pretentiously quoted – reveals how little Bogdanovich understands his vastly superior predecessors.' – *Robert Asahina, New Leader*

'The crudest, stupidest, unfunniest farce of this or any other year.' – *John Simon, New York*

A Night at the Opera****
US 1935 96m bw
MGM (Irving Thalberg)
V, L

Three zanies first wreck, then help an opera company.

Certainly among the best of the Marxian extravaganzas, and the first to give them a big production to play with as well as musical interludes by other than themselves for a change of pace. The mix plays beautifully.

w George S. Kaufman, Morrie Ryskind d Sam Wood ph Merritt Gerstad *md* Herbert Stothart

Groucho, Chico, Harpo (Zeppo absented himself from here on), *Margaret Dumont*, Kitty Carlisle, Allan Jones, Walter Woolf King, *Sig Rumann*

'Corking comedy with the brothers at par and biz chances excellent . . . songs in a Marx picture are generally at a disadvantage because they're more or less interruptions, the customers awaiting the next laugh.' – *Variety*

A Night in Casablanca**
US 1946 85m bw
David L. Loew

Three zanies rout Nazi refugees in a North African hotel.

The last authentic Marxian

extravaganza; it starts uncertainly, builds to a fine sustained frenzy, then peters out in some overstretched airplane acrobatics.

w Joseph Fields, Roland Kibbee, Frank Tashlin   *d* Archie Mayo *ph* James Van Trees   *m* Werner Janssen   *pd* Duncan Cramer

Groucho, Chico, Harpo, Sig Rumann, Lisette Verea, Charles Drake, Lois Collier, Dan Seymour

KORNBLOW (Groucho Marx): 'I don't mind being killed, but I resent hearing it from a character whose head comes to a point.'

KORNBLOW: 'From now on the essence of this hotel will be speed. If a customer asks you for a three-minute egg, give it to him in two minutes. If he asks you for a two-minute egg, give it to him in one minute. If he asks you for a one-minute egg, give him the chicken and let him work it out for himself.'

BEATRICE (Lisette Verea): 'My name's Beatrice Ryner. I stop at the hotel.'

KORNBLOW: 'My name's Ronald Kornblow. I stop at nothing.'

'It is beside the main point to add that it isn't one of their best movies; for the worst they might ever make would be better worth seeing than most other things I can think of.' – *James Agee*

Night Owls*
US 1930 20m bw
Hal Roach

A policeman wanting to record an arrest bribes two tramps to burgle a house.

The stars at their most hilariously incompetent, unable even to get through a doorway efficiently.

w Leo McCarey, H. M. Walker *d* James Parrott

Laurel and Hardy, Edgar Kennedy, James Finlayson

Night Shift

US   1982   106m   Technicolor
Warner/Ladd (Brian Grazer)
L

A weary financial analyst becomes a morgue attendant and finds himself involved with gangsters and pimps.

Unattractive comedy that outstays its welcome, which wasn't very enthusiastic in the first place.

w Lowell Ganz, Babaloo Mandel
d Ron Howard   ph James Crabe
m Burt Bacharach   pd Jack Collis

Henry Winkler, Michael Keaton, Shelley Long, Gina Hecht

The Night They Raided Minsky's**

US   1968   99m   DeLuxe
UA/Tandem (Norman Lear)
GB title: The Night They Invented Striptease

Various human problems are posed and solved during a night at a burlesque theatre.

Marvellous kaleidoscopic ragbag of brilliant fragments which unfortunately don't cohere in the mind into a really memorable film, though it gives detailed pleasure on every viewing.

w Arnold Schulman, Sidney Michaels, Norman Lear
book Rowland Barber   d William Friedkin   ph Andrew Laszlo
m Charles Strouse   pd William Eckart, Jean Eckar   ch Danny Daniels
narrator Rudy Vallee

Jason Robards, Britt Ekland, Norman Wisdom, Forrest Tucker, Joseph Wiseman, Bert Lahr, Harry Andrews, Denholm Elliott, Elliott Gould, Jack Burns

'The Fanny Brice country stunningly brought to life – every face a snapshot of yesterday.' – Alexander Walker
'It's lightweight and disorganized; it's a shambles; yet a lot of it is charming, and it has a wonderful seedy chorus line – a row of pudgy girls with faces like slipped discs.' – Pauline Kael, New Yorker
'A brilliant pastiche of classic American burlesque on the lower east side in the twenties.' – Time
'An entire way of life is encapsulated' – Morning Star

A Night to Remember*

US   1943   91m   bw
Columbia (Samuel Bischoff)

A Greenwich Village mystery-writing couple try to solve a murder.

Reasonably sparkling comedy whodunnit with a zany tinge.

w Richard Flournoy, Jack Henley
d Richard Wallace   ph Joseph Walker   md Morris Stoloff
m Werner Heymann

Loretta Young, Brian Aherne, Jeff Donnell, William Wright, Sidney Toler, Gale Sondergaard, Donald MacBride, Lee Patrick, Blanche Yurka

'A first-rate gloom chaser.' – Picture Show

Nine to Five*

US   1980   110m   DeLuxe
TCF/IPC (Bruce Gilbert)
L

Three office women plot to get rid of their boss, and nearly make it.

Sporadically agreeable comedy somewhat reminiscent of Sturges' Unfaithfully Yours.

w Colin Higgins, Patricia Resnick
d Colin Higgins   ph Reynaldo

Villalobos *m* Charles Fox
pd Dean Mitzner

Jane Fonda, Dolly Parton, Lily Tomlin, Dabney Coleman, Sterling Hayden, Elizabeth Wilson, Henry Jones

'An effective escapist feast with lotsa funny physical schtick.' – *Variety*
AAN: title song (Dolly Parton)

1941*
US 1979 118m Metrocolor
Panavision
Columbia/Universal/A-Team (John Milius)
V, L

Just after Pearl Harbor, a stray Japanese submarine terrorizes Hollywood.

Absurdly over-budgeted manic farce which substitutes noise for wit and slapstick for comedy; it fails on every level.

w Robert Zemeckis, Bob Gale
d Steven Spielberg *ph* William A. Fraker *m* John Williams
pd Dean Edward Mitzner

Dan Aykroyd, Ned Beatty, John Belushi, Lorraine Gary, Murray Hamilton, Christopher Lee, Tim Matheson, Toshiro Mifune, Warren Oates, Robert Stack, Elisha Cook Jnr

'So overloaded with visual humour of rather monstrous nature that the feeling emerges that once you've seen ten explosions, you've seen them all.' – *Variety*
'Aimed at young audiences, who deserve better fun.' – *New Yorker*
'Its sheer relentless physicality, its elaborately orchestrated pointlessness on every other level, make it probably the purest demonstration of what it means to have two of the all-time commercial blockbusters to one's record and one's hands firmly on the fantasy machine.' – *Richard Combs, MFB*
'Spielberg intended it as "a stupidly outrageous celebration of paranoia" . . . audiences found it curiously unfunny and elephantine.' – *Les Keyser, Hollywood in the Seventies*
AAN: William A. Fraker

'The picture that kids the commissars!'
'Garbo laughs!'
'Don't pronounce it – see it!'
Ninotchka*
US 1939 110m bw
MGM (Ernst Lubitsch)
V, L

A Paris playboy falls for a communist emissary sent to sell some crown jewels.

Sparkling comedy on a theme which has been frequently explored; delicate pointing and hilarious character comedy sustain this version perfectly until the last half hour, when it certainly sags; but it remains a favourite Hollywood example of this genre.

w Charles Brackett, Billy Wilder, Walter Reisch, story Melchior Lengyel
d Ernst Lubitsch *ph* William Daniels *m* Werner Heymann

Greta Garbo, Melvyn Douglas, Sig Rumann, Alexander Granach, Felix Bressart, Ina Claire, Bela Lugosi
PROLOGUE: This picture takes place in Paris in those wonderful days when a siren was a brunette and not an alarm – and if a Frenchman turned out the light it was not on account of an air raid!
NINOTCHKA (Greta Garbo): 'I must have a complete report of your negotiations and a detailed expense account.'
BULJANOFF (Felix Bressart): 'No, non, Ninotchka. Don't ask for it. There is an old Turkish proverb that says, if

something smells bad, why put your nose in it?'

NINOTCHKA: 'And there is an old Russian saying, the cat who has cream on his whiskers had better find good excuses.'

NINOTCHKA: 'The last mass trials were a great success. There are going to be fewer but better Russians.'

'High calibre entertainment for adult audiences, and a top attraction for the key de-luxers.' – *Variety*
'The Lubitsch style, in which much was made of subtleties – glances, finger movements, raised eyebrows – has disappeared. Instead we have a hard, brightly lit, cynical comedy with the wisecrack completely in control.' – *John Baxter, 1968*

† William Powell and Robert Montgomery were formerly considered for the Melvyn Douglas role.
AAN: best picture; script; story; Greta Garbo

'He was a hit and run lover ... personally, he preferred a cigarette to any dame!'
No Man of Her Own*
US   1932   98m   bw
Paramount

A big-time gambler marries a local girl on a bet and tries to keep her innocent of his activities.

Star romantic comedy drama, quite professionally assembled and played.

w Maurine Watkins, Milton H. Gropper   *d* Wesley Ruggles
ph Leo Tover

Clark Gable, Carole Lombard, Dorothy Mackaill, Grant Mitchell, George Barbier, Elizabeth Patterson, J. Farrell MacDonald

'Entertaining film with national appeal.' – *Variety*

'Just about everything that the ordinary picture fan looks for: drama, romance, comedy, strong build-ups, exciting climaxes, a fine line of human interest.' – *Film Daily*

No, My Darling Daughter
GB   1961   96m   bw
Rank/Five Star/Betty E. Box-Ralph Thomas

Chaos ensues when a tycoon's daughter is thought to be eloping with an American boy friend.

Clumsy comedy with moments of brightness provided by the actors.

w Frank Harvey   *play* A Handful of Tansy *by* Harold Brooke, Kay Bannerman   *d* Ralph Thomas
ph Ernest Steward   *m* Norrie Paramor

Michael Redgrave, Michael Craig, . Roger Livesey, Kad Fulton, Juliet Mills, Renee Houston, Joan Sims, Peter Butterworth

No Sex Please, We're British
GB   1973   91m   Technicolor
Columbia/BHP (John R. Sloan)
V

Confusion ensues when a wrongly addressed parcel of dirty postcards arrives at a bank.

Fairly lively farce with everything from mistaken identity to falling trousers.

w Anthony Marriott, Johnnie Mortimer, Brian Cooke
play Anthony Marriott, Alistair Foot   *d* Cliff Owen   *ph* Ken Hodges   *m* Eric Rogers

Ronnie Corbett, Arthur Lowe, Beryl Reid, Ian Ogilvy, Susan Penhaligon, David Swift, Michael Bates

No Time for Sergeants
US 1958 111m bw
Warner (Mervyn Le Roy)
L

Adventures of a hillbilly army conscript.

Heavy-handed adaptation of the stage success, a real piece of filmed theatre with not much sparkle to it.

w John Lee Mahin   play Ira Levin   novel Mac Hyman
d Mervyn Le Roy   ph Harold Rosson   m Ray Heindorf

Andy Griffith, William Fawcett, Murray Hamilton, Nick Adams, Myron McCormick, Bartlett Robinson

Noises Off
US 1992 104m Technicolor
Warner/Touchstone/Touchstone Pacific Partners I/Amblin (Frank Marshall)

The American cast of a British sex comedy suffer a series of disasters, on-stage and off, during a pre-Broadway tour.

Brave though misguided attempt to transfer to the screen an intensely theatrical work, depending on live performance for its effect. It begins well but soon ceases to amuse.

w Marty Kaplan   play Michael Frayn   d Peter Bogdanovich
ph Tim Suhrstedt   m Phil Marshall   pd Norman Newberry
ed Lisa Day

Carol Burnett, Michael Caine, Denholm Elliott, Julie Hagerty, Marilu Henner, Mark Linn-Baker, Christopher Reeve, John Ritter, Nicollette Sheridan

'Serves up plenty of laughs, and in many ways it stands as a model transfer of a play to the screen.' – Variety
'If I say that I laughed till I cried, I have a dreadful fear the words will be ripped out and stuck on the poster. But I did.' – Nigel Andrews, Financial Times
'On screen, Noises Off fails in the only way that films can fail – bit by bit. But utterly.' – Adam Mars-Jones, Independent

Not with My Wife You Don't
US 1966 119m Technicolor
Warner/Fernwood/Reynard (Norman Panama, Joel Freeman)

A Korean war veteran is furious when an old rival turns up in London and again makes eyes at his wife.

Extraordinarily flat star comedy of cross and double cross among friends.

w Norman Panama, Larry Gelbart, Peter Barnes   d Norman Panama
ph Charles Lang, Paul Beeson
m Johnny Williams

Tony Curtis, George C. Scott, Virna Lisi, Carroll O'Connor, Richard Eastham

'About as frothy as a tin of dehydrated milk.' – MFB
'It has all the verve, subtlety and sophistication of its title.' – Judith Crist

Nothing but Trouble
US 1944 70m bw
MGM (B. F. Ziedman)
V

A chef and butler accidentally prevent a poison plot against a young king.

Feebly-devised star comedy, their last for a big studio.

w Russel Rouse, Ray Golden
d Sam Taylor   ph Charles Salerno Jnr   m Nathaniel Shilkret

Stan Laurel, Oliver Hardy, Mary Boland, Henry O'Neill, David Leland

Nothing but Trouble

US   1991   94m   Technicolor
Warner/Applied Action (Robert K. Weiss)
V, L

A New York couple find themselves
stranded in a village where a
centenarian judge has absolute rule.

Exceedingly dismal comedy, in which
a group of self-indulgent comedians,
having been given a great deal of rope,
proceed to hang themselves; it is not
a pretty sight.

wd Dan Aykroyd   *story* Peter
Aykroyd   *ph* Dean Cundey
m Michael Kamen   *pd* William
Sandell   *ed* Malcolm Campbell,
James Symons

Chevy Chase, Dan Aykroyd, John
Candy, Demi Moore, Valri Bromfield,
Taylor Negron, Bertila Damas,
Raymond J. Barry, Brian Doyle-
Murray, Peter Aykroyd

'Astonishingly poor effort . . . one of
the longest 94 minutes on record.' –
Variety
'Combines absolute failure as a
comedy with a surprisingly
interesting and disgusting vision of
grotesque America.' – *Kim Newman,
Sight and Sound*

Nothing Sacred***

US   1937   77m   Technicolor
David O. Selznick

A girl thought to be dying of a rare
disease is built up by the press into a
national heroine; but the diagnosis
was wrong.

Hollywood's most bitter and hilarious
satire, with crazy comedy elements
and superb wisecracks; a historical
monument of screen comedy,
though its freshness at the time can't
now be recaptured.

w Ben Hecht,   *story* Letter to the Editor

by James H. Street   *d* William
Wellman   *ph* W. Howard
Greene   *m* Oscar Levant

*Carole Lombard, Fredric March, Walter
Connolly,* Charles Winninger, Sig
Rumann, Frank Fay, Maxie
Rosenbloom, Margaret Hamilton,
Hedda Hopper, Monty Woolley,
Hattie McDaniel, Olin Howland, John
Qualen

DOCTOR (Charles Winninger): 'I'll
tell you briefly what I think of
newspapermen. The hand of God,
reaching down into the mire, couldn't
elevate one of them to the depths of
degradation.'

EDITOR (Walter Connolly): 'I am
sitting here, Mr Cook, toying with the
idea of cutting out your heart and
stuffing it – like an olive!'

'Hit comedy . . . will be one of the big
grossers of the year.' – *Variety*
'Because it does hold up a mirror,
even though a distorting mirror, to a
very real world of ballyhoo and cheap
sensationalism, the pleasure to be
obtained from it is something more
than the usual mulish guffaw.' –
Spectator

† Refashioned in 1953 as a stage
musical, *Hazel Flagg*, with Jule Styne;
this in turn became a Martin and
Lewis comedy *Living It Up* (Jerry Lewis
in the Carole Lombard part).

The Nude Bomb

US   1980   94m   Technicolor
Universal/Time-Life Films (Jennings Lang)
L
aka: *The Return of Maxwell Smart*

An incompetent secret agent chases a
missile launching villain.

Curious and unsatisfactory attempt to
revive a twenty-year-old TV situation
comedy minus half its personnel.

w Arne Sultan, Bill Dana, Leonard B.

Stern *d* Clive Donner *ph* Harry L. Wolf *m* Lalo Schifrin *pd* William Tuntke *ed* Walter Hannemann

Don Adams, Sylvia Kristel, Dana Elcar, Rhonda Fleming, Andrea Howard, Norman Lloyd

'Fans of the vidshow will derive much more enjoyment by crowding round their television sets with a bowl of popcorn watching *Get Smart* reruns.' – *Variety*.

Nuns on the Run
GB 1990 92m Technicolor
Palace/Handmade Films (Michael White)
V, L

Two petty criminals disguise themselves as nuns to escape capture.

Broad, slapstick comedy that provides scant amusement, although it went down well in America.

wd Jonathan Lynn *ph* Michael Garfath *m* Hidden Faces

pd Simon Holland *ed* David Martin

Eric Idle, Robbie Coltrane, Camille Coduri, Janet Suzman, Doris Hare, Lila Kaye, Robert Patterson, Robert Morgan, Winston Dennis, Tom Hickey

The Nutty Professor
US 1963 107m Technicolor
Paramount/Jerry Lewis (Ernest D. Glucksman)
L

An eccentric chemistry professor discovers an elixir which turns him into a pop idol.

Long dreary comedy which contains patches of its star at somewhere near his best; but even *Dr Jekyll and Mr Hyde* is funnier.

w Jerry Lewis, Bill Richmond *d* Jerry Lewis *ph* W. Wallace Kelley *m* Walter Scharf

Jerry Lewis, Stella Stevens, Howard Morris, Kathleen Freeman

O. C. and Stiggs

US 1987 109m Metrocolor
MGM (Robert Altman, Peter Newman)

Two teenagers spend their summer
playing practical jokes, particularly
on their obnoxious neighbour.

Tedious comedy with an air
of desperate improvisation
about it.

w Donald Cantrell, Ted Mann
story Tod Carroll, Ted Mann
d Robert Altman *ph* Pierre
Mignot *m* King Sunny Ade and
his African Beats *pd* Scott
Bushnell *ed* Elizabeth Kling

Daniel H. Jenkins, Neill Barry, Paul
Dooley, Jane Curtin, Jon Cryer, Ray
Walston, Louis Nye, Tina Louise,
Dennis Hopper, Melvin Van
Peebles

'Smile while you're makin' it
Laugh while you're takin' it
Even though you're fakin' it
Nobody's gonna know . . .'

O Lucky Man**

GB 1973 174m Eastmancolor
Warner/Memorial/Sam (Michael Medwin,
Lindsay Anderson)

The odyssey of a trainee salesman
who after a while as an international
financier settles down to be a do-
gooder.

Modern revue-style version of
Candide/Decline and Fall; very hit or
miss in style and effect, and hellishly
overlong, but with good things along
the way.

w David Sherwin *d* Lindsay
Anderson *ph* Miroslav
Ondricek *m* Alan Price
pd Jocelyn Herbert

*Malcolm McDowell, Arthur Lowe, Ralph
Richardson*, Rachel Roberts, Helen
Mirren, Mona Washbourne, Dandy
Nichols

'A sort of mod *Pilgrim's Progress*.' –
New Yorker

Ocean's Eleven*

US 1960 128m Technicolor
  Panavision
Warner/Dorchester (Lewis Milestone)
L

A gang of friends plan to rob a Las
Vegas casino.

Self-indulgent and overlong caper
comedy which marked Hollywood's
entry into a subsequently much
overworked field. In this case the plot
stops all too frequently for guest spots
and in-jokes.

w Harry Brown, Charles Lederer
d Lewis Milestone *ph* William H.
Daniels *m* Nelson Riddle

Frank Sinatra, Peter Lawford, Sammy
Davis Jnr, Richard Conte, Dean
Martin, Angie Dickinson, Cesar
Romero, Joey Bishop, Patrice
Wymore, Akim Tamiroff, Henry Silva,
Ilka Chase

The Odd Couple**
US 1968 105m Technicolor
Panavision
Paramount (Howard W. Koch)
L

A fussy divorce-shocked newswriter moves in with his sloppy sportscaster friend, and they get on each other's nerves.

Straight filming of a funny play which sometimes seems lost on the wide screen, but the performances are fine.

w Neil Simon, *play* Neil Simon
d Gene Saks *ph* Robert B. Hauser *m* Neal Hefti

Jack Lemmon, Walter Matthau, John Fiedler, Herb Edelman, David Sheiner, Larry Haines, Monica Evans, Carole Sheely, Iris Adrian

OSCAR (Walter Matthau): 'I can't take it anymore, Felix. I'm crackin' up. Everything you do irritates me. And when you're not here, the things I know you're gonna do when you come in irritate me. You leave me little notes on my pillow. I told you 158 times I cannot stand little notes on my pillow. "We are all out of cornflakes, F.U." It took me three hours to figure out that F.U. was Felix Ungar. It's not your fault, Felix. It's a rotten combination, that's all.'
AAN: Neil Simon

Oh Dad, Poor Dad, Mamma's Hung You in the Closet and I'm Feelin' So Sad
US 1966 86m Technicolor
Paramount/Seven Arts (Ray Stark, Stanley Rubin)

A dead father helps his son to get married despite his mother's influence to the contrary.

Zany black comedy which never really worked on the stage, let alone the screen.

w Ian Bernard *play* Arthur Kopit *d* Richard Quine
ph Geoffrey Unsworth *m* Neal Hefti

Rosalind Russell, Jonathan Winters, Robert Morse, Hugh Griffith, Barbara Harris, Lionel Jeffries, Cyril Delevanti, Hiram Sherman

'It's an almighty laugh!'
Oh, God*
US 1977 104m Technicolor
Warner (Jerry Weintraub)
V, L

A bewildered supermarket manager is enlisted by God to prove to the world that it can only work if people try.

Overlong but generally amiable reversion to the supernatural farces of the forties: its success seems to show that people again need this kind of comfort.

w Larry Gelbart *novel* Avery Corman *d* Carl Reiner *ph* Victor Kemper *m* Jack Elliott

George Burns, John Denver, Ralph Bellamy, Donald Pleasence, Teri Garr, William Daniels, Barnard Hughes, Paul Sorvino, Barry Sullivan, Dinah Shore, Jeff Corey, David Ogden Stiers

'Undeniably funny and almost impossible to dislike.' – *Tom Milne, MFB*
'Basically a single-joke movie: George Burns is God in a football cap.' – *Pauline Kael, New Yorker*
AAN: Larry Gelbart

Oh God Book Two
US 1980 94m Technicolor
Warner (Gilbert Cates)
V

God enlists a child to remind people that he is still around.

Crass sequel with sentiment replacing jokes.

w Josh Greenfeld, Hal Goldman, Fred S. Fox, Seaman Jacobs, Melissa Miller d Gilbert Cates ph Ralph Woolsey m Charles Fox pd Preston Ames ed Peter E. Bergher

George Burns, Suzanne Pleshette, David Birney, Louanne, Howard Duff, Hans Conried, Wilfrid Hyde White

Oh God, You Devil
US 1984 96m Technicolor
Warner (Robert M. Sherman)
V, L

A struggling musician sells his soul to the devil in exchange for success.

A comic version of Faust, appended to the two films in which George Burns played God; he now puts on the other hat to fairly, but not very, comic effect.

w Andrew Bergman d Paul Bogart ph King Baggot m David Shire pd Peter Wooley ed Andy Zall

George Burns, Ted Wass, Ron Silver, Roxanne Hart, Eugene Roche

Oh Heavenly Dog
US 1980 103m DeLuxe
Mulberry Square/TCF

A private eye is reincarnated as a dog and solves his own murder.

Witless fantasy comedy, an uncredited remake of You Never Can Tell which also rates as a Benji movie with curious additions of sex and profanity. A total muddle.

w Rod Browning, Joe Camp d Joe Camp

Chevy Chase, Jane Seymour, Omar Sharif, Robert Morley, Alan Sues

Oh Mr Porter****
GB 1937 84m bw
GFD/Gainsborough (Edward Black)

The stationmaster of an Irish halt catches gun-runners posing as ghosts.

Marvellous star comedy showing this trio of comedians at their best, and especially Hay as the seedy incompetent. The plot is borrowed from The Ghost Train, but each line and gag brings its own inventiveness. A delight of character comedy and cinematic narrative.

w Marriott Edgar, Val Guest, J. O. C. Orton, story Frank Launder d Marcel Varnel ph Arthur Crabtree md Louis Levy

Will Hay, Moore Marriott, Graham Moffatt, Dave O'Toole, Dennis Wyndham

'That rare phenomenon: a film comedy without a dud scene.' – Peter Barnes, 1964
'Behind it lie the gusty uplands of the British music hall tradition, whose rich soil the British film industry is at last beginning to exploit.' – Basil Wright

Okay for Sound*
GB 1937 85m bw
GFD/Gainsborough (Edward Black)

The Crazy Gang runs amok in a film studio.

Patchy farce with music hall talents of the time.

w Marriott Edgar, Val Guest, R. P. Weston, Bert Lee d Marcel Varnel ph Jack Cox md Louis Levy

Bud Flanagan, Chesney Allen, Jimmy Nervo, Teddy Knox, Charlie Naughton, Jimmy Gold, Fred Duprez,

Enid Stamp-Taylor, Graham Moffatt, Meinhart Maur, H. F. Maltby, Peter Dawson, The Radio Three, The Sherman Fisher Girls

Old Mother Riley

This Irish washerwoman with flailing arms and a nice line in invective was a music hall creation of Arthur Lucan, a variation of a pantomime dame. His wife Kitty Macshane played Mother Riley's daughter, and despite personal difficulties they were top of the bill for nearly 30 years. Their first film was *Stars on Parade*, a collection of music-hall acts, in 1935.

The films were very cheaply made and the padding is difficult to sit through, but Lucan at his best is a superb comedian: they were made for small independent companies such as Butcher's and usually directed by Maclean Rogers.

1937: OLD MOTHER RILEY
1938: OLD MOTHER RILEY IN PARIS
1939: OLD MOTHER RILEY MP, OLD MOTHER RILEY JOINS UP
1940: OLD MOTHER RILEY IN BUSINESS, OLD MOTHER RILEY'S GHOSTS
1941: OLD MOTHER RILEY'S CIRCUS
1942: OLD MOTHER RILEY IN SOCIETY
1943: OLD MOTHER RILEY DETECTIVE
1943: OLD MOTHER RILEY OVERSEAS
1944: OLD MOTHER RILEY AT HOME
1945: OLD MOTHER RILEY HEADMISTRESS
1947: OLD MOTHER RILEY'S NEW VENTURE
1949: OLD MOTHER RILEY'S JUNGLE TREASURE
1952: MOTHER RILEY MEETS THE VAMPIRE

Oliver the Eighth
US 1933 20m bw
Hal Roach

Ollie goes on a blind date, and the lady turns out to be homicidal.

Star farce which never quite rises to the occasion; pleasant fooling but no more.

w anon *d* Lloyd French

Laurel and Hardy, Mae Busch, Jack Barty

On the Beat
GB 1962 105m bw
Rank (Hugh Stewart)

A Scotland Yard car park attendant manages to capture some crooks and become a policeman.

Busy but flat comedy vehicle, never very likeable.

w Jack Davies *d* Robert Asher
ph Geoffrey Faithfull *m* Philip Green

Norman Wisdom, Jennifer Jayne, Raymond Huntley, David Lodge

On the Buses
GB 1971 88m Technicolor
EMI/Hammer (Ronald Woolfe, Ronald Chesney)
V

Women drivers cause trouble at a bus depot.

Grotesque, ham-handed farce from a TV series which was sometimes funny; this is merely vulgar.

w Ronald Woolfe, Ronald

Chesney   *d* Harry Booth
ph Mark MacDonald   *m* Max Harris

Reg Varney, Doris Hare, Anna Karen,
Michael Robbins, Stephen Lewis

† *Mutiny on the Buses* followed in 1972
and *Holiday on the Buses* in 1973. Both
were deplorably witless.

On the Fiddle*
GB   1961   97m   bw
Anglo-Amalgamated/S. Benjamin Fisz
US title: *Operation Snafu*

A wide boy and a slow-witted gypsy
have comic and other adventures in
the RAF.

Curious mixture of farce and action,
more on American lines than British,
but quite entertainingly presented.

w Harold Buchman   *novel Stop at a
Winner* by R. F. Delderfield   *d* Cyril
Frankel   *ph* Ted Scaife
m Malcolm Arnold

Alfred Lynch, Sean Connery, Cecil
Parker, Wilfrid Hyde White, Kathleen
Harrison, Alan King, Eleanor
Summerfield, Eric Barker, Terence
Longdon, John Le Mesurier, Harry
Locke

On the Riviera**
US   1951   90m   Technicolor
TCF (Sol C. Siegel)

A cabaret artist is persuaded to pose
as a philandering businessman.

Remake of *Folies Bergère* and *That
Night in Rio* (see also *On the Double*);
disliked at the time and accused of
tastelessness, it now seems smarter
and funnier than comparable films of
its era.

w Valentine Davies, Phoebe and
Henry Ephron   *d* Walter Lang
ph Leon Shamroy   *m* Alfred

Newman   *ad* Lyle Wheeler, Leland
Fuller

Danny Kaye, Corinne Calvet, Gene
Tierney, Marcel Dalio, Jean Murat
AAN: Alfred Newman; art direction

Once Around**
US   1991   114m   colour
Universal/Cinecom (Amy Robinson, Griffin
  Dunne)
V, L

Urged by her loving family to marry,
a thirtyish woman chooses as a
husband a brash and vulgar salesman
who does not win their approval.

Perceptive drama of the swings and
roundabouts of marital and family
life.

w Malia Scotch Marmo   *d* Lasse
Hallstrom   *ph* Theo Van De
Sande   *m* James Horner
ad David Gropman   *ed* Andrew
Monsheim

Richard Dreyfuss, Holly Hunter,
Danny Aiello, Laura San Giacomo,
Gena Rowlands, Roxanne Hart,
Griffin Dunne

'An intelligently engaging domestic
comedy-drama.' – *Variety*

Once Upon a Crime
US   1992   94m   Technicolor
Entertainment/Troublemakers/Dino De
  Laurentiis

Two Americans in Europe, hoping to
collect a reward for finding a valuable
dog, are suspected of murdering the
animal's owner.

Hysterically unamusing comedy,
performed in a frantic style.

w Charles Shyer, Nancy Myers, Steve
Kluger   *story* Rodolfo Sonego
d Eugene Levy   *ph* Giuseppe
Rotunno   *m* Richard Gibbs

pd Pier Luigi Basile   *ed* Patrick Kennedy

John Candy, James Belushi, Cybill Shepherd, Sean Young, Richard Lewis, Ornella Muti, Giancarlo Giannini, George Hamilton, Joss Ackland

'An overacted, unfunny, unexciting comedy-thriller.' – *Philip French, Observer*
'The film gives the impression of having been assembled, at great haste and in a state of panic, from bits and pieces left over from several other "international comedies".' – *Philip Kemp, Sight and Sound*
'Abysmal comedy.' – *Variety*

† A remake of *Crimen*, directed by Mario Camerini in 1960.

Once Upon a Honeymoon*
US   1942   116m   bw
RKO (Leo McCarey)

An American radio correspondent and an ex-burlesque queen cheat the Nazis – and her husband – in Europe during World War II.

Smooth but curious mixture of comedy and drama, a satisfactory but unmemorable star vehicle.

w Sheridan Gibney, Leo McCarey *d* Leo McCarey   *ph* George Barnes   *m* Robert Emmett Dolan

Cary Grant, Ginger Rogers, Walter Slezak, Albert Dekker, Albert Bassermann, Ferike Boros, Harry Shannon

'The attempt to play for both laughs and significance against a terrifying background of Nazi aggression is on the whole a little disappointing.' – *Newsweek*

One Good Turn
US   1931   20m   bw
Hal Roach
V(C)

Two odd-job men see their benefactress rehearsing a play, and think she is really being evicted.

Moderate star comedy with nice moments.

w H. M. Walker   *d* James W. Horne

Laurel and Hardy, Mary Carr, Billy Gilbert

One Good Turn
GB   1954   90m   bw
GFD/Two Cities (Maurice Cowan)

An orphan stays on to become an odd job man, and tries to raise money to buy an old car.

The star's second comedy is an almost unmitigated disaster, disjointed and depending too much on pathos.

w Maurice Cowan, John Paddy Carstairs, Ted Willis   *d* John Paddy Carstairs   *ph* Jack Cox   *m* John Addison

Norman Wisdom, Joan Rice, Shirley Abicair, Thora Hird, William Russell, Richard Caldicot

'Gayest screen event of the year!'
One Hour with You***
US   1932   84m   bw
Paramount (Ernst Lubitsch)

The affairs of a philandering Parisian doctor.

Superbly handled comedy of manners in Lubitsch's most inventive form, handled by a most capable cast. Unique entertainment of a kind which is, alas, no more.

w Samson Raphaelson,   play *Only a Dream* by Lothar Schmidt   *d* George

Cukor, Ernst Lubitsch   ph Victor
Milner   m Oscar Straus, Richard
Whiting   ly Leo Robin   ad Hans
Dreier

Maurice Chevalier, Jeanette MacDonald,
Genevieve Tobin, Roland Young,
Charles Ruggles, George Barbier

'Sure fire if frothy screen fare, cinch
b.o. at all times.' – Variety
'A brand new form of musical
entertainment . . . he has mixed verse,
spoken and sung, a smart and satiric
musical background, asides to the
audience, and sophisticated dialogue,
as well as lilting and delightful
songs . . . The result is something so
delightful that it places the circle of
golden leaves jauntily upon the
knowing head of Hollywood's most
original director.' – Philadelphia
Inquirer

† A remake of Lubitsch's silent success
The Marriage Circle.
AAN: best picture

One Touch of Venus*
US   1948   82m   bw
Universal/Lester Cowan

In a fashionable department store, a
statue of Venus comes to life and falls
for a window dresser.

Pleasant satirical comedy, watered
down from the Broadway original.

w Harry Kurnitz, Frank Tashlin
play S. J. Perelman, Ogden Nash
d William A. Seiter   ph Franz
Planer   songs Kurt Weill
ad Bernard Herzbrun, Emrich
Nicholson

Ava Gardner, Robert Walker, Eve
Arden, Dick Haymes, Olga San Juan,
Tom Conway

One, Two, Three**
US   1961   115m   bw   Panavision
United Artists/Mirisch/Pyramid (Billy
   Wilder)
L

An executive in West Berlin is trying
to sell Coca Cola to the Russians
while preventing his boss's daughter
from marrying a communist.

Back to Ninotchka territory, but this
time the tone is that of a wild farce
which achieves fine momentum in
stretches but also flags a lot in
between, teetering the while on the
edge of taste.

w Billy Wilder, I. A. L. Diamond
play Ferenc Molnar   d Billy
Wilder   ph Daniel Fapp   m André
Previn

James Cagney, Horst Buchholz, Arlene
Francis, Pamela Tiffin, Lilo Pulver,
Howard St John, Leon Askin

'A sometimes bewildered, often
wonderfully funny exercise in nonstop
nuttiness.' – Time
'This first-class featherweight farce is
a serious achievement.' – Stanley
Kauffmann
AAN: Daniel Fapp

One Way Pendulum
GB   1964   85m   bw
UA/Woodfall (Michael Deeley)

A suburban clerk leads a dream
existence; his son teaches speak-
your-weight machines to sing, while
he sets an imaginary murder trial in
motion.

A nonsense play (which has many
adherents) resists the literalness of the
camera eye.

w N. F. Simpson   play N. F.
Simpson   d Peter Yates   ph Denys
Coop   m Richard Rodney Bennett

Eric Sykes, George Cole, Julia Foster,
Jonathan Miller, Peggy Mount,
Alison Leggatt, Mona Washbourne

'A comedy for anyone who's ever had a
mother.'

Only the Lonely
US   1991   104m   DeLuxe
TCF/Hughes Entertainment (John Hughes,
   Hunt Lowry)
V, L

A mother-dominated cop falls in love
with a shy beautician at his
neighbourhood undertakers.

Soft-centred, sentimental drama that
lacks the courage to be convincing.

wd Chris Columbus   ph Julio
Macat   m Maurice Jarre   pd John
Muto   ch Monica Devereux
ed Raja Gosnell

John Candy, Maureen O'Hara, Ally
Sheedy, Anthony Quinn, James
Belushi, Kevin Dunn, Milo O'Shea,
Bert Remsen, Macaulay Culkin

† It was Maureen O'Hara's first film
for 20 years.

Only Two Can Play***
GB   1962   106m   bw
British Lion/Vale (Launder and Gilliat)
V

A much married assistant librarian in
a Welsh town has an abortive affair
with a councillor's wife.

Well characterized and generally
diverting 'realistic' comedy which
slows up a bit towards the end but
contains many memorable sequences
and provides its star's last good
character performance.

w Bryan Forbes,   novel That
Uncertain Feeling by Kingsley Amis
d Sidney Gilliat   ph John Wilcox
m Richard Rodney Bennett
ad Albert Witherick

Peter Sellers, Mai Zetterling, Virginia
Maskell, Richard Attenborough,
Raymond Huntley, John Le Mesurier,
Kenneth Griffith

'It has a kind of near-truth which is
at once hilarious and faintly macabre.'
– Dilys Powell

Only When I Larf*
GB   1968   103m   Eastmancolor
Paramount/Beecord (Len Deighton, Brian
   Duffy, Hugh Attwooll)

The adventures of three confidence
tricksters.

Quite likeable but unmemorable 'with
it' comedy of the sixties; the tricks
are more amusing than the
characterization.

w John Salmon   novel Len
Deighton   d Basil Dearden
ph Anthony Richmond   m Ron
Grainer

Richard Attenborough, David
Hemmings, Alexandra Stewart,
Nicholas Pennell, Melissa Stribling,
Terence Alexander, Edric Connor,
Calvin Lockhart, Clifton Jones

Ooh, You Are Awful*
GB   1972   97m   Eastmancolor
British Lion/Quintain (E. M. Smedley Aston)
V
US title: Get Charlie Tully

A London con man seeks a fortune,
the clue to which is tattooed on the
behind of one of several girls.

Amusing star vehicle with plenty of
room for impersonations and
outrageous jokes.

w John Warren, John Singer
d Cliff Owen   ph Ernest Stewart
m Christopher Gunning

Dick Emery, Derren Nesbitt, Ronald

Fraser, Pat Coombs, William Franklyn, Brian Oulton, Norman Bird

Operation Bullshine

GB   1959   84m   Technicolor
ABPC

In 1942, complications ensue when an ATS private suspects her husband of infidelity.

Flabby army comedy with a few laughs.

w Anne Burnaby, Rupert Lang, Gilbert Gunn   d Gilbert Gunn

Donald Sinden, Barbara Murray, Carole Lesley, Ronald Shiner, Naunton Wayne, Daniel Massey, Dora Bryan

Operation Mad Ball*

US   1957   105m   bw
Columbia (Jed Harris)

American troops in Normandy are forbidden to fraternize with nurses, but a clandestine dance is arranged.

Madcap army farce which keeps promising to be funnier than it is.

w Arthur Carter, Jed Harris, Blake Edwards   play Arthur Carter   d Richard Quine   ph Charles Lawton Jnr   m George Duning

Jack Lemmon, Ernie Kovacs, Kathryn Grant, Mickey Rooney, James Darren, Arthur O'Connell

Operation Petticoat*

US   1959   124m   Eastmancolor
Universal/Granart (Robert Arthur)
L

During World War II, a crippled submarine is refloated by fair means and foul, and a party of nurses is taken aboard.

Flabby comedy with good moments, but not many.

w Stanley Shapiro, Maurice Richlin   story Paul King, Joseph Stone   d Blake Edwards
ph Russell Harlan   m David Rose

Cary Grant, Tony Curtis, Joan O'Brien, Dina Merrill, Gene Evans, Arthur O'Connell, Richard Sargent

'Grant is a living lesson in getting laughs without lines.' – Variety
AAN: story and screenplay

Oscar

US   1991   109m   Technicolor
Warner/Touchstone/Silver Screen Partners IV (Leslie Belzberg)
V, L

A gangster who is trying to reform attempts to sort out the marital problems of his daughters.

Leaden attempt at a screwball comedy, and one that sinks under its own witlessness.

w Michael Barrie, Jim Mulholland   play Claude Magnier   d John Landis   ph Mac Ahlberg   m Elmer Bernstein   pd Bill Kenney   ed Dale Beldin, Michael R. Miller

Sylvester Stallone, Ornella Muti, Kirk Douglas, Peter Riegert, Chazz Palminteri, Vincent Spano, Marisa Tomei, Tim Curry, Don Ameche, Yvonne DeCarlo, Linda Gray

'Zany farce generates a fair share of laughs but still probably remains too creaky a conceit for modern audiences to go for in a big way.' – Variety

† Magnier's play was first filmed in France in 1967, directed by Eduardo Molinaro and starring Louis de Funes.

'Meet Larry the Liquidator. Arrogant. Greedy. Self-centered. Ruthless. You gotta love the guy.'

Other People's Money*
US 1991 101m Technicolor
Warner/Yorktown (Norman Jewison, Ric Kidney)
V, L

A selfish asset-stripper attempts to take over an old-established company and its attractive young lawyer.

Entertaining comedy of the conflict between big-city and small-town values in the modern manner: that is, greed wins.

w Alvin Sargent play Jerry Sterner d Norman Jewison ph Haskell Wexler m David Newman pd Philip Rosenberg ed Lou Lombardo, Michael Pacek, Hubert de la Bouillerie

Danny DeVito, Gregory Peck, Penelope Ann Miller, Piper Laurie, Dean Jones, R. D. Call, Mo Gaffney, Bette Henritze

Our Hospitality***
US 1923 70m approx (24 fps) bw silent
Metro/Buster Keaton (Joseph M. Schenck)
V, L

Around 1850, a southerner returns home to claim his bride and finds himself in the middle of a blood feud.

Charming rather than hilarious star comedy with a splendid ancient train and at least one incredible stunt by the star.

w Jean Havez, Joseph Mitchell, Clyde Bruckman d Buster Keaton, Jack Blystone ph Elgin Lessley, Gordon Jennings

Buster Keaton, Natalie Talmadge, Joe Keaton, Buster Keaton Jnr

'A novelty mélange of dramatics, low comedy, laughs and thrills . . . one of the best comedies ever produced.' – Variety

Our Miss Fred*
GB 1972 96m Technicolor
EMI/Willis World Wide (Josephine Douglas)

In World War II France, an actor escapes in women's clothes when his troupe is captured by the Nazis.

A carefully nurtured vehicle for Britain's top female impersonator somehow doesn't come off; celluloid both constrains his range and reveals his inadequacies.

w Hugh Leonard d Bob Kellett ph Dick Bush m Peter Greenwell

Danny La Rue, Alfred Marks, Lance Percival, Lally Bowers, Frances de la Tour, Walter Gotell

Our Relations***
US 1936 65m bw
Hal Roach/Stan Laurel Productions
V, V(C), L

Two sailors entrusted with a diamond ring get mixed up with their long lost and happily married twin brothers.

A fast-moving comedy which contains some of Laurel and Hardy's most polished work as well as being their most satisfying production.

w Richard Connell, Felix Adler, Charles Rogers, Jack Jevne story The Money Box by W. W. Jacobs d Harry Lachman ph Rudolph Maté

Stan Laurel, Oliver Hardy, James Finlayson, Alan Hale, Sidney Toler, Daphne Pollard, Iris Adrian, Noel Madison, Ralf Harolde, Arthur Housman

Our Wife*

US 1931 20m bw
Hal Roach

Stan helps Ollie to elope.

Good standard star comedy with a
rather disappointing third sequence
as three people try to get into a car
designed for one.

w H. M. Walker   d James W. Horne

Laurel and Hardy, James Finlayson,
Jean London

Out Cold

US 1989 92m CFI
Hemdale (George G. Braunstein, Ron
  Hamady)
V, L

Believing that he has inadvertently
killed his partner, a butcher covers
up the crime with the help of the
widow, who is the real murderer.

Limp comedy that quickly runs out of
ideas.

w Leonard Glasser, George Malko
d Malcolm Mowbray   ph Tony
Pierce-Roberts   m Michel
Colombier   pd Linda Pearl
ed Dennis M. Hill

John Lithgow, Teri Garr, Randy
Quaid, Bruce McGill, Lisa Blount, Alan
Blumenfeld, Morgan Paull, Barbara
Rhoades

Out of the Blue

US 1947 86m bw
Eagle Lion

A Greenwich village artist thinks a girl
who has passed out in his apartment
is dead, and tries to hide the body.

Tasteless and very unfunny farce.

w Vera Caspary, Walter Bullock,
Edward Eliscu   d Leigh Jason

George Brent, Carole Landis, Ann
Dvorak, Turhan Bey, Virginia Mayo,
Elizabeth Patterson, Julia Dean,
Richard Lane

The Out of Towners*

US 1970 98m Movielab
Paramount/Jalem (Paul Nathan)

An executive and his wife fly into
New York for an interview, but their
encounter with the city is a mounting
series of traumatic disasters.

A love-hate relationship with a city
demonstrated by a resident is
something of an in-joke and becomes
increasingly hysterical and
unsympathetic, but there are bright
moments in this company.

w Neil Simon   d Arthur Hiller
ph Andrew Laszlo   m Quincy
Jones

Jack Lemmon, Sandy Dennis

Outrageous Fortune*

US 1987 100m DeLuxe
Touchstone/Interscope (Ted Field, Robert
  Cort)
V, L

Two disparate women are in love with
the same man, who is wanted by the
CIA and the KGB.

Chase comedy with sex elements and
plenty going on: old-fashioned jokes
wrapped up in a modern package.

w Leslie Dixon   d Arthur Hiller
ph David M. Walsh   m Alan
Silvestri   pd James D. Vance

Shelley Long, Bette Midler, Peter
Coyote, Robert Prosky, John Schuck

'Really a risqué film for a conservative
audience.' – Daily Variety

Over the Brooklyn Bridge

US 1983 106m Metrocolor
Golan-Globus

Misadventures of a family-ridden Jewish restaurant owner in New York.

Frantic ethnic comedy with an unsympathetic hero.

w Arnold Somkin   d Menahem Golan

Elliott Gould, Margaux Hemingway, Sid Caesar, Shelley Winters, Burt Young, Carol Kane

'The film's lip service to liberalism is offset by a blatantly sexist storyline.' – Ruth Baumgarten, MFB

Overboard
US 1987 112m colour
UIP/MGM (Alexandra Rose, Anthea Sylbert)
V, L

An heiress suffering from amnesia is claimed as a wife by a carpenter with three kids.

Mild amusement is provided by a predictable comedy.

w Leslie Dixon   d Garry Marshall   ph John A. Alonzo
m Alan Silvestri   ad James Shanahan, Jim Dultz   ed Dov Hoenig, Sonny Baskin

Goldie Hawn, Kurt Russell, Edward Herrmann, Katherine Helmond, Roddy McDowall, Michael Hagerty, Jeffrey Wiseman

'When she starts mixing business with pleasure, she goes out of business'
The Owl and the Pussycat*
US 1970 96m Eastmancolor Panavision
Columbia/Rastar (Ray Stark)
V

A bookstore assistant reports a fellow tenant for prostitution, and when she is evicted she moves in with him.

Wacky, bawdy double act which starts promisingly but outstays its welcome. A solid step forward in permissiveness, with kinky behaviour as well as four-letter words.

w Buck Henry   play Bill Manhoff   d Herbert Ross
ph Harry Stradling, Andrew Laszlo   m Richard Halligan

Barbra Streisand, George Segal, Robert Klein, Allen Garfield

'If computers ever turn out romantic comedies, the results will look like this.' – Stanley Kauffmann

Pack Up Your Troubles*
US 1931 68m bw
Hal Roach
V

Two World War I veterans try to look after their late pal's orphan daughter.

Patchy comedy vehicle in which too many gags are not fully thought out or timed.

w H. M. Walker   *d* George Marshall, Ray McCarey   *ph* Art Lloyd

Stan Laurel, Oliver Hardy, Donald Dillaway, Mary Carr, Charles Middleton, Dick Cramer, James Finlayson, Tom Kennedy, Billy Gilbert

The Paleface*
US 1948 91m Technicolor
Paramount (Robert L. Welch)

Calamity Jane undertakes an undercover mission against desperadoes, and marries a timid dentist as a cover.

Splendid wagon train comedy Western with the stars in excellent form.

w *Edmund Hartman, Frank Tashlin* *d* Norman Z. McLeod   *ph* Ray Rennahan   *m* Victor Young

Bob Hope, Jane Russell, Robert Armstrong, Iris Adrian, Robert Watson, Jack Searle, Joe Vitale, Clem Bevans, Charles Trowbridge

† Sequel: *Son of Paleface* (qv); remake, *The Shakiest Gun in the West* (1968).

AA: song 'Buttons and Bows' (*m* Jay Livingston, *ly* Ray Evans)

The Palm Beach Story*
US 1942 88m bw
Paramount (Paul Jones)

The wife of a penurious engineer takes off for Florida to set her sights on a millionaire.

Flighty comedy, inconsequential in itself, but decorated with scenes, characters and zany touches typical of its creator, here at his most brilliant if uncontrolled.

wd *Preston Sturges*   *ph* Victor Milner   *m* Victor Young

Claudette Colbert, Joel McCrea, Rudy Vallee, Mary Astor, Sig Arno, Robert Warwick, Torben Meyer, Jimmy Conlin, William Demarest, Jack Norton, Robert Greig, Roscoe Ates, Chester Conklin, Franklin Pangborn, Alan Bridge, *Robert Dudley*
  HACKENSACKER (Rudy Vallee): 'That's one of the tragedies of this life, that the men most in need of a beating up are always enormous.'
  WEENIE KING (Robert Dudley): 'Anyway, I'd be too old for you. Cold are the hands of time that creep along relentlessly, destroying slowly but without pity that which yesterday was young. Alone, our memories resist this disintegration and grow more

lovely with the passing years. That's hard to say with false teeth.'

'Surprises and delights as though nothing of the kind had been known before . . . farce and tenderness are combined without a fault.' – *William Whitebait*
'Minus even a hint of the war . . . packed with delightful absurdities.' – *Variety*

Palm Springs Weekend

US   1963   100m   Technicolor
Warner (Michael Hoey)

Various holidaymakers at Palm Springs get romantically involved.

Youth-oriented farce, better produced than most but basically a depressing experience.

w Earl Hamner Jnr   *d* Norman Taurog   *ph* Harold Lipstein   *m* Frank Perkins

Troy Donahue, Ty Hardin, Connie Stevens, Stefanie Powers, Robert Conrad, Jack Weston, Andrew Duggan

'As P. T. Barnum put it, "There's a sucker born every minute".'

Paper Moon**

US   1973   103m   bw
Paramount/Saticoy (Peter Bogdanovich)

In the American midwest in the thirties, a bible salesman and a plain little girl make a great con team.

Unusual but overrated comedy, imperfectly adapted from a very funny book, with careful but disappointing period sense and photography. A lot more style and gloss was required.

w Alvin Sargent   *novel* Addie Pray by *Joe David Brown*   *d* Peter Bogdanovich   *ph* Laszlo Kovacs   *m* popular songs and recordings

Ryan O'Neal, Tatum O'Neal, Madeline Kahn, John Hillerman

'I've rarely seen a film that looked so unlike what it was about.' – *Stanley Kauffmann*
'At its best the film is only mildly amusing, and I'm not sure I could recall a few undeniable highlights if pressed on the point.' – *Gary Arnold*
'Bogdanovich once again deploys the armoury of nostalgia with relentless cunning to evoke the threadbare side of American life forty years ago . . . one of those rare movies which engages at least two of the senses.' – *Benny Green, Punch*
'It is so enjoyable, so funny, so touching that I couldn't care less about its morals.' – *Daily Telegraph*

AA: Tatum O'Neal
AAN: Alvin Sargent; Madeline Kahn

Parade*

France/Sweden   1974   85m   Technicolor
Gray Film/Sveriges Radio

Jacques Tati introduces a series of acts in a small-scale circus.

Pleasant, sometimes boring variety show, to be included in the Tati canon for completeness; it does include some of his unique pieces of mime.

wd Jacques Tati

'A curious, unresolved *envoi*.' – *John Pym, MFB*
'Moments of great good humour and flashes of incomparable magic.' – *Sight and Sound*

Pardon Mon Affaire*

France   1977   108m   Eastmancolor
Gaumont/La Guéville (Daniel Deschamps)
aka: *Un Eléphant Ça Trompe Enormément*

A middle-aged married man discovers

that he is a very unsuccessful adulterer.

Unsubtle comedy that was successful in France, though it does not travel well.

w Jean-Loup Dabadie, Yves Robert   *d* Yves Robert   *ph* René Mathelin   *m* Vladimir Cosma   *ad* Jean-Pierre Kohut-Svelko   *ed* Gérard Pollicand

Jean Rochefort, Claude Brasseur, Guy Bedos, Victor Lanoux, Danielle Delorme, Anny Duperey

† The film was remade by Hollywood as *The Woman In Red* (qv), directed by Gene Wilder.

Pardon Us*
US   1931   55m   bw
Hal Roach
V, V(C), L
aka: *Jailbirds*

Two zany bootleggers find themselves in and out of prison.

Patchy star comedy which finds the boys on the whole not in quite their best form.

w H. M. Walker   *d* James Parrott   *ph* Jack Stevens

Stan Laurel, Oliver Hardy, Wilfred Lucas, Walter Long, James Finlayson

'Their first full-length, with not over two reels of value.' – *Variety*

Parenthood**
US   1989   99m   DeLuxe
Panavision
UIP/Imagine Entertainment (Brian Grazer)
V, L

Three generations of fathers and sons try to come to terms with each other.

Expertly packaged, frequently funny, sometimes accurate, but more often

sentimental, study of paternal relationships (maternal relationships are defined in terms of the absence of a father).

w Lowell Ganz, Babaloo Mandel   *d* Ron Howard   *ph* Donald McAlpine   *m* Randy Newman   *pd* Todd Hallowell   *ed* Michael Hill, Daniel Hanley

Steve Martin, Tom Hulce, Rick Moranis, Martha Plimpton, Keanu Reeves, Jason Robards, Mary Steenburgen, Dianne Wiest
AAN: Dianne Wiest

Parents
US   1988   82m   colour
Vestron/Parents Productions (Bonnie Palef-Woolf)
L

A child in small-town America of the 1950s discovers that his parents are cannibals.

Black comedy all the more unsettling because of its resolutely suburban setting.

w Christopher Hawthorne   *d* Bob Balaban   *ph* Ernest Day, Robin Vidgeon   *m* Angelo Badalamenti, Jonathan Elias   *ad* Andris Hausmanis   *ed* Bill Pankow

Randy Quaid, Mary Beth Hurt, Sandy Dennis, Bryan Madorsky, Juno Mills-Cockell, Kathryn Grody, Deborah Rush, Graham Jarvis

Paris Holiday*
US   1957   101m   Technirama
UA/Tolda (Bob Hope)

An American comedian meets a French one in Paris, and both have narrow escapes because their script contains the clue to a gang of counterfeiters.

Amiable location romp with the stars in pretty good form.

w Edmund Beloin, Dean Riesner
d Gerd Oswald   ph Roger Hubert
m Joseph J. Lilley

Bob Hope, Fernandel, Anita Ekberg, Martha Hyer, André Morell, Maurice Teynac, Jean Murat, Preston Sturges

Paris When It Sizzles
US   1963   110m   Technicolor
Paramount (Richard Quine, George Axelrod)

A film writer tries out several script ideas with his secretary as heroine and himself as hero or villain.

As a French film called La Fête à Henriette this was a charming whimsy, but Hollywood made it heavy-handed and boring, especially as no one in it seems to be having much fun.

w George Axelrod
screenplay Julien Duvivier, Henri Jeanson   d Richard Quine
ph Charles Lang Jnr   m Nelson Riddle

William Holden, Audrey Hepburn, Grégoire Aslan, Noel Coward, Raymond Bussières

'The new script embalms the original instead of reviving it.' – Stanley Kauffmann, New Republic

The Party*
US   1968   98m   DeLuxe
Panavision
UA/Mirisch/Geoffrey (Blake Edwards)
L

An accident-prone Indian actor is accidentally invited to a swank Hollywood party and wrecks it.

Would-be Tatiesque comedy of disaster, occasionally well-timed but far too long for all its gloss.

w Blake Edwards, Tom and Frank Waldman   d Blake Edwards
ph Lucien Ballard   m Henry Mancini   pd Fernando Carrere

Peter Sellers, Claudine Longet, Marge Champion, Fay McKenzie, Steve Franken, Buddy Lester

'One thing the old movie makers did know is that two reels is more than enough of this stuff.' – Wilfred Sheed
'It is only rarely that one laughs or even smiles; mostly one just chalks up another point for ingenuity.' – Tom Milne

The Passionate Plumber
US   1932   73m   bw
MGM

A woman hires a professional lover to fend off the man she really loves but thinks she shouldn't have.

Much revamped farce version of a comedy made straight in 1927 and 1942. All flopped, but this is the worst.

w Laurence E. Johnson   play Her Cardboard Lover by Frederick Lonsdale   d Edward Sedgwick

Buster Keaton, Jimmy Durante, Irene Purcell, Polly Moran, Gilbert Roland, Mona Maris, Maude Eburne

'Another lay-me-down-to-sleeper for box offices.' – Variety

Passport to Pimlico**
GB   1949   84m   bw
Ealing (E. V. H. Emmett)

Part of a London district is discovered to belong to Burgundy, and the inhabitants find themselves free of rationing restrictions.

A cleverly detailed little comedy which inaugurated the best period of

Ealing, its preoccupation with suburban man and his foibles. Not exactly satire, but great fun, and kindly with it.

w T. E. B. Clarke   *d* Henry Cornelius   *ph* Lionel Banes   *m* Georges Auric

Stanley Holloway, *Margaret Rutherford*, Basil Radford, Naunton Wayne, Hermione Baddeley, John Slater, Paul Dupuis, Jane Hylton, Raymond Huntley, Betty Warren, Barbara Murray, Sidney Tafler

† The film was based on a genuine news item. The Canadian government presented to the Netherlands the room in which Princess Juliana was to bear a child.
AAN: T. E. B. Clarke

'Not much meat on her, but what there is is cherce!'

Pat and Mike**
US   1952   95m   bw
MGM (Lawrence Weingarten)

A small-time sports promoter takes on a female intellectual multi-champion.

A comedy which amuses because of its star playing, but doesn't really develop. All very easy going, with guest appearances from sporting personalities.

w Ruth Gordon, Garson Kanin   *d* George Cukor   *ph* William Daniels   *m* David Raksin

Spencer Tracy, Katharine Hepburn, Aldo Ray, William Ching, Sammy White, Jim Backus, Phyllis Povah

'They do not, like the Lunts, give the impression of a rigid calculated effect; rather, they complement and stimulate each other.' – *MFB*
AAN: script

'He wants YOU to have his baby!'

Paternity
US   1981   93m   Movielab
Paramount (Jerry Tokofsky)
L

A middle-aged bachelor decides to father a son via a hired mother, who will then return the child to him.

Tastelessly up-dated Hollywood romance with predictable complications. Not worth sitting through.

w Charlie Peters   *d* David Steinberg   *ph* Bobby Byrne   *m* David Shire

Burt Reynolds, Beverly D'Angelo, Norman Fell, Paul Dooley, Elizabeth Ashley, Lauren Hutton, Juanita Moore

The Patsy
US   1964   101m   Technicolor
Paramount/Jerry Lewis (E. J. Glucksman)
V

Hollywood executives try to mould a bellboy to replace a deceased comedian.

A few mildly funny scenes scarcely atone for a long raucous comedy in which the star upstages his betters.

wd Jerry Lewis   *ph* Wallace Kelley   *m* David Raksin

Jerry Lewis, Everett Sloane, Peter Lorre, John Carradine, Phil Harris, Hans Conried, Ina Balin

Peggy Sue Got Married**
US   1986   104m   DeLuxe
Tri-Star/Rastar (Paul R. Gurian)
V, L

A disillusioned woman goes to her 25th high school reunion and finds herself reliving her young life.

It plays like an extended *Twilight Zone*,

but with plenty of interesting details to back up an excellent leading performance.

w Jerry Leichtling, Arlene Sarner *d* Francis Coppola *ph* Jordan Cronenweth *m* John Barry *pd* Dean Tavoularis *ed* Barry Malkin

Kathleen Turner, Nicolas Cage, Barry Miller, Catherine Hicks, Maureen O'Sullivan, Leon Ames, Helen Hunt, Don Murray, Barbara Harris, Kevin J. O'Connor

'Provocative, well acted, stylish and uneven.' – *Variety*
AAN: Jordan Cronenweth; Theodora Van Runkle (costumes); Kathleen Turner

Percy
GB 1971 103m Eastmancolor
Anglo EMI/Welbeck (Betty E. Box)
V

After an unfortunate accident, a young man undergoes a successful penis transplant, and sets out to discover who the donor was.

Barrage of phallic jokes, some quite funny, but mostly as witless as the whole idea.

w Hugh Leonard *novel* Raymond Hitchcock *d* Ralph Thomas *ph* Ernest Steward *m* Ray Davies

Hywel Bennett, Elke Sommer, *Denholm Elliott*, Britt Ekland, Cyd Hayman

Percy's Progress
GB 1974 101m Eastmancolor
EMI (Betty E. Box)
V

A chemical causes impotence in all males except the owner of the first transplanted penis.

Percy dug deep, but this is really the bottom of the barrel.

w Sid Colin *d* Ralph Thomas *ph* Tony Imi *m* Tony Macauley

Leigh Lawson, Elke Sommer, Denholm Elliott, Judy Geeson, Harry H. Corbett, Vincent Price, Adrienne Posta, Julie Ege, James Booth

Perfect Day*
US 1929 20m bw
Hal Roach
V

Various problems delay a family's departure for a picnic.

Technically a most adept star comedy but its repetition can annoy.

w Hal Roach, Leo McCarey, H. M. Walker *d* James Parrott

Laurel and Hardy, Edgar Kennedy

† The picnic was originally to have occupied the second reel, but the departure gags swelled to occupy the entire footage.

The Perfect Furlough
US 1958 93m Eastmancolor
Cinemascope
U-I (Robert Arthur)
GB title: *Strictly for Pleasure*

To help morale at a remote Arctic army unit, one of the men is selected to enjoy the perfect leave in Paris on behalf of the others.

Amiable farce which entertains while it's on but is quickly forgotten.

w Stanley Shapiro *d* Blake Edwards *ph* Philip Lathrop *m* Frank Skinner

Tony Curtis, Janet Leigh, Elaine Stritch, Keenan Wynn, Troy Donahue, King Donovan, Linda Cristal

Perfectly Normal*

Canada   1990   105m   colour
Palace/Bialystock & Bloom/Téléfilm
   Canada/BSB/Skyhost/British Screen
   (Michael Burns)
V, L

An ice hockey-playing brewery
worker teams up with a dubious chef
to open an operatic restaurant.

Bizarre comedy of eccentric lives in a
small-town setting.

w Eugene Lipinski, Paul
Quarrington   d Yves Simoneau
ph Alain Dostie   m Richard
Gregoire   pd Anne Pritchard
ed Ronald Sanders

Robbie Coltrane, Michael Riley,
Deborah Duchene, Eugene Lipinski,
Jack Nichols, Elizabeth Harpur,
Patricia Gage, Kenneth Welsh

'The movie is too eager to be loved,
but has its moments.' –Philip French,
Observer

The Perils of Pauline*

US   1947   96m   Technicolor
Paramount (Sol C. Siegel)

The career of silent serial queen Pearl
White.

An agreeable recreation of old time
Hollywood, with plenty of slapstick
chases but a shade too much
sentiment also.

w P. J. Wolfson   d George
Marshall   ph Ray Rennahan
md Robert Emmett Dolan

Betty Hutton, John Lund, Billy de
Wolfe, William Demarest, Constance
Collier, Frank Faylen, William
Farnum, Paul Panzer, Snub Pollard,
Creighton Hale, Chester Conklin,
James Finlayson, Hank Mann, Bert
Roach, Francis McDonald, Chester
Clute

'People who can accept such stuff as
solid gold have either forgotten a lot,
or never knew first-rate slapstick
when they saw it, twenty or thirty
years ago, when it was one of the
wonders of the world.' – James Agee
AAN: song 'I Wish I Didn't Love You
So' (m/ly Frank Loesser)

Personal Property*

US   1937   84m   bw
MGM (John W. Considine Jnr)
GB title: The Man in Possession

An American widow in England, in
financial straits, falls for the bailiff sent
to keep an eye on her.

Moderate star comedy which still
amuses.

w Hugh Mills, Ernest Vajda
play The Man in Possession by H. M.
Harwood   d W. S. Van Dyke II
ph William Daniels   m Franz
Waxman

Jean Harlow, Robert Taylor, Reginald
Owen, Una O'Connor, Henrietta
Crosman, E. E. Clive, Cora
Witherspoon, Barnett Parker

'Harmless boudoir farce, for the
undergraduates.' – Variety

'Honeymoon's over – time to get married!'
Pete 'n Tillie*

US   1972   100m   Technicolor
   Panavision
Universal (Julius J. Epstein)

The tragi-comic marriage of two
eccentrics.

Curious: plain drama treated as
comedy, with surprisingly satisfactory
results, but not an example to be
followed.

w Julius J. Epstein   novel Witch's
Milk by Peter de Vries   d Martin
Ritt   ph John Alonzo   m John T.
Williams

Walter Matthau, Carol Burnett,
Geraldine Page, René Auberjonois,
Barry Nelson, Henry Jones

'For the most part an amusing,
moving, sentimental comedy. The
wisecracks stay on this side of human
possibility — that is, we don't feel, as
we do so often with Neil Simon, that
the characters have private gag writers
in their homes.' – *Stanley Kauffmann*
AAN: Julius J. Epstein; Geraldine
Page

Petulia*
US 1968 105m Technicolor
Warner/Petersham (Raymond Wagner)

A doctor's life is disrupted by his
meeting and loving a kooky girl who
has family problems.

Swinging London melodrama which
happens to be set in San Francisco. All
very flashy, and occasionally arresting
or well acted, but adding up to
nothing.

w Lawrence B. Marcus *novel Me
and the Arch Kook Petulia* by John
Haase *d* Richard Lester
ph Nicolas Roeg *m* John Barry

George C. Scott, Julie Christie,
Richard Chamberlain, Joseph Cotten,
Arthur Hill, Shirley Knight, Kathleen
Widdoes, Pippa Scott

'A sad and savage comment on the
ways we waste our time and ourselves
in upper-middle-class America.' –
Richard Schickel
'A soulless, arbitrary, attitudinizing
piece of claptrap.' – *John Simon*

'Uncle Leo's bedtime story for you older
tots! The things they do among the playful
rich – oh, boy!'

The Philadelphia Story****
US 1940 112m bw
MGM (Joseph L. Mankiewicz)

A stuffy heiress, about to be married
for the second time, turns human and
returns gratefully to number one.

Hollywood's most wise and sparkling
comedy, with a script which is even an
improvement on the original play.
Cukor's direction is so discreet you
can hardly sense it, and all the
performances are just perfect.

*w Donald Ogden Stewart,   play Philip
Barry d George Cukor ph Joseph
Ruttenberg m Franz Waxman
ad Cedric Gibbons*

*Katharine Hepburn, Cary Grant, James
Stewart, Ruth Hussey, Roland Young,
John Halliday, Mary Nash, Virginia
Weidler, John Howard, Henry Daniell*

'There are just not enough
superlatives sufficiently to appreciate
this show.' – *Hollywood Reporter*
'An exceptionally bright job of
screenplay writing . . . though films
like this do little to advance the art of
motion pictures, they may help to
convince some of the more discerning
among cultural slugabeds that when
movies want to turn their hand to
anything, they can turn it.' – *Otis
Ferguson*

† Cary Grant donated his salary to war
relief.

AA: Donald Ogden Stewart; James
Stewart
AAN: best picture; George Cukor;
Katharine Hepburn; Ruth Hussey

The Pickwick Papers*
GB 1952 115m bw
George Minter (Bob McNaught)
V

Various adventures of the Pickwick
Club culminate in Mrs Bardell's suit for
breach of promise.

Flatly conceived and loosely
constructed Dickensian comedy;

good humour and lots of well-known faces do not entirely atone for lack of artifice.

wd Noel Langley   *ph* Wilkie Cooper   *m* Antony Hopkins   *ad* Fred Pusey

James Hayter, James Donald, Donald Wolfit, Hermione Baddeley, Hermione Gingold, Kathleen Harrison, *Nigel Patrick,* Alexander Gauge, Lionel Murton

'As welcome as the sun in the morning and as British as a cup of tea.' – *Daily Mirror*

A Piece of the Action
US   1977   135m   Metrocolor
Warner/First Artists/Verdon (Melville Tucker)

Crooks are blackmailed into helping rebellious adolescents.

A black version, at immense length, of the hoodlum comedies in which the Dead End Kids so often featured. Not badly made, but out of date without being nostalgic.

w Charles Blackwell   *story* Timothy March   *d* Sidney Poitier   *ph* Don Morgan   *m* Curtis Mayfield

Sidney Poitier, James Earl Jones, Bill Cosby, Denise Nicholas, Hope Clarke, Tracy Reed, Jason Evers, Marc Lawrence

Pillow Talk**
US   1959   110m   Eastmancolor Cinemascope
Universal/Arwin (Ross Hunter, Martin Melcher)

Two people who can't stand each other fall in love via a party line.

Slightly elephantine romantic comedy which nevertheless contains a number of funny scenes and was notable for starting off the Hudson-Day partnership and a run of similar comedies which survived the sixties.

w Stanley Shapiro, Maurice Richlin, Russell Rouse, Clarence Greene   *d* Michael Gordon   *ph* Arthur E. Arling   *m* Frank de Vol   *ad* Richard H. Riedel

Doris Day, Rock Hudson, Tony Randall, Thelma Ritter, Nick Adams, Julia Meade, Allen Jenkins, Marcel Dalio, Lee Patrick

AA: Stanley Shapiro, Maurice Richlin, Russell Rouse, Clarence Greene
AAN: Frank de Vol; Doris Day; Thelma Ritter; art direction

Pink Cadillac*
US   1989   122m   Technicolor
Warner/Malpaso (David Valdes)
V

A bounty hunter goes in search of a mother who has disappeared with her baby and a pink Cadillac containing $250,000 belonging to a bunch of neo-Nazis.

Amiable, if somewhat aimless, comedy with unsubtle performances.

w John Eskow   *d* Buddy Van Horn   *ph* Jack N. Green   *m* Steve Dorff   *pd* Edward C. Carfagno   *ed* Joel Cox

Clint Eastwood, Bernadette Peters, Timothy Carhart, John Dennis Johnston, Michael Des Barres, Geoffrey Lewis

The Pink Panther**
US   1963   113m   Technirama
UA/Mirisch (Martin Jurow)
V, L

An incompetent *Sûreté* inspector is in Switzerland on the trail of a jewel thief called The Phantom.

Sporadically engaging mixture of pratfalls, *Raffles*, and *Monsieur Hulot*, all dressed to kill and quite palatable for the uncritical.

w Maurice Richlin, Blake Edwards
d Blake Edwards   ph Philip Lathrop   m Henry Mancini
ad Fernando Carrere
animation De Patie-Freleng

David Niven, Peter Sellers, Capucine, Claudia Cardinale, Robert Wagner, Brenda de Banzie, Colin Gordon

† Inspector Clouseau later became a cartoon character and also provoked five sequels: *A Shot in the Dark*, *Inspector Clouseau*, *The Return of the Pink Panther*, *The Pink Panther Strikes Again* and *The Revenge of the Pink Panther*.
AAN: Henry Mancini

The Pink Panther Strikes Again*
GB   1976   103m   DeLuxe
    Panavision
United Artists/Amjo (Blake Edwards)
V, L

After a nervous breakdown, Chief Inspector Dreyfus builds up a vast criminal organization devoted to the extermination of Inspector Clouseau.

Zany pratfall farce with signs of over-confidence since the success of *The Return of the Pink Panther*. But some gags are funny, despite a rather boring star.

w Frank Waldman, Blake Edwards   d Blake Edwards
ph Harry Waxman   m Henry Mancini

Peter Sellers, Herbert Lom, Colin Blakely, Leonard Rossiter, Lesley-Anne Down, Burt Kwouk
AAN: song 'Come To Me' (m Henry Mancini, ly Don Black)

The Pink Telephone
France   1975   93m   colour
Gaumont International/Les Productions 2000 (Alain Poire)
aka: Le Téléphone Rose

An old-fashioned, provincial businessman becomes involved with an expensive Parisian call-girl.

Satire on big business, sexual politics and middle-aged angst that runs out of steam before the end.

w Francis Véber   d Edouard Molinaro   ph Gérard Hameline
m Vladimir Cosma   pd Robert Sussfeld, Michel Choquet   ed Robert and Monique Isnardon

Mireille Darc, Pierre Mondy, Michel Lonsdale, Daniel Ceccaldi, Françoise Prevost, Gérard Hérold

Pirates
France/Tunisia   1986   124m
    Eclaircolor   Panavision
Cannon/Carthago/Accent Dominco (Tarak Ben Ammar)

A British buccaneer, cast adrift on a raft, is taken aboard a Spanish galleon and causes mayhem.

A disaster from a director who should never be allowed to attempt comedy. This one is revolting when it is not a crashing bore.

w Gerard Brach, Roman Polanski
d Roman Polanski   ph Witold Sobocinski   m Philippe Garde

Walter Matthau, Damien Thomas, Richard Pearson, Roy Kinnear, Ferdy Mayne, Charlotte Lewis

† The galleon, which cost 8 million dollars, was not wasted. It was given to the municipality of Cannes and became a tourist attraction.
AAN: costumes (Anthony Powell)

Plaff! Or Too Afraid of Life*

Cuba 1988 92m colour
Metro/ICAIC (Ricardo Avila)
original title: Desmasiado Miedo A La Vida,
   O Plaff

A superstitious mother tries to get rid
of her scientific daughter-in-law.

Deliberately ramshackle political
comedy – the beginning of the film is
kept to the end – which is not without
a certain surrealist charm.

w Daniel Chavarría, Juan Carlos
Tabío   d Juan Carlos Tabío
ph Julio Valdés   ad Raúl Oliva
ed Roberto Bravo, Osvaldo M.
Donatien

Daysi Granados, Thais Valdés, Luis
Alberto Garcia, Raúl Pamares, Alicia
Bustamente, Jorge Cao

'A wittily cynical exercise in
alienation which oozes awkwardness
and provokes uncomfortable
laughter.' – MFB

Planes, Trains and Automobiles*

US 1987 93m colour
UIP/Paramount (John Hughes)
V, L

An advertising executive, trying to get
home for Thanksgiving, finds many
obstacles hampering his progress,
including an insufferable companion.

Cheerful farce that allows some room
for characterization.

wd John Hughes   ph Don
Peterman   m Ira Newborn
pd John W. Corso   ed Paul Hirsch

Steve Martin, John Candy, Michael
McKean, Kevin Bacon, Dylan Baker,
Carol Bruce, Olivia Burnette, Diana
Douglas, William Windom

Play It Again Sam*

US 1972 86m Technicolor
   Panavision
Paramount/APJAC/Rollins-Joffe (Arthur P.
   Jacobs)
V, L

A neurotic film critic is abandoned by
his wife and seeks fresh
companionship, with help from the
shade of Humphrey Bogart.

Random comedy for star fans, mainly
quite lively and painless.

w Woody Allen   play Woody
Allen   d Herbert Ross   ph Owen
Roizman   m Billy Goldenberg

Woody Allen, Diane Keaton, Jerry
Lacy, Susan Anspach

The Player***

US 1992 124m DeLuxe
Guild/Avenue (David Brown, Michael
   Tolkin, Nick Wechsler)
V

A Hollywood studio executive gets
away with murder.

A deft and dazzling satire on the film
industry – witty, surprising and
intelligent.

w Michael Tolkin   novel Michael
Tolkin   d Robert Altman
ph Jean Lepine   m Thomas
Newman   pd Stephen Altman
ed Geraldine Peroni

Tim Robbins, Greta Scacchi, Fred
Ward, Whoopi Goldberg, Peter
Gallagher, Brion James, Cynthia
Stevenson, Vincent D'Onofrio, Dean
Stockwell, Richard E. Grant, Sydney
Pollack

'The movie has the exhilarating
nonchalance of the director's
seventies classics, and its tone is
volatile, elusive: with breathtaking
assurance, it veers from

psychological-thriller suspense to goofball comedy to icy satire.' – *Terrence Rafferty, New Yorker*

† The film featured more than 60 stars playing themselves, including Harry Belafonte, James Coburn, Peter Falk, Teri Garr, Angelica Huston, Jack Lemmon, Nick Nolte, Burt Reynolds, Julia Roberts, Susan Sarandon, Rod Steiger and Bruce Willis.
AAN: Robert Altman; Michael Tolkin; Geraldine Peroni

Playtime*

France   1968   152m
   Eastmancolor   70mm
Specta Films (René Silvera)
V

Hulot and a group of American tourists are bewildered by life in an airport, a business block and a restaurant.

Incredibly extended series of sketches, none of which is devastatingly funny. The irritation is that the talent is clearly there but needs control.

w Jacques Tati, Jacques Lagrange
d Jacques Tati   *ph* Jean Badal, Andreas Winding   *m* Francis Lemarque   *pd* Eugène Roman

Jacques Tati, Barbara Dennek, Jacqueline Lecomte, Henri Piccoli

'Tati still seems the wrong distance from his audience: not so far that we cannot see his gifts, not close enough so that they really touch.' – *Stanley Kauffmann*
'How sad that the result of all this, though it includes a great deal of intermittent pleasure, comes at times so dangerously close to boredom.' – *Brenda Davies, MFB*
'A series of brilliant doodles by an artist who has earned the right to indulge himself on such a scale.' – *Alexander Walker*

Plaza Suite*

US   1971   114m   Technicolor
Paramount (Howard B. Koch)
L

Three sketches set in the same suite at New York's Plaza Hotel, with Walter Matthau appearing in all three but in different character.

A highly theatrical entertainment which was bound to seem flattened on the screen, but emerges with at least some of its laughs intact.

w Neil Simon   *play* Neil Simon
d Arthur Hiller   *ph* Jack Marta
m Maurice Jarre

Walter Matthau, Maureen Stapleton, Barbara Harris, Lee Grant, Louise Sorel

† In the play, Maureen Stapleton played all three female roles.

Please Don't Eat the Daisies

US   1960   111m   Metrocolor
   Panavision
MGM (Joe Pasternak)

The family of a drama critic move to the country.

Thin, obvious comedy, all dressed up but with nowhere to go.

w Isobel Lennart   *book* Jean Kerr   *d* Charles Walters
ph Robert Bronner   *m* David Rose

Doris Day, David Niven, Janis Paige, Spring Byington, Patsy Kelly, Richard Haydn, Jack Weston, John Harding, Margaret Lindsay

Please Sir

GB   1971   101m   Eastmancolor
Rank/LWI/Leslie Grade (Andrew Mitchell)

The masters and pupils of Fenn Street school go on an annual camp.

Grossly inflated, occasionally funny big-screen version of the TV series.

w John Esmonde, Bob Larbey
d Mark Stuart   *ph* Wilkie
Cooper   *m* Mike Vickers

*John Alderton, Deryck Guyler, Joan
Sanderson, Noel Howlett, Eric Chitty,
Richard Davies*

The Plot Against Harry
US   1969   81m   bw
Electric/Contemporary/King Screen
  (Robert Young, Michael Roemer)

Out of jail on parole, a gangster finds
that business and his family are not
what they were.

Put on the shelf for twenty years
before its eventual release and hailed
by some as a comic masterpiece, it
turns out to be a moderately amusing
movie that shows its age.

wd Michael Roemer   *ph* Robert
Young   *m* Frank Lewin
ad Howard Mandel   *ed* Maurice
Schell

Martin Priest, Ben Lang, Maxine
Woods, Henry Nemo, Jacques Taylor,
Jean Leslie, Ellen Herbert, Sandra
Kazan

'Harry's wit looks less deadpan than
stone dead.' – *Kevin Jackson,
Independent*

Pocketful of Miracles
US   1961   136m   Technicolor
  Panavision
UA/Franton (Frank Capra)

Kindly gangsters help an old apple
seller to persuade her long lost
daughter that she is a lady of means.

Boring, overlong remake of *Lady for a
Day*, showing that Capra's touch
simply doesn't work on the wide
screen, that his themes are dated
anyway, and that all the fine character
actors in Hollywood are a liability
unless you find them something to do.

w Hal Kanter, Harry Tugend
scenario Robert Riskin
story Damon Runyon   *d* Frank
Capra   *ph* Robert Bronner
m Walter Scharf

Bette Davis, Glenn Ford, Hope Lange,
Arthur O'Connell, Peter Falk, Thomas
Mitchell, Edward Everett Horton,
Sheldon Leonard, Barton MacLane,
Jerome Cowan, Fritz Feld, Snub
Pollard, David Brian, Ann-Margret,
John Litel, Jay Novello, Willis
Bouchey, George E. Stone, Mike
Mazurki, Jack Elam, Mickey
Shaughnessy, Peter Mann, Frank
Ferguson

'The effect is less one of whimsy than
of being bludgeoned to death with a
toffee apple.' – *Peter John Dyer*
'The story has enough cracks in it for
the syrup to leak through.' – *Playboy*
AAN: title song (*m* James Van Heusen,
ly Sammy Cahn); Peter Falk

'Call them what you like. Just don't call
them when you're in trouble!'
Police Academy
US   1984   96m   Technicolor
Paul Maslansky/Ladd Company/Warner
  Brothers
V, L

The mayor of an American city lifts all
restrictions on entry to the police force.

Appallingly unfunny series of snippets
about police training, like an
American Carry On with few jokes
leading to a punch line and occasional
resorting to dirty bits.

w Neal Israel, Pat Proft, Hugh
Wilson   *d* Hugh Wilson

Steve Guttenberg, Kim Cattrall, G. W.
Bailey, Bubba Smith, Donovan Scott,
George Gaynes

'Hit or miss comic juvenilia . . . pure

popcorn fantasy fodder.' – *Paul Taylor, MFB*

Police Academy 2: Their First Assignment
US 1985 87m Technicolor
Warner/Ladd (Paul Maslansky)
V

The new recruits foil attempts from an ambitious lieutenant to take over command.

An unambitious and dull sequel.

w Barry Blaustein, David Sheffield
d Jerry Paris *ph* James Crabe
m Robert Folk *pd* Trevor
Williams *ed* Bob Wyman

Steve Guttenberg, Bubba Smith,
David Graf, Michael Winslow, Art
Metrano, Marion Ramsey, George
Gaynes

Police Academy 3: Back in Training
US 1986 82m colour
Warner (Paul Maslansky)
V

Rival police academies vie for survival.

Plodding comedy that recycles a few familiar, unfunny routines.

w Gene Quintano *d* Jerry Paris
ph Robert Saad *m* Robert Folk
pd Trevor Williams *ed* Bud Malin

Steve Guttenberg, Bubba Smith,
David Graf, Michael Winslow, Marion
Ramsey, Leslie Easterbrook, George
Gaynes, Bobcat Goldthwait, Art
Metrano

Police Academy 4: Citizens on Patrol
US 1987 87m colour
Warner (Paul Maslansky)
V

A police commandant attempts to involve ordinary people in law enforcement.

A feeble comedy that makes it impossible to understand the apparent popularity of this turgid series.

w Gene Quintano *d* Jim Drake
ph Robert Saad *m* Robert Folk
pd Trevor Williams *ed* David
Rawlins

Steve Guttenberg, Bubba Smith,
David Graf, Michael Winslow, Sharon
Stone, Leslie Easterbrook, Bobcat
Goldthwait, George Gaynes

'Carries the banner of tasteless humor . . . to new heights of insipidness.' – *Variety*

Police Academy 5: Assignment: Miami Beach
US 1988 90m colour
Warner (Paul Maslansky)
V

Cops on holiday in Miami help foil a gang of jewel thieves.

Witlessness reaches a new low in a comedy devoid of laughs.

w Stephen J. Curwick *d* Alan
Myerson *ph* Jim Pergola
m Robert Folk *pd* Trevor
Williams *ed* Hubert de la
Bouillerie

Matt McCoy, Janet Jones, George
Gaynes, G. W. Bailey, Rene
Auberjonois, Bubba Smith, David
Graf, Michael Winslow, Leslie
Easterbook

Police Academy 6: City Under Siege
US 1989 84m Technicolor
Warner (Paul Maslansky)
V, L

The police squad track down a criminal mastermind responsible for a massive crime wave.

Farcical, broadly acted comedy that does raise an occasional smile.

w Stephen J. Curwick   d Peter Bonerz   ph Charles Rosher Jr m Robert Folk   pd Tho E. Azzari ed Hubert de la Bouillerie

Bubba Smith, David Graf, Michael Winslow, Leslie Easterbrook, Marion Ramsey, Lance Kinsey, Matt McCoy, Bruce Mahler, G. W. Bailey, George Gaynes, Kenneth Mars

Poor Little Rich Girl*
US   1936   79m   bw
TCF (Darryl F. Zanuck)

A child is separated from her father and joins a radio singing act.

Pleasing star vehicle with all the expected elements, adapted from a Mary Pickford vehicle of 1917.

w Sam Hellman, Gladys Lehman, Harry Tugend   d Irving Cummings   ph John Seitz songs Mack Gordon, Harry Revel

Shirley Temple, Jack Haley, Alice Faye, Gloria Stuart, Michael Whalen, Sara Haden, Jane Darwell, Claude Gillingwater, Henry Armetta

'In the tradition of the great religious epics, Ben Hur, The Greatest Story Ever Told and 9½ Weeks, comes a film that breaks all Ten Commandments and a few laws of nature.'

The Pope Must Die
GB   1991   99m   colour
Palace/Michael White/Miramax/British Film/
   Film Four (Stephen Woolley)
V
US title: The Pope Must Diet

Through an error, a former car mechanic, rock singer and inept priest becomes Pope and tries to clean up a Vatican infiltrated by the Mafia.

Farcical and misfiring comedy, a poor

attempt at a parody of gangster films.

w Peter Richardson, Pete Richens d Peter Richardson   ph Frank Gell   m Anne Dudley, Jeff Beck pd John Ebden   ed Katharine Wenning

Robbie Coltrane, Beverly D'Angelo, Herbert Lom, Alex Rocco, Paul Bartel, Balthazar Getty, William Hootkins, Robert Stephens, Annette Crosbie, Steve O'Donnell, John Sessions

Popi*
US   1969   113m   DeLuxe
UA/Leonard Films (Herbert B. Leonard)

Adventures of a cheerful inhabitant of New York's Puerto Rican ghetto.

Ethnic comedy-drama of the kind that has since found its way in abundance into American TV series. Very competently done for those who like it, e.g. Puerto Ricans.

w Tina and Lester Pine   d Arthur Hiller   ph Ross Lowell m Dominic Frontière

Alan Arkin, Rita Moreno, Miguel Alejandro, Ruben Figuero

'An appropriately disenchanted view of an immigrant's struggling ambitions in the Promised Land.' – Richard Combs.

Poppy*
US   1936   74m   bw
Paramount (Paul Jones)

An itinerant medicine-seller sets up his stall in a small town where his daughter falls in love with the mayor's son.

Clumsily but heavily plotted vehicle for W. C. Fields, who as usual has great moments but seems to rob the show of its proper pace.

w Waldemar Young, Virginia Van

Upp   *play* Dorothy Donnelly
d A. Edward Sutherland
ph William Mellor   *m* Frederick
Hollander

W. C. Fields, Rochelle Hudson, Richard
Cromwell, Granville Bates, Catherine
Doucet, Lynne Overman, Maude
Eburne

'Antique hokum trussed up for a
Fields vehicle.' – *Literary Digest*
'To watch Mr Fields, as Dickensian as
anything Dickens ever wrote, is a
form of escape for poor human
creatures: we who are haunted by
pity, by fear, by our sense of right and
wrong, who are tongue-tied by
conscience, watch with envious love
this free spirit robbing the gardener
of ten dollars, cheating the country
yokels by his own variant of the three-
card trick, faking a marriage
certificate, and keeping up all the
time, in the least worthy and the most
embarrassing circumstances, his
amazing flow of inflated sentiments.'
– *Graham Greene, The Spectator*

Porky's

Canada   1982   98m   colour
Melvin Simon/Astral Bellevue Pathe/Porky's
   Productions/(Don Carmody, Bob
   Clark)
V, L

In Florida in the early fifties, high
school boys try to get into a local
brothel.

Ghastly teenage goings-on taking
cinema bad taste just about as far as it
will get.

wd Bob Clark   *ph* Reginald H.
Morris   *m* Carl Zittrer, Paul Zaza
pd Reuben Freed

Dan Monahan, Mark Herrier, Wyatt
Knight, Roger Wilson, Kim Cattrall,
Art Hindle, Wayne Maunder, Alex
Karras, Nancy Parsons.

'It is difficult to say which is the more
depressing: the technical expertise
with which this mind-numbing tripe
has been put together, or its great
success at the US box office.' – *Jo
Imeson, MFB*
'One of those movies that makes you
weep for the state of the
contemporary commercial cinema –
and, even more, for the gullibility of
the public that pays to see it.' –
Margaret Hinxman, Daily Mail

† *Porky's 2* followed in 1983 and was
even worse. 1985 brought *Porky's
Revenge*, about which there is nothing
to be said.

Porridge*

GB   1979   93m   Eastmancolor
Black Lion/Witzend
V

Old lags at Slade Prison try to arrange
an escape for a first offender.

Genial expansion of a successful TV
series to the big screen; alas, as usual
the material is stretched to snapping
point, and the welcome irony of the
original becomes sentimentality. Still,
the film is a valuable record of
memorable characters.

w Dick Clement, Ian La Frenais
d Dick Clement   *ph* Bob Huke
md Terry Oates

*Ronnie Barker, Richard Beckinsale,
Fulton Mackay, Brian Wilde, Peter
Vaughan*, Geoffrey Bayldon, Julian
Holloway

Pot o' Gold

US   1941   87m   bw
Globe/James Roosevelt
GB title: *The Golden Hour*

A radio giveaway show finds work for
idle musicians.

Thin Capraesque comedy which needed more determined handling.

w Walter de Leon   *d* George Marshall   *ph* Hal Mohr   *md* Lou Forbes

James Stewart, Paulette Goddard, Horace Heidt, Charles Winninger, Mary Gordon, Frank Melton, Jed Prouty

The President's Analyst*
US   1967   104m   Technicolor Panavision
Paramount/Panpiper (Stanley Rubin)

A psychiatrist who has been asked to treat the president is pursued by spies of every nationality.

Wild political satirical farce which finally unmasks as its chief villain the telephone company. Laughs along the way, but it's all rather too much.

wd Theodore J. Flicker   *ph* William A. Fraker   *m* Lalo Schifrin
pd Pato Guzman

James Coburn, Godfrey Cambridge, Severn Darden, Joan Delaney, Pat Harrington, Eduard Franz, Will Geer

Press for Time
GB   1966   102m   Eastmancolor
Rank/Ivy/Titan (Robert Hartford Davis, Peter Newbrook)
V

The prime minister's grandson is a newspaper seller, and is quietly promoted to be a journalist in a seaside town where it is thought he can do no harm.

The star's last comedy in his original style; competent but nothing special.

w Norman Wisdom, Eddie Leslie
novel Yea Yea Yea by Angus McGill
d Robert Asher   *ph* Peter Newbrook   *m* Mike Vickers

Norman Wisdom, Derek Bond, Angela Browne, Derek Francis, Noel Dyson, Peter Jones, David Lodge

The Prince and the Showgirl*
GB   1957   117m   Technicolor
Warner/Marilyn Monroe Productions (Laurence Olivier)
V

In London for the 1911 coronation, a Ruritanian prince picks up a chorus girl and they come to understand and respect each other.

Heavy-going comedy, rich in production values but weak in dramatic style and impact.

w Terence Rattigan   *play* The Sleeping Prince by Terence Rattigan
d Laurence Olivier   *ph* Jack Cardiff   *m* Richard Addinsell
pd Roger Furse   *ad* Carmen Dillon

Laurence Olivier, Marilyn Monroe, Sybil Thorndike, Richard Wattis, Jeremy Spenser, Esmond Knight, Rosamund Greenwood, Maxine Audley

The Princess Comes Across*
US   1936   76m   bw
Paramount (Arthur Hornblow Jnr)

A starstruck Brooklyn girl makes a transatlantic liner voyage disguised as a princess, and finds herself involved in a murder mystery.

Zany comedy thriller with plenty of jokes.

w Walter de Leon, Frances Martin, Frank Butler, Don Hartman, Philip MacDonald   *novel* Louis Lucien Rogger   *d* William K. Howard
ph Ted Tetzlaff   *m* Phil Boutelje

Carole Lombard, Fred MacMurray, Alison Skipworth, Douglass Dumbrille, William Frawley, Porter Hall, George Barbier, Lumsden Hare,

Sig Rumann, Mischa Auer, Tetsu Komai

'And you think you've got problems?'
The Prisoner of Second Avenue*
US   1975   98m   Technicolor
  Panavision
Warner (Melvin Frank)
L

A New York clerk and his wife are driven to distraction by the problems of urban living.

Gloomier-than-usual (from this author) collection of one-liners which almost turns into a psychopathic melodrama and causes its amiable leading players to overact horrendously.

w Neil Simon   play Neil Simon
d Melvin Frank   ph Philip Lathrop   m Marvin Hamlisch

Jack Lemmon, Anne Bancroft, Gene Saks, Elizabeth Wilson

The Prisoner of Zenda
US   1979   108m   Technicolor
Universal (Walter Mirisch)

Palpably uneasy version of the above which teeters between comedy and straight romance, with barely a moment of real zest creeping in. The star is way off form in both roles.

w Dick Clement, Ian La Frenais
d Richard Quine   ph Arthur Ibbetson   m Henry Mancini
pd John J. Lloyd

Peter Sellers, Lynne Frederick, Lionel Jeffries, Elke Sommer, Gregory Sierra, Stuart Wilson, Jeremy Kemp, Catherine Schell, Simon Williams, Norman Rossington, John Laurie

'Flatly directed, leadenly unfunny.' –
Paul Taylor, MFB

Private Benjamin
US   1980   110m   Technicolor
Warner/Hawn-Myers-Shyer-Miller
V, L

A well-heeled Jewish widow, at a crossroads in her life, joins the army.

Half-assed attempt at combining slapstick, character study, sentiment, sex and a recruiting poster. Some funny moments don't really make it worth sitting through.

w Nancy Meyers, Charles Shyer, Harvey Miller   d Howard Zieff
ph David M. Walsh   m Bill Conti

Goldie Hawn, Eileen Brennan, Armand Assante, Robert Webber, Sam Wanamaker, Barbara Barrie, Harry Dean Stanton
AAN: screenplay; Goldie Hawn; Eileen Brennan (supporting actress)

A Private Function**
GB   1984   94m   colour
Handmade (Mark Shivas)

In 1947 Yorkshire, a doctor and his family secretly fatten an unlicensed pig.

Sharply-detailed comedy typical of its author, but less likeable than many.

w Alan Bennett   d Malcolm Mowbray   ph Tony Pierce-Roberts   m John Du Prez
pd Stuart Walker   ed Barrie Vince

Michael Palin, Maggie Smith, Denholm Elliott, Richard Griffiths, Tony Haygarth, Liz Smith, John Normington

BFA: Maggie Smith; Liz Smith (supporting actress); Denholm Elliott (supporting actor)

The Private Life of Sherlock Holmes***
GB 1970 125m DeLuxe Panavision
UA/Phalanx/Mirisch/Sir Nigel (Billy Wilder)
V

A secret Watson manuscript reveals cases in which Sherlock Holmes became involved with women.

What started as four stories is reduced to two, one brightly satirical and the other no more than a careful and discreet recreation, with the occasional jocular aside, of the flavour of the stories themselves. A very civilized and pleasing entertainment except for the hurried rounding-off which is a let-down.

w Billy Wilder, I. A. L. Diamond d Billy Wilder ph Christopher Challis m Miklos Rozsa ad Alexander Trauner

Robert Stephens, Colin Blakely, Genevieve Page, Clive Revill, Christopher Lee, Catherine Lacey, Stanley Holloway

'Affectionately conceived and flawlessly executed.' – NFT, 1974
'Wilder's least embittered film, and by far his most moving. Great.' – Time Out, 1984

Privates on Parade*
GB 1982 113m colour
Handmade (Simon Relph)

Farcical and serious incidents in the lives of an army concert party in 1948 Singapore.

Rather heavy-going comedy with much bad language and an overdose of effeminacy; on the whole no funnier than It Ain't Half Hot, Mum.

w Peter Nichols play Peter Nichols d Michael Blakemore ph Ian Wilson m Denis King

John Cleese, Denis Quilley, Michael Elphick, Nicola Pagett, Bruce Payne, Joe Melia

Private's Progress***
GB 1956 97m bw
British Lion/Charter (Roy Boulting)
V

An extremely innocent young national serviceman is taught a few army dodges and becomes a dupe for jewel thieves.

Celebrated army farce with satirical pretensions; when released it had something to make everyone in Britain laugh.

w Frank Harvey, John Boulting, novel Alan Hackney d John Boulting ph Eric Cross m John Addison

Ian Carmichael, Terry-Thomas, Richard Attenborough, Dennis Price, Peter Jones, William Hartnell, Thorley Walters, Ian Bannen, Jill Adams, Victor Maddern, Kenneth Griffith, Miles Malleson, John Le Mesurier

Prizzi's Honor*
US 1985 129m DeLuxe
ABC/John Foreman
V, L

Male and female hired killers for Mafia families fall in love but are assigned to 'hit' each other.

Critically lauded but puzzling and unsatisfactory black comedy which takes far too long to get going, is muddled in narrative, and leaves an unpleasant taste.

w Richard Condon, Janet Roach novel Richard Condon d John Huston ph Andrzej Bartkowiak m Alex North pd Dennis Washington ed Rudi and Kaja Fehr

Jack Nicholson, Kathleen Turner, Robert

Loggia, William Hickey, John Randolph, *Anjelica Huston*

'Certainly one of the most curious films to kick off the summer season by an American major.' – *Variety*

AA: Anjelica Huston (supporting actress)
AAN: best picture; direction; Jack Nicholson; William Hickey; adapted screenplay; editing

BFA: adapted screenplay

Problem Child
US 1990 81m DeLuxe
UIP/Universal/Imagine Entertainment
  (Robert Simonds)
V, L

A badly behaved boy is adopted by a small-town couple.

Broadly played, predictable comedy of mayhem and misunderstandings.

w Scott Alexander, Larry Karaszewski *d* Dennis Dugan *ph* Peter Lyons Collister *m* Miles Goodman *pd* George Costello *ed* Daniel Hanley, Michael Hill

John Ritter, Jack Warden, Michael Oliver, Gilbert Gottfried, Amy Yasbeck, Michael Richards, Peter Jurasik, Charlotte Akin

'Universal took a step in the right direction by whittling it down to just 81 minutes but didn't go far enough. The studio should have excised another 75 minutes and released this unbelievable mess as a short.' – *Variety*

'Now, Junior has a brand new friend. He's bad. She's worse.'
Problem Child 2
US 1991 91m DeLuxe
UIP/Universal/Imagine (Robert Simonds)
V

An ill-behaved boy decides that his father should marry the mother of his friend, a badly behaved girl.

Nasty-minded, witless slapstick with an anal fixation.

w Scott Alexander, Larry Karaszewski *d* Brian Levant *ph* Peter Smokler *m* David Kitay *pd* Maria Caso *ed* Lois Freeman-Fox, Robert P. Seppey

John Ritter, Michael Oliver, Jack Warden, Laraine Newman, Amy Yasbeck, Ivyann Schwan, Gilbert Gottfried, Paul Wilson

'No seam of bad taste is left unmined as the screenwriters sink to impossibly low depths in pursuit of anything vaguely resembling a laugh.' – *Mark Salisbury, Empire*

The Producers*
US 1968 88m Pathecolor
Avco /Springtime/Crossbow (Sidney
  Glazier)
L

A Broadway producer seduces elderly widows to obtain finance for his new play, sells 25,000 per cent in the expectation that it will flop, and is horrified when it succeeds.

Dismally unfunny satire except for the play itself, *Springtime for Hitler*, which is neatly put down. This has, however, become a cult film, so that criticism is pointless.

wd Mel Brooks *ph* Joseph Coffey *m* John Morris

Zero Mostel, Gene Wilder, Kenneth Mars, Estelle Winwood, Renee Taylor, Dick Shawn

'Over and over again promising ideas are killed off, either by over-exposure or bad timing.' – *Tom Milne*
'An almost flawless triumph of bad

taste, unredeemed by wit or style.' –
Arthur Schlesinger Jnr

AA: Mel Brooks (as writer)
AAN: Gene Wilder

Professor Beware*
US   1938   93m   bw
Paramount

A staid professor finds himself on the
run across America in pursuit of an
Egyptian artefact.

Slow-starting comedy with only
moments of the comedian at his best.

w Delmer Daves, Jack
Cunningham   *story* Crampton
Harris, Francis M. and Marian B.
Cockrell   *d* Elliott Nugent
ph Archie Stout

Harold Lloyd, Phyllis Welch,
Raymond Walburn, Lionel Stander,
William Frawley, Thurston Hall, Cora
Witherspoon, Sterling Holloway

'Both Lloyd and the audience are out
of breath after 3000 miles cross
country, but most of it is exhaustion
from laughing.' – *Variety*

'There's something funny going on in the
world of diplomacy!'
Protocol
US   1984   96m   Technicolor
Warner (Anthea Sylbert)
V, L

A cocktail waitress thwarts an
assassination and becomes a career
diplomat.

Star comedy with Something to Say
and not much to laugh at; a step down
even from *Private Benjamin*.

w Buck Henry   *d* Herbert Ross
ph William A. Fraker   *m* Basil
Poledouris   *pd* Bill Malley
ed Paul Hirsch

Goldie Hawn, Chris Sarandon, Gail

Strickland, Richard Romanus, André
Gregory, Cliff de Young

Prudence and the Pill*
GB   1968   92m   DeLuxe
TCF/Kenneth Harper, Ronald Kahn

A girl borrows her mother's
contraceptive pills and replaces them
with aspirin, causing no end of
complications.

Self-consciously naughty sex comedy
with a long dénouement and some
stiff patches to affect one's enjoyment
of the brighter moments.

w Hugh Mills   *play* Hugh Mills
d Fielder Cook   *ph* Ted Moore
m Bernard Ebbinghouse

David Niven, Deborah Kerr, Edith
Evans, Keith Michell, Robert Coote,
Irina Demick, Joyce Redman, Judy
Geeson

'Everybody winds up pregnant to
clutter the earth, apparently, with
people as obnoxious as their
progenitors.' – *Judith Crist*

The Punch and Judy Man*
GB   1962   96m   bw
(ABP) Macconkey (Gordon L. T. Scott)
V

A seashore children's entertainer tries
and fails to establish himself as an
important citizen.

Melancholy comedy of failure which
did not please its star's adherents and
indeed just missed the style it was
seeking.

w Philip Oakes, Tony Hancock
d Jeremy Summers   *ph* Gilbert
Taylor   *m* Derek Scott, Don Banks

Tony Hancock, Sylvia Syms, Ronald
Fraser, Barbara Murray, John Le
Mesurier, Hugh Lloyd

The Pure Hell of St Trinian's*

GB · 1960 94m bw
Hallmark/Tudor (Frank Launder, Sidney
  Gilliat)

After the girls burn down St Trinian's,
a dubious headmaster offers to create
a new school for them.

Bright comedy performances from
some of the best of character actors
add a gloss to familiar material.

w Frank Launder, Sidney Gilliat, Val
Valentine   d Frank Launder
ph Gerald Gibbs   m Malcolm
Arnold   ed Thelma Connell

Cecil Parker, Joyce Grenfell, George
Cole, Thorley Walters, Irene Handl,
Eric Barker, Dennis Price, Raymond
Huntley, Julie Alexander

The Purple Rose of Cairo*

US 1984 82m DeLuxe
Orion/Jack Rollins-Charles H. Joffe (Robert
  Greenhut)
V, L

In the thirties, a film-struck woman is
confronted in reality by the hero of
her dreams.

Amusing but slight comedy: several
good jokes, but in sum no more than
an elongated sketch.

wd Woody Allen   ph Gordon
Willis   m Dick Hyman   pd Stuart
Wurtzel   ed Susan E. Morse

Mia Farrow, Jeff Daniels, Danny
Aiello, Dianne Wiest, Van Johnson,
Zoe Caldwell, John Wood, Milo
O'Shea

BFA: best picture, original
screenplay

The Pursuit of D. B. Cooper

US 1981 100m Metrocolor
Polygram (Daniel Wigutow, Michael
  Taylor)
L

A skyjacker bails out with his loot and
is chased by various people after the
reward.

Fantasy variation on a real case which
was never solved; of no interest
whatever despite the talent involved.

w Jeffrey Alan Fiskin   book Free
Fall by J. D. Reed   d Roger
Spottiswoode (also John
Frankenheimer, Buzz Kulik)
ph Harry Stradling   m James
Horner   pd Preston Ames

Robert Duvall, Treat Williams,
Kathryn Harrod, Ed Flanders, Paul
Gleason, R. G. Armstrong

'Doubtless a law-enforcement ploy to
lure the skyjacker out of hiding:
surely after seeing this mess he will
want to surface and sue somebody.'
– Variety

Putting Pants on Philip*

US 1927 20m bw silent
Hal Roach

A respectable man meets his randy
Scottish nephew who wears nothing
under his kilt.

Early star comedy, allegedly their first
as a team but before their more
recognizable characteristics had
developed. Not at all bad in its way,
though developing into one long
chase.

w H. M. Walker   d Clyde
Bruckman

Laurel and Hardy, Sam Lufkin,
Harvey Clark

Quackser Fortune Has a Cousin in the Bronx*

US 1970 90m Eastmancolor
UMC (John H. Cushingham)

An Irish layabout strikes up an acquaintance with an American student.

Likeable if plotless Dublin comedy, pleasantly photographed.

w Gabriel Walsh d Waris Hussein ph Gil Taylor m Michael Dress

Gene Wilder, Margot Kidder, Eileen Colgen, Seamus Ford

Queen of the Road

Australia 1984 96m colour
JNP (James Davern)

A daughter inherits trouble when she takes over her father's truck haulage business.

A dull comedy of mishap and misadventure, interspersed with country and western songs and relying for the most part on the old joke (though it may be new to Australia) that women are poor drivers.

w Tom Mitchell d Bruce Best ph Joseph Pickering m Mike Perjanik ad Michael Ralph ed Zsolt Kollanyi

Joanne Samuel, Amanda Muggleton, Shane Worthington, Jonathan Sweet, Chris Hession

Quick Change

US 1990 88m DuArt
Panavision
Warner/Devoted (Robert Greenhut, Bill Murray)
V, L

Two men and a woman stage a flawless bank robbery and then have trouble making their getaway from New York.

Farcical comedy taken at a decorous pace and with the joke of an escalating series of disasters too often mistimed to produce any amusement.

w Howard Franklin novel Jay Cronley d Howard Franklin, Bill Murray ph Michael Chapman m Randy Edelman ad Speed Hopkins ed Alan Heim

Bill Murray, Geena Davis, Randy Quaid, Jason Robards, Bob Elliott, Kimberleigh Aarn, Ron Ryan, Brian McConnachie, Jack Gilpin

Quick Let's Get Married

US 1965 100m colour
Golden Eagle (William Marshall)
aka: The Confession, Seven Different Ways

The voice of a sneak thief in a ruined church is taken by an unwed mother as a miracle.

Downright peculiar mishmash wasting interesting stars; an independent production by Rogers and husband in Jamaica.

w Allen Scott   *d* William Dieterle   *ph* Robert Bronner   *m* Michael Colicchio

Ginger Rogers, Ray Milland, Barbara Eden, Walter Abel, Cecil Kellaway, Elliott Gould, Michael Ansara, David Hurst

The Quiet Man***

US   1952   129m   Technicolor
Republic/Argosy (John Ford, Merian C. Cooper)
V, L

An Irish village version of *The Taming of the Shrew*, the tamer being an ex-boxer retired to the land of his fathers and in need of a wife. Archetypal John Ford comedy, as Irish as can be, with everything but leprechauns and the Blarney Stone on hand.

Despite some poor sets the film has a gay swing to it, much brawling vigour and broad comedy, while the actors all give their roistering best.

w Frank Nugent,   *story* Maurice Walsh   *d* John Ford   *ph* Winton C. Hoch, Archie Stout   *m* Victor Young

John Wayne, Maureen O'Hara, Barry Fitzgerald, Victor McLaglen, Ward Bond, Mildred Natwick, Francis Ford, Arthur Shields, Eileen Crowe, Sean McClory, Jack McGowran

'Ford's art and artifice . . . are employed to reveal a way of life – stable, rooted, honourable, purposeful in nature's way, and thereby rhythmic. Everyone is an individual, yet everyone and everything has a place.' – *Henry Hart, Films in Review*

AA: John Ford; Winton C. Hoch, Archie Stout
AAN: best picture; Frank Nugent; Victor McLaglen

Quiet Wedding***

GB   1940   80m   bw
Paramount/Conqueror (Paul Soskin)

Middle-class wedding preparations are complicated by family guests.

A semi-classic British stage comedy is admirably filmed with a splendid cast.

w Terence Rattigan, Anatole de Grunwald,   *play* Esther McCracken   *d* Anthony Asquith

Margaret Lockwood, Derek Farr, *A. E. Matthews, Marjorie Fielding, Athene Seyler, Peggy Ashcroft,* Margaretta Scott, Frank Cellier, Roland Culver, Jean Cadell, David Tomlinson, Bernard Miles

'A completely unpretentious and charming film, the components of which are as delicately balanced as the mechanism of a watch.' – *New York Times*
'No subtlety of glance, movement or dialogue has been missed, no possible highlight omitted.' – *MFB*

† Production was halted five times when bombs fell on the studio.

†† Remade as *Happy is the Bride* (qv).

R

Rabbit Test
US   1978   84m   colour
Avco Embassy (Edgar Rosenberg)
L

A man becomes pregnant.

Dreary and tasteless film, the nadir of comedy.

w Jay Redack, Joan Rivers   *d* Joan Rivers   *ph* Lucien Ballard   *m* Peter Carpenter, Mike Post   *ad* Robert Kinoshita   *ed* Stanford C. Allen

Billy Crystal, Joan Prather, Alex Rocco, Doris Roberts, Edward Ansara, Imogene Coca, Jane Connell, Keene Curtis, Roddy McDowall, Sheree North, Joan Rivers

The Rachel Papers
GB   1989   95m   colour
Virgin/Initial Film and Television/Longfellow Pictures (Andrew S. Karsch)
V

A would-be Oxford University student has an on-and-off affair with an American girl.

Bungled attempt at a contemporary comedy of manners.

wd Damian Harris   *novel* Martin Amis   *ph* Alex Thomson   *m* Chaz Jankel, David Storrs   *pd* Andrew McAlpine   *ed* David Martin

Dexter Fletcher, Ione Skye, Jonathan Pryce, James Spader, Bill Paterson, Shirley Anne Field, Michael Gambon,

Lesley Sharp, Jared Harris, Aubrey Morris

Radio Days**
US   1987   85m   DuArt
Orion (Robert Greenhut)
V, L

At the beginning of World War II, families near New York are affected by what they hear on the radio.

Shapeless montage of funny bits, best appreciated by those who lived through the time at somewhere near the place.

wd Woody Allen   *ph* Carlo Di Palma   *m/ed* Dick Hyman   *pd* Santo Loquasto   *ed* Susan E. Morse

Mia Farrow, Dianne Wiest, Seth Green, Julie Kavner, Josh Mostel, Michael Tucker, Wallace Shawn

'One of his most purely entertaining pictures.' – *Daily Variety*
AAN: best original screenplay; art direction (Speed Hopkins)

Rafferty and the Gold Dust Twins
US   1975   92m   Technicolor Panavision
Warner/Gruskoff-Venture-Linson

A drifter encounters two female vagrants who force him at gunpoint to drive them to New Orleans and get him into various adventures.

Indulgent and unattractive 'road'

movie which despite occasional amusing incident gets nowhere very slowly.

w John Kaye   d Dick Richards
ph Ralph Woolsey   m Artie Butler

Alan Arkin, Sally Kellerman, MacKenzie Phillips, Alex Rocco, Charlie Martin Smith, Harry Dean Stanton, John McLiam

A Rage in Harlem**
GB 1991 108m DeLuxe
Palace/Miramax (Stephen Woolley, Kerry Boyle)
V, L

In 1950s Harlem, a gullible undertaker's assistant gives refuge to a gangster's mistress with a trunkful of gold.

Lively, entertaining, fast-paced tongue-in-cheek thriller.

w John Toles-Bey, Bobby Crawford   novel Chester Himes
d Bill Duke   ph Toyomichi Kurita   m Elmer Bernstein
pd Steven Legler   ed Curtis Clayton

Forest Whitaker, Gregory Hines, Robin Givens, Zakes Mokae, Danny Glover, Badja Djola, John Toles-Bey, Ron Taylor, Samm-Art Williams

'Many will be turned off by the excessive bloodshed, but the fine cast keeps the pic watchable.' – Variety
'Enjoyable though it is, Bill Duke's mix of brisk action, sexy innuendo and cameo-studded comedy takes considerable liberties with the spirit of Himes' Harlem.' – Jonathan Romney, Sight and Sound

Rain or Shine*
US 1930 90m bw
Columbia (Harry Cohn)

A circus performer puts on a one-man show in an attempt to stop it from closing.

A musical comedy translated to the screen without its songs as a showcase for the acrobatic, slack-wire and juggling talents of its star, a Broadway comedian famous for his wide smile and nonsense patter.

w Jo Swerling, Dorothy Howell
musical comedy: James Gleason, Maurice Marks   d Frank Capra
ph Joe Walker
md Bakaleinikoff   ed Maurice Wright

Joe Cook, Louise Fazenda, Joan Peers, William Collier Jnr, Tom Howard

Raising Arizona*
US 1987 94m DuArt
Circle Films/TCF
V, L

In the American heartlands, a petty crook falls for the lady cop who regularly checks him into jail.

Zany collection of incidents which scarcely welds itself into a story but offers a few laughs along the way.

w Ethan and Joel Coen   d Joel Coen

Nicolas Cage, Holly Hunter, Trey Wilson, John Goodman, William Forsythe

The Rake's Progress*
GB 1945 123m bw
GFD/Individual (Frank Launder, Sidney Gilliat)
US title: Notorious Gentleman

The career of a cheerful ne'er-do-well playboy of the thirties.

The road to ruin played for light comedy, with silly endpapers in which, quite out of character, the rake becomes a war hero. Generally good production, witty script.

w Frank Launder, Sidney Gilliat *story* Val Valentine *d* Sidney Gilliat *ph* Wilkie Cooper *m* William Alwyn *pd* David Rawnsley

Rex Harrison, Lilli Palmer, Margaret Johnston, Godfrey Tearle, Griffith Jones, Guy Middleton, Jean Kent, Marie Lohr, Garry Marsh, David Horne, Alan Wheatley

† In the American version Harrison crowned the Martyrs' Memorial not with a chamber pot but with a top hat.

Rally Round the Flag Boys
US 1958 106m DeLuxe
Cinemascope
TCF (Leo McCarey)
V

A small community protests at the siting nearby of a missile base.

Raucous service and sex comedy which becomes frenetic without ever being very funny.

w Claude Binyon, Leo McCarey *novel* Max Shulman *d* Leo McCarey *ph* Leon Shamroy *m* Cyril Mockridge

Paul Newman, Joanne Woodward, Joan Collins, Jack Carson, Dwayne Hickman, Tuesday Weld, Gale Gordon, Murvyn Vye

Reaching for the Moon
US 1931 90m bw
United Artists (Douglas Fairbanks)

On a transatlantic liner, a new cocktail has a sensational effect on a mild-mannered hero.

Very flimsy comedy with songs and some athletic stunts for its hero.

wd Edmund Goulding *ph* Ray June *song* Irving Berlin

Douglas Fairbanks, Bebe Daniels, Edward Everett Horton, Claud Allister, Jack Mulhall, Bing Crosby

'Not a smash entry, but should do moderately and perhaps a little better than that.' – *Variety*

Real Life*
US 1979 99m colour
Paramount (Penelope Spheeris)

A self-centred film-maker moves in with an average family in order to make a documentary about them.

Clever satire on a certain style of television programme, but the joke is over-stretched.

w Albert Brooks, Monica Johnson, Harry Shearer *d* Albert Brooks *ph* Eric Saarinen *m* Mort Lindsay *ad* Linda Marder, Linda Spheeris *ed* David Finfer

Albert Brooks, Charles Grodin, Frances Lee McCain, J. A. Preston, Matthew Tobin, Jennings Lang

Real Men
US 1987 96m Metrocolor
United Artists (Martin Bregman)

An unpredictable CIA agent recruits a timid insurance clerk to deliver a message to friendly aliens while rival agents attempt to kill them both.

Dim though frenetic comedy that provides nothing but tedium.

wd Dennis Feldman *ph* John A. Alonzo *m* Miles Goodman *ad* William J. Cassidy, James Allen *ed* Malcolm Campbell, Glenn Farr

James Belushi, John Ritter, Barbara Barrie, Bill Morey, Isa Andersen, Gale Barle, Mark Herrier

Rebecca's Daughters*

GB/Germany 1991 97m colour
Mayfair/Palace/Rebecca's Daughters/
    Astralma Erste Filmproduktions/Delta/
    BBC Wales/British Screen (Chris
    Sievernich)
V

In the 19th century, Welsh farmers
form gangs dressed in women's clothes
to protest against unfair toll-gate
charges imposed by the local
aristocracy.

Ramshackle caper, ripely performed
and occasionally amusing.

w Guy Jenkin, Karl Francis
story based on a screenplay by Dylan
Thomas   d Karl Francis   ph Russ
Walker   m Rachel Portman
pd Ray Price   ed Roy Sharman

Peter O'Toole, Paul Rhys, Joely
Richardson, Keith Allen, Simon
Dormandy, Dafydd Hywel, Sue
Roderick

'An irresistible period romp.' – Variety

The Rebel*

GB 1960 105m Technicolor
Associated British (W. A. Whitaker)
US title: Call Me Genius

A suburban businessman goes to Paris
to become an artist.

A kind of farcical The Moon and
Sixpence, insufficiently well tailored
to the requirements of a very
specialized comic, but occasionally
diverting none the less.

w Alan Simpson, Ray Galton
d Robert Day   ph Gilbert
Taylor   m Frank Cordell

Tony Hancock, George Sanders, Paul
Massie, Margit Saad, Grégoire Aslan,
Dennis Price, Irene Handl, Mervyn
Johns, Peter Bull, John Le Mesurier,
Nanette Newman, Oliver Reed, John
Wood

'The more prosaic the setting, the
funnier Hancock seems; transplanted
into a conventionally silly screen art
world, he is submerged among the
other grotesques.' – Penelope Houston

The Reivers*

US 1969 111m Technicolor
    Panavision
Cinema Center/Duo/Solar (Irving Ravetch)

In Mississippi at the turn of the
century a hired hand borrows the new
family auto for a trip into Memphis
with the grandson of the family and
a black stablehand.

Pleasant but insubstantial yarn of
more gracious days; most attractive
to look at, it entertains gently without
ever reaching a point.

w Irving Ravetch, Harriet Frank
Jnr   novel William Faulkner
d Mark Rydell   ph Richard Moore
m John Williams

Steve McQueen, Sharon Farrell, Will
Geer, Rupert Crosse, Mitch Vogel,
Michael Constantine, Juano
Hernandez, Clifton James
AAN: John Williams; Rupert Crosse

The Reluctant Débutante*

US 1958 96m Metrocolor
    Cinemascope
MGM/Avon (Pandro S. Berman)

A noble couple have difficulty in
steering their American-educated
daughter through the intricacies of
the London season.

A slight but pleasing British comedy
has become a rather strident example
of lend-lease, but still affords minor
pleasures.

w William Douglas Home
play William Douglas Home

d Vincente Minnelli   *ph* Joseph Ruttenberg   *md* Eddie Warner *ad* Jean d'Aubonne

Rex Harrison, Kay Kendall, Sandra Dee, Peter Myers, Angela Lansbury, John Saxon, Diane Clare

Reluctant Heroes*
GB   1951   80m   bw
Byron (Henry Halstead)
V

Comedy of national servicemen and their misdemeanours.

Simple-minded army farce which was popular for years as play and film.

w Colin Morris   *play* Colin Morris   *d* Jack Raymond *ph* James Wilson

Brian Rix, Ronald Shiner, Derek Farr, Christine Norden, Larry Noble

Remember the Night*
US   1940   94m   bw
Paramount (Mitchell Leisen)

An assistant district attorney takes a lady shoplifter home with him for Christmas.

Eccentric but winning blend of comedy, romance and drama, deftly mixed by master chefs.

w Preston Sturges   d Mitchell Leisen   ph Ted Tetzlaff *m* Frederick Hollander

Barbara Stanwyck, Fred MacMurray, Beulah Bondi, Elizabeth Patterson, Sterling Holloway, Paul Guilfoyle, Willard Robertson

'Rarely has such a theme been so smoothly advanced and so pleasantly played out to so sensible and credible a conclusion.' – *New York Times*

Rentadick
GB   1972   94m   Eastmancolor
Rank/Paradine/Virgin (Ned Sherrin)

Incompetent private eyes become involved in the battle for a deadly nerve gas.

Ineffective crazy comedy which never takes shape, preferring to aim barbs of satire in all directions.

w John Wells, John Fortune   *d* Jim Clark   *ph* John Coquillon   *m* Carl Davis

James Booth, Richard Briers, Julie Ege, Donald Sinden

Repossessed
US   1990   84m   CFI
Guild/First Class films (Steve Wizan)
V, L

Attempting an exorcism on television, a priest struggles to control a demon intent on possessing the entire viewing audience.

Raucous parody of *The Exorcist*, crammed with jokes, most of them juvenile.

wd Bob Logan   *ph* Michael D. Margulies   *m* Charles Fox *pd* Shay Austin   *ed* Jeff Freeman

Linda Blair, Ned Beatty, Leslie Nielsen, Anthony Starke, Thom J. Sharp, Lana Schwab

'Clunking, but the jokes are just about numerous enough to stifle the groans.' – *Sight and Sound*

Restless Natives
GB   1985   89m   Technicolor
Thorn EMI/Oxford Film Company (Rick Stevenson)
V

Two young idlers set up as modern highwaymen, robbing American visitors on coach tours; to their surprise, they become a tourist attraction.

Irritatingly patchy and amoral comedy which wastes a potentially interesting idea.

w Ninian Dunnett   d Michael Hoffman   ph Oliver Stapleton   m Stuart Adamson   pd Adrienne Atkinson   ed Sean Barton

Vincent Friell, Joe Mullaney, Teri Lally, Ned Beatty, Robert Urquhart

The Return of Captain Invincible
Australia   1982   91m
   Eastmancolor   Panavision
Seven Keys/Willarra

An American superhero is discovered in the back streets of Sydney, a down-and-out drunk; but his skills are needed for the fight against Mr Midnight.

Occasionally agreeable spoof which for most of its length is too frantic.

w Steven E. De Souza, Andrew Gaty   d Philippe Mora

Alan Arkin, Christopher Lee, Kate Fitzpatrick, Bill Hunter, Michael Pate, John Bluthal

The Return of the Pink Panther*
GB   1974   113m   DeLuxe
   Panavision
UA/Jewel/Pimlico/Mirisch/Geoffrey (Blake Edwards)
V, L

When the Pink Panther diamond — national treasure of the Eastern state of Lugash — is once again stolen, bungling Inspector Clouseau is called in.

Rehash of jokes from The Pink Panther (qv), not bad in parts but a rather tedious whole.

w Frank Waldman, Blake Edwards   d Blake Edwards   ph Geoffrey Unsworth   m Henry Mancini

Peter Sellers, Christopher Plummer, Herbert Lom, Catherine Schell, Peter Arne, Peter Jeffrey, Grégoire Aslan, David Lodge, Graham Stark

'The film never comes fully to the boil, but simmers in a series of self-contained, self-destructing little set pieces.' — Richard Combs
'The first film in history to be upstaged by its own credit titles.' — Benny Green, Punch

Reuben, Reuben*
US   1982   101m   CFI colour
Saltair/Taft (Walter Shenson)

A drunken British poet upsets a New England community.

Oddball comedy at which one laughs without much enthusiasm.

w Julius J. Epstein   play Spofford by Herman Shumlin   novel Peter de Vries   d Robert Ellis Miller   ph Peter Stein   m Billy Goldenberg   pd Peter Larkin

Tom Conti, Kelly McGillis, Roberts Blossom, Cynthia Harris, Joel Fabiani
AAN: Tom Conti; adaptation

The Revenge of the Pink Panther
US   1978   98m   Technicolor
   Panavision
UA/Blake Edwards
V, L

Inspector Clouseau tracks down a drug-smuggling industrialist.

Feeble addition to a series which was always too pleased with itself.

w Frank Waldman, Ron Clarke, Blake Edwards   d Blake Edwards   ph Ernie Day   m Henry Mancini

Peter Sellers, Herbert Lom, Robert

Webber, Dyan Cannon, Burt Kwouk, Paul Stewart, Robert Loggia, Graham Stark

Rhubarb
US 1951 94m bw
Paramount (Perlberg-Seaton)

A millionaire leaves his fortune, including a baseball team, to a wild ginger cat, which means problems for his publicity agent.

Typical scatty farce of the early fifties, held together by the splendid performance of the disdainful feline in the title role rather than by any special merit in the handling.

w Dorothy Reid, Francis Cockrill novel H. Allen Smith d Arthur Lubin ph Lionel Lindon m Van Cleave

Ray Milland, Jan Sterling, Gene Lockhart, William Frawley

Rhubarb
GB 1969 37m Technicolor
ABPC/Avalon

Various village notables congregate on the golf course.

Virtually silent comedy (nobody says anything but 'rhubarb') which could have been very funny with better jokes. A TV remake in 1979 was however much worse.

wd Eric Sykes

Harry Secombe, Eric Sykes, Jimmy Edwards, Hattie Jacques, Gordon Rollins, Graham Stark, Kenneth Connor

Ride 'Em Cowboy
US 1941 82m bw
Universal (Alex Gottlieb)

Two hot dog vendors find themselves working on an Arizona dude ranch.

Slick but routine comedy star vehicle with no outstanding sequences.

w True Boardman, John Grant d Arthur Lubin ph John W. Boyle m Frank Skinner songs Don Raye, Gene de Paul

Bud Abbott, Lou Costello, Dick Foran, Anne Gwynne, Samuel S. Hinds, Richard Lane, Johnny Mack Brown, Ella Fitzgerald

Riding High*
US 1950 112m bw
Paramount (Frank Capra)

An easygoing racing man forsakes the chance of wealth to train his beloved horse for the Imperial Derby.

The director's familiar ingredients – farce, sentimentality, fast cutting, nice people and a lot of noise – seem a shade too tried and tested in this remake of his 1934 success Broadway Bill. Despite the cast, the result is only moderately entertaining.

w Robert Riskin d Frank Capra ph George Barnes, Ernest Laszlo m James Van Heusen ly Johnny Burke

Bing Crosby, Coleen Gray, Charles Bickford, Raymond Walburn, James Gleason, Oliver Hardy, Frances Gifford, William Demarest, Ward Bond, Clarence Muse, Percy Kilbride, Harry Davenport, Margaret Hamilton, Douglass Dumbrille, Gene Lockhart

'Those that live on the edge sometimes fall.'
Riff-Raff**
GB 1990 95m colour
BFI/Parallax (Sally Hibbin)
V, L

Labourers on a building site take revenge on their employers when one of them is killed in an accident.

Successful blend of wit and

naturalism, although the overlapping dialogue in many regional accents can be hard to follow at times.

w Bill Jesse   *d* Ken Loach
ph Barry Ackroyd   *m* Stewart Copeland   *pd* Martin Johnson
ed Jonathan Morris

Robert Carlyle, Emer McCourt, Jimmy Coleman, George Moss, Ricky Tomlinson, David Finch, Richard Belgrave, Ade Sapara, Derek Young, Bill Moores

'A wonderfully entertaining account of life on the margins in London that combines laughter and tears, delivering its message in an intimate and subtle way.' – *Screen International*

† The film was turned down by Britain's major distributors. It received a limited release after winning an award as the best European film of the year and receiving the International Critics Prize at the Cannes Film Festival.

The Rise and Rise of Michael Rimmer
GB   1970   101m   Technicolor
Warner/David Frost (Harry Fine)

An efficiency expert takes over an advertising agency and is soon an MP, a cabinet minister, and PM.

Satirical comedy which quickly goes overboard and is only occasionally funny; it does, however, mark the final death throes of the swinging sixties, and the changeover to *Monty Python*.

w Peter Cook, John Cleese, Kevin Billington, Graham Chapman
d Kevin Billington   *ph* Alex Thompson   *m* John Cameron

Peter Cook, John Cleese, Arthur Lowe, Denholm Elliott, Ronald Fraser, Vanessa Howard, George A. Cooper, Harold Pinter, James Cossins, Roland Culver, Dudley Foster, Julian Glover, Dennis Price, Ronnie Corbett

Rising Damp
GB   1980   98m   colour
ITC/Black Lion (Roy Skeggs)
V

The amorous and conniving landlord of a slum boarding house develops a passion for one of his tenants.

A useful reminder of a TV sitcom worth remembering, but handicapped by restriction of action, paucity of plot and the overlength usual in film versions of such things, not to mention the premature death of its original co-star Richard Beckinsale.

w Eric Chappell   *d* Joe McGrath
ph Frank Watts   *m* David Lindup

Leonard Rossiter, Frances de la Tour, Don Warrington, Denholm Elliott, Christopher Strauli

'Joel was a perfectly ordinary high-school virgin with two perfectly ordinary obsessions: SEX and MONEY'
Risky Business
US   1983   99m   Technicolor
Tisch-Avnet/Geffen
V, L

A 17-year-old is left in charge of his parents' house and fills it with pimps and prostitutes . . . a lucrative business.

Would-be outrageous teenage comedy which is pretty well made but soon wears out its welcome.

wd Paul Brickman

Tom Cruise, Rebecca de Mornay, Joe Pantoliano, Richard Masur, Bronson Pinchot, Curtis Armstrong, Nicholas Pryor

Rita, Sue and Bob Too*

GB 1987 95m Eastmancolor
Mainline/Umbrella/British Screen/Film Four
(Sandy Lieberson)

Schoolgirl babysitters are introduced
to sex by their employer on the way
home.

Raunchy yet appealing study of
British attitudes to sex, in the
tradition of *Letter to Brezhnev*.

w Andrea Dunbar   plays *The Arbour*
and *Rita, Sue And Bob Too* by Andrea
Dunbar   d Alan Clarke   ph Ivan
Strasburg   m Michael Kamen
pd Len Huntingford   ed Stephen
Singleton

Michelle Holmes, Siobhan Finneran,
George Costigan, Lesley Sharp

The Ritz*

US 1976 90m Technicolor
Warner/Courtyard (Denis O'Dell)
L

A comedy of mistaken identities in a
gay New York turkish bath.

An adaptation of a stage success which
doesn't seem nearly as funny as it
thinks it is; but some of it does work.

w Terrance McNally   play Terrance
McNally   d Richard Lester
ph Paul Wilson   m Ken Thorne
pd Phillip Harrison

Jack Weston, Rita Moreno, Jerry Stiller,
Kaye Ballard, Bessie Love, George
Coulouris, F. Murray Abraham, Treat
Williams

THE 'ROAD' SERIES:
Road to Singapore*

US 1940 84m bw
Paramount (Harlan Thompson)

Two rich playboys swear off women
until they quarrel over a Singapore
maiden.

The first Hope-Crosby-Lamour 'road'
picture is basically a light romantic
comedy and quite forgettable; the
series got zanier as it progressed.

w Don Hartman, Frank Butler
story Harry Hervey   d Victor
Schertzinger   ph William C.
Mellor   m Victor Young

Bing Crosby, Bob Hope, Dorothy
Lamour, Charles Coburn, Judith
Barrett, Anthony Quinn, Jerry
Colonna

'A deft blend of romance and comedy,
songs and fisticuffs.' – *Picture Show*
'Two of the most congenially
harmonized performances caught by
the camera in recent years.' – *Motion
Picture Herald*

† The script was originally designed
for Fred MacMurray and Jack Oakie,
who weren't available; then for Burns
and Allen, who turned it down.

Road to Zanzibar**

US 1941 92m bw
Paramount (Paul Jones)

The trio on safari in Africa, with
Hellzapoppin gags breaking in and an
anything-goes atmosphere.

w Frank Butler, Don Hartman
d Victor Schertzinger   ph Ted
Tetzlaff   m Victor Young
songs Johnny Burke, Jimmy Van
Heusen

Hope, Crosby, Lamour, Una Merkel,
Eric Blore, Luis Alberni, Douglass
Dumbrille

'The funniest thing I've seen on the
screen in years. Years.' – *Otis Ferguson*

Road to Morocco**

US 1942 83m bw
Paramount (Paul Jones)

Hollywood Arab palaces, a captive

princess, topical gags and talking camels.

w Frank Butler, Don Hartman
d David Butler   ph William C.
Mellor   md Victor Young
songs Johnny Burke, Jimmy Van
Heusen

Hope, Crosby, Lamour, Anthony
Quinn, Dona Drake

'A bubbly spontaneous entertainment
without a semblance of sanity.' –
Variety
'It would be difficult to find a screen
pantomime with better wartime
credentials.' – Kine Weekly
'This is the screwiest picture I've ever
been in.' – Camel
AAN: script

Road to Utopia**
US 1945 89m bw
Paramount (Paul Jones)
V, L

The Klondike gold rush, with all the
previous gag styles in good order,
capped by a cheeky epilogue and
constant explanatory narration by
Robert Benchley.

w Norman Panama, Melvin Frank
d Hal Walker   ph Lionel Lindon
m Leigh Harline   songs Johnny
Burke, Jimmy Van Heusen

Hope, Crosby, Lamour, Douglass
Dumbrille, Hillary Brooke, Jack La Rue
AAN: script

Road to Rio**
US 1947 100m bw
Paramount (Daniel Dare)

Guest stars are given their head, plot
intrudes again in the shape of a
hypnotized heiress, and the style is
more constrained (but still funny).

w Edmund Beloin, Jack Rose
d Norman Z. McLeod   ph Ernest

Laszlo   md Robert Emmett
Dolan   songs Johnny Burke, Jimmy
Van Heusen

Hope, Crosby, Lamour, Gale
Sondergaard, Frank Faylen, the Wiere
Brothers, the Andrews Sisters

'Enough laughs to pass the time easily
and to remind you how completely,
since sound came in, the American
genius for movie comedy has
disintegrated.' – James Agee
AAN: Robert Emmett Dolan

Road to Bali*
US 1952 91m Technicolor
Paramount (Harry Tugend)

In and around the South Seas, with
colour making the sets obvious and
the gags only tediously funny.

The team's zest was also flagging.

w Frank Butler, Hal Kanter, William
Morrow   d Hal Walker
ph George Barnes   md Joseph J.
Lilley   songs Johnny Burke, Jimmy
Van Heusen

Hope, Crosby, Lamour, Murvyn Vye,
Peter Coe

Road to Hong Kong
GB 1962 91m bw
UA/Melnor (Melvin Frank)

Curious, slightly dismal-looking
attempt to continue the series in a
British studio and on a low budget.

A few good gags, but it's all very tired
by now, and the space fiction plot
makes it seem more so.

w Norman Panama, Melvin Frank
d Norman Panama   ph Jack
Hildyard   m Robert Farnon
pd Roger Furse

Hope, Crosby, Lamour, Joan Collins,
Robert Morley, Walter Gotell, Felix
Aylmer and guests Peter Sellers, David

Niven, Frank Sinatra, Dean Martin, Jerry Colonna

Robin and the Seven Hoods*
US   1964   123m   Technicolor
Panavision
Warner/PC (Howard W. Koch, William H. Daniels)
V, L

A spoof of the Robin Hood legend set in gangland Chicago of the twenties.

Too flabby by far to be as funny as it thinks it is, this farrago of cheerful jokes has effective moments and lively routines, but most of them are nearly swamped by flat treatment and the wide screen.

w David Schwartz   d Gordon Douglas   ph William H. Daniels
m Nelson Riddle   songs Sammy Cahn, James Van Heusen

Frank Sinatra, Dean Martin, Bing Crosby, Sammy Davis Jnr, Peter Falk, Barbara Rush, Edward G. Robinson, Victor Buono, Barry Kelley, Jack La Rue, Allen Jenkins, Sig Rumann, Hans Conried
AAN: Nelson Riddle; song 'My Kind of Town' (m James Van Heusen, ly Sammy Cahn)

Rock a Bye Baby
US   1958   107m   Technicolor
Vistavision
Paramount (Jerry Lewis)

A film star asks her devoted schoolday admirer to look after her triplets by a secret marriage.

Tasteless jazzing-up of The Miracle of Morgan's Creek by talents distinctly unsympathetic.

wd Frank Tashlin   ph Haskell Boggs   m Walter Scharf

Jerry Lewis, Marilyn Maxwell, Reginald Gardiner, Salvatore

Baccaloni, Hans Conried, Isobel Elsom, James Gleason, Isa Moore, Connie Stevens

Rock 'n' Roll High School*
US   1979   93m   colour
New World (Michael Finnell)

High-school students rebel against an oppressive principal.

A tongue-in-cheek, sometimes self-conscious update of a 1950s rock movie, retaining and enjoying every cliché.

w Russ Dvonch, Joseph McBride, Richard Whitley   story Allan Arkush, Joe Dante   d Allan Arkush   ph Dean Cundey   m The Ramones   ad Marie Kordus
ed Larry Bock, Gail Werbin

P. J. Soles, Vincent Van Patten, Clint Howard, Dey Young, Mary Woronov, Paul Bartel, Dick Miller, Grady Sutton

Rockets Galore
GB   1958   94m   Technicolor
Rank/Relph and Dearden
US title: Mad Little Island

The Scottish island of Todday resists the installation of a rocket-launching site.

Amiable but disappointingly listless sequel to Whisky Galore.

w Monja Danischewsky   d Michael Relph   ph Reg Wyer   m Cedric Thorpe Davie

Jeannie Carson, Donald Sinden, Roland Culver, Noel Purcell, Ian Hunter, Duncan Macrae, Jean Cadell, Carl Jaffe, Gordon Jackson, Catherine Lacey

The Rocky Horror Picture Show**
GB   1975   100m   Eastmancolor
TCF (Michael White)
V

A couple, whose car breaks down on a dark and stormy night, take refuge in an old, dark mansion where a mad scientist is trying to make the perfect man.

A spoof of horror and science-fiction movies, based on a hit musical, and notable mainly for the high-energy performance of Tim Curry, repeating his stage success as a transvestite transsexual from Transylvania.

w Richard O'Brien, Jim Sharman play The Rocky Horror Show by Richard O'Brien   d Jim Sharman   ph Peter Suschitzky m Richard O'Brien   pd Brian Thomson   ed Graeme Clifford

Tim Curry, Susan Sarandon, Barry Bostwick, Richard O'Brien, Patricia Quinn, Little Nell, Jonathan Adams, Peter Hinwood, Meatloaf, Charles Gray

'A self-consciously slick rendition of the original material, shorn of the song reprises, staged and performed with evident delight in having larger and more lavish sets to move around in.' – Tony Rayns, MFB
'A quite wonderful mixture of spoof horror and sci-fi.' – Empire

† The film was a failure on its first release but later became a cult phenomenon at midnight screenings, with audiences dressed as the characters and chanting their dialogue.

Roman Holiday**
US   1953   118m   bw
Paramount (William Wyler)
V, L

A princess on an official visit to Rome slips away incognito and falls in love with a newspaperman.

Wispy, charming, old-fashioned

romantic comedy shot in Rome and a little obsessed by the locations; one feels that a studio base would have resulted in firmer control of the elements. The stars, however, made it memorable.

w Ian McLellan Hunter, John Dighton   d William Wyler ph Franz Planer, Henri Alekan m Georges Auric   ad Hal Pereira, Walter Tyler   ed Robert Swink

Gregory Peck, Audrey Hepburn, Eddie Albert, Hartley Power, Harcourt Williams

'While Capra, or in a different way Lubitsch, could have made something wholly enjoyable from it, it would seem that Wyler's technique is now too ponderously inflexible for such lightweight material.' – MFB

† Dalton Trumbo, then a blacklisted writer, was the actual author of the original story, although Ian McLellan Hunter received the credit for it.

AA: original story (Ian McLellan Hunter); Audrey Hepburn; costumes (Edith Head)
AAN: best picture; script; William Wyler; photography; Eddie Albert; art direction; editing

Romanoff and Juliet*
US   1961   103m   Technicolor
U-I/Pavla (Peter Ustinov)

Both Americans and Russians woo the tiny country of Concordia, and war threatens while the ambassadors' children fall in love.

Despite the author's wit this pattern comedy became something of a bore as a stylized stage piece, and the film is not smartly enough handled to be anything but a yawn; the humour never becomes cinematic.

wd Peter Ustinov   play Peter

Ustinov   *ph* Robert Krasker
m Mario Nascimbene
ad Alexander Trauner

Peter Ustinov, Sandra Dee, John
Gavin, Akim Tamiroff, Tamara
Shayne, John Phillips, Alix Talton,
Peter Jones

Romantic Comedy

US 1983 102m Metrocolor
MGM-UA/Taft Entertainment/The Mirisch
  Corporation (Walter Mirisch, Morton
  Gottlieb)

A Broadway playwright and a New
England schoolteacher have a creative
partnership that is more personal than
professional.

Tedious film version of a play which
wallows in autobiography.

w Bernard Slade   *play* Bernard
Slade   *d* Arthur Hiller   *ph* David
M. Walsh   *m* Marvin Hamlisch
pd Alfred Sweeney

Dudley Moore, Mary Steenburgen,
Frances Sternhagen, Janet Eilber,
Robyn Douglass, Ron Leibman

'When a movie's production notes
wax lyrical about the pile of the living
room carpet, one senses that they're
in trouble.' – *Nick Roddick, MFB*

Room Service*

US 1938 78m bw
RKO (Pandro S. Berman)
V, L

Penniless theatricals find ways of
staying in a hotel until they can find
a backer.

Claustrophobic Broadway farce
unsuitably adapted for the Marx
Brothers, who are constrained by
having to play characters with a
passing resemblance to human beings.

w Morrie Ryskind   *play* John

Murray, Allen Boretz   *d* William A.
Seiter   *ph* Russell Metty   *m* Roy
Webb

Groucho, Chico, Harpo, Lucille Ball,
Donald MacBride, Frank Albertson, Ann
Miller, Philip Loeb

'A natural for the box office . . . the
change of pace is a good idea.' –
Variety
'It should also be noted . . . that there
is a scene in which a turkey is chased
around a room. Not everybody will
care for this.' – *MFB*

† Remade as *Step Lively* (qv).

Rosalie Goes Shopping

West Germany 1989 93m colour
Mainline/Pelemele (Percy Adlon, Eleonore
  Adlon)
V

A German housewife, living in
Arizona with her large family, uses
credit card frauds to keep them
supplied with the good things of life.

Slight comedy of consumerism that
relies too heavily on the charm of its
performers.

w Percy Adlon, Eleonore Adlon,
Christopher Doherty   *d* Percy
Adlon   *ph* Bernd Heinl
ad Stephen Lineweaver   *ed* Heiko
Hinders

Marianne Sägebrecht, Brad Davis,
Judge Reinhold, William Harlander,
Erika Blumberger, Patricia
Zehentmayr, John Hawkes, Alex
Winter, Courtney Kraus

Rotten to the Core

GB 1965 88m bw Panavision
BL-Tudor (The Boulting Brothers)

Ex-convicts plan an army payroll
robbery.

Routine caper comedy, unsuitably

widescreened, with a few good jokes along the way.

w Jeffrey Dell, Roy Boulting, John Warren, Len Heath   d John Boulting   ph Freddie Young   m Michael Dress

Anton Rodgers, *Thorley Walters*, Eric Sykes, Kenneth Griffith, Charlotte Rampling, Ian Bannen, Avis Bunnage, Raymond Huntley

† The original title, *Rotten to the Corps*, was more apt but plainly seemed too subtle.

Roxanne*
US   1987   107m   DeLuxe
Columbia/Michael Rachmil, Daniel Melnick
V, L

An ugly man writes love letters for his friend . . . but true love will find a way.

Zany modernization of Rostand's *Cyrano de Bergerac*, funny in spots but way overlong.

w Steve Martin   d Fred Schepisi
ph Ian Baker   m Bruce Smeaton   pd Jack DeGovia

Steve Martin, Daryl Hannah, Rick Rossovich, Shelley Duvall, John Kapelos, Fred Willard, Michael J. Pollard

'The low down story of a high class gal!'
Roxie Hart**
US   1942   72m   bw
TCF (Nunnally Johnson)

A twenties showgirl confesses for the sake of publicity to a murder of which she is innocent.

Crowded Chicago burlesque which now seems less funny than it did but is full of smart moments.

w *Nunnally Johnson*,   play *Chicago* by Maurine Watkins   d *William*

Wellman   ph *Leon Shamroy*
m Alfred Newman

Ginger Rogers, George Montgomery, *Adolphe Menjou*, Lynne Overman, Nigel Bruce, Spring Byington, Sara Allgood, William Fawley

DEDICATION: To all the beautiful women in the world who have shot their husbands full of holes out of pique.

'A masterpiece of form, of ensemble acting, of powerhouse comedy and scripting.' – *NFT, 1974*
'Why then, am I not in the aisles all the time? Is it possible that Ginger Rogers, by overplaying the brainless little creature, destroys some of the plausibility and therefore some of the fun? Maybe; I can offer no other explanation of my moments of repose, straight-faced and in my stall.' – *Dilys Powell*

† The play was also filmed in 1927 under its original title, with Phyllis Haver.

Royal Flash
GB   1975   118m   Technicolor
TCF/Two Roads (David V. Picker, Denis O'Dell)

A Victorian bully and braggart has various adventures in Europe and Ruritania.

A rather unsatisfactory romp which takes pot shots at every 19th-century person and object in the encyclopaedia, but is never as funny as it intends to be.

w George Macdonald Fraser
novel George Macdonald Fraser
d Richard Lester   ph Geoffrey Unsworth   m Ken Thorpe
pd Terence Marsh

Malcolm McDowell, Oliver Reed, Alan Bates, Florinda Bolkan, Britt

Ekland, Lionel Jeffries, Tom Bell, Joss
Ackland, Leon Greene, Richard
Hurndall, Alastair Sim, Michael
Hordern

'Five comedy stars in a five-star comedy!'
Ruggles of Red Gap**
US   1935   90m   bw
Paramount (Arthur Hornblow Jnr)

A British butler has a startling effect
on the family of an American rancher
who takes him out west.

A famous comedy which seemed
hilarious at the time but can now be
seen as mostly composed of flat spots;
the performances however are worth
remembering.

w Walter de Leon, Harlan Thompson,
Humphrey Pearson   novel Harry
Leon Wilson   d Leo McCarey
ph Alfred Gilks

*Charles Laughton, Mary Boland, Charles
Ruggles, ZaSu Pitts, Roland Young,
Leila Hyams, James Burke, Maude
Eburne, Lucien Littlefield*

'Plenty of marquee strength, and
dynamite on the inside. An A1
comedy.' – *Variety*
'A sane, witty, moving and quite
unusual picture of Anglo-American
relations.' – *C. A. Lejeune*
'The most heart-warming comedy of
the season . . . there is about it a
sympathetic and even a patriotic
quality which is touching.' – *Literary
Digest*
'The archetypal film they don't make
any more, partly because comedy has
now grown too raucous to favour the
quiet drollery of players like Charlie
Ruggles and Mary Boland, partly
because even McCarey himself had
trouble after the thirties separating
sentiment from sentimentality.' –
Time Out, 1980

† Remade as *Fancy Pants* (qv).

AAN: best picture

The Ruling Class*
GB   1972   155m   DeLuxe
Keep Films (Jules Buck, Jack Hawkins)

The fetishistic Earl of Gurney is
succeeded by his mad son Jack who
believes he is God.

An overlong satirical play with
brilliant patches is hamfistedly filmed
but boasts some bright performances.
The hits are as random as the misses,
however.

w Peter Barnes   play Peter
Barnes   d Peter Medak   ph Ken
Hodges   m John Cameron

Peter O'Toole, Harry Andrews, *Arthur
Lowe, Alastair Sim*, Coral Browne,
Michael Bryant

'This irritating and unsatisfying film is
worth being irritated and unsatisfied
by.' – *Stanley Kauffmann*
AAN: Peter O'Toole

A Run for Your Money*
GB   1949   83m   bw
Ealing (Leslie Norman)

Welsh Rugby supporters have various
adventures on their one day in
London.

Slight, bright, British chase comedy
with characterizations as excellent as
they are expected.

w Richard Hughes, Charles Frend,
Leslie Norman   d Charles
Frend   ph Douglas Slocombe
m Ernest Irving

Alec Guinness, Meredith Edwards,
Moira Lister, Donald Houston,
Hugh Griffith, Clive Morton, Joyce
Grenfell

Ruthless People*
US 1986 93m DeLuxe
Touchstone/Silver Screen Partners/
 Wagner-Lancaster
V, L

Comic kidnappers find they have on
their hands a troublesome woman
whose husband won't pay for her
return.

Raucous comedy which packs a few
good laughs before wearing out its
welcome.

w Dane Launer d Jim Abrahams,
David and Jerry Zucker ph Jan
DeBont m Michel Colombier

Danny DeVito, Bette Midler, Judge
Reinhold, Helen Slater, Anita Morris,
Bill Pulman

S

□ □ □ □ □

S.O.B.

US 1981 121m Metrocolor
Panavision
Lorimar/Geoffrey (Blake Edwards, Tony
Adams)
L

A Hollywood director goes bananas
when his much-touted epic is a
fiasco, and decides to remake it as a
sex picture.

Tasteless, vulgar and unfunny
comedy, with everybody shouting at
once and most of the jokes about
vomiting, farting and funerals. Julie
Andrews, who is made to bare her
breasts, could surely use it as grounds
for divorce.

wd Blake Edwards *ph* Harry
Stradling *m* Henry Mancini

Julie Andrews, Richard Mulligan,
Robert Preston, William Holden, Robert
Vaughn, Robert Webber, Larry
Hagman, Shelley Winters, Marisa
Berenson, Loretta Swit, Craig Stevens,
Robert Loggia

'One feels that this in-house comedy
was in some way intended as a purge
and not an entertainment.' – *John
Pym, MFB*
'At best the humour is cheap and at
worst unnecessarily vulgar.' –
Margaret Hinxman, Daily Mail

† S.O.B., it seems, stands no longer for
Son Of a Bitch but for Standard
Operational Bullshit.

Sabrina*

US 1954 113m bw
Paramount (Billy Wilder)
GB title: *Sabrina Fair*

The chauffeur's daughter is wooed by
both her brother employers.

Superior comedy, rather uneasily cast.

w Billy Wilder *play* Samuel
Taylor *d* Billy Wilder *ph* Charles
Lang Jnr *m* Frederick
Hollander *ad* Hal Pereira, Walter
Tyler

Humphrey Bogart, William Holden,
Audrey Hepburn, Walter Hampden,
John Williams, Martha Hyer, Joan
Vohs, Marcel Dalio

'This is never less than a glittering
entertainment, but somehow a
certain measure of lead has found its
way into the formula.' – *Time*

† Cary Grant was sought for the role
played by Bogart.
AAN: Billy Wilder (as writer and
director); Charles Lang Jnr; Audrey
Hepburn; art direction

The Sad Sack

US 1957 98m bw Vistavision
Paramount (Paul Nathan)

Adventures of an army misfit.

Resistible star comedy.

w Edmund Beloin, Nate Monaster
cartoon George Baker *d* George

Marshall   *ph* Loyal Griggs
m Walter Scharf

Jerry Lewis, David Wayne, Phyllis
Kirk, Peter Lorre, Joe Mantell, Gene
Evans, George Dolenz, Liliane
Montevecchi, Shepperd Strudwick

Safety Last***
US 1923 70m (24 fps) bw
  silent
Harold Lloyd
V

A small-town boy goes to the big city
and to impress his girl friend enters a
contest to climb a skyscraper.

Marvellous star comedy which set a
new standard not only in sight gags
but in the comedy-thrill stunts which
became Lloyd's stock-in-trade.

w Harold Lloyd, Sam Taylor, Tim
Whelan, Hal Roach   *d* Sam Taylor,
Fred Newmeyer   *ph* Walter Lundin

Harold Lloyd, Mildred Davis, Noah
Young

Sailor Beware
US 1952 103m bw
Paramount/Hal B. Wallis

Martin and Lewis in the navy.

Unlovable star antics.

w James Allardice, Martin Rackin
play Kenyon Nicholson, Charles
Robinson   *d* Hal Walker
ph Daniel L. Fapp   *m* Joseph J.
Lilley

Dean Martin, Jerry Lewis, Corinne
Calvet, Marion Marshall, Robert
Strauss, Leif Erickson

Sailor Beware*
GB 1956 80m bw
Romulus (Jack Clayton)
US title: *Panic in the Parlor*

A young sailor has trouble with his
mother-in-law-to-be.

Plain but adequate film version of a
successful lowbrow stage farce about
an archetypal female dragon.

w Philip King, Falkland L. Cary
play Philip King, Falkland L. Cary
d Gordon Parry   *ph* Douglas
Slocombe   *m* Peter Akister

Peggy Mount, Esma Cannon, Cyril Smith,
Shirley Eaton, Ronald Lewis

'It's the music-hall mother-in-law
joke inflated to gigantic proportions.'
– *The Times*

'The story of the longest-run date in the
history of non-marriage!'
Same Time, Next Year*
US 1978 119m colour
Universal/Walter Mirisch, Robert Mulligan
L

An illicit affair is carried on for
twenty-five years, the couple
confining themselves to one annual
meeting in a hotel.

Careful film version of a smash
Broadway comedy; the flimsiness of
the premise is well concealed, but it
remains a one-set play.

w Bernard Slade   *play* Bernard
Slade   *d* Robert Mulligan
ph Robert Surtees   *m* Marvin
Hamlisch   *pd* Henry Bumstead

Ellen Burstyn, Alan Alda
AAN: Bernard Slade; Robert Surtees;
Ellen Burstyn; song 'The Last Time I
Felt Like This' (*m* Marvin Hamlisch, *ly*
Alan and Marilyn Bergman)

The Sandwich Man*
GB 1966 95m Eastmancolor
Rank/Titan (Peter Newbrook)

In the course of a walking day around
London a sandwich man encounters

many of his eccentric acquaintances.

Spurned when it was first released, this comedy variety show, mostly in mime, can now be seen to be of a kind popularized by TV, and may have been simply ahead of its time. It certainly seems funnier than it did.

w Michael Bentine, Robert Hartford-Davis   *d* Robert Hartford-Davis   *ph* Peter Newbrook   *m* Mike Vickers

Michael Bentine, Dora Bryan, Suzy Kendall, Norman Wisdom, Harry H. Corbett, Bernard Cribbins, Ian Hendry, Stanley Holloway, Alfie Bass, Diana Dors, Ron Moody, Wilfrid Hyde White, Donald Wolfit, Max Bacon, Fred Emney, Frank Finlay, Peter Jones, Michael Medwin, Ronnie Stevens, John Le Mesurier, Sidney Tafler, John Junkin, Warren Mitchell

Saps at Sea
US   1940   60m   bw
Hal Roach
V, V(C)

Ollie needs a rest after working in a horn factory, so he and Stan take a boating holiday but are kidnapped by a gangster.

Disappointing star comedy with gags too few and too long drawn out.

w Charles Rogers, Harry Langdon, Gil Pratt, Felix Adler   *d* Gordon Douglas   *ph* Art Lloyd   *m* Marvin Hatley

Stan Laurel, Oliver Hardy, James Finlayson, Dick Cramer, Ben Turpin

Say Anything . . .*
US   1989   100m   DeLuxe
TCF (Polly Platt)
V, L

A student whose ambition it is to become a kick-boxer dates a beautiful and brainy girl, to the distress of her father.

Better than average teenage romance, deft and sometimes witty.

wd Cameron Crowe   *ph* Laszlo Kovacs   *m* Richard Gibbs, Anne Dudley, Nancy Wilson   *pd* Mark Mansbridge   *ed* Richard Marks

John Cusack, Ione Skye, John Mahoney, Lili Taylor, Amy Brooks, Pamela Segall, Jason Gould, Joan Cusack, Lois Chiles

Scandalous!
GB   1984   92m   Technicolor
Hemdale/Raleigh/Angeles Cinema Investors   (Arlene Sellers, Alex Winitsky)

A TV reporter becomes involved with two con artists, who seem to have some connection with the murder of his wife.

Frantic black comedy which never even begins to be funny.

w Rob Cohen, John Byrum   *d* Rob Cohen   *ph* Jack Cardiff   *m* Dave Grusin   *pd* Peter Mullins

Robert Hays, John Gielgud, Pamela Stephenson, M. Emmet Walsh, Nancy Wood, Jim Dale

'They're making a spook-tacle of themselves!'
Scared Stiff
US   1953   108m   bw
Paramount (Hal B. Wallis)

Night-club entertainers get involved with a girl who has inherited a spooky castle off the Cuban coast.

Stretched-out remake of *The Ghost Breakers*; the last half hour, being closest to the original, is the most nearly funny.

w Herbert Baker, Walter de Leon   *d* George Marshall, Ed Simmons,

Norman Lear   ph Ernest Laszlo
md Joseph J. Lilley

Dean Martin, Jerry Lewis, Lizabeth
Scott, Carmen Miranda, George
Dolenz, Dorothy Malone, William
Ching, Jack Lambert

Scavenger Hunt
US   1979   116m   DeLuxe
TCF/Melvin Simon

A rich man leaves a fortune to the
member of his family who can collect
most of the useless objects in a list
provided.

Depressing cheapjack imitation of
Kramer's *It's a Mad Mad Mad Mad
World*, which itself was not free from
fault.

w Steven A. Vail, Henry Harper
d Michael Schultz   ph Ken
Lamkin   m Billy Goldenberg

Richard Benjamin, James Coco,
Scatman Crothers, Cloris Leachman,
Cleavon Little, Roddy McDowall,
Robert Morley, Richard Mulligan,
Tony Randall, Dirk Benedict, Vincent
Price

'Loud, obnoxious, and above all
unfunny.' – *Variety*

Scenes from a Mall
US   1990   87m   DuArt
   Panavision
Warner/Touchstone/Silver Screen Partners
   IV (Paul Mazursky)
V, L

Preparing to celebrate their sixteenth
wedding anniversary, a Los Angeles
couple confess their recent affairs
while on a shopping spree.

An unsuccessful comic teaming in a
wordy celebration of conspicuous
consumption.

w Roger L. Simon, Paul Mazursky

d Paul Mazursky   ph Fred
Murphy   m Marc Shaiman
pd Pato Guzman   ed Stuart Pappé

Bette Midler, Woody Allen, Bill Irwin,
Daren Firestone, Rebecca Nickels, Paul
Mazursky

Scenes from the Class Struggle in Beverly Hills
US   1989   103m   CFI
Rank/North Street Films/Cinecom
   Entertainment (Amir J. Malin, Ira
   Deutchman)

Two servants bet that they can seduce
the other's mistress, both of whom
have sexual problems of their own.

Bed-hopping black-tinged comedy
that never goes quite far enough to be
funny.

w Bruce Wagner   story Paul Bartel,
Bruce Wagner   d Paul Bartel
ph Steven Fierberg   m Stanley
Myers   pd Alex Tavoularis
ed Alan Toomayan

Jacqueline Bisset, Ray Sharkey, Mary
Woronov, Robert Beltran, Ed Begley
Jr, Wallace Shawn, Arnetia Walker,
Paul Bartel, Paul Mazursky, Rebecca
Schaeffer

School for Scoundrels*
GB   1960   94m   bw
ABP/Guardsman (Hal E. Chester)
V

A failure reports to the College of
One-Upmanship and his life is
transformed.

Amusing trifle, basically a series of
sketches by familiar comic actors.

w Patricia Mayes, Hal E. Chester
books Stephen Potter   d Robert
Hamer   ph Erwin Hillier   m John
Addison

Ian Carmichael, Alastair Sim, Terry-

Thomas, Janette Scott, Dennis Price, Peter Jones, Edward Chapman, John Le Mesurier

Schtonk!

Germany 1992 111m colour
Artificial Eye/Bavarian Film/WDR (Gunter Rohrbach, Helmut Dietl)

A forger decides to fake Hitler's diaries to sell to a collector of Nazi memorabilia and enlists the aid of a journalist.

The heavy-handed farcical treatment of an hilarious true story provides little amusement, although it was a great success in its home country.

w Helmut Dietl, Ulrich Limmer d Helmut Dietl ph Xaver Schwarzenberger m Konstantin Wecker ad Götz Weidner, Benedikt Herforth ed Tanja Schmidbauer

Götz George, Uwe Ochsenknecht, Christiane Hörbiger, Rolf Hoppe, Dagmar Manzel, Veronica Ferres, Rosemarie Fendel

'This crude, overacted account of the Hitler diaries scandal is largely of sociological interest, an occasion for sporadic chuckles rather than sustained laughter.' – *Philip French, Observer*
AAN: Foreign language film

Scram!*

US 1932 20m bw
Hal Roach
V

Two vagrants are ordered out of town but by a series of misadventures are found drunk with the judge's wife.

Generally sprightly star comedy culminating in a marathon laughing session.

w H. M. Walker d Ray McCarey

Laurel and Hardy, Arthur Housman, Rychard Cramer, Vivien Oakland

Scrooged*

US 1988 101m Technicolor
Paramount/Mirage (Richard Donner, Art Linson)
V, L

Updated version of Dickens's *A Christmas Carol*, centring on the president of a New York television company.

Energetic and sometimes genuinely scary seasonal entertainment for modern kids.

w Mitch Glazer, Michael O'Donoghue d Richard Donner ph Michael Chapman m Danny Elfman pd J. Michael Riva

Bill Murray, Karen Allen, John Forsythe, Robert Mitchum, John Housman, Lee Majors

Seagulls over Sorrento

GB 1954 92m bw
MGM (John Boulting)
US title: *Crest of the Wave*

Life on a naval research station on a small Scottish island.

A long-running British service comedy has been Americanized to little effect, but it remains just about watchable.

w Frank Harvey, Roy Boulting play Hugh Hastings d Roy Boulting ph Gilbert Taylor m Miklos Rozsa

Gene Kelly, John Justin, Bernard Lee, Sidney James, Jeff Richards, Patric Doonan, Patrick Barr

The Secret Life of an American Wife**

US 1968 92m DeLuxe
TCF/Charlton (George Axelrod)

A bored suburban housewife sets out to seduce a movie star.

Sympathetic comedy of sixties suburban manners.

wd George Axelrod   *ph* Leon Shamroy · *m* Billy May

Walter Matthau, Anne Jackson, Patrick O'Neal, Edy Williams

'Both a first-class satire on American mores and a compassionate study of wish-fulfilment.' – *NFT, 1970*

The Secret Life of Walter Mitty**
US 1947 110m Technicolor
Samuel Goldwyn

A mother's boy dreams of derring-do, and eventually life catches up with fiction.

This pleasantly remembered star comedy, though it never had much to do with Thurber, can now be seen to have missed most of its opportunities, though the nice moments do tend to compensate.

w Ken Englund, Everett Freeman *story* James Thurber   *d* Norman Z. McLeod   *ph* Lee Garmes *m* David Raksin

Danny Kaye, Virginia Mayo, Boris Karloff, Florence Bates, Fay Bainter, *Thurston Hall*, Ann Rutherford, Gordon Jones, Reginald Denny

The Secret of My Success*
US 1987 110m DeLuxe
Universal/Rastar (Herbert Ross)
V, L

A country cousin in New York is determined to hit the big time.

An amiable melange of familiar situations with just a touch of *Midnight Cowboy* and a sharp edge to some of the writing; but not enough to keep its star at the top.

w Jim Cash, Jack Epps, A. J. Carothers   *d* Herbert Ross *ph* Carlo Di Palma   *m* David Foster

Michael J. Fox, Helen Slater, Richard Jordan, Margaret Whitton, John Pankow, Christopher Murney

'A bedroom farce with a leaden touch, a corporate comedy without teeth.' – *Daily Variety*

'It's not who you con – it's how you do it!'
The Secret War of Harry Frigg
US 1967 109m Techniscope
Universal/Albion (Hal E. Chester)

In 1943 a private engineers the escape of five captured generals.

Unattractive war comedy; slow, uninventive and overlong.

w Peter Stone, Frank Tarloff *d* Jack Smight   *ph* Russell Metty   *m* Carlo Rustichelli

Paul Newman, *John Williams*, Sylva Koscina, Andrew Duggan, Tom Bosley, Charles D. Gray, Vito Scotti, James Gregory

See How They Run
GB 1955 84m bw
Winwell (BL)

A country vicarage gets lively when several miscreants pretend to be the vicar.

Reliable stage farce which doesn't get the laughs on screen.

w Leslie Arliss, Philip King, Val Valentine   *play* Philip King *d* Leslie Arlis

Ronald Shiner, Greta Gynt, James Hayter, Wilfrid Hyde White, Dora Bryan, Richard Wattis, Viola Lyel

See No Evil, Hear No Evil
US   1989   102m   Technicolor
Columbia TriStar (Marvin Worth)
V, L

Suspected of murder, two friends, one deaf and the other blind, go in pursuit of the real killer.

Halting comedy that is not worth watching.

w Earl Barret, Arne Sultan, Eliot Wald, Andrew Kurtzman, Gene Wilder   story Earl Barret, Arne Sullivan, Marvin Worth   d Arthur Hiller   ph Victor J. Kemper   m Stewart Copeland   pd Robert Gundlach   ed Robert C. Jones

Richard Pryor, Gene Wilder, Joan Severance, Kevin Spacey, Alan North, Anthony Zerbe, Louis Giambalvo, Kirsten Childs

Seems Like Old Times*
US   1980   102m   Metrocolor
Columbia/Ray Stark
L

An innocently involved bank robber takes refuge with his ex-wife, a lady lawyer married to the district attorney.

Nostalgic farce which doesn't quite live up to the old skills and often bogs down in talk. Funny moments, though.

w Neil Simon   d Jay Sandrich   ph David M. Walsh   m Marvin Hamlisch   pd Gene Callahan

Goldie Hawn, Chevy Chase, Charles Grodin, Robert Guillaume, Harold Gould, George Grizzard

Semi-Tough*
US   1977   107m   DeLuxe
UA/David Merrick
V

The manager's daughter decides between two star members of a football team.

Rambling satiric comedy which takes jabs at various states of mind in America today, notably the fashionable forms of self-help therapy. Much of it comes off quite well.

w Walter Bernstein   novel Dan Jenkins   d Michael Ritchie   ph Charles Rosher Jnr   m Jerry Fielding

Burt Reynolds, Kris Kristofferson, Jill Clayburgh, Bert Convy, Robert Preston, Lotte Lenya, Roger E. Mosley

The Senator Was Indiscreet*
US   1947   95m   bw
U-I (Nunnally Johnson)
GB title: Mr Ashton Was Indiscreet

A foolish politician determines to become president and hires a press agent.

Satirical political farce which hurls its shafts wide and doesn't seem to mind how few of them hit.

w Charles MacArthur   story Edwin Lanham   d George S. Kaufman   ph William Mellor   m Daniele Amfitheatrof

William Powell, Ella Raines, Peter Lind Hayes, Ray Collins, Arleen Whelan, Allen Jenkins, Hans Conried, Charles D. Brown

Send Me No Flowers*
US   1964   100m   Technicolor
U-I/Martin Melcher (Harry Keller)

A hypochondriac mistakenly thinks he is dying and tries to provide another spouse for his wife.

A timeworn farcical situation is handled in the glossy Doris Day manner; it all starts quite brightly but gradually fizzles out.

w Julius Epstein   *play* Norman
Barrasch, Carroll Moore   *d* Norman
Jewison   *ph* Daniel Fapp
m Frank de Vol   *ad* Alexander
Golitzen, Robert Clatworthy

Doris Day, Rock Hudson, Tony
Randall, Paul Lynde, Clint Walker, Hal
March, Edward Andrews

The Seniors
US   1977   87m   Metrocolor
CSI (Stanley Shapiro, Carter De Haven)

Four college students discover a way
to become rich by making
prostitution respectable.

Exploitative comedy, mixing teenage
wish-fulfilment with black but
unfunny farce.

w Stanley Shapiro   *d* Rod
Amateau   *ph* Robert Jessup
ed Guy Scarpitta

Jeffrey Byron, Gary Imhoff, Dennis
Quaid, Lou Richards, Rocky
Flintermann, Priscilla Barnes, Alan
Reed

'The funniest foul-up of the space age!'
Sergeant Deadhead
US   1965   89m   CFI colour
AIP

An army sergeant is accidentally sent
into orbit and undergoes a personality
change.

Clumsy comedy partially redeemed by
its supporting players.

w Louis M. Heyward   *d* Norman
Taurog

Frankie Avalon, Deborah Walley,
Fred Clark, Cesar Romero, Eve
Arden, Gale Gordon, Buster
Keaton, Harvey Lembeck, John
Ashley

Serial*
US   1980   91m   Movielab
Paramount/Sidney Beckerman

Well-heeled Californians in a high
suburban community go in for various
cults and fashions.

Amusing satire on everything from
Peyton Place to *Bob and Carol and Ted
and Alice*. Just a little late in coming,
that's all.

w Rich Eustis, Michael Elias
novel Cyra McFadden   *d* Bill
Persky   *ph* Rexford Metz   *m* Lalo
Schifrin

Martin Mull, Tuesday Weld, Jennifer
McAllister, Sam Chew Jnr, Sally
Kellerman, Nita Talbot, Bill Macy,
Christopher Lee, Pamela Bellwood,
Peter Bonerz, Tom Smothers

Seven Chances**
US   1925   69m (24 fps)   bw
    silent
Buster Keaton/Joseph M. Schenck

A meek young man finds that he is to
inherit seven million dollars if he is
married within a few hours.

Slim and rather slow comedy which
builds to a fine climax as the hero is
pursued first by hordes of women and
then by rolling boulders.

w Clyde Bruckman, Jean Havez,
Joseph A. Mitchell   *play* Roi Cooper
Megrue   *d* Buster Keaton
ph Elgin Lessley, Byron Houck

Buster Keaton, Ruth Dwyer, Ray
Barnes, Snitz Edwards

† The rocks sequence, which makes
the film, was added only after a
disappointing sneak preview.

The Seven Little Foys*
US   1955   95m   Technicolor
    Vistavision
Paramount (Jack Rose)

The story of a family vaudeville act.

Routine showbiz biopic, a little heavy on the syrup.

w Melville Shavelson, Jack Rose
d Melville Shavelson ph John F. Warren md Joseph J. Lilley

Bob Hope, Milly Vitale, George Tobias, Angela Clarke, Herbert Heyes, *James Cagney* as George M. Cohan
AAN: script

The Seven Per Cent Solution
US 1976 114m Technicolor
Universal (Herbert Ross)
L

Dr Watson lures Sherlock Holmes to Vienna so that Professor Freud can cure him of persecution complex and cocaine addiction.

Drearily serious spoof with only a glimmer of the required style and a totally miscast Holmes.

w Nicholas Meyer *novel* Nicholas Meyer d Herbert Ross
ph Oswald Morris m John Addison pd Ken Adam

Nicol Williamson, Robert Duvall, Alan Arkin, Vanessa Redgrave, Laurence Olivier, Jeremy Kemp, Samantha Eggar, Joel Grey, Charles Gray, Georgia Brown, Regine

'Sorrily botched all-star extravaganza.' – *Sight and Sound*
'Comes into the category of hit and myth . . . A heavyweight spoof in which Sherlock Holmes is placed under hypnosis by Sigmund Freud. The audience is then placed under hypnosis by director Herbert Ross.' – *Michael Billington, Illustrated London News*
AAN: script

The Seven Year Itch*
US 1955 105m DeLuxe
 Cinemascope
TCF (Charles K. Feldman, Billy Wilder)
V, L

A married man has a fling with the girl upstairs.

An amusing theatrical joke, with dream sequences like revue sketches, is really all at sea on the big screen, especially as the affair remains unconsummated, but direction and performances keep the party going more or less.

w Billy Wilder, George Axelrod
play George Axelrod d Billy Wilder ph Milton Krasner
m Alfred Newman

Tom Ewell, Marilyn Monroe, Sonny Tufts, Evelyn Keyes, Robert Strauss, Oscar Homolka, Marguerite Chapman, Victor Moore

Sex and the Single Girl
US 1964 114m Technicolor
Warner/Richard Quine/Reynard (William T. Orr)

A journalist worms his way into the life of a lady sexologist in order to unmask her – but guess what.

Coy sex comedy with noise substituting for wit and style, all pretence being abandoned in a wild chase climax.

w Joseph Heller, David R. Schwarz *book* Helen Gurley Brown d Richard Quine
ph Charles Lang Jnr m Neal Hefti

Natalie Wood, Tony Curtis, Henry Fonda, Lauren Bacall, Mel Ferrer, Fran Jeffries, Edward Everett Horton, Otto Kruger

'For those willing to devote two hours of their lives to a consideration of Natalie Wood's virginity.' — *Judith Crist, 1973*

Sextette*
US   1978   91m   Metrocolor
Briggs and Sullivan (Warren G. Toub)

The honeymoon of a Hollywood film star is interrupted by her previous husbands.

An amazing last stab at her old métier by an 86-year-old ex-star. It doesn't work, of course, and most of it is embarrassing, but the attempt is in itself remarkable.

w Herbert Baker   *play* Mae West   *d* Ken Hughes   *ph* James Crabe   *m* Artie Butler

Mae West, Tony Curtis, Ringo Starr, Dom de Luise, Timothy Dalton, George Hamilton, Alice Cooper, Rona Barrett, Walter Pidgeon, George Raft

Shadows and Fog*
US   1991   86m   bw
Columbia TriStar/Orion (Jack Rollins, Charles Joffe)

In a town where a circus has come to visit, a timid individual is forced by his neighbours to join vigilantes trying to trap a murderer.

An occasionally witty excursion into the world of German expressionist movies of the 20s.

wd Woody Allen   *ph* Carlo Di Palma   *m* Kurt Weill   *pd* Santo Loquasto   *ed* Susan E. Morse

Woody Allen, Mia Farrow, John Malkovich, Madonna, Donald Pleasence, Lily Tomlin, Jodie Foster, Kathy Bates, John Cusack, Kate Nelligan, Julie Kavner, Fred Gwynne

'Is Allen confronting his inability to treat history, or anything else, as tragedy rather than farce? The film is a serious joke, possibly reflecting on German re-unification, and it has an unpleasant aftertaste.' — *Philip French, Observer*

Shag
GB   1988   100m   colour
Palace/Hemdale (Stephen Woolley, Julia Chasman)
V, L

Four girls go to the beach for fun and boys.

Set in the 1960s, it is an attempt, successful enough in its inane way, to revive the style of the teen movies of the time.

w Robin Swicord, Lanier Laney, Terry Sweeney   *d* Zelda Barron   *ph* Peter MacDonald   *pd* Buddy Cone   *ed* Laurence Mery Clark

Phoebe Cates, Scott Coffey, Bridget Fonda, Annabeth Gish, Page Hannah, Robert Rusler, Tyrone Power III, Jeff Yagher

Shampoo*
US   1975   110m   Technicolor
Columbia/Persky-Bright/Vista (Warren Beatty)
V, L

A Beverly Hills hairdresser seduces his most glamorous clients.

Ugly little sex farce with few laughs but much dashing about and bad language. Its setting on election eve 1968 has made some people think it a political satire.

w Robert Towne, Warren Beatty   *d* Hal Ashby   *ph* Laszlo Kovacs   *m* Paul Simon

Warren Beatty, Julie Christie, Lee

Grant, Goldie Hawn, Jack Warden, Tony Bill, Jay Robinson

'It has the bursting-with-talent but fuzziness-of-effect aspect of a movie made by a group of friends for their own amusement.' – *Richard Combs*

AA: Lee Grant
AAN: script; Jack Warden

She Couldn't Say No
US   1952   89m   bw
RKO (Robert Sparks)
GB title: *Beautiful But Dangerous*

An heiress returns to the town of her childhood to distribute anonymous gifts to those who had helped her.

Moderate Capraesque comedy which doesn't quite come off.

w D. D. Beauchamp, William Bowers, Richard Flournoy   d Lloyd Bacon   ph Harold J. Wild   m Roy Webb

Jean Simmons, Robert Mitchum, Arthur Hunnicutt, Edgar Buchanan, Wallace Ford, Raymond Walburn

She Done Him Wrong***
US   1933   68m   bw
Paramount (William Le Baron)

A lady saloon keeper of the Gay Nineties falls for the undercover cop who is after her.

As near undiluted Mae West as Hollywood ever came: fast, funny, melodramatic and pretty sexy; also a very atmospheric and well-made movie.

w Mae West,   play Diamond Lil by Mae West (with help on the scenario from Harry Thew, John Bright)
d Lowell Sherman   ph Charles Lang   songs Ralph Rainger (m), Leo Robin (ly)

Mae West, Cary Grant, Owen Moore,

Gilbert Roland, Noah Beery, David Landau, Rafaela Ottiano, Rochelle Hudson, Dewey Robinson

'Only alternative to a strong drawing cast, nowadays if a picture wants business, is strong entertainment. This one has neither.' – *Variety*
AAN: best picture

She-Devil
US   1989   99m   DuArt
Rank/Orion (Jonathan Brett, Susan Seidelman)
V, L

An unattractive housewife takes her revenge when her husband leaves her for a glamorous romantic novelist.

Unsuccessful and bland adaptation of the sour comedy of the original.

w Barry Strugatz, Mark R. Burns
novel The Life and Loves of a She-Devil by Fay Weldon   d Susan Seidelman   ph Oliver Stapleton
m Howard Shore   pd Santo Loquasto   ed Craig McKay

Meryl Streep, Roseanne Barr, Ed Begley Jr, Sylvia Miles, Linda Hunt, Elisabeth Peters, Bryan Larkin, A. Martinez

The Sheep Has Five Legs*
France   1954   96m   bw
Raoul Ploquin
original title: *Le Mouton a Cinq Pattes*

A town seeking publicity tries to bring together the five quintuplet grandsons of its oldest inhabitant.

Mildly saucy star vehicle which was in fact most notable for introducing Fernandel to an international audience.

w Albert Valentin   d Henri Verneuil   ph Armand Thirard   m Georges Van Parys

Fernandel, Françoise Arnoul,
Delmont, Paulette Dubost, Louis de
Funès
AAN: original story

Sherlock Junior**
US   1924   45m (24 fps)   bw
   silent
Metro/Buster Keaton (Joseph M. Schenck)
V

A film projectionist, unjustly accused
of stealing a watch, has dreams of
being a great detective.

Fast-moving, gag-filled comedy
which ranks among its star's best.

w Clyde Bruckman, Jean Havez,
Joseph Mitchell   d/ed Buster
Keaton   ph Elgin Lessley, Byron
Houck

Buster Keaton, Kathryn McGuire,
Ward Crane, Joseph Keaton

She's Gotta Have It
US   1986   84m   bw/colour
40 Acres And A Mule Filmworks (Shelton
   J. Lee)
V

Three men woo the same woman.

Smart, but ultimately tiresome,
comedy as the men explain one-by-
one and then together why each
would make the perfect lover.

wd Spike Lee   ph Ernest
Dickerson   m Bill Lee   pd Wynn
Thomas   ed Spike Lee

Tracy Camilla Jones, Tommy Redmon
Hicks, John Canada Terrell, Raye
Dowell, Joie Lee, Spike Lee

She's Out of Control
US   1989   95m   CFI
Columbia TriStar/Weintraub
   Entertainment (Stephen Deutsch)
V, L

A widower follows the advice of a
psychiatrist in trying to control the
sex life of his teenage daughter.

Lifeless and singularly witless comedy.

w Seth Winston, Michael J.
Nathanson   d Stan Dragoti
ph Donald Peterman   m Alan
Silvestri   pd David L. Snyder
ed Dov Hoenig

Tony Danza, Catherine Hicks, Wallace
Shawn, Dick O'Neill, Ami Dolenz,
Laura Mooney, Derek McGrath, Dana
Ashbrook

'The movie begins shakily and ends
feebly, but, in between, is often sharp
and funny.' – Philip French, Observer

The Shiralee*
GB   1957   99m   bw
Ealing (Jack Rix)

An Australian swagman leaves his
wife and takes to the road with his
small daughter.

Episodic character comedy-drama
throwing a fairly sharp light on the
Australian scene.

w Neil Paterson, Leslie Norman
novel D'Arcy Niland   d Leslie
Norman   ph Paul Beeson   m John
Addison

Peter Finch, Dana Wilson, Elizabeth
Sellars, George Rose, Russell Napier,
Niall MacGinnis, Tessie O'Shea

Shirley Valentine**
US   1989   108m   Technicolor
UIP/Paramount (Lewis Gilbert)
V, L

A bored housewife abandons her
husband to enjoy a holiday romance
in Greece.

Enjoyably old-fashioned movie, with
some entertaining monologues on
her narrow existence from its heroine.

w Willy Russell   *play* Willy
Russell   *d* Lewis Gilbert   *ph* Alan
Hune   *m* Willy Russell, George
Hatzinassios   *pd* John Stoll
ed Lesley Walker

Pauline Collins, Tom Conti, Julia
McKenzie, Alison Steadman, Joanna
Lumley, Sylvia Sims, Bernard Hill
AAN: Pauline Collins

'Trust me, I'm a doctor.'
Shock Treatment
GB 1982 95m Technicolor
TCF (John Goldstone)

An innocent young couple are
trapped on a bizarre TV game show.

A sort of sequel to *The Rocky Horror
Show* (qv), featuring the same hapless
hero and heroine, but lacking any
spark of originality. It also failed to
attract its predecessor's cult following.

w Richard O'Brien, Jim Sharman
d Jim Sharman   *ph* Mike
Molloy   *m* Richard Hartley, Richard
O'Brien   *pd* Brian Thomson
ed Richard Bedford

Jessica Harper, Cliff De Young,
Richard O'Brien, Patricia Quinn,
Charles Gray, Nell Campbell, Ruby
Wax, Barry Humphries, Rik Mayall

The Shop around the Corner**
US 1940 97m bw
MGM (Ernst Lubitsch)

In a Budapest shop, the new
floorwalker and a girl who dislikes him
find they are pen pals.

Pleasant period romantic comedy
which holds no surprises but is
presented with great style.

*w Samson Raphaelson,
play* Nikolaus Laszlo   *d Ernst
Lubitsch   ph* William Daniels
m Werner Heymann

James Stewart, Margaret Sullavan,
Frank Morgan, Joseph Schildkraut,
Sara Haden, *Felix Bressart*, William
Tracy

'It's not pretentious but it's a beautiful
job of picture-making, and the people
who did it seem to have enjoyed doing
it just as much as their audiences will
enjoy seeing it.' – *James Shelley
Hamilton*
'An agreeably bittersweet example of
light entertainment.' – *Charles Higham,
1972*
'One of the most beautifully acted and
paced romantic comedies ever made in
this country.' – *New Yorker, 1978*

† Remade as *In the Good Old
Summertime* (qv).

'Getting killed isn't as easy as it looks'
Short Time
US 1987 102m colour
Rank/Gladden Entertainment/Touchstone
  (Todd Black)
V, L

Discovering he has a fatal disease and
wanting to die on active service so his
family can collect on his insurance
policy, an ageing cop volunteers for
dangerous assignments.

A comedy suffering from a terminal
lack of laughs.

w John Blumenthal, Michael
Berry   *d* Gregg Champion
ph John Connor   *m* Ira
Newborn   *pd* Michael Bolton
ed Frank Morriss

Dabney Coleman, Matt Frewer, Teri
Garr, Barry Corbin, Joe Pantoliano,
Xander Berkeley, Rob Roy

A Shot in the Dark*
US 1964 101m DeLuxe
  Panavision
UA/Mirisch/Geoffrey (Blake Edwards)
V, L

A woman is accused of shooting her lover; accident-prone Inspector Clouseau investigates.

Further adventures of the oafish, Tatiesque clodhopper from *The Pink Panther;* mildly funny for those in the mood for pratfalls.

w Blake Edwards, William Peter Blatty   *d* Blake Edwards
ph Christopher Challis   *m* Henry Mancini   *pd* Michael Stringer

Peter Sellers, Elke Sommer, George Sanders, Herbert Lom, Tracy Reed, Graham Stark

Shoulder Arms*

US   1918   24m (24 fps)   bw
silent
Charles Chaplin/First National

A soldier in the trenches dreams of winning the war single-handedly.

A comedy which meant a great deal at the time of its release but now provides precious little to laugh at.

wd Charles Chaplin   *ph* Rollie Totheroh

Charles Chaplin, Edna Purviance, Sydney Chaplin, Henry Bergman, Albert Austin

Show People

US   1928   80m at 24 fps   bw
silent
MGM

A naïve young actress makes it in Hollywood.

Historically important comedy with cameo appearances by many stars of the time.

w Wanda Tuchock, Agnes Christine Johnston, Lawrence Stallings

d King Vidor Marion Davies, William Haines

'It was not sex it was good!'

Sibling Rivalry

US   1990   88m   colour
First Independent/Castle Rock/Nelson
V, L

Complications ensue after an unhappy wife, advised by her sister to have an affair, goes to bed with her sister's husband.

Broad farce of marital upset that causes an occasional smile.

w Martha Goldhirsh   *d* Carl Reiner   *ph* Reynaldo Villalobos
m Jack Elliott   *pd* Jeannine C. Oppewall   *ed* Bud Molin

Kirstie Alley, Bill Pullman, Carrie Fisher, Jami Gertz, Scott Bakula, Frances Sternhagen, John Randolph, Sam Elliott, Ed O'Neill, Paul Benedict

'In opting for romantic comedy rather than the black variety, the picture has grave problems of mood which are never resolved.' – *Philip French, Observer*

Silent Movie*

US   1976   87m   DeLuxe
TCF/Crossbow (Michael Hertzberg)
V, L

An alcoholic producer gets the idea that a silent movie would be a great novelty, and tries to get stars to take part.

Fairly lively spoof with the talents concerned in variable form. The shortage of laughter made it a hit in the seventies, but at no time does it approach the Keaton or Laurel and Hardy level.

w Mel Brooks, Ron Clark, Rudy de Luca, Barry Levinson   *d* Mel Brooks   *ph* Paul Lohmann
m John Morris

Mel Brooks, Marty Feldman, Dom De Luise, Bernardette Peters, Sid Caesar, Harold Gould, Fritz Feld, Harry Ritz, Henny Youngman *guest stars* Anne Bancroft, Paul Newman, Burt Reynolds, James Caan, Liza Minnelli, Marcel Marceau

† Marcel Marceau utters the only word in the movie, which is *'Non'*.

Silver Bears
GB 1977 113m Technicolor
EMI/Raleigh (Martin Schute)

A Las Vegas money man invests money in various European outlets and makes a killing.

Extraordinarily complex financial jape which tries the patience of all but financiers.

w Peter Stone *novel* Paul Erdman *d* Ivan Passer
ph Anthony Richmond *m* Claude Bolling

Michael Caine, Louis Jourdan, Cybill Shepherd, Stephane Audran, David Warner, Tom Smothers, Martin Balsam, Charles Gray

Silver Streak*
US 1976 113m DeLuxe
TCF/Martin Ransohoff, Frank Yablans
V, L

On a trans-continental train, a young publisher discovers a murder and is at the mercy of the culprits.

Rather like an update of a Bob Hope comedy-thriller with a whiff of sex, this amiable spoof goes on too long, brings in a second comic too late, and ends with fashionable but irrelevant violence.

w Colin Higgins *d* Arthur Hiller
ph David M. Walsh *m* Henry Mancini *pd* Alfred Sweeney

Gene Wilder, Jill Clayburgh, Richard Pryor, Patrick McGoohan, Ned Beatty, Clifton James, Ray Walston, Richard Kiel

'Nineteen-seventies performers are trapped in this fake thirties mystery comedy, which is so inept you can't even get angry.' – *New Yorker*

Simon*
US 1980 97m Technicolor
Warner/Orion (Louis A. Stroller, Martin Bregman)

Corrupt scientists brainwash a psychology professor into thinking he's from another planet.

Solemn comic fantasy which doesn't seem to make much of a point and only superficially entertains, but is well made and well acted.

wd Marshall Brickman *ph* Adam Holender *m* Stanley Silverman
pd Stuart Wurtzel

Alan Arkin, Madeline Kahn, Austin Pendleton, Judy Graubert, William Finley, Fred Gwynne

Simon and Laura*
GB 1955 91m Technicolor Vistavision
GFD/Group Films (Teddy Baird)

The actors who play husband and wife in a TV series are married in reality and hate each other, a fact that shows in the live Christmas episode.

Adequate film of a reasonably sophisticated West End comedy; good lines and performances.

w Peter Blackmore *play* Alan Melville *d* Muriel Box
ph Ernest Steward *m* Benjamin Frankel

Peter Finch, Kay Kendall, Ian Carmichael, Alan Wheatley, Richard

Wattis, Muriel Pavlow, Maurice
Denham, Hubert Gregg

Sing As We Go***
GB 1934 80m bw
ATP (Basil Dean)

An unemployed millgirl gets various
holiday jobs in Blackpool.

A splendid, pawky star vehicle which
is also the best picture we have of
industrial Lancashire in the thirties.
Great fun.

w J. B. Priestley, Gordon Wellesley
d Basil Dean ph Robert G. Martin

Gracie Fields, John Loder, Frank
Pettingell, Dorothy Hyson, Stanley
Holloway

'We have an industrial north that is
bigger than Gracie Fields running
around a Blackpool fun fair.' – C. A.
Lejeune

Sir Henry at Rawlinson End
GB 1980 71m bw
Charisma (Tony Stratton Smith)

A grossly eccentric English aristocrat
lays a family ghost.

Weirdly isolated, semi-professional
comedy with elements of everything
from Ealing to Monty Python.

w Vivien Stanshall, Steve Roberts
radio play Vivien Stanshall d Steve
Roberts ph Martin Bell
m Vivian Stanshall pd Alistair
Bowtell ed Chris Rose

Trevor Howard, Patrick Magee,
Denise Coffey, J. G. Devlin, Vivian
Stanshall

'No Sex. No Booze. No Men. No Way.'

Sister Act*
US 1992 100m Technicolor
Buena Vista/Touchstone/Touchwood
   Pacific Partners (Teri Schwartz)
V

A singer on the run from the Mafia
takes refuge in a convent and
transforms its choir.

Cheerful and modest comedy, though
lacking in wit and with a plot that
makes little sense. It was the surprise
hit of 1992, ranking fourth at the
box-office.

w Joseph Howard d Emile
Ardolino ph Adam Greenberg
m Marc Shaiman pd Jackson
DeGovia ed Richard Halsey

Whoopi Goldberg, Maggie Smith,
Kathy Najimy, Wendy Makkena, Mary
Wickes, Harvey Keitel, Bill Nunn,
Robert Miranda, Richard Portnow

'The film isn't a divine comedy, and
it's not satisfyingly profane either. But
it generates a few laughs. It's got a
good beat, and you can dance to it.'
– Michael Sragow, New Yorker
'Offers the kind of cute, synthetic
uplift usually found in television
commercials and casts its nun
characters as walking sight gags
rather than real people.' – Janet
Maslin, New York Times
'A truly awful film, pretending to be
audacious but in fact pandering to
every facile assumption in the book.'
– Derek Malcolm, Guardian

Sitting Ducks
US 1978 88m DeLuxe
Sunny Side Up (Meira Atta Dor)

Two men steal a fortune and abscond
to Miami with two women who turn
out to have a contract on them.

Endlessly talkative sex comedy from a

practitioner who scorns built-up gags. The kind of movie that puts people off movies.

wd Henry Jaglom   *ph* Paul Glickman   *m* Richard Romanus

Michael E. Jaglom, Zack Norman, Patrice Townsend, Irene Forrest, Richard Romanus, Henry Jaglom

Sitting Pretty***
US   1948   84m   bw
TCF (Samuel G. Engel)

A young couple acquire a most unusual male baby sitter, a self-styled genius who sets the neighbourhood on its ears by writing a novel about it.

Out of the blue, a very funny comedy which entrenched Clifton Webb as one of Hollywood's great characters and led to two sequels, *Mr Belvedere Goes to College* and *Mr Belvedere Rings the Bell* (qv).

w F. Hugh Herbert,   *novel* Belvedere by Gwen Davenport   *d* Walter Lang   *ph* Norbert Brodine
m Alfred Newman

Clifton Webb, Robert Young, Maureen O'Hara, *Richard Haydn*, Louise Allbritton, Ed Begley, Randy Stuart, Larry Olsen
AAN: Clifton Webb

'Pray they never have to rescue YOU...!'
Ski Patrol
US   1989   92m   DeLuxe
Entertainment/Epic/Sarlui/Diamant/Paul Maslansky (Phillip B. Goldfine, Donald L. West)
V, L

A developer attempts to sabotage the safety record of a ski resort.

Broad farce in the style of the *Police Academy* series and no funnier.

w Steven Long Mitchell, Craig W. Van Sickle   *d* Richard Correll
ph John Stephens   *m* Bruce Miller   *pd* Fred Weiler   *ed* Scott Wallace

Roger Rose, Yvette Nipar, T. K. Carter, Leslie Jordan, Paul Feig, Sean Gregory Sullivan, Tess, George Lopez, Ray Walston

Ski School
Canada   1991   88m   colour
Movie Store Entertainment/Rose & Ruby (Damian Lee)

Rival groups of skiers try to sabotage each other.

Crass comedy that is mainly an excuse for ski stunts and the cavortings of skimpily clad bimbos.

w David Mitchell   *d* Damian Lee   *ph* Curtis Petersen, Roxanne Di Santo   *m* Steven Hunter
ad Craig MacMillan   *ed* Robert Gordon

Dean Cameron, Tom Breznahan, Patrick Laborteaux, Mark Thomas Miller, Darlene Vogel, Charlie Spradling

Skidoo
US   1968   98m   Technicolor Panavision
Paramount/Sigma (Otto Preminger)

Active and reformed gangsters get involved with hippies and preach universal love.

Abysmal mishmash with top talent abused; clearly intended as satirical farce, but in fact one of the most woebegone movies ever made.

w Doran William Cannon   *d* Otto Preminger   *ph* Leon Shamroy
m Harry Nilsson

Jackie Gleason, Carol Channing,

Groucho Marx, Frankie Avalon, Fred Clark, Michael Constantine, Frank Gorshin, John Philip Law, Peter Lawford, Burgess Meredith, George Raft, Cesar Romero, Mickey Rooney

'Unspeakable.' – *Michael Billington, Illustrated London News*

Skin Deep
US 1989 101m Technicolor Panavision
Braveworld/Fox/Morgan Creek/BECO (Tony Adams)
V

A best-selling author devotes his time to booze and women.

Shallow comedy too much in love with its unprepossessing hero.

wd Blake Edwards *ph* Isidore Mankofsky *pd* Rodger Maus *ed* Robert Pergament

John Ritter, Vincent Gardenia, Alyson Reed, Joel Brooks, Julianne Phillips, Chelsea Field, Peter Donat, Don Gordon, Nina Foch

'Edwards' undeniable personal obsessions are winding up as bland, uniform, nothing-in-particular films like this.' – *Kim Newman, MFB*

Slacker**
US 1991 97m colour
Feature/Detour (Richard Linklater)

In Austin, Texas, young people wandering the streets confide to the camera their odd beliefs and attitudes, including the avoidance of careers.

Leisurely, lackadaisical feature of oddballs that exerts a certain bemused fascination.

wd Richard Linklater *ph* Lee Daniel *m* Buffalo Gals, Triangle Mallet Apron, The Texas

Instruments *ad* Debbie Pastor *ed* Scott Rhodes

Richard Linklater, Rudy Basquez, Jean Caffeine, Jan Hockey, Stephan Hockey, Mark James

'A film of quirky, unpredictable and oddly poetic charm.' – *Philip Kemp, Sight and Sound*
'One of the freshest independent films to come along in some time, but because of its non-narrative, non-characterization approach, film won't be to all tastes.' – *Variety*

Slap Shot*
US 1977 124m Technicolor
Universal/Robert J. Wunsch, Stephen Friedman
V, L

The wily player-coach of a fading ice hockey team finds ways, including dirty play, of keeping it going.

Violent, foul-mouthed comedy which works as it goes but leaves a bad taste in the mouth.

w Nancy Dowd *d* George Roy Hill *ph* Victor Kemper, Wallace Worsley *md* Elmer Bernstein

Paul Newman, Michael Ontkean, Lindsay Crouse, Jennifer Warren, Strother Martin

'Fast, noisy, profane . . . gets you laughing, all right, but you don't necessarily enjoy yourself.' – *New Yorker*
'Both indulgent and moralizing, the self-consciously racy script ends up looking merely opportunistic.' – *Time Out*

'A love story about two people who hate each other!'

Sleeper**
US   1973   88m   DeLuxe
UA/Jack Rollins, Charles Joffe (Jack Grossberg)
V, L

A health food store owner is deep frozen after an operation and wakes two hundred years in the future.

Predictable star vehicle with an agreeable string of bright gags.

w *Woody Allen, Marshall Brickman*
d Woody Allen   ph David M. Walsh   m Woody Allen   pd Dale Hennesy

Woody Allen, Diane Keaton, John Beck, Mary Gregory

'Verbal and visual gags rain down like hailstones.' – *Michael Billington, Illustrated London News*

'Her heart belongs to daddy, and she calls everybody daddy!'
Slightly Honorable
US   1940   85m   bw
UA/Walter Wanger (Tay Garnett)

Lawyer partners set out to break a crime syndicate.

Fair crime thriller which can't decide whether it's comedy or drama.

w John Hunter Lay, Robert Tallman, Ken Englund   *novel Send Another Coffin* by F. G. Presnell   d Tay Garnett   ph Merritt Gerstad
m Werner Janssen

Pat O'Brien, Broderick Crawford, Edward Arnold, Eve Arden, Claire Dodd, Ruth Terry, Bernard Nedell, Alan Dinehart, Douglass Dumbrille, Ernest Truex

'The story skips along without deftness between serious drama and comedy, and winds up in the aggregate as a whatisit.' – *Variety*

Slither*
US   1972   96m   Metrocolor
MGM/Talent Associates/Jack Sher

An ex-con, some gangsters, and a few mobile homes are involved in a chase across California for some hidden loot.

Wackily with-it comedy-thriller ranging from violence to slapstick, the former always undercut into the latter. Pretty funny, once you get the idea.

w W. D. Richter   d Howard Zieff
ph Laszlo Kovacs   m Tom McIntosh

James Caan, Peter Boyle, Sally Kellerman, Louise Lasser

The Smallest Show on Earth*
GB   1957   81m   bw
British Lion/Launder and Gilliat (Michael Relph)
US title: *Big Time Operators*

Two young marrieds inherit a decayed cinema and make it pay.

Amiable caricature comedy with plenty of obvious jokes and a sentimental attachment to old cinemas but absolutely no conviction, little plot, and a very muddled sense of the line between farce and reality.

w William Rose, John Eldridge
d Basil Dearden   ph Douglas Slocombe   m William Alwyn

Bill Travers, Virginia McKenna, Margaret Rutherford, Bernard Miles, Peter Sellers, Leslie Phillips, Francis de Wolff

Smashing Time
GB   1967   96m   Eastmancolor
Paramount/Partisan/Carlo Ponti (Ray Millichip)

Two north country girls have farcical adventures in swinging London, including paint squirting and pie throwing.

Horrendous attempt to turn two unsuitable actresses into a female Laurel and Hardy; plenty of coarse vigour but no style or sympathy.

w George Melly   *d* Desmond Davis   *ph Manny Wynn   m* John Addison

Rita Tushingham, Lynn Redgrave, Ian Carmichael, Anna Quayle, Michael York, Irene Handl, Jeremy Lloyd

Smile*
US   1975   113m   DeLuxe
UA (Michael Ritchie)

A bird's eye view of the Young Miss America pageant in a small California town.

A witty series of sketches in the form of a drama-documentary or satirical mosaic. Highly polished fun for those who can stay the course.

w Jerry Belson   d Michael Ritchie ph Conrad Hall   *m* various

Bruce Dern, Barbara Feldon, Michael Kidd, Geoffrey Lewis, Nicholas Pryor

'A beady, precise, technically skilful movie.' – *Michael Billington, Illustrated London News*

Smiles of a Summer Night**
Sweden   1955   105m   bw
Svensk Filmindustri
original title: *Sommarnattens Leende*

A country lawyer meets again a touring actress who was once his mistress, and accepts an invitation for him and his young wife to stay at her mother's country home for a weekend.

Comedy of high period manners with

an admirable detached viewpoint and elegant trappings. It later formed the basis of Stephen Sondheim's *A Little Night Music*, a stage musical which was later filmed.

wd Ingmar Bergman   *ph* Gunnar Fischer   *m* Erik Nordgren

Gunnar Bjornstrand, Eva Dahlbeck, Ulla Jacobsson, Harriet Andersson, Margit Carlquist, Naima Wifstrand, Jarl Kulle

'His intimate and roguish romance will break your heart – with love and laughter!'

The Smiling Lieutenant**
US   1931   88m   bw
Paramount (Ernst Lubitsch)

A Viennese guards officer leaves his mistress to become consort to a visiting princess.

A sophisticated soufflé in Lubitsch's best style, naughty but quite nice, with visual effects largely replacing dialogue.

w Ernest Vajda, Samson Raphaelson   *operetta* A Waltz Dream   *d* Ernst Lubitsch *ph* George Folsey   *md* Adolph Deutsch   *m* Oscar Straus

Maurice Chevalier, Miriam Hopkins, Claudette Colbert, Charles Ruggles, George Barbier, Elizabeth Patterson

'Will delight smart audiences and figures to be liked well enough by the average fan. A good but not a smash picture.' – *Variety*
'All the shrewd delights that were promised in *The Love Parade* all realized with an economy and sureness that give it a luster which no other American-made comedy satire has achieved. One must look to *Le Million* to find its peer.' – *Richard Watts, New York Post*
AAN: best picture

Smokey and the Bandit*

US   1977   97m   Technicolor
Universal/Rastar (Robert L. Levy)
V

A Georgia bootlegger on a mission picks up a girl in distress and is chased by her irate sheriff fiancé.

Frantic chase comedy full of car crashes and low lines: a surprise box-office smash.

w James Lee Barrett, Charles Shyer, Alan Mandel   d Hal Needham
ph Bobby Byrne   m Bill Justis, Jerry Reed, Art Feller

Burt Reynolds, Jackie Gleason, Sally Field, Jerry Reed, Mike Henry, Pat McCormick, Paul Williams

Smokey and the Bandit II

US   1980   101m   Technicolor
Universal/Rastar/Mort Engelberg
GB title: Smokey and the Bandit Ride Again

A trucker is hired to take a pregnant elephant to the Republican convention.

More mindless chasing and crashing, with even less wit than before and rather more wholesale destruction.

w Jerry Belson, Brock Yates   d Hal Needham   ph Michael Butler
md Snuff Garrett

Burt Reynolds, Jackie Gleason, Sally Field, Jerry Reed, Dom DeLuise, Paul Williams

Smokey and the Bandit III

US   1983   88m   Technicolor
Mort Engelberg/Universal

Sheriff Justice mistakes an innocent driver for his old enemy.

A rather random car chase movie, obviously the last of a short line.

w Stuart Birnbaum, David Dashev

d Dick Lowry   ph James Pergola
m Larry Cansler   ad Ron Hobbs
ed Byron Brandt, David Blewitt, Christopher Greenbury

Jackie Gleason, Jerry Reed, Mike Henry, Pat McCormick, Burt Reynolds (for a cameo)

'A patchwork of arbitrary mayhem.' – Variety

'There's only one thing that can keep them apart – the seven-foot thing she's married to!'

So Fine

US   1981   91m   Technicolor
Warner/Lobell – Bergman (Mike Lobell)

A professor of literature trying to save his father from gangsters becomes involved in strange adventures.

Weirdly titled action comedy which tries to be far too clever for its own good.

wd Andrew Bergman   ph James A. Contner   m Ennio Morricone

Ryan O'Neal, Jack Warden, Mariangela Melato, Richard Kiel, Fred Gwynne, Mike Kellin

'A visual insult, crudely lighted and framed, and jumping out at you.' – Pauline Kael, New Yorker

Soapdish*

US   1991   97m   Technicolor
UIP/Paramount (Aaron Spelling, Alan Greisman)
V, L

A jealous co-star tries to sabotage the popularity of America's most popular star of a daily soap-opera.

Fitfully amusing parody of a TV soap, but one that failed to find much of an audience.

w Robert Harling, Andrew Bergman   d Michael Hoffman

ph Ueli Steiger   m Alan Silvestri
pd Eugenio Zanetti   ed Garth
Craven

Sally Field, Kevin Kline, Robert
Downey Jnr, Whoopi Goldberg, Carrie
Fisher, Cathy Moriarty, Teri Hatcher,
Paul Johansson, Elisabeth Shue,
Garry Marshall

'An amiable comedy with enough
one-liners to keep the chuckles coming
regularly.' – Sight and Sound

Soft Beds, Hard Battles.
GB   1973   107m   colour
Rank/Charter (John Boulting)
US title: Undercovers Hero

Inhabitants of a Paris brothel help to
win World War II.

Ragbag of poor sketches and dirty
jokes, with the star in several
ineffective roles including Hitler.

w Leo Marks, Roy Boulting   d Roy
Boulting   ph Gil Taylor   m Neil
Rhoden

Peter Sellers, Lila Kedrova, Curt
Jurgens, Gabriella Licudi, Jenny
Hanley

'A Motorvated Comedy.'
'They're going to make it. Nothing will stop
them now...'
Soft Top, Hard Shoulder*
GB   1992   95m   colour
Feature/Road Movie Productions (Richard
   Holmes)

An unsuccessful Scottish artist living
in London has 36 hours to drive to
Glasgow in his ancient car so that he
can share in the family fortune; on
the way he picks up a female hitch-
hiker.

Amiable, soft-centred road movie
with an affection for eccentricity.

w Peter Capaldi   d Stefan

Schwartz   ph Henry Braham
m Chris Rea   pd Sonja Klaus
ed Derek Trigg

Peter Capaldi, Frances Barber,
Catherine Russell, Jeremy Northam,
Richard Wilson, Peter Ferninando,
Simon Callow, Phyllis Logan

'The initial novelty of this particular
roadshow ultimately pales.' – Empire

Some Kind of Hero
US   1981   97m   Movielab
Paramount (Howard W. Koch)
V, L

After six years as a prisoner of the
Vietcong, an army veteran returns
home to find his life no bed of roses.

Weird mixture of comedy and
melodrama which simply doesn't jell,
especially when it tries to get earnest.
d James Kirkwood, Robert Boris
novel James Kirkwood   d Michael
Pressman   ph King Baggot
m Patrick Williams   ad James L.
Schoppe   ed Christopher
Greenbury

Richard Pryor, Margot Kidder, Ray
Sharkey, Ronny Cox, Lynne Moody,
Olivia Cole

Some Kind of Wonderful
US   1987   95m   Technicolor
   Panavision
Paramount (John Hughes)
V, L

Girl meets boy, boy meets another
girl, boy loses girl, boy gets first girl.

Teen romance pandering to its target
audience: all adults are stupid and
repressive and maturity and wisdom
are to be found among the young. Its
appeal will be limited to the
immature.

w John Hughes   d Howard
Deutch   ph Jan Kiesser

m Stephen Hague, John Musser
pd Josan Russo   *ed* Bud Smith,
Scott Smith

Eric Stoltz, Mary Stuart Masterson,
Craig Sheffer, John Ashton, Lea
Thompson, Elias Koteas, Maddie
Corman

Some Like It Hot***
US 1959 122m bw
UA/Mirisch (Billy Wilder)
V, L

Two unemployed musicians
accidentally witness the St Valentine's
Day Massacre and flee to Miami
disguised as girl musicians.

Overstretched but sporadically very
funny comedy which constantly flogs
its central idea to death and then
recovers with a smart line or situation.
It has in any case become a milestone
of film comedy.

w Billy Wilder, I. A. L. Diamond
d Billy Wilder   *ph* Charles Lang
Jnr   *m* Adolph Deutsch   *ad* Ted
Howarth

*Jack Lemmon, Tony Curtis, Marilyn
Monroe, Joe E. Brown*, George Raft, Pat
O'Brien, Nehemiah Persoff, George E.
Stone, Joan Shawlee

'A comedy set in the Prohibition era,
with transvestism, impotence, role
confusion, and borderline inversion –
and all hilariously innocent, though
always on the brink of really
disastrous *double-entendre*.' – *Pauline
Kael*
'Most of the time Billy Wilder's new
piece – a farce blacker than is common
on the American screen – whistles
along at a smart, murderous pace.' –
Dilys Powell
'Hectic slapstick, smartass movie
pardies, sexist stereotyping, crass
one-liners, and bad taste galore.' –
Time Out, 1984

AAN: script; Billy Wilder (as director);
Charles Lang Jnr; Jack Lemmon; art
direction

Son of Paleface*
US 1952 95m Technicolor
(Paramount) Bob Hope (Robert L. Welch)

A tenderfoot and a government agent
compete for the attentions of a lady
bandit.

Gagged-up sequel to *The Paleface;*
much of the humour now seems self-
conscious and dated in the *Road*
tradition which it apes, but there are
still moments of delight.

w Frank Tashlin, Joseph Quillan,
Robert L. Welch   *d* Frank
Tashlin   *ph* Harry J. Wild   *m* Lyn
Murray

Bob Hope, Roy Rogers, Jane Russell,
Trigger, Douglass Dumbrille, Harry
Von Zell, Bill Williams, Lloyd
Corrigan
AAN: song 'Am I in Love' (*m/ly* Jack
Brooks)

Sons of the Desert****
US 1934 68m bw
Hal Roach
V, L
GB title: *Fraternally Yours*

Stan and Ollie want to go to a Chicago
convention, but kid their wives that
they are going on a cruise for health
reasons.

Archetypal Laurel and Hardy comedy,
unsurpassed for gags, pacing and
sympathetic characterization.

w Frank Craven, Byron Morgan
d William A. Seiter   *ph* Kenneth
Peach

Stan Laurel, Oliver Hardy, Charlie Chase,
Mae Busch, Dorothy Christie

Soul Man

US 1986 101m Technicolor
Panavision
New World (Steve Tisch)
V, L

A white student tans his skin to win
a black scholarship to law school.

Despite its premise, basically a farce of
mistaken identities rather than a
treatment of racism.

w Carol Black   d Steve Miner
ph Jeffrey Jur   m Tom Scott
pd Greg Fonseca   ed David Finfer

C. Thomas Howell, Rae Dawn Chong,
Arye Gross, Melora Hardin, James B.
Sikking, Leslie Nielsen, James Earl
Jones

A Southern Yankee*

US 1948 90m bw
MGM (Paul Jones)
GB title: My Hero

During the Civil War a southern
bellboy masquerades as a spy and
finds himself behind enemy lines.

A rather feeble reworking of Buster
Keaton's The General, with some
excellent gags supervised by the
master himself.

w Harry Tugend   d Edward
Sedgwick   ph Ray June
m David Snell

Red Skelton, Brian Donlevy, Arlene
Dahl, George Coulouris, Lloyd Gough,
John Ireland, Minor Watson, Charles
Dingle

Spaceballs

US 1987 96m Metrocolor
MGM/UA (Mel Brooks, Ezra Swerdlow)
V

A ruthless race is out to steal the air
supply from the planet Druidia.

Flabby spoof of Star Wars, without any
funny ideas.

w Mel Brooks, Thomas Meehan,
Ronny Graham   d Mel Brooks
ph Nick McLean   m John
Morris   pd Terence Marsh
ed Conrad Buff IV

Mel Brooks, John Candy, Rick
Moranis, Bill Pullman, Daphne Zuniga,
Dom DeLuise, John Hurt

'At its worst, it displays a colossal ego
at work and humour better left to
home movies.' – Daily Variety

Spaced Invaders

US 1989 100m CFI
Medusa/Smart Egg Pictures (Luigi Cingolani)
V, L

A spaceship load of inept Martians
mistakenly try to conquer the Earth.

Inane spoof of the current cycle of
science fiction films.

w Patrick Read Johnson, Scott
Alexander   d Patrick Read
Johnson   ph James L. Carter
m David Russo   pd Tony
Tremblay   ed Seth Gaven, Daniel
Bross

Douglas Barr, Royal Dano, Ariana
Richards, J. J. Anderson, Gregg Berger,
Fred Applegate, Patrika Darbo

Spare a Copper*

GB 1940 77m bw
Ealing

A police war reservist catches
saboteurs.

One of the last good Formby
comedies, with everything percolating
as it should.

w Roger MacDougall, Austin
Melford, Basil Dearden   d John
Paddy Carstairs

George Formby, Dorothy Hyson,
Bernard Lee, John Warwick, John
Turnbull, George Merritt

Sparrows Can't Sing

GB 1962 94m bw
Elstree/Carthage (Donald Taylor)
V

Returning after two years at sea, a sailor searches for his wife and threatens vengeance on her lover.

Relentlessly caricatured cockney comedy melodrama, too self-conscious to be effective, and not at all likeable anyway.

w Stephen Lewis, Joan Littlewood
d Joan Littlewood   ph Mac
Greene   m James Stevens

James Booth, Barbara Windsor, Roy Kinnear, Avis Bunnage, George Sewell, Barbara Ferris, Murray Melvin, Arthur Mullard

Spies Like Us

US 1985 109m Technicolor
Warner (Brian Grazer, George Folsey Jnr)
V, L

Bumbling bureaucrats are mistakenly chosen for a spy mission.

Inept attempts at humour fall flat throughout this dreary venture, which is as though Hope and Crosby had set out on the road to Morocco without a script.

w Dan Aykroyd, Lowell Ganz, Babaloo Mandel   d John Landis
ph Robert Paynter   m Elmer Bernstein   pd Peter Murton
ed Malcolm Campbell

Chevy Chase, Dan Aykroyd, Steve Forrest, Donna Dixon, Bruce Davison, William Prince, Bernie Casey

Spite Marriage*

US 1929 77m (24 fps) bw
silent
MGM/Buster Keaton (Lawrence Weingarten)

A tailor's assistant loves an actress, who marries him to spite someone else.

For a Keaton comedy from his great period, this is remarkably thin on invention, and its pleasures, though undeniable, are minor.

w Richard Schayer, Lew Lipton
d Edward Sedgwick   ph Reggie Lanning

Buster Keaton, Dorothy Sebastian, Edward Earle, Leila Hyams

'She was the woman of his dreams. She had large dark eyes, a beautiful smile, and a great pair of fins.'

Splash!*

US 1984 110m Technicolor
Touchstone/Buena Vista (Brian Grazer)
V, L

A New York wholesaler on holiday off Cape Cod falls in love with a mermaid.

A kind of updated and mildly sexed-up *Miranda:* occasionally funny but far too long.

w Lowell Ganz, Babaloo Mandel, Bruce Jay Friedman, Brian Grazer
d Ron Howard   ph Don Peterman   m Lee Holdridge

Tom Hanks, Daryl Hannah, Eugene Levy, John Candy, Dody Goodman, Shecky Greene, Richard B. Shull, Howard Morris

'A typically Disney subject trying to be grown up.' – *Kim Newman, MFB*
'The picture is frequently on the verge of being more wonderful than it is . . . more lyrical, a little wilder.' – *Pauline Kael, New Yorker*
AAN: screenplay

'It's the business.'

Spotswood*

Australia 1991 95m colour
Feature/Meridian/Smiley (Richard Brennan,
Timothy White)

An English time-and-motion expert
investigates a ramshackle shoe factory.

Pleasant comedy in the Ealing
tradition of the little man against
uncaring bureaucracy.

w Max Dann, Andrew Knight
d Mark Joffe   ph Ellery Ryan
m Ricky Fataar   pd Chris
Kennedy   ed Nicholas Beauman

Anthony Hopkins, Ben Mendelsohn,
Alwyn Kurts, Bruno Lawrence, Angela
Punch McGregor, Russell Crowe, Toni
Colette

'Glides along with a dry wit, a keen
visual sense and a kindly heart.' – *Geoff
Brown, The Times*

Spring and Port Wine

GB 1970 101m Technicolor
EMI/Memorial (Michael Medwin)
V

A Lancashire family runs into trouble
when stern father insists that teenage
daughter should eat a meal she
refuses.

A popular old-fashioned stage
comedy which simply doesn't work
on film, partly from being set in a too-
real town (Bolton) and partly because
of a miscast lead.

w Bill Naughton   play Bill
Naughton   d Peter Hammond
ph Norman Warwick   m Douglas
Gamley   pd Reece Pemberton

James Mason, Diana Coupland, Susan
George, Rodney Bewes, Hannah
Gordon, Adrienne Posta, Arthur
Lowe

Spring in Park Lane**

GB 1948 92m bw
Imperadio/Herbert Wilcox

A diamond merchant's niece falls for
a footman who just happens to be an
impoverished lord in disguise.

Flimsy but highly successful romantic
comedy which managed to get its
balance right and is still pretty
entertaining, much more so than its
sequel *Maytime in Mayfair*.

w Nicholas Phipps,   play *Come Out of
the Kitchen* by Alice Duer Miller
d Herbert Wilcox   ph Max
Greene   m Robert Farnon

*Anna Neagle, Michael Wilding, Tom
Walls, Nicholas Phipps, Peter Graves,
Marjorie Fielding, Nigel Patrick, Lana
Morris*

'A never-failing dream of Olde
Mayfaire and its eternally funny
butlers and maids, its disguised lords
and ladies.' – *Richard Winnington*
'A gag comedy which absolutely
sparkles.' – *Picture Show*
'The best comedy any British studio
has produced for more years than I
care to remember.' – *News of the World*

The Spy with a Cold Nose

GB 1966 93m Eastmancolor
Paramount/Associated London/Embassy
(Robert Porter)

A fashionable vet is blackmailed by
MI5 into inserting a radio transmitter
into a bulldog.

Rather painful, overacted and
overwritten farce full of obvious jokes
masquerading as satire.

w Ray Galton, Alan Simpson
d Daniel Petrie   ph Kenneth
Higgins   m Riz Ortolani

*Lionel Jeffries, Laurence Harvey,
Daliah Lavi, Eric Sykes, Eric Portman,*

Colin Blakely, Denholm Elliott, Robert Flemyng, Paul Ford, Bernard Lee, June Whitfield, Bernard Archard

S*P*Y*S

GB 1974 100m Technicolor
Dymphana/C-W/American Film Properties (Irwin Winkler, Robert Chartoff)
V

Clumsy CIA agents in Paris come across a list of KGB agents in China.

Surprisingly dull and unfashionable parade of comic spy clichés; the talents involved obviously intended something closer to M*A*S*H.

w Malcolm Marmorstein, Lawrence J. Cohen, Fred Freeman　d Irwin Kershner　ph Gerry Fisher　m John Scott

Elliott Gould, Donald Sutherland, Zouzou, Joss Ackland, Kenneth Griffith, Vladek Sheybal

'Seems to have arrived several years too late to find its true niche.' – *Sight and Sound*

The Square Peg*

GB 1958 89m bw
Rank (Hugh Stewart)

An army recruit finds he is the double of a German general.

Slam-bang star slapstick, shorter than usual and with a few jokes that can't fail.

w Jack Davies　d John Paddy Carstairs　ph Jack Cox　m Philip Green

Norman Wisdom, Honor Blackman, Edward Chapman, Campbell Singer, Hattie Jacques, Brian Worth, Terence Alexander

Stage Door***

US 1937 93m bw
RKO (Pandro S. Berman)
L

Life in a New York theatrical boarding house for girls.

Melodramatic, sharply comedic, always fascinating slice of stagey life from a Broadway hit; the performances alone make it worth preserving.

w Morrie Ryskind, Anthony Veiller, play Edna Ferber, George S. Kaufman　d Gregory La Cava　ph Robert de Grasse　m Roy Webb　ad Van Nest Polglase

Katharine Hepburn, Ginger Rogers, Adolphe Menjou, Gail Patrick, Constance Collier, Andrea Leeds, Lucille Ball, Samuel S. Hinds, Jack Carson, Franklin Pangborn, Eve Arden

'It is a long time since we have seen so much feminine talent so deftly handled.' – *Otis Ferguson*
'Zest and pace and photographic eloquence.' – *Frank S. Nugent, New York Times*
'A rare example of a film substantially improving on a stage original and a remarkably satisfying film on all levels.' – *NFT, 1973*
'One of the flashiest, most entertaining comedies of the 30s, even with its tremolos and touches of heartbreak.' – *Pauline Kael, 70s*
AAN: best picture; script; Gregory La Cava; Andrea Leeds

Stand Up Virgin Soldiers

GB 1977 90m Technicolor
Warner/Greg Smith/Maidenhead

More sexual adventures of National Servicemen in Singapore in 1950.

The Virgin Soldiers had a certain

authenticity behind the fooling; this is a bawdy romp, and not a very efficient one.

w Leslie Thomas   *novel* Leslie Thomas   *d* Norman Cohen *ph* Ken Hodges   *m* Ed Welch

Nigel Davenport, Robin Askwith, George Layton, Robin Nedwell, Warren Mitchell, John Le Mesurier, Edward Woodward, Irene Handl

Star Spangled Rhythm***
US   1942   99m   bw
Paramount (Joseph Sistrom)

The doorman of Paramount Studios pretends to his sailor son that he is a big producer.

Frenetic farce involving most of the talent on Paramount's payroll and culminating in an 'impromptu' show staged for the navy. A good lighthearted glimpse of wartime Hollywood.

w Harry Tugend   *d* George Marshall   *ph* Leo Tover, Theodor Sparkuhl   *md* Robert Emmett Dolan   *songs* Johnny Mercer, Harold Arlen

Betty Hutton, Eddie Bracken, *Victor Moore*, *Walter Abel*, Anne Revere, Cass Daley, Gil Lamb, Macdonald Carey, Bob Hope, Bing Crosby, Paulette Goddard, Veronica Lake, Dorothy Lamour, Vera Zorina, Fred MacMurray, Ray Milland, Lynne Overman, Franchot Tone, Dick Powell, *Walter Dare Wahl and Co, Cecil B. de Mille*, *Preston Sturges*, Alan Ladd, Rochester, Katherine Dunham, Susan Hayward
AAN: Robert Emmett Dolan; song 'That Old Black Magic' (*m* Harold Arlen, *ly* Johnny Mercer)

Stardust Memories*
US   1980   88m   bw
UA/Jack Rollins, Charles H. Joffe
L

An increasingly melancholy comedian attends a retrospective of his work and is plagued by real and imaginary fears.

A plainly autobiographical work which, while amusing and moving in spots, makes it doubtful that the writer/director/star can even now shake off his obsessions.

wd Woody Allen   *ph* Gordon Willis   *m* Dick Hyman

Woody Allen, Charlotte Rampling, Jessica Harper, Marie-Christine Barrault, Tony Roberts, Helen Hanft

'Its posturing pyrotechnics seem more the symptom of a crisis than its controlled expression.' – *Gilbert Adair*, *MFB*

Stars and Bars
US   1988   94m   DuArt/DeLuxe
Columbia (Sandy Lieberson)
V, L

Cliché Englishman's encounters with stereotyped Americans in search for long-lost Renoir painting.

w William Boyd   *novel* William Boyd   *d* Pat O'Connor   *ph* Jerzy Zielinski   *m* Stanley Myers *pd* Leslie Dilley, Stuart Craig *ed* Michael Bradsell

Daniel Day-Lewis, Harry Dean Stanton, Martha Plimpton, Joan Cusack

'Unhappy mixture of farce and misdirected satire.' – *Variety*

Start the Revolution without Me*
US   1969   90m   Technicolor
Warner/Norbud (Norman Lear)

Two sets of twins get mixed up at the court of Louis XVI.

Historical spoof of the kind subsequently made familiar by Mel Brooks; the script might have suited Abbott and Costello better than these two actors.

w Fred Freeman, Lawrence J. Cohen   d Bud Yorkin   ph Jean Tournier   m John Addison

Donald Sutherland, Gene Wilder, Hugh Griffith, Jack McGowran, Billie Whitelaw, Victor Spinetti, Ewa Aulin

Starting Over*
US 1979 106m Movielab
Paramount/Century Associates (Alan J. Pakula, James L. Brooks)
L

A divorced man nearly goes back to his wife but finally plumps for a nursery school teacher.

Plain-speaking sex comedy-drama with accomplished stars giving rather more than the script is worth.

w James L. Brooks   novel Dan Wakefield   d Alan J. Pakula
ph Sven Nykvist   m Marvin Hamlisch   pd George Jenkins

Burt Reynolds, Jill Clayburgh, Candice Bergen, Charles Durning, Austin Pendleton
AAN: Jill Clayburgh, Candice Bergen

'The face was his ... the body was his ... but suddenly, Hello, Charlie!'
The Statue
GB 1970 89m Eastmancolor
Cinerama/Josef Shaftel (Anis Nohra)

A languages professor is embarrassed when his sculptress wife makes an immense nude statue of him – with someone else's private parts.

Strained phallic comedy which

doesn't even make the most of its one joke.

w Alec Coppel, Denis Norden
d Rod Amateau   ph Piero Portalupi   m Riz Ortolani

David Niven, Virna Lisi, Robert Vaughn, Ann Bell, John Cleese, Hugh Burden

Stay Tuned
US 1992 87m Technicolor
Warner/Morgan Creek (James G. Robinson)

A couple are trapped in a cable television system run by the Devil.

An unsuccessful send-up of obsessive television viewing, mainly because it picks targets, such as Wayne's World, that are beyond parody.

w Tom S. Parker, Jim Jennewein
d Peter Hyams   ph Peter Hyams   m Bruce Broughton
pd Philip Harrison   sp Rhythm and Hues Inc.   ed Peter E. Berger

John Ritter, Pam Dawber, Jeffrey Jones, David Thom, Heather McComb, Bob Dishy

'High class trash ... redeemed by a manic script, good special effects and production values.' – Sheila Johnston, Independent
'A picture with nothing for everybody.' – Variety

Steamboat Bill Jnr*
US 1928 71m (24 fps) bw silent
UA/Buster Keaton/Joseph Schenck

A student takes over his father's old Mississippi steamboat, and wins the daughter of his rival.

Rather flat comedy redeemed by a magnificent cyclone climax.

w Carl Harbaugh, Buster Keaton

□ [

d Charles Riesner   *ph* J.
Devereaux Jennings, Bert Haines

Buster Keaton, Ernest Torrence,
Marion Byron

Steelyard Blues

US   1972   92m   Technicolor
Warner/S. B. Productions (Tony Bill,
   Michael and Julia Phillips)

An ex-con and his call-girl friend are
an embarrassment to his DA brother.

Bits and pieces of anti-establishment
comedy are tacked on to a thin plot;
a few of them work.

w David S. Ward   *d* Alan
Myerson   *ph* Laszlo Kovacs, Steven
Larner   *m* Nick Gravenites

Donald Sutherland, Jane Fonda, Peter
Boyle, Howard Hesseman

Steptoe and Son

GB   1972   98m   Technicolor
EMI/Associated London Films (Aida Young)
V

Harold gets married, mislays his wife
but thinks he is a father.

Strained attempt to transfer the TV
rag-and-bone comedy (which in the
US became *Sanford and Son*) to the big
screen. Not the same thing at all.

w Ray Galton, Alan Simpson
d Cliff Owen   *ph* John Wilcox
m Roy Budd, Jack Fishman

Wilfrid Brambell, Harry H. Corbett,
Carolyn Seymour, Arthur Howard,
Victor Maddern

† *Steptoe and Son Ride Again*, which
followed in 1973, was even more
crude and out of character.

Sticky Fingers

US   1988   88m   DuArt
Virgin/Hightop/Spectrafilm (Catlin Adams,
   Melanie Mayron)

Two struggling musicians spend a
fortune left with them for safe
keeping by a drug dealer.

Lacklustre comedy without enough
wit to keep it alive.

w Catlin Adams, Melanie Mayron
d Catlin Adams   *ph* Gary
Thieltges   *m* Gary Chang   *ed* Bob
Reitano

Helen Slater, Melanie Mayron,
Danitra Vance, Eileen Brennan,
Carol Kane, Loretta Devine, Stephen
McHattie, Christopher Guest

'All it takes is a little confidence!'
The Sting**

US   1973   129m   Technicolor
Universal/Richard Zanuck, David Brown
   (Tony Bill, Michael S. Phillips)
V, L

In twenties Chicago, two con men
stage an elaborate revenge on a big
time gangster who caused the death
of a friend.

Bright, likeable, but overlong,
unconvincingly studio-set and casually
developed comedy suspenser cashing
in on star charisma but riding to
enormous success chiefly on its tinkly
music and the general lack of simple
entertainment.

w David S. Ward   *d George Roy
Hill*   *ph* Robert Surtees   *m* Scott
Joplin (arranged by Marvin
Hamlisch)   *ad* Henry Bumstead

Paul Newman, *Robert Redford*, Robert
Shaw, Charles Durning, Ray
Walston, Eileen Brennan

'A visually claustrophobic,
mechanically plotted movie that's
meant to be a roguishly charming
entertainment.' – *New Yorker*
'It demonstrates what can happen
when a gifted young screenwriter has
the good fortune to fall among

□ □

professionals his second time out.' –
Judith Crist

'A testament to the value of blue eyes
and bright smiles.' – *Les Keyser,
Hollywood in the Seventies*

AA: best picture; David S. Ward;
George Roy Hill; Marvin Hamlisch
AAN: Robert Surtees; Robert
Redford

Stir Crazy
US 1980 111m Metrocolor
Columbia/Hannah Weinstein
V, L

Two New Yorkers heading for
California to try their luck are
wrongly convicted of a bank robbery
but plan escape from prison.

Extended farce giving rather too free
rein to its stars' potential for mugging,
and polishing up every prison gag in
the book.

w Bruce Jay Friedman *d* Sidney
Poitier *ph* Fred Schuler *m* Tom
Scott *pd* Alfred Sweeney

Gene Wilder, Richard Pryor, George
Stanford Brown, Jobeth Williams

A Stitch in Time
GB 1963 94m bw
Rank (Hugh Stewart)

A butcher's boy goes into hospital and
falls for a nurse.

Thin star slapstick; all one can say is
that it's marginally preferable to Jerry
Lewis.

w Jack Davies *d* Robert Asher
ph Jack Asher *m* Philip Green

Norman Wisdom, Edward Chapman,
Jerry Desmonde, Jeanette Sterke, Jill
Melford

Stolen Kisses*
France 1968 91m Eastmancolor
Films du Carrosse/Artistes Associés
   (Marcel Berbert)
original title: *Baisers Volés*

An ineffective young man can find
neither work nor love.

A pleasing, rather sad little comedy
which has almost the feel of a
Keaton; but one is not quite sure at
the end what its creator intended.

w François Truffaut, Claude de
Givray, Bernard Revon *d* François
Truffaut *ph* Denys Clerval
m Antoine Duhamel

Jean-Pierre Léaud, Delphine Seyrig,
Michel Lonsdale, Claude Jade
AAN: best foreign film

The Stooge
US 1952 100m bw
Paramount/Hal B. Wallis

In 1930 a conceited song and dance
man fails to realize that his moronic
stooge is the act's real attraction.

Typical, and particularly resistible,
Martin and Lewis concoction:
whenever one thinks of laughing, a
dollop of sentimentality comes along
and promptly quashes the idea.

w Fred Finkelhoffe, Martin Rackin
d Norman Taurog *ph* Daniel L.
Fapp *m* Joseph J. Lilley

Dean Martin, Jerry Lewis, Polly
Bergen, Marie McDonald, Eddie
Mayehoff, Marion Marshall, Richard
Erdman

Stop! Or My Mom Will Shoot
US 1992 87m DeLuxe
UIP/Universal/Northern Lights (Ivan
   Reitman, Joe Medjuck, Michael C.
   Gross)
V

The mother of a Los Angeles cop helps him solve a murder and get back together with his girlfriend.

Lamentable comedy, a failed attempt to extend Stallone's narrow range.

w Blake Snyder, William Osborne, William Davies   d Roger Spottiswoode   ph Frank Tidy   m Alan Silvestri   pd Charles Rosen   ed Mark Conte, Lois Freeman-Fox

Sylvester Stallone, Estelle Getty, JoBeth Williams, Roger Rees, Martin Ferrero, Gailard Sartain, Dennis Burkley

'One of those Hollywood films in which the flimsiest of plots buckles under the most obvious of concepts.' – Lizzie Franke, Sight and Sound

Storm in a Teacup*
GB   1937   87m   bw
Alexander Korda/Victor Saville

A national sensation ensues when a Scottish provost fines an old lady for not licensing her dog, and she refuses to pay.

Early Ealing-type comedy, a bit emaciated by later standards.

w Ian Dalrymple, Donald Bull play Sturm in Wasserglass by Bruno Frank   d Ian Dalrymple, Victor Saville   ph Max Greene   m Frederic Lewis

Vivien Leigh, Rex Harrison, Cecil Parker, Sara Allgood, Ursula Jeans, Gus McNaughton, Arthur Wontner

'Dreams do come true ... sometimes.'
Straight Talk
US   1992   91m   Technicolor
Warner/Hollywood/Sandollar (Robert Chartoff, Fred Berner)

An Arkansas dance teacher goes to Chicago to become a TV agony aunt.

Mundane romantic comedy tailored to the personality of Dolly Parton.

w Craig Bolotin, Patricia Resnick   d Barnet Kellman   ph Peter Sova   m Brad Fiedel   pd Jeffrey Townsend   ed Michael Tronick

Dolly Parton, James Woods, Griffin Dunne, Michael Madsen, Deirdre O'Connell, John Sayles, Teri Hatcher, Spalding Gray, Jerry Orbach, Philip Bosco

'Glib but sunny romantic comedy ... should be a B.O. winner.' – Variety

Strange Brew
US   1983   90m   colour
MGM (Louis M. Silverstein)

Two dim-witted, beer-swilling Canadian brothers visit the Elsinore brewery in search of free drinks and, with the aid of some lunatics, thwart a plan to take over the world.

Offbeat but unamusing comedy, based on two characters from the SCTV Network television comedy series and borrowing much of its plot from Hamlet.

w Rick Moranis, Dave Thomas, Steven De Jarnatt   d Dave Thomas, Rick Moranis   ph Steven Poster   m Charles Fox   pd David L. Snyder   ed Patrick McMahon

Dave Thomas, Rick Moranis, Max Von Sydow, Paul Dooley, Lynne Griffin, Angus MacInnes, Tom Harvey, Douglas Campbell

Strictly Ballroom***
Australia   1992   94m   Eastmancolor
Rank/M&A/Australian Film Finance Corp. (Tristam Miall)
V

A would-be champion ballroom

dancer, who incurs the wrath of the establishment by improvising his own steps, searches for a new partner in tune with his ideas.

Exuberant, charming, witty romance acted and directed with style and verve.

w Baz Luhrmann, Craig Pearce play N.I.D.A. stage production devised by its original cast story Baz Luhrmann, Andrew Bovell d Baz Luhrmann ph Steve Mason m David Hirschfelder pd Catherine Martin ch John 'Cha Cha' O'Connell, Paul Mercurio ed Jill Bilcock

Paul Mercurio, Tara Morice, Bill Hunter, Pat Thomson, Gia Carides, Peter Whitford, Barry Otto, John Hannan, Sonia Kruger, Kris McQuade, Antonio Vargas, Armonia Benedito

'Bright, breezy and immensely likable musical-comedy.' – Variety

'Today's army needs men of courage – honesty – integrity – ambition. Instead, they got John Winger . . .'

Stripes
US 1981 106m Metrocolor
Columbia (Ivan Reitman, Dan Goldberg)
V, L

Sergeant Hulka tries to train a platoon of misfit volunteers.

Ancient army wheezes dressed up with fashionable black comedy and sex, but no funnier than Carry On Sergeant.

w Len Blum, Dan Goldberg, Harold Ramis d Ivan Reitman ph Bill Butler m Elmer Bernstein

Bill Murray, Harold Ramis, Warren Oates, P. J. Soles, John Larroquette, Sean Young

Stroker Ace
US 1983 96m Technicolor
  Panavision
Universal/Warner (Hank Moonjean)

A top racing car driver is sponsored by the owner of a chain of fast-food restaurants.

Tediously leering comedy, with Reynolds repeating his over-familiar role as a macho ladies' man.

w Hugh Wilson, Hal Needham novel Stand On It by William Neely, Robert K. Ottum d Hal Needham ph Nick McLean m Al Capps ad Paul Peters ed Carl Kress, William Gordean

Burt Reynolds, Ned Beatty, Jim Nabors, Parker Stevenson, Loni Anderson

The Strong Man*
US 1926 75m approx (24 fps)
  bw (colour sequence) silent
First National/Harry Langdon

A war veteran returns and searches the city for his female penfriend.

Quite charming star comedy, probably Langdon's best.

w Frank Capra, Arthur Ripley, Hal Conklin, Robert Eddy d Frank Capra ph Elgin Lessley, Glenn Kershner

Harry Langdon, Gertrude Astor, Tay Garnett

'He's an intergalactic Super Hero whose quest is to rid the Universe of evil-doers and combat the forces of darkness . . . But sometimes you gotta come down to Earth.'

Suburban Commando
US 1991 DeLuxe
Entertainment/New Line (Howard Gottfried)
V

An alien bounty-hunter takes a holiday on Earth and lodges with a suburban family.

Amiable, juvenile, low-brow comedy of no particular originality or distinction.

w Frank Capello   d Burt Kennedy   ph Patrick J. Swovelin   pd Ivo Cristante, C. J. Strawn   sp creature effects: Steve Johnson's XFX Productions   ed Sonny Baskin

Hulk Hogan, Christopher Lloyd, Shelley Duvall

'A sort of sickly lovechild of Star Wars (whose effects are reproduced on the cheap, and whose music is repeatedly plagiarized) and Kindergarten Cop.' – Adam Mars-Jones, Independent

Such Good Friends*
US 1971 102m Movielab
Paramount/Sigma (Otto Preminger)

A successful man has a mysterious illness and his wife enlists help from his friends.

Satirical parable which alternates between sex comedy and medical exposé; generally heavy-going but with good moments.

w Elaine May   novel Lois Gould   d Otto Preminger   ph Gayne Rescher   m Thomas Z. Shepherd

Dyan Cannon, James Coco, Jennifer O'Neil, Nina Foch, Laurence Luckinbill, Ken Howard, Burgess Meredith, Louise Lasser, Sam Levene, Rita Gam, Nancy Guild

Sugarbaby**
West Germany 1984 87m colour
Electric/Pelemele film/BMI/Bayerischen Rundfunks (Eleonore Adlon)
original title: Zuckerbaby

A fat woman pursues a handsome, married train driver whom she loves.

Enjoyable and witty romantic comedy.

wd Percy Adlon   ph Johanna Heer   m Dreier, Franz Erlmeier, Fritz Köstler, Paul Würges Combo   pd Matthias Heller   ed Jean-Claude Piroue

Marianne Sägebrecht, Eisi Gulp, Toni Berger, Manuela Denz, Will Spindler, Hans Stadlbauer

'There's no speed limit and no brake When Sullivan travels with Veronica Lake!'
Sullivan's Travels****
US 1941 90m bw
Paramount (Paul Jones)

A Hollywood director tires of comedy and goes out to find real life.

Marvellously sustained tragi-comedy which ranges from pratfalls to the chain gang and never loses its grip or balance.

wd Preston Sturges   ph John Seitz   m Leo Shuken

Joel McCrea, Veronica Lake, Robert Warwick, William Demarest, Franklin Pangborn, Porter Hall, Byron Foulger, Eric Blore, Robert Greig, Torben Meyer, Jimmy Conlin, Margaret Hayes
   DEDICATION: 'To all the funny men and clowns who have made people laugh.'

'A brilliant fantasy in two keys – slapstick farce and the tragedy of human misery.' – James Agee
'The most witty and knowing spoof of Hollywood movie-making of all time.' – Film Society Review
'A deftly sardonic apologia for Hollywood make-believe.' – New York Times
'Reflecting to perfection the mood of wartime Hollywood, it danced on the

grave of thirties social cinema.' – *Eileen Bowser, 1969*

Sunnyside*

US   1919   27m approx (24 fps)
  bw   silent
First National/Charles Chaplin

The overworked odd job man at a country hotel has a pastoral dream.

Very mildly funny star comedy which was intended as a satire on the D. W. Griffith/Charles Ray type of rural drama then popular. It doesn't work in this vein either.

wd Charles Chaplin   *ph* Rollie Totheroh

Charles Chaplin, Edna Purviance, Tom Wilson, Albert Austin, Henry Bergman

Sunset

US   1988   107m   Technicolor
  Panavision
Columbia/Tri-Star/ML Delphi (Tony Adams)

In Hollywood as an adviser to a studio making a film of his life, Wyatt Earp teams up with cowboy star Tom Mix to solve a murder.

A comedy-thriller that misfires.

wd Blake Edwards   *story* Rod Amateau   *ph* Anthony B. Richmond   *m* Henry Mancini
pd Rodger Maus   *ed* Robert Pergament

Bruce Willis, James Garner, Malcolm McDowell, Mariel Hemingway, Kathleen Quinlan, Jennifer Edwards, Patricia Hodge, Richard Bradford, M. Emmet Walsh, Joe Dallesandro

'For the price of a movie, you'll feel like a million!'

The Sunshine Boys*

US   1975   111m   Metrocolor
MGM/Rastar (Ray Stark)
V, L

Two feuding old vaudeville comedians come together for a television spot, and ruin it.

Over-extended sketch in which one main role is beautifully underplayed, the other hammed up, and the production lacks any kind of style. The one-liners are good, though.

w Neil Simon   *play* Neil Simon
d Herbert Ross   *ph* David M. Walsh   *md* Harry V. Lojewski

Walter Matthau, *George Burns*, Richard Benjamin, Carol Arthur

'It's just shouting, when it needs to be beautifully timed routines.' – *New Yorker*
'They feud with ill-matched resources, and the movie's visual delights vanish with the title sequence.' – *Sight and Sound*

† George Burns stepped in when Jack Benny became ill and died.

AA: George Burns
AAN: Neil Simon; Walter Matthau

Sunstruck

Australia   1972   92m
  Eastmancolor
Immigrant (Jack Neary, James Grafton)

A shy Welsh schoolmaster emigrates to the Australian outback.

Simple-minded, uninspired, predictable family comedy for star fans.

w Stan Mars   *d* James Gilbert
ph Brian West   *m* Peter Knight

Harry Secombe, Maggie Fitzgibbon, John Meillon, Dawn Lake

'The judge sentenced slumlord Louis Kritski to six months in his own building. He would have been better off in jail.'

The Super
US 1991 85m colour
Largo/JVC (Charles Gordon)
V

A New York landlord is forced to live in one of his slum properties.

A misfiring movie, comic when it should be serious, and sentimental the rest of the time.

w Sam Simon   d Rod Daniel
ph Bruce Surtees   m Miles Goodman   pd Kristi Zea   ed Jack Hofstra

Joe Pesci, Vincent Gardenia, Madolyn Smith-Osborne, Ruben Blades, Stacey Travis, Carole Shelley, Paul Benjamin

'A lesson, perhaps, that those movies that fail to get a theatrical release do, with the occasional exception, deserve the direct-to-video treatment.' – Empire

† The film was released direct to video in Britain.

The Supergrass
GB 1985 105m colour
Recorded Releasing
V

The police unwisely believe that a boaster can lead them to a drug ring.

For those who enjoy the somewhat remote satirical humour of Channel 4's The Comic Strip.

w Pete Richens, Peter Richardson
d Peter Richardson

Adrian Edmondson, Jennifer Saunders, Peter Richardson, Dawn French

Supersnooper
Italy/US 1981 94m Technicolor
Columbia/Trans-Cinema TV (Maximilian Wolkoff)
aka: Super Fuzz

A Miami cop develops superhuman powers after being exposed to radiation.

Stolid comedy with poor special effects.

w Sergio Corbucci, Sabatino Giuffini   d Sergio Corbucci
ph Silvano Ippoliti   m La Bionda   pd Marco Dentici
ed Eugene Ballaby

Terence Hill, Ernest Borgnine, Joanne Dru, Marc Lawrence, Julie Gordon, Lee Sandman

Support Your Local Gunfighter
US 1971 92m DeLuxe
UA/Cherokee/Brigade (Burt Kennedy)
V

A con man jumps a train at a small mining town and is mistaken for a dreaded gunfighter.

Disappointing sequel to the following; just a couple of good jokes.

w James Edward Grant   d Burt Kennedy   ph Harry Stradling Jnr   m Jack Elliott, Allyn Ferguson

James Garner, Suzanne Pleshette, Joan Blondell, Jack Elam, Chuck Connors, Harry Morgan, Marie Windsor, Henry Jones, John Dehner

Support Your Local Sheriff**
US 1968 92m Technicolor
UA/Cherokee (William Bowers)
V

Gold is found near a Western village, and the resulting influx of desperate characters causes problems for the sheriff.

Amusing comedy, drawing on many Western clichés.

w William Bowers d Burt Kennedy ph Harry Stradling Jnr m Jeff Alexander

James Garner, Joan Hackett, Walter Brennan, Jack Elam, Henry Morgan, Bruce Dern, Henry Jones

'It rejuvenates a stagnating genre by combining just the right doses of parody and affectionate nostalgia.' – *Jan Dawson*

Suppose They Gave a War and Nobody Came

US 1969 114m DeLuxe
Engel – Auerbach/ABC (Fred Engel)

Three accident-prone PROs try to give the army a good name in a town which wishes it would go away; they eventually cause panic by arriving at a dance in a tank.

Muddled farce which may have hoped to be satire.

w Don McGuire, Hal Captain d Hy Averback ph Burnett Guffey m Jerry Fielding

Tony Curtis, Brian Keith, Ernest Borgnine, Ivan Dixon, Suzanne Pleshette, *Tom Ewell*, Bradford Dillman, Arthur O'Connell, Robert Emhardt, John Fiedler, Don Ameche

The Sure Thing

US 1985 94m DeLuxe
Roger Birnbaum/Monument/Embassy
V, L

Two uneasy couples travel west to California for Christmas.

Slightly unsettling youth comedy which, in the form of *It Happened One Night*, seems to be saying that friendship is more important than sex.

w Steven L. Bloom, Jonathan Roberts d Rob Reiner

John Cusack, Daphne Zuniga, Anthony Edwards, Boyd Gaines, Tim Robbins, Lisa Jane Persky, Viveca Lindfors

'Two sounds clash: old wine being poured into new bottles, and familiar barrels being scraped.' – *Philip French, Observer*

Surrender

US 1987 95m TVC colour
Cannon (Aaron Spelling, Alan Greisman)

A writer with a history of unsatisfactory relationships with women falls for an artist who has had similar experiences with men.

Lacklustre attempt at a romantic comedy, taken at a snail's pace and with dialogue that fails to sparkle.

wd Jerry Belson ph Juan-Ruiz Anchia m Michel Colombier pd Lily Kilvert ed Wendy Greene Bricmont

Sally Field, Michael Caine, Steve Guttenberg, Peter Boyle, Jackie Cooper, Julie Kavner, Louise Lasser

The Survivors

US 1983 102m Metrocolor
Columbia-Delphi-Rastar-William Sackheim

An executive and a gas station attendant, both potential victims of a hit man, take refuge in the snowy mountains of Vermont.

Bewilderingly unfocused black comedy with some pleasant barbs along the way.

w Michael Leeson d Michael Ritchie ph Billy Williams m Paul Chihara pd Gene Callahan ed Richard A. Harris

Walter Matthau, Robin Williams,
Jerry Reed, James Wainwright,
Kristen Vigard, Annie McEnroe

Susan Slept Here

US 1954 98m Technicolor
RKO (Harriet Parsons)

The Hollywood scriptwriter of a film
about youth problems agrees to look
after a delinquent teenage girl.

Skittish, would-be piquant comedy;
quite unattractive.

w Alex Gottlieb   d Frank
Tashlin   ph Nicholas Musuraca
md Leigh Harline   songs Jack
Lawrence, Richard Myers

Dick Powell, Debbie Reynolds, Anne
Francis, Glenda Farrell, Alvy Moore,
Horace MacMahon
AAN: song 'Hold My Hand'

Sweet Liberty

US 1986 107m colour
Universal/Martin Bregman
L

A college professor is disgusted as he
watches the Hollywood filming of his
historical novel.

A good idea surprisingly wasted: the
plot turns to tedium before the half-
way mark.

wd Alan Alda   ph Frank Tidy
m Bruce Broughton   pd Ben
Edwards   ed Michael Economou

Alan Alda, Michael Caine, Michelle
Pfeiffer, Lillian Gish, Bob Hoskins, Saul
Rubinek, Lois Chiles, Lise Hilboldt

Swimming to Cambodia**

US 1987 87m colour
  Panavision
Mainline/Cinecom International/The
  Swimming Co (R. A. Shafransky)
V

An actor who played a bit part in The
Killing Fields reminisces about his
experiences in Thailand.

Witty and fascinating one-man show,
skilfully filmed.

w Spalding Gray   d Jonathan
Demme   ph John Bailey
m Laurie Anderson   pd Sandy
McLeod   ed Carol Littleton

Spalding Gray

Swing High Swing Low**

US 1937 97m bw
Paramount (Arthur Hornblow Jnr)

A talented trumpeter goes on a bender
but is rescued by his wife.

Backstage comedy-drama, a
beautifully cinematic version of a
very tedious story also filmed as Dance
of Life (1929) and When My Baby Smiles
at Me (1948).

w Virginia Van Upp, Oscar
Hammerstein II   play Burlesque by
George Manker Walters, Arthur
Hopkins   d Mitchell Leisen
ph Ted Tetzlaff   md Boris
Morros   m Victor Young

Carole Lombard, Fred MacMurray,
Charles Butterworth, Jean Dixon,
Dorothy Lamour, Harvey Stephens,
Franklin Pangborn, Anthony Quinn

'No reason to believe it won't jam 'em
at the gate . . . it's a cinch for the
younger trade, and will satisfy general
audience standards.' – Variety
'Enough concentrated filmcraft to fit
out half a dozen of those gentlemen
who are always dashing around in an
independent capacity making just the
greatest piece of cinema ever.' – Otis
Ferguson

The Swinger

US 1966 81m Technicolor
Paramount/George Sidney

When a girl writer's wholesome stories are rejected, she pretends to have a naughty past.

With-it comedy which audiences preferred to be without.

w Lawrence Roman   *d* George Sidney   *ph* Joseph Biroc   *m* Marty Paich

Ann-Margret, Tony Franciosa, Robert Coote, Yvonne Romain, Horace MacMahon, Nydia Westman

'A hectically saucy mixture of lechery, depravity, perversion, voyeurism and girlie magazines . . . a heavy, witless pudding.' – *MFB*

The Swissmakers
Switzerland   1978   108m
  Eastmancolor
Lyssy/Rex/Willora/Schoch/Ecco

Cases of a department investigating applicants for naturalization.

Amusing satirical comedy which presumably has more bite in its home territory.

w Rolf Lyssy and Christa Maerker *d* Rolf Lyssy

Walo Luond, Emil Steinberger, Beatrice Kessler

'For a ladykiller like Steve there was a fate worse than death: when he got to heaven they sent him back . . . with some modifications . . . It's tough being a woman in a man's world.'

Switch
US   1991   103m   Technicolor
  Panavision
Columbia TriStar/Odyssey-Regency/HBO/
  Cinema Plus/LP/Beco (Tony Adams)
V, L

Murdered by old flames, a male chauvinist is sent back to Earth as a woman and told that he can live again

if he can find a woman who likes him.

Bizarre farce that relies on the most obvious of sex-change jokes.

wd Blake Edwards   *ph* Dick Bush   *m* Henry Mancini *pd* Rodger Maus   *ed* Robert Pergament

Ellen Barkin, Jimmy Smits, JoBeth Williams, Lorraine Bracco, Tony Roberts, Perry King, Bruce Martin Payne, Lysette Anthony, Victoria Mahoney

'A talented cast is wasted on a witless script.' – *Sunday Telegraph*

Switching Channels*
US   1988   105m   colour
Rank (Martin Ransohoff)
V

A television reporter, leaving to be married, agrees to undertake one last assignment.

The third remake of *The Front Page*, this does not match the classic *His Girl Friday*, which, like this version, changed the sex of the hero, but it provides some amusement.

w Jonathan Reynolds   *play The Front Page* by Ben Hecht, Charles MacArthur   *d* Ted Kotcheff *ph* François Protat   *m* Michel Legrand   *pd* Anne Pritchard *ed* Thom Noble

Kathleen Turner, Burt Reynolds, Christopher Reeve, Ned Beatty, Henry Gibson, George Newbern, Al Waxman, Ken James

The System
GB   1964   90m   bw
British Lion/Bryanston/Kenneth Shipman
US title: *The Girl-Getters*

Seaside layabouts have a system for

collecting and sharing rich girl visitors, but one of the latter traps the leader at his own game.

Adequate sexy showcase for some looming talents; all very unattractive, but smoothly directed in a number of imitated styles.

w Peter Draper   *d Michael Winner   ph Nicolas Roeg   m* Stanley Black

Oliver Reed, Jane Merrow, Barbara Ferris, Julia Foster, Ann Lynn, Guy Doleman, Andrew Ray, David Hemmings, John Alderton, Derek Nimmo, Harry Andrews

'A modest, skilful, charming, inconsequential, and fairly dishonest little picture, to be enjoyed and deprecated in roughly equal measure.' – *John Simon*

Take Her, She's Mine*
US 1963 98m DeLuxe
Cinemascope
TCF (Henry Koster)

A lawyer protects his teenage
daughter from boys and causes.

Routine Hollywood family comedy
with some laughs and an agreeable
cast.

w Nunnally Johnson   *play* Phoebe
and Henry Ephron   *d* Henry
Koster   *ph* Lucien Ballard
m Jerry Goldsmith

James Stewart, Sandra Dee, Robert
Morley, Audrey Meadows, Philippe
Forquet, John McGiver

Take the Money and Run
US 1968 85m Technicolor
Palomar (Charles H. Joffe)
V, L

A social misfit becomes a bungling
crook.

A torrent of middling visual gags, not
the star's best vehicle.

wd Woody Allen   *ph* Lester
Shorr   *m* Marvin Hamlisch

Woody Allen, Janet Margolin, Marcel
Hillaire

Taking Care of Business
US 1990 108m Technicolor

Warner/Hollywood Pictures/Silver Screen
Partners IV (Geoffrey Taylor)
V, L
GB title: *Filofax*

A thief assumes the identity of an
advertising executive whose Filofax he
acquires.

Slow-moving comedy that fails to get
much mileage from its tired central
idea.

w Jill Mazursky, Jeffrey Abrams
d Arthur Hiller   *ph* David M.
Walsh   *m* Stewart Copeland
pd Jon Hutman   *ed* William
Reynolds

James Belushi, Charles Grodin, Anne
DeSalvo, Loryn Locklin, Stephen
Elliott, Hector Elizondo, Veronica
Hamel

'Hiller brings his usual dogged
persistence to bear, but it would take
an alchemist's touch to turn *Filofax*
into comic gold.' – *Geoff Brown, Sight
and Sound*

Taking Off**
US 1971 92m Movielab
Universal (Alfred W. Crown, Michael
Hausman)

Suburban parents seek their errant
daughter among the hippies, and
gradually lose their own inhibitions.

Slight, formless, but amusing revue-style comment by a Czech director on the American scene.

w Milos Forman, John Guare, Jean-Claude Carrière, John Klein d Milos Forman ph Miroslav Ondricek

Lynn Carlin, Buck Henry, Linnea Heacock

The Talk of the Town***
US 1942 118m bw
Columbia (George Stevens, Fred Guiol)
V, L

A girl loves both a suspected murderer and the lawyer who defends him.

Unusual mixture of comedy and drama, delightfully handled by three sympathetic stars.

w Irwin Shaw, Sidney Buchman d George Stevens ph Ted Tetzlaff m Frederick Hollander ad Lionel Banks, Rudolph Sternad ed Otto Meyer

Ronald Colman, Cary Grant, Jean Arthur, Edgar Buchanan, Glenda Farrell, Charles Dingle, Emma Dunn, Rex Ingram

'A rip-roaring, knock-down-and-drag-out comedy about civil liberties.' – John T. McManus
'Well tuned and witty, at its best when it sticks to the middle ground between farce and melodrama. The chief fault of the script is its excessive length and the fact that a standard lynching mob climax is followed by a prolonged anti-climax.' – Newsweek
'I can't take my lynching so lightly, even in a screwball. Still, I am all for this kind of comedy and for players like Arthur and Grant, who can mug more amusingly than most scriptwriters can write.' – Manny Farber
'Did the authors think they were writing a Shavian comedy of ideas? The ideas are garbled and silly, but the people are so pleasant that the picture manages to be quite amiable and high-spirited.' – Pauline Kael, 70s
'I knew it was going to come off all along: it didn't have that element of hazard in it. It was more of an understood flight with a take-off time and an arrival time and not too much headwind.' – George Stevens

† Two endings were filmed: the eventual choice of mate for Miss Arthur was determined by audience reaction at previews.
AAN: best picture; original story (Sidney Harmon); script; Ted Tetzlaff; Frederick Hollander; art direction; Otto Meyer

The Tall Guy
GB 1989 92m Eastmancolor
Virgin/LWT/Working Title (Tim Bevan)
V, L

The stooge to a sadistic comedian tries for stardom on his own.

Lamentably unfunny comedy, ponderously directed.

w Richard Curtis d Mel Smith ph Adrian Biddle m Peter Brewis pd Grant Hicks ed Dan Rae

Jeff Goldblum, Emma Thompson, Rowan Atkinson, Geraldine James, Emil Wolk, Kim Thomson, Harold Innocent, Anna Massey

Tall Story
US 1960 91m bw
Warner/Mansfield (Joshua Logan)
L

A college basketball player faces various kinds of trouble when he marries.

Dislikeable campus comedy with leading players miscast.

w Julius J. Epstein novel The

Homecoming Game by Howard
Nemoor   *d* Joshua Logan
ph Ellsworth Fredericks   *m* Cyril
Mockridge

Anthony Perkins, Jane Fonda, Ray
Walston, Anne Jackson, Marc
Connelly, Murray Hamilton,
Elizabeth Patterson

Tamahine

GB   1962   95m   Technicolor
    Cinemascope
ABP (John Bryan)

The headmaster of a boys' school is
visited by his glamorous half-caste
Polynesian cousin.

Simple-minded school comedy with
predictable situations.

w Denis Cannan   *novel* Thelma
Niklaus   *d* Philip Leacock
ph Geoffrey Unsworth   *m* Malcolm
Arnold

John Fraser, Nancy Kwan, Dennis
Price, Derek Nimmo, Justine Lord,
James Fox, Coral Browne, Michael
Gough, Allan Cuthbertson

The Taming of the Shrew*

US   1929   68m   bw
United Artists/Pickford/Elton

A condensed version of the play
which did not do much in its day for
its stars' then declining reputations,
but can now be watched with a fair
measure of enjoyment.

w William Shakespeare, 'with
additional dialogue by Sam
Taylor'   *d* Sam Taylor   *ph* Karl
Struss   *pd* William Cameron
Menzies, Laurence Irving

Douglas Fairbanks, Mary Pickford,
Edwin Maxwell, Joseph Cawthorn,
Clyde Cook, Dorothy Jordan

† A 'widescreen' version was issued in
1976.

'In the war between the sexes, there
always comes a time to surrender
unconditionally!'

The Taming of the Shrew*

US   1967   122m   Technicolor
    Panavision
Columbia/Royal/FAI (Richard McWhorter)
V, L

Petruchio violently tames his
shrewish wife.

Busy version of one of Shakespeare's
more proletarian comedies; the
words in this case take second place
to violent action and rioting colour.

w Suso Cecchi d'Amico, Paul Dehn,
Franco Zeffirelli   *d* Franco
Zeffirelli   *ph* Oswald Morris,
Luciano Trasatti   *m* Nino Rota

Richard Burton, Elizabeth Taylor,
Michael York, Michael Hordern,
Cyril Cusack, Alfred Lynch, Natasha
Pyne, Alan Webb, Victor Spinetti

'As entertainment *Kiss Me Kate* is
infinitely better but then Cole Porter
was a real artist and Burton is a
culture vulture.' – *Wilfrid Sheed*
'The old warhorse of a comedy has
been spanked into uproarious life.' –
Hollis Alpert

Tampopo**

Japan   1986   117m   colour
    Panavision
Itami Productions/New Century Producers
    (Juzo Itami, Yashushi Tamaoki, Seigo
    Hosogoe)
V, L

Encouraged by a truck driver, a
woman learns to become the best of
noodle cooks.

Witty, affectionate, episodic
celebration of food as nourishment,

pleasure and aid to sexual enjoyment, contained within a parody of film genres, notably the Western.

wd Juzo Itami *ph* Masaki Tamura *m* Kinihiko Murai *ad* Takeo Kimura *ed* Akira Suzuki

Tsutomu Yamazaki, Nobuko Miyamoto, Koji Yakuso, Ken Watanabe, Rikiya Yasouka

'You haven't met her yet and she already hates you.'
Tatie Danielle**
France 1990 112m colour
Palace/Téléma/FR3/Les Productions du
  Champ Poirer/Sofica (Charles Gassot)
V, L

A malicious elderly woman creates problems when she moves in with her nephew's family.

Sharp and enjoyable black comedy.

w Florence Quentin *d* Etienne Chatillez *ph* Philippe Welt *m* Gabriel Yared *pd* Geoffroy Larcher *ed* Catherine Renault

Tsilla Chelton, Catherine Jacob, Isabelle Nanty, Neige Dolsky, Eric Pratt, Laurence Février, Virgine Pradal

'A tart comedy providing welcome Gallic relief to the saccharine Hollywood-endorsed stereotypes of the elderly as armchair dispensers of love and bromides.' — *Variety*

Teachers
US 1984 106m Metrocolor
MGM-UA (Aaron Russo)

A burnt-out teacher is drawn back to his ideas despite, or because of, apparent lunacy in the administration.

Wildly unconsidered black comedy which takes stabs at everything and hits nothing.

w W. R. McKinney *d* Arthur Hiller *ph* David M. Walsh *m* Sandy Gibson *pd* Richard MacDonald *ed* Don Zimmermann

Nick Nolte, JoBeth Williams, Judd Hirsch, Ralph Macchio, Richard Mulligan, Allen Garfield, Royal Dano

Teacher's Pet*
US 1958 120m bw Vistavision
Paramount/Perlberg-Seaton (William Perlberg)

A tough city editor falls for a lady professor of journalism and enrols as a student.

Overlong one-joke comedy which quickly reneges on its early promise; but the principals play up divertingly.

w Fay and Michael Kanin *d* George Seaton *ph* Haskell Boggs *m* Roy Webb

Clark Gable, Doris Day, Gig Young, Mamie Van Doren, Nick Adams
AAN: Fay and Michael Kanin; Gig Young

The Teahouse of the August Moon*
US 1956 123m Metrocolor
  Cinemascope
MGM (Jack Cummings)

Okinawa 1944: a wily interpreter helps American troops succumb to the oriental way of life.

Adequate, well-acted screen version of a Broadway comedy which succeeded largely because of its theatricality. A few good jokes remain.

w John Patrick *play* John Patrick *d* Daniel Mann *ph* John Alton *m* Saul Chaplin

Marlon Brando, Glenn Ford, Eddie Albert, *Paul Ford,* Michiko Kyo, Henry Morgan

'Just when he thought it was safe to go back in the water...'

'10'

US 1979 122m Metrocolor
Panavision
Warner/Orion/Geoffrey (Blake Edwards, Tony Adams)
V, L

A sex-mad middle-aged composer marks his girls from one to ten according to their performance.

Randy farce which struck some, but not all, audiences as the funniest thing since sliced bread.

wd Blake Edwards   *ph* Frank Stanley   *m* Henry Mancini
pd Rodger Maus

Dudley Moore, Julie Andrews, Bo Derek, Robert Webber, Dee Wallace, Sam Jones
AAN: Henry Mancini; song 'It's Easy to Say' (*m* Henry Mancini, *ly* Robert Wells)

The Tender Trap*

US 1955 111m Eastmancolor
Cinemascope
MGM (Lawrence Weingarten)

A smart New York agent has a way with women which annoys his friend; but Casanova gets his come-uppance when he sets his sights on an apparently naïve young actress.

Thin comedy with agreeable moments, not helped by the wide screen.

w Julius J. Epstein   *play* Max Shulman, Robert Paul Smith
d Charles Walters   *ph* Paul Vogel   *m* Jeff Alexander

Frank Sinatra, Debbie Reynolds, David Wayne, Celeste Holm, Lola Albright, Carolyn Jones
AAN: title song (*m* James Van Heusen, *ly* Sammy Cahn)

Tenue de Soirée*

France 1986 85m
Eastmancolor   Panavision
Hachette Première/DD Productions/Cine Valse/Philippe Dussart
GB title: *Evening Dress*

A husky burglar seduces the puny husband of a couple he involves in his criminal activities.

Anti-bourgeois comedy that tries too hard to be outrageous. Michel Blanc won the award for best actor at the Cannes Film Festival in 1986 for his performance as the timid husband.

wd Bertrand Blier   *ph* Jean Penzer   *m* Serge Gainsbourg
pd Theobald Meurisse   *ed* Claudine Merlin

Gérard Depardieu, Michel Blanc, Miou-Miou, Michel Creton, Jean-François Stevenin, Mylène Demongeot, Caroline Sihol, Jean-Yves Berteloot, Bruno Cremer

That Certain Feeling

US 1956 102m Technicolor
Vistavision
Paramount (Melvin Frank, Norman Panama)

An arrogant comic strip artist loses his touch and hires a 'ghost' – the ex-husband of his secretary/fiancée.

Arid comedy from a mild Broadway play, totally miscast and lacking any kind of interest.

w Norman Panama, Melvin Frank, I. A. L. Diamond, William Altman
play King of Hearts by Jean Kerr, Eleanor Brooke   *d* Norman Panama, Melvin Frank   *ph* Loyal Griggs
m Joseph J. Lilley

Bob Hope, George Sanders, Eva Marie Saint, Pearl Bailey, Al Capp

'When A No No Girl Meets A Go Go Man
– Wham!!!'

That Lucky Touch
GB   1975   93m   Technicolor
Rank/Gloria (Dimitri de Grunwald)

During NATO war games in Brussels,
a lady correspondent falls for an arms
dealer.

Dim romantic farce which gives the
impression of emanating from a dog-
eared script written for the kind of
stars who no longer shine.

w John Briley   story Moss Hart
d Christopher Miles   ph Douglas
Slocombe   m John Scott

Roger Moore, Susannah York, Lee J.
Cobb, Shelley Winters, Jean-Pierre
Cassel, Raf Vallone, Sydne Rome,
Donald Sinden

That Touch of Mink**
US   1962   99m   Eastmancolor
  Panavision
U-I/Granley/Arwin/Nob Hill (Stanley
  Shapiro, Martin Melcher)
V

Bachelor tycoon pursues virginal
secretary.

Jaded sex comedy (or what passed for
it in nudge-nudge 1962) enlivened
by practised star performances and
smart timing.

w Stanley Shapiro, Nate Monaster
d Delbert Mann   ph Russell
Metty   m George Duning

Cary Grant, Doris Day, Gig Young, Audrey
Meadows, Dick Sargent, John Astin

'Too often there's a hampering
second-hand air about situation and
joke. Throughout, the determination
is to keep faith with the American sex
mythology at all costs.' – Jack Pitman,
Variety
AAN: script

That Uncertain Feeling*
US   1941   84m   bw
UA/Sol Lesser (Ernst Lubitsch)

A wife with insomnia and hiccups
befriends a wacky concert pianist
who proceeds to move into her home.

Although Lubitsch had made this
story before, as the silent Kiss Me Again,
the elements didn't really jell in this
version, which seemed silly rather
than funny.

w Donald Ogden Stewart, Walter
Reisch   play Divorçons by Victorien
Sardou, Emile de Najac   d Ernst
Lubitsch   ph George Barnes
m Werner Heymann
pd Alexander Golitzen

Merle Oberon, Melvyn Douglas,
Burgess Meredith, Alan Mowbray,
Olive Blakeney, Harry Davenport, Eve
Arden, Sig Rumann

'Gay entertainment.' – Picture Show
AAN: Werner Heymann

'Boy! do we need it now!'
That's Entertainment**
US   1974   137m   Metrocolor
  70mm (blown up)/scope
MGM (Daniel Melnick, Jack Haley Jnr)
V, L

Fred Astaire, Gene Kelly, Elizabeth
Taylor, James Stewart, Bing Crosby,
Liza Minnelli, Donald O'Connor,
Debbie Reynolds, Mickey Rooney
and Frank Sinatra introduce
highlights from MGM's musical past.

A slapdash compilation which was
generally very big at the box-office
and obviously has fascinating
sequences, though the narration is
sloppily sentimental and the later
wide-screen sequences let down the
rest.

wd Jack Haley Jnr   ph various
m various

Principal stars as above plus Judy Garland, Esther Williams, Eleanor Powell, Clark Gable, Ray Bolger

'While many ponder the future of MGM, none can deny that it has one hell of a past.' – *Variety*
'It is particularly gratifying to get the key sequences from certain movies without having to sit through a fatuous storyline.' – *Michael Billington, Illustrated London News*
'No other film in town offers such a harvest of undiluted joy.' – *Sunday Express*

That's Entertainment Part Two**
US 1976 133m Metrocolor
70mm (blown up)/scope
MGM (Saul Chaplin, Daniel Melnick)
V, L

More of the above, introduced by Fred Astaire and Gene Kelly, with comedy and drama sequences as well as musical. *d* Gene Kelly *titles* Saul Bass *ph* various

Principal stars as above plus Jeanette MacDonald, Nelson Eddy, the Marx Brothers, Laurel and Hardy, Jack Buchanan, Judy Garland, Ann Miller, Mickey Rooney, Oscar Levant, Louis Armstrong, etc

That's Life!
US 1986 102m DeLuxe
Panavision
Columbia/Paradise Cove/Ubilam (Tony Adams)

An architect touching sixty, with a sick wife, pours out all his fears of old age and mortality.

Blake Edwards exposing himself again; the movie was even shot in his own house. Somewhat embarrassing to watch, and overwrought, it does have a few good moments.

w Milton Wexler, Blake Edwards

d Blake Edwards *ph* Anthony Richmond *m* Henry Mancini

Jack Lemmon, Julie Andrews, Sally Kellerman, Robert Loggia, Jennifer Edwards
AAN: song 'Life in a Looking Glass' (Mancini, Leslie Bricusse)

That's My Wife*
US 1929 20m bw silent
Hal Roach

Stan dresses up as Ollie's wife to impress his rich uncle.

Lesser-known star comedy which well sustains its basic joke and includes some splendidly timed farce in a restaurant.

w Leo McCarey, H. M. Walker *d* Lloyd French

Laurel and Hardy, Vivien Oakland, William Courtright

Theatre Royal
GB 1943 92m bw
British National

A revue and a theatre are saved by a sentimental prop man.

Shapeless star comedy with music; not their best.

w Bud Flanagan, Austin Melford, Geoffrey Orme *d* John Baxter

Bud Flanagan and Chesney Allen, Peggy Dexter, Lydia Sherwood, Horace Kenney, Marjorie Rhodes, Finlay Currie

Their First Mistake**
US 1932 20m bw
Hal Roach
V

Ollie decides to improve his marriage by adopting a baby, only to find that his wife has left him.

Sublimely silly but endearing star comedy with brilliant passages of imbecilic conversation followed by well-timed farce.

w H. M. Walker *d* George Marshall (who also plays a bit)

Laurel and Hardy, Mae Busch

Their Purple Moment
US 1928 20m bw silent
Hal Roach

Stan and Ollie go out on the town, only to discover that Stan's wife has replaced his money with grocery coupons.

Minor star comedy with efficient but predictable restaurant scenes ending in a pie fight.

w H. M. Walker *d* James Parrott

Laurel and Hardy, Anita Garvin, Kay Deslys

Themroc**
France 1972 110m Eastmancolor
The Other Cinema/Filmanthrope/FDL (Jean-Claude Bourlat)

A depressed worker in a dead-end job suddenly breaks free of all his restrictions, making love to his sister and demolishing the walls of his apartment.

An exuberant anti-authoritarian comedy, in which normal dialogue is replaced by an invented language of grunts and whistles.

wd Claude Faraldo *ph* Jean-Marc Ripert *ad* C. Lamarque *ed* Noun Serra

Michel Piccoli, Béatrice Romand, Marilu Tolo, Francesca R. Coluzzi, Patrick Dewaere, Miou-Miou

'Succeeds in being poetic without being arty and, by using laughter as a critical tactic, in suggesting that revolution in a puritanical society ought to take a hedonistic form.' – *Jan Dawson, MFB*

There Goes the Bride
GB 1980 91m Eastmancolor
Lonsdale (Martin Schute, Ray Cooney)
V

A harassed advertising executive suffers hallucinations about a lifesize cardboard cut-out of a twenties flapper.

Embarrassingly witless and plotless revamp of innumerable better comedies in the Topper tradition; it has to be seen to be believed.

w Terence Marcel, Ray Cooney
play Ray Cooney, John Chapman
d Terence Marcel *ph* James
Devis *m* Harry Robinson
pd Peter Mullins

Tom Smothers, Twiggy, Sylvia Syms, Martin Balsam, Michael Whitney, Geoffrey Sumner, Hermione Baddeley, Phil Silvers, Broderick Crawford, Jim Backus

'The whole thing would be laughable if it weren't so unfunny.' – *Gilbert Adair, MFB*

There Was a Crooked Man*
GB 1960 107m bw
UA/Knightsbridge (John Bryan)

An ex-safecracker outwits the crooked mayor of an industrial town.

Semi-happy attempt to humanize a knockabout clown; good supporting performances and production.

w Reuben Ship *d* Stuart Burge
ph Arthur Ibbetson *m* Kenneth V. Jones

Norman Wisdom, Andrew

Cruickshank, Alfred Marks, Susanna York, Reginald Beckwith

There Was a Crooked Man*
US 1970 126m Technicolor
Panavision
Warner Seven Arts (Joseph L. Mankiewicz)
L

In 1883 Arizona a murderer tries to escape from jail and recover hidden loot but is constantly thwarted by the sheriff who arrested him, now a warden.

Curious black comedy melodrama with lots of talent going nowhere in particular; hard to endure as a whole but with entertaining scenes.

w David Newman, Robert Benton
d Joseph L. Mankiewicz   ph Harry
Stradling Jnr   m Charles Strouse
ad Edward Carrere

Kirk Douglas, Henry Fonda, Hume Cronyn, Warren Oates, Burgess Meredith, John Randolph, Arthur O'Connell, Martin Gabel, Alan Hale

'This example of commercialized black comedy nihilism seems to have been an evil two-year-old, and it has been directed in the Grand Rapids style of moviemaking.' – *Pauline Kael, New Yorker*

There's a Girl in My Soup*
GB 1970 96m Eastmancolor
Columbia/Ascot (John Boulting)
V

A randy TV personality finds himself outplotted by a waif he picks up.

Flimsy screen version of a long-running sex comedy; some laughs, but the star is uncomfortably miscast.

w Terence Frisby   play Terence
Frisby   d Roy Boulting
ph Harry Waxman   m Mike D'Abo

Peter Sellers, Goldie Hawn, Tony Britton, Nicky Henson, John Comer, Diana Dors, Judy Campbell

They All Laughed*
US 1982 115m Movielab
Time-Life/Moon (George Morfogen, Blaine Novak)

Three agency detectives fall in and out of love in the course of their duties.

It has the air of a somewhat misshapen and Americanized *La Ronde*, with added suggestions of *On the Town*, but it adds up to very little and provides only a few laughs on the way.

wd Peter Bogdanovich   ph Robby
Muller   m various

Audrey Hepburn, Ben Gazzara, John Ritter, Dorothy Stratten, Colleen Camp, Patti Hansen, George Morfogen, Blaine Novak

'One tires of long looks that speak volumes, of endless successions of meeting cute.' – *John Pym, MFB*

They Go Boom
US 1929 20m bw
Hal Roach

Stan's nocturnal efforts to cure Ollie's cold nearly bring down the house about their ears.

Average, rather protracted star comedy.

w Leo McCarey, H. M. Walker
d James Parrott

Laurel and Hardy, Charlie Hall

They Got Me Covered*
US 1943 93m bw
Samuel Goldwyn

An incompetent foreign correspondent inadvertently breaks up a spy ring in Washington.

One of Hope's better and most typical comedy-thriller vehicles.

w Harry Kurnitz   d David Butler   ph Rudolph Maté   m Leigh Harline

Bob Hope, Dorothy Lamour, Otto Preminger, Lenore Aubert, Eduardo Ciannelli, Marion Martin, Donald Meek, Donald MacBride, Walter Catlett, John Abbott, Florence Bates, Philip Ahn

The Thief Who Came to Dinner
US   1973   105m   DeLuxe
Warner/Tandem (Bud Yorkin)

A computer analyst determines to become a jewel thief.

Tedious comedy aping the *Raffles* school but saddled with a complex plot and listless script.

w Walter Hill   novel Terence L. Smith   d Bud Yorkin   ph Philip Lathrop   m Henry Mancini

Ryan O'Neal, Jacqueline Bisset, Warren Oates, Jill Clayburgh, Charles Cioffi

Things Are Tough All Over
US   1982   92m   Metrocolor
Panavision
Columbia/C & C Brown (Howard Brown)
V, L

Two layabouts are hired by Arabs to drive a limousine containing five million dollars to Las Vegas.

Dire and inane comedy, full of racist jokes.

w Cheech Marin, Tommy Chong   d Thomas K. Avildsen   ph Bobby Byrne   m Gaye Delorme   pd Richard Tom Sawyer   ed Dennis Dolan

Richard 'Cheech' Marin, Tommy Chong, Shelby Fields, Rikki Marin, Evelyn Guerrero, John Steadman, Rip Taylor

Things Change**
US   1988   100m   DuArt
Columbia TriStar/Filmhaus (Michael Hausman)
V, L

An incompetent crook is given the task of guarding for a week an elderly shoemaker who has agreed to go to jail in place of the leading gangster he resembles.

Gently comic anecdote, delicately played.

w David Mamet, Shel Silverstein   d David Mamet   ph Juan Ruiz Anchia   m Alaric Jans   pd Michael Merritt   ed Trudy Ship

Don Ameche, Joe Mantegna, Robert Prosky, J. J. Johnston, Ricky Jay, Mike Nussbaum, Jack Wallace, Dan Conway

Thirty Is a Dangerous Age, Cynthia
GB   1967   84m   Technicolor
Columbia/Walter Shenson

A timid night-club pianist has trouble with women but sells his first musical.

Mild star vehicle for a very mild star, basically a few thin sketches, frantically overdirected.

w Dudley Moore, Joe McGrath, John Wells   d Joe McGrath   ph Billy Williams   m Dudley Moore   titles Richard Williams

Dudley Moore, Eddie Foy Jnr, Suzy Kendall, John Bird, Duncan Macrae, Patricia Routledge, John Wells

This Happy Feeling
US   1958   92m   Eastmancolor
Cinemascope
U-I (Ross Hunter)

An ageing actor is invigorated by a mild affair with his secretary.

Flat romantic comedy: the bubbles obstinately refuse to rise.

wd Blake Edwards *play For Love or Money* by F. Hugh Herbert
ph Arthur E. Arling *m* Frank Skinner

Curt Jurgens, Debbie Reynolds, John Saxon, Alexis Smith, *Mary Astor, Estelle Winwood*

'It's 10 p.m. Do you know where your mother is?'

This Is My Life**
US 1992 94m DeLuxe
TCF (Lynda Obst)

A mother with two young daughters tries to make it as a stand-up comedian.

Sharply observed movie with a tough comic edge about the problems and conflicts between daughters and a working mother.

w Nora Ephron, Delia Ephron
novel This Is Your Life by Meg Wolitzer *d* Nora Ephron
ph Bobby Byrne *m* Carly Simon *pd* David Chapman
ed Robert Reitano

Julie Kavner, Samantha Mathis, Gaby Hoffman, Carrie Fisher, Dan Aykroyd, Bob Nelson, Marita Geraghty

'Intimate, honestly rendered film looks likely to score some emotional points with the working parents it speaks to, but a funny but frank teen sex scene may somewhat erode its potential as family fare.' – *Variety*
'Woefully unfunny. If comedy is all about timing then Ephron's directorial watch needs winding.' – *Stephen Amidon, Financial Times*

This Is Spinal Tap**
US 1984 82m CFI colour
Mainline/Embassy (Karen Murphy)
V, L

Adventures of a British heavy metal rock group on tour in America.

Witty, wickedly accurate satire that skewers the pretensions of rock musicians and their hangers-on, done in documentary style.

w Christopher Guest, Michael McKean, Harry Shearer, Rob Reiner *d* Rob Reiner *ph* Peter Smokler *m* Christopher Guest, Michael McKean, Harry Shearer, Rob Reiner *pd* Dryan Jones
ed Robert Leighton

Christopher Guest, Michael McKean, Harry Shearer, Rob Reiner, R. J. Parnell, David Kaff, Tony Hendra, Bruno Kirby

This Thing Called Love*
US 1941 98m bw
Columbia (William Perlberg)
GB title: *Married But Single*

A lady executive insists on proving that marriage is best if the partners start out just good friends.

Amusing comedy which at the time seemed a little saucy, and got itself banned by the Legion of Decency.

w George Seaton, Ken Englund, P. J. Wolfson *d* Alexander Hall
ph Joseph Walker *md* Morris Stoloff *m* Werner Heyman

Rosalind Russell, Melvyn Douglas, Binnie Barnes, Allyn Joslyn, Gloria Dickson, Lee J. Cobb, Gloria Holden, Don Beddoe

'One of those laborious forties comedies in which the independent-minded woman has no common sense.' – *New Yorker, 1979*

Thoroughly Modern Millie*

US   1967   138m   Technicolor
Universal (Ross Hunter)

In the twenties, a young girl comes to
New York, becomes thoroughly
modern, falls for her boss, and has
various adventures unmasking a
white slave racket centring on a
Chinese laundry.

Initially most agreeable but
subsequently very patchy spoof of
twenties fads and films, including a
Harold Lloyd thrill sequence which
just doesn't work and a comedy
performance from Beatrice Lillie
which does. Tunes and performances
are alike variable.

w Richard Morris   d George Roy
Hill   ph *Russell Metty*   md André
Previn, Joseph Gershenson   ch Joe
Layton   *songs* various   m Elmer
Bernstein   ad Alexander Golitzen,
George Webb

Julie Andrews, Mary Tyler Moore, *John
Gavin*, James Fox, Carol Channing,
Beatrice Lillie, Jack Soo, Pat Morita,
Anthony Dexter

'What a nice 65-minute movie is
buried therein!' – *Judith Crist*

AA: Elmer Bernstein
AAN: André Previn, Joseph
Gershenson; title song (m James Van
Heusen, ly Sammy Cahn); Carol
Channing

Those Daring Young Men in Their Jaunty Jalopies

US/Italy/France   1969   125m
   Technicolor   Panavision
Paramount/Dino de Laurentiis/Marianne
   (Ken Annakin, Basil Keys)
V
GB title: Monte Carlo or Bust

Accidents befall various competitors
in the Monte Carlo Rally.

Rough-edged imitation of *The Great
Race* and *Those Magnificent Men in Their
Flying Machines*, much feebler than
either but with the waste of a big
budget well in evidence.

w Jack Davies, Ken Annakin
d Ken Annakin   ph Gabor
Pogany   m Ron Goodwin

Peter Cook, Dudley Moore, Tony
Curtis, Bourvil, Walter Chiari, Terry-
Thomas, Gert Frobe, Susan
Hampshire, Jack Hawkins, Eric Sykes

Those Endearing Young Charms

US   1945   81m   bw
RKO

An air corps mechanic loves a
shopgirl.

Nothing to remember about this light
star time-passer.

w Jerome Chodorov   *play* Edward
Chodorov   d Lewis Allen

Robert Young, Laraine Day, Bill
Williams, Ann Harding, Marc
Cramer, Anne Jeffries

'Well played, well directed, and not
quite interesting enough to be worth
the time it takes.' – *James Agee*

Those Magnificent Men in Their Flying Machines, or How I Flew from London to Paris in 25 hours and 11 Minutes**

GB   1965   133m   Technicolor
   Todd-AO
TCF (Stan Marguilies, Jack Davies)
V, L

In 1910, a newspaper owner sponsors
a London to Paris air race.

Long-winded, generally agreeable
knockabout comedy with plenty to
look at but far too few jokes to sustain
it.

w Jack Davies, Ken Annakin   d Ken

Annakin   ph Christopher Challis
m Ron Goodwin   pd Tom Morahan

Sarah Miles, Stuart Whitman, Robert
Morley, Eric Sykes, Terry-Thomas,
James Fox, Alberto Sordi, Gert Frobe,
Jean-Pierre Cassel, Karl Michael
Vogler, Irina Demich, Benny Hill,
Flora Robson, Sam Wanamaker, Red
Skelton, Fred Emney, Cicely
Courtneidge, Gordon Jackson, John
Le Mesurier, Tony Hancock, William
Rushton

'There is many a likely gag, but none
that survives the second or third
reprise. It could have been a good bit
funnier by being shorter: the winning
time is 25 hours 11 minutes, and by
observing some kind of neo-
Aristotelian unity the film seems to
last exactly as long.' – *John Simon*
AAN: script

Those Were the Days*
GB   1934   80m   bw
BIP (Walter C. Mycroft)

In the nineties, a magistrate seeks
out his teenage stepson in a music
hall.

Lively comedy which is valuable as
giving the screen's best re-creation of
an old-time music hall.

*w Fred Thompson, Frank Miller,
Frank Launder, Jack Jordan
play The Magistrate* by Arthur Wing
Pinero   *d Thomas Bentley
ph Otto Kanturek   md Idris Lewis*

Will Hay, John Mills, Iris Hoey,
Angela Baddeley, Claud Allister,
George Graves, Jane Carr, H. F.
Maltby

† Music hall acts include Gaston and
Andrée, Lily Morris, G. H. Elliott, Sam
Curtis, Frank Boston and Betty

A Thousand Clowns*
US   1965   115m   bw
UA/Harell (Fred Coe)

A New Yorker who has abdicated
from work leads a cheerful, useless
life with his young nephew, but the
school board have their doubts.

Imitative nonconformist comedy with
frequent reminiscences of older, better
plays such as *You Can't Take It with
You.* Good lines occasionally make
themselves felt, but the overall effect
is patchy, the lead is miscast, and the
location montages only emphasize the
basic one-room set.

w Herb Gardner,   play Herb
Gardner   *d* Fred Coe   *ph* Arthur
J. Ornitz   *m* Don Walker

Jason Robards, Martin Balsam, Barry
Gordon, Barbara Harris, *William
Daniels,* Gene Saks

AA: Martin Balsam
AAN: best picture; Herb Gardner; Don
Walker

The Three Ages*
US   1923   80m approx   bw
   silent
Joseph Schenck/Metro

Three stories parodying Griffith's
Intolerance.

The star's first feature film, not his
strongest, is saved by the final chases.

*w Clyde Bruckman, Jean Havez,
Joseph Mitchell   d* Buster Keaton,
Eddie Cline

Buster Keaton, Wallace Beery,
Margaret Leahy, Joe Roberts

Three Amigos
US   1986   105m   Technicolor
Orion (Lorne Michaels, George Folsey Jr)
V

Three wimpish cowboy stars find

themselves hired to defend a desert town from a bandit.

Weak take-off of *The Magnificent Seven*, with performances that grate.

w Steve Martin, Lorne Michaels, Randy Newman *d* John Landis *ph* Ronald W. Browne *m* Elmer Bernstein *pd* Richard Sawyer *ed* Malcolm Campbell

Chevy Chase, Steve Martin, Martin Short, Patrice Martinez, Alfonso Arau

Three for Bedroom C
US 1952 74m Natural Color
Brenco (Edward L. Alperson Jnr)

Confusion reigns on a train when a film star takes a compartment booked for a Harvard scientist.

Inept farce which never rises above mediocrity and coasts along well below it.

wd Milton H. Bren *ph* Ernest Laszlo *m* Heinz Roemheld

Gloria Swanson, Fred Clark, James Warren, Hans Conried, Steve Brodie, Margaret Dumont

Three Fugitives*
US 1989 96m Metrocolor
Warner/Touchstone/Silver Screen Partners IV (Lauren Shuler-Donner)
V, L

An ex-convict, trying to reform, is forced to go on the run with an inept bank robber and his small daughter.

A chase farce that piles up the absurdities with diminishing effect.

wd Francis Veber *ph* Haskell Wexler *m* David McHugh *pd* Rick Carter *ed* Bruce Green

Nick Nolte, Martin Short, Sarah Rowland Doroff, James Earl Jones, Alan Ruck, Kenneth McMillan, David Arnott, Bruce McGill

Three in the Attic
US 1968 90m Pathecolor
AIP-Hermes (Richard Wilson)

A college Casanova is locked in an attic by three girls who seduce him by rota until he cries for mercy.

One of the first outspoken comedies of the sexual revolution, but not a particularly funny one.

w Stephen Yafa *novel Paxton Quigley's Had the Course* by Stephen Yafa *d* Richard Wilson *ph* J. Burgi Contner *m* Chad Stuart

Chris Jones, Yvette Mimieux, Judy Pace, Maggie Turett, Nan Martin

'They changed her diapers – she changed their lives!'
Three Men and a Baby
US 1987 102m DeLuxe
Touchstone/Silver Screen III (Ted Field, Robert W. Cort)
V, L

Three swinging bachelors find a baby on their doorstep.

Slight comedy, given some momentum by a heroin-dealing subplot, which proved surprisingly successful with audiences thanks to energetic playing.

w James Orr, Jim Cruickshank *d* Leonard Nimoy *ph* Adam Greenberg *m* Marvin Hamlisch *pd* Peter Larkin

Tom Selleck, Steve Guttenberg, Ted Danson, Nancy Travis

† Remake of the more thoughtful and elegant *Trois Hommes et un Couffin* of 1985, whose director Coline Serreau was to have directed the US version but backed out.

Three Men and a Cradle*

France 1985 107m colour
UKFD/Floch Film/Soprofilm/TF1 Films
   (Jean-François Lepetit)
original title: *Trois Hommes et un Couffin*

Three bachelors fall for a baby left on
their doorstep by a former girl-friend.

Amusing comedy of role reversal
which was remade by Hollywood as
the glossier *Three Men and a Baby*.

wd Coline Serreau *ph* Jean-Yves
Éscoffier, Jean-Jacques Bouhon
pd Yvan Maussion   *ed* Catherine
Renault

Roland Giraud, Michel Boujenah,
André Dussollier, Philippine Leroy
Beaulieu

Three Men and a Little Lady

US 1990 100m
Touchstone/Jean François LePetit-
   Interscope Communications (Ted Field,
   Robert W. Cort)
V, L

Three bachelors prevent the mother
of the child they 'adopted' marrying an
Englishman.

Dire sequel to *Three Men and a Baby*,
notably silly in its depiction of
England as a backward rural country
inhabited entirely by eccentrics.

w Charlie Peters   *story* Sara
Parriott, Josann McGibbon   *d* Emilio
Ardolino   *ph* Adam Greenberg
m James Newton Howard
pd Stuart Wurtzel   *ad* David M.
Haber   *ed* Michael A. Stevenson

Tom Selleck, Steve Guttenberg, Ted
Danson, Nancy Travis, Robin
Weisman, Christopher Cazenove,
Sheila Hancock, Fiona Shaw

'Thinking people will be hard-pressed
to find a single interesting moment in
this relentlessly predictable fantasy.' –
Variety

Three Men in a Boat

GB 1956 94m Eastmancolor
   Cinemascope
Romulus (Jack Clayton)

In the 1890s, misadventures befall
three men holidaying on the Thames.

Flabby burlesque of a celebrated
comic novel whose style is never
even approached.

w Hubert Gregg, Vernon Harris
novel Jerome K. Jerome   *d* Ken
Annakin   *ph* Eric Cross   *m* John
Addison   *ad* John Howell

David Tomlinson, Jimmy Edwards,
Laurence Harvey, Shirley Eaton,
Robertson Hare, Jill Ireland, Lisa
Gastoni, Martita Hunt, A. E. Matthews,
Ernest Thesiger, Adrienne Corri

† A previous version in 1933 starred
William Austin, Edmond Breon and
Billy Milton; directed by Graham
Cutts for ATP.

'Move over, Casanova!'

Three on a Couch

US 1966 109m Technicolor
Columbia/Jerry Lewis Productions (Jerry
   Lewis)

An artist tries to cure the sexual hang-
ups of his psychiatrist fiancée's three
female patients.

Intolerably lengthy and witless
comedy.

w Bob Ross, Samuel A. Taylor, Arne
Sultan, Marvin Worth   *d* Jerry
Lewis

Jerry Lewis, Janet Leigh, James Best,
Mary Ann Mobley, Gila Golan, Leslie
Parrish, Kathleen Freeman, Fritz Feld

'A long drag through stock situations.'
– *MFB*

'Unintentionally unfunny.' – *Leonard Maltin*

'Stay on your own couch and don't bother with Jerry's.' – *Steven Scheuer*

The Thrill of it All*
US 1963 104m Eastmancolor
U-I/Ross Hunter/Arwin (Ross Hunter, Marty Melcher)

The wife of a gynaecologist becomes an advertising model, and work pressures disrupt her marriage.

Glossy matrimonial farce which starts brightly but eventually flags and becomes exhausting. Its better jokes linger in the memory.

w Carl Reiner   *d* Norman Jewison   *ph* Russell Metty
m Frank de Vol

Doris Day, James Garner, Arlene Francis, Edward Andrews, Reginald Owen, Zasu Pitts, Elliot Reid

'Pleasantly reminiscent of some of the screwball comedies of the thirties.' – *MFB*

Throw Momma from the Train*
US 1987 88m DeLuxe
Orion (Larry Brezner)
V, L

After seeing *Strangers on a Train*, a student tries to persuade his professor to 'swap' murders.

Cheerful black comedy-cum-homage to Hitchcock.

w Stu Silver   *d* Danny DeVito
ph Barry Sonnenfeld   *m* David Newman   *pd* Ida Random

Danny DeVito, Billy Crystal, Anne Ramsey, Kim Greist, Kate Mulgrew

'Very clever and engaging from beginning to end.' – *Variety*
AAN: Anne Ramsey

Thunder and Lightning
US 1977 93m DeLuxe
TCF (Roger Corman)

An independent maker of moonshine whiskey finds himself in competition with his girlfriend's father.

Action-filled comedy, mainly consisting of car and boat chases and crashes.

w William Hjortsberg   *d* Corey Allen   *ph* James Pergola   *m* Andy Stein   *ed* Anthony Redman

David Carradine, Kate Jackson, Roger C. Carmel, Sterling Holloway, Ed Barth

A Tiger's Tale
US 1987 97m colour
Entertainment/Atlantic (Peter Douglas)
L

A middle-aged woman becomes pregnant as a result of an affair with a high-school student.

Dire comedy with no visible or audible wit.

wd Peter Douglas   *novel* Love and Other Natural Disasters by Allen Hanney III   *ph* Tony Pierce-Roberts   *m* Lee Holdridge
pd Shay Austin   *ed* David Campling

Ann-Margret, C. Thomas Howell, Charles Durning, Kelly Preston, William Zabka, Ann Wedgeworth, James Noble

Till Death Us Do Part*
GB 1968 100m Eastmancolor
British Lion/Associated London Films (Jon Pennington)
V

From the thirties to the sixties with loud-mouthed, bigoted Londoner Alf Garnett.

Unremarkable and frequently misguided opening-up of a

phenomenally successful TV series, adapted for the US as *All in the Family*. The original cast wades cheerfully enough through a bitty script; the sequel, *The Alf Garnett Saga*, defeated them.

w Johnny Speight   *d* Norman Cohen   *ph* Harry Waxman   *m* Wilfrid Burns

Warren Mitchell, Dandy Nichols, Anthony Booth, Una Stubbs, Liam Redmond, Bill Maynard, Sam Kydd, Brian Blessed

Tillie and Gus*
US   1933   61m   bw
Paramount (Douglas MacLean)

Two middle-aged cardsharps return home, help their niece and nephew win an inheritance, and come first in a paddleboat race.

Jumbled comedy with good moments and a rousing climax.

w Walter de Leon, Francis Martin   *d* Francis Martin   *ph* Benjamin Reynolds

W. C. Fields, Alison Skipworth, Baby Le Roy, Jacqueline Wells, Clifford Jones, Clarence Wilson, Edgar Kennedy, Barton MacLane

'Very funny in spots, but not enough spots.' – *Variety*

The Time of Their Lives*
US   1946   82m   bw
Universal (Val Burton)

Revolutionary ghosts haunt a country estate.

Unusual, quite effective Abbott and Costello vehicle with the comedians not playing as a team.

w Val Burton, Walter de Leon, Bradford Ropes, John Grant

d Charles Barton   *ph* Charles Van Enger   *m* Milton Rosen

Bud Abbott, Lou Costello, Marjorie Reynolds, Binnie Barnes, Gale Sondergaard, John Shelton

Tin Men**
US   1987   112m   DeLuxe
Touchstone/Silver Screen Partners II (Mark Johnson)

In 1960s Baltimore, two aluminium salesmen have a series of feuds.

A comedy enjoyable not for its plot but for its authentic period backgrounds and characters.

wd Barry Levinson   ph Peter Sova   *m* David Steele   *pd* Peter Jamison   *ed* Stu Linder

Richard Dreyfuss, Danny DeVito, Barbara Hershey, John Mahoney, Jackie Gayle, Stanley Brock

The Titfield Thunderbolt***
GB   1952   84m   Technicolor
Ealing (Michael Truman)
V

When a branch railway line is threatened with closure, the villagers take it over as a private concern.

Undervalued on its release in the wake of other Ealing comedies, this now seems among the best of them as well as an immaculate colour production showing the England that is no more; the script has pace, the whole thing is brightly polished and the action works up to a fine climactic frenzy.

w T. E. B. Clarke   d Charles Crichton   *ph* Douglas Slocombe   *m* Georges Auric

Stanley Holloway, George Relph, John Gregson, Godfrey Tearle, *Edie Martin*, Naunton Wayne, Gabrielle Brune,

Hugh Griffith, Sidney James, Jack McGowran, Ewan Roberts, Reginald Beckwith

To Be or Not to Be****
US   1942   99m   bw
Alexander Korda/Ernst Lubitsch

Warsaw actors get involved in an underground plot and an impersonation of invading Nazis, including Hitler.

Marvellous free-wheeling entertainment which starts as drama and descends through romantic comedy and suspense into farce; accused of bad taste at the time, but now seen as an outstanding example of Hollywood moonshine, kept alight through sheer talent and expertise.

w Edwin Justus Mayer,   story Ernst Lubitsch, Melchior Lengyel
d Ernst Lubitsch   ph Rudolph Maté   m Werner Heymann
ad Vincent Korda

Jack Benny, Carole Lombard, Robert Stack, *Stanley Ridges, Felix Bressart, Lionel Atwill, Sig Rumann, Tom Dugan,* Charles Halton
    TURA in disguise (Jack Benny): 'That great, great Polish actor Joseph Tura – you must have heard of him.'
    ERHARDT (Sig Rumann): 'Ah, yes . . . what he did to Shakespeare, we are now doing to Poland!'
    ERHARDT (and others): 'So they call me Concentration Camp Erhardt!'

'The comedy is hilarious, even when it is hysterically thrilling.' – *Commonweal*
'As effective an example of comic propaganda as *The Great Dictator* and far better directed.' – *Charles Higham, 1972*
'Based on an indiscretion, but undoubtedly a work of art.' – *James Agee*

'In any other medium it would be acknowledged as a classic to rank with *The Alchemist* or *A Modest Proposal*.' – *Peter Barnes*
'Lubitsch's comic genius and corrosive wit are displayed at every turn.' – *John Baxter*
'The actual business at hand . . . is nothing less than providing a good time at the expense of Nazi myth . . . Lubitsch distinguishes the film's zanier moments with his customary mastery of sly humour and innuendo, and when the story calls for outright melodrama he is more than equal to the occasion.' – *Newsweek*
AAN: Werner Heymann

To Be or Not to Be
US   1983   107m   DeLuxe
TCF/Brooksfilms (Mel Brooks)
V

Flat-footed remake of the above, with stagey sets, unconvincing acting (including the unnecessary addition of a gay dresser) and a leading comedian who won't stay still in case his lack of style should be noticed.

w Thomas Meehan, Ronnie Graham   *d* Alan Johnson
ph Gerald Hirschfeld   *m* John Morris   *pd* Terence Marsh

Mel Brooks, Anne Bancroft, Tim Matheson, Charles Durning, Jose Ferrer, George Gaynes, Christopher Lloyd, James Haake
AAN: Charles Durning

To Paris with Love
GB   1954   78m   Technicolor
GFD/Two Cities (Anthony Darnborough)

A middle-aged widower and his son go to Paris on holiday and devise matrimonial plans for each other.

Thin, disappointing taradiddle which is short but seems long.

w Robert Buckner   *d* Robert Hamer   *ph* Reg Wyer   *m* Edwin Astley

Alec Guinness, Vernon Gray, Odile Versois, Jacques François, Elina Labourdette, Austin Trevor

'The general impression is somehow too aimless, too muted.' – *Gavin Lambert*
'John Davis came on the set one day and said: Give us some pratfalls, Alec, give us some laughs. I realized there and then that I was not going to fit in.' – *Alec Guinness*

Tom, Dick and Harry**
US 1941 86m bw
RKO (Robert Sisk)

A girl daydreams about her three boy friends, but can't make up her mind.

Brightly-handled comedy which became a minor classic but does seem to have faded a little. Remade as *The Girl Most Likely* (qv).

w Paul Jarrico   *d* Garson Kanin
ph Merrit Gerstad   *m* Roy Webb

Ginger Rogers, Burgess Meredith, Alan Marshal, George Murphy, *Phil Silvers*, Joe Cunningham, Jane Seymour, Lenore Lonergan

'Foot by foot the best made picture of this year.' – *Otis Ferguson*
AAN: Paul Jarrico

'The whole world loves him!'
Tom Jones***
GB 1963 129m Eastmancolor
UA/Woodfall (Tony Richardson)
V

In 18th-century England a foundling is brought up by the squire and marries his daughter after many adventures.

Fantasia on Old England, at some distance from the original novel, with the director trying every possible jokey approach against a meticulously realistic physical background.

Despite trade fears, the *Hellzapoppin* style made it an astonishing box-office success (the sex helped), though it quickly lost its freshness and was much imitated.

w John Osborne,   *novel* Henry Fielding   *d* Tony Richardson
ph Walter Lassally, Manny Wynn
m John Addison   *pd* Ralph Brinton

Albert Finney, Susannah York, Hugh Griffith, Edith Evans, Joan Greenwood, Diane Cilento, George Devine, Joyce Redman, David Warner, Wilfrid Lawson, Freda Jackson, Rachel Kempson

'Uncertainty, nervousness, muddled method . . . desperation is writ large over it.' – *Stanley Kauffmann*
'Much of the time it looks like a home movie, made with sporadic talent by a group with more enthusiasm than discipline.' – *Tom Milne*
'It is as though the camera had become a method actor: there are times when you wish you could buy, as on certain juke boxes, five minutes' silence . . . Obviously a film which elicits such lyric ejaculations from the reviewers cannot be all good.' – *John Simon*
'I just felt I was being used. I wasn't involved . . . I was bored most of the time.' – *Albert Finney*

† The narrator was Michael MacLiammoir.

AA: best picture; John Osborne; Tony Richardson; John Addison
AAN: Albert Finney; Hugh Griffith; Edith Evans; Diane Cilento; Joyce Redman

Too Many Crooks*

GB 1958 87m bw
Rank/Mario Zampi

Incompetent crooks plot a kidnapping.

Agreeable farce with black edges and an excellent chase sequence.

w Michael Pertwee   d Mario Zampi   ph Stan Pavey   m Stanley Black

Terry-Thomas, George Cole, Brenda de Banzie, Bernard Bresslaw, Sidney James, Joe Melia, Vera Day, John Le Mesurier

Tootsie**

US 1982 116m colour
Columbia/Mirage/Punch (Sydney Pollack)
V, L

An out-of-work actor pretends to be a woman in order to get a job in a soap opera.

As with Genevieve and Whisky Galore, an unlikely comedy subject makes an instant classic. It's all in the handling.

w Larry Gelbart, Murray Shisgal, story Don McGuire   d Sydney Pollack   ph Owen Roizman   m Dave Grusin   pd Peter Larkin   ed Frederick and William Steinkamp

Dustin Hoffman, Jessica Lange, Teri Garr, Dabney Coleman, Charles Durning, Sydney Pollack, George Gaynes

AA: Jessica Lange
AAN: best picture; Dustin Hoffman; Teri Garr; Sydney Pollack as director; original screenplay; cinematography; editing; song, 'It Might Be You' (m Dave Grusin, ly Alan Bergman, Marilyn Bergman); sound

BFA: Dustin Hoffman

Top Secret*

GB 1952 94m bw
ABP (Mario Zampi)
US title: Mr Potts Goes to Moscow

A sanitary engineer, mistaken for a spy, is kidnapped to Moscow when his blueprints are taken for atomic secrets.

Farcical satire full of chases and lavatory humour; much of it comes off nicely.

w Jack Davies, Michael Pertwee   d Mario Zampi   ph Stan Pavey   m Stanley Black

George Cole, Oscar Homolka, Nadia Gray, Frederick Valk, Wilfrid Hyde White, Geoffrey Sumner, Ronald Adam

Top Secret!

US 1984 90m Metrocolor
Paramount/Kingsmere (Jon Davison, Hunt Lowry)
V

An American rock star in Germany gets involved with spies of both sides.

Dull spoof from the folks who gave us Airplane! A very few sight gags stand out among the dross.

w Jim Abrahams, David Zucker, Jerry Zucker, Martyn Burke   d Jim Abrahams, David Zucker, Jerry Zucker   ph Christopher Challis   m Maurice Jarre   pd Peter Lamont

Val Kilmer, Lucy Gutteridge, Peter Cushing, Jeremy Kemp, Warren Clarke, Michael Gough, Omar Sharif, Christopher Villiers

'Too far over the top to retain any comic sense of the targets it sets out to lampoon. The overwhelming impression is of a Mad magazine strip in a particularly poor week.' – Martyn Auty, MFB

Topper**

US 1937 96m bw
(MGM) Hal Roach (Milton H. Bren)

A stuffy banker is haunted by the ghosts of his sophisticated friends the Kirbys, who are visible only to him.

Influential supernatural farce, still pretty funny and deftly acted though a shade slow to get going.

w Jack Jevne, Eric Hatch, Eddie Moran *novel* The Jovial Ghosts by Thorne Smith *d* Norman Z. McLeod *ph* Norbert Brodine *md* Arthur Morton

Cary Grant, Constance Bennett, Roland Young, Billie Burke, Alan Mowbray, Eugene Pallette, Arthur Lake, Hedda Hopper

'How substantial the fan support will be is difficult to anticipate . . . None of the other films of similar theme aroused more than mild enthusiasm among a small group who patronize the arty theatres and talk about pictures in terms of art expression . . . Effort to excuse the story's absurdities on the theory that the intent is farce comedy does not entirely excuse the production from severe rebuke. Fact also that the living dead are always facetious may be shocking to sensibilities. Some of the situations and dialogue offend conventional good taste.' – *Variety*
AAN: Roland Young

Topper Returns**

US 1941 87m bw
Hal Roach

A girl ghost helps Topper solve her own murder.

Spirited supernatural farce which spoofs murder mysteries, spooky houses, frightened servants, dumb cops, etc, in a pacy, accomplished and generally delightful manner.

w Jonathan Latimer, Gordon Douglas, with additional dialogue by Paul Gerard Smith *d* Roy del Ruth *ph* Norbert Brodine *m* Werner Heyman

Roland Young, Joan Blondell, Eddie Anderson, Carole Landis, Dennis O'Keefe, *H. B. Warner,* Billie Burke, *Donald McBride,* Rafaela Ottiano

'Ectoplasm runs riot and blazes a trail of hilarity from 5th Avenue to the French Riviera!'

Topper Takes a Trip*

US 1939 85m bw
Hal Roach

Ghostly Mrs Kirby helps Topper to save his wife from a Riviera philanderer.

Mildly pleasant follow-up, with a dog replacing Cary Grant who had become too expensive.

w Eddie Moran, Jack Jevne, Corey Ford *d* Norman Z. McLeod *ph* Norbert Brodine *m* Hugo Friedhofer

Constance Bennett, Roland Young, Billie Burke, Alan Mowbray, Verree Teasdale, Franklin Pangborn, Alexander D'Arcy

'Dandy comedy sequel . . . can't miss at the b.o. . . . the original ended up a fine money-maker . . . no doubt one a year about Topper would be welcomed by exhibitors.' – *Variety*

Touch and Go

GB 1955 85m Technicolor
Ealing (Seth Holt)
L
US title: The Light Touch

A family has doubts about its decision to emigrate to Australia.

Very mild comedy which fails to engage sympathy because the characters don't seem real.

w William Rose   *d* Michael Truman   *ph* Douglas Slocombe   *m* John Addison

Jack Hawkins, Margaret Johnston, June Thorburn, John Fraser, Roland Culver, Alison Leggatt, James Hayter

'They had the perfect love affair. Until they fell in love!'
A Touch of Class**
GB   1973   106m   Technicolor Panavision
Avco/Brut/Gordon Films (Melvin Frank)

A married American businessman in London has a hectic affair with a dress designer.

Amiable and very physical sex farce with hilarious highlights and a few longueurs between; the playing keeps it above water.

w Melvin Frank, Jack Rose   *d* Melvin Frank   *ph* Austin Dempster   *m* John Cameron

Glenda Jackson, George Segal, Paul Sorvino, Hildegarde Neil

'Machine-tooled junk.' – *William S. Pechter*
'Brightly performed and quite engaging until it fades into vapid variations on a one-joke theme.' – *Sight and Sound*

AA: Glenda Jackson
AAN: best picture; script; John Cameron; song 'All That Love Went to Waste' (*m* George Barrie, *ly* Sammy Cahn)

A Touch of the Sun
GB   1956   80m   bw
Eros/Raystro (Raymond Stross)

A hall porter is left a fortune but after living it up for a while returns to his old hotel which is on the rocks.

Limp comedy vehicle.

w Alfred Shaughnessy   *d* Gordon Parry   *ph* Arthur Grant   *m* Eric Spear

Frankie Howerd, Ruby Murray, Dorothy Bromiley, Gordon Harker, Reginald Beckwith, Richard Wattis, Dennis Price, Alfie Bass, Willoughby Goddard

Tough Guys
US   1986   104m   DeLuxe Panavision
Touchstone/Silver Screen/Brynal (Joe Wizan)

The last train robbers are released from prison after 30 years, and, finding that an old people's home is not for them, return to their old ways.

Slackly written caper comedy with two former stars in their seventh teaming.

w James Orr, Jim Cruickshank   *d* Jeff Kanew   *ph* King Baggot   *m* James Newton Howard

Burt Lancaster, Kirk Douglas, Charles Durning, Alexis Smith, Eli Wallach

'The most exciting screen event of all time!'
Tovarich**
US   1937   98m   bw
Warner (Robert Lord)

A royal Russian husband and wife flee the revolution to Paris and take jobs as servants in an eccentric household.

A lively comedy of its time; though many of the jokes now seem obvious, the playing preserves its essential quality.

w Casey Robinson   *play adaptation* Robert E. Sherwood   *original* Jacques Deval   *d* Anatole

Litvak   *ph* Charles Lang   *m* Max
Steiner

*Claudette Colbert, Charles Boyer, Basil
Rathbone,* Anita Louise, Melville
Cooper, Isabel Jeans, Maurice
Murphy, Morris Carnovsky, Gregory
Gaye, Montagu Love, Fritz Feld

'A yarn of charming and finely shaded
characterizations. Both humour and
heart appeal spring from intimate
acquaintance with the background
and motives of each player. Class
production, magnet for first runs.' –
Variety

The Toy
US   1983   102m   colour
Columbia/Rastar (Phil Feldman)
L

A black janitor is hired as a toy for a
millionaire's nine-year-old son.

Feeble attempt to translate a 1976
French film by Francis Veber. The
few laughs are laughs of
embarrassment.

w Carol Sobieski   *d* Richard
Donner   *ph* Laszlo Kovacs
m Patrick Williams   *pd* Charles
Rosen

Richard Pryor, Jackie Gleason, Ned
Beatty, Scott Schwarz, Teresa Ganzel,
Wilfrid Hyde-White, Tony King

'Tasteless in implication, flavourless in
execution.' – *Sight and Sound*

'Laughter Is A State of Mind.'
Toys
US   1992   121m   CFI colour
TCF (Mark Johnson, Barry Levinson)

An uptight army officer inherits a toy
factory and switches production from
cuddly toys to increasingly aggressive
ones.

Visually splendid but otherwise totally
incoherent movie.

w Valerie Curtin, Barry Levinson
d Barry Levinson   *ph* Adam
Greenberg   *m* Hans Zimmer, Trevor
Horn   *pd* Ferdinando Scarfiotti
ed Stu Linder

Robin Williams, Michael Gambon,
Joan Cusack, Robin Wright, LL Cool
J, Donald O'Connor, Jack Warden

'Only a filmmaker with Barry
Levinson's clout would have been so
indulged to create such a sprawling,
seemingly unsupervised mess . . . It
will be hard to top as the season's
major clunker.' – *Variety*
'A disaster . . . It is quite unlike
anything Levinson has done before,
and it is sincerely to be hoped that he
never does anything like it again.' –
Derek Malcolm, Guardian
AAN: Ferdinando Scarfiotti; Albert
Wolsky (costume design)

Trading Places**
US   1983   116m   Technicolor
Paramount/Landis-Folsey (Aaron Russo)
V, L

Two rich men arrange a wager on the
effects of environment over heredity,
and arrange for a con man and a
stockbroker to change places.

Surprisingly witty comedy, which
while not aspiring to great heights,
and marred by a few excesses, brought
a refreshing breath of air to a
declining genre.

w Timothy Harris, Herschel
Weingrod   *d John Landis*
ph Robert Paynter   *m* Elmer
Bernstein   *pd* Gene Rudolf

Dan Aykroyd, Eddie Murphy, *Ralph
Bellamy, Don Ameche,* Denholm Elliott,
Jamie Lee Curtis, Kristin Holby

'Proof positive that the genuine American populist comedy can still attract attention.' – *John Pym, MFB*

BFA: Jamie Lee Curtis, Denholm Elliott
AAN: Elmer Bernstein

Traffic*
France/Italy   1970   96m
  Eastmancolor
Corona/Gibe/Selenia (Robert Dorfman)

The designer of a camping car has various little accidents on the way from the works to a show.

Rambling comedy with understated jokes and an almost invisible star.

w Jacques Tati, Jacques Legrange
d Jacques Tati (with Bert Haanstra)   *ph* Edouard Van Den Enden, Marcel Weiss   *m* Charles Dumont

Jacques Tati

Trail of the Pink Panther
GB   1982   97m   Technicolor
  Panavision
MGM-UA/Titan (Blake Edwards, Tony Adams)
V

Inspector Clouseau is reported missing at sea and a television reporter interviews those who had known him.

Flimsy, necrophiliac excuse for a movie, with a star cast clearly failing to make bricks without straw two years after the nominal star's death.

w Frank and Tom Waldman, Blake Edwards, Geoffrey Edwards
d Blake Edwards   *ph* Dick Bush
m Henry Mancini   *pd* Peter Mullins   *ed* Alan Jones

Peter Sellers, Joanna Lumley, Herbert Lom, David Niven, Richard Mulligan, Capucine, Robert Loggia, Harvey Korman, Burt Kwouk, Graham Stark, Leonard Rossiter, Peter Arne, Ronald Fraser

The Tramp*
US   1915   20m approx (24 fps)
  bw   silent
Mutual

A tramp saves a girl from crooks, is wounded and cared for by her, deliriously happy – until her lover arrives.

Fairly funny star comedy, the first with sentimental touches and the origin of the into-the-sunset fade-out.

wd Charles Chaplin   *ph* Rollie Totheroh

Charles Chaplin, Edna Purviance, Bud Jamison, Leo White, Lloyd Bacon

Tramp Tramp Tramp*
US   1926   65m approx (24 fps)
  bw   silent
Harry Langdon

Harry enters a cross-country walking contest in order to impress his girl.

Well-staged peripatetic comedy, the star's first feature.

w Frank Capra, Tim Whelan, Hal Conklin, Gerald Duffy, Murray Roth, J. Frank Holliday   *d* Harry Edwards

Harry Langdon, Joan Crawford, Alec B. Francis

Travels with My Aunt*
US   1972   109m   Metrocolor
  Panavision
MGM (Robert Fryer, James Cresson)

A staid bank accountant is landed in a series of continental adventures by his eccentric life-loving aunt.

Busy but fairly disastrous adaptation

HALLIWELL'S GUIDE TO THE BEST COMEDIES

of a delightful novel, ruined by ceaseless chatter, lack of characterization, shapeless incident and an absurdly caricatured central performance.

w Jay Presson Allen, Hugh Wheeler   *novel* Graham Greene   *d* George Cukor   *ph* Douglas Slocombe   *m* Tony Hatch   *pd* John Box

Maggie Smith, *Alec McCowen*, Lou Gossett, Robert Stephens, Cindy Williams

'It seems to run down before it gets started.' – *New Yorker, 1977*
AAN: Douglas Slocombe; Maggie Smith

Tremors**
US   1989   96m   DeLuxe
UIP/Universal/No Frills/Brent Maddock, S. S. Wilson
L

Giant man-eating worms threaten a small Western town.

Enjoyable monster movie in the style of 50s films, which manages to be both funny and suspenseful.

w S. S. Wilson, Brent Maddock, Ron Underwood   *d* Ron Underwood   *ph* Alexander Gruszynski   *m* Ernest Troost   *pd* Ivo Cristante   *ed* O. Nicholas Brown

Kevin Bacon, Fred Ward, Finn Carter, Michael Gross, Reba McEntire, Bobby Jacoby, Charlotte Stewart, Tony Genaro

'Shrewdly, unpretentiously written, energetically directed and played with high comic conviction, *Tremors* is bound to become a cult classic.' – *Richard Schickel, Time*

Tristana***
Spain/Italy/France   1970   105m   Eastmancolor
Academy/Connoisseur/Epoca/Talia/Selenia/Les Films Corona (Juan Estelrich)
V

An impoverished, womanizing aristocrat seduces his young ward and pays the price for his action.

Complex black comedy of obsessive behaviour which also mocks religion and other forms of consolation.

w Luis Buñuel, Julio Alejandro   *novel* Benito Pérez Galdós   *d* Luis Buñuel   *ph* José F. Aguayo   *ad* Enrique Alarcón   *ed* Pedro Del Rey

Catherine Deneuve, Fernando Rey, Franco Nero, Lola Gaos, Antonio Casas, Jesús Fernández

'It is Buñuel at his most majestic.' – *Tom Milne, MFB*

Troop Beverly Hills
US   1989   106m   Metrocolor
Columbia TriStar/Weintraub Entertainment/Fries Entertainment (Ava Ostern Fries, Martin Mickelson, Peter MacGregor-Scott)
V, L

A wealthy mother transforms her daughter's disintegrating Girl Scout troop by giving them badges in shopping and other consumer activities.

A broad and far from sparkling comedy which emphasises that it is best to be born rich.

w Pamela Norris, Margaret Grieco Oberman   *story* Ava Ostern Fries   *d* Jeff Kanew   *ph* Donald E. Thorin   *m* Randy Edelman, Lou Hemsey   *pd* Robert F. Boyle   *ed* Mark Melnick

Shelley Long, Craig T. Nelson, Betty Thomas, Mary Gross, Stephanie Beacham, David Gautreaux, Karen Kopins, Dinah Lacey, Shelley Morrison

Trop Belle pour Toi!*

France 1989 91m colour
Artificial Eye/Cine Valse/DD Productions/ Orly Films/SEDIF/TF1 (Bernard Marescot)
V(W), L
aka: Too Beautiful For You

A successful car salesman with a beautiful wife begins an affair with his homely secretary.

Mildly amusing romantic comedy, for all that it seems no more than a heterosexual variation on Blier's Tenue De Soirée.

wd Bertrand Blier   ph Philippe Rousselot   m Schubert
ad Theobald Meurisse   ed Claudine Merlin

Gérard Depardieu, Josiane Balasko, Carole Bouquet, Roland Blanche, François Cluzet, Didier Benureau, Philippe Loffredo

Trouble Brewing*

GB 1939 87m bw
ATP

A newspaper printer catches counterfeiters.

Lively star comedy.

w Anthony Kimmins, Angus MacPhail and Michael Hogan
d Anthony Kimmins

George Formby, Googie Withers, Gus MacNaughton, Joss Ambler, Martita Hunt, Garry Marsh, Ronald Shiner, C. Denier Warren, Basil Radford

Trouble in Paradise****

US 1932 86m bw
Paramount (Ernst Lubitsch)
V

Jewel thieves insinuate themselves into the household of a rich Parisienne, and one falls in love with her.

A masterpiece of light comedy, with sparkling dialogue, innuendo, great performances and masterly cinematic narrative. For connoisseurs, it can't be faulted, and is the masterpiece of American sophisticated cinema.

w Samson Raphaelson, Grover Jones play The Honest Finder by Laszlo Aladar   d Ernst Lubitsch
ph Victor Milner   m W. Franke Harling

Herbert Marshall, Miriam Hopkins, Kay Francis, Edward Everett Horton, Charles Ruggles, C. Aubrey Smith, Robert Greig, Leonid Kinskey

'Swell title, poor picture. Better for the class houses than the subsequents.' – Variety
'One of the gossamer creations of Lubitsch's narrative art . . . it would be impossible in this brief notice to describe the innumerable touches of wit and of narrative skill with which it is unfolded.' – Alexander Bakshy
'A shimmering, engaging piece of work . . . in virtually every scene a lively imagination shines forth.' – New York Times
'An almost continuous musical background pointed up and commented on the action. The settings were the last word in modernistic design.' – Theodor Huff, 1948

Trouble in Store*

GB 1953 85m bw
GFD/Two Cities (Maurice Cowan)
V

A stock assistant causes chaos in a department store.

First, simplest and best of the Wisdom farces.

w John Paddy Carstairs, Maurice Cowan, Ted Willis   *d* John Paddy Carstairs   *ph* Ernest Steward   *m* Mischa Spoliansky

Norman Wisdom, Jerry Desmonde, Margaret Rutherford, Moira Lister, Derek Bond, Lana Morris, Megs Jenkins, Joan Sims

Trouble in the Glen

GB   1954   91m   Trucolor
Republic/Wilcox-Neagle (Stuart Robertson)

An Argentinian laird in a Scottish glen causes ill-feeling.

Heavy-handed Celtic comedy whose predictability and sentimentality could have been forgiven were it not for the most garish colour ever seen.

w Frank S. Nugent   *novel* Maurice Walsh   *d* Herbert Wilcox   *ph* Max Greene   *m* Victor Young

Margaret Lockwood, Orson Welles, Forrest Tucker, Victor McLaglen, John McCallum, Eddie Byrne, Archie Duncan, Moultrie Kelsall

The Trouble with Angels

US   1966   112m   Pathecolor
Columbia/William Frye

Two mischievous new pupils cause trouble at a convent school.

Fun with the nuns, for addicts only.

w Blanche Hanalis   *novel* Life with Mother Superior by Jane Trahey
d Ida Lupino   *ph* Lionel Lindon   *m* Jerry Goldsmith

Rosalind Russell, Hayley Mills, June Harding, Marge Redmond, Binnie

Barnes, Gypsy Rose Lee, Camilla Sparv, Mary Wickes, Margalo Gillmore

'A relentless series of prankish escapades.' – *MFB*

True Confession**

US   1937   85m   bw
Paramount (Albert Lewin)

A fantasy-prone girl confesses to a murder she didn't commit, and her upright lawyer husband defends her.

Archetypal crazy comedy with fine moments despite longueurs and a lack of cinematic inventiveness. Remade as *Cross My Heart* (qv).

w Claude Binyon   *play Mon Crime* by Louis Verneuil, George Berr   *d* Wesley Ruggles   *ph* Ted Tetzlaff   *m* Frederick Hollander

Carole Lombard, Fred MacMurray, *John Barrymore*, Una Merkel, Porter Hall, Edgar Kennedy, Lynne Overman, Fritz Feld, *Irving Bacon*

'Not a big bet but a favourable enough one . . . it just falls short of being a smash.' – *Variety*
'The best comedy of the year.' – *Graham Greene*

True Identity

USA   1991   93m   Technicolor
Warner/Touchstone/Silver Screen Partners IV/Sandollar (Carol Baum, Teri Schwartz)
V

On the run from the Mafia, a black actor disguises himself as a white man.

A star vehicle that, despite an engaging central performance, failed, due to a weak script.

w Andy Breckman   *d* Charles Lane   *ph* Tom Ackerman

m Marc Marder   *pd* John DeCuir
Jnr   *ed* Kent Beyda

Lenny Henry, Frank Langella, Charles
Lane, J. T. Walsh, Anne-Marie
Johnson, Andreas Katsulas, Michael
McKean, Peggy Lipton

'Mild comedy that works best as a
showcase for Lenny Henry.' —*New
York Times*

'If All You Want To Do Is Have A Good
Time... Why Get Married?'

True Love
US 1989 100m DuArt
Oasis/UA (Richard Guay, Shelley Houis)

A young Italian-American couple in
the Bronx prepare for their marriage,
she with determination, he with
reluctance.

Well-observed, low-budget comedy
with a ring of truth about it.

w Nancy Savoca, Richard Guay
d Nancy Savoca   *ph* Lisa
Rinzler   *pd* Lester W. Cohen
ed John Tintori

Annabella Sciorra, Ron Eldard, Aida
Turturro, Roger Rignack, Star Jasper,
Michael J. Wolfe, Kelly Cinnante,
Rick Shapiro

True Stories*
US 1986 89m DuArt
Warner/Edward R. Pressman/Gary Kurfirst
V, L

A narrator introduces people from the
town of Virgil, Texas.

A curious entertainment which plays
like a whimsical update of Thornton
Wilder's *Our Town*, though without
the subtlety.

w Stephen Tobolowsky, Beth Henley,
David Byrne   *d* David Byrne
ph Ed Lachman   *m* David Byrne

David Byrne, John Goodman, Annie

McEnroe, Jo Harvey Allen, Spalding
Gray, Alix Elias, Swoosie Kurtz

'The story is just a trick to get your
attention. It opens the door and lets
the real movie in.' – *David Byrne*

'A slightly twisted comedy.'

Trust**
GB/USA 1990 106m colour
Palace/Zenith/True Fiction/Film Four (Bruce
  Weiss)
V, L

A pregnant teenager meets a moody,
grenade-carrying electronics expert
and takes him home with her.

Off-beat film that examines
motherhood and marriage with a
beady eye.

wd Hal Hartley   *ph* Michael
Spiller   *m* Phillip Reed   *pd* Dan
Ouellette   *ed* Nick Gomez

Adrienne Shelly, Martin Donovan,
Marritt Nelson, John MacKay, Edie
Falco, Gary Sauer, Matt Malloy

Tugboat Annie**
US 1933 88m bw
MGM (Harry Rapf)

An elderly waterfront lady and her
boozy friend smooth out the path of
young love.

Hilarious and well-loved comedy
vehicle for two great stars of the
period.

w Zelda Sears, Eve Greene
stories Norman Reilly Raine
d Mervyn Le Roy   *ph* Gregg Toland

Marie Dressler, Wallace Beery, Robert
Young, Maureen O'Sullivan, Willard
Robertson, Paul Hurst

'One of those rare naturals in the
picture business – a flicker that sells
itself immediately the stars' names go
into the lights.' – *Variety*

'A bare outline of the story cannot convey the note of mother love that runs through it, the laughs, the pathos.' – *Picturegoer*

'They're having a secret love affair. Only fifty thousand listeners know about it.'

Tune In Tomorrow*
US 1990 104m colour
Hobo/Polar/Odyssey/Cinecom (John Fielder, Mark Tarlov)
V
GB title: *Aunt Julia and The Scriptwriter*

A writer of a daily radio serial manipulates an affair between a young journalist and his older aunt to provide material for his scripts.

A comedy at the expense of soap operas and the original novel.

w William Boyd *novel Aunt Julia and The Scriptwriter* by Mario Vargas Llosa d Jon Amiel ph Robert Stevens m Wynton Marsalis pd Jim Clay, James L. Schoppe ed Peter Boyle

Barbara Hershey, Keanu Reeves, Peter Falk, Bill McCutheon, Patricia Clarkson, Richard Portnow, Jerome Dempsey

'A sharp-fanged novel has been turned into an ingratiating puppy walking on its hind legs.' – *Philip French, Observer*

Turtle Diary*
GB 1985 97m Technicolor
CBS/United British Artists/Britannic (Richard Johnson)

Two self-admitted eccentrics take it upon themselves to release turtles from captivity in the London Zoo.

Mainly ineffective character comedy, memorable only for fragments of dialogue and acting.

w Harold Pinter *novel* Russell

Hoban d John Irvin ph Peter Hannan m Geoffrey Burgon pd Leo Austin ed Peter Tanner

Glenda Jackson, Ben Kingsley, Richard Johnson, Michael Gambon, Rosemary Leach, Eleanor Bron, Harriet Walter, Nigel Hawthorne, Michael Aldridge

The Tuttles of Tahiti
US 1942 91m bw
RKO (Sol Lesser)

The Tuttles have one ambition: to do no work.

A negative prospect even for a light comedy, and this one rapidly sinks under a welter of flat dialogue.

w S. Lewis Meltzer, Robert Carson, James Hilton *novel No More Gas* by Charles Noordhof, James Norman Hall d Charles Vidor

Charles Laughton, Jon Hall, Victor Francen, Peggy Drake, Florence Bates

The Twelve Chairs
US 1970 93m Movielab
UMC/Crossbow (Michael Hertzberg)
L

A Russian bureaucrat chases twelve dining chairs, in one of which is hidden the family jewels.

Tedious Mel Brooks romp with not too many laughs, from a yarn better handled in *Keep Your Seats Please* and *It's in the Bag*, from both of which he might have learned something about comedy timing.

w Mel Brooks *novel* Ilya Ilf, Evgeny Petrov d Mel Brooks ph Dorde Nikolic m John Morris

Ron Moody, Frank Langella, Dom De Luise, Bridget Brice, Diana Coupland, Mel Brooks

'In the end it runs out of both steam

and jokes.' – *Michael Billington,
Illustrated London News*

Twelve Plus One

Italy/France 1969 108m
Technicolor
CEF/COFCI (Claude Giroux, Edward J.
Pope)
original title: *Una su 13*; aka: *The Twelve
Chairs*

After he sells some chairs inherited
from his aunt, a barber discovers that
one of them contains a fortune and
sets out to retrieve it.

Broad farce that wastes the talents of
its cast, though it contains a bizarrely
enjoyable moment by Welles as a
barnstorming actor giving a ham
performance of *Dr Jekyll and Mr Hyde*.

w Marc Behm, Dennis Norden,
Nicolas Gessner *novel Twelve Chairs*
by Ilf and Petrov *d* Nicolas
Gessner *ph* Giuseppe
Ruzzolini *m* Stelvio Cipriani
ed Giancarlo Cappelli

Sharon Tate, Vittorio Gassman, Orson
Welles, Vittoria De Sica, Terry-
Thomas, Mylene Demongeot,
Grégoire Aslan, Tim Brooke-Taylor,
Lionel Jeffries

Twentieth Century**

US 1934 91m bw
Columbia (Howard Hawks)
V

A temperamental Broadway producer
trains an untutored actress, but when
a star she proves a match for him.

Though slightly lacking in pace, this is
a marvellously sharp and memorable
theatrical burlesque, and the second
half, set on the train of the title,
reaches highly agreeable peaks of
insanity.

w *Ben Hecht, Charles MacArthur,*

play *Napoleon of Broadway* by Charles
Bruce Millholland *d* Howard
Hawks *ph* Joseph August

John Barrymore, Carole Lombard,
Roscoe Karns, Walter Connolly,
Ralph Forbes, *Etienne Girardot*, Charles
Lane, Edgar Kennedy

'Probably too smart for general
consumption . . . a long shot for
grosses outside the large cities that
boast a cosmopolitan clientele.' –
Variety
'Notable as the first comedy in which
sexually attractive, sophisticated stars
indulged in their own slapstick instead
of delegating it to their inferiors.' –
Andrew Sarris, 1963
'In the role of Jaffe John Barrymore
fits as wholly and smoothly as a
banana in a skin.' – *Otis Ferguson*

Twice in a Lifetime

US 1985 117m colour
Yorkin Company/Bud Yorkin
V

A man turns fifty and decides to make
a clean break with his family.

Comedy drama of the mid-life crisis:
nothing new.

w Colin Welland *play Kisses at 50*
by Colin Welland *d* Bud Yorkin
ph Nick McLean *m* Pat Metheny,
Paul McCartney *pd* William
Creber *ed* Robert Jones

Gene Hackman, Ellen Burstyn, Ann-
Margret, Amy Madigan, Ally Sheedy
AAN: Amy Madigan (supporting
actress)

Twice round the Daffodils

GB 1962 89m bw
Anglo Amalgamated/GHW (Peter Rogers)

Comic and serious episodes in the
lives of male patients at a TB
sanatorium.

Acceptable broadening, almost in *Carry On* style, of a modestly successful play.

w Norman Hudis   *play Ring for Catty* by Patrick Cargill, Jack Beale   *d* Gerald Thomas   *ph* Alan Hume   *m* Bruce Montgomery

Juliet Mills, Donald Sinden, Donald Houston, Kenneth Williams, Ronald Lewis, Joan Sims, Andrew Ray, Lance Percival, Jill Ireland, Sheila Hancock, Nanette Newman

Twice Two
US   1933   20m   bw
Hal Roach
V, V(C)

Stan and Ollie have each married the other's twin sister . . .

Strained and laboured trick comedy in which neither the double exposures nor the gags quite come off.

w Stan Laurel   *d* James Parrott

Laurel and Hardy

Twins*
US   1988   107m   DeLuxe
UIP/Universal (Ivan Reitman)
V, L

A 36-year-old man, bred in a genetic experiment as the perfect man, discovers that he has a less-than-perfect twin brother.

Amusing, if sometimes ponderous, comedy with the joke depending on the physical disparity of its two protagonists.

w William Davies, William Osborne, Timothy Harris, Herschel Weingrod   *d* Ivan Reitman   *ph* Andrzej Bartkowiak   *m* Georges Delerue, Randy Edelman   *pd* James D. Bissel   *ed* Sheldon Kahn, Donn Cambern

Arnold Schwarzenegger, Danny DeVito, Kelly Preston, Chloe Webb, Bonnie Bartlett, Marshall Bell, Trey Wilson, David Caruso, Hugh O'Brien

Two for the Road*
GB   1966   113m   DeLuxe   Panavision
TCF/Stanley Donen
L

An architect and his wife motoring through France recall the first twelve years of their relationship.

Fractured, fashionable light romantic comedy dressed up to seem of more significance than the gossamer thing it really is; and some of the gossamer has a Woolworth look.

w Frederic Raphael   *d* Stanley Donen   *ph Christopher Challis*   *m* Henry Mancini

Albert Finney, Audrey Hepburn. Eleanor Bron, William Daniels, Claude Dauphin

'The facile, comic bits set off audience expectations which are then betrayed, and the clever, bitter stuff just seems sour.' – *Pauline Kael, New Yorker*
AAN: Frederic Raphael

Two for the Seesaw
US   1962   120m   bw   Panavision
UA/Seesaw/Mirisch/Argyle/Talbot (Robert Wise)

A New York dance instructress has a tempestuous affair with an Omaha attorney on the verge of divorce.

Serious comedy or light drama, meticulously detailed but immensely long for its content and too revealing of its stage origins.

w Isobel Lennart   *play* William Gibson   *d* Robert Wise   *ph* Ted McCord   *m* André Previn   *ad* Boris Leven

Robert Mitchum, Shirley Maclaine
AAN: Ted McCord; song 'Second
Chance' (*m* André Previn, *ly* Dory
Langdon)

The Two Lives of Mattia Pascal**

Italy/West Germany   1984   118m
   colour
RAI/Excelsior Cinematografica/Cinecitta/
   Antenne 2/Telemunchen/RTVE/RTS1/
   Channel 4 (Silvia D'Amico Bendico,
   Carlo Cucci)
original title: *Le Due Vite di Mattia Pascal*

Cheated out of his inheritance and
humiliated by his wife, a man adopts
a new identity.

Witty, dark comedy of a personality
crisis.

w Suso Cecchi D'Amico, Ennio De
Concini, Amanzo Todini, Mario
Monicelli   *novel Il Fu Mattia Pascal*
by Luigi Pirandello   *d* Mario
Monicelli   *ph* Camillo Bazzoni
m Nicola Piovani   *ad* Lorenzo
Baraldi   *ed* Ruggero Mastroianni

Marcello Mastroianni, Flavio Bucci,
Laura Morante, Laura Del Sol, Nestor
Garay, Alessandro Haber, Carlo
Bagno, Rosalia Maggio, Senta Berger,
Bernard Blier

Two of a Kind

US   1983   87m   DeLuxe
TCF (Roger M. Rothstein, Joe Wizan)
L

Four angels propose that Earth be
spared from a second flood if two
arbitrarily chosen human beings can
be seen to perform a great sacrifice
for each other.

Curious reversion to angelic comedies
of the thirties and forties. Lacking the
right measures of wit and whimsy, it
is totally unsuccessful.

wd John Herzfeld   *ph* Fred
Koenekamp, Warren Rothenberger
md Patrick Williams   *pd* Albert
Brenner

John Travolta, Olivia Newton-John,
Charles Durning, Oliver Reed,
Beatrice Straight, Scatman Crothers

'It feels as if it must be a remake of
something . . .' – Sheila Johnston, MFB

Two Tars****

US   1928   20m   bw   silent
Hal Roach
V

Two sailors in an old banger cause a
traffic jam and a consequent escalation
of violence.

Marvellous elaboration of a tit-for-tat
situation, with the stars already at their
technical best.

w Leo McCarey, H. M. Walker
d James Parrott

Laurel and Hardy, Edgar Kennedy,
Charley Rogers

Two Way Stretch**

GB   1960   87m   bw
British Lion/Shepperton (M. Smedley
   Aston)

Three convicts break jail to rob a
maharajah.

Amusing comedy with good
performances and situations,
unofficially borrowed in part from
Convict 99.

w John Warren, Len Heath   *d* Robert
Day   *ph* Geoffrey Faithfull
m Ken Jones

Peter Sellers, *Lionel Jeffries,* Wilfrid
Hyde White, Bernard Cribbins, David
Lodge, Maurice Denham, Beryl Reid,
Liz Fraser, Irene Handl, George
Woodbridge

Unaccustomed as We Are

US 1929 20m bw silent
Hal Roach
V(C)

Ollie takes a friend home to dinner, but his wife walks out, leaving him to get into all kinds of trouble.

The team's first sound comedy, rather hesitant in its use of the new medium. The story was later reworked as the last half hour of *Blockheads*.

w Leo McCarey and H. M. Walker
d Lewis R. Foster

Laurel and Hardy, Edgar Kennedy, Mae Busch, Thelma Todd

Uncle Benjamin

France 1969 90m Eastmancolor
Gaumont International (Robert Sussfeld, Roger Debelmas)
original title: *Mon Oncle Benjamin*

A rakish country doctor tries to seduce the virginal daughter of the local innkeeper.

A Gallic attempt at the bawdy zest of *Tom Jones*, often coarse in tone and closer to the *Carry On* films in style.

w André Couteaux, Jean-François Hauduro, Edouard Molinaro
d Edouard Molinaro *ph* Alain Levent *m* Jacques Brel, François Rauber *ed* Robert and Monique Isnardon

Jacques Brel, Claude Jade, Rosy Varte, Bernard Alane, Paul Frankeur, Alfred Adam, Bernard Blier

Uncle Buck*

US 1989 100m DeLuxe
UIP/Universal (John Hughes, Tom Jacobson)
V, L

A good-natured but slobbish layabout straightens out his sister's warring children and learns to love domesticity.

Rambling, moderately enjoyable comedy, although it is not far removed from a television sit-com.

wd John Hughes *ph* Ralph Bode *m* Ira Newborn *pd* John W. Corso *ed* Lou Lombardo, Tom Lombardo, Peck Prior

John Candy, Jean Louisa Kelly, Gaby Hoffman, Macauley Culkin, Amy Madigan, Elaine Bromka, Garrett M. Brown

Under the Rainbow

US 1981 95m colour
Orion/Warner

Nazis and midgets mingle backstage while *The Wizard of Oz* is being filmed.

Zany fantasy which someone must have thought was a good idea. Wrong.

w Pat McCormick, Harry Hurwitz, Martin Smith, Pat Bradley, Fred Bauer *d* Steve Rash

Chevy Chase, Carrie Fisher, Billy Barty, Eve Arden, Joseph Maher

† The film allegedly cost 20 million dollars and took eight.

Under the Yum Yum Tree
US 1963 110m Eastmancolor
Columbia/Sonnis/Swift (Frederick Brisson)

Two college students have a trial marriage in an apartment block with a lecherous landlord.

Coy, non-erotic and extremely tedious comedy which runs out of jokes after reel one.

w Lawrence Roman, David Swift
d David Swift   ph Joseph Biroc
m Frank de Vol

Jack Lemmon, Carol Lynley, Dean Jones, Imogene Coca, Edie Adams, Paul Lynde, Robert Lansing

Unfaithfully Yours**
US 1948 105m bw
TCF (Preston Sturges)
L

An orchestral conductor believes his wife is unfaithful, and while conducting a concert thinks of three different ways of dealing with the situation.

A not entirely happy mixture of romance, farce, melodrama and wit, but in general a pretty entertaining concoction and the last major film of its talented writer-director.

wd Preston Sturges   ph Victor Milner   m Alfred Newman

Rex Harrison, Linda Darnell, Barbara Lawrence, Rudy Vallee, Kurt Kreuger, Lionel Stander, Edgar Kennedy, Al Bridge, Julius Tannen, Torben Meyer, Robert Greig

'Harrison discovers more ways of tripping over a telephone cable than one can count, and his efforts to falsify evidence through a recalcitrant tape recorder are as funny as anything thought up by Clair in A Nous La Liberté or by Chaplin in Modern Times.' – Basil Wright, 1972

† The Rex Harrison character is named Sir Alfred de Carter and is meant to be Sir Thomas Beecham. (In America the equivalent of Beecham's Pills is Carter's Little Liver Pills.)

† † The pieces of music played are as follows:

For murder: the Semiramide Overture by Rossini
For surrender: the Venusberg music from Tannhäuser, by Wagner
For Russian roulette: Francesca da Rimini by Tchaikovsky

Unfaithfully Yours
US 1983 96m DeLuxe
TCF (Marvin Worth, Joe Wizan)
L

Modernized and simplified version of the above, with only one plot instead of three.

This proves to be an advantage, and the film does deliver some laughs.

w Valerie Curtin, Barry Levinson, Robert Klane   d Howard Zieff
ph David M. Walsh   m Bill Conti   pd Albert Brenner

Dudley Moore, Nastassja Kinski, Armand Assante, Albert Brooks, Cassie Yates, Richard Libertini, Richard B. Shull

Up in Arms**
US 1944 106m Technicolor
Samuel Goldwyn

A hypochondriac joins the army.

Loose, generally pleasant introductory vehicle for Danny Kaye.

w Don Hartman, Robert Pirosh, Allen Boretz   d Elliott Nugent   ph Ray Rennahan   md Ray Heindorf, Louis Forbes

Danny Kaye, Dinah Shore, Constance Dowling, Dana Andrews, Louis Calhern, Lyle Talbot

'Not since Greta Garbo made her bow has there been anything so terrific as the inimitable Danny, one of the most exhilarating and spontaneous personalities in film history.' – *New York Daily Mirror*
AAN: song 'Now I Know' (*m* Harold Arlen, *ly* Ted Koehler); Ray Heindorf, Louis Forbes

Up in Smoke
US   1978   86m   colour
Paramount (Lou Adler, Lou Lombardo)

Two dopeheads from a rock band go in search of pot so that they can play.

Direly unamusing; the slapstick is badly timed and the humour infantile. Stoned or sober, Cheech and Chong are the least funny comedy team since The Three Stooges.

w Tommy Chong, Cheech Marin   d Lou Adler   ph Gene Polito   ad Leon Ericksen   ed Scott Conrad, Lou Lombardo

Cheech Marin, Tommy Chong, Strother Martin, Edie Adams, Stacy Keach, Tom Skerritt

'The humor is like dogface underclass humor – but without the resentment of the officers. And Cheech and Chong are so gracefully dumb-assed that if you're in a relaxed mood you can't help laughing at them.' – *Pauline Kael, New Yorker*

Up in the World
GB   1956   91m   bw
Rank (Hugh Stewart)

A window cleaner becomes friendly with a boy millionaire.

Slow and unattractive comedy star vehicle.

w Jack Davies, Henry Blyth, Peter Blackmore   d John Paddy Carstairs   ph Jack Cox   m Philip Green

Norman Wisdom, Martin Caridia, Jerry Desmonde, Maureen Swanson, Ambrosine Philpotts, Colin Gordon

Up Pompeii
GB   1971   90m   Technicolor
EMI/Associated London Films (Ned Sherrin)
V

A wily slave outwits Nero and escapes the eruption of Vesuvius.

Yawnmaking spinoff of a lively TV comedy series: the jokes just lie there, and die there.

w Sid Colin   d Bob Kellett   ph Ian Wilson   m Carl Davis

Frankie Howerd, Patrick Cargill, Michael Hordern, Barbara Murray, Lance Percival, Bill Fraser, Adrienne Posta

† Sequels: *Up the Front, Up the Chastity Belt* (qv).

Up the Chastity Belt*
GB   1971   94m   Technicolor
EMI/Associated London Films (Ned Sherrin)
V

Medieval adventures of the serf Lurkalot and his master Sir Coward de Custard.

Patchy pantomime which doesn't

always have the courage of its own slapdash vulgarity.

w Sid Colin, Ray Galton, Alan Simpson   d Bob Kellett   ph Ian Wilson   m Carl Davis

Frankie Howerd, Graham Crowden, Bill Fraser, Roy Hudd, Hugh Paddick, Anna Quayle, Eartha Kitt, Dave King, Fred Emney

Up the Creek*
GB 1958 83m bw
  HammerScope
Byron (Henry Halsted)

A none-too-bright naval lieutenant is assigned command of a broken-down shore establishment.

Cheeky remake of Oh Mr Porter. Jokes fair, atmosphere cheerful and easy-going.

wd Val Guest   ph Arthur Grant

David Tomlinson, Peter Sellers, Wilfrid Hyde White, Vera Day, Tom Gill, Michael Goodliffe, Reginald Beckwith, Lionel Jeffries

† Sequel: Further Up the Creek.

Up the Sandbox
US 1972 98m Technicolor
Barwood/First Artists (Robert Chartoff, Irwin Winkler)
L

A professor's wife finds she is pregnant again and fantasizes about her future life.

Muddled comedy-drama with little point and less entertainment value.

w Paul Zindel   novel Anne Richardson Roiphe   d Irwin Kershner   ph Gordon Willis, Andy Marton   m Billy Goldenberg   ad Harry Horner

Barbra Streisand, David Selby, Ariane Heller, Jane Hoffman

'A magical mystery tour through the picture book mind of one Manhattan housewife.' – Richard Combs

Uptown Saturday Night*
US 1974 104m Technicolor
Warner/Verdon/First Artists (Melville Tucker)
V

Three friends pursue crooks who have inadvertently stolen a winning lottery ticket.

Witless but high-spirited star comedy for blacks, with a variety of sordid backgrounds.

w Richard Wesley   d Sidney Poitier   ph Fred J. Koenekamp   m Tom Scott

Sidney Poitier, Bill Cosby, Harry Belafonte, Flip Wilson, Roscoe Lee Browne, Richard Pryor, Rosalind Cash, Paula Kelly

'If it had been filmed with a white cast this collection of atrophied comedy routines would have been indistinguishable from a Monogram farce of the forties.' – David McGillivray

Used Cars*
US 1980 111m Metrocolor
Columbia (Bob Gale)

For the love of his boss's daughter, a fast-talking car salesman saves a used-car lot from being taken over by a mean-spirited rival.

Vigorous broad comedy, amusing enough if you're feeling indulgent.

w Robert Zemeckis, Bob Gale   d Robert Zemeckis   ph Donald M. Morgan   m Patrick Williams   pd Peter M. Jamison   ed Michael Kahn

Kurt Russell, Gerrit Graham, Frank McRae, Deborah Harmon, Jack Russell

'A classic screwball fantasy – a neglected modern comedy that's like a more restless and visually high-spirited version of the W. C. Fields pictures.' – *Pauline Kael, New Yorker*

□ □ □ □ □ □

Very Important Person**
GB 1961 98m bw
Rank/Independent Artists (Julian Wintle,
  Leslie Parkyn)
US title: *A Coming-Out Party*

A senior British scientist is caught by
the Nazis and has to be rescued.

Very satisfactory British comedy with
a few suspense scenes; POW fare with
a difference.

w Jack Davies   *d* Ken Annakin
ph Ernest Steward   *m* Reg Owen

James Robertson Justice, Stanley Baxter,
Leslie Phillips, Eric Sykes, Richard
Wattis, Colin Gordon

Vice Versa*
GB 1947 111m bw
Rank/Two Cities (Peter Ustinov, George
  H. Brown)

A magic stone enables an unhappy
Victorian boy to change places with
his pompous father.

Funny moments can't disguise the
fact that this overlong comedy is a bit
of a fizzle, its talented creator not
being a film-maker. A pity, as British
films have so rarely entered the
realms of fancy.

wd Peter Ustinov   *novel* F. Anstey

Roger Livesey, Kay Walsh, Anthony
Newley, *James Robertson Justice*, David
Hutcheson, Petula Clark, Joan Young

'A repository of English oddities.' –
John Russell Taylor

Vice Versa
US 1988 98m colour
Columbia (Dick Clement, Ian La Frenais)
V, L

A father and his 11-year-old son find
their minds transplanted into the
other's body by a magic skull.

One of the last and certainly the least
of the mid-1980s cycle of role
swapping movies.

w Dick Clement, Ian La Frenais
d Brian Gilbert   *ph* King
Baggott   *m* David Shire   *pd* Jim
Schoppe   *ed* David Garfield

Judge Reinhold, Fred Savage, Corinne
Bohrer, Swoosie Kurtz, David Profal,
Jane Kaczmerek, Gloria Gifford

Victor/Victoria*
GB 1982 134m Technicolor
  Panavision
MGM/Peerford/Ladbroke Entertainments/
  Blake Edwards
V, L

In 1934 Paris, a girl singer becomes
successful when she poses as a female
impersonator, but it causes
complications in her love life.

The story was previously filmed more
innocuously as a Jessie Matthews
vehicle, *First a Girl*; Edwards makes it
a sexually harping, grotesque low

comedy, but there are pleasurable moments.

wd Blake Edwards, from the German film of 1933 *Viktor und Viktoria* (*wd* Reinhold Schunzel)   *ph* Dick Bush   *m* Henry Mancini *pd* Rodger Maus

Julie Andrews, James Garner, *Robert Preston*, Lesley Anne Warren, Alex Karras, John Rhys-Davies, Graham Stark

'An audience pleaser in the worst sense.' – *New Yorker*
'Edwards' idea of European sophistication and Gallic naughtiness is seen throughout to be depressingly crude, parochial and second-hand, based on old American farces and reprises of his own Clouseau routines.' – *Sunday Times*

AA: original song score (Henry Mancini, Leslie Bricusse)
AAN: Julie Andrews; Robert Preston; Lesley Ann Warren; screenplay (adaptation); costume design; art direction

Vintage Wine
GB   1935   90m   bw
Gaumont-British/Real Art (Julius Hagen)

A 62-year-old widower upsets his family by marrying a young girl.

Amiable boulevard comedy transferred to the screen in a stagey fashion but providing a vehicle for the well-honed comic skills of Seymour Hicks.

w H. Fowler Mear, Seymour Hicks, Ashley Dukes   *play Der Ewige Jüngling* by Alexander Engel *d* Henry Edwards   *ph* Sydney Blyth   *md* W. L. Trytel   *ad* James A. Carter   *ed* Ralph Kemplen

Seymour Hicks, Claire Luce, Eva Moore, Judy Gunn, Miles Malleson, Kynaston Reeves, A. Bromley Davenport, Michael Shepley

'Sooner or later they're going to get it!'
The Virgin Soldiers
GB   1969   96m   Technicolor
Columbia/Carl Foreman (Leslie Gilliat, Ned Sherrin)
V

Serio-comic adventures of recruits in the British army in 1960 Singapore.

Autobiographical fragments, mostly from below the belt, sharply observed and often very funny.

w John Hopkins   *novel* Leslie Thomas   *d* John Dexter   *ph* Ken Higgins   *m* Peter Greenwell

Hywel Bennett, Nigel Patrick, *Lynn Redgrave*, Nigel Davenport, *Rachel Kempson*, Michael Gwynn, Tsai Chin

'A kind of monstrous mating of *Private's Progress* and *The Family Way*, with bits of *The Long and the Short and the Tall* thrown in for good measure.' – *David Pirie*

† Sequel 1977: *Stand Up Virgin Soldiers.*

Viridiana
Spain/Mexico   1961   91m   bw
Uninci/Films 59/Gustavo Alatriste (Munoz Suay)

A novice about to take her vows is corrupted by her wicked uncle and installs a load of beggars in his house.

Often hilarious surrealist melodrama packed with shades of meaning, most of them sacrilegious. A fascinating film to watch.

w Luis Buñuel, Julio Alajandro *d* Luis Buñuel   *ph* José F. Agayo

Silvia Pinal, Francisco Rabal, Fernando Rey

'One of the cinema's few major philosophical works.' – *Robert Vas*

'They Weren't Born Yesterday!'
Les Visiteurs*
France 1993 107m colour
Arrow/Gaumont/France3/Alpilles/Amigo (Alain Terzain)

A knight and his servant are transported from the twelfth century to the modern day.

Broad farce that will appeal to lovers of Carry On films.

w Christian Claiver, Jean-Marc Poir d Jean-Marc Poir

Christian Clavier, Jean Reno, Valrie Lemercier, Marie-Anne Chazel, Christian Bujeau, Isabelle Nanty, Didier Pain

'People fall over a lot, or hit each other, or shout very loud.' – *Sight and Sound*

† The film was the biggest success of 1993 in France, taking twice as much at the box-office as the No 2 film, *Jurassic Park*.

Viva Max
US 1969 93m Eastmancolor
Commonwealth United/Mark Carliner

A Mexican general marches his troops into Texas and seizes the Alamo.

Flat comedy with mildly amusing passages but too much noise, bluster and sentiment.

w Elliott Baker *novel* James Lehrer d Jerry Paris ph Jack Richards m Hugo Montenegro

Peter Ustinov, *John Astin*, Pamela Tiffin, Jonathan Winters, Keenan Wynn, Henry Morgan, Alice Ghostley

Vivacious Lady*
US 1938 90m bw
RKO (George Stevens)

A night-club singer marries a botany professor and has trouble with his parents.

Pleasant romantic comedy for two popular stars.

w P. J. Wolfson, Ernest Pagano
d George Stevens ph Robert de Grasse m Roy Webb

Ginger Rogers, James Stewart, Charles Coburn, Beulah Bondi, James Ellison, Frances Mercer, Franklin Pangborn, Grady Sutton, Jack Carson

'A good-natured, unpretentiously entertaining comedy.' – *New Yorker*
AAN: Robert de Grasse

Volere Volare*
Italy 1991 92m colour
Metro/Italtoons (Ernesto di Sarro, Mario Cecchi Gori, Vittorio Cecchi Gori)
V, L

A sound engineer who dubs animated films finds himself changing into a cartoon character as he becomes involved with a psycho-sexual prostitute.

Witty and inventive comedy that mixes live action and animation to amusing effect.

wd Maurizio Nichetti, Guido Manuli ph Mario Battistoni
ad Maria Pio Angelini ed Rita Rossi

Maurizio Nichetti, Angela Finocchiaro, Mariella Valentina, Patrizio Roversi

'An offbeat fable for adults. Pic's expensive technical bravura is more impressive than the comedy.' – *Variety*

The Wackiest Ship in the Army
US   1960   99m   Technicolor
  Cinemascope
Columbia/Fred Kohlmar

In the South Pacific during World War II a decrepit sailing ship with an inexperienced crew manages to confuse Japanese patrols and land a scout behind enemy lines.

Slapstick war comedy with fragments of action; effect rather muddled.

wd Richard Murphy   *story* Herbert Carlson   *ph* Charles Lawton   *m* George Duning

Jack Lemmon, Ricky Nelson, John Lund, Chips Rafferty, Tom Tully, Joby Baker, Warren Berlinger, Richard Anderson

Wake Me When It's Over
US   1960   126m   DeLuxe
  Cinemascope
TCF/Mervyn Le Roy

Soldiers holding a Pacific island build a de luxe hotel from surplus war material.

Aptly-titled army farce on the lines of *The Teahouse of the August Moon* but constructed from inferior material. Yawningly tedious.

w Richard Breen   *novel* Howard Singer   *d* Mervyn Le Roy   *ph* Leon Shamroy   *m* Cyril Mockridge

Ernie Kovacs, Dick Shawn, Jack Warden, Margo Moore, Nobu McCarthy, Don Knotts, Robert Emhardt

Walk, Don't Run*
US   1966   114m   Technicolor
  Panavision
Columbia/Granley (Sol C. Siegel)

In Tokyo during the Olympics accommodation is hard to find, and two men move in with a girl.

Witless reprise of *The More the Merrier*, notable only for the Tokyo backgrounds and for Cary Grant's farewell appearance.

w Sol Saks   *d* Charles Walters   *ph* Harry Stradling   *m* Quincy Jones

Cary Grant, Samantha Eggar, Jim Hutton, *John Standing*, Miiko Taka

'Too long as are most comedies today, it seems to take its title far too literally; but there are several very funny sequences, a jaunty score, and the unflawed elegance of Mr Grant.'
– *Arthur Knight*

The Waltz of the Toreadors*
GB   1962   105m   Technicolor
Rank Wintle-Parkyn (Peter de Sarigny)

A lecherous retired general finds his past creeping up on him and loses his young mistress to his son.

Lukewarm adaptation of a semi-classic comedy, disastrously

translated to English setting and characters.

w Wolf Mankowitz   *play* Jean Anouilh   *d* John Guillermin   *ph* John Wilcox   *m* Richard Addinsell   *pd* Wilfrid Shingleton

Peter Sellers, Margaret Leighton, Dany Robin, John Fraser, Cyril Cusack, Prunella Scales

Waltzes from Vienna
GB   1933   80m   bw
Gaumont (Tom Arnold)
US title: *Strauss's Great Waltz*

A romance of the Strausses.

There is very little music and very little Hitchcock in this extremely mild romantic comedy.

w Alma Reville, Guy Bolton *play* Guy Bolton   *d* Alfred Hitchcock   *ph* Glen MacWilliams

Jessie Matthews, Esmond Knight, Frank Vosper, Fay Compton, Edmund Gwenn, Robert Hale, Hindle Edgar

'I hate this sort of thing. Melodrama is the only thing I can do.' – *Alfred Hitchcock*

The War between Men and Women
US   1972   105m   Technicolor Panavision
National General/Jalem/Llenroc/4D (Danny Arnold)

A half-blind cartoonist marries a divorcee and is troubled by her ex-husband.

Semi-serious comedy vaguely based on Thurber, but not so that you'd notice, apart from the blind hero; generally neither funny nor affecting.

w Mel Shavelson, Danny Arnold, based on the writings of James Thurber   *d* Melville Shavelson

ph Charles F. Wheeler   *m* Marvin Hamlisch   *pd* Stan Jolley

Jack Lemmon, Barbara Harris, Jason Robards Jnr, Herb Edelman, Lisa Gerritsen

'Once in a lifetime comes a motion picture that makes you feel like falling in love all over again. This is not that movie.'

The War of the Roses*
US   1989   116m   DeLuxe
Fox/Gracie Films (James L. Brooks, Arnon Milchan)
V

A couple who decide to divorce fight to the death over who gets the house.

Rancorous comedy, sometimes amusing but too mean-spirited for many laughs.

w Michael Leeson   *novel* Warren Adler   *d* Danny DeVito   *ph* Stephen H. Burum   *m* David Newman   *pd* Ida Random   *ed* Lynzee Klingman

Michael Douglas, Kathleen Turner, Danny DeVito, Marianne Sägebrecht, Sean Astin, Heather Fairfield, G. D. Spradlin, Trenton Teigen, Bethany McKinney

Watch It, Sailor
GB   1961   81m   bw
Columbia/Cormorant/Hammer (Maurice Cowan)

A sailor about to be married receives a paternity accusation.

Glum farce with wasted talent.

w Falkland Cary, Phillip King *play* Falkland Cary, Phillip King *d* Wolf Rilla   *ph* Arthur Grant *m* Douglas Gamley   *ad* Bernard Robinson, Don Mingaye   *ed* James Needs, Alfred Cox

Dennis Price, Marjorie Rhodes, Irene

Handl, Liz Fraser, Vera Day, John
Meillon, Cyril Smith

Watch the Birdie
US 1950 71m bw
MGM (Harry Ruskin)

A photographer meets a rich girl and
saves her from a crook.

Unhappy remake of Buster Keaton's
The Cameraman, enlivened by a chase
finale, but not helped by the star
playing three members of the same
family.

w Ivan Tors, Devery Freeman, Harry
Ruskin   d Jack Donohue
ph Paul C. Vogel   m George Stoll

Red Skelton, Arlene Dahl, Ann Miller,
Leon Ames, Pamela Britton, Richard
Rober

Water*
GB 1985 95m colour
HandMade (Ian La Frenais)

Chaos comes to a Caribbean island
when industrialists check it for mineral
springs.

Hysterical comedy which never
develops a single line for long, and
quickly wears out its welcome.

w Dick Clement, Ian La Frenais, Bill
Bersky   d Dick Clement
ph Douglas Slocombe   m Mike
Moran

Michael Caine, Valerie Perrine,
Brenda Vaccaro, Leonard Rossiter,
Billy Connolly, Fred Gwynne,
Maureen Lipman

Watermelon Man
US 1970 100m Technicolor
Columbia/Johanna (John B. Bennett)

A bigoted insurance salesman wakes
up one morning to find he has turned
into a black man.

Spasmodically funny racial comedy,
compromised by the impossibility of
a black man playing white even with
heavy make-up.

w Herman Raucher   d Melvin Van
Peebles   ph W. Wallace Kelley
m Melvin Van Peebles

Godfrey Cambridge, Estelle Parsons,
Howard Caine, Mantan Moreland

Way Back Home
US 1932 81m bw
RKO

Problems of a Maine preacher.

Unintentionally hilarious farrago of
dark deeds in a small town, from a
radio serial.

w Jane Murfin   d William A. Seiter

Phillips Lord, Bette Davis, Effie
Palmer, Bennett Kilpack, Frank
Albertson, Mrs Phillips Lord

Way Out West****
US 1937 66m bw
Hal Roach (Stan Laurel)
V, V(C), L

Laurel and Hardy come to Brushwood
Gulch to deliver the deed to a gold
mine.

Seven reels of perfect joy, with the
comedians at their very best in
brilliantly-timed routines, plus two
song numbers as a bonus.

w Jack Jevne, Charles Rogers, James
Parrott, Felix Adler   d James
Horne   ph Art Lloyd, Walter
Lundin   m Marvin Hatley

Stan Laurel, Oliver Hardy, James
Finlayson, Sharon Lynne, Rosina
Lawrence

'Thin returns indicated . . . for added
feature on duallers.' – *Variety*
'Not only one of their most perfect

films, it ranks with the best screen comedy anywhere.' – *David Robinson, 1962*

'The film is leisurely in the best sense; you adjust to a different rhythm and come out feeling relaxed as if you'd had a vacation.' – *New Yorker, 1980*

AAN: Marvin Hatley

'You'll laugh. You'll cry. You'll hurl.'

Wayne's World
US 1992 95m Technicolor
UIP/Paramount (Lorne Michaels)
V

A ramshackle cable TV show, put together by two girl- and rock-obsessed teenagers, is given big-time exposure by a sleazy TV executive.

Tedious teen comedy, based on characters developed for the *Saturday Night Live* TV show, which long outstays its welcome. It was, though, one of 1992's surprise hits, ranking sixth at the US box-office and doing well in Europe.

w Mike Myers, Bonnie Turner, Terry Turner *d* Penelope Spheeris
ph Theo Van de Sande *m* J. Peter Robinson *pd* Gregg Fonseca
ed Malcolm Campbell

Mike Myers, Dana Carvey, Rob Lowe, Tia Carrere, Brian Doyle-Murray, Lara Flynn Boyle, Michael DeLuise, Dan Bell

'Aggressively pitched at a young white male audience, feature is unlikely to appeal to mainstream moviegoers . . . Even for fans of the TV comics, the laugh-to-running-time ratio is extremely low.' – *Variety*

Wayne's World 2*
US 1993 94m DeLuxe
UPI/Paramount (Lorne Michaels)

In a dream, Wayne is told to organise Waynestock, the ultimate rock concert.

The mixture much the same as the first, but funnier.

w Mike Myers, Bonnie Turner, Terry Turner *d* Stephen Surjik

Mike Myers, Dana Carvey, Christopher Walken, Tia Carrere, Kim Basinger, Ralph Brown, Olivia D'Abo, James Hong, Lee Tergeson

'A puerile, misguided and loathsome effort . . . NOT!' – *Variety*

A Wedding*
US 1978 125m DeLuxe
TCF/Lion's Gate (Thommy Thompson, Robert Altman)

Two families converge for a fashionable wedding, but the day is beset by calamities.

Wide-ranging satirical comedy which despite excellent moments goes on far too long, is rather too black, and is sabotaged by the director's *penchant* for having fourteen people talking at the same time. An exhausting experience.

w John Considine, Patricia Resnick, Allan Nicholls, Robert Altman
d Robert Altman *ph* Charles Rosher *md* Tom Walls

Carol Burnett, Paul Dooley, Amy Stryker, Mia Farrow, Peggy Ann Garner, Lillian Gish, Nina Van Pallandt, Vittorio Gassman, Howard Duff, Desi Arnaz Jnr, Dina Merrill, Geraldine Chaplin, Viveca Lindfors, Lauren Hutton, John Cromwell

Wedding Rehearsal
GB 1932 84m bw
Ideal/London Films/Alexander Korda

A Guards officer foils his grandmother's plans to get him

married by finding suitors for all the young ladies offered.

Frail comedy with unsure technique.

w Helen Gardom   *story* Lajos Biro, George Grossmith   *d* Alexander Korda   *ph* Leslie Rowson *m* Kurt Schroeder   *ad* O. F. Werndorff, Vincent Korda *ed* Harold Young

Roland Young, George Grossmith, John Loder, Lady Tree, Wendy Barrie, Maurice Evans, Joan Gardner, Merle Oberon, Kate Cutler, Edmund Breon

Weekend at Bernie's
US   1989   99m   DuArt
Fox/Gladden (Victor Drai)
V, L

Two minor executives, fearing that they will be blamed when they discover the murdered body of their boss on a weekend visit to his beach house, pretend that he is still alive.

Black farce that manages occasionally to amuse.

w Robert Klane   *d* Ted Kotcheff *ph* François Protat   *m* Andy Summers   *pd* Peter Jamison *ed* Joan E. Chapman

Andrew McCarthy, Jonathan Silverman, Catherine Mary Stewart, Terry Kiser, Don Calfa, Catherine Parks, Eloise Broady, Ted Kotcheff

Weird Science
US   1985   94m   Technicolor
Universal (Joel Silver)
V, L

Teenage science students create a woman from a computer.

Sex-obsessed frolics which go nowhere.

wd John Hughes   *ph* Matthew F.

Leonetti, Joseph Calloway   *m* Ira Newborn   *pd* John W. Corso *ed* Mark Warner, Christopher Lebenzon, Scott Wallace

Anthony Michael Hall, Kelly Le Brock, Ilan Mitchell-Smith, Bill Paxton, Robert Downey

We're No Angels*
US   1954   106m   Technicolor
    Vistavision
Paramount (Pat Duggan)
V, L

Three escaped Devil's Island convicts help a downtrodden storekeeper and his family to outwit a scheming relative.

Whimsical, overstretched period comedy suffering from miscasting but with some pleasantries along the way.

w Ranald MacDougall   *play La Cuisine des Anges* by Albert Husson *d* Michael Curtiz   *ph* Loyal Griggs   *m* Frederick Hollander

Humphrey Bogart, *Peter Ustinov*, Aldo Ray, Joan Bennett, Basil Rathbone, Leo G. Carroll, John Smith

We're No Angels
US   1989   106m   Technicolor
    Panavision
UIP/Paramount (Art Linson)
L

Convicts on the run disguise themselves as priests and take refuge in a monastery.

Dismal remake that suggests its stars have little talent for comedy.

w David Mamet   *play La Cuisine des Anges* by Albert Husson   *d* Neil Jordan   *ph* Philippe Rousselot *m* George Fenton   *pd* Wolf Kroeger   *ed* Mick Audsley, Joke Van Wijk

Robert De Niro, Sean Penn, Demi Moore, Hoyt Axton, Bruno Kirby, Ray McAnally, James Russo, Wallace Shawn, John C. Reilly, Jay Brazeau

We're Not Married*
US 1952 85m bw
TCF (Nunnally Johnson)

Six couples find that they were never legally married.

Amiable, smartly-played compendium of sketches on a familiar theme.

w Nunnally Johnson   d Edmund Goulding   ph Leo Tover   m Cyril Mockridge

Ginger Rogers, Fred Allen, Victor Moore, Paul Douglas, Eve Arden, Marilyn Monroe, David Wayne, Louis Calhern, Zsa Zsa Gabor, Mitzi Gaynor, Eddie Bracken, James Gleason, Jane Darwell

What about Bob?*
US 1991 99m Technicolor
Warner/Touchstone/Touchwood Pacific Partners I (Laura Ziskin)
V, L

A disturbed patient moves in on holidaying psychiatrist and his equally disturbed family.

Intermittently amusing black comedy.

w Tom Schulman   story Alvin Sargent, Laura Ziskin   d Frank Oz   ph Michael Ballhaus   m Miles Goodman   pd Les Dilley   ed Anne V. Coates

Bill Murray, Richard Dreyfuss, Julie Hagerty, Charlie Korsmo, Kathryn Erbe, Tom Aldredge, Susan Willis

'Frank Oz proves that he's a director with just the mean sense of humor these bland times desperately need.' – Richard Schickel, Time

What Did You Do in the War, Daddy?
US 1966 115m DeLuxe Panavision
UA/Mirisch/Geoffrey (Owen Crump, Blake Edwards)

In 1943, an Italian town surrenders readily to the Americans providing its wine festival and football match can take place.

Silly war comedy with insufficient jokes for its wearisome length. The performances are bright enough.

w William Peter Blatty   d Blake Edwards   ph Philip Lathrop   m Henry Mancini

James Coburn, Dick Shawn, Sergio Fantoni, Giovanni Ralli, Aldo Ray, Harry Morgan, Carroll O'Connor, Leon Askin

What Have I Done to Deserve This?*
Spain 1984 101m colour
Metro/Tesauro/Kaktus (Tadeo Villabla)
original title: Que He Hecho Yo Para Merecer Esto?

A slum family falls apart, to the indifference of the busy mother, who takes drugs to keep her awake as she works hard as a cleaner.

Fast-paced inconsequential black comedy, lacking any internal coherence as it rushes from one tasteless joke to another.

wd Pedro Almodóvar   ph Angel Luis Fernandez   m Bernardo Bonezzi   ed Jose Solcedo

Carmen Maura, Luis Hostalot, Angel De Andres-Lopez, Gonzalo Suarez, Veronica Forque, Juan Martinez, Miguel Angel Harranz

'Almodóvar is an underground theatre clown. He may not know how to make anything stay with you

– he may not even care to. He just likes to put on a show. Some of the vignettes might be comedy classics if their timing weren't so sloppy.' – *Pauline Kael, New Yorker*

What, No Beer?

US 1933 65m bw
MGM

A barber rushes to be first on the market with beer after its legalization, but finds himself premature and at odds with gangsters.

Topical farce ending in a slapstick mêlée.

w Carey Wilson, Jack Cluett, Robert E. Hopkins   d Edward Sedgwick

Buster Keaton, Jimmy Durante, Rosco Atcs, Phyllis Barry, John Miljan, Henry Armetta

'A commercial little laugh picture.' – *Variety*

What Price Glory?*

US 1952 111m Technicolor
TCF (Sol C. Siegel)
V

In 1917 France Captain Flagg and Sergeant Quirt spar for the same girl.

Stagey remake of the celebrated silent film and play; watchable if not exactly inspired.

w Phoebe and Henry Ephron
play Maxwell Anderson, Lawrence Stallings   d John Ford   ph Joe MacDonald   m Alfred Newman

James Cagney, Dan Dailey, Corinne Calvet, William Demarest, Robert Wagner, Marisa Pavan, James Gleason

What's New Pussycat?

US/France 1965 108m
Technicolor
UA/Famous Artists (Charles K. Feldman)

A fashion editor is distracted by beautiful girls.

Zany sex comedy with many more misses than hits, a product of the wildly swinging sixties when it was thought that a big budget and stars making fools of themselves would automatically ensure a success.

w Woody Allen   d Clive Donner   ph Jean Badal   m Burt Bacharach

Peter O'Toole, Peter Sellers, Woody Allen, Ursula Andress, Romy Schneider, Capucine, Paula Prentiss

'Unfortunately for all concerned, to make something enjoyably dirty a lot of taste is required.' – *John Simon*
AAN: title song (*m* Burt Bacharach, *ly* Hal David)

What's So Bad About Feeling Good?

US 1965 94m Technicolor
Universal (George Seaton)

A 'happy virus' is carried into New York by a toucan, and affects the lives of various people.

Flimsy pretext for a comedy, further hampered by a less than sparkling script. The actors have their moments.

w George Seaton, Robert Pirosh
d George Seaton   ph Ernesto Caparros   m Frank de Vol

George Peppard, Mary Tyler Moore, Dom De Luise, John McMartin, Susan St James, Don Stroud, Charles Lane

What's Up, Doc?**

US 1972 94m Technicolor
Warner/Saticoy (Peter Bogdanovich)
V, L

In San Francisco, an absent-minded young musicologist is troubled by the attentions of a dotty girl who gets him involved with crooks and a series of accidents.

Madcap comedy, a pastiche of several thirties originals. Spectacular slapstick and willing players are somewhat let down by exhausted patches and a tame final reel.

w Buck Henry, David Newman, Robert Benton d Peter Bogdanovich ph Laszlo Kovacs m Artie Butler pd Polly Pratt

Barbra Streisand, Ryan O'Neal, Kenneth Mars, Austin Pendleton, Madeleine Kahn, Mabel Albertson, Sorrell Booke

'A comedy made by a man who has seen a lot of movies, knows all the mechanics, and has absolutely no sense of humour. Seeing it is like shaking hands with a joker holding a joy buzzer: the effect is both presumptuous and unpleasant.' – Jay Cocks

'It's all rather like a 19th-century imitation of Elizabethan blank verse drama.' – Stanley Kauffmann

'It freely borrows from the best screen comedy down the ages but has no discernible style of its own.' – Michael Billington, Illustrated London News

What's Up, Tiger Lily?*

US 1966 80m Eastmancolor Tohoscope
Benedict/Toho (Woody Allen)
V

A Japanese agent searches for the world's greatest egg salad recipe.

Woody Allen and his American cast re-dub a Japanese spy film to create an off-beat comedy that is amusing in fits and starts.

w Kazuo Yamada, Woody Allen and others d Senkichi Taniguchi m Jack Lewis, The Lovin' Spoonful ed Richard Krown

Tatsua Mihashi, Mie Hama, Akiko Wakabayashi, Tadeo Nakamuru, Susumu Kurobe, Woody Allen, Frank Buxton, Len Maxwell, Louise Lasser, Mickey Rose

'The jokes get rather desperate, but there are enough wildly sophomoric ones to keep this pop stunt fairly amusing until about midway.' – Pauline Kael, New Yorker

When Comedy Was King***

US 1959 84m bw
Robert Youngson Productions

Valuable compilation of silent comedy sequences, with the high print quality and poor commentary to be expected from this source. Extracts include Buster Keaton in Cops, Laurel and Hardy in Big Business, and a Fatty Arbuckle comedy.

ed Robert Youngson

When Harry Met Sally***

US 1989 95m DuArt
Palace/Castle Rock/Nelson Entertainment (Rob Reiner, Andrew Scheinman)
V, L

Over a period of 12 years, a couple meet occasionally to debate whether there can be friendship without sex between a man and a woman.

Deft, witty romantic comedy.

w Nora Ephron d Rob Reiner ph Barry Sonnenfeld m Harry Connick Jr and others pd Jane Musky ed Robert Leighton

Billy Crystal, Meg Ryan, Carrie Fisher, Bruno Kirby, Steven Ford, Lisa Jane Persky, Michelle Nicastro

AAN: Nora Ephron

When We Are Married*
GB 1942 98m bw
British National (John Baxter)

In 1890s Yorkshire, three couples celebrating their silver wedding are told they were never legally married.

A very funny play smartly filmed with a superb cast of character actors.

w Austin Melford, Barbara K. Emery   play J. B. Priestley
d Lance Comfort   ph James Wilson

Raymond Huntley, Marian Spencer, Lloyd Pearson, Olga Lindo, Ernest Butcher, Ethel Coleridge, Sydney Howard, Barry Morse, Lesley Brook, Marjorie Rhodes, Charles Victor, Cyril Smith, George Carney

Where the Boys Are
US 1960 99m Metrocolor
Cinemascope
MGM/Euterpe (Joe Pasternak)

Four college girls spend the Easter vacation near a Florida military post in search of conquests.

Mindless, frothy youth musical, quite smoothly done.

w George Wells   novel Glendon Swarthout   d Henry Levin
ph Robert Bronner   m George Stoll

George Hamilton, Dolores Hart, Paula Prentiss, Jim Hutton, Yvette Mimieux, Connie Francis, Frank Gorshin, Chill Wills, Barbara Nichols

Where the Boys Are
US 1984 94m colour
ITC/TriStar (Allan Carr)
L

The 1960 musical becomes a teenage sex movie.

Neither version has much to do with the original novel.

w Stu Krieger, Jeff Burkhart   d Hy Averback   ph James A. Contner   m Sylvester Levay
ed Melvin Shapiro, Bobbie Shapiro

Lisa Hartman, Lorna Luft, Wendy Schaal, Lynn-Holly Johnson, Russel Todd, Howard McGillin

'A travesty . . . insufferably coy.' – Tom Milne, MFB

Where the Buffalo Roam
US 1980 98m Technicolor
Panavision
Universal (Art Linson)

A drug-crazed journalist takes a trip through Nixon's America.

Frenetic, rarely funny comedy, based on the work of self-styled 'gonzo journalist' Hunter S. Thompson.

w John Kaye   d Art Linson
ph Tak Fujimoto   m Mal Young   pd Richard Sawyer
ed Christopher Greenburg

Peter Boyle, Bill Murray, Bruno Kirby, Rene Auberjonois, R. G. Armstrong, Rafael Campos, Leonard Frey

Where the Heart Is*
US 1990 94m Technicolor
Buena Vista/Touchstone (John Boorman)
V, L

A tycoon orders his children to leave their life of luxury and live in a slum tenement.

Domestic comedy with some heavy-handed humour that is never funny enough to be entertaining.

w John Boorman, Telsche Boorman   d John Boorman
ph Peter Suschitzky   m Peter

Martin   *pd* Carol Spier   *ed* Ian Crafford

Dabney Coleman, Uma Thurman, Joanna Cassidy, Crispin Glover, Suzy Amis, Christopher Plummer

Where There's a Will*
GB   1936   81m   bw
Gainsborough (Edward Black, Sidney Gilliat)

A seedy education expert sponges on his rich relations but redeems himself by rounding up gangsters at a Christmas party.

Rather slapdash star comedy with very good scenes along the way.

w Will Hay, Robert Edmunds, Ralph Spence   *d* William Beaudine   *ph* Charles Van Enger   *md* Louis Levy

Will Hay, Hartley Power, Gibb McLaughlin, Graham Moffatt, Norma Varden, Gina Malo

'If you laugh yourself sick at this picture – sue Bob Hope!'

Where There's Life
US   1947   75m   bw
Paramount (Paul Jones)

A timid New Yorker turns out to be heir to the throne of a Ruritanian country, and is harassed by spies of both sides.

Mild star comedy with slow patches.

w Allen Boretz, Melville Shavelson   *d* Sidney Lanfield   *ph* Charles Lang Jnr   *m* Irwin Talbot

Bob Hope, Signe Hasso, William Bendix, George Coulouris

Where Were You When the Lights Went Out?*
US   1968   94m   Metrocolor
Panavision
MGM (Everett Freeman, Martin Melcher)

New York's famous electrical blackout in 1965 has its effect on the life of a musical comedy star.

Cheerful sex farce with intriguing beginnings; the later confinement to one set is just a bit harmful.

w Everett Freeman, Karl Tunberg   *play* Claude Magnier   *d* Hy Averback   *ph* Ellsworth Fredericks   *m* Dave Grusin

Doris Day, Terry-Thomas, Patrick O'Neal, Robert Morse, Lola Albright, Jim Backus, Ben Blue

Where's Charley?*
GB   1952   97m   Technicolor
Warner

An Oxford undergraduate impersonates the rich aunt of his best friend.

Slow and rather stately musical version of the famous farce *Charley's Aunt*, unsatisfactorily shot on a mixture of poor sets and sunlit Oxford locations; worth cherishing for the ebullient performance of its over-age star.

w John Monks Jnr   *play* Brandon Thomas (via stage musical)   *book* George Abbott   *d* David Butler   *ph* Erwin Hillier   *ch* Michael Kidd   *m* Frank Loesser

Ray Bolger, Robert Shackleton, Mary Germaine, Allyn McLerie, Margaretta Scott, Horace Cooper

Where's Poppa?*
US   1970   82m   DeLuxe
Jerry Tokovsky/Marvin Worth

A Jewish lawyer's aged mother

constantly harms his love life, and he considers various means of getting rid of her.

Much-censored black comedy which might have been funnier in a complete form. Even so, it has its moments.

w Robert Klane   *novel* Robert Klane   *d* Carl Reiner   *ph* Jack Priestly   *m* Jack Elliott

George Segal, Ruth Gordon, Trish Van Devere, Ron Leibman

W.H.I.F.F.S.
US 1975 92m Technicolor Panavision
Brut (C. O. Erickson)
V
GB title: *C.A.S.H.*

An impotent army veteran finds that a criminal career, helped by stolen army gas, helps his sex life.

Over-the-top comedy with vaguely anti-war and anti-pollution leanings.

w Malcolm Marmorstein   *d* Ted Post   *ph* David M. Walsh   *m* John Cameron

Elliott Gould, Eddie Albert, Harry Guardino, Godfrey Cambridge, Jennifer O'Neill

† Rather typical of the film was its ambiguous catch line: 'The biggest bang in history!'
AAN: song 'Now That We're in Love' (*m* George Barrie, *ly* Sammy Cahn)

Whisky Galore****
GB 1948 82m bw
Ealing (Monja Danischewsky)
V
US title: *Tight Little Island*

During World War II, a ship full of whisky is wrecked on a small Hebridean island, and the local

customs and excise man has his hands full.

Marvellously detailed, fast-moving, well-played and attractively photographed comedy which firmly established the richest Ealing vein.

w Compton Mackenzie, Angus Macphail   *novel* Compton Mackenzie   *d* Alexander Mackendrick   *ph* Gerald Gibbs   *m* Ernest Irving

Basil Radford, Joan Greenwood, Jean Cadell, Gordon Jackson, James Robertson Justice, Wylie Watson, John Gregson, Morland Graham, Duncan Macrae, Catherine Lacey, Bruce Seton, Henry Mollinson, Compton Mackenzie, A. E. Matthews

'Brilliantly witty and fantastic, but wholly plausible.' – *Sunday Chronicle*

'It Ain't Easy Being This Good.'
White Men Can't Jump**
US 1992 112m DeLuxe
TCF (Don Miller, David Lester)
V

Two baseball hustlers – one white, one black – team up to part the unwary from their money.

Crisply performed, enjoyable caper with something to say about relationships between races.

wd Ron Shelton   *ph* Russell Boyd   *m* Bennie Wallace   *pd* Dennis Washington   *ed* Paul Seydor

Wesley Snipes, Woody Harrelson, Rosie Perez, Tyra Ferrell, Cylk Cozart, Kadeem Hardison, Ernest Harden Jnr

'As fast, buoyant and full of feinting rubato as basketball itself.' – *Nigel Andrews, Financial Times*
'With a remarkable lack of soap-box

oratory, Shelton's film manages to catch the prevailing tone of American race relations, to show us what urban America really looks like, and to depict the moral quandaries that poverty inevitably forces on its victims.' – *Henry Sheehan, Sight and Sound*

Who Done It?

US 1942 77m bw
Universal (Alex Gottlieb)

Soda jerks in a New York radio station catch a murderer.

So-so comedy thriller, fatally lacking atmosphere (and good jokes).

w Stanley Roberts, Edmund Joseph, John Grant   d Erle C. Kenton
ph Charles Van Enger   m Frank Skinner

Bud Abbott, Lou Costello, William Gargan, Louise Allbritton, Patric Knowles, Don Porter, Jerome Cowan, William Bendix, Mary Wickes, Thomas Gomez

Who Done It?

GB 1956 85m bw
Ealing (Michael Relph, Basil Dearden)

An ice-rink sweeper sets up as a private eye and captures a ring of spies.

Lively but disappointing film debut for a star comic whose screen personality proved too bland.

w T. E. B. Clarke   d Basil Dearden   ph Otto Heller
m Philip Green

Benny Hill, Belinda Lee, David Kossoff, Garry Marsh, Ernest Thesiger, Thorley Walters

Who Framed Roger Rabbit***

US 1988 103m Rank Color/
Metrocolor/DeLuxe
Warner/Touchstone/Amblin (Robert Watts, Frank Marshall)
V, L

Cartoon characters become involved in Dashiell Hammett-style whodunnit.

Criticisms of thin plotting are irrelevant: the seamless integration of animation and live-action enchanted audiences.

w Jeffrey Price, Peter S. Seaman
book Who Censored Roger Rabbit? by Gary K. Wold   d Robert Zemeckis   ph Dean Cundey
m Alan Silvestri   pd Elliot Scott
animation Richard Williams
ed Arthur Schmidt

Bob Hoskins, Christopher Lloyd, Joanna Cassidy, Stubby Kaye
voices Charles Fleischer, Kathleen Turner, Amy Irving, Lou Hirsch, Mel Blanc

'A deplorable development in the possibilities of animation – and a melancholy waste of the gifts of one of our most gifted actors.' – *Dilys Powell*

AA: Arthur Schmidt; visual effects
AAN: Dean Cundey; art direction

Who Was That Lady?*

US 1960 115m bw
Columbia/Ansark/George Sidney (Norman Krasna)

A professor seen kissing a student persuades a friend to tell his wife that they are both FBI agents on duty. Foreign spies believe them . . .

Agreeably wacky comedy with a strained and prolonged middle section leading to a totally zany climax.

w Norman Krasna   play Norman Krasna   d George Sidney

ph Harry Stradling   *m* André Previn

Tony Curtis, Dean Martin, Janet Leigh, James Whitmore, John McIntire, Barbara Nichols, Larry Keating

Wholly Moses

US   1980   109m   Metrocolor
   Panavision
Columbia/David Begelman
L

A shepherd hears God talking to Moses, and thinks he himself has been ordained to set his people free.

Inept and tasteless biblical spoof which must set back by about ten years the reputations of all connected with it.

w Guy Thomas   *d* Gary Weis

Dudley Moore, James Coco, Paul Sand, Jack Gilford, Dom DeLuise, John Houseman, Madeleine Kahn

'Deadly dullness of both writing and execution render pointless any attempt to single out blame for misfire, which leaves many talented performers flailing about in desperate attempts to generate laughs.' – *Variety*

Whoops Apocalypse

GB   1986   91m   Eastmancolor
ITC (Brian Eastman)
V

First woman president of the US tries to avert nuclear attack.

Frenetic but pathetic attempt at *Dr Strangelove* for the 80s.

w Andrew Marshall, David Renwick   *d* Tom Bussmann
ph Ron Robson   *m* Patrick Gowers   *pd* Tony Noble   *ed* Peter Boyle

Loretta Swit, Peter Cook, Rik Mayall, Ian Richardson, Alexei Sayle, Herbert Lom

Who's Harry Crumb?

US   1989   90m   Technicolor
Columbia TriStar/NBC (Arnon Milchan)
V

An incompetent, accident-prone private detective investigates the kidnapping of a millionaire's daughter.

Broad, slapstick comedy that offers occasional pleasures.

w Robert Conte, Peter Martin Wortmann   *d* Paul Flaherty
ph Stephen M. Katz   *m* Michel Colombier   *pd* Trevor Williams
ed Danford B. Greene, Scott Conrad

John Candy, Jeffrey Jones, Annie Potts, Tim Thomerson, Barry Corbin, Shawnee Smith, Valri Bromfield, Doug Steckler, Renee Coleman

Who's Minding the Mint?*

US   1967   97m   Technicolor
Columbia/Norman Maurer

An employee of the US mint and his friends find a means of printing bills at night.

Smartly-made action comedy with good performances.

w R. S. Allen, Harvey Bullock
d Howard Morris   *ph* Joseph Biroc   *m* Lalo Schifrin

Jim Hutton, Dorothy Provine, Milton Berle, Joey Bishop, Bob Denver, Walter Brennan, Victor Buono, Jack Gilford

Who's Minding the Store?*

US   1963   90m   Technicolor
Paramount/York/Jerry Lewis (Paul Jones)

An accident-prone young man gets a job in a department store.

Better-than-average star comedy, slapstick being allowed precedence over sentimentality.

w Frank Tashlin, Harry Tugend
d Frank Tashlin   ph W. Wallace Kelley   m Joseph J. Lilley

Jerry Lewis, Jill St John, Agnes Moorehead, John McGiver, Ray Walston, Nancy Kulp

Who's That Girl?

US 1987 94m Technicolor
Warner/Peter Guber, Jon Peters, Roger Birnbaum
V

A mild lawyer finds an ex-jailbird starlet his hardest client to handle.

Muddled 'realistic' comedy which starts at screaming pitch and stays there.

w Andrew Smith, Ken Finkleman
d James Foley   ph Jan DeBont
ed Pembroke J. Herring

Madonna, Griffin Dunne, Haviland Morris, John McMartin, Robert Swan, Drew Pilsbury

'What's lacking is pure and simple good humour.' – Variety

Wild West*

GB 1992 100m Metrocolor
Initial/Channel 4/British Screen (Eric Fellner)

Young Asians, living in London and dreaming of stardom, form a country and western band.

Engagingly energetic comedy of cultural misunderstandings and fantasies.

w Harwant Bains   d David Attwood   ph Nic Knowland
m Dominic Miller   pd Caroline Hanania   ed Martin Walsh

Naveen Andrews, Sarita Choudhury,

Ronny Jhutti, Ravi Kapoor, Ameet Chana, Bhasker, Lalita Ahmed, Shaun Scott

'Mangy and artless, this boisterous low-budgeter generates plenty of good laughs and gets lots of mileage from its comic, knowing observations about a vibrant British sub-culture.' – Variety

Wildcats

US 1986 107m Technicolor
Warner (Anthea Sylbert)
V, L

A girl is appointed football coach at a ghetto school, and of course works wonders.

Silly comedy with few laughs and not much plot development.

w Ezra Sacks   d Michael Ritchie
ph Donald E. Thorin   m Hawk Wolinski, James Newton Howard
pd Boris Leven   ed Richard A. Harris

Goldie Hawn, Swoosie Kurtz, Robyn Lively, Brandy Gold, James Keach, Bruce McGill, M. Emmet Walsh

The Wildcats of St Trinian's

GB 1980 91m Technicolor
Wildcat (E. M. Smedley-Aston)

The awful schoolgirls get unionized, and kidnap an Arab's daughter to gain attention.

Crude and belated tailpiece to a series which was never very satisfactory. (See The Belles of . . . , Blue Murder at . . . , The Pure Hell of . . . , The Great St Trinian's Train Robbery.)

wd Frank Launder   ph Ernest Steward   m James Kenelm Clarke

Sheila Hancock, Michael Hordern, Joe

Melia, Thorley Walters, Rodney
Bewes, Maureen Lipman, Ambrosine
Philpotts

Will Success Spoil Rock Hunter?
US   1957   95m   Eastmancolor
Cinemascope
TCF (Frank Tashlin)
GB title: *Oh! For a Man!*

A timid advertising executive is touted
for a publicity stunt as the world's
greatest lover.

A too-wild satire on TV commercials:
less frenzied direction and gag-writing
would have prised more humour from
the situations.

w Frank Tashlin   *play* George
Axelrod   *d* Frank Tashlin
ph Joe MacDonald   *m* Cyril
Mockridge

Jayne Mansfield, Tony Randall, Betsy
Drake, Joan Blondell, John Williams,
Henry Jones, Mickey Hargitay

Willie and Phil
US   1980   116m   DeLuxe
TCF (Paul Mazursky, Tony Ray)

Two men and a woman enjoy a
variable *ménage à trois* throughout the
seventies.

Curious attempt at an American *Jules
et Jim*; not badly done if you have to
do it, but why do it?

wd Paul Mazursky   *ph* Sven
Nykvist   *m* Claude Bolling

Michael Ontkean, Margot Kidder, Ray
Sharkey

'Truffaut's film existed both in the real
world and in a world of the
imagination. Mazursky's has no
imagination and doesn't even touch a
passable form of reality.' – *Sunday
Times*

Wilt
GB   1989   93m   Eastmancolor
Rank/LWT/Picture Partnership (Brian
Eastman)
V

A polytechnic lecturer is suspected of
having murdered his wife by an inept
police inspector.

A low farce which, briskly directed,
affords moderate amusement.

w Andrew Marshall, David
Renwick   *novel* Tom Sharpe
d Michael Tuchner   *ph* Norman
Langley   *m* Anne Dudley
pd Leo Austin   *ed* Chris Blunden

Griff Rhys Jones, Mel Smith, Alison
Steadman, Diana Quick, Jeremy
Clyde, Roger Allam, David Ryall,
Roger Lloyd Pack, Dermot Crowley,
John Normington

The Witches of Eastwick**
US   1987   118m   Technicolor
Warner/Guber-Peters/Kennedy Miller
V, L

Three divorcees on the make are
seduced by the devil.

Horny fantasy, impeccably played,
though it could have been shorter.

w Michael Cristofer   *novel* John
Updike   *d* George Miller
ph Vilmos Zsigmond   *m* John
Williams   *pd* Polly Platt

Jack Nicholson, Cher, Susan Sarandon,
Michelle Pfeiffer, Veronica Cartwright,
Richard Jenkins
AAN: John Williams

With Six You Get Egg Roll
US   1968   99m   DeLuxe
Panavision
Cinema Center/Arwin (Martin Melcher)

A widow with three sons marries a
widower with one daughter.

Quite a bright and inventive family comedy.

w Gwen Bagni, Paul Dubov
d Howard Morris   ph Ellsworth Fredericks, Harry Stradling Jnr
m Robert Mersey

Doris Day, Brian Keith, Pat Carroll, Barbara Hershey

Withnail and I*
GB 1987 108m colour
Recorded Releasing/HandMade Films (Paul M. Heller)
V

In the 60s in Britain two out-of-work actors settle in a dilapidated country cottage.

Deliberately seedy comedy which settles down as a study of character and contrives to be hard to forget.

wd Bruce Robinson   ph Peter Hannan   m David Dundas
pd Michael Pickwoad   ed Alan Strachan

Richard E. Grant, Paul McGann, Richard Griffiths, Ralph Brown, Michael Elphick

Without a Clue
US 1988 107m CFI
Rank/ITC (Marc Stirdivant)
V, L

Dr Watson hires a failed actor to impersonate Sherlock Holmes, a fictional character he has invented to hide his own abilities as a detective.

The mystery is that anyone should have released this witless spoof.

w Gary Murphy, Larry Strawther
d Thom Eberhardt   ph Alan Hume   m Henry Mancini
pd Brian Ackland-Snow, Martyn Hebert   ed Peter Tanner

Michael Caine, Ben Kingsley, Jeffrey Jones, Lysette Anthony, Paul Freeman, Nigel Davenport, Pat Keen, Peter Cook, Tim Killick

Without Love*
US 1945 111m bw
MGM (Lawrence Weingarten)

The housing shortage in wartime Washington causes a widow to allow a scientist to move in with her, quite platonically.

Altered version of a popular play; rather long-drawn-out and disappointing considering the talent on hand.

w Donald Ogden Stewart
play Philip Barry   d Harold S. Bucquet   ph Karl Freund
m Bronislau Kaper

Spencer Tracy, Katharine Hepburn, Lucille Ball, Keenan Wynn, Carl Esmond, Patricia Morison, Felix Bressart, Gloria Grahame

'One of those glossy conversation pieces that MGM does up so handsomely.' – Rose Pelswick

Without Reservations
US 1946 101m bw
RKO/Jesse L. Lasky

A famous woman writer heads for Hollywood by train and meets a marine who seems ideal for her male lead.

Would-be zany romantic comedy à la It Happened One Night; doesn't quite come off.

w Andrew Solt   d Mervyn Le Roy   ph Milton Krasner   m Roy Webb

Claudette Colbert, John Wayne, Don Defore, Phil Brown, Frank Puglia

The Woman in Red*
US   1984   86m   DeLuxe
Orion (Victor Drai)
V, L

A middle-aged married man has
fantasies of infidelity.

Moderately successful transfer to
America of a French comedy success.

wd Gene Wilder, from the film *Un
Eléphant Ça Trompe Enormement* by
Jean-Loup Dabadie, Yves Robert
ph Fred Schuler   m John Morris
pd David L. Snyder   ed Christopher
Greenbury

Gene Wilder, Charles Grodin, Joseph
Bologna, Judith Ivey, Gilda Radner

AA: song 'I Just Called to Say I Love
You' (Stevie Wonder)

A Woman of Distinction
US   1950   85m   bw
Columbia (Buddy Adler)

The lady dean of a New England
school falls for a British astronomer.

Pratfall farce for ageing stars. No go.

w Charles Hoffman   d Edward
Buzzell   ph Joseph Walker
md Morris Stoloff   m Werner
Heymann

Rosalind Russell, Ray Milland,
Edmund Gwenn, Janis Carter, Mary
Jane Saunders, Francis Lederer,
Jerome Courtland

Woman of the Year*
US   1942   114m   bw
MGM (Joseph L. Mankiewicz)
L

A sports columnist marries a lady
politician; they have nothing in
common but love.

Simple, effective, mildly sophisticated
comedy which allows two splendid

stars, in harness for the first time, to
do their thing to the general benefit.

w *Ring Lardner Jnr, Michael Kanin*
d *George Stevens*   ph Joseph
Ruttenberg   m Franz Waxman

Spencer Tracy, Katharine Hepburn, Fay
Bainter, Reginald Owen, William
Bendix, Dan Tobin, Minor Watson,
Roscoe Karns

'Between them they have enough
charm to keep any ball rolling.' –
William Whitebait

AA: script
AAN: Katharine Hepburn

'It's a great big wonderful woman's world
because men are in it!'
Woman's World**
US   1954   94m   Technicolor
   Cinemascope
TCF (Charles Brackett)

Three top salesmen and their wives
are summoned to New York by the
boss, who seeks to choose a new
general manager.

Amusing, superficial pattern comedy-
drama for an all-star cast, backed by
all-round technical competence.

w Claude Binyon, Mary Loos,
Richard Sale   d Jean Negulesco
ph Joe MacDonald   m Cyril
Mockridge

Clifton Webb, Lauren Bacall, Van Heflin,
June Allyson, Fred MacMurray,
Arlene Dahl, Cornel Wilde, Elliott
Reid, Margalo Gillmore

'135 women with men on their minds!'
The Women**
US   1939   132m   bw
   (Technicolor sequence)
MGM (Hunt Stromberg)

A New York socialite gets a divorce
but later thinks better of it.

Bitchy comedy drama distinguished by an all-girl cast ('135 women with men on their minds'). An over-generous slice of real theatre, skilfully adapted, with rich sets, plenty of laughs, and some memorable scenes between the fighting ladies.

w Anita Loos, Jane Murfin play Clare Boothe *d* George Cukor *ph* Oliver T. Marsh, Joseph Ruttenberg *m* Edward Ward, David Snell

Norma Shearer, Joan Crawford, *Rosalind Russell*, Mary Boland, Paulette Goddard, Joan Fontaine, Lucile Watson, Phyllis Povah, Virginia Weidler, Ruth Hussey, Margaret Dumont, Marjorie Main, Hedda Hopper

'Smash hit of solid proportions for extended runs and heavy profits . . . a strong woman entry but still has plenty of spicy lines and situations for the men.' – *Variety*
'A mordant, mature description of the social decay of one corner of the American middle class.' – *Time*
'So marvellous that we believe every Hollywood studio should make at least one thoroughly nasty picture a year.' – *New York Times*
'Whether you go or not depends on whether you can stand Miss Shearer with tears flowing steadily in all directions at once, and such an endless damn back fence of cats.' – *Otis Ferguson*

Women on the Verge of a Nervous Breakdown**

Spain 1988 89m Eastmancolor
Rank/El Deseo/Lauren Film/Orion (Agustin Almodóvar)
V, L
original title: *Mujeres al borde de un ataque de nervios*

Three women approach crack-up as their lives entangle: a demented wife whose husband has abandoned her, her husband's estranged mistress, a temperamental actress, and the actress's friend, who has fallen in love with a terrorist.

Frenetic, fashionable farce that manages to amuse most of the time.

wd Pedro Almodóvar *ph* Jose Luis Alcaine *m* Bernardo Bonezzi *ed* Jose Salcedo

Carmen Maura, Antonio Banderas, Julieta Serrano, Maria Barranco, Rossy de Palma, Guillermo Montesinos, Kiti Manver

'The best to be said for *Women on the Verge* is that Almodóvar makes a good interior decorator.' – *Mark Finch, MFB*
AAN: best foreign film

Won Ton Ton, the Dog Who Saved Hollywood

US 1976 92m colour
Paramount/David V. Picker, Arnold Schulman, Michael Winner

In twenties Hollywood, a lost Alsatian dog becomes a movie star but later suffers some ups and downs before being reunited with his mistress.

Scatty, unlikeable comedy with too frantic a pace, apparently in desperation at the dearth of funny lines and situations. The sixty 'guest stars' barely get a look in; the director seems to think (erroneously) that their appearance makes some kind of point even though they have nothing to do. Altogether, an embarrassment.

w Arnold Schulman, Cy Howard *d* Michael Winner *ph* Richard H. Kline *m* Neal Hefti

Madeleine Kahn, Art Carney, Bruce Dern, Ron Leibman; and Dennis Morgan, William Demarest, Virginia Mayo, Rory Calhoun, Henry Wilcoxon, Ricardo Montalban, Jackie

Coogan, Johnny Weissmuller, Aldo Ray, Ethel Merman, Joan Blondell, Yvonne de Carlo, Andy Devine, Broderick Crawford, Richard Arlen, Jack La Rue, Dorothy Lamour, Phil Silvers, Gloria de Haven, Stepin Fetchit, Rudy Vallee, George Jessel, Ann Miller, Janet Blair, the Ritz Brothers, Victor Mature, Fernando Lamas, Cyd Charisse, Huntz Hall, Edgar Bergen, Peter Lawford, Regis Toomey, Alice Faye, Milton Berle, John Carradine, Walter Pidgeon, etc

'The film tries to conceal its deficiencies in comic ideas and comic skill by doing everything at the pace of a clockwork toy with a too-tight spring.' – *Dave Robinson, Times*

Wonder Man**
US 1945 97m Technicolor
Samuel Goldwyn

A mild-mannered student is persuaded by the ghost of his dead twin to avenge his murder.

Smooth, successful mixture of *Topper*, a night-club musical, a gangster drama and the star's own brand of fooling; this is possibly his best vehicle after *The Court Jester*.

w Don Hartman, Melville Shavelson, *Philip Rapp story* Arthur Sheekman *d* Bruce Humberstone *ph* Victor Milner, William Snyder *md* Louis Forbes, Ray Heindorf *sp* John Fulton

Danny Kaye, Vera-Ellen, Virginia Mayo, Steve Cochran, S. Z. Sakall, Allen Jenkins, Ed Brophy, Donald Woods, Otto Kruger, Richard Lane, Natalie Schaefer
AAN: Louis Forbes, Ray Heindorf; song 'So in Love' (*m* David Rose, *ly* Leo Robin)

Working Girl**
US 1988 113m DuArt
Fox (Douglas Wick)
V, L

A secretary outsmarts her female boss in business and love.

Glossy comedy that owes much to the performances of its leading actors.

w Kevin Wade *d* Mike Nichols *ph* Michael Ballhaus *m* Carly Simon *pd* Patrizia von Brandenstein *ed* Sam O'Steen, Richard Nord

Harrison Ford, Sigourney Weaver, Melanie Griffith, Alec Baldwin, Joan Cusack, Philip Bosco, Nora Dunn, Oliver Platt, James Lally, Olympia Dukakis

AA: best song
AAN: best picture; Mike Nicholls; Melanie Griffith; Joan Cusack

The World of Henry Orient**
US 1964 106m DeLuxe
Panavision
UA/Pan Arts (Jerome Hellman)

Two rich 14-year-old New York girls build fantasies around a concert pianist.

Charming, immaculately mounted, refreshingly unusual but overlong comedy.

w Nora and Nunnally Johnson *novel* Nora Johnson *d* George Roy Hill *ph* Boris Kaufman, Arthur J. Ornitz *m* Elmer Bernstein *pd* James Sullivan

Tippy Walker, Merri Spaeth, Peter Sellers, Angela Lansbury, Paula Prentiss, Phyllis Thaxter, Tom Bosley, Bibi Osterwald

The World's Greatest Lover
US 1977 89m DeLuxe
TCF (Gene Wilder)

In the twenties, a rival studio starts a search for a man to surpass Valentino.

Imitative slapstick extravaganza in which anything goes but hardly anything pleases.

wd Gene Wilder   *ph* Gerald Hirschfeld   *m* John Morris

Gene Wilder, Carol Kane, Dom DeLuise, Fritz Feld

'Infantile humour for young, slow kids who want everything pounded at them.' – *Pauline Kael, New Yorker*

† The film carries a credit to Federico Fellini, 'for encouragement at the right time'.

Worm's Eye View
GB   1951   77m   bw
ABFD/Byron (Henry Halsted)

Incidents in the lives of a group of RAF billetees.

Plotless comedy from a highly successful stage romp; plainly made and empty-headed but not disagreeable.

w R. F. Delderfield   *play* R. F. Delderfield   *d* Jack Raymond   *ph* James Wilson   *m* Tony Lowry, Tony Fones

Ronald Shiner, Garry Marsh, Diana Dors, Eric Davis, John Blythe

The Wrong Arm of the Law*
GB   1962   94m   bw
Romulus/Robert Verlaise (Aubrey Baring, E. M. Smedley Aston)

London gangsters plan retaliation against Australian interlopers, and offer Scotland Yard a temporary truce.

Forgettable but pretty funny crook comedy in the British vein, with pacy script and excellent comedy timing.

w Ray Galton, Alan Simpson, John Antrobus   *screenplay* Len Heath, John Warren   *d* *Cliff Owen* *ph* Ernest Steward   *m* Richard Rodney Bennett

Peter Sellers, Lionel Jeffries, Bernard Cribbins, Davy Kaye, Nanette Newman, Bill Kerr, John Le Mesurier

The Wrong Box*
GB   1966   110m   Technicolor
Columbia/Salamander (Bryan Forbes)

Two elderly Victorian brothers are the last survivors of a tontine (an involved form of lottery) and try to murder each other.

Well-intentioned and star-studded black farce in which the excellent period trappings and stray jokes completely overwhelm the plot.

w Larry Gelbart, Burt Shevelove *novel* Robert Louis Stevenson, Lloyd Osbourne   *d* Bryan Forbes *ph* *Gerry Turpin*   *m* John Barry *ad* Ray Simm

Ralph Richardson, John Mills, Michael Caine, *Wilfrid Lawson*, Nanette Newman, Peter Cook, Dudley Moore, Peter Sellers, Tony Hancock, Thorley Walters, Cicely Courtneidge, Irene Handl, John Le Mesurier, Gerald Sim, Norman Bird, Tutte Lemkow

'A slapdash affair in which anything goes, irrespective of whether or not it fits.' – *Tom Milne*

Xala*
Senegal 1974 123m colour
Filmi Domireew/Société Nationale
    Cinématographique (Paulin Soumanou
    Vieyra)
GB title: *The Curse*

A leading businessman is humiliated
when he finds that he is unable to
consummate his marriage to his third
wife.

Exuberant satire on corruption and a
clash of cultures: tribal and urban,
African and European, revolutionary
and colonial, feminine and
masculine, rich and poor.

wd Ousmane Sembène
novel Ousmane Sembène
ph Georges Caristan, Orlando R.
Lopez, Seydina D. Gaye, Farba Seck
m Samba Diabare Samb
ed Florence Eymon

Thierno Lege, Miriam Niang, Seune
Samb, Fatim Diagne, Younouss
Seye, Moustapha Toure, Dieynaba
Niang

'A picture filled with swashbucklers, privateers, public floggings, saucy tarts, looney lords, beggars, queens, and even a very jolly Roger!'

Yellowbeard

US 1983 96m DeLuxe
Orion/Seagoat (Carter de Haven Jnr)
V, L

Farcical adventures of a 17th-century pirate captain.

A spoofy saga in deliberately bad taste, this ragbag of old gags and new unpleasantness sank rapidly to the bottom of the box-office barrel.

w Graham Chapman, Peter Cook, Bernard McKenna *d* Mel Damski *ph* Gerry Fisher *m* John Morris *pd* Joseph R. Jennings

Graham Chapman, Peter Boyle, Cheech and Chong, Peter Cook, Marty Feldman, Michael Hordern, Eric Idle, Madeline Kahn, James Mason, John Cleese, Kenneth Mars, Spike Milligan, Susannah York, Beryl Reid, Ferdy Mayne, Peter Bull

'The atrocious script and haphazard direction elicit generally embarrassing performances from all concerned.' – *Kim Newman, MFB*

Yokel Boy

US 1942 69m bw
Republic (Robert North)
GB title: *Hitting the Headlines*

A film buff from the sticks comes to Hollywood and gets involved with production.

Spoofy comedy which doesn't come off despite the talent around.

w Isabel Dawn *story* Russel Rouse (the legit musical by Lew Brown was thrown away, together with the songs) *d* Joseph Santley

Eddie Foy Jnr, Joan Davis, Albert Dekker, Alan Mowbray, Roscoe Karns, Mikhail Rasumny, Marc Lawrence, Tom Dugan

You Can't Cheat an Honest Man*

US 1939 79m bw
Universal (Lester Cowan)

Trials and tribulations of a circus owner.

Flat, desultory and generally disappointing comedy vehicle for an irresistible star combination.

w George Marion Jnr, Richard Mack, Everett Freeman *story* Charles Bogle (W. C. Fields) *d* George Marshall *ph* Milton Krasner *m* Charles Previn

W. C. Fields, Edgar Bergen (with Charlie McCarthy and Mortimer Snerd), Constance Moore, Mary Forbes, Thurston Hall, Charles Coleman, Edward Brophy

'Fairly amusing but lacks sustained overall interest.' – *Variety*

You Can't Have Everything*

US 1937 99m bw
TCF (Lawrence Schwab)

A failed play is turned into a musical.

Lively backstage comedy with good moments.

w Harry Tugend, Jack Yellen, Karl Tunberg d Norman Taurog ph Lucien Andriot md David Buttolph songs Mack Gordon, Harry Revel

Alice Faye, the Ritz Brothers, Don Ameche, Charles Winninger, Gypsy Rose Lee, Tony Martin, Arthur Treacher, Louis Prima, Tip Tap and Toe, Wally Vernon

'An expert piecing together of story, melody, blackouts, night club specialties and production numbers.'
– Variety

You Can't Take It with You**

US 1938 127m bw
Columbia (Frank Capra)
L

The daughter of a highly eccentric New York family falls for a rich man's son.

A hilarious, warm and witty play is largely changed into a tirade against big business, but the Capra expertise is here in good measure and the stars all pull their weight.

w Robert Riskin play George S. Kaufman, Moss Hart d Frank Capra ph Joseph Walker m Dimitri Tiomkin ed Gene Havlik

Jean Arthur, Lionel Barrymore, James Stewart, Edward Arnold, Spring Byington, Mischa Auer, Ann Miller, Samuel S. Hinds, Donald Meek, H. B. Warner, Halliwell Hobbes, Mary Forbes, Dub Taylor, Lillian Yarbo, Eddie Anderson, Harry Davenport

GRANDPA VANDERHOF (Lionel Barrymore) offering a prayer: 'Well, sir, here we are again. We had a little trouble, but that's not your fault. You spread the milk of human kindness, and if some of it gets curdled, that's our look-out. Anyway, things have turned out fine. Alice is going to marry Tony. The Kirbys are going to live with us for a while. And everybody on the block is happy. We've all got our health – and as far as anything else is concerned, we'll leave it up to you. Thank you.'

'The comedy is wholly American, wholesome, homespun, human, appealing, and touching in turn.' – Variety
'Shangri-La in a frame house.' – Otis Ferguson

AA: best picture; Frank Capra
AAN: Robert Riskin; Joseph Walker; Spring Byington; Gene Havlik

You Must Be Joking*

GB 1965 100m bw
Columbia/Ameran (Charles H. Schneer)

Assorted army personnel vie in an extended initiative test.

Slam-bang location comedy with more hits than misses: cheerful entertainment.

w Alan Hackney d Michael Winner ph Geoffrey Unsworth m Laurie Johnson

Terry-Thomas, Lionel Jeffries, Michael Callan, Gabriella Licudi, Denholm Elliott, Lee Montague, Bernard Cribbins, Wilfrid Hyde White, James Robertson Justice, Richard Wattis, James Villiers

Young Doctors in Love

US 1982 95m Metrocolor
TCF/ABC (Jerry Bruckheimer)

Goings-on in a modern hospital.

Spoof soap opera in the wake of *Airplane* but seeming more like a flat edition of *Carry On*.

w Michael Elias, Rich Eustis *d* Garry Marshall *ph* Don Peterman *m* Maurice Jarre

Michael McKean, Sean Young, Harry Dean Stanton, Patrick MacNee, Hector Elizondo, Dabney Coleman

Young Einstein
Australia 1988 91m colour
Warner/Serious Productions (Yahoo
 Serious, Warwick Ross, David Roach)
V, L

Einstein discovers the theory of relativity, falls in love with Marie Curie, and then invents the surfboard, the electric guitar and rock 'n' roll.

A smash-hit in its native land, it is a ramshackle, slapstick comedy that, relatively speaking, does not travel well.

w Yahoo Serious, David Roach *d* Yahoo Serious *ph* Jeff Darling *m* William Motzing, Martin Armiger, Tommy Tycho *ad* Steve Marr, Laurie Faen, Colin Gibson, Ron Highfield *ed* Yahoo Serious

Yahoo Serious, Odile Le Clezio, John Howard, Peewee Wilson, Su Cruikshank

'A film which manages to be innocuous and appalling at the same time.' – *MFB*

Young Frankenstein**
US 1974 108m bw
TCF/Gruskoff/Venture/Jouer/Crossbow
 (Michael Gruskoff)
V, L

Young Frederick Frankenstein, a brain

surgeon, goes back to Transylvania and pores over his grandfather's notebooks.

The most successful of Mel Brooks' parodies, *Mad Magazine* style; the gleamingly reminiscent photography is the best of it, the script being far from consistently funny, but there are splendid moments.

w Gene Wilder, Mel Brooks *d* Mel Brooks *ph* Gerald Hirschfeld *m* John Morris *ad* Dale Hennesy

Gene Wilder, Marty Feldman, Madeleine Kahn, *Peter Boyle*, Cloris Leachman, Kenneth Mars, Gene Hackman, Richard Haydn
AAN: script

The Young in Heart***
US 1938 91m bw
David O. Selznick

A family of charming confidence tricksters move in on a rich old lady but she brings out the best in them.

Delightful, roguish romantic comedy, perfectly cast and pacily handled.

w Paul Osborn, Charles Bennett novel The Gay Banditti by I. A. R. Wylie *d Richard Wallace ph* Leon Shamroy *m* Franz Waxman

Douglas Fairbanks Jnr, Janet Gaynor, Roland Young, Billie Burke, Minnie Dupree, Paulette Goddard, Richard Carlson, Henry Stephenson

'Sentimental drama, vastly touching and entertaining . . . has everything to ensure box office success.' – *Variety*
'It comes as a gentle breeze in the hurricane of hurly burly comedies that have hurtled across the screen of late.' – *Motion Picture Herald*
AAN: Leon Shamroy; Franz Waxman

You're a Big Boy Now*

US   1967   96m   Eastmancolor
Warner Seven Arts (William Fadiman)

A young assistant librarian discovers
girls.

Freewheeling semi-surrealist comedy
with exhilarating moments and the
inevitable letdowns associated with
this kind of campy high style.

wd Francis Ford Coppola
novel David Benedictus   *ph* Andy
Laszlo   *m* Bob Prince

Peter Kastner, Elizabeth Hartman,
Geraldine Page, Julie Harris, Rip
Torn, Tony Bill, Karen Black, Michael
Dunn

'A half-kooky, half-sweetly-innocent
comedy . . . which is wonderfully
photogenic from a young director's
point of view.' – *Judith Crist*
AAN: Geraldine Page

You're Darn Tootin'***

US   1929   20m   bw   silent
Hal Roach

Two musicians get into trouble at
work, in their digs and in the street.

Star comedy which though early in
their teaming shows Stan and Ollie at
their best in a salt shaker routine and
in a surreal pants-ripping contest.

w H. M. Walker   *d* Edgar Kennedy

Laurel and Hardy, Agnes Steele

You're in the Army Now**

US   1941   79m   bw
Warner (Ben Stoloff)

Two incompetent vacuum cleaner
salesmen accidentally join the army.

An excellent vehicle for two star
comedians who have often suffered
from poor material, with a silent-
comedy-style climax involving a house
on wheels.

w Paul Gerard Smith, George
Beatty   *d* Lewis Seiler   *ph* James
Van Trees   *m* Howard Jackson

*Jimmy Durante, Phil Silvers, Donald
MacBride*, Jane Wyman, Regis Toomey

You're Telling Me*

US   1934   66m   bw
Paramount

A small-town inventor meets a
princess and makes the social grade.

Meaninglessly-titled star vehicle
which is often defiantly unamusing
but does include the famous golf
routine.

w Walter de Leon, Paul M. Jones
d Erle C. Kenton   *ph* Alfred
Gilks   *m* Arthur Johnston

W. C. Fields, Larry 'Buster' Crabbe,
Joan Marsh, Adrienne Ames, Louise
Carter

'The kind of comedy that Chaplin
used to do in two reels, but stretched
out like Carnera's suspenders to run
an even six.' – *Variety*

Z

Zapped!

US 1982 98m CFI
Thunder Associates
L

A high-school boffin discovers his own telekinetic powers, by which he is able to tear everyone's clothes off at the senior prom.

Mild adolescent smut, half-way between *Porky's* and the unbearable Disney comedies of the sixties.

w Bruce Rubin, Robert J. Rosenthal   *d* Robert J. Rosenthal

Scott Baio, Willie Aames, Robert Mandan, Scatman Crothers

Zazie dans le Métro**

France 1960 88m Eastmancolor
Nouvelles Editions (Irène Leriche)
V

A naughty little girl has a day in Paris and causes chaos.

Inventive little comedy which almost turns into a French *Hellzapoppin*, with everybody chasing or fighting everybody else.

wd Louis Malle   *novel* Raymond Queneau   *ph* Henri Raichi   *m* Fiorenzo Capri

Catherine Demongeot, Philippe Noiret, Vittorio Caprioli

'There is something not quite innocent or healthy about this film.' – *Bosley Crowther*

Zelig**

US 1983 79m (including about 5m of credits) bw/colour
Orion/Rollins-Joffe (Robert Greenhut)
V

A parody documentary tracing a chameleon-like nonentity who contrives to have been associated with all the major events of the 20th century.

The central idea is more elusive than appealing, and the mid-section of psychiatric consultation is downright dull, but considerable amusement derives from the technical trickery which puts Woody Allen in pictorial association with Hitler, Roosevelt and Eugene O'Neill. In all, an after-dinner treat for the intellectuals.

wd Woody Allen   *ph* Gordon Willis   *m* Dick Hyman   *pd* Mel Bourne

Woody Allen, Mia Farrow

'We can all admire the brilliance and economy with which it is made. But is it funny enough? I take leave to doubt it.' – *Derek Malcolm, Guardian*
'*Citizen Kane* miraculously transformed into side-splitting comedy.' – *New York Times*
'The movie is a technical masterpiece, but in artistic and comic terms, only pretty good.' – *Roger Ebert*
AAN: cinematography; costume design

Zenobia

US   1939   83m   bw
Hal Roach
V
GB title: *Elephants Never Forget*

A small-town doctor finds himself looking after a performing elephant.

Very mild small-town comedy made during a break-up in the Laurel and Hardy contract.

w Corey Ford, Arnold Belgard, Walter De Leon   *d* Gordon Douglas
ph Karl Struss   *m* Marvin Hatley

Oliver Hardy, Harry Langdon, Jean Parker, Billie Burke, Alice Brady, James Ellison, Stepin Fetchit, Hattie McDaniel

Zéro de Conduite**

France   1933   45m approx   bw
Gaumont/Franco Film/Aubert
V

Boys return from the holiday to a nasty little boarding school, where the headmaster is an unpleasant dwarf and all the staff are hateful. A revolution breaks out . . .

A clear forerunner of *If . . .* and one of the most famous of surrealist films, though it pales beside Buñuel and is chiefly valuable for being funny.

wd Jean Vigo   *ph* Boris Kaufman
m Maurice Jaubert

Jean Dasté, Louis Lefébvre, Gilbert Pruchon, le nain Delphin

'One of the most poetic films ever made and one of the most influential.' – *New Yorker, 1978*

'Zany! Zexy! Zensational!'

Zorro the Gay Blade

US   1981   93m   DeLuxe
Melvin Simon (George Hamilton, C. O. Erickson)

Zorro, the masked avenger, not only pretends to be a fop but is one. Luckily he has a twin brother.

Abysmal attempt to do for Zorro what *Love at First Bite* did for Dracula.

w Hal Dresner   *d* Peter Medak
ph John A. Alonzo   *m* Max Steiner themes

George Hamilton, Lauren Hutton, Brenda Vaccaro, Ron Leibman, James Booth

'A wonderful giddy farce.' – *Pauline Kael*

This is Orson Welles

Orson Welles and Peter Bogdanovich

This is the book that Welles ultimately considered his auto-biography, but it's a memoir like no other. At once accessible, entertaining and revealing, Welles and Bogdanovich's collaboration is an unforgettable collection of penetrating, fascinating and often hilarious conversations undertaken over many years, on both sides of the Atlantic. With *This is Orson Welles* the master illusionist and self-confessed 'faker', in his own words, 'puts the record straight'.

'The Art of Bogdanovich's interrogation conceals itself in the ease of good friends talking, yet it elicits from Welles answers which show us his position and his character under the arc-light thrown upon them by his brilliant tongue . . . Such humorous charm is captivating'   Philip Glazebrook, *Spectator*

'This is a book you must beg, borrow or steal . . . Welles pulls no punches: reading it is like being a privileged guest at his table, savouring that inimitable voice, as the pearls drop in abundance'
                    Bryan Forbes, *Mail on Sunday*

'Fascinating. A treasure-trove of insights'   John Lahr

'Welles at his roaring best'   *New York Times Book Review*

ISBN 0 00 638232 0

Laurence Olivier

A Biography

Donald Spoto

'Rivetingly interesting, admirably researched and exquisitely written – an altogether wonderful book'   Sir John Gielgud

'A work of subtle critical insight, warm, human, and always highly readable'   *New Statesman*

In the first biography of Laurence Olivier to appear since his death, Donald Spoto reveals the man behind the mask of the flamboyant, heroic actor. Based on meticulous research and many previously unpublished documents, this is the first full portrait of our greatest man of the theatre.

Chaplin
His Life and Art
David Robinson

'Unlikely ever to be surpassed.' *Spectator*

In just a few short years Charles Chaplin revolutionized the language of cinema and became the most universally loved performer of all time. But who was the man that dazzled and perplexed his adoring public? Perfectionist, playboy or workaholic? Spokesman for the poor or playmate of the international rich? Calculating or compassionate?

Only this definitive biography answers such contradictory and intriguing questions – the only one to be written with full access to the Chaplin archives – in which David Robinson provides a uniquely documented record of the working methods and extraordinary life of the mercurial genius of early cinema.

'An indispensable work for all concerned with the history of the cinema.' *Sunday Times*

'A classic piece of film biography which is also the fascinating story of a brilliant, perverse, courageous man, indisputably one of the great artists of the twentieth century.'
Lindsay Anderson, *Tatler*

ISBN 0 586 08544 0

Halliwell's Filmgoer's Companion
10th Edition

Edited by John Walker

Halliwell's Filmgoer's Companion is unique as the only complete encyclopedia of movie people from cinema's silent monochrome beginnings to the colourful, wide-screen present. Packed with biographical profiles of actors, directors, producers, writers, cinematographers, film editors and other key personnel, definitions of technical terms, notes on the studios, movements and national film industries, the *Companion* is the one indispensable guide for anyone with an interest in films, from the dedicated film buff and movie star fan to the late-night TV film addict.

All existing entries are fully up-dated and over 1,000 new entries added for the 10th Edition.

'The *Companion* is everything people say it is. It is indispensable; it is a bargain at the price; it is one of the most fascinating books you ever saw' – Benny Green, *Spectator*

ISBN 0 586 09174 2